Algorithms

Jeff Erickson

oth edition (pre-publication draft) — December 30, 2018
½th edition (pre-publication draft) — April 9, 2019
1st paperback edition — June 13, 2019

1 2 3 4 5 6 7 8 9 — 27 26 25 24 23 22 21 20 **19**

ISBN: 978-1-792-64483-2 (paperback)

Download this book at http://jeffe.cs.illinois.edu/teaching/algorithms/
or http://algorithms.wtf
or https://archive.org/details/Algorithms-Jeff-Erickson

Please report errors at https://github.com/jeffgerickson/algorithms

Portions of our programming are mechanically reproduced,
and we now begin our broadcast day.

For Kim, Kay, and Hannah
with love and admiration

And for Erin
with thanks
for breaking her promise

Incipit prologus in libro alghoarismi de practica arismetrice.

— Ioannis Hispalensis [John of Seville?],
Liber algorismi de pratica arismetrice (c.1135)

Shall I tell you, my friend, how you will come to understand it?
Go and write a book upon it.

— Henry Home, Lord Kames (1696–1782),
in a letter to Sir Gilbert Elliot

The individual is always mistaken. He designed many things, and drew in other
persons as coadjutors, quarrelled with some or all, blundered much, and
something is done; all are a little advanced, but the individual is always mistaken.
It turns out somewhat new and very unlike what he promised himself.

— Ralph Waldo Emerson, "Experience", *Essays, Second Series* (1844)

What I have outlined above is the content of a book the realization of whose basic
plan and the incorporation of whose details would perhaps be impossible; what I
have written is a second or third draft of a preliminary version of this book

— Michael Spivak, preface of the first edition of
Differential Geometry, Volume I (1970)

Preface

About This Book

This textbook grew out of a collection of lecture notes that I wrote for various algorithms classes at the University of Illinois at Urbana-Champaign, which I have been teaching about once a year since January 1999. Spurred by changes of our undergraduate theory curriculum, I undertook a major revision of my notes in 2016; this book consists of a subset of my revised notes on the most fundamental course material, mostly reflecting the algorithmic content of our new required junior-level theory course.

Prerequisites

The algorithms classes I teach at Illinois have two significant prerequisites: a course on discrete mathematics and a course on fundamental data structures. Consequently, this textbook is probably not suitable for most students as a *first* course in data structures and algorithms. In particular, I assume at least passing familiarity with the following specific topics:

- **Discrete mathematics:** High-school algebra, logarithm identities, naive set theory, Boolean algebra, first-order predicate logic, sets, functions, equivalences, partial orders, modular arithmetic, recursive definitions, trees (as abstract objects, not data structures), graphs (vertices and edges, not function plots).

- **Proof techniques:** direct, indirect, contradiction, exhaustive case analysis, and induction (especially "strong" and "structural" induction). Chapter o uses induction, and whenever Chapter $n-1$ uses induction, so does Chapter n.

- **Iterative programming concepts:** variables, conditionals, loops, records, indirection (addresses/pointers/references), subroutines, recursion. I do not assume fluency in any particular programming language, but I do assume experience with at least one language that supports both indirection and recursion.

- **Fundamental abstract data types:** scalars, sequences, vectors, sets, stacks, queues, maps/dictionaries, ordered maps/dictionaries, priority queues.

- **Fundamental data structures:** arrays, linked lists (single and double, linear and circular), binary search trees, at least one form of *balanced* binary search tree (such as AVL trees, red-black trees, treaps, skip lists, or splay trees), hash tables, binary heaps, and most importantly, the difference between this list and the previous list.

- **Fundamental computational problems:** elementary arithmetic, sorting, searching, enumeration, tree traversal (preorder, inorder, postorder, level-order, and so on).

- **Fundamental algorithms:** elementary algorism, sequential search, binary search, sorting (selection, insertion, merge, heap, quick, radix, and so on), breadth- and depth-first search in (at least binary) trees, and most importantly, the difference between this list and the previous list.

- **Elementary algorithm analysis:** Asymptotic notation (o, O, Θ, Ω, ω), translating loops into sums and recursive calls into recurrences, evaluating simple sums and recurrences.

- **Mathematical maturity:** facility with abstraction, formal (especially recursive) definitions, and (especially inductive) proofs; writing and following mathematical arguments; recognizing and avoiding syntactic, semantic, and/or logical nonsense.

The book *briefly* covers some of this prerequisite material when it arises in context, but more as a reminder than a good introduction. For a more thorough overview, I strongly recommend the following freely available references:

- Margaret M. Fleck. *Building Blocks for Theoretical Computer Science*. Version 1.3 (January 2013) or later available from http://mfleck.cs.illinois.edu/building-blocks/.
- Eric Lehman, F. Thomson Leighton, and Albert R. Meyer. *Mathematics for Computer Science*. June 2018 revision available from https://courses.csail.mit.edu/6.042/spring18/. (I strongly recommend searching for the most recent revision.)
- Pat Morin. *Open Data Structures*. Edition 0.1Gβ (January 2016) or later available from http://opendatastructures.org/.
- Don Sheehy. *A Course in Data Structures and Object-Oriented Design*. February 2019 or later revision available from https://donsheehy.github.io/datastructures/.

Additional References

Please do not restrict yourself to this or any other single reference. Authors and readers bring their own perspectives to any intellectual material; no instructor "clicks" with every student, or even with every very strong student. Finding the author that most effectively gets *their* intuition into *your* head takes some effort, but that effort pays off handsomely in the long run.

The following references have been particularly valuable sources of intuition, examples, exercises, and inspiration; this is not meant to be a complete list.

- Alfred V. Aho, John E. Hopcroft, and Jeffrey D. Ullman. *The Design and Analysis of Computer Algorithms*. Addison-Wesley, 1974. (I used this textbook as an undergraduate at Rice and again as a masters student at UC Irvine.)
- Boaz Barak. *Introduction to Theoretical Computer Science*. Textbook draft, most recently revised June 2019. (Not your grandfather's theoretical CS textbook, and so much the better for it; the fact that it's free is a delightful bonus.)
- Thomas Cormen, Charles Leiserson, Ron Rivest, and Cliff Stein. *Introduction to Algorithms*, third edition. MIT Press/McGraw-Hill, 2009. (I used the first edition as a teaching assistant at Berkeley.)
- Sanjoy Dasgupta, Christos H. Papadimitriou, and Umesh V. Vazirani. *Algorithms*. McGraw-Hill, 2006. (Probably the closest in content to this book, but considerably less verbose.)
- Jeff Edmonds. *How to Think about Algorithms*. Cambridge University Press, 2008.
- Michael R. Garey and David S. Johnson. *Computers and Intractability: A Guide to the Theory of NP-Completeness*. W. H. Freeman, 1979.

- Michael T. Goodrich and Roberto Tamassia. *Algorithm Design: Foundations, Analysis, and Internet Examples*. John Wiley & Sons, 2002.
- Jon Kleinberg and Éva Tardos. *Algorithm Design*. Addison-Wesley, 2005. Borrow it from the library if you can.
- Donald Knuth. *The Art of Computer Programming*, volumes 1–4A. Addison-Wesley, 1997 and 2011. (My parents gave me the first three volumes for Christmas when I was 14. Alas, I didn't actually read them until *much* later.)
- Udi Manber. *Introduction to Algorithms: A Creative Approach*. Addison-Wesley, 1989. (I used this textbook as a teaching assistant at Berkeley.)
- Ian Parberry. *Problems on Algorithms*. Prentice-Hall, 1995 (out of print). Downloadable from https://larc.unt.edu/ian/books/free/license.html after you agree to make a small charitable donation. Please honor your agreement.
- Robert Sedgewick and Kevin Wayne. *Algorithms*. Addison-Wesley, 2011.
- Robert Endre Tarjan. *Data Structures and Network Algorithms*. SIAM, 1983.
- Class notes from my own algorithms classes at Berkeley, especially those taught by Dick Karp and Raimund Seidel.
- Lecture notes, slides, homeworks, exams, video lectures, research papers, blog posts, StackExchange questions and answers, podcasts, and full-fledged MOOCs made freely available on the web by innumerable colleagues around the world.

About the Exercises

Each chapter ends with several exercises, most of which I have used at least once in a homework assignment, discussion/lab section, or exam. The exercises are *not* ordered by increasing difficulty, but (generally) clustered by common techniques or themes. Some problems are annotated with symbols as follows:

- ♥Red hearts indicate particularly challenging problems; many of these have appeared on qualifying exams for PhD students at Illinois. A small number of *really* hard problems are marked with ♥large hearts.

- ♦Blue diamonds indicate problems that require familiarity with material from later chapters, but thematically belong where they are. Problems that require familiarity with *earlier* material are not marked, however; the book, like life, is cumulative.

- ♣Green clubs indicate problems that require familiarity with material outside the scope of this book, such as finite-state machines, linear algebra, probability, or planar graphs. These are rare.

- ♠Black spades indicate problems that require a significant amount of grunt work and/or coding. These are rare.

- ★Orange stars indicate that you are eating Lucky Charms that were manufactured before 1998. Ew.

These exercises are designed as opportunities to practice, not as targets for their own sake. The goal of each problem is not to solve that specific problem, but to exercise a certain set of skills, or to practice solving a certain *type* of problem. Partly for this reason, I don't provide solutions to the exercises; the solutions are not the point. In particular, there is no "instructor's manual"; if you can't solve a problem yourself, you probably shouldn't assign it to your students. That said, you can probably find solutions to whatever homework problems I've assigned *this* semester on the web page of whatever course I'm teaching. And nothing is stopping *you* from writing an instructor's manual!

Steal This Book!

This book is published under a Creative Commons Licence that allows you to use, redistribute, adapt, and remix its contents *without my permission,* as long as you point back to the original source. A complete electronic version of this book is freely available at any of the following locations:

- The book web site: http://jeffe.cs.illinois.edu/teaching/algorithms/
- The mnemonic shortcut: http://algorithms.wtf
- The bug-report site: https://github.com/jeffgerickson/algorithms
- The Internet Archive: https://archive.org/details/Algorithms-Jeff-Erickson

The book web site also contains several hundred pages of additional lecture notes on related and more advanced material, as well as a near-complete archive of past homeworks, exams, discussion/lab problems, and other teaching resources. Whenever I teach an algorithms class, I revise, update, and sometimes cull my teaching materials, so you may find more recent revisions on the web page of whatever course I am currently teaching.

Whether you are a student or an instructor, you are more than welcome to use any subset of this textbook or my other lecture notes in your own classes, without asking my permission—that's why I put them on the web! However, please also cite this book, either by name or with a link back to http://algorithms.wtf; this is *especially* important if you are a student, and you use my course materials to help with your homework. (Please also check with your instructor.)

However, if you are an instructor, I strongly encourage you to supplement these with additional material *that you write yourself.* Writing the material yourself will strengthen your mastery and in-class presentation of the material, which will in turn improve your students' mastery of the material. It will also get you past the frustration of dealing with the parts of this book that you don't like. All textbooks are ~~crap~~ imperfect, and this one is no exception.

Finally, **please make whatever you write freely, easily, and globally available on the open web**—not hidden behind the gates of a learning management system or some other type of paywall—so that students and instructors elsewhere can benefit from your unique insights. In particular, if you develop useful resources that directly complement this textbook, such as slides, videos, or solution manuals, please let me know so that I can add links to your resources from the book web site.

Acknowledgments

This textbook draws heavily on the contributions of countless algorithms students, teachers, and researchers. In particular, I am immensely grateful to more than three thousand Illinois students who have used my lecture notes as a primary reference, offered useful (if sometimes painful) criticism, and suffered through some truly awful early drafts. Thanks also to many colleagues and students around the world who have used these notes in their own classes and have sent helpful feedback and bug reports.

I am particularly grateful for the feedback and contributions (especially exercises) from my amazing teaching assistants:

> Aditya Ramani, Akash Gautam, Alex Steiger, Alina Ene, Amir Nayyeri, Asha Seetharam, Ashish Vulimiri, Ben Moseley, Brad Sturt, Brian Ensink, Chao Xu, Charlie Carlson, Chris Neihengen, Connor Clark, Dan Bullok, Dan Cranston, Daniel Khashabi, David Morrison, Ekta Manaktala, Erin Wolf Chambers, Gail Steitz, Gio Kao, Grant Czajkowski, Hsien-Chih Chang, Igor Gammer, Jacob Laurel, John Lee, Johnathon Fischer, Junqing Deng, Kent Quanrud, Kevin Milans, Kevin Small, Konstantinos Koiliaris, Kyle Fox, Kyle Jao, Lan Chen, Mark Idleman, Michael Bond, Mitch Harris, Naveen Arivazhagen, Nick Bachmair, Nick Hurlburt, Nirman Kumar, Nitish Korula, Patrick Lin, Phillip Shih, Rachit Agarwal, Reza Zamani-Nasab, Rishi Talreja, Rob McCann, Sahand Mozaffari, Shalan Naqvi, Shripad Thite, Spencer Gordon, Srihita Vatsavaya, Subhro Roy, Tana Wattanawaroon, Umang Mathur, Vipul Goyal, Yasu Furakawa, and Yipu Wang.

I've also been helped tremendously by many discussions with faculty colleagues at Illinois: Alexandra Kolla, Cinda Heeren, Edgar Ramos, Herbert Edelsbrunner, Jason Zych, Kim Whittlesey, Lenny Pitt, Madhu Parasarathy, Mahesh Viswanathan, Margaret Fleck, Shang-Hua Teng, Steve LaValle, and especially Chandra Chekuri, Ed Reingold, and Sariel Har-Peled.

Of course this book owes a great debt to the people who taught me this algorithms stuff in the first place: Bob Bixby and Michael Pearlman at Rice; David Eppstein, Dan Hirschberg, and George Lueker at Irvine; and Abhiram Ranade, Dick Karp, Manuel Blum, Mike Luby, and Raimund Seidel at Berkeley.

I stole the first iteration of the overall course structure, and the idea to write up my own lecture notes in the first place, from Herbert Edelsbrunner; the idea of turning a subset of my notes into a book from Steve LaValle; and several components of the book design from Robert Ghrist.

Caveat Lector!

Of course, none of those people should be blamed for any flaws in the resulting book. Despite many rounds of revision and editing, this book contains several mistakes, bugs, gaffes, omissions, snafus, kludges, typos, mathos, grammaros, thinkos, brain farts, poor design decisions, historical inaccuracies, anachronisms, inconsistencies, exaggerations, dithering, blather, distortions, oversimplifications, redundancy, logorrhea, nonsense, garbage, cruft, junk, and outright lies, **all of which are entirely Steve Skiena's fault.**

I maintain an issue tracker at https://github.com/jeffgerickson/algorithms, where readers like you can submit bug reports, feature requests, and general feedback on the book. Please let me know if you find an error of any kind, whether mathematical, grammatical, historical, typographical, cultural, or otherwise, whether in the main text, in the exercises, or in my other course materials. (Steve is unlikely to care.) Of course, all other feedback is also welcome!

Enjoy!

— Jeff

It is traditional for the author to magnanimously accept the blame for whatever deficiencies remain. I don't. Any errors, deficiencies, or problems in this book are somebody else's fault, but I would appreciate knowing about them so as to determine who is to blame.
— Steven S. Skiena, *The Algorithm Design Manual* (1997)

No doubt this statement will be followed by an annotated list of all textbooks, and why each one is crap.
— Adam Contini, MetaFilter, January 4, 2010

Table of Contents

Hinc incipit algorismus. *Haec algorismus ars praesens dicitur in qua*
talibus indorum fruimur bis quinque figuris 0. 9. 8. 7. 6. 5. 4. 3. 2. 1.

— Friar Alexander de Villa Dei, *Carmen de Algorismo* (c. 1220)

You are right to demand that an artist engage his work consciously,
but you confuse two different things:
solving the problem and correctly posing the question.

— Anton Chekhov, in a letter to A. S. Suvorin (October 27, 1888)

The more we reduce ourselves to machines in the lower things,
the more force we shall set free to use in the higher.

— Anna C. Brackett, *The Technique of Rest* (1892)

And here I am at 2:30 a.m. writing about technique, in spite of a strong conviction
that the moment a man begins to talk about technique that's proof that he is fresh
out of ideas.

— Raymond Chandler, letter to Erle Stanley Gardner (May 5, 1939)

Good men don't need rules.
Today is not the day to find out why I have so many,

— The Doctor [Matt Smith], "A Good Man Goes to War", *Doctor Who* (2011)

0

Introduction

0.1 What is an algorithm?

An algorithm is an explicit, precise, unambiguous, mechanically-executable sequence of elementary instructions, usually intended to accomplish a specific purpose. For example, here is an algorithm for singing that annoying song "99 Bottles of Beer on the Wall", for arbitrary values of 99:

$\text{BottlesOfBeer}(n)$:
 For $i \leftarrow n$ down to 1
  Sing "*i bottles of beer on the wall, i bottles of beer,*"
  Sing "*Take one down, pass it around, $i - 1$ bottles of beer on the wall.*"

 Sing "*No bottles of beer on the wall, no bottles of beer,*"
 Sing "*Go to the store, buy some more, n bottles of beer on the wall.*"

The word "algorithm" does *not* derive, as algorithmophobic classicists might guess, from the Greek roots *arithmos* (ἀριθμός), meaning "number", and *algos* (ἄλγος), meaning "pain". Rather, it is a corruption of the name of the 9th century Persian scholar Muḥammad ibn Mūsā al-Khwārizmī.[1] Al-Khwārizmī is perhaps best known as the writer of the treatise *Al-Kitāb al-mukhtaṣar fīhīsāb al-ğabr wa'l-muqābala*,[2] from which the modern word *algebra* derives. In a different treatise, al-Khwārizmī described the modern decimal system for writing and manipulating numbers—in particular, the use of a small circle or *ṣifr* to represent a missing quantity—which had been developed in India several centuries earlier. The methods described in this latter treatise, using either written figures or counting stones, became known in English as *algorism* or *augrym*, and its figures became known in English as *ciphers*.

Although both place-value notation and al-Khwārizmī's works were already known by some European scholars, the "Hindu-Arabic" numeric system was popularized in Europe by the medieval Italian mathematician and tradesman Leonardo of Pisa, better known as Fibonacci. Thanks in part to his 1202 book *Liber Abaci*,[3] written figures began to replace the counting table (then known as an *abacus*) and finger arithmetic[4] as the preferred platform for calculation[5] in Europe in the 13th century—*not* because written decimal figures were easier to learn or use, but because they provided an audit trail. Ciphers became common in Western Europe only with the advent of movable type, and truly ubiquitous only after cheap paper became plentiful in the early 19th century.

Eventually the word *algorism* evolved into the modern *algorithm*, via folk etymology from the Greek *arithmos* (and perhaps the previously mentioned *algos*).[6] Thus, until very recently, the word *algorithm* referred exclusively

---

[1]"Mohammad, father of Adbdulla, son of Moses, the Kwārizmian". Kwārizm is an ancient city, now called Khiva, in the Khorezm Province of Uzbekistan.

[2]"The Compendious Book on Calculation by Completion and Balancing"

[3]While it is tempting to translate the title *Liber Abaci* as "The Book of the Abacus", a more accurate translation is "The Book of Calculation". Both before and after Fibonacci, the Italian word *abaco* was used to describe anything related to numerical calculation—devices, methods, schools, books, and so on—much in the same way that "computer science" is used today in English, or as the Chinese phrase for "operations research" translates literally as "the study of using counting rods".

[4]☞ Reckoning with *digits*! ☜

[5]The word *calculate* derives from the Latin word *calculus*, meaning "small rock", referring to the stones on a counting table, or as Chaucer called them, *augrym stones*. In 440BCE, Herodotus wrote in his *Histories* that "The Greeks write and calculate (λογίζεσθαι ψήφοις, literally 'reckon with pebbles') from left to right; the Egyptians do the opposite. Yet they say that their way of writing is toward the right, and the Greek way toward the left." (Herodotus is strangely silent on which end of the egg the Egyptians ate first.)

[6]Some medieval sources claim that the Greek prefix "algo-" means "art" or "introduction". Others claim that algorithms were invented by a Greek philosopher, or a king of India, or perhaps a king of Spain, named "Algus" or "Algor" or "Argus". A few, possibly including Dante Alighieri, even identified the inventor with the mythological Greek shipbuilder and eponymous argonaut. It's unclear whether any of these risible claims were intended to be historically accurate, or merely mnemonic.

to mechanical techniques for place-value arithmetic using "Arabic" numerals. People trained in the fast and reliable execution of these procedures were called *algorists* or *computators*, or more simply, *computers*.

0.2 Multiplication

Although they have been a topic of formal academic study for only a few decades, algorithms have been with us since the dawn of civilization. Descriptions of step-by-step arithmetic computation are among the earliest examples of written human language, long predating the expositions by Fibonacci and al-Khwārizmī, or even the place-value notation they popularized.

Lattice Multiplication

The most familiar method for multiplying large numbers, at least for American students, is the **lattice algorithm**. This algorithm was popularized by Fibonacci in *Liber Abaci*, who learned it from Arabic sources including al-Khwārizmī, who in turn learned it from Indian sources including Brahmagupta's 7th-century treatise *Brāhmasphuṭasiddhānta*, who may have learned it from Chinese sources. The oldest surviving descriptions of the algorithm appear in *The Mathematical Classic of Sunzi*, written in China between the 3rd and 5th centuries, and in Eutocius of Ascalon's commentaries on Archimedes' *Measurement of the Circle*, written around 500CE, but there is evidence that the algorithm was known much earlier. Eutocius credits the method to a lost treatise of Apollonius of Perga, who lived around 300BCE, entitled *Okytokion* (Ὠκυτόκιον).[7] The Sumerians recorded multiplication tables on clay tablets as early as 2600BCE, suggesting that they may have used the lattice algorithm.[8]

The lattice algorithm assumes that the input numbers are represented as explicit strings of digits; I'll assume here that we're working in base ten, but the algorithm generalizes immediately to any other base. To simplify notation,[9] the

---

[7]Literally "medicine that promotes quick and easy childbirth"! Pappus of Alexandria reproduced several excerpts of *Okytokion* about 200 years before Eutocius, but his description of the lattice multiplication algorithm (if he gave one) is *also* lost.

[8]There is ample evidence that ancient Sumerians calculated accurately with extremely large numbers using their base-60 place-value numerical system, but I am not aware of any surviving record of the actual methods they used. In addition to standard multiplication and reciprocal tables, tables listing the squares of integers from 1 to 59 have been found, leading some math historians to conjecture that Babylonians multiplied using an identity like $xy = ((x+y)^2 - x^2 - y^2)/2$. But this trick only works when $x + y < 60$; history is silent on how the Babylonians might have computed x^2 when $x \geq 60$.

[9]but at the risk of inflaming the historical enmity between Greece and Egypt, or Lilliput and Blefuscu, or Macs and PCs, or people who think zero is a natural number and people who are wrong

input consists of a pair of arrays $X[0..m-1]$ and $Y[0..n-1]$, representing the numbers

$$x = \sum_{i=0}^{m-1} X[i] \cdot 10^i \quad \text{and} \quad y = \sum_{j=0}^{n-1} Y[j] \cdot 10^j,$$

and similarly, the output consists of a single array $Z[0..m+n-1]$, representing the product

$$z = x \cdot y = \sum_{k=0}^{m+n-1} Z[k] \cdot 10^k.$$

The algorithm uses addition and *single-digit* multiplication as primitive operations. Addition can be performed using a simple for-loop. In practice, single-digit multiplication is performed using a lookup table, either carved into clay tablets, painted on strips of wood or bamboo, written on paper, stored in read-only memory, or memorized by the computator. The entire lattice algorithm can be summarized by the formula

$$x \cdot y = \sum_{i=0}^{m-1} \sum_{j=0}^{n-1} \left(X[i] \cdot Y[j] \cdot 10^{i+j} \right).$$

Different variants of the lattice algorithm evaluate the partial products $X[i] \cdot Y[j] \cdot 10^{i+j}$ in different orders and use different strategies for computing their sum. For example, in *Liber Abaco*, Fibonacci describes a variant that considers the mn partial products in increasing order of significance, as shown in modern pseudocode below.

FIBONACCIMULTIPLY($X[0..m-1], Y[0..n-1]$):
 $hold \leftarrow 0$
 for $k \leftarrow 0$ to $n+m-1$
   for all i and j such that $i+j = k$
     $hold \leftarrow hold + X[i] \cdot Y[j]$
   $Z[k] \leftarrow hold \bmod 10$
   $hold \leftarrow \lfloor hold/10 \rfloor$
 return $Z[0..m+n-1]$

Fibonacci's algorithm is often executed by storing all the partial products in a two-dimensional table (often called a "tableau" or "grate" or "lattice") and then summing along the diagonals with appropriate carries, as shown on the right in Figure 0.1. American elementary-school students are taught to multiply one factor (the "multiplicand") by each digit in the other factor (the "multiplier"), writing down all the multiplicand-by-digit products before adding them up, as shown on the left in Figure 0.1. This was also the method described by Eutocius, although he fittingly considered the multiplier digits from left to right, as shown in Figure 0.2. Both of these variants (and several others) are described and illustrated side by side in the anonymous 1458 textbook *L'Arte dell'Abbaco*, also known as the *Treviso Arithmetic*, the first *printed* mathematics book in the West.

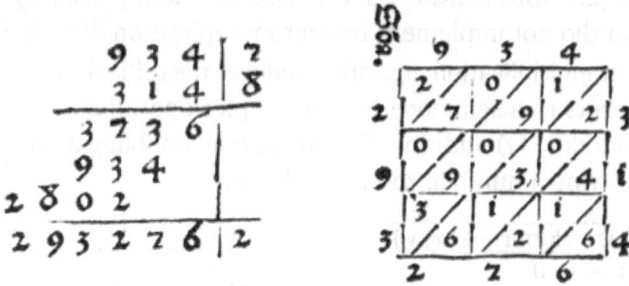

Figure 0.1. Computing $934 \times 314 = 293276$ using "long" multiplication (with error-checking by casting out nines) and "lattice" multiplication, from *L'Arte dell'Abbaco* (1458). (See Image Credits at the end of the book.)

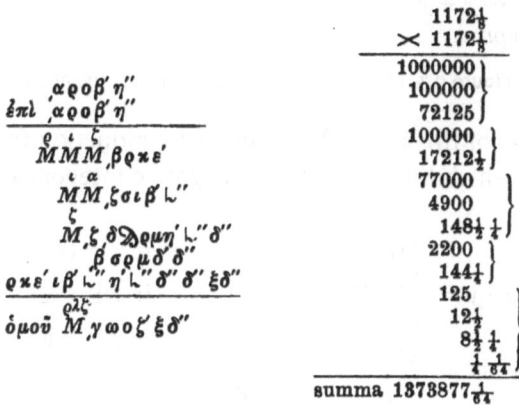

Figure 0.2. Eutocius's 6th-century calculation of $1172\frac{1}{8} \times 1172\frac{1}{8} = 1373877\frac{1}{64}$, in his commentary on Archimedes' *Measurement of the Circle*, transcribed (left) and translated into modern notation (right) by Johan Heiberg (1891). (See Image Credits at the end of the book.)

All of these variants of the lattice algorithm—and other similar variants described by Sunzi, al-Khwārizmī, Fibonacci, *L'Arte dell'Abbaco*, and many other sources—compute the product of any m-digit number and any n-digit number in $O(mn)$ *time*; the running time of every variant is dominated by the number of single-digit multiplications.

Duplation and Mediation

The lattice algorithm is not the oldest multiplication algorithm for which we have direct recorded evidence. An even older and arguably simpler algorithm, which does not rely on place-value notation, is sometimes called *Russian peasant multiplication, Ethiopian peasant multiplication,* or just **peasant multiplication**. A variant of this algorithm was copied into the Rhind papyrus by the Egyptian scribe Ahmes around 1650BCE, from a document he claimed was (then) about 350 years old.[10] This algorithm was still taught in elementary schools in Eastern Europe in the late 20th century; it was also commonly used by early digital computers that did not implement integer multiplication directly in hardware.

The peasant multiplication algorithm reduces the difficult task of multiplying arbitrary numbers to a sequence of four simpler operations: (1) determining parity (even or odd), (2) addition, (3) *duplation* (doubling a number), and (4) *mediation* (halving a number, rounding down).

PEASANTMULTIPLY(x, y):
  $prod \leftarrow 0$
  while $x > 0$
    if x is odd
      $prod \leftarrow prod + y$
    $x \leftarrow \lfloor x/2 \rfloor$
    $y \leftarrow y + y$
  return $prod$

x	y		$prod$
			0
123	$+456$	$=$	456
61	$+912$	$=$	1368
30	~~1824~~		
15	$+3648$	$=$	5016
7	$+7296$	$=$	12312
3	$+14592$	$=$	26904
1	$+29184$	$=$	56088

Figure 0.3. Multiplication by duplation and mediation

The correctness of this algorithm follows by induction from the following recursive identity, which holds for all non-negative integers x and y:

$$x \cdot y = \begin{cases} 0 & \text{if } x = 0 \\ \lfloor x/2 \rfloor \cdot (y + y) & \text{if } x \text{ is even} \\ \lfloor x/2 \rfloor \cdot (y + y) + y & \text{if } x \text{ is odd} \end{cases}$$

Arguably, this recurrence *is* the peasant multiplication algorithm. Don't let the iterative pseudocode fool you; the algorithm is fundamentally recursive!

As stated, PEASANTMULTIPLY performs $O(\log x)$ parity, addition, and mediation operations, but we can improve this bound to $O(\log \min\{x, y\})$ by swapping the two arguments when $x > y$. Assuming the numbers are represented using any reasonable place-value notation (like binary, decimal, Babylonian hexagesimal, Egyptian duodecimal, Roman numeral, Chinese counting rods, bead positions on an abacus, and so on), each operation requires at most $O(\log(xy)) = O(\log \max\{x, y\})$ single-digit operations, so the overall running time of the algorithm is $O(\log \min\{x, y\} \cdot \log \max\{x, y\}) = O(\log x \cdot \log y)$.

---

[10]The version of this algorithm actually used in ancient Egypt does not use mediation or parity, but it does use comparisons. To avoid halving, the algorithm pre-computes two tables by repeated doubling: one containing all the powers of 2 not exceeding x, the other containing the same powers of 2 multiplied by y. The powers of 2 that sum to x are then found by greedy subtraction, and the corresponding entries in the other table are added together to form the product.

In other words, this algorithm requires $O(mn)$ *time* to multiply an m-digit number by an n-digit number; up to constant factors, this is the same running time as the lattice algorithm. This algorithm requires (a constant factor!) more paperwork to execute by hand than the lattice algorithm, but the necessary primitive operations are arguably easier for humans to perform. In fact, the two algorithms are equivalent when numbers are represented in binary.

Compass and Straightedge

Classical Greek geometers identified numbers (or more accurately, *magnitudes*) with line segments of the appropriate length, which they manipulated using two simple mechanical tools—the compass and the straightedge—versions of which had already been in common use by surveyors, architects, and other artisans for centuries. Using *only* these two tools, these scholars reduced several complex geometric constructions to the following primitive operations, starting with one or more identified reference points.

- Draw the unique line passing through two distinct identified points.
- Draw the unique circle centered at one identified point and passing through another.
- Identify the intersection point (if any) of two lines.
- Identify the intersection points (if any) of a line and a circle.
- Identify the intersection points (if any) of two circles.

In practice, Greek geometry students almost certainly drew their constructions on an *abax* (ἄβαξ), a table covered in dust or sand.[11] Centuries earlier, Egyptian surveyors carried out many of the same constructions using ropes to determine straight lines and circles on the ground.[12] However, Euclid and other Greek geometers presented compass and straightedge constructions as precise mathematical *abstractions*—points are *ideal* points; lines are *ideal* lines; and circles are *ideal* circles.

Figure 0.4 shows an algorithm, described in Euclid's *Elements* about 2500 years ago, for multiplying or dividing two magnitudes. The input consists of four distinct points A, B, C, and D, and the goal is to construct a point Z such that $|AZ| = |AC||AD|/|AB|$. In particular, if we define $|AB|$ to be our unit of length, then the algorithm computes the product of $|AC|$ and $|AD|$.

Notice that Euclid first defines a new primitive operation RIGHTANGLE by (as modern programmers would phrase it) writing a subroutine. The correctness

---

[11]The written numerals 1 through 9 were known in Europe at least two centuries before Fibonacci's *Liber Abaci* as "gobar numerals", from the Arabic word *ghubār* meaning dust, ultimately referring to the Indian practice of performing arithmetic on tables covered with sand. The Greek word ἄβαξ is the origin of the Latin *abacus*, which also originally referred to a sand table.

[12]Remember what "geometry" means? Democritus would later refer to these Egyptian surveyors, somewhat derisively, as *arpedonaptai* (ἀρπεδονάπται), meaning "rope-fasteners".

⟨⟨*Construct the line perpendicular to ℓ passing through P.*⟩⟩
RIGHTANGLE(ℓ, P):
    Choose a point $A \in \ell$
    $A, B \leftarrow$ INTERSECT(CIRCLE(P, A), ℓ)
    $C, D \leftarrow$ INTERSECT(CIRCLE(A, B), CIRCLE(B, A))
    return LINE(C, D)

⟨⟨*Construct a point Z such that* $|AZ| = |AC||AD|/|AB|$.⟩⟩
MULTIPLYORDIVIDE(A, B, C, D):
    $\alpha \leftarrow$ RIGHTANGLE(LINE(A, C), A)
    $E \leftarrow$ INTERSECT(CIRCLE(A, B), α)
    $F \leftarrow$ INTERSECT(CIRCLE(A, D), α)
    $\beta \leftarrow$ RIGHTANGLE(LINE(E, C), F)
    $\gamma \leftarrow$ RIGHTANGLE(β, F)
    return INTERSECT(γ, LINE(A, C))

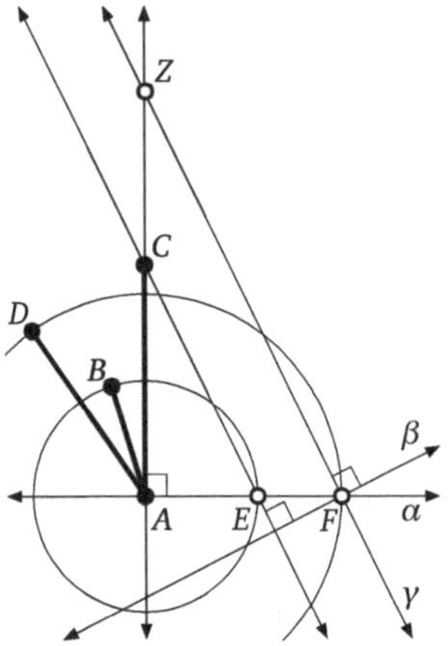

Figure 0.4. Multiplication by compass and straightedge.

of the algorithm follows from the observation that triangles ACE and AZF are similar. The second and third lines of the main algorithm are ambiguous, because α intersects any circle centered at A at *two* distinct points, but the algorithm is actually correct no matter which intersection points are chosen for E and F.

Euclid's algorithm reduces the problem of multiplying two magnitudes (lengths) to a series of primitive compass-and-straightedge operations. These operations are difficult to implement precisely on a modern digital computer, but Euclid's algorithm wasn't *designed* for a digital computer. It was designed for the Platonic Ideal Geometer, wielding the Platonic Ideal Compass and the Platonic Ideal Straightedge, who could execute each operation perfectly in constant time *by definition.* In this model of computation, MULTIPLYORDIVIDE runs in $O(1)$ time!

0.3 Congressional Apportionment

Here is another real-world example of an algorithm of significant political importance. Article I, Section 2 of the United States Constitution requires that

> Representatives and direct Taxes shall be apportioned among the several States which may be included within this Union, according to their respective Numbers.... The Number of Representatives shall not exceed one for every thirty Thousand, but each State shall have at Least one Representative....

Because there are only a finite number of seats in the House of Representatives, *exact* proportional representation requires either shared or fractional representatives, neither of which are legal. As a result, over the next several decades, many different apportionment algorithms were proposed and used to round the ideal fractional solution fairly. The algorithm actually used today, called

the **Huntington-Hill method** or the **method of equal proportions**, was first
suggested by Census Bureau statistician Joseph Hill in 1911, refined by Harvard
mathematician Edward Huntington in 1920, adopted into Federal law (2 U.S.C.
§2a) in 1941, and survived a Supreme Court challenge in 1992.[13]

The Huntington-Hill method allocates representatives to states one at a
time. First, in a preprocessing stage, each state is allocated one representative.
Then in each iteration of the main loop, the next representative is assigned
to the state with the highest *priority*. The priority of each state is defined
to be $P/\sqrt{r(r+1)}$, where P is the state's population and r is the number of
representatives already allocated to that state.

The algorithm is described in pseudocode in Figure 0.5. The input consists of
an array $Pop[1..n]$ storing the populations of the n states and an integer R equal
to the total number of representatives; the algorithm assumes $R \geq n$. (Currently,
in the United States, $n = 50$ and $R = 435$.) The output array $Rep[1..n]$ records
the number of representatives allocated to each state.

$\text{ApportionCongress}(Pop[1..n], R):$
    $PQ \leftarrow \text{NewPriorityQueue}$

    ⟨⟨*Give every state its first representative*⟩⟩
    for $s \leftarrow 1$ to n
        $Rep[s] \leftarrow 1$
        $\text{Insert}\left(PQ, s, Pop[i]/\sqrt{2}\right)$

    ⟨⟨*Allocate the remaining $n - R$ representatives*⟩⟩
    for $i \leftarrow 1$ to $n - R$
        $s \leftarrow \text{ExtractMax}(PQ)$
        $Rep[s] \leftarrow Rep[s] + 1$
        $priority \leftarrow Pop[s]/\sqrt{Rep[s](Rep[s]+1)}$
        $\text{Insert}(PQ, s, priority)$

    return $Rep[1..n]$

Figure 0.5. The Huntington-Hill apportionment algorithm

This implementation of Huntington-Hill uses a priority queue that supports
the operations NewPriorityQueue, Insert, and ExtractMax. (The actual
law doesn't say anything about priority queues, of course.) The output of the
algorithm, and therefore its correctness, does not depend *at all* on how this

---

[13]Overruling an earlier ruling by a federal district court, the Supreme Court unanimously
held that *any* apportionment method adopted in good faith by Congress is constitutional (*United
States Department of Commerce v. Montana*). The current congressional apportionment algorithm
is described in gruesome detail at the U.S. Census Department web site http://www.census.gov/
topics/public-sector/congressional-apportionment.html. A good history of the apportionment
problem can be found at http://www.thirty-thousand.org/pages/Apportionment.htm. A report
by the Congressional Research Service describing various apportionment methods is available at
http://www.fas.org/sgp/crs/misc/R41382.pdf.

priority queue is implemented. The Census Bureau uses a sorted array, stored in a single column of an Excel spreadsheet, which is recalculated from scratch at every iteration. You (should have) learned a more efficient implementation in your undergraduate data structures class.

Similar apportionment algorithms are used in multi-party parliamentary elections around the world, where the number of seats allocated to each party is supposed to be proportional to the number of votes that party receives. The two most common are the *D'Hondt method*[14] and the *Webster–Sainte-Laguë method*,[15] which respectively use priorities $P/(r+1)$ and $P/(2r+1)$ in place of the square-root expression in Huntington-Hill. The Huntington-Hill method is essentially unique to the United States House of Representatives, thanks in part to the constitutional requirement that each state must be allocated at least one representative.

0.4 A Bad Example

As a prototypical example of a sequence of instructions that is *not* actually an algorithm, consider "Martin's algorithm":[16]

BeAMillionaireAndNeverPayTaxes():
  Get a million dollars.
  If the tax man comes to your door and says, *"You have never paid taxes!"*
    Say *"I forgot."*

Pretty simple, except for that first step; it's a doozy! A group of billionaire CEOs, Silicon Valley venture capitalists, or New York City real-estate hustlers might consider this an algorithm, because for them the first step is both unambiguous and trivial,[17] but for the rest of us poor slobs, Martin's procedure is too vague to be considered an actual algorithm. On the other hand, this is a perfect example of a **reduction**—it *reduces* the problem of being a millionaire and never paying taxes to the "easier" problem of acquiring a million dollars. We'll see reductions over and over again in this book. As hundreds of businessmen and politicians have demonstrated, if you know how to solve the easier problem, a reduction tells you how to solve the harder one.

---

[14]developed by Thomas Jefferson in 1792, used for U.S. Congressional apportionment from 1792 to 1832, rediscovered by Belgian mathematician Victor D'Hondt in 1878, and refined by Swiss physicist Eduard Hagenbach-Bischoff in 1888.

[15]developed by Daniel Webster in 1832, used for U.S. Congressional apportionment from 1842 to 1911, rediscovered by French mathematician André Sainte-Laguë in 1910, and rediscovered again by German physicist Hans Schepers in 1980.

[16]Steve Martin, "You Can Be A Millionaire", *Saturday Night Live*, January 21, 1978. Also appears on *Comedy Is Not Pretty*, Warner Bros. Records, 1979.

[17]Something something secure quantum blockchain deep-learning something.

Martin's algorithm, like some of our previous examples, is not the kind of algorithm that computer scientists are used to thinking about, because it is phrased in terms of operations that are difficult for computers to perform. This book focuses (almost!) exclusively on algorithms that can be reasonably implemented on a standard digital computer. Each step in these algorithms is either directly supported by common programming languages (such as arithmetic, assignments, loops, or recursion) or something that you've already learned how to do (like sorting, binary search, tree traversal, or singing "n Bottles of Beer on the Wall").

0.5 Describing Algorithms

The skills required to effectively *design and analyze* algorithms are entangled with the skills required to effectively *describe* algorithms. At least in my classes, a complete description of any algorithm has four components:

- **What:** A precise specification of the problem that the algorithm solves.
- **How:** A precise description of the algorithm itself.
- **Why:** A proof that the algorithm solves the problem it is supposed to solve.
- **How fast:** An analysis of the running time of the algorithm.

It is not necessary (or even advisable) to *develop* these four components in this particular order. Problem specifications, algorithm descriptions, correctness proofs, and time analyses usually evolve simultaneously, with the development of each component informing the development of the others. For example, we may need to tweak the problem description to support a faster algorithm, or modify the algorithm to handle a tricky case in the proof of correctness. Nevertheless, *presenting* these components separately is usually clearest for the reader.

As with any writing, it's important to aim your descriptions at the right audience; I recommend writing for a competent but skeptical programmer *who is not as clever as you are*. Think of yourself six months ago. As you develop any new algorithm, you will naturally build up lots of intuition about the problem and about how your algorithm solves it, and your informal reasoning will be guided by that intuition. But anyone *reading* your algorithm later, or the code you derive from it, won't share your intuition or experience. Neither will your compiler. Neither will you six months from now. All they will have is your written description.

Even if you never have to explain your algorithms to anyone else, it's still important to develop them with an audience in mind. Trying to communicate clearly forces you to *think* more clearly. In particular, writing for a *novice* audience, who will interpret your words *exactly* as written, forces you to work through fine details, no matter how "obvious" or "intuitive" your high-level ideas may seem at the moment. Similarly, writing for a *skeptical* audience forces you to develop robust arguments for correctness and efficiency, instead of trusting your intuition or your intelligence.[18]

I cannot emphasize this point enough: **Your primary job as an algorithm designer is *teaching other people* how and why your algorithms work.** If you can't communicate your ideas to other human beings, they may as well not exist. Producing correct and efficient executable code is an important but secondary goal. Convincing yourself, your professors, your (prospective) employers, your colleagues, or your students that you are smart is at best a distant third.

Specifying the Problem

Before we can even start developing a new algorithm, we have to agree on what problem our algorithm is supposed to solve. Similarly, before we can even start *describing* an algorithm, we have to *describe* the problem that the algorithm is supposed to solve.

Algorithmic problems are often presented using standard English, in terms of real-world objects. It's up to us, the algorithm designers, to restate these problems in terms of formal, abstract, *mathematical* objects—numbers, arrays, lists, graphs, trees, and so on—that we can reason about formally. We must also determine if the problem statement carries any hidden assumptions, and state those assumptions explicitly. (For example, in the song "n Bottles of Beer on the Wall", n is always a non-negative integer.[19])

We may need to refine our specification as we develop the algorithm. For example, our algorithm may require a particular input representation, or produce a particular output representation, that was left unspecified in the original informal problem description. Or our algorithm might actually solve a *more general* problem than we were originally asked to solve. (This is a common feature of recursive algorithms.)

The specification should include just enough detail that someone else could *use* our algorithm as a black box, without knowing how or why the algorithm actually works. In particular, we must describe the type *and meaning* of each input parameter, and exactly how the eventual output depends on the input parameters. On the other hand, our specification should *deliberately hide* any details that are *not* necessary to use the algorithm as a black box. Let that which does not matter truly slide.

---

[18]In particular, I assume that *you* are a skeptical novice!

[19]I've never heard anyone sing "$\sqrt{2}$ Bottles of Beer on the Wall." Occasionally I *have* heard set theorists singing "$\aleph_0$ bottles of beer on the wall", but for some reason they always gave up before the song was over.

For example, the lattice and duplation-and-mediation algorithms both solve the same problem: Given two non-negative integers x and y, each represented as an array of digits, compute the product $x \cdot y$, also represented as an array of digits. To someone *using* these algorithms, the choice of algorithm is completely irrelevant. On the other hand, the Greek straightedge-and-compass algorithm solves a *different problem*, because the input and output values are represented by line segments instead of arrays of digits.

Describing the Algorithm

Computer programs are concrete representations of algorithms, but algorithms are *not* programs. Rather, algorithms are abstract mechanical procedures that can be implemented in *any* programming language that supports the underlying primitive operations. The idiosyncratic syntactic details of your favorite programming language are utterly irrelevant; focusing on these will only distract you (and your readers) from what's *really* going on.[20] A good algorithm description is closer to what we should write in the *comments* of a real program than the code itself. Code is a poor medium for storytelling.

On the other hand, a plain English prose description is usually not a good idea either. Algorithms have lots of idiomatic structure—especially conditionals, loops, function calls, and recursion—that are far too easily hidden by unstructured prose. Colloquial English is full of ambiguities and shades of meaning, but algorithms must be described as unambiguously as possible. Prose is a poor medium for precision.

In my opinion, the clearest way to present an algorithm is using a combination of *pseudo*code and structured English. Pseudocode uses the *structure* of formal programming languages and mathematics to break algorithms into primitive steps; the primitive steps themselves can be written using mathematical notation, pure English, or an appropriate mixture of the two, *whatever is clearest*. Well-written pseudocode reveals the internal structure of the algorithm but hides irrelevant implementation details, making the algorithm easier to understand, analyze, debug, and implement.

---

[20]This is, of course, a matter of religious conviction. Armchair linguists argue incessantly over the *Sapir-Whorf hypothesis*, which states (more or less) that people think only in the categories imposed by their languages. According to an extreme formulation of this principle, some concepts in one language simply cannot be understood by speakers of other languages, not just because of technological advancement—How would you translate "jump the shark" or "Fortnite streamer" into Aramaic?—but because of inherent structural differences between languages and cultures. For a more skeptical view, see Steven Pinker's *The Language Instinct*. There is admittedly some strength to this idea when applied to different programming paradigms. (What's the Y combinator, again? How do templates work? What's an Abstract Factory?) Fortunately, those differences are too subtle to have any impact on the material in *this* book. For a compelling counterexample, see Chris Okasaki's monograph *Functional Data Structures* and its more recent descendants.

Whenever we describe an algorithm, our description should include every detail necessary to fully specify the algorithm, prove its correctness, and analyze its running time. At the same time, it should *exclude* any details that are *not* necessary to fully specify the algorithm, prove its correctness, and analyze its running time. (Slide.) At a more practical level, our description should allow a competent but skeptical programmer *who has not read this book* to quickly and correctly implement the algorithm in *their* favorite programming language, *without understanding why it works*.

I don't want to bore you with the rules I follow for writing pseudocode, but I must caution against one especially pernicious habit. **Never** describe repeated operations informally, as in "Do [this] first, then do [that] second, **and so on**." or "Repeat **this process** until [something]". As anyone who has taken one of those frustrating "What comes next in this sequence?" tests already knows, describing the first few steps of an algorithm says little or nothing about what happens in later steps. If your algorithm has a loop, write it as a loop, and explicitly describe what happens in an *arbitrary* iteration. Similarly, if your algorithm is recursive, write it recursively, and explicitly describe the case boundaries and what happens in each case.

0.6 Analyzing Algorithms

It's not enough just to write down an algorithm and say "Behold!" We must also convince our audience (and ourselves!) that the algorithm actually does what it's supposed to do, and that it does so efficiently.

Correctness

In some application settings, it is acceptable for programs to behave correctly most of the time, on all "reasonable" inputs. Not in this book; we require algorithms that are *always* correct, for *all possible* inputs. Moreover, we must *prove* that our algorithms are correct; trusting our instincts, or trying a few test cases, isn't good enough. Sometimes correctness is truly obvious, especially for algorithms you've seen in earlier courses. On the other hand, "obvious" is all too often a synonym for "wrong". Most of the algorithms we discuss in this course require real work to prove correct. In particular, correctness proofs usually involve induction. We *like* induction. Induction is our *friend*.[21]

Of course, before we can formally prove that our algorithm does what it's supposed to do, we have to formally describe what it's supposed to do!

---

[21]If induction is *not* your friend, you will have a hard time with this book.

Running Time

The most common way of ranking different algorithms for the same problem is by how quickly they run. Ideally, we want the fastest possible algorithm for any particular problem. In many application settings, it is acceptable for programs to run efficiently most of the time, on all "reasonable" inputs. Not in this book; we require algorithms that *always* run efficiently, even in the worst case.

But how do we measure running time? As a specific example, how long does it take to sing the song BOTTLESOFBEER(n)? This is obviously a function of the input value n, but it also depends on how quickly you can sing. Some singers might take ten seconds to sing a verse; others might take twenty. Technology widens the possibilities even further. Dictating the song over a telegraph using Morse code might take a full minute per verse. Downloading an mp3 over the Web might take a tenth of a second per verse. Duplicating the mp3 in a computer's main memory might take only a few microseconds per verse.

What's important here is how the singing time changes as n grows. Singing BOTTLESOFBEER($2n$) requires about twice much time as singing BOTTLESOF-BEER(n), no matter what technology is being used. This is reflected in the asymptotic singing time $\Theta(n)$.

We can measure time by counting how many times the algorithm executes a certain instruction or reaches a certain milestone in the "code". For example, we might notice that the word "beer" is sung three times in every verse of BOTTLESOFBEER, so the number of times you sing "beer" is a good indication of the total singing time. For this question, we can give an exact answer: BOTTLESOFBEER(n) mentions beer exactly $3n + 3$ times.

Incidentally, there are *lots* of songs with quadratic singing time. This one is probably familiar to most English-speakers:

```
NDAYSOFCHRISTMAS(gifts[2 .. n]):
    for i ← 1 to n
        Sing "On the ith day of Christmas, my true love gave to me"
        for j ← i down to 2
            Sing "j gifts[j],"
        if i > 1
            Sing "and"
        Sing "a partridge in a pear tree."
```

The input to NDAYSOFCHRISTMAS is a list of $n-1$ gifts, represented here as an array. It's quite easy to show that the singing time is $\Theta(n^2)$; in particular, the singer mentions the name of a gift $\sum_{i=1}^{n} i = n(n+1)/2$ times (counting the partridge in the pear tree). It's also easy to see that during the first n days of Christmas, my true love gave to me exactly $\sum_{i=1}^{n} \sum_{j=1}^{i} j = n(n+1)(n+2)/6 = \Theta(n^3)$ gifts.

Other quadratic-time songs include "Old MacDonald Had a Farm", "There Was an Old Lady Who Swallowed a Fly", "Hole in the Bottom of the Sea", "Green Grow the Rushes O", "The Rattlin' Bog", "The Court Of King Caractacus","The Barley-Mow", "If I Were Not Upon the Stage", "Ist das nicht ein Schnitzelbank?",[22]"Il Pulcino Pio", "Minkurinn í hænsnakofanum", "Echad Mi Yodea", and "Το κοκοράκι". For more examples, consult your favorite preschooler.

Alouette(*lapart*[1..*n*]):
    Chantez « *Alouette, gentille alouette, alouette, je te plumerai.* »
    pour tout *i* de 1 à *n*
        Chantez « *Je te plumerai* **lapart**[*i*]. *Je te plumerai* **lapart**[*i*]. »
        pour tout *j* de *i* à 1 ⟨⟨*à rebours*⟩⟩
            Chantez « *Et* **lapart**[*j*]*! Et* **lapart**[*j*]*!* »
        Chantez « *Alouette! Alouette! Aaaaaa...* »
        Chantez « *...alouette, gentille allouette, alouette, je te plumerai.* »

A few songs have even more bizarre singing times. A fairly modern example is "The TELNET Song" by Guy Steele, which actually takes $\Theta(2^n)$ time to sing the first *n* verses; Steele recommended $n = 4$. Finally, there are some songs that *never* end.[23]

Except for "The TELNET Song", all of these songs are most naturally expressed as a small set of nested loops, so their ~~running~~ singing times can be computed using nested summations. The running time of a *recursive* algorithm is more easily expressed as a recurrence. For example, the peasant multiplication algorithm can be expressed recursively as follows:

$$x \cdot y = \begin{cases} 0 & \text{if } x = 0 \\ \lfloor x/2 \rfloor \cdot (y + y) & \text{if } x \text{ is even} \\ \lfloor x/2 \rfloor \cdot (y + y) + y & \text{if } x \text{ is odd} \end{cases}$$

Let $T(x, y)$ denote the number of parity, addition, and mediation operations required to compute $x \cdot y$. This function satisfies the recursive inequality $T(x, y) \leq T(\lfloor x/2 \rfloor, 2y) + 2$ with base case $T(0, y) = 0$. Techniques described in the next chapter imply the upper bound $T(x, y) = O(\log x)$.

Sometimes the running time of an algorithm depends on a particular implementation of some underlying data structure of subroutine. For example, the Huntington-Hill apportionment algorithm ApportionCongress runs in $O(N + RI + (R - n)E)$ time, where N denotes the running time of NewPriority-Queue, I denotes the running time of Insert, and E denotes the running time

---

[22] Ja, das ist Otto von Schnitzelpusskrankengescheitmeyer!
[23] They just go on and on, my friend.

of EXTRACTMAX. Under the reasonable assumption that $R \geq 2n$ (on average, each state gets at least two representatives), we can simplify this bound to $O(N + R(I + E))$. The precise running time depends on the implementation of the underlying priority queue. The Census Bureau implements the priority queue as an unsorted array, which gives us $N = I = \Theta(1)$ and $E = \Theta(n)$, so the Census Bureau's implementation of APPORTIONCONGRESS runs in $O(Rn)$ *time*. However, if we implement the priority queue as a binary heap or a heap-ordered array, we have $N = \Theta(1)$ and $I = E = O(\log n)$, so the overall algorithm runs in $O(R \log n)$ time.

Finally, sometimes we are interested in computational resources other than time, such as space, number of coin flips, number of cache or page faults, number of inter-process messages, or the number of gifts my true love gave to me. These resources can be analyzed using the same techniques used to analyze running time. For example, lattice multiplication of two n-digit numbers requires $O(n^2)$ space if we write down all the partial products before adding them, but only $O(n)$ space if we add them on the fly.

Exercises

0. Describe and analyze an efficient algorithm that determines, given a legal arrangement of standard pieces on a standard chess board, which player will win at chess from the given starting position if both players play perfectly. *[Hint: There is a trivial one-line solution!]*

♥1. (a) Identify (or write) a song that requires $\Theta(n^3)$ time to sing the first n verses.

   (b) Identify (or write) a song that requires $\Theta(n \log n)$ time to sing the first n verses.

   (c) Identify (or write) a song that requires some other weird amount of time to sing the first n verses.

2. Careful readers might complain that our analysis of songs like "n Bottles of Beer on the Wall" or "The n Days of Christmas" is overly simplistic, because larger numbers take longer to sing than shorter numbers. More generally, because there are only so many words of a given length, larger sets of words necessarily contain longer words.[24] We can more accurately estimate singing time by counting the number of *syllables* sung, rather than the number of *words*.

   (a) How long does it take to sing the integer n?

---

[24] Ja, das ist das Subatomarteilchenbeschleunigungsnaturmäßigkeitsuntersuchungsmaschine!

(b) How long does it take to sing "n Bottles of Beer on the Wall"?

(c) How long does it take to sing "The n Days of Christmas"?

As usual, express your answers in the form $O(f(n))$ for some function f.

3. The cumulative drinking song "The Barley Mow" has been sung throughout the British Isles for centuries. The song has many variants; Figure 0.6 contains pseudolyrics for one version traditionally sung in Devon and Cornwall, where *vessel*[i] is the name of a vessel that holds 2^i ounces of beer.[25]

BarleyMow(n):
  "Here's a health to the barley-mow, my brave boys,"
  "Here's a health to the barley-mow!"

  "We'll drink it out of the jolly brown bowl,"
  "Here's a health to the barley-mow!"
  "Here's a health to the barley-mow, my brave boys,"
  "Here's a health to the barley-mow!"

  for $i \leftarrow 1$ to n
    "We'll drink it out of the vessel[i], boys,"
    "Here's a health to the barley-mow!"
    for $j \leftarrow i$ downto 1
      "The vessel[j],"
    "And the jolly brown bowl!"
    "Here's a health to the barley-mow!"
    "Here's a health to the barley-mow, my brave boys,"
    "Here's a health to the barley-mow!"

Figure 0.6. "The Barley Mow".

(a) Suppose each name *vessel*[i] is a single word, and you can sing four words a second. How long would it take you to sing BarleyMow(n)? (Give a tight asymptotic bound.)

(b) If you want to sing this song for arbitrarily large values of n, you'll have to make up your own vessel names. To avoid repetition, these names must become progressively longer as n increases. Suppose *vessel*[n] has

---

[25]In practice, the song uses some subset of the following vessels; nipperkin, quarter-gill, half-a-gill, gill, quarter-pint, half-a-pint, pint, quart, pottle, gallon, half-anker, anker, firkin, half-barrel/kilderkin, barrel, hogshead, pipe/butt, tun, well, river, and ocean. With a few exceptions (especially at the end), every vessel in this list has twice the volume of its predecessor. Irish and Scottish versions of the song have slightly different lyrics, and they usually switch to people (barmaid, landlord, drayer, and so on) after "gallon".

An early version of the song entitled "Give us once a drink" appears in the play *Jack Drum's Entertainment (or the Comedie of Pasquill and Katherine)* written by John Marston around 1600. ("Giue vs once a drinke for and the black bole. Sing gentle Butler *bally moy*!") There is some disagreement whether Marston wrote the "high Dutch Song" specifically for the play, whether "bally moy" is a mondegreen for "barley mow" or vice versa, or whether it's actually the same song at all. These discussions are best had over n bottles of beer.

$\Theta(\log n)$ syllables, and you can sing six syllables per second. Now how long would it take you to sing BARLEYMOW(n)? (Give a tight asymptotic bound.)

(c) Suppose each time you mention the name of a vessel, you actually drink the corresponding amount of beer: one ounce for the jolly brown bowl, and 2^i ounces for each *vessel*[i]. Assuming for purposes of this problem that you are at least 21 years old, *exactly* how many ounces of beer would you drink if you sang BARLEYMOW(n)? (Give an *exact* answer, not just an asymptotic bound.)

4. Recall that the input to the Huntington-Hill algorithm APPORTIONCONGRESS is an array *Pop*[$1 .. n$], where *Pop*[i] is the population of the ith state, and an integer R, the total number of representatives to be allotted. The output is an array *Rep*[$1 .. n$], where *Rep*[i] is the number of representatives allotted to the ith state by the algorithm.

The Huntington-Hill algorithm is sometimes described in a way that avoids the use of priority queues entirely. The top-level algorithm "guesses" a positive real number D, called the *divisor*, and then runs the following subroutine to compute an apportionment. The variable q is the ideal *quota* of representatives allocated to a state for the given divisor D; the actual number of representatives allocated is always either $\lceil q \rceil$ or $\lfloor q \rfloor$.

```
HHGUESS(Pop[1 .. n], R, D):
    reps ← 0
    for i ← 1 to n
        q ← Pop[i]/D
        if q · q < ⌈q⌉ · ⌊q⌋
            Rep[i] ← ⌊q⌋
        else
            Rep[i] ← ⌈q⌉
        reps ← reps + Rep[i]
    return reps
```

There are three possibilities for the final return value *reps*. If *reps* $< R$, we did not allocate enough representatives, which (at least intuitively) means our divisor D was too small. If *reps* $> R$, we allocated too many representatives, which (at least intuitively) means our divisor D was too large. Finally, if *reps* $= R$, we can return the array *Rep*[$1 .. n$] as the final apportionment. In practice, we can compute a valid apportionment (with *reps* $= R$) by calling HHGUESS with a small number of integer divisors close to the *standard* divisor $D = P/R$.

In the following problems, let $P = \sum_{i=1}^{n} Pop[i]$ denote the total population of all n states, and assume that $n \le R \le P$.

(a) Show that calling HHGUESS with the standard divisor $D = P/R$ does *not* necessarily yield a valid apportionment.

(b) Prove that if HHGUESS returns the same value of *reps* for two different divisors D and D', it also computes the same allocation $Rep[1..n]$ for both of those divisors.

(c) Prove that if HHGUESS returns the correct value R, it computes the same allocation $Rep[1..n]$ as our earlier algorithm APPORTIONCONGRESS.

(d) Prove that a "correct" divisor D does not necessarily exist! That is, describe inputs $Pop[1..n]$ and R, where $n \leq R \leq P$, such that for *every* real number $D > 0$, the number of representatives allocated by HHGUESS is not equal to R. [*Hint: What happens if we change $<$ to $\leq$ in the fourth line of HHGUESS?*]

The control of a large force is the same principle as the control of a few men:
it is merely a question of dividing up their numbers.

— Sun Zi, *The Art of War* (c. 400CE), translated by Lionel Giles (1910)

Our life is frittered away by detail.... Simplify, simplify.

— Henry David Thoreau, *Walden* (1854)

Now, don't ask me what Voom is. I never will know.
But, boy! Let me tell you, it DOES clean up snow!

— Dr. Seuss [Theodor Seuss Geisel], *The Cat in the Hat Comes Back* (1958)

Do the hard jobs first. The easy jobs will take care of themselves.

— attributed to Dale Carnegie

1

Recursion

1.1 Reductions

Reduction is the single most common technique used in designing algorithms. Reducing one problem X to another problem Y means to write an algorithm for X that uses an algorithm for Y as a black box or subroutine. Crucially, the correctness of the resulting algorithm for X cannot depend in any way on *how* the algorithm for Y works. The only thing we can assume is that the black box solves Y correctly. The inner workings of the black box are simply *none of our business*; they're somebody else's problem. It's often best to literally think of the black box as functioning purely by magic.

For example, the peasant multiplication algorithm described in the previous chapter reduces the problem of multiplying two arbitrary positive integers to three simpler problems: addition, mediation (halving), and parity-checking. The algorithm relies on an abstract "positive integer" data type that supports those three operations, but the correctness of the multiplication algorithm does not depend on the precise data representation (tally marks, clay tokens, Babylonian hexagesimal, quipu, counting rods, Roman numerals, finger positions, augrym stones, gobar numerals, binary, negabinary, Gray code, balanced ternary, phinary, quater-imaginary, . . .), or on the precise implementations of those operations. Of course, the *running time* of the multiplication algorithm depends on the *running time* of the addition, mediation, and parity operations, but that's a separate issue from *correctness*. Most importantly, we can create a more efficient multiplication algorithm just by switching to a more efficient number representation (from tally marks to place-value notation, for example).

Similarly, the Huntington-Hill algorithm reduces the problem of apportioning Congress to the problem of maintaining a priority queue that supports the operations INSERT and EXTRACTMAX. The abstract data type "priority queue" is a black box; the correctness of the apportionment algorithm does not depend on any specific priority queue data structure. Of course, the *running time* of the apportionment algorithm depends on the *running time* of the INSERT and EXTRACTMAX algorithms, but that's a separate issue from the *correctness* of the algorithm. The beauty of the reduction is that we can create a more efficient apportionment algorithm by simply swapping in a new priority queue data structure. Moreover, the designer of that data structure does not need to know or care that it will be used to apportion Congress.

When we design algorithms, we may not know exactly how the basic building blocks we use are implemented, or how our algorithms might be used as building blocks to solve even bigger problems. That ignorance is uncomfortable for many beginners, but it is both unavoidable and extremely useful. Even when you do know precisely how your components work, it is often *extremely* helpful to pretend that you don't.

1.2 Simplify and Delegate

Recursion is a particularly powerful kind of reduction, which can be described loosely as follows:

- If the given instance of the problem can be solved directly, solve it directly.
- Otherwise, reduce it to one or more **simpler instances of the same problem**.

If the self-reference is confusing, it may be helpful to imagine that someone else is going to solve the simpler problems, just as you would assume for other types of reductions. I like to call that someone else the **Recursion Fairy**. Your *only* task is to *simplify* the original problem, or to solve it directly when simplification is either unnecessary or impossible; the Recursion Fairy will solve all the simpler subproblems for you, using Methods That Are None Of Your Business So *Butt*

Out.[1] Mathematically sophisticated readers might recognize the Recursion Fairy by its more formal name: the **Induction Hypothesis**.

There is one mild technical condition that must be satisfied in order for any recursive method to work correctly: There must be no infinite sequence of reductions to simpler and simpler instances. Eventually, the recursive reductions must lead to an elementary **base case** that can be solved by some other method; otherwise, the recursive algorithm will loop forever. The most common way to satisfy this condition is to reduce to one or more **smaller** instances of the same problem. For example, if the original input is a skreeble with n glurps, the input to each recursive call should be a skreeble with strictly less than n glurps. Of course this is impossible if the skreeble has no glurps at all—You can't have negative glurps; that would be silly!—so in that case we must grindlebloff the skreeble using some other method.

We've already seen one instance of this pattern in the peasant multiplication algorithm, which is based directly on the following recursive identity.

$$x \cdot y = \begin{cases} 0 & \text{if } x = 0 \\ \lfloor x/2 \rfloor \cdot (y + y) & \text{if } x \text{ is even} \\ \lfloor x/2 \rfloor \cdot (y + y) + y & \text{if } x \text{ is odd} \end{cases}$$

The same recurrence can be expressed algorithmically as follows:

```
PEASANTMULTIPLY(x, y):
    if x = 0
        return 0
    else
        x' ← ⌊x/2⌋
        y' ← y + y
        prod ← PEASANTMULTIPLY(x', y')    ⟨⟨Recurse!⟩⟩
        if x is odd
            prod ← prod + y
        return prod
```

A lazy Egyptian scribe could execute this algorithm by computing x' and y', *asking a more junior scribe to multiply x' and y'*, and then possibly adding y to the junior scribe's response. The junior scribe's problem is simpler because $x' < x$, and repeatedly decreasing a positive integer eventually leads to 0. How the junior scribe actually computes $x' \cdot y'$ is none of the senior scribe's business (and it's none of your business, either).

---

[1] When I was an undergraduate, I attributed recursion to "elves" instead of the Recursion Fairy, referring to the Brothers Grimm story about an old shoemaker who leaves his work unfinished when he goes to bed, only to discover upon waking that elves ("Wichtelmänner") have finished everything overnight. Someone more entheogenically experienced than I might recognize these Rekursionswichtelmänner as Terence McKenna's "self-transforming machine elves".

1.3 Tower of Hanoi

The Tower of Hanoi puzzle was first published—as an actual physical puzzle!—by the French teacher and recreational mathematician Édouard Lucas in 1883,[2] under the pseudonym "N. Claus (de Siam)" (an anagram of "Lucas d'Amiens"). The following year, Henri de Parville described the puzzle with the following remarkable story:[3]

> In the great temple at Benares[4]... beneath the dome which marks the centre of the world, rests a brass plate in which are fixed three diamond needles, each a cubit high and as thick as the body of a bee. On one of these needles, at the creation, God placed sixty-four discs of pure gold, the largest disc resting on the brass plate, and the others getting smaller and smaller up to the top one. This is the Tower of Bramah. Day and night unceasingly the priests transfer the discs from one diamond needle to another according to the fixed and immutable laws of Bramah, which require that the priest on duty must not move more than one disc at a time and that he must place this disc on a needle so that there is no smaller disc below it. When the sixty-four discs shall have been thus transferred from the needle on which at the creation God placed them to one of the other needles, tower, temple, and Brahmins alike will crumble into dust, and with a thunderclap the world will vanish.

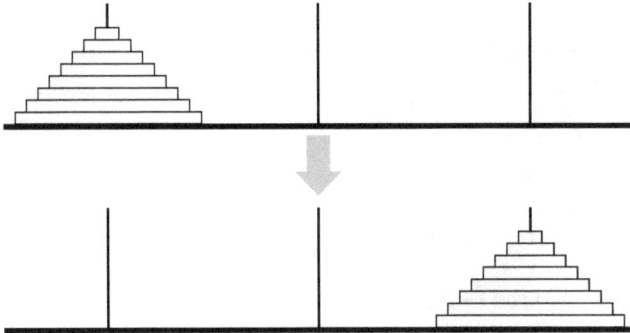

Figure 1.1. The (8-disk) Tower of Hanoi puzzle

Of course, as good computer scientists, our first instinct on reading this story is to substitute the variable n for the hardwired constant 64. And because most physical instances of the puzzle are made of wood instead of diamonds and gold, I will call the three possible locations for the disks "pegs" instead of

---

[2]Lucas later claimed to have invented the puzzle in 1876.

[3]This English translation is taken from W. W. Rouse Ball's 1892 book *Mathematical Recreations and Essays*.

[4]The "great temple at Benares" is almost certainly the Kashi Vishvanath Temple in Varanasi, Uttar Pradesh, India, located approximately 2400km west-north-west of Hà Nội, Việt Nam, where the fictional N. Claus supposedly resided. Coincidentally, the French Army invaded Hanoi in 1883, the same year Lucas released his puzzle, ultimately leading to its establishment as the capital of French Indochina.

"needles". How can we move a tower of n disks from one peg to another, using a third spare peg as an occasional placeholder, without ever placing a disk on top of a smaller disk?

As N. Claus (de Siam) pointed out in the pamphlet included with his puzzle, the secret to solving this puzzle is to think recursively. Instead of trying to solve the entire puzzle at once, let's concentrate on moving just the largest disk. We can't move it at the beginning, because all the other disks are in the way. So first we have to move those $n - 1$ smaller disks to the spare peg. Once that's done, we can move the largest disk directly to its destination. Finally, to finish the puzzle, we have to move the $n - 1$ smaller disks from the spare peg to their destination.

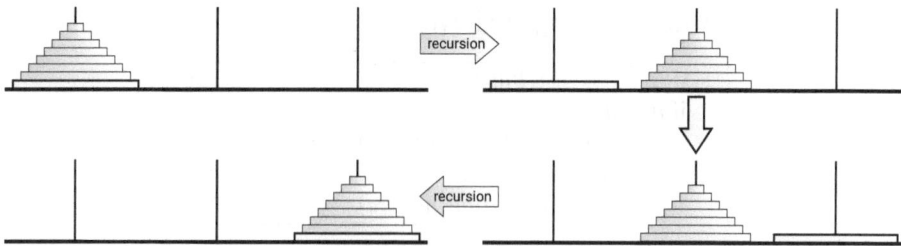

Figure 1.2. The Tower of Hanoi algorithm; ignore everything but the bottom disk.

So now all we have to figure out is how to—

NO!! STOP!!

That's it! We're done! We've successfully reduced the n-disk Tower of Hanoi problem to two instances of the $(n - 1)$-disk Tower of Hanoi problem, which we can gleefully hand off to the Recursion Fairy—or to carry Lucas's metaphor further, to the junior monks at the temple. *Our* job is finished. If we didn't trust the junior monks, we wouldn't have hired them; let them do their job in peace.

Our reduction does make one subtle but extremely important assumption: *There is a largest disk.* Our recursive algorithm works for any *positive* number of disks, but it breaks down when $n = 0$. We must handle that case using a different method. Fortunately, the monks at Benares, being good Buddhists, are quite adept at moving zero disks from one peg to another in no time at all, by doing nothing.

Figure 1.3. The vacuous base case for the Tower of Hanoi algorithm. There is no spoon.

It may be tempting to think about how all those smaller disks move around—or more generally, what happens when the recursion is unrolled—but really, don't do it. For most recursive algorithms, unrolling the recursion is neither necessary nor helpful. Our *only* task is to reduce the problem instance we're given to one or more simpler instances, or to solve the problem directly if such a reduction is impossible. Our recursive Tower of Hanoi algorithm is trivially correct when $n = 0$. For any $n \geq 1$, the Recursion Fairy correctly moves the top $n - 1$ disks (more formally, the Inductive Hypothesis implies that our recursive algorithm correctly moves the top $n - 1$ disks) so our algorithm is correct.

The recursive Hanoi algorithm is expressed in pseudocode in Figure 1.4. The algorithm moves a stack of n disks from a source peg (*src*) to a destination peg (*dst*) using a third temporary peg (*tmp*) as a placeholder. Notice that the algorithm correctly does nothing at all when $n = 0$.

$$
\begin{array}{l}
\underline{\text{HANOI}(n, src, dst, tmp):} \\
\quad \text{if } n > 0 \\
\quad\quad \text{HANOI}(n - 1, src, tmp, dst) \quad \langle\!\langle \textit{Recurse!}\rangle\!\rangle \\
\quad\quad \text{move disk } n \text{ from } src \text{ to } dst \\
\quad\quad \text{HANOI}(n - 1, tmp, dst, src) \quad \langle\!\langle \textit{Recurse!}\rangle\!\rangle
\end{array}
$$

Figure 1.4. A recursive algorithm to solve the Tower of Hanoi

Let $T(n)$ denote the number of moves required to transfer n disks—the running time of our algorithm. Our vacuous base case implies that $T(0) = 0$, and the more general recursive algorithm implies that $T(n) = 2T(n-1) + 1$ for any $n \geq 1$. By writing out the first several values of $T(n)$, we can easily guess that $T(n) = 2^n - 1$; a straightforward induction proof implies that this guess is correct. In particular, moving a tower of 64 disks requires $2^{64} - 1 = 18,446,744,073,709,551,615$ individual moves. Thus, even at the impressive rate of one move per second, the monks at Benares will be at work for approximately 585 billion years ("plus de *cinq milliards de siècles*") before tower, temple, and Brahmins alike will crumble into dust, and with a thunderclap the world will vanish.

1.4 Mergesort

Mergesort is one of the earliest algorithms designed for general-purpose stored-program computers. The algorithm was developed by John von Neumann in 1945, and described in detail in a publication with Herman Goldstine in 1947, as one of the first non-numerical programs for the EDVAC.[5]

---

[5] Goldstine and von Neumann actually described an non-recursive variant now usually called bottom-up mergesort. At the time, large data sets were sorted by special-purpose machines—almost all built by IBM—that manipulated punched cards using variants of binary radix sort. Von

1. Divide the input array into two subarrays of roughly equal size.

2. Recursively mergesort each of the subarrays.

3. Merge the newly-sorted subarrays into a single sorted array.

Input:	S	O	R	T	I	N	G	E	X	A	M	P	L		
Divide:	S	O	R	T	I	N	G	E	X	A	M	P	L		
Recurse Left:	I	N	O	R	S	T	G	E	X	A	M	P	L		
Recurse Right:	I	N	O	R	S	T	A	E	G	L	M	P	X		
Merge:	A	E	G	I	L	M	N	O	P	R	S	T	X		

Figure 1.5. A mergesort example.

The first step is completely trivial—just divide the array size by two—and we can delegate the second step to the Recursion Fairy. All the real work is done in the final merge step. A complete description of the algorithm is given in Figure 1.6; to keep the recursive structure clear, I've extracted the merge step into an independent subroutine. The merge algorithm is also recursive—identify the first element of the output array, and then recursively merge the rest of the input arrays.

```
MERGESORT(A[1..n]):
    if n > 1
        m ← ⌊n/2⌋
        MERGESORT(A[1..m])        ⟨⟨Recurse!⟩⟩
        MERGESORT(A[m+1..n])      ⟨⟨Recurse!⟩⟩
        MERGE(A[1..n], m)
```

```
MERGE(A[1..n], m):
    i ← 1;  j ← m+1
    for k ← 1 to n
        if j > n
            B[k] ← A[i];  i ← i+1
        else if i > m
            B[k] ← A[j];  j ← j+1
        else if A[i] < A[j]
            B[k] ← A[i];  i ← i+1
        else
            B[k] ← A[j];  j ← j+1
    for k ← 1 to n
        A[k] ← B[k]
```

Figure 1.6. Mergesort

Correctness

To prove that this algorithm is correct, we apply our old friend induction twice, first to the MERGE subroutine then to the top-level MERGESORT algorithm.

Lemma 1.1. *MERGE correctly merges the subarrays* $A[1..m]$ *and* $A[m+1..n]$, *assuming those subarrays are sorted in the input.*

Neumann argued (successfully!) that because the EDVAC could sort faster than IBM's dedicated sorters, "without human intervention or need for additional equipment", the EDVAC was an "all purpose" machine, and special-purpose sorting machines were no longer necessary.

Proof: Let $A[1..n]$ be any array and m any integer such that the subarrays $A[1..m]$ and $A[m+1..n]$ are sorted. We prove that for all k from 0 to n, the last $n-k-1$ iterations of the main loop correctly merge $A[i..m]$ and $A[j..n]$ into $B[k..n]$. The proof proceeds by induction on $n-k+1$, the number of elements remaining to be merged.

If $k > n$, the algorithm correctly merges the two empty subarrays by doing absolutely nothing. (This is the base case of the inductive proof.) Otherwise, there are four cases to consider for the kth iteration of the main loop.

- If $j > n$, then subarray $A[j..n]$ is empty, so $\min\big(A[i..m] \cup A[j..n]\big) = A[i]$.
- If $i > m$, then subarray $A[i..m]$ is empty, so $\min\big(A[i..m] \cup A[j..n]\big) = A[j]$.
- Otherwise, if $A[i] < A[j]$, then $\min\big(A[i..m] \cup A[j..n]\big) = A[i]$.
- Otherwise, we must have $A[i] \geq A[j]$, and $\min\big(A[i..m] \cup A[j..n]\big) = A[j]$.

In all four cases, $B[k]$ is correctly assigned the smallest element of $A[i..m] \cup A[j..n]$. In the two cases with the assignment $B[k] \leftarrow A[i]$, the Recursion Fairy correctly merges—sorry, I mean the Induction Hypothesis implies that the last $n-k$ iterations of the main loop correctly merge $A[i+1..m]$ and $A[j..n]$ into $B[k+1..n]$. Similarly, in the other two cases, the Recursion Fairy also correctly merges the rest of the subarrays. □

Theorem 1.2. *MERGESORT correctly sorts any input array $A[1..n]$.*

Proof: We prove the theorem by induction on n. If $n \leq 1$, the algorithm correctly does nothing. Otherwise, the Recursion Fairy correctly sorts—sorry, I mean the induction hypothesis implies that our algorithm correctly sorts the two smaller subarrays $A[1..m]$ and $A[m+1..n]$, after which they are correctly MERGEd into a single sorted array (by Lemma 1.1). □

Analysis

Because the MERGESORT algorithm is recursive, its running time is naturally expressed as a recurrence. MERGE clearly takes $O(n)$ time, because it's a simple for-loop with constant work per iteration. We immediately obtain the following recurrence for MERGESORT:

$$T(n) = T\big(\lceil n/2 \rceil\big) + T\big(\lfloor n/2 \rfloor\big) + O(n).$$

As in most divide-and-conquer recurrences, we can safely strip out the floors and ceilings (using a technique called *domain transformations* described later in this chapter), giving us the simpler recurrence $T(n) = 2T(n/2) + O(n)$. The "all levels equal" case of the recursion tree method (also described later in this chapter) immediately implies the closed-form solution $T(n) = O(n \log n)$. Even if you are not (yet) familiar with recursion trees, you can verify the solution $T(n) = O(n \log n)$ by induction.

1.5 Quicksort

Quicksort is another recursive sorting algorithm, discovered by Tony Hoare in 1959 and first published in 1961. In this algorithm, the hard work is splitting the array into smaller subarrays *before* recursion, so that merging the sorted subarrays is trivial.

1. Choose a *pivot* element from the array.

2. Partition the array into three subarrays containing the elements smaller than the pivot, the pivot element itself, and the elements larger than the pivot.

3. Recursively quicksort the first and last subarrays.

Input:	S	O	R	T	I	N	G	E	X	A	M	P	L
Choose a pivot:	S	O	R	T	I	N	G	E	X	A	M	P	L
Partition:	A	G	O	E	I	N	L	M	P	T	X	S	R
Recurse Left:	A	E	G	I	L	M	N	O	P	T	X	S	R
Recurse Right:	A	E	G	I	L	M	N	O	P	R	S	T	X

Figure 1.7. A quicksort example.

More detailed pseudocode is given in Figure 1.8. In the PARTITION subroutine, the input parameter p is the index of the pivot element in the unsorted array; the subroutine partitions the array and returns the new index of the pivot element. There are many different efficient partitioning algorithms; the one I'm presenting here is attributed to Nico Lomuto.[6] The variable ℓ counts the number of items in the array that are ℓess than the pivot element.

```
QUICKSORT(A[1..n]):
    if (n > 1)
        Choose a pivot element A[p]
        r ← PARTITION(A, p)
        QUICKSORT(A[1..r − 1])    ⟨⟨Recurse!⟩⟩
        QUICKSORT(A[r + 1..n])    ⟨⟨Recurse!⟩⟩
```

```
PARTITION(A[1..n], p):
    swap A[p] ⟷ A[n]
    ℓ ← 0                        ⟨⟨#items < pivot⟩⟩
    for i ← 1 to n − 1
        if A[i] < A[n]
            ℓ ← ℓ + 1
            swap A[ℓ] ⟷ A[i]
    swap A[n] ⟷ A[ℓ + 1]
    return ℓ + 1
```

Figure 1.8. Quicksort

Correctness

Just like mergesort, proving that QUICKSORT is correct requires two separate induction proofs: one to prove that PARTITION correctly partitions the array, and

---

[6]Hoare proposed a more complicated "two-way" partitioning algorithm that has some practical advantages over Lomuto's algorithm. On the other hand, Hoare's partitioning algorithm is one of the places off-by-one errors go to die.

the other to prove that QUICKSORT correctly sorts *assuming* PARTITION is correct. To prove PARTITION is correct, we need to prove the following loop invariant: At the end of each iteration of the main loop, everything in the subarray $A[1..\ell]$ is ℓess than $A[n]$, and nothing in the subarray $A[\ell+1..i]$ is less than $A[n]$. I'll leave the remaining straightforward but tedious details as exercises for the reader.

Analysis

The analysis of quicksort is also similar to that of mergesort. PARTITION clearly runs in $O(n)$ time, because it's a simple for-loop with constant work per iteration. For QUICKSORT, we get a recurrence that depends on r, the *rank* of the chosen pivot element:

$$T(n) = T(r-1) + T(n-r) + O(n)$$

If we could somehow always magically choose the pivot to be the *median* element of the array A, we would have $r = \lceil n/2 \rceil$, the two subproblems would be as close to the same size as possible, the recurrence would become

$$T(n) = T(\lceil n/2 \rceil - 1) + T(\lfloor n/2 \rfloor) + O(n) \le 2T(n/2) + O(n),$$

and we'd have $T(n) = O(n \log n)$ using either the recursion tree method or the even simpler "Oh yeah, we already solved that recurrence for mergesort" method.

In fact, as we will see later in this chapter, we *can* actually locate the median element in an unsorted array in linear time, but the algorithm is fairly complicated, and the hidden constant in the $O(\cdot)$ notation is large enough to make the resulting sorting algorithm impractical. In practice, most programmers settle for something simple, like choosing the first or last element of the array. In this case, r can take any value between 1 and n, so we have

$$T(n) = \max_{1 \le r \le n} \left(T(r-1) + T(n-r) + O(n) \right).$$

In the worst case, the two subproblems are completely unbalanced—either $r = 1$ or $r = n$—and the recurrence becomes $T(n) \le T(n-1) + O(n)$. The solution is $T(n) = O(n^2)$.

Another common heuristic is called "median of three"—choose three elements (usually at the beginning, middle, and end of the array), and take the median of those three elements as the pivot. Although this heuristic is somewhat more efficient in practice than just choosing one element, especially when the array is already (nearly) sorted, we can still have $r = 2$ or $r = n-1$ in the worst case. With the median-of-three heuristic, the recurrence becomes $T(n) \le T(1) + T(n-2) + O(n)$, whose solution is still $T(n) = O(n^2)$.

Intuitively, the pivot element should "usually" fall somewhere in the middle of the array, say with rank between $n/10$ and $9n/10$. This observation suggests that the "average-case" running time should be $O(n \log n)$. Although this intuition can be formalized, the most common formalization makes the completely unrealistic assumption that all permutations of the input array are equally likely. Real world data *may* be random, but it is not random in any way that we can predict in advance, and it is *certainly* not uniform![7]

Occasionally people also consider "best case" running time for some reason. We won't.

1.6 The Pattern

Both mergesort and quicksort follow a general three-step pattern called *divide and conquer*:

1. **Divide** the given instance of the problem into several *independent smaller* instances of *exactly* the same problem.
2. **Delegate** each smaller instance to the Recursion Fairy.
3. **Combine** the solutions for the smaller instances into the final solution for the given instance.

If the size of any instance falls below some constant threshold, we abandon recursion and solve the problem directly, by brute force, in constant time.

Proving a divide-and-conquer algorithm correct almost always requires induction. Analyzing the running time requires setting up and solving a recurrence, which usually (but unfortunately not always!) can be solved using recursion trees.

1.7 Recursion Trees

So what are these "recursion trees" I keep talking about? Recursion trees are a simple, general, pictorial tool for solving divide-and-conquer recurrences. A recursion tree is a rooted tree with one node for each recursive subproblem. The *value* of each node is the amount of time spent on the corresponding subproblem *excluding* recursive calls. Thus, the overall running time of the algorithm is the sum of the values of all nodes in the tree.

To make this idea more concrete, imagine a divide-and-conquer algorithm that spends $O(f(n))$ time on non-recursive work, and then makes r recursive

---

[7]On the other hand, if we choose the pivot index p uniformly at random, then QUICKSORT runs in $O(n \log n)$ time *with high probability*, for *every* possible input array. The key difference is that the randomness is controlled by our algorithm, not by the All-Powerful Malicious Adversary who gives us input data after reading our code. The analysis of randomized quicksort is unfortunately outside the scope of this book, but you can find relevant lecture notes at http://algorithms.wtf/.

calls, each on a problem of size n/c. Up to constant factors (which we can hide in the $O(\,)$ notation), the running time of this algorithm is governed by the recurrence

$$T(n) = r\,T(n/c) + f(n).$$

The root of the recursion tree for $T(n)$ has value $f(n)$ and r children, each of which is the root of a (recursively defined) recursion tree for $T(n/c)$. Equivalently, a recursion tree is a complete r-ary tree where each node at depth d contains the value $f(n/c^d)$. (Feel free to assume that n is an integer power of c, so that n/c^d is always an integer, although in fact this doesn't matter.)

In practice, I recommend drawing out the first two or three levels of the tree, as in Figure 1.9.

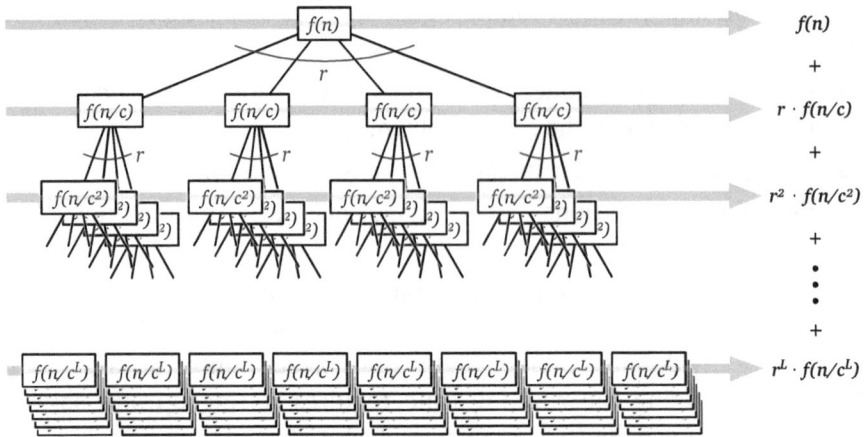

Figure 1.9. A recursion tree for the recurrence $T(n) = r\,T(n/c) + f(n)$

The leaves of the recursion tree correspond to the base case(s) of the recurrence. Because we're only looking for asymptotic bounds, the precise base case doesn't actually matter; we can safely assume $T(n) = 1$ for all $n \le n_0$, where n_0 is an arbitrary positive constant. In particular, we can choose whatever value of n_0 is most convenient for our analysis. For this example, I'll choose $n_0 = 1$.

Now $T(n)$ is the sum of all values in the recursion tree; we can evaluate this sum by considering the tree level-by-level. For each integer i, the ith level of the tree has exactly r^i nodes, each with value $f(n/c^i)$. Thus,

$$T(n) = \sum_{i=0}^{L} r^i \cdot f(n/c^i) \qquad (\Sigma)$$

where L is the depth of the tree. Our base case $n_0 = 1$ immediately implies $L = \log_c n$, because $n/c^L = n_0 = 1$. It follows that the number of leaves in the recursion tree is exactly $r^L = r^{\log_c n} = n^{\log_c r}$. Thus, the last term in the level-by-level sum (Σ) is $n^{\log_c r} \cdot f(1) = O(n^{\log_c r})$, because $f(1) = O(1)$.

There are three common cases where the level-by-level series (Σ) is especially easy to evaluate:

- **Decreasing:** If the series *decays exponentially*—every term is a constant factor smaller than the previous term—then $T(n) = O(f(n))$. In this case, the sum is dominated by the value at the root of the recursion tree.

- **Equal:** If all terms in the series are equal, we immediately have $T(n) = O(f(n) \cdot L) = O(f(n) \log n)$. (The constant c vanishes into the $O(\ )$ notation.)

- **Increasing:** If the series *grows exponentially*—every term is a constant factor larger than the previous term—then $T(n) = O(n^{\log_c r})$. In this case, the sum is dominated by the number of leaves in the recursion tree.

In the first and third cases, only the largest term in the geometric series matters; all other terms are swallowed up by the $O(\cdot)$ notation. In the decreasing case, we don't even have to compute L; the asymptotic upper bound would still hold if the recursion tree were infinite!

As an elementary example, if we draw out the first few levels of the recursion tree for the (simplified) mergesort recurrence $T(n) = 2T(n/2) + O(n)$, we discover that all levels are equal, which immediately implies $T(n) = O(n \log n)$.

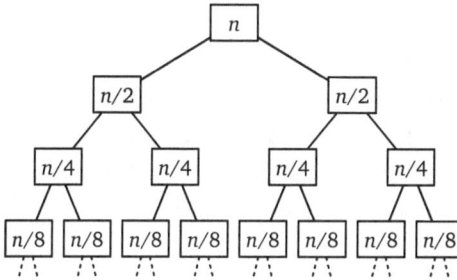

Figure 1.10. The recursion tree for mergesort

The recursion tree technique can also be used for algorithms where the recursive subproblems have different sizes. For example, if we could somehow implement quicksort so that the pivot *always* lands in the middle third of the sorted array, the worst-case running time would satisfy the recurrence

$$T(n) \leq T(n/3) + T(2n/3) + O(n).$$

This recurrence might look scary, but it's actually pretty tame. If we draw out a few levels of the resulting recursion tree, we quickly realize that the sum of values on any level is *at most* n—deeper levels might be missing some nodes—and the entire tree has depth $\log_{3/2} n = O(\log n)$. It immediately follows that $T(n) = O(n \log n)$. (Moreover, the number of *full* levels in the recursion tree is $\log_3 n = \Omega(\log n)$, so this conservative analysis can be improved by at most a constant factor, which for our purposes means not at all.) The fact that the recursion tree is unbalanced simply doesn't matter.

As a more extreme example, the worst-case recurrence for quicksort $T(n) = T(n-1) + T(1) + O(n)$ gives us a completely unbalanced recursion tree, where one child of each internal node is a leaf. The level-by-level sum doesn't fall into any of our three default categories, but we can still derive the solution $T(n) = O(n^2)$ by observing that every level value is at most n and there are at most n levels. (Again, this conservative analysis is tight, because $n/2$ levels each have value at least $n/2$.)

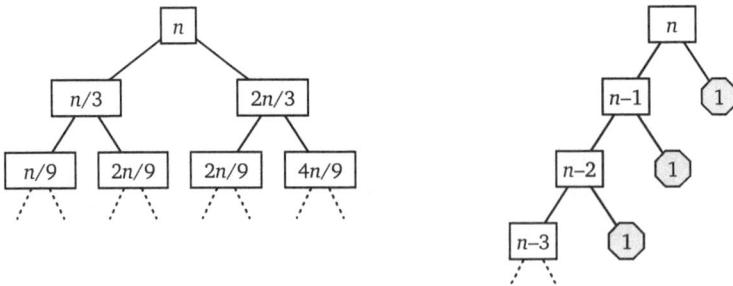

Figure 1.11. Recursion trees for quicksort with good pivots (left) and with worst-case pivots (right)

♥Ignoring Floors and Ceilings Is Okay, Honest

Careful readers might object that our analysis brushes an important detail under the rug. The running time of mergesort doesn't *really* obey the recurrence $T(n) = 2T(n/2) + O(n)$; after all, the input size n might be odd, and what could it possibly mean to sort an array of size $42\frac{1}{2}$ or $17\frac{7}{8}$? The actual mergesort recurrence is somewhat messier:

$$T(n) = T(\lceil n/2 \rceil) + T(\lfloor n/2 \rfloor) + O(n).$$

Sure, we could check that $T(n) = O(n \log n)$ using induction, but the necessary calculations would be awful. Fortunately, there is a simple technique for removing floors and ceilings from recurrences, called *domain transformation*.

- First, because we are deriving an upper bound, we can safely overestimate $T(n)$, once by pretending that the two subproblem sizes are equal, and again to eliminate the ceiling:[8]

$$T(n) \leq 2T(\lceil n/2 \rceil) + n \leq 2T(n/2 + 1) + n.$$

---

[8]Formally, we are treating T as a function over the *reals*, not just over the integers, that satisfies the given recurrence with the base case $T(n) = C$ for all $n \leq n_0$, for some real numbers $C \geq 0$ and $n_0 > 0$ whose values don't matter. If n happens to be an integer, then $T(n)$ coincides with the running time of an algorithm on an input of size n, but that doesn't matter, either.

- Second, we define a new function $S(n) = T(n + \alpha)$, choosing the constant α so that $S(n)$ satisfies the simpler recurrence $S(n) \leq 2S(n/2) + O(n)$. To find the correct constant α, we derive a recurrence for S from our given recurrence for T:

$$
\begin{aligned}
S(n) &= T(n + \alpha) & &\text{[definition of } S\text{]} \\
&\leq 2T(n/2 + \alpha/2 + 1) + n + \alpha & &\text{[recurrence for } T\text{]} \\
&= 2S(n/2 - \alpha/2 + 1) + n + \alpha & &\text{[definition of } S\text{]}
\end{aligned}
$$

Setting $\alpha = 2$ simplifies this recurrence to $S(n) \leq 2S(n/2) + n + 2$, which is exactly what we wanted.

- Finally, the recursion tree method implies $S(n) = O(n \log n)$, and therefore

$$
T(n) = S(n - 2) = O((n - 2)\log(n - 2)) = O(n \log n),
$$

exactly as promised.

Similar domain transformations can be used to remove floors, ceilings, and even lower order terms from *any* divide and conquer recurrence. But now that we realize this, we don't need to bother grinding through the details ever again! From now on, faced with any divide-and-conquer recurrence, I will silently brush floors and ceilings and lower-order terms under the rug, and I encourage you to do the same.

♥1.8 Linear-Time Selection

During our discussion of quicksort, I claimed in passing that we can find the median of an unsorted array in linear time. The first such algorithm was discovered by Manuel Blum, Bob Floyd, Vaughan Pratt, Ron Rivest, and Bob Tarjan in the early 1970s. Their algorithm actually solves the more general problem of selecting the kth smallest element in an n-element array, given the array and the integer k as input, using a variant of an algorithm called *quickselect* or *one-armed quicksort*. Quickselect was first described by Tony Hoare in 1961, literally on the same page where he first published quicksort.

Quickselect

The generic quickselect algorithm chooses a pivot element, partitions the array using the same PARTITION subroutine as QUICKSORT, and then recursively searches *only one* of the two subarrays, specifically, the one that contains the kth smallest element of the original input array. Pseudocode for quickselect is given in Figure 1.12.

```
QUICKSELECT(A[1..n], k):
    if n = 1
        return A[1]
    else
        Choose a pivot element A[p]
        r ← PARTITION(A[1..n], p)

        if k < r
            return QUICKSELECT(A[1..r − 1], k)
        else if k > r
            return QUICKSELECT(A[r + 1..n], k − r)
        else
            return A[r]
```

Figure 1.12. Quickselect, or one-armed quicksort

This algorithm has two important features. First, just like quicksort, the correctness of quickselect does not depend on how the pivot is chosen. Second, even if we really only care about selecting *medians* (the special case $k = n/2$), Hoare's recursive strategy requires us to consider the more general selection problem; the median of the input array $A[1..n]$ is almost never the median of either of the two smaller subarrays $A[1..r − 1]$ or $A[r + 1..n]$.

The worst-case running time of QUICKSELECT obeys a recurrence similar to QUICKSORT. We don't know the value of r, or which of the two subarrays we'll recursively search, so we have to assume the worst.

$$T(n) \leq \max_{1 \leq r \leq n} \max \{T(r − 1), T(n − r)\} + O(n)$$

We can simplify the recurrence slightly by letting ℓ denote the length of the recursive subproblem:

$$T(n) \leq \max_{0 \leq \ell \leq n−1} T(\ell) + O(n)$$

If the chosen pivot element is always either the smallest or largest element in the array, the recurrence simplifies to $T(n) = T(n − 1) + O(n)$, which implies $T(n) = O(n^2)$. (The recursion tree for this recurrence is just a simple path.)

Good pivots

We could avoid this quadratic worst-case behavior if we could *somehow* magically choose a **good** pivot, meaning $\ell \leq \alpha n$ for some constant $\alpha < 1$. In this case, the recurrence would simplify to

$$T(n) \leq T(\alpha n) + O(n).$$

This recurrence expands into a decreasing geometric series, which is dominated by its largest term, so $T(n) = O(n)$. (Again, the recursion tree is just a simple path. The constant in the $O(n)$ running time depends on the constant α.)

In other words, if we could somehow quickly find an element that's even *close* to the median in linear time, we could find the *exact* median in linear time. So now all we need is an Approximate Median Fairy. The Blum-Floyd-Pratt-Rivest-Tarjan algorithm chooses a good quickselect pivot by **recursively** computing the median of a carefully-chosen subset of the input array. The Approximate Median Fairy is just the Recursion Fairy in disguise!

Specifically, we divide the input array into $\lceil n/5 \rceil$ *blocks*, each containing exactly 5 elements, except possibly the last. (If the last block isn't full, just throw in a few ∞s.) We compute the median of each block by brute force, collect those medians into a new array $M[1..\lceil n/5 \rceil]$, and then *recursively* compute the median of this new array. Finally, we use the median of the block medians (called "*mom*" in the pseudocode below) as the quickselect pivot.

MOMSELECT($A[1..n], k$):
  if $n \le 25$ ⟨⟨or whatever⟩⟩
     use brute force
  else
     $m \leftarrow \lceil n/5 \rceil$
     for $i \leftarrow 1$ to m
         $M[i] \leftarrow$ MEDIANOFFIVE($A[5i - 4 .. 5i]$)   ⟨⟨*Brute force!*⟩⟩
     $mom \leftarrow$ MOMSELECT($M[1..m], \lfloor m/2 \rfloor$)   ⟨⟨*Recursion!*⟩⟩

     $r \leftarrow$ PARTITION($A[1..n], mom$)

     if $k < r$
         return MOMSELECT($A[1..r-1], k$)   ⟨⟨*Recursion!*⟩⟩
     else if $k > r$
         return MOMSELECT($A[r+1..n], k-r$)   ⟨⟨*Recursion!*⟩⟩
     else
         return *mom*

MOMSELECT uses recursion for two different purposes; the first time to choose a pivot element (*mom*), and the second time to search through the entries on one side of that pivot.

Analysis

But why is this fast? The first key insight is that **the median of medians is a good pivot.** Mom is larger than $\lfloor \lceil n/5 \rceil/2 \rfloor - 1 \approx n/10$ block medians, and each block median is larger than two other elements in its block. Thus, mom is bigger than at least $3n/10$ elements in the input array; symmetrically, mom is smaller than at least $3n/10$ elements. Thus, in the worst case, the second recursive call searches an array of size at most $7n/10$.

We can visualize the algorithm's behavior by drawing the input array as a $5 \times \lceil n/5 \rceil$ grid, which each column represents five consecutive elements. For purposes of illustration, imagine that we sort every column from top down, and then we sort the columns by their middle element. (Let me emphasize that *the algorithm does not actually do this!*) In this arrangement, the median-of-medians is the element closest to the center of the grid.

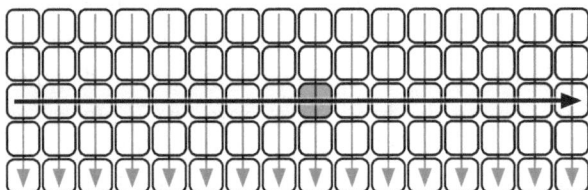

The left half of the first three rows of the grid contains $3n/10$ elements, each of which is smaller than mom. If the element we're looking for is larger than mom, our algorithm will throw away *everything* smaller than mom, including those $3n/10$ elements, before recursing. Thus, the input to the recursive subproblem contains at most $7n/10$ elements. A symmetric argument implies that if our target element is smaller than mom, we discard at least $3n/10$ elements larger than mom, so the input to our recursive subproblem has at most $7n/10$ elements.

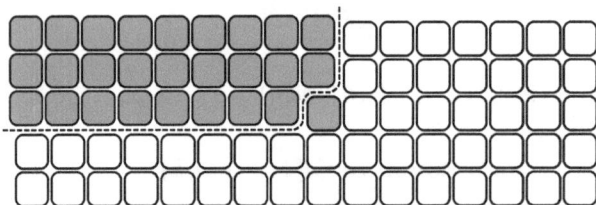

Okay, so mom is a good pivot, but our algorithm still makes *two* recursive calls instead of just one; how do we prove linear time? The second key insight is that the *total* size of the two recursive subproblems is a constant factor smaller than the size of the original input array. The worst-case running time of the algorithm obeys the recurrence

$$T(n) \le T(n/5) + T(7n/10) + O(n).$$

If we draw out the recursion tree for this recurrence, we observe that the total work at each level of the recursion tree is at most $9/10$ the total work at the previous level. Thus, the level sums decay exponentially, giving us the solution $T(n) = O(n)$. (Again, the fact that the recursion tree is unbalanced is completely immaterial.) Hooray! Thanks, Mom!

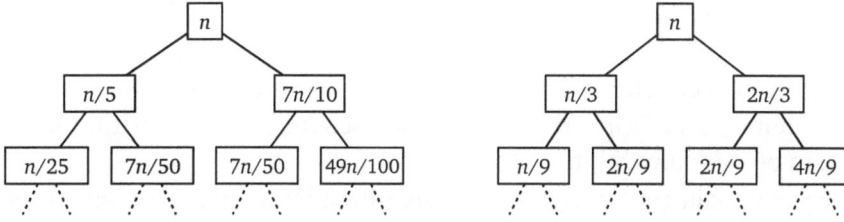

Figure 1.13. The recursion trees for MomSelect and a similar selection algorithm with blocks of size 3

Sanity Checking

At this point, many students ask about that magic constant 5. Why did we choose that particular block size? The answer is that 5 is the smallest odd block size that gives us exponential decay in the recursion-tree analysis! (Even block sizes introduce additional complications.) If we had used blocks of size 3 instead, the running-time recurrence would be

$$T(n) \le T(n/3) + T(2n/3) + O(n).$$

We've seen this recurrence before! Every level of the recursion tree has total value *at most n*, and the depth of the recursion tree is $\log_{3/2} n = O(\log n)$, so the solution to this recurrence is $T(n) \le O(n \log n)$. (Moreover, this analysis is tight, because the recursion tree has $\log_3 n$ complete levels.) Median-of-medians selection using 3-element blocks is no faster than sorting.

Finer analysis reveals that the constant hidden by the $O( )$ notation is quite large, even if we count only comparisons. Selecting the median of 5 elements requires at most 6 comparisons, so we need at most $6n/5$ comparisons to set up the recursive subproblem. Naïvely partitioning the array after the recursive call would require $n - 1$ comparisons, but we already know $3n/10$ elements larger than the pivot and $3n/10$ elements smaller than the pivot, so partitioning actually requires only $2n/5$ additional comparisons. Thus, a more precise recurrence for the worst-case number of comparisons is

$$T(n) \le T(n/5) + T(7n/10) + 8n/5.$$

The recursion tree method implies the upper bound

$$T(n) \le \frac{8n}{5} \sum_{i \ge 0} \left(\frac{9}{10} \right)^i = \frac{8n}{5} \cdot 10 = 16n.$$

In practice, median-of-medians selection is not as slow as this worst-case analysis predicts—getting a worst-case pivot at every level of recursion is incredibly unlikely—but it is still slower than sorting for even moderately large arrays.[9]

---

[9] In fact, the right way to choose the pivot element in practice is to choose it *uniformly at random*. Then the expected number of comparisons required to find the median is at most $4n$. See my randomized algorithms lecture notes at http://algorithms.wtf for more details.

1.9 Fast Multiplication

In the previous chapter, we saw two ancient algorithms for multiplying two n-digit numbers in $O(n^2)$ time: the grade-school lattice algorithm and the Egyptian peasant algorithm.

Maybe we can get a more efficient algorithm by splitting the digit arrays in half and exploiting the following identity:

$$(10^m a + b)(10^m c + d) = 10^{2m} ac + 10^m (bc + ad) + bd$$

This recurrence immediately suggests the following divide-and-conquer algorithm to multiply two n-digit numbers x and y. Each of the four sub-products ac, bc, ad, and bd is computed recursively, but the multiplications in the last line are *not* recursive, because we can multiply by a power of ten by shifting the digits to the left and filling in the correct number of zeros, all in $O(n)$ time.

$\underline{\text{SPLITMULTIPLY}(x, y, n):}$
  if $n = 1$
      return $x \cdot y$
  else
      $m \leftarrow \lceil n/2 \rceil$
      $a \leftarrow \lfloor x/10^m \rfloor$; $b \leftarrow x \bmod 10^m$ $\langle\!\langle x = 10^m a + b \rangle\!\rangle$
      $c \leftarrow \lfloor y/10^m \rfloor$; $d \leftarrow y \bmod 10^m$ $\langle\!\langle y = 10^m c + d \rangle\!\rangle$
      $e \leftarrow \text{SPLITMULTIPLY}(a, c, m)$
      $f \leftarrow \text{SPLITMULTIPLY}(b, d, m)$
      $g \leftarrow \text{SPLITMULTIPLY}(b, c, m)$
      $h \leftarrow \text{SPLITMULTIPLY}(a, d, m)$
      return $10^{2m} e + 10^m (g + h) + f$

Correctness of this algorithm follows easily by induction. The running time for this algorithm follows the recurrence

$$T(n) = 4T(\lceil n/2 \rceil) + O(n).$$

The recursion tree method transforms this recurrence into an *increasing* geometric series, which implies $T(n) = O(n^{\log_2 4}) = O(n^2)$. In fact, this algorithm multiplies each digit of x with each digit of y, just like the lattice algorithm. So I guess that didn't work. Too bad. It was a nice idea.

In the mid-1950s, Andrei Kolmogorov, one of the giants of 20th century mathematics, publicly conjectured that there is *no* algorithm to multiply two n-digit numbers in subquadratic time. Kolmogorov organized a seminar at Moscow University in 1960, where he restated his "n^2 conjecture" and posed several related problems that he planned to discuss at future meetings. Almost exactly a week later, a 23-year-old student named Anatoliĭ Karatsuba presented Kolmogorov with a remarkable counterexample. According to Karatsuba himself,

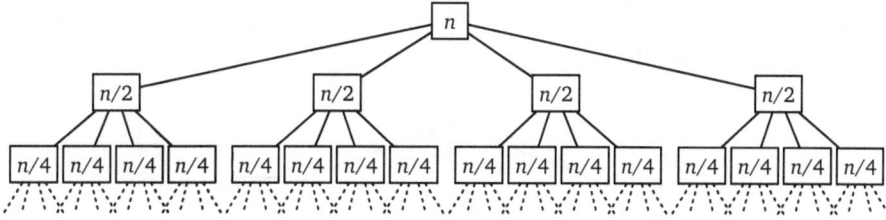

Figure 1.14. The recursion tree for naïve divide-and-conquer multiplication

> After the seminar I told Kolmogorov about the new algorithm and about the disproof of the n^2 conjecture. Kolmogorov was very agitated because this contradicted his very plausible conjecture. At the next meeting of the seminar, Kolmogorov himself told the participants about my method, and at that point the seminar was terminated.

Karatsuba observed that the middle coefficient $bc + ad$ can be computed from the other two coefficients ac and bd using only *one* more recursive multiplication, via the following algebraic identity:

$$ac + bd - (a - b)(c - d) = bc + ad$$

This trick lets us replace the four recursive calls in the previous algorithm with only three recursive calls, as shown below:

$$
\begin{aligned}
&\underline{\text{FastMultiply}(x, y, n):} \\
&\quad \text{if } n = 1 \\
&\quad\quad \text{return } x \cdot y \\
&\quad \text{else} \\
&\quad\quad m \leftarrow \lceil n/2 \rceil \\
&\quad\quad a \leftarrow \lfloor x/10^m \rfloor; \quad b \leftarrow x \bmod 10^m \quad\quad \langle\!\langle x = 10^m a + b \rangle\!\rangle \\
&\quad\quad c \leftarrow \lfloor y/10^m \rfloor; \quad d \leftarrow y \bmod 10^m \quad\quad \langle\!\langle y = 10^m c + d \rangle\!\rangle \\
&\quad\quad e \leftarrow \text{FastMultiply}(a, c, m) \\
&\quad\quad f \leftarrow \text{FastMultiply}(b, d, m) \\
&\quad\quad g \leftarrow \text{FastMultiply}(a - b, c - d, m) \\
&\quad\quad \text{return } 10^{2m} e + 10^m (e + f - g) + f
\end{aligned}
$$

The running time of Karatsuba's FastMultiply algorithm follows the recurrence

$$T(n) \leq 3T(\lceil n/2 \rceil) + O(n)$$

Once again, the recursion tree method transforms this recurrence into an increasing geometric series, but the new solution is only $T(n) = O(n^{\log_2 3}) = O(n^{1.58496})$, a significant improvement over our earlier quadratic time bound.[10]

---

[10]My presentation simplifies the actual history slightly. In fact, Karatsuba proposed an algorithm based on the formula $(a + b)(c + d) - ac - bd = bc + ad$. This algorithm also runs in $O(n^{\lg 3})$ time, but the actual recurrence is slightly messier: $a - b$ and $c - d$ are still m-digit numbers, but $a + b$ and $c + d$ might each have $m + 1$ digits. The simplification presented here is due to Donald Knuth.

Karatsuba's algorithm arguably launched the design and analysis of algorithms as a formal field of study.

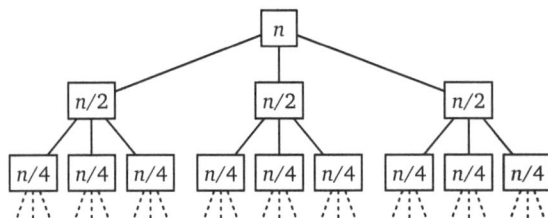

Figure 1.15. The recursion tree for Karatsuba's divide-and-conquer multiplication algorithm

We can take Karatsuba's idea even further, splitting the numbers into more pieces and combining them in more complicated ways, to obtain even faster multiplication algorithms. Andrei Toom discovered an infinite family of algorithms that split any integer into k parts, each with n/k digits, and then compute the product using only $2k - 1$ recursive multiplications; Toom's algorithms were further simplified by Stephen Cook in his PhD thesis. For any fixed k, the Toom-Cook algorithm runs in $O(n^{1+1/(\lg k)})$ time, where the hidden constant in the $O(\cdot)$ notation depends on k.

Ultimately, this divide-and-conquer strategy led Gauss (yes, really) to the discovery of the **Fast Fourier transform**.[11] The basic FFT algorithm itself runs in $O(n \log n)$ time; however, using FFTs for integer multiplication incurs some small additional overhead. The first FFT-based integer multiplication algorithm, published by Arnold Schönhage and Volker Strassen in 1971, runs in $O(n \log n \log \log n)$ time. Schönhage-Strassen remained the theoretically fastest integer multiplication algorithm for several decades, before Martin Fürer discovered the first of a long series of technical improvements. Finally, in 2019, David Harvey and Joris van der Hoeven published an algorithm that runs in $O(n \log n)$ time.[12]

1.10 Exponentiation

Given a number a and a positive integer n, suppose we want to compute a^n. The standard naïve method is a simple for-loop that performs $n - 1$ multiplications by a:

---

[11]See http://algorithms.wtf for lecture notes on Fast Fourier transforms.

[12]Schönhage-Strassen is actually the fastest algorithm *in practice* for multiplying integers with more than about 75000 digits; the more recent algorithms of Fürer, Harvey, van der Hoeven, and others would be faster "in practice" only for integers with more digits than there are particles in the universe.

```
SlowPower(a, n):
    x ← a
    for i ← 2 to n
        x ← x · a
    return x
```

This iterative algorithm requires n multiplications.

The input parameter a could be an integer, or a rational, or a floating point number. In fact, it doesn't need to be a number at all, as long as it's something that we know how to multiply. For example, the same algorithm can be used to compute powers modulo some finite number (an operation commonly used in cryptography algorithms) or to compute powers of matrices (an operation used to evaluate recurrences and to compute shortest paths in graphs). Because we don't know what kind of object we're multiplying, we *can't* know how much time a single multiplication requires, so we're forced to analyze the running time in terms of the number of multiplications.

There is a much faster divide-and-conquer method, originally proposed by the Indian prosodist Piṅgala in the 2nd century BCE, which uses the following simple recursive formula:

$$a^n = \begin{cases} 1 & \text{if } n = 0 \\ (a^{n/2})^2 & \text{if } n > 0 \text{ and } n \text{ is even} \\ (a^{\lfloor n/2 \rfloor})^2 \cdot a & \text{otherwise} \end{cases}$$

```
PiṅgalaPower(a, n):
    if n = 1
        return a
    else
        x ← PiṅgalaPower(a, ⌊n/2⌋)
        if n is even
            return x · x
        else
            return x · x · a
```

The total number of multiplications performed by this algorithm satisfies the recurrence $T(n) \le T(n/2) + 2$. The recursion-tree method immediately give us the solution $T(n) = O(\log n)$.

A nearly identical exponentiation algorithm can also be derived directly from the Egyptian peasant multiplication algorithm from the previous chapter, by replacing addition with multiplication (and in particular, replacing duplation with squaring).

$$a^n = \begin{cases} 1 & \text{if } n = 0 \\ (a^2)^{n/2} & \text{if } n > 0 \text{ and } n \text{ is even} \\ (a^2)^{\lfloor n/2 \rfloor} \cdot a & \text{otherwise} \end{cases}$$

$$\boxed{\begin{array}{l} \textsc{PeasantPower}(a, n):\\ \quad \text{if } n = 1\\ \qquad \text{return } a\\ \quad \text{else if } n \text{ is even}\\ \qquad \text{return } \textsc{PeasantPower}(a^2, n/2)\\ \quad \text{else}\\ \qquad \text{return } \textsc{PeasantPower}(a^2, \lfloor n/2 \rfloor) \cdot a \end{array}}$$

This algorithm—which might reasonably be called "squaring and mediation"—also performs only $O(\log n)$ multiplications.

Both of these algorithms are asymptotically optimal; any algorithm that computes a^n *must* perform at least $\Omega(\log n)$ multiplications, because each multiplication at most doubles the largest power computed so far. In fact, when n is a power of two, both of these algorithms require exactly $\log_2 n$ multiplications, which is *exactly* optimal. However, there are slightly faster methods for other values of n. For example, PiṅgalaPower and PeasantPower each compute a^{15} using six multiplications, but in fact only five multiplications are necessary:

- Piṅgala: $a \rightarrow a^2 \rightarrow a^3 \rightarrow a^6 \rightarrow a^7 \rightarrow a^{14} \rightarrow a^{15}$
- Peasant: $a \rightarrow a^2 \rightarrow a^4 \rightarrow a^8 \rightarrow a^{12} \rightarrow a^{14} \rightarrow a^{15}$
- Optimal: $a \rightarrow a^2 \rightarrow a^3 \rightarrow a^5 \rightarrow a^{10} \rightarrow a^{15}$

It is a long-standing open question whether the absolute minimum number of multiplications for a given exponent n can be computed efficiently.

Exercises

Tower of Hanoi

1. Prove that the original recursive Tower of Hanoi algorithm performs *exactly* the same sequence of moves—the same disks, to and from the same pegs, in the same order—as each of the following non-recursive algorithms. The pegs are labeled 0, 1, and 2, and our problem is to move a stack of n disks from peg 0 to peg 2 (as shown on page 24).

   (a) If n is even, swap pegs 1 and 2. At the ith step, make the only legal move that avoids peg $i \bmod 3$. If there is no legal move, then all disks are on peg $i \bmod 3$, and the puzzle is solved.

   (b) For the first move, move disk 1 to peg 1 if n is even and to peg 2 if n is odd. Then repeatedly make the only legal move that involves a different disk from the previous move. If no such move exists, the puzzle is solved.

   (c) Pretend that disks $n + 1$, $n + 2$, and $n + 3$ are at the bottom of pegs 0, 1, and 2, respectively. Repeatedly make the only legal move that satisfies the following constraints, until no such move is possible.

- Do not place an odd disk directly on top of another odd disk.
- Do not place an even disk directly on top of another even disk.
- Do not undo the previous move.

(d) Let $\rho(n)$ denote the smallest integer k such that $n/2^k$ is not an integer. For example, $\rho(42) = 2$, because $42/2^1$ is an integer but $42/2^2$ is not. (Equivalently, $\rho(n)$ is one more than the position of the least significant 1 in the binary representation of n.) Because its behavior resembles the marks on a ruler, $\rho(n)$ is sometimes called the *ruler function*.

```
RulerHanoi(n):
    i ← 1
    while ρ(i) ≤ n
        if n − i is even
            move disk ρ(i) forward      ⟨⟨0 → 1 → 2 → 0⟩⟩
        else
            move disk ρ(i) backward     ⟨⟨0 → 2 → 1 → 0⟩⟩
        i ← i + 1
```

2. The Tower of Hanoi is a relatively recent descendant of a much older mechanical puzzle known as the Chinese linked rings, Baguenaudier, Cardan's Rings, Meleda, Patience, Tiring Irons, Prisoner's Lock, Spin-Out, and many other names. This puzzle was already well known in both China and Europe by the 16th century. The Italian mathematician Luca Pacioli described the 7-ring puzzle and its solution in his unpublished treatise *De Viribus Quantitatis*, written between 1498 and 1506;[13] only a few years later, the Ming-dynasty poet Yang Shen described the 9-ring puzzle as "a toy for women and children". The puzzle is apocryphally attributed to a 2nd-century Chinese general, who gave the puzzle to his wife to occupy her time while he was away at war.

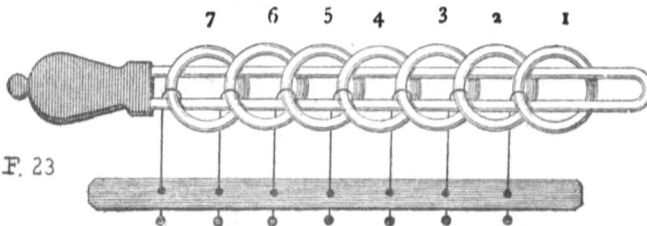

Figure 1.16. The 7-ring Baguenaudier, from *Récréations Mathématiques* by Édouard Lucas (1891) (See Image Credits at the end of the book.)

---

[13]*De Viribus Quantitatis* [*On the Powers of Numbers*] is an important early work on recreational mathematics and perhaps the oldest surviving treatise on magic. Pacioli is better known for *Summa de Aritmetica*, a near-complete encyclopedia of late 15th-century mathematics, which included the first description of double-entry bookkeeping.

The Baguenaudier puzzle has many physical forms, but one of the most common consists of a long metal loop and several rings, which are connected to a solid base by movable rods. The loop is initially threaded through the rings as shown in Figure 1.16; the goal of the puzzle is to remove the loop.

More abstractly, we can model the puzzle as a sequence of bits, one for each ring, where the ith bit is 1 if the loop passes through the ith ring and 0 otherwise. (Here we index the rings from right to left, as shown in Figure 1.16.) The puzzle allows two legal moves:

- You can always flip the 1st (= rightmost) bit.

- If the bit string ends with exactly z 0s, you can flip the $(z + 2)$th bit.

The goal of the puzzle is to transform a string of n 1s into a string of n 0s. For example, the following sequence of 21 moves solves the 5-ring puzzle:

$$11111 \xrightarrow{1} 11110 \xrightarrow{3} 11010 \xrightarrow{1} 11011 \xrightarrow{2} 11001 \xrightarrow{1} 11000$$

$$\xrightarrow{5} 01000 \xrightarrow{1} 01001 \xrightarrow{2} 01011 \xrightarrow{1} 01010 \xrightarrow{3} 01110$$

$$\xrightarrow{1} 01111 \xrightarrow{2} 01101 \xrightarrow{1} 01100 \xrightarrow{4} 00100 \xrightarrow{1} 00101$$

$$\xrightarrow{2} 00111 \xrightarrow{1} 00110 \xrightarrow{3} 00010 \xrightarrow{1} 00011 \xrightarrow{2} 00001 \xrightarrow{1} 00000$$

⬥(a) Call a sequence of moves *reduced* if no move is the inverse of the previous move. Prove that for any non-negative integer n, there is *exactly one* reduced sequence of moves that solves the n-ring Baguenaudier puzzle. [Hint: This problem is much easier if you're already familiar with graphs.]

(b) Describe an algorithm to solve the Baguenaudier puzzle. Your input is the number of rings n; your algorithm should print a reduced sequence of moves that solves the puzzle. For example, given the integer 5 as input, your algorithm should print the sequence 1, 3, 1, 2, 1, 5, 1, 2, 1, 3, 1, 2, 1, 4, 1, 2, 1, 3, 1, 2, 1.

(c) *Exactly* how many moves does your algorithm perform, as a function of n? Prove your answer is correct.

3. A less familiar chapter in the Tower of Hanoi's history is its brief relocation of the temple from Benares to Pisa in the early 13th century.[14] The relocation was organized by the wealthy merchant-mathematician Leonardo Fibonacci, at the request of the Holy Roman Emperor Frederick II, who had heard reports of the temple from soldiers returning from the Crusades. The Towers of Pisa and their attendant monks became famous, helping to establish Pisa as a dominant trading center on the Italian peninsula.

---

[14]Portions of this story are actually true.

Unfortunately, almost as soon as the temple was moved, one of the diamond needles began to lean to one side. To avoid the possibility of the leaning tower falling over from too much use, Fibonacci convinced the priests to adopt a more relaxed rule: ***Any number of disks on the leaning needle can be moved together to another needle in a single move.*** It was still forbidden to place a larger disk on top of a smaller disk, and disks had to be moved one at a time *onto* the leaning needle or between the two vertical needles.

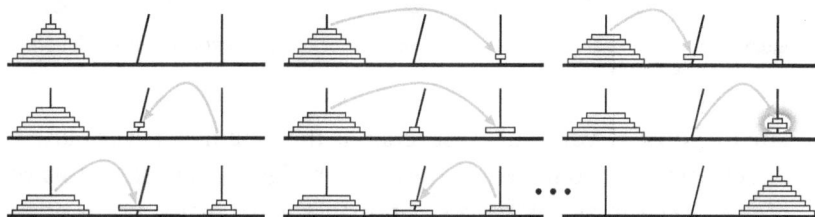

Figure 1.17. The Towers of Pisa. In the fifth move, two disks are taken off the leaning needle.

Thanks to Fibonacci's new rule, the priests could bring about the end of the universe somewhat faster from Pisa than they could from Benares. Fortunately, the temple was moved from Pisa back to Benares after the newly crowned Pope Gregory IX excommunicated Frederick II, making the local priests less sympathetic to hosting foreign heretics with strange mathematical habits. Soon afterward, a bell tower was erected on the spot where the temple once stood; it too began to lean almost immediately.

Describe an algorithm to transfer a stack of n disks from one *vertical* needle to the other *vertical* needle, using the smallest possible number of moves. *Exactly* how many moves does your algorithm perform?

4. Consider the following restricted variants of the Tower of Hanoi puzzle In each problem, the pegs are numbered 0, 1, and 2, and your task is to move a stack of n disks from peg 0 to peg 2, exactly as in problem 1.

   (a) Suppose you are forbidden to move any disk directly between peg 1 and peg 2; *every* move must involve peg 0. Describe an algorithm to solve this version of the puzzle in as few moves as possible. *Exactly* how many moves does your algorithm make?

♣♥(b) Suppose you are only allowed to move disks from peg 0 to peg 2, from peg 2 to peg 1, or from peg 1 to peg 0. Equivalently, suppose the pegs are arranged in a circle and numbered in clockwise order, and you are only allowed to move disks counterclockwise. Describe an algorithm to solve this version of the puzzle in as few moves as possible. How many moves does your algorithm make?

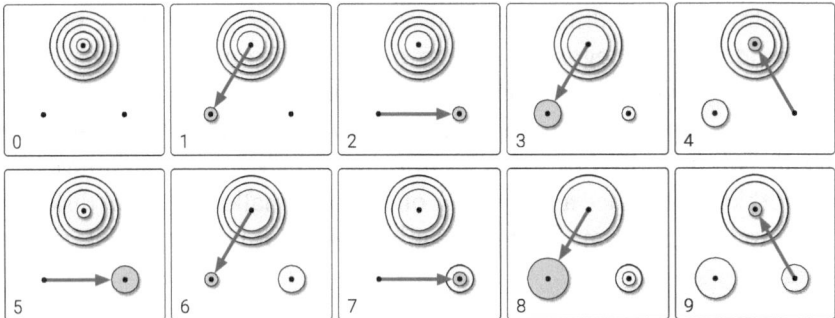

Figure 1.18. The first several moves in a counterclockwise Towers of Hanoi solution.

♠♥(c) Finally, suppose your only restriction is that you may never move a disk directly from peg 0 to peg 2. Describe an algorithm to solve this version of the puzzle in as few moves as possible. How many moves does your algorithm make? [*Hint: Matrices! This variant is considerably harder to analyze than the other two.*]

5. Consider the following more complex variant of the Tower of Hanoi puzzle The puzzle has a row of k pegs, numbered from 1 to k. In a single turn, you are allowed to move the smallest disk on peg i to either peg $i-1$ or peg $i+1$, for any index i; as usual, you are not allowed to place a bigger disk on a smaller disk. Your mission is to move a stack of n disks from peg 1 to peg k.

    (a) Describe a recursive algorithm for the case $k = 3$. *Exactly* how many moves does your algorithm make? (This is exactly the same as problem 4(a).)

    (b) Describe a recursive algorithm for the case $k = n+1$ that requires at most $O(n^3)$ moves. [*Hint: Use part (a).*]

    ♥(c) Describe a recursive algorithm for the case $k = n+1$ that requires at most $O(n^2)$ moves. [*Hint: Don't use part (a).*]

    ♥(d) Describe a recursive algorithm for the case $k = \sqrt{n}$ that requires at most a polynomial number of moves. (Which polynomial??)

    ♥(e) Describe and analyze a recursive algorithm for arbitrary n and k. How small must k be (as a function of n) so that the number of moves is bounded by a polynomial in n?

Recursion Trees

6. Use recursion trees to solve each of the following recurrences.

$$A(n) = 2A(n/4) + \sqrt{n} \quad B(n) = 2B(n/4) + n \quad C(n) = 2C(n/4) + n^2$$
$$D(n) = 3D(n/3) + \sqrt{n} \quad E(n) = 3E(n/3) + n \quad F(n) = 3F(n/3) + n^2$$
$$G(n) = 4G(n/2) + \sqrt{n} \quad H(n) = 4H(n/2) + n \quad I(n) = 4I(n/2) + n^2$$

7. Use recursion trees to solve each of the following recurrences.

(j) $J(n) = J(n/2) + J(n/3) + J(n/6) + n$

(k) $K(n) = K(n/2) + 2K(n/3) + 3K(n/4) + n^2$

(l) $L(n) = L(n/15) + L(n/10) + 2L(n/6) + \sqrt{n}$

♥8. Use recursion trees to solve each of the following recurrences.

(m) $M(n) = 2M(n/2) + O(n \log n)$

(n) $N(n) = 2N(n/2) + O(n / \log n)$

(p) $P(n) = \sqrt{n} P(\sqrt{n}) + n$

(q) $Q(n) = \sqrt{2n} Q(\sqrt{2n}) + \sqrt{n}$

Sorting

9. Suppose you are given a stack of n pancakes of different sizes. You want to sort the pancakes so that smaller pancakes are on top of larger pancakes. The only operation you can perform is a *flip*—insert a spatula under the top k pancakes, for some integer k between 1 and n, and flip them all over.

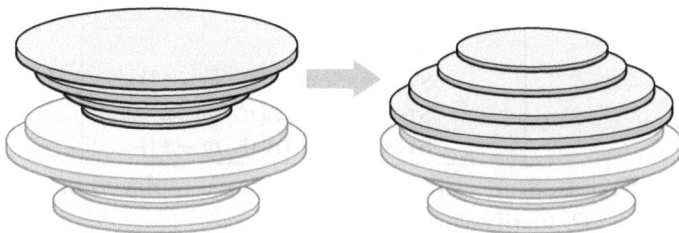

Figure 1.19. Flipping the top four pancakes.

(a) Describe an algorithm to sort an arbitrary stack of n pancakes using $O(n)$ flips. *Exactly* how many flips does your algorithm perform in the worst case?[15] [*Hint: This problem has nothing to do with the Tower of Hanoi.*]

---

[15]The *exact* worst-case optimal number of flips required to sort n pancakes (either burned or unburned) is an long-standing open problem; just do the best you can.

(b) For every positive integer n, describe a stack of n pancakes that requires $\Omega(n)$ flips to sort.

(c) Now suppose one side of each pancake is burned. Describe an algorithm to sort an arbitrary stack of n pancakes, so that the burned side of every pancake is facing down, using $O(n)$ flips. *Exactly* how many flips does your algorithm perform in the worst case?

10. Recall that the *median-of-three* heuristic examines the first, last, and middle element of the array, and uses the median of those three elements as a quicksort pivot. Prove that quicksort with the median-of-three heuristic requires $\Omega(n^2)$ time to sort an array of size n in the worst case. Specifically, for any integer n, describe a permutation of the integers 1 through n, such that in every recursive call to median-of-three-quicksort, the pivot is always the second smallest element of the array. Designing this permutation requires intimate knowledge of the PARTITION subroutine.

(a) As a warm-up exercise, assume that the PARTITION subroutine is *stable*, meaning it preserves the existing order of all elements smaller than the pivot, and it preserves the existing order of all elements smaller than the pivot.

♥(b) Assume that the PARTITION subroutine uses the specific algorithm listed on page 29, which is *not* stable.

11. (a) Hey, Moe! Hey, Larry! Prove that the following algorithm actually sorts its input!

```
StoogeSort(A[0 .. n − 1]) :
    if n = 2 and A[0] > A[1]
        swap A[0] ↔ A[1]
    else if n > 2
        m = ⌈2n/3⌉
        StoogeSort(A[0 .. m − 1])
        StoogeSort(A[n − m .. n − 1])
        StoogeSort(A[0 .. m − 1])
```

(b) Would STOOGESORT still sort correctly if we replaced $m = \lceil 2n/3 \rceil$ with $m = \lfloor 2n/3 \rfloor$? Justify your answer.

(c) State a recurrence (including the base case(s)) for the number of comparisons executed by STOOGESORT.

(d) Solve the recurrence, and prove that your solution is correct. *[Hint: Ignore the ceiling.]*

(e) Prove that the number of *swaps* executed by STOOGESORT is at most $\binom{n}{2}$.

12. The following cruel and unusual sorting algorithm was proposed by Gary Miller:

```
CRUEL(A[1..n]):
    if n > 1
        CRUEL(A[1..n/2])
        CRUEL(A[n/2+1..n])
        UNUSUAL(A[1..n])
```

```
UNUSUAL(A[1..n]):
    if n = 2
        if A[1] > A[2]                          ⟨⟨the only comparison!⟩⟩
            swap A[1] ↔ A[2]
    else
        for i ← 1 to n/4                        ⟨⟨swap 2nd and 3rd quarters⟩⟩
            swap A[i+n/4] ↔ A[i+n/2]
        UNUSUAL(A[1..n/2])                     ⟨⟨recurse on left half⟩⟩
        UNUSUAL(A[n/2+1..n])                   ⟨⟨recurse on right half⟩⟩
        UNUSUAL(A[n/4+1..3n/4])               ⟨⟨recurse on middle half⟩⟩
```

The comparisons performed by this algorithm do not depend at all on the values in the input array; such a sorting algorithm is called **oblivious**. Assume for this problem that the input size n is always a power of 2.

(a) Prove by induction that CRUEL correctly sorts any input array. [Hint: Consider an array that contains $n/4$ 1s, $n/4$ 2s, $n/4$ 3s, and $n/4$ 4s. Why is this special case enough?]

(b) Prove that CRUEL would *not* correctly sort if we removed the for-loop from UNUSUAL.

(c) Prove that CRUEL would *not* correctly sort if we swapped the last two lines of UNUSUAL.

(d) What is the running time of UNUSUAL? Justify your answer.

(e) What is the running time of CRUEL? Justify your answer.

13. An **inversion** in an array $A[1..n]$ is a pair of indices (i, j) such that $i < j$ and $A[i] > A[j]$. The number of inversions in an n-element array is between 0 (if the array is sorted) and $\binom{n}{2}$ (if the array is sorted backward). Describe and analyze an algorithm to count the number of inversions in an n-element array in $O(n \log n)$ time. [Hint: Modify mergesort.]

14. (a) Suppose you are given two sets of n points, one set $\{p_1, p_2, \ldots, p_n\}$ on the line $y = 0$ and the other set $\{q_1, q_2, \ldots, q_n\}$ on the line $y = 1$. Create a set of n line segments by connect each point p_i to the corresponding point q_i. Describe and analyze a divide-and-conquer algorithm to determine how many pairs of these line segments intersect, in $O(n \log n)$ time. [Hint: See the previous problem.]

(b) Now suppose you are given two sets $\{p_1, p_2, \ldots, p_n\}$ and $\{q_1, q_2, \ldots, q_n\}$ of n points on the unit circle. Connect each point p_i to the corresponding point q_i. Describe and analyze a divide-and-conquer algorithm to determine how many pairs of these line segments intersect in $O(n \log^2 n)$ time. [*Hint: Use your solution to part (a).*]

♥(c) Describe an algorithm for part (b) that runs in $O(n \log n)$ time. [*Hint: Use your solution from part (b)!*]

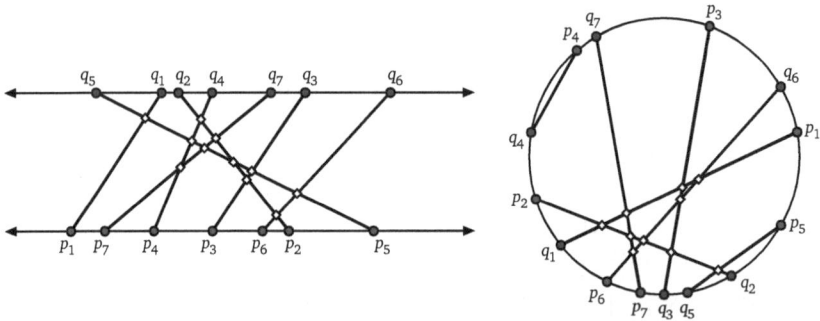

Figure 1.20. Eleven intersecting pairs of segments with endpoints on parallel lines, and ten intersecting pairs of segments with endpoints on a circle.

15. (a) Describe an algorithm that sorts an input array $A[1..n]$ by calling a subroutine SQRTSORT(k), which sorts the subarray $A[k+1..k+\sqrt{n}]$ in place, given an arbitrary integer k between 0 and $n-\sqrt{n}$ as input. (To simplify the problem, assume that $\sqrt{n}$ is an integer.) Your algorithm is *only* allowed to inspect or modify the input array by calling SQRTSORT; in particular, your algorithm must not directly compare, move, or copy array elements. How many times does your algorithm call SQRTSORT in the worst case?

♣(b) Prove that your algorithm from part (a) is optimal up to constant factors. In other words, if $f(n)$ is the number of times your algorithm calls SQRTSORT, prove that no algorithm can sort using $o(f(n))$ calls to SQRTSORT.

(c) Now suppose SQRTSORT is implemented recursively, by calling your sorting algorithm from part (a). For example, at the second level of recursion, the algorithm is sorting arrays roughly of size $n^{1/4}$. What is the worst-case running time of the resulting sorting algorithm? (To simplify the analysis, assume that the array size n has the form 2^{2^k}, so that repeated square roots are always integers.)

Selection

16. Suppose we are given a set S of n items, each with a *value* and a *weight*. For any element $x \in S$, we define two subsets

- $S_{<x}$ is the set of elements of S whose value is less than the value of x.
- $S_{>x}$ is the set of elements of S whose value is more than the value of x.

For any subset $R \subseteq S$, let $w(R)$ denote the sum of the weights of elements in R. The **weighted median** of R is any element x such that $w(S_{<x}) \le w(S)/2$ and $w(S_{>x}) \le w(S)/2$.

Describe and analyze an algorithm to compute the weighted median of a given weighted set in $O(n)$ time. Your input consists of two unsorted arrays $S[1..n]$ and $W[1..n]$, where for each index i, the ith element has value $S[i]$ and weight $W[i]$. You may assume that all values are distinct and all weights are positive.

17. (a) Describe an algorithm to determine in $O(n)$ time whether an arbitrary array $A[1..n]$ contains more than $n/4$ copies of any value.

    (b) Describe and analyze an algorithm to determine, given an arbitrary array $A[1..n]$ and an integer k, whether A contains more than k copies of any value. Express the running time of your algorithm as a function of both n and k.

    Do not use hashing, or radix sort, or any other method that depends on the precise input values, as opposed to their order.

18. Describe an algorithm to compute the median of an array $A[1..5]$ of distinct numbers using at most 6 comparisons. Instead of writing pseudocode, describe your algorithm using a **decision tree**: A binary tree where each internal node contains a comparison of the form "$A[i] \gtrless A[j]$?" and each leaf contains an index into the array.

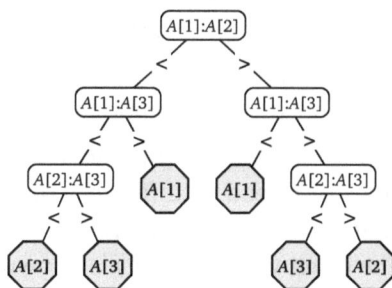

Figure 1.21. Finding the median of a 3-element array using at most 3 comparisons

19. Consider the generalization of the Blum-Floyd-Pratt-Rivest-Tarjan Mom-Select algorithm shown in Figure 1.22, which partitions the input array into $\lceil n/b \rceil$ blocks of size b, instead of $\lceil n/5 \rceil$ blocks of size 5, but is otherwise identical.

```
MOM_b SELECT(A[1..n], k):
    if n ≤ b²
        use brute force
    else
        m ← ⌈n/b⌉
        for i ← 1 to m
            M[i] ← MEDIANOFB(A[b(i − 1) + 1 .. bi])
        mom_b ← MOM_b SELECT(M[1 .. m], ⌊m/2⌋)
        r ← PARTITION(A[1 .. n], mom_b)
        if k < r
            return MOM_b SELECT(A[1 .. r − 1], k)
        else if k > r
            return MOM_b SELECT(A[r + 1 .. n], k − r)
        else
            return mom_b
```

Figure 1.22. A parametrized family of selection algorithms; see problem 19.

(a) State a recurrence for the running time of MOM$_b$SELECT, assuming that b is a constant (so the subroutine MEDIANOFB runs in $O(1)$ time). In particular, how do the sizes of the recursive subproblems depend on the constant b? Consider even b and odd b separately.

(b) What is the worst-case running time of MOM$_1$SELECT? [*Hint: This is a trick question.*]

♣♥(c) What is the worst-case running time of MOM$_2$SELECT? [*Hint: This is an unfair question!*]

♥(d) What is the worst-case running time of MOM$_3$SELECT? Finding an upper bound on the running time is straightforward; the hard part is showing that this analysis is actually tight. [*Hint: See problem 10.*]

♥(e) What is the worst-case running time of MOM$_4$SELECT? Again, the hard part is showing that the analysis cannot be improved.[16]

(f) For any constants $b \geq 5$, the algorithm MOM$_b$SELECT runs in $O(n)$ time, but different values of b lead to different constant factors. Let $M(b)$ denote the minimum number of comparisons required to find the median of b numbers. The exact value of $M(b)$ is known only for $b \leq 13$:

b	1	2	3	4	5	6	7	8	9	10	11	12	13
$M(b)$	0	1	3	4	6	8	10	12	14	16	18	20	23

---

[16]The median of four elements is either the second smallest or the second largest. In 2014, Ke Chen and Adrian Dumitrescu proved that if we modify MOM$_4$SELECT to find second-smallest elements when $k < n/2$ and second-largest elements when $k > n/2$, the resulting algorithm runs in $O(n)$ time! See their paper "Select with Groups of 3 or 4 Takes Linear Time" (WADS 2015, arXiv:1409.3600) for details.

For each b between 5 and 13, find an upper bound on the running time of $\text{Mom}_b\text{Select}$ of the form $T(n) \le \alpha_b n$ for some explicit constant α_b. (For example, on page 39 we showed that $\alpha_5 \le 16$.)

(g) Which value of b yields the smallest constant α_b? *[Hint: This is a trick question!]*

20. Prove that the variant of the Blum-Floyd-Pratt-Rivest-Tarjan Select algorithm shown in Figure 1.23, which uses an extra layer of small medians to choose the main pivot, runs in $O(n)$ time.

$\underline{\text{MomomSelect}(A[1\mathbin{..}n], k):}$
   if $n \le 81$
      use brute force
   else
      $m \leftarrow \lceil n/3 \rceil$
      for $i \leftarrow 1$ to m
         $M[i] \leftarrow \text{MedianOf3}(A[3i-2\mathbin{..}3i])$
      $mm \leftarrow \lceil m/3 \rceil$
      for $j \leftarrow 1$ to mm
         $Mom[j] \leftarrow \text{MedianOf3}(M[3j-2\mathbin{..}3j])$
      $momom \leftarrow \text{MomomSelect}(Mom[1\mathbin{..}mm], \lfloor mm/2 \rfloor)$
      $r \leftarrow \text{Partition}(A[1\mathbin{..}n], momom)$
      if $k < r$
         return $\text{MomomSelect}(A[1\mathbin{..}r-1], k)$
      else if $k > r$
         return $\text{MomomSelect}(A[r+1\mathbin{..}n], k-r)$
      else
         return $momom$

Figure 1.23. Selection by median of moms; see problem 20).

---

21. (a) Suppose we are given two sorted arrays $A[1\mathbin{..}n]$ and $B[1\mathbin{..}n]$. Describe an algorithm to find the median element in the union of A and B in $\Theta(\log n)$ time. You can assume that the arrays contain no duplicate elements.

(b) Suppose we are given two sorted arrays $A[1\mathbin{..}m]$ and $B[1\mathbin{..}n]$ and an integer k. Describe an algorithm to find the kth smallest element in $A \cup B$ in $\Theta(\log(m+n))$ time. For example, if $k = 1$, your algorithm should return the smallest element of $A \cup B$.) *[Hint: Use your solution to part (a).]*

♥(c) Now suppose we are given *three* sorted arrays $A[1\mathbin{..}n]$, $B[1\mathbin{..}n]$, and $C[1\mathbin{..}n]$, and an integer k. Describe an algorithm to find the kth smallest element in $A \cup B \cup C$ in $O(\log n)$ time.

(d) Finally, suppose we are given a two dimensional array $A[1..m, 1..n]$ in which every row $A[i, \cdot]$ is sorted, and an integer k. Describe an algorithm to find the kth smallest element in A as quickly as possible. How does the running time of your algorithm depend on m? [*Hint: Solve problem 16 first.*]

Arithmetic

22. In 1854, archaeologists discovered Sumerians clay tablets, carved around 2000BCE, that list the squares of integers up to 59. This discovery led some scholars to conjecture that ancient Sumerians performed multiplication by reduction to squaring, using an identity like $x \cdot y = (x^2 + y^2 - (x - y)^2)/2$. Unfortunately, those same scholars are silent on how the Sumerians supposedly squared larger numbers. Four thousand years later, we can finally rescue these Sumerian mathematicians from their lives of drudgery through the power of recursion!

(a) Describe a variant of Karatsuba's algorithm that squares any n-digit number in $O(n^{\lg 3})$ time, by reducing to squaring three $\lceil n/2 \rceil$-digit numbers. (Karatsuba actually did this in 1960.)

(b) Describe a recursive algorithm that squares any n-digit number in $O(n^{\log_3 6})$ time, by reducing to squaring six $\lceil n/3 \rceil$-digit numbers.

♥(c) Describe a recursive algorithm that squares any n-digit number in $O(n^{\log_3 5})$ time, by reducing to squaring only *five* $(n/3 + O(1))$-digit numbers. [*Hint: What is $(a + b + c)^2 + (a - b + c)^2$?*]

23. (a) Describe and analyze a variant of Karatsuba's algorithm that multiplies any m-digit number and any n-digit number, for any $n \geq m$, in $O(nm^{\lg 3 - 1})$ time.

(b) Describe an algorithm to compute the decimal representation of 2^n in $O(n^{\lg 3})$ time, using the algorithm from part (a) as a subroutine. (The standard algorithm that computes one digit at a time requires $\Theta(n^2)$ time.)

(c) Describe a divide-and-conquer algorithm to compute the decimal representation of an arbitrary n-bit binary number in $O(n^{\lg 3})$ time. [*Hint: Watch out for an extra log factor in the running time.*]

♥(d) Suppose we can multiply two n-digit numbers in $O(M(n))$ time. Describe an algorithm to compute the decimal representation of an arbitrary n-bit binary number in $O(M(n) \log n)$ time. [*Hint: The analysis is the hard part; use a domain transformation.*]

24. Consider the following classical recursive algorithm for computing the factorial $n!$ of a non-negative integer n:

> FACTORIAL(n):
>   if $n = 0$
>   return 1
>   else
>   return $n \cdot$ FACTORIAL($n - 1$)

(a) How many multiplications does this algorithm perform?

(b) How many bits are required to write $n!$ in binary? Express your answer in the form $\Theta(f(n))$, for some familiar function $f(n)$. [Hint: $(n/2)^{n/2} < n! < n^n$.]

(c) Your answer to (b) should convince you that the number of multiplications is *not* a good estimate of the actual running time of FACTORIAL. We can multiply any k-digit number and any l-digit number in $O(k \cdot l)$ time using either the lattice algorithm or duplation and mediation. What is the running time of FACTORIAL if we use this multiplication algorithm as a subroutine?

(d) The following recursive algorithm also computes the factorial function, but using a different grouping of the multiplications:

> FALLING(n, m):   ⟨⟨Compute $n!/(n - m)!$⟩⟩
>   if $m = 0$
>   return 1
>   else if $m = 1$
>   return n
>   else
>   return FALLING($n, \lfloor m/2 \rfloor$) $\cdot$ FALLING($n - \lfloor m/2 \rfloor, \lceil m/2 \rceil$)

What is the running time of FALLING(n, n) if we use grade-school multiplication? [Hint: As usual, ignore the floors and ceilings.]

(e) Describe and analyze a variant of Karatsuba's algorithm that multiplies any k-digit number and any l-digit number, for any $k \geq l$, in $O(k \cdot l^{\lg 3 - 1}) = O(k \cdot l^{0.585})$ time.

▼(f) What are the running times of FACTORIAL(n) and FALLING(n, n) if we use the modified Karatsuba multiplication from part (e)?

25. The **greatest common divisor** of two positive integer x and y, denoted $\gcd(x, y)$, is the largest integer d such that both x/d and y/d are integers. Euclid's *Elements*, written around 300BCE, describes the following recursive algorithm to compute $\gcd(x, y)$: [17]

---

[17] Euclid's algorithm is sometimes incorrectly described as the oldest recursive algorithm, or even the oldest *nontrivial* algorithm, even though the Egyptian duplation and mediation algorithm—which is both nontrivial and recursive—predates Euclid by at least 1500 years.

```
EUCLIDGCD(x, y):
    if x = y
        return x
    else if x > y
        return EUCLIDGCD(x − y, y)
    else
        return EUCLIDGCD(x, y − x)
```

(a) Prove that EUCLIDGCD correctly computes $\gcd(x, y)$.[18] Specifically:

    i. Prove that EUCLIDGCD(x, y) divides both x and y.

    ii. Prove that every divisor of x and y is a divisor of EUCLIDGCD(x, y).

(b) What is the worst-case running time of EUCLIDGCD(x, y), as a function of x and y? (Assume that computing $x − y$ requires $O(\log x + \log y)$ time.)

(c) Prove that the following algorithm also computes $\gcd(x, y)$:

```
FASTEUCLIDGCD(x, y):
    if y = 0
        return x
    else if x > y
        return FASTEUCLIDGCD(y, x mod y)
    else
        return FASTEUCLIDGCD(x, y mod x)
```

(d) What is the worst-case running time of FASTEUCLIDGCD(x, y), as a function of x and y? (Assume that computing $x \bmod y$ takes $O(\log x \cdot \log y)$ time.)

(e) Prove that the following algorithm also computes $\gcd(x, y)$:

```
BINARYGCD(x, y):
    if x = y
        return x
    else if x and y are both even
        return 2 · BINARYGCD(x/2, y/2)
    else if x is even
        return BINARYGCD(x/2, y)
    else if y is even
        return BINARYGCD(x, y/2)
    else if x > y
        return BINARYGCD((x − y)/2, y)
    else
        return BINARYGCD(x, (y − x)/2)
```

[18] Euclid did not do this. Proposition 1 in *Elements* Book VII states that if EUCLIDGCD$(x, y) = 1$, then x and y are relatively prime (that is, $\gcd(x, y) = 1$), but the proof only considers the special case $x \bmod (y \bmod (x \bmod y)) = 1$. Proposition 2 states that if x and y are *not* relatively prime, then EUCLIDGCD$(x, y) = \gcd(x, y)$, but the proof only considers the special cases $\gcd(x, y) = y$ and $\gcd(x, y) = y \bmod (x \bmod y)$. Finally, these two Propositions do not make a complete proof that EUCLIDGCD is correct. Don't be like Euclid.

(f) What is the worst-case running time of BINARYGCD(x, y), as a function of x and y? (Assume that computing $x - y$ takes $O(\log x + \log y)$ time, and computing $z/2$ requires $O(\log z)$ time.)

Arrays

26. Suppose you are given a $2^n \times 2^n$ checkerboard with one (arbitrarily chosen) square removed. Describe and analyze an algorithm to compute a tiling of the board by without gaps or overlaps by **L**-shaped tiles, each composed of 3 squares. Your input is the integer n and two n-bit integers representing the row and column of the missing square. The output is a list of the positions and orientations of $(4^n - 1)/3$ tiles. Your algorithm should run in $O(4^n)$ time. [*Hint: First prove that such a tiling always exists.*]

27. You are a visitor at a political convention (or perhaps a faculty meeting) with n delegates; each delegate is a member of exactly one political party. It is impossible to tell which political party any delegate belongs to; in particular, you will be summarily ejected from the convention if you ask. However, you can determine whether any pair of delegates belong to the *same* party by introducing them to each other. Members of the same political party always greet each other with smiles and friendly handshakes; members of different parties always greet each other with angry stares and insults.[19]

    (a) Suppose more than half of the delegates belong to the same political party. Describe an efficient algorithm that identifies all members of this majority party.

    (b) Now suppose there are more than two parties, but one party has a *plurality*: more people belong to that party than to any other party. Present a practical procedure to precisely pick the people from the plurality political party as parsimoniously as possible, presuming the plurality party is composed of at least p people. Pretty please.

28. Smullyan Island has three types of inhabitants: *knights* always speak the truth; *knaves* always lie; and *normals* sometimes speak the truth and sometimes don't. Everyone on the island knows everyone else's name and type (knight, knave, or normal). You want to learn the type of every inhabitant.

    You can ask any inhabitant to tell you the type of any other inhabitant. Specifically, if you ask "Hey X, what is Y's type?" then X will respond as follows:

---

[19] Real-world politics is much messier than this simplified model, but this is a theory book!

- If X is a knight, then X will respond with Y's correct type.
- If X is a knave, then X could respond with *either* of the types that Y is *not*.
- If X is a normal, then X could respond with *any* of the three types.

The inhabitants will ignore any questions not of this precise form; in particular, you may not ask an inhabitant about their own type. Asking the same inhabitant the same question multiple times always yields the same answer, so there's no point in asking any question more than once.

(a) Suppose you know that a strict majority of inhabitants are knights. Describe an efficient algorithm to identify the type of every inhabitant.

(b) Prove that if at most half the inhabitants are knights, it is impossible to determine the type of every inhabitant.

29. Most graphics hardware includes support for a low-level operation called *blit*, or **block transfer**, which quickly copies a rectangular chunk of a pixel map (a two-dimensional array of pixel values) from one location to another. This is a two-dimensional version of the standard C library function memcpy().

    Suppose we want to rotate an $n \times n$ pixel map 90° clockwise. One way to do this, at least when n is a power of two, is to split the pixel map into four $n/2 \times n/2$ blocks, move each block to its proper position using a sequence of five blits, and then recursively rotate each block. (Why five? For the same reason the Tower of Hanoi puzzle needs a third peg.) Alternately, we could *first* recursively rotate the blocks and *then* blit them into place.

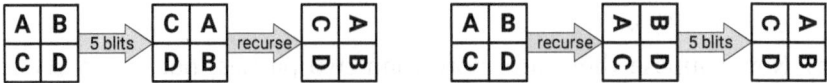

Figure 1.24. Two algorithms for rotating a pixel map.

(a) Prove that both versions of the algorithm are correct when n is a power of 2.

(b) *Exactly* how many blits does the algorithm perform when n is a power of 2?

(c) Describe how to modify the algorithm so that it works for arbitrary n, not just powers of 2. How many blits does your modified algorithm perform?

(d) What is your algorithm's running time if a $k \times k$ blit takes $O(k^2)$ time?

(e) What if a $k \times k$ blit takes only $O(k)$ time?

30. An array $A[0..n-1]$ of n distinct numbers is **bitonic** if there are unique indices i and j such that $A[(i-1) \bmod n] < A[i] > A[(i+1) \bmod n]$ and

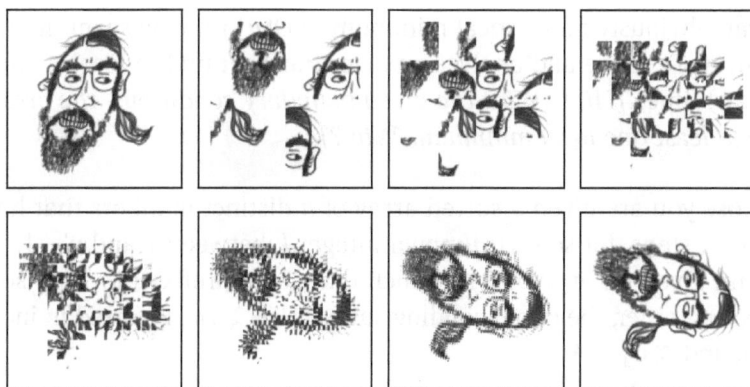

Figure 1.25. The first rotation algorithm (blit then recurse) in action. (See Image Credits at the end of the book.)

$A[(j-1) \bmod n] > A[j] < A[(j+1) \bmod n]$. In other words, a bitonic sequence either consists of an increasing sequence followed by a decreasing sequence, or can be circularly shifted to become so. For example,

4	6	9	8	7	5	1	2	3

is bitonic, but

3	6	9	8	7	5	1	2	4

is *not* bitonic.

Describe and analyze an algorithm to find the *smallest* element in an n-element bitonic array in $O(\log n)$ time. You may assume that the numbers in the input array are distinct.

31. Suppose we are given an array $A[1 .. n]$ of n distinct integers, which could be positive, negative, or zero, sorted in increasing order so that $A[1] < A[2] < \cdots < A[n]$.

    (a) Describe a fast algorithm that either computes an index i such that $A[i] = i$ or correctly reports that no such index exists.

    (b) Suppose we know in advance that $A[1] > 0$. Describe an even faster algorithm that either computes an index i such that $A[i] = i$ or correctly reports that no such index exists. *[Hint: This is **really** easy.]*

32. Suppose we are given an array $A[1 .. n]$ with the special property that $A[1] \geq A[2]$ and $A[n-1] \leq A[n]$. We say that an element $A[x]$ is a *local minimum* if it is less than or equal to both its neighbors, or more formally, if $A[x-1] \geq A[x]$ and $A[x] \leq A[x+1]$. For example, there are six local minima in the following array:

9	7	7	2	1	3	7	5	4	7	3	3	4	8	6	9
	▲		▲					▲		▲	▲			▲	

We can obviously find a local minimum in $O(n)$ time by scanning through the array. Describe and analyze an algorithm that finds a local minimum in $O(\log n)$ time. [*Hint: With the given boundary conditions, the array **must** have at least one local minimum. Why?*]

33. Suppose you are given a sorted array of n distinct numbers that has been *rotated* k steps, for some **unknown** integer k between 1 and $n - 1$. That is, you are given an array $A[1..n]$ such that some prefix $A[1..k]$ is sorted in increasing order, the corresponding suffix $A[k + 1..n]$ is sorted in increasing order, and $A[n] < A[1]$.

    For example, you might be given the following 16-element array (where $k = 10$):

    | 9 | 13 | 16 | 18 | 19 | 23 | 28 | 31 | 37 | 42 ‖ 1 | 3 | 4 | 5 | 7 | 8 |

    (a) Describe and analyze an algorithm to compute the unknown integer k.

    (b) Describe and analyze an algorithm to determine if the given array contains a given number x.

34. At the end of the second act of the action blockbuster *Fast and Impossible XIII¾: The Last Guardians of Expendable Justice Reloaded*, the villainous Dr. Metaphor hypnotizes the entire Hero League/Force/Squad, arranges them in a long line at the edge of a cliff, and instructs each hero to shoot the closest taller heroes to their left and right, at a prearranged signal.

    Suppose we are given the heights of all n heroes, in order from left to right, in an array $Ht[1..n]$. (To avoid salary arguments, the producers insisted that no two heroes have the same height.) Then we can compute the Left and Right targets of each hero in $O(n^2)$ time using the following brute-force algorithm.

    ```
    WHOTARGETSWHOM(Ht[1..n]):
        for j ← 1 to n
            ⟨⟨Find the left target L[j] for hero j⟩⟩
            L[j] ← NONE
            for i ← 1 to j − 1
                if Ht[i] > Ht[j]
                    L[j] ← i

            ⟨⟨Find the right target R[j] for hero j⟩⟩
            R[j] ← NONE
            for k ← n down to j + 1
                if Ht[k] > Ht[j]
                    R[j] ← k
        return L[1..n], R[1..n]
    ```

(a) Describe a divide-and-conquer algorithm that computes the output of WHOTARGETSWHOM in $O(n \log n)$ time.

(b) Prove that at least $\lfloor n/2 \rfloor$ of the n heroes are targets. That is, prove that the output arrays $R[0..n-1]$ and $L[0..n-1]$ contain at least $\lfloor n/2 \rfloor$ distinct values (other than NONE).

(c) Alas, Dr. Metaphor's diabolical plan is successful. At the prearranged signal, all the heroes simultaneously shoot their targets, and all targets fall over the cliff, apparently dead. Metaphor repeats his dastardly experiment over and over; after each massacre, he forces the remaining heroes to choose new targets, following the same algorithm, and then shoot their targets at the next signal. Eventually, only the shortest member of the Hero Crew/Alliance/Posse is left alive.[20]

Describe and analyze an algorithm to compute the number of rounds before Dr. Metaphor's deadly process finally ends. For full credit, your algorithm should run in $O(n)$ time.

35. You are a contestant on the hit game show "Beat Your Neighbors!" You are presented with an $m \times n$ grid of boxes, each containing a unique number. It costs $100 to open a box. Your goal is to find a box whose number is larger than its neighbors in the grid (above, below, left, and right). If you spend less money than any of your opponents, you win a week-long trip for two to Las Vegas and a year's supply of Rice-A-Roni™, to which you are hopelessly addicted.

(a) Suppose $m = 1$. Describe an algorithm that finds a number that is bigger than either of its neighbors. How many boxes does your algorithm open in the worst case?

♥(b) Suppose $m = n$. Describe an algorithm that finds a number that is bigger than any of its neighbors. How many boxes does your algorithm open in the worst case?

♣♥(c) Prove that your solution to part (b) is optimal up to a constant factor.

36. (a) Let $n = 2^\ell - 1$ for some positive integer ℓ. Suppose someone claims to hold an unsorted array $A[1..n]$ of *distinct* ℓ-bit strings; thus, exactly one ℓ-bit string does *not* appear in A. Suppose further that the *only* way we can access A is by calling the function FETCHBIT(i, j), which returns the jth bit of the string $A[i]$ in $O(1)$ time. Describe an algorithm to find the missing string in A using only $O(n)$ calls to FETCHBIT.

---

[20] In the thrilling final act, Retcon the Squirrel, the last surviving member of the Hero Team/Group/Society, saves everyone by traveling back in time and retroactively replacing the other $n-1$ heroes with lifelike balloon sculptures. So, yeah, basically it's *Avengers: Endgame*.

♥(b) Now suppose $n = 2^\ell - k$ for some positive integers k and ℓ, and again we are given an array $A[1 .. n]$ of *distinct* ℓ-bit strings. Describe an algorithm to find the k strings that are missing from A using only $O(n \log k)$ calls to FetchBit.

Trees

37. For this problem, a *subtree* of a binary tree means any connected subgraph. A binary tree is *complete* if every internal node has two children, and every leaf has exactly the same depth. Describe and analyze a recursive algorithm to compute the *largest complete subtree* of a given binary tree. Your algorithm should return both the root and the depth of this subtree. See Figure 1.26 for an example.

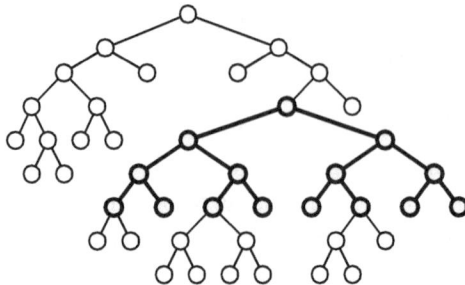

Figure 1.26. The largest complete subtree of this binary tree has depth 3.

38. Let T be a binary tree with n vertices. Deleting any vertex v splits T into at most three subtrees, containing the left child of v (if any), the right child of v (if any), and the parent of v (if any). We call v a **central** vertex if each of these smaller trees has at most $n/2$ vertices. See Figure 1.27 for an example.

Describe and analyze an algorithm to find a central vertex in an arbitrary given binary tree. [*Hint: First prove that every tree has a central vertex.*]

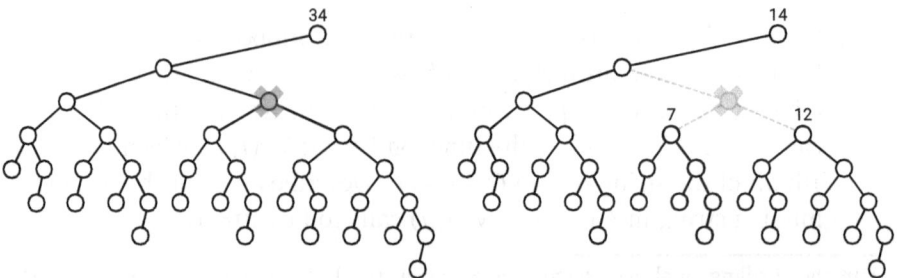

Figure 1.27. Deleting a central vertex in a 34-node binary tree, leaving subtrees with 14, 7, and 12 nodes.

39. (a) Professor George O'Jungle has a 27-node binary tree, in which every node is labeled with a unique letter of the Roman alphabet or the character **&**. Preorder and postorder traversals of the tree visit the nodes in the following order:

    - Preorder: I Q J H L E M V O T S B R G Y Z K C A & F P N U D W X
    - Postorder: H E M L J V Q S G Y R Z B T C P U D N F W & X A K O I

    Draw George's binary tree.

    (b) Recall that a binary tree is *full* if every non-leaf node has exactly two children.

    i. Describe and analyze a recursive algorithm to reconstruct an arbitrary *full* binary tree, given its preorder and postorder node sequences as input.

    ii. Prove that there is no algorithm to reconstruct an *arbitrary* binary tree from its preorder and postorder node sequences.

    (c) Describe and analyze a recursive algorithm to reconstruct an *arbitrary* binary tree, given its preorder and *inorder* node sequences as input.

    (d) Describe and analyze a recursive algorithm to reconstruct an arbitrary binary *search* tree, given only its preorder node sequence.

    ♥(e) Describe and analyze a recursive algorithm to reconstruct an arbitrary binary *search* tree, given only its preorder node sequence, *in $O(n)$ time*.

    In parts (b)–(e), assume that all keys are distinct and that the input is consistent with at least one binary tree.

40. Suppose we have n points scattered inside a two-dimensional box. A *kd-tree*[21] recursively subdivides the points as follows. If the box contains no points in its interior, we are done. Otherwise, we split the box into two smaller boxes with a *vertical* line, through a median point inside the box (*not* on its boundary), partitioning the points as evenly as possible. Then we recursively build a kd-tree for the points in each of the two smaller boxes, *after rotating them 90 degrees*. Thus, we alternate between splitting vertically and splitting horizontally at each level of recursion. The final empty boxes are called *cells*.

---

[21] The term "kd-tree" (pronounced "kay *dee* tree") was originally an abbreviation for "k-dimensional tree", but modern usage ignores this etymology, in part because nobody in their right mind would *ever* use the letter k to denote dimension instead of the *obviously* superior d. Etymological consistency would require calling the data structure in this problem a "2d-tree" (or perhaps a "2-d tree"), but the standard nomenclature is now "two-dimensional kd-tree". See also: B-tree (maybe), alpha shape, beta skeleton, epsilon net, Potomac River, Mississippi River, Lake Michigan, Lake Tahoe, Manhattan Island, La Brea Tar Pits, Sahara Desert, Mount Kilimanjaro, South Vietnam, East Timor, the Milky Way Galaxy, the City of Townsville, and self-driving automobiles.

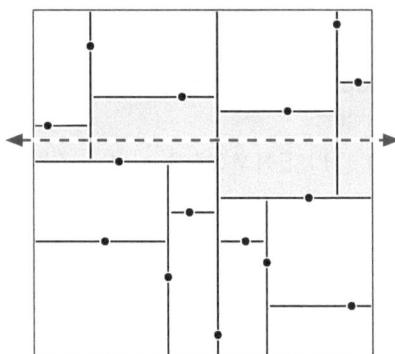

Figure 1.28. A kd-tree for 15 points. The dashed line crosses the four shaded cells.

(a) How many cells are there, as a function of n? Prove your answer is correct.

(b) In the worst case, *exactly* how many cells can a horizontal line cross, as a function of n? Prove your answer is correct. Assume that $n = 2^k - 1$ for some integer k. *[Hint: There is more than one function f such that $f(16) = 4$.]*

(c) Suppose we are given n points stored in a kd-tree. Describe and analyze an algorithm that counts the number of points above a horizontal line (such as the dashed line in the figure) as quickly as possible. *[Hint: Use part (b).]*

(d) Describe an analyze an efficient algorithm that counts, given a kd-tree containing n points, the number of points that lie inside a rectangle R with horizontal and vertical sides. *[Hint: Use part (c).]*

♥41. Bob Ratenbur, a new student in CS 225, is trying to write code to perform preorder, inorder, and postorder traversals of binary trees. Bob sort-of understands the basic idea behind the traversal algorithms, but whenever he actually tries to implement them, he keeps mixing up the recursive calls. Five minutes before the deadline, Bob frantically submits code with the following structure:

PREORDER(v):	INORDER(v):	POSTORDER(v):
if $v =$ NULL	if $v =$ NULL	if $v =$ NULL
return	return	return
else	else	else
print *label(v)*	███ORDER(*left(v)*)	███ORDER(*left(v)*)
███ORDER(*left(v)*)	print *label(v)*	███ORDER(*right(v)*)
███ORDER(*right(v)*)	███ORDER(*right(v)*)	print *label(v)*

Each ███ in this pseudocode hides one of the prefixes PRE, IN, or POST. Moreover, each of the following function calls appears exactly once in Bob's submitted code:

$$\text{PreOrder}(\textit{left}(v)) \qquad \text{PreOrder}(\textit{right}(v))$$
$$\text{InOrder}(\textit{left}(v)) \qquad \text{InOrder}(\textit{right}(v))$$
$$\text{PostOrder}(\textit{left}(v)) \qquad \text{PostOrder}(\textit{right}(v))$$

Thus, there are precisely 36 possibilities for Bob's code. Unfortunately, Bob accidentally deleted his source code after submitting the executable, so neither you nor he knows which functions were called where.

Now suppose you are given the output of Bob's traversal algorithms, executed on some **unknown** binary tree T. Bob's output has been helpfully parsed into three arrays $Pre[1..n]$, $In[1..n]$, and $Post[1..n]$. You may assume that these traversal sequences are consistent with exactly one binary tree T; in particular, the vertex labels of the unknown tree T are distinct, and every internal node in T has exactly two children.

(a) Describe an algorithm to reconstruct the unknown tree T from the given traversal sequences.

(b) Describe an algorithm that either reconstructs Bob's code from the given traversal sequences, or correctly reports that the traversal sequences are consistent with more than one set of algorithms.

For example, given the input

$$Pre[1..n] = [\text{H A E C B I F G D}]$$
$$In[1..n] = [\text{A H D C E I F B G}]$$
$$Post[1..n] = [\text{A E I B F C D G H}]$$

your first algorithm should return the following tree:

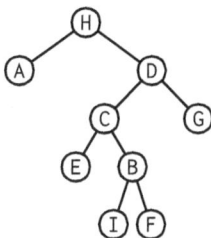

and your second algorithm should reconstruct the following code:

PreOrder(v):	InOrder(v):	PostOrder(v):
if $v = $ Null	if $v = $ Null	if $v = $ Null
return	return	return
else	else	else
print $label(v)$	PostOrder($left(v)$)	InOrder($left(v)$)
PreOrder($left(v)$)	print $label(v)$	InOrder($right(v)$)
PostOrder($right(v)$)	PreOrder($right(v)$)	print $label(v)$

♥42. Let T be a binary tree whose nodes store distinct numerical values. Recall that T is a **binary search tree** if and only if either (1) T is empty, or (2) T satisfies the following recursive conditions:

- The left subtree of T is a binary search tree.
- All values in the left subtree are smaller than the value at the root.
- The right subtree of T is a binary search tree.
- All values in the right subtree are larger than the value at the root.

Consider the following pair of operations on binary trees:

- **Rotate** an arbitrary node upward.[22]

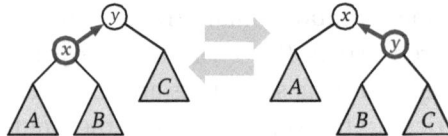

- **Swap** the left and right subtrees of an arbitrary node.

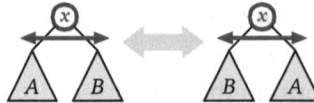

In both of these operations, some, all, or none of the subtrees A, B, and C could be empty.

(a) Describe an algorithm to transform an *arbitrary* n-node binary tree with distinct node values into a binary search tree, using at most $O(n^2)$ rotations and swaps. Figure 1.29 shows a sequence of eight operations that transforms a five-node binary tree into a binary search tree.

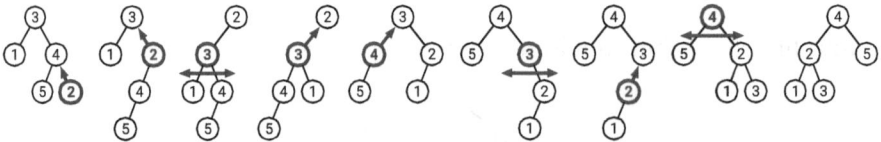

Figure 1.29. "Sorting" a binary tree: rotate 2, rotate 2, swap 3, rotate 3, rotate 4, swap 3, rotate 2, swap 4.

Your algorithm is not allowed to directly modify parent or child pointers, create new nodes, or delete old nodes; the *only* way to modify the tree is through rotations and swaps.

On the other hand, you may *compute* anything you like for free, as long as that computation does not modify the tree; the running time of your algorithm is *defined* to be the number of rotations and swaps that it performs.

♥(b) Describe an algorithm to transform an arbitrary n-node binary tree into a binary search tree, using at most $O(n \log n)$ rotations and swaps.

---

[22]Rotations preserve the inorder sequence of nodes in a binary tree. Partly for this reason, rotations are used to maintain several types of balanced binary search trees, including AVL trees, red-black trees, splay trees, scapegoat trees, and treaps. See http://algorithms.wtf for lecture notes on most of these data structures.

(c) Prove that any n-node binary *search* tree can be transformed into any other binary *search* tree with the same node values, using only $O(n)$ rotations (and *no* swaps).

♥(d) **Open problem:** Either describe an algorithm to transform an arbitrary n-node binary tree into a binary search tree using only $O(n)$ rotations and swaps, or prove that no such algorithm is possible. *[Hint: I don't think it's possible.]*

Where, however, the ambiguity cannot be cleared up, either by the rule of faith or by
the context, there is nothing to hinder us to point the sentence according to any
method we choose of those that suggest themselves.

— Augustine of Hippo, *De doctrina Christiana* (397CE)
Translated by Marcus Dods (1892)

I dropped my dinner, and ran back to the laboratory. There, in my excitement,
I tasted the contents of every beaker and evaporating dish on the table. Luckily for
me, none contained any corrosive or poisonous liquid.

— Constantine Fahlberg on his discovery of saccharin,
Scientific American (1886)

The greatest challenge to any thinker is stating the problem
in a way that will allow a solution.

— attributed to Bertrand Russell

When you come to a fork in the road, take it.

— Yogi Berra (giving directions to his house)

2

Backtracking

This chapter describes another important recursive strategy called **backtracking**. A backtracking algorithm tries to construct a solution to a computational problem incrementally, one small piece at a time. Whenever the algorithm needs to decide between multiple alternatives to the next component of the solution, it recursively evaluates *every* alternative and then chooses the best one.

2.1 N Queens

The prototypical backtracking problem is the classical **n Queens Problem**, first proposed by German chess enthusiast Max Bezzel in 1848 (under his pseudonym "Schachfreund") for the standard 8×8 board and by François-Joseph Eustache Lionnet in 1869 for the more general $n \times n$ board. The problem is to place n queens on an $n \times n$ chessboard, so that no two queens are attacking each other.

For readers not familiar with the rules of chess, this means that no two queens are in the same row, the same column, or the same diagonal.

Figure 2.1. Gauss's first solution to the 8 queens problem, represented by the array $[5, 7, 1, 4, 2, 8, 6, 3]$

In a letter written to his friend Heinrich Schumacher in 1850, the eminent mathematician Carl Friedrich Gauss wrote that one could easily confirm Franz Nauck's claim that the Eight Queens problem has 92 solutions by trial and error in a few hours. (*"Schwer ist es übrigens nicht, durch ein methodisches Tatonniren sich diese Gewissheit zu verschaffen, wenn man 1 oder ein paar Stunden daran wenden will."*) His description *Tatonniren* comes from the French *tâtonner*, meaning to feel, grope, or fumble around blindly, as if in the dark.

Gauss's letter described the following recursive strategy for solving the n-queens problem; the same strategy was described in 1882 by the French recreational mathematician Édouard Lucas, who attributed the method to Emmanuel Laquière. We place queens on the board one row at a time, starting with the top row. To place the rth queen, we methodically try all n squares in row r from left to right in a simple for loop. If a particular square is attacked by an earlier queen, we ignore that square; otherwise, we tentatively place a queen on that square and *recursively* grope for consistent placements of the queens in later rows.

Figure 2.2 shows the resulting algorithm, which recursively enumerates *all* complete n-queens solutions that are consistent with a given partial solution. Following Gauss, we represent the positions of the queens using an array $Q[1..n]$, where $Q[i]$ indicates which square in row i contains a queen. When PLACEQUEENS is called, the input parameter r is the index of the first empty row, and the prefix $Q[1..r-1]$ contains the positions of the first $r-1$ queens. In particular, to compute all n-queens solutions with no restrictions, we would call PLACEQUEENS($Q[1..n]$, 1). The outer for-loop considers all possible placements of a queen on row r; the inner for-loop checks whether a candidate placement of row r is consistent with the queens that are already on the first $r-1$ rows.

The execution of PLACEQUEENS can be illustrated using a **recursion tree**. Each node in this tree corresponds to a recursive subproblem, and thus to a legal partial solution; in particular, the root corresponds to the empty board

```
PLACEQUEENS(Q[1..n], r):
    if r = n + 1
        print Q[1..n]
    else
        for j ← 1 to n
            legal ← TRUE
            for i ← 1 to r − 1
                if (Q[i] = j) or (Q[i] = j + r − i) or (Q[i] = j − r + i)
                    legal ← FALSE
            if legal
                Q[r] ← j
                PLACEQUEENS(Q[1..n], r + 1)        ⟨⟨Recursion!⟩⟩
```

Figure 2.2. Gauss and Laquière's backtracking algorithm for the n queens problem.

(with $r = 0$). Edges in the recursion tree correspond to recursive calls. Leaves correspond to partial solutions that cannot be further extended, either because there is already a queen on every row, or because every position in the next empty row is attacked by an existing queen. The backtracking search for complete solutions is equivalent to a depth-first search of this tree.

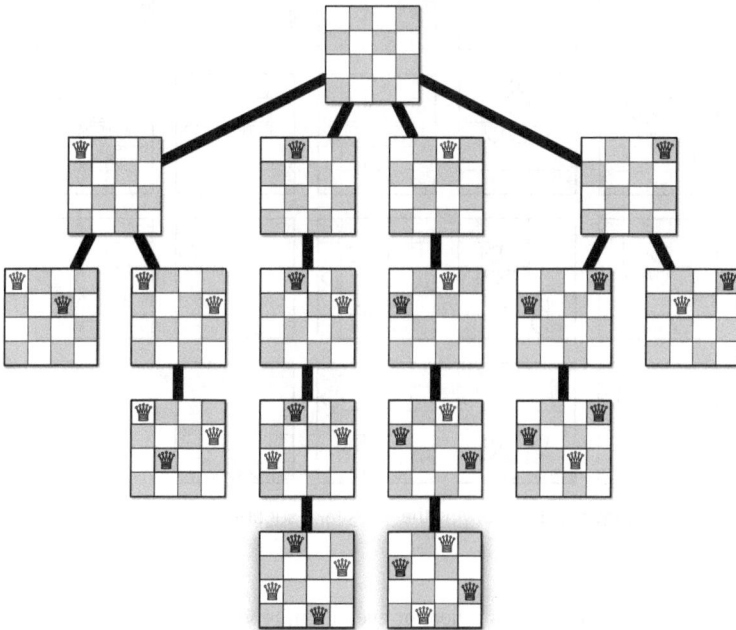

Figure 2.3. The complete recursion tree of Gauss and Laquière's algorithm for the 4 queens problem.

2.2 Game Trees

Consider the following simple two-player game[1] played on an $n \times n$ square grid with a border of squares; let's call the players Horace Fahlberg-Remsen and Vera Rebaudi.[2] Each player has n tokens that they move across the board from one side to the other. Horace's tokens start in the left border, one in each row, and move *hor*izontally to the right; symmetrically, Vera's tokens start in the top border, one in each column, and move *ver*tically downward. The players alternate turns. In each of his turns, Horace either *moves* one of his tokens one step to the right into an empty square, or *jumps* one of his tokens over exactly one of Vera's tokens into an empty square two steps to the right. If no legal moves or jumps are available, Horace simply passes. Similarly, Vera either moves or jumps one of her tokens downward in each of her turns, unless no moves or jumps are possible. The first player to move all their tokens off the edge of the board wins. (It's not hard to prove that as long as there are tokens on the board, at least one player can legally move, and therefore someone eventually wins.)

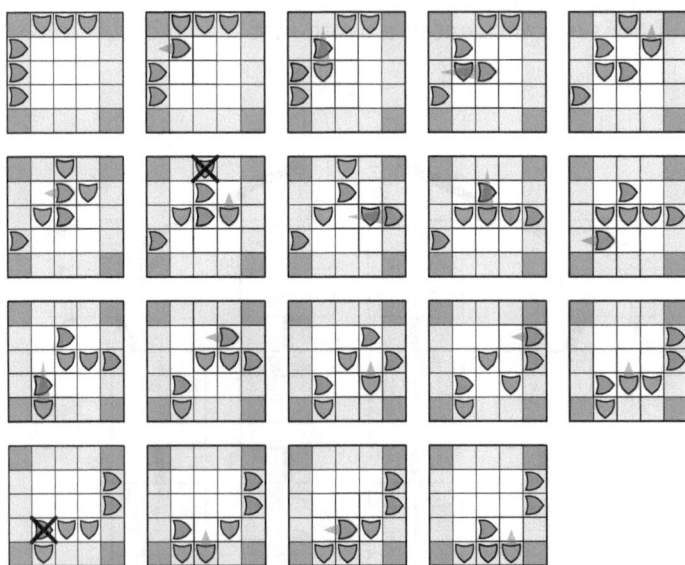

Figure 2.4. Vera wins the 3 × 3 fake-sugar-packet game.

---

[1] I don't know what this game is called, or even if I'm reporting the rules correctly; I learned it (or something like it) from Lenny Pitt, who recommended playing it with fake-sugar packets at restaurants.

[2] Constantin Fahlberg and Ira Remsen synthesized saccharin for the first time in 1878, while Fahlberg was a postdoc in Remsen's lab investigating coal tar derivatives. In 1900, Ovidio Rebaudi published the first chemical analysis of *ka'a he'ê*, a medicinal plant cultivated by the Guaraní for more than 1500 years, now more commonly known as *Stevia rebaudiana*.

Unless you've seen this game before[3], you probably don't have any idea how to play it well. Nevertheless, there is a relatively simple backtracking algorithm that can play this game—or any two-player game without randomness or hidden information that ends after a finite number of moves—*perfectly*. That is, if we drop you into the middle of a game, and it is *possible* to win against another perfect player, the algorithm will tell you how to win.

A **state** of the game consists of the locations of all the pieces and the identity of the current player. These states can be connected into a *game tree*, which has an edge from state x to state y if and only if the current player in state x can legally move to state y. The root of the game tree is the initial position of the game, and every path from the root to a leaf is a complete game.

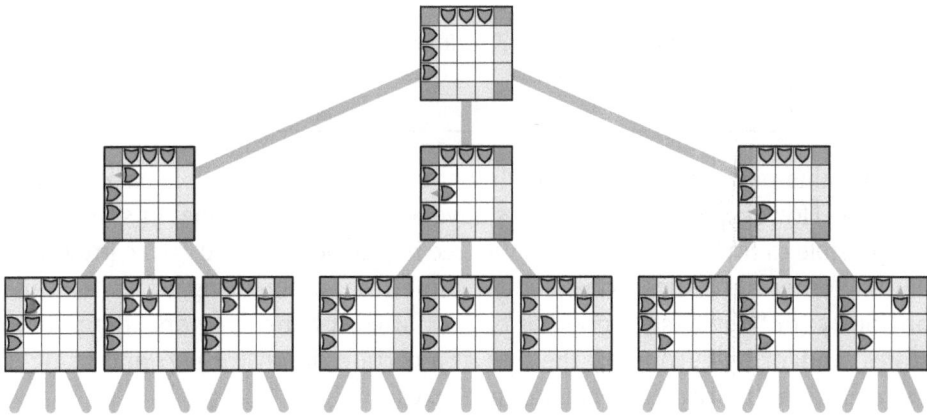

Figure 2.5. The first two levels of the fake-sugar-packet game tree.

To navigate through this game tree, we recursively define a game state to be **good** or **bad** as follows:

- A game state is *good* if either the current player has already won, or if the current player can move to a bad state for the opposing player.

- A game state is *bad* if either the current player has already lost, or if every available move leads to a good state for the opposing player.

Equivalently, a non-leaf node in the game tree is good if it has at least one bad child, and a non-leaf node is bad if all its children are good. By induction, any player that finds the game in a good state on their turn can win the game, even if their opponent plays perfectly; on the other hand, starting from a bad state, a player can win only if their opponent makes a mistake. This recursive definition was proposed by Ernst Zermelo in 1913.[4]

---

[3]If you have, please tell me where!

[4]In fact, Zermelo considered the more subtle class of games that have a finite number of states, but that allow infinite sequences of moves. (Zermelo defined infinite play to be a draw.)

This recursive definition immediately suggests the following recursive back-tracking algorithm to determine whether a given game state is good or bad. At its core, this algorithm is just a depth-first search of the game tree; equivalently, the game tree is the recursion tree of the algorithm! A simple modification of this backtracking algorithm finds a good move (or even all possible good moves) if the input is a good game state.

PLAYANYGAME(X, *player*):
    if *player* has already won in state X
        return GOOD
    if *player* has already lost in state X
        return BAD
    for all legal moves $X \rightsquigarrow Y$
        if PLAYANYGAME(Y, ¬*player*) = BAD
            return GOOD   ⟨⟨$X \rightsquigarrow Y$ is a good move⟩⟩
    return BAD   ⟨⟨There are no good moves⟩⟩

All game-playing programs are ultimately based on this simple backtracking strategy. However, since most games have an enormous number of states, it is not possible to traverse the entire game tree in practice. Instead, game programs employ other heuristics[5] to *prune* the game tree, by ignoring states that are obviously (or "obviously") good or bad, or at least better or worse than other states, and/or by cutting off the tree at a certain depth (or *ply*) and using a more efficient heuristic to evaluate the leaves.

2.3 Subset Sum

Let's consider a more complicated problem, called SUBSETSUM: Given a set X of positive integers and *target* integer T, is there a subset of elements in X that add up to T? Notice that there can be more than one such subset. For example, if $X = \{8, 6, 7, 5, 3, 10, 9\}$ and $T = 15$, the answer is TRUE, because the subsets $\{8, 7\}$ and $\{7, 5, 3\}$ and $\{6, 9\}$ and $\{5, 10\}$ all sum to 15. On the other hand, if $X = \{11, 6, 5, 1, 7, 13, 12\}$ and $T = 15$, the answer is FALSE.

There are two trivial cases. If the target value T is zero, then we can immediately return TRUE, because the empty set is a subset of *every* set X, and the elements of the empty set add up to zero.[6] On the other hand, if $T < 0$, or if $T \neq 0$ but the set X is empty, then we can immediately return FALSE.

For the general case, consider an arbitrary element $x \in X$. (We've already handled the case where X is empty.) There is a subset of X that sums to T if and only if one of the following statements is true:

---

[5]A heuristic is an algorithm that doesn't work. (Except in practice. Sometimes. Maybe.)
[6]... because what else could they add up to?

- There is a subset of X that *includes* x and whose sum is T.
- There is a subset of X that *excludes* x and whose sum is T.

In the first case, there must be a subset of $X \setminus \{x\}$ that sums to $T - x$; in the second case, there must be a subset of $X \setminus \{x\}$ that sums to T. So we can solve SUBSETSUM(X, T) by reducing it to two simpler instances: SUBSETSUM$(X \setminus \{x\}, T - x)$ and SUBSETSUM$(X \setminus \{x\}, T)$. The resulting recursive algorithm is shown below.

⟨⟨*Does any subset of X sum to T?*⟩⟩
SUBSETSUM(X, T):
 if $T = 0$
   return TRUE
 else if $T < 0$ or $X = \varnothing$
   return FALSE
 else
   $x \leftarrow$ any element of X
   with $\leftarrow$ SUBSETSUM$(X \setminus \{x\}, T - x)$ ⟨⟨*Recurse!*⟩⟩
   wout $\leftarrow$ SUBSETSUM$(X \setminus \{x\}, T)$ ⟨⟨*Recurse!*⟩⟩
   return (*with* $\vee$ *wout*)

Correctness

Proving this algorithm correct is a straightforward exercise in induction. If $T = 0$, then the elements of the empty subset sum to T, so TRUE is the correct output. Otherwise, if T is negative or the set X is empty, then no subset of X sums to T, so FALSE is the correct output. Otherwise, if there is a subset that sums to T, then either it contains $X[n]$ or it doesn't, and the Recursion Fairy correctly checks for each of those possibilities. Done.

Analysis

In order to analyze the algorithm, we have to describe a few implementation details more precisely. To begin, let's assume that the input set X is given as an array $X[1 .. n]$.

 The previous recursive algorithm allows us to choose *any* element $x \in X$ in the main recursive case. Purely for the sake of efficiency, it is helpful to choose an element x such that the remaining subset $X \setminus \{x\}$ has a concise description, which can be computed quickly, so that setting up the recursive calls requires minimal overhead. Specifically, we will let x be the last element $X[n]$; then the subset $X \setminus \{x\}$ is stored in the prefix $X[1 .. n - 1]$. Passing a complete *copy* of this prefix to the recursive calls would take too long—we need $\Theta(n)$ time just to make the copy—so instead, we push only two values: a reference to the array (or its starting address) and the length of the prefix. (Alternatively, we could avoid passing a reference to X to *every* recursive call by making X a global variable.)

```
⟨⟨Does any subset of X[1..i] sum to T?⟩⟩
SUBSETSUM(X, i, T):
    if T = 0
        return TRUE
    else if T < 0 or i = 0
        return FALSE
    else
        with  ← SUBSETSUM(X, i−1, T −X[i])    ⟨⟨Recurse!⟩⟩
        wout ← SUBSETSUM(X, i−1, T)           ⟨⟨Recurse!⟩⟩
        return (with ∨ wout)
```

With these implementation choices, the running time $T(n)$ of our algorithm satisfies the recurrence $T(n) \le 2T(n-1) + O(1)$. The solution $T(n) = O(2^n)$ follows easily using either recursion trees or the even simpler "Oh yeah, we already solved this recurrence for the Tower of Hanoi" method. In the worst case—for example, when T is larger than the sum of all elements of X—the recursion tree for this algorithm is a complete binary tree with depth n, and the algorithm considers all 2^n subsets of X.

Variants

With only minor changes, we can solve several variants of SUBSETSUM. For example, Figure 2.6 shows an algorithm that actually *constructs* a subset of X that sums to T, if one exists, or returns the error value NONE if no such subset exists; this algorithm uses exactly the same recursive strategy as our earlier decision algorithms. This algorithm also runs in $O(2^n)$ time; the analysis is simplest if we assume a set data structure that allows us to insert a single element in $O(1)$ time (for example, a linked list), but in fact the running time is still $O(2^n)$ even if insertion requires $O(n)$ time (for example, a *sorted* linked list). Similar variants allow us to count subsets that sum to a particular value, or choose the *best* subset (according to some other criterion) that sums to a particular value.

Most other problems that are solved by backtracking have this property: the same recursive strategy can be used to solve many different variants of the same problem. For example, it is easy to modify the recursive strategy described in the previous section, which determines whether a given game position is good or bad, to instead return a good move, or a list of all good moves. For this reason, when we *design* backtracking algorithms, we should aim for the simplest possible variant of the problem, computing a number or even a single boolean instead of more complex information or structure.

⟨⟨*Return a subset of $X[1..i]$ that sums to T*⟩⟩
⟨⟨*or NONE if no such subset exists*⟩⟩
CONSTRUCTSUBSET(X, i, T):
   if $T = 0$
      return $\varnothing$
   if $T < 0$ or $n = 0$
      return NONE
   $Y \leftarrow$ CONSTRUCTSUBSET($X, i-1, T$)
   if $Y \neq$ NONE
      return Y
   $Y \leftarrow$ CONSTRUCTSUBSET($X, i-1, T-X[i]$)
   if $Y \neq$ NONE
      return $Y \cup \{X[i]\}$
   return NONE

Figure 2.6. A recursive backtracking algorithm for the construction version of SUBSETSUM.

2.4 The General Pattern

Backtracking algorithms are commonly used to make a *sequence of decisions*, with the goal of building a recursively defined structure satisfying certain constraints. Often (but not always) this goal structure is itself a sequence. For example:

- In the n-queens problem, the goal is a sequence of queen positions, one in each row, such that no two queens attack each other. For each row, the algorithm *decides* where to place the queen.

- In the game tree problem, the goal is a sequence of legal moves, such that each move is as good as possible for the player making it. For each game state, the algorithm *decides* the best possible next move.

- In the SUBSETSUM problem, the goal is a sequence of input elements that have a particular sum. For each input element, the algorithm *decides* whether to include it in the output sequence or not.

(Hang on, why is the goal of *subset* sum finding a *sequence*? That was a deliberate design decision. We imposed a convenient ordering on the input set—by representing it using an array, as opposed to some other more amorphous data structure—that we can exploit in our recursive algorithm.)

In each recursive call to the backtracking algorithm, we need to make **exactly one** decision, and our choice must be consistent with all previous decisions. Thus, each recursive call requires not only the portion of the input data we have not yet processed, but also a suitable summary of the decisions we have already made. For the sake of efficiency, the summary of past decisions should be as small as possible. For example:

- For the *n*-queens problem, we must pass in not only the number of empty rows, but the positions of all previously placed queens. Here, unfortunately, we must remember our past decisions in complete detail.

- For the game tree problem, we only need to pass in the current state of the game, including the identity of the next player. We don't need to remember *anything* about our past decisions, because who wins from a given game state does not depend on the moves that created that state.[7]

- For the SUBSETSUM problem, we need to pass in both the remaining available integers and the remaining target value, which is the original target value minus the *sum* of the previously chosen elements. Precisely which elements were previously chosen is unimportant.

When we design new recursive backtracking algorithms, we must figure out *in advance* what information we will need about past decisions *in the middle of the algorithm*. If this information is nontrivial, our recursive algorithm might need to solve a more general problem than the one we were originally asked to solve. (We've seen this kind of generalization before: To find the *median* of an unsorted array in linear time, we derived an algorithm to select the *k*th smallest element for *arbitrary k*.)

Finally, once we've figured out what recursive problem we *really* need to solve, we solve that problem by **recursive brute force**: Try *all* possibilities for the next decision that are consistent with past decisions, and let the Recursion Fairy worry about the rest. No being clever here. No skipping "obviously" stupid choices. Try everything. You can make the algorithm faster later.

2.5 Text Segmentation (*Interpunctio Verborum*)

Suppose you are given a string of letters representing text in some foreign language, but without any spaces or punctuation, and you want to break this string into its individual constituent words. For example, you might be given the following passage from Cicero's famous oration in defense of Lucius Licinius Murena in 62BCE, in the standard *scriptio continua* of classical Latin:[8]

---

[7]Many games *appear* to violate this independence condition. For example, the standard rules of both chess and checkers allow a player to declare a draw if the same arrangement of pieces occurs three times, and the Chinese rules for go simply forbid repeating any earlier arrangement of stones. Thus, for these games, a game state formally includes not only the current positions of the pieces but the entire history of previous moves.

[8]In·fact·most·classical·Latin·manuscripts·separated·words·with·small·dots·called·*interpuncts*. Interpunctuation all but disappeared by the 3rd century in favor of *scriptio continua*. Empty spaces between words were introduced by Irish monks in the 8th century and slowly spread across Europe over the next several centuries. *Scriptio continua* survives in early 21st-century English in the form of URLs and hashtags. #octotherps4lyfe

PRIMVSDIGNITASINTAMTENVISCIENTIANONPOTEST
ESSERESENIMSVNTPARVAEPROPEINSINGVLISLITTERIS
ATQVEINTERPVNCTIONIBUSVERBORVMOCCVPATAE

A fluent Latin reader would parse this string (in modern orthography) as *Primus dignitas in tam tenui scientia non potest esse; res enim sunt parvae, prope in singulis litteris atque interpunctionibus verborum occupatae.*[9] Text segmentation is not only a problem in classical Latin and Greek, but in several modern languages and scripts including Balinese, Burmese, Chinese, Japanese, Javanese, Khmer, Lao, Thai, Tibetan, and Vietnamese. Similar problems arise in segmenting unpunctuated English text into sentences,[10] segmenting text into lines for typesetting, speech and handwriting recognition, curve simplification, and several types of time-series analysis. For purposes of illustration, I'll stick to segmenting sequences of letters in the modern English alphabet into modern English words.

Of course, some strings can be segmented in several different ways; for example, BOTHEARTHANDSATURNSPIN can be decomposed into English words as either BOTH·EARTH·AND·SATURN·SPIN or BOT·HEART·HANDS·AT·URNS·PIN, among many other possibilities. For now, let's consider an extremely simple segmentation problem: Given a string of characters, can it be segmented into English words *at all*?

To make the problem concrete (and language-agnostic), let's assume we have access to a subroutine IsWord(w) that takes a string w as input, and returns True if w is a "word", or False if w is not a "word". For example, if we are trying to decompose the input string into palindromes, then a "word" is a synonym for "palindrome", and therefore IsWord(ROTATOR) = True but IsWord(PALINDROME) = False.

Just like the SubsetSum problem, the *input* structure is a sequence, this time containing letters instead of numbers, so it is natural to consider a decision process that consumes the input characters in order from left to right. Similarly, the *output* structure is a sequence of words, so it is natural to consider a process that produces the output words in order from left to right. Thus, jumping into the middle of the segmentation process, we might imagine the following picture:

BLUE	STEM	UNIT	ROBOT	HEARTHANDSATURNSPIN

---

[9] Loosely translated: "First of all, dignity in such paltry knowledge is impossible; this is trivial stuff, mostly concerned with individual letters and the placement of points between words." Cicero was openly mocking the legal expertise of his friend(!) and noted jurist Servius Sulpicius Rufus, who had accused Murena of bribery, after Murena defeated Rufus in election for consul. Murena was acquitted, thanks in part to Cicero's acerbic defense, although he was almost certainly guilty. #librapondo #nunquamestfidelis

[10] St. Augustine's *De doctrina Christiana* devotes an entire chapter to removing ambiguity from Latin scripture by adding punctuation.

Here the black bar separates our past decisions—splitting the first 17 letters into four words—from the portion of the input string that we have not yet processed.

The next stage in our imagined process is to **decide** where the next word in the output sequence ends. For this specific example, there are four possibilities for the next output word—HE, HEAR, HEART, and HEARTH. We have *no idea* which of these choices, if any, is consistent with a complete segmentation of the input string. We could be "smart" at this point and try to *figure out* which choices are good, but that would require *thinking*! Instead, let's "stupidly" try every possibility by brute force, and let the Recursion Fairy do all the real work.

- First *tentatively* accept HE as the next word, and let the Recursion Fairy make the rest of the decisions.

BLUE	STEM	UNIT	ROBOT	HE	ARTHANDSATURNSPIN

- Then *tentatively* accept HEAR as the next word, and let the Recursion Fairy make the rest of the decisions.

BLUE	STEM	UNIT	ROBOT	HEAR	THANDSATURNSPIN

- Then *tentatively* accept HEART as the next word, and let the Recursion Fairy make the rest of the decisions.

BLUE	STEM	UNIT	ROBOT	HEART	HANDSATURNSPIN

- Finally, *tentatively* accept HEARTH as the next word, and let the Recursion Fairy make the rest of the decisions.

BLUE	STEM	UNIT	ROBOT	HEARTH	ANDSATURNSPIN

As long as the Recursion Fairy reports success at least once, we report success. On the other hand, if the Recursion Fairy *never* reports success—in particular, if the set of possible next words is empty—then we report failure.

None of our past decisions affect which choices are available now; all that matters is the suffix of characters that we have not yet processed. In particular, several different sequences of past decisions could lead us to the same suffix, but they all leave us with exactly the same set of choices for that suffix.

BLUE	STEM	UNIT	ROBOT	HEARTHANDSATURNSPIN

BLUEST	EMU	NITRO	BOT	HEARTHANDSATURNSPIN

Thus, we can simplify our picture of the recursive process by discarding *everything* left of the black bar:

HEARTHANDSATURNSPIN

We are now left with a simple and natural backtracking strategy: *Select the first output word, and recursively segment the rest of the input string.*

To get a complete recursive algorithm, we need a base case. Our recursive strategy breaks down when we reach the end of the input string, because there is no next word. Fortunately, the empty string has a unique segmentation into zero words!

Putting all the pieces together, we arrive at the following simple recursive algorithm:

$$
\begin{array}{l}
\underline{\text{Splittable}(A[1..n]):} \\
\quad \text{if } n = 0 \\
\qquad \text{return True} \\
\quad \text{for } i \leftarrow 1 \text{ to } n \\
\qquad \text{if IsWord}(A[1..i]) \\
\qquad\quad \text{if Splittable}(A[i+1..n]) \\
\qquad\qquad \text{return True} \\
\quad \text{return False}
\end{array}
$$

Index Formulation

In practice, passing arrays as input parameters is rather slow; we should really find a more compact way to describe our recursive subproblems. *For purposes of designing the algorithm*, it's incredibly useful to treat the original input array as a global variable, and then reformulate the problem and the algorithm in terms of array indices instead of explicit subarrays.

For our string segmentation problem, the argument of any recursive call is always a **suffix** $A[i..n]$ of the original input array. So if we treat the input array $A[1..n]$ as a global variable, we can reformulate our recursive problem as follows:

> Given an index i, find a segmentation of the suffix $A[i..n]$.

To describe our algorithm, we need two boolean functions:

- For any indices i and j, let $\text{IsWord}(i, j) = \text{True}$ if and only if the substring $A[i..j]$ is a word. (We're assuming this function is given to us.)
- For any index i, let $Splittable(i) = \text{True}$ if and only if the suffix $A[i..n]$ can be split into words. (This is the function we need to implement.)

For example, $\text{IsWord}(1, n) = \text{True}$ if and only if the entire input string is a single word, and $Splittable(1) = \text{True}$ if and only if the entire input string can be segmented. Our earlier recursive strategy gives us the following recurrence:

$$
Splittable(i) = \begin{cases}
\text{True} & \text{if } i > n \\
\displaystyle\bigvee_{j=i}^{n} \bigl(\text{IsWord}(i, j) \wedge Splittable(j+1)\bigr) & \text{otherwise}
\end{cases}
$$

This is *exactly* the same algorithm as we saw earlier; the only thing we've changed is the notation. The similarity is even more apparent if we rewrite the recurrence in pseudocode:

$\langle\langle$*Is the suffix $A[i..n]$ Splittable?*$\rangle\rangle$
SPLITTABLE(i):
    if $i > n$
        return TRUE
    for $j \leftarrow i$ to n
        if ISWORD(i, j)
            if SPLITTABLE($j + 1$)
                return TRUE
    return FALSE

Although it may look like a trivial notational difference, using index notation instead of array notation is an important habit, not only to speed up backtracking algorithms in practice, but for developing dynamic programming algorithms, which we discuss in the next chapter.

♥Analysis

It should come as no surprise that most backtracking algorithms have exponential worst-case running times. Analyzing the precise running times of many of these algorithms requires techniques that are beyond the scope of this book. Fortunately, most of the backtracking algorithms we will encounter *in this book* are only intermediate results on the way to more efficient algorithms, which means their exact worst-case running time is not actually important. (First make it work; then make it fast.)

But just for fun, let's analyze the running time of our recursive algorithm SPLITTABLE. Because we don't know what ISWORD is doing, we can't know how long each call to ISWORD takes, so we're forced to analyze the running time in terms of the number of calls to ISWORD.[11] SPLITTABLE calls ISWORD on every prefix of the input string, and *possibly* calls itself recursively on every suffix of the output string. Thus, the "running time" of SPLITTABLE obeys the scary-looking recurrence

$$T(n) \leq \sum_{i=0}^{n-1} T(i) + O(n)$$

This really isn't as bad as it looks, especially once you've seen the trick.

First, we replace the $O(n)$ term with an explicit expression αn, for some unknown (and ultimately unimportant) constant α. Second, we conservatively

---

[11]In fact, as long as ISWORD runs in *polynomial* time, SPLITTABLE runs in $O(2^n)$ time.

assume that the algorithm actually makes every possible recursive call.[12] Then we can transform the "full history" recurrence into a "limited history" recurrence by subtracting the recurrence for $T(n-1)$, as follows:

$$T(n) = \sum_{i=0}^{n-1} T(i) + \alpha n$$

$$T(n-1) = \sum_{i=0}^{n-2} T(i) + \alpha(n-1)$$

$$\implies T(n) - T(n-1) = T(n-1) + \alpha$$

This final recurrence simplifies to $T(n) = 2T(n-1) + \alpha$. At this point, we can confidently guess (or derive via recursion trees, or remember from our Tower of Hanoi analysis) that $T(n) = O(2^n)$; indeed, this upper bound is not hard to prove by induction from the original full-history recurrence.

Moreover, this analysis is tight. There are exactly 2^{n-1} possible ways to segment a string of length n—each input character either ends a word or doesn't, except the last input character, which always ends the last word. In the worst case, our SPLITTABLE algorithm explores each of these 2^{n-1} possibilities.

Variants

Now that we have the basic recursion pattern in hand, we can use it to solve many different variants of the segmentation problem, just as we did for the SUBSETSUM problem. Here I'll describe just one example; more variations are considered in the exercises. As usual, the original input to our problem is an array $A[1..n]$.

If a string can be segmented in more than one sequence of words, we may want to find the *best* segmentation according to some criterion; conversely, if the input string cannot be segmented into words, we may want to compute the best segmentation we can find, rather than merely reporting failure. To meet both of these goals, suppose we have access to a second function SCORE that takes a string as input and returns a numerical value. For example, we might assign higher scores to longer or more common words, lower scores to shorter or more obscure words, slightly negative scores for minor spelling errors, and more negative scores to obvious non-words. Our goal is to find a segmentation that maximizes the sum of the scores of the segments.

---

[12]This assumption is wildly conservative for English *word* segmentation, since most strings of letters are not English words, but *not* for the similar problem of segmenting sequences of English *words* into grammatically correct English *sentences*. Consider, for example, a sequence of n copies of the word "buffalo", or n copies of the work "police", or n copies of the word "can", for any positive integer n. (At the Moulin Rouge, dances that are preservable in metal cylinders by other dances have the opportunity to fire dances that happen in prison restroom trash receptacles.)

For any index i, let $MaxScore(i)$ denote the maximum score of any segmentation of the suffix $A[i..n]$; we need to compute $MaxScore(1)$. This function satisfies the following recurrence:

$$MaxScore(i) = \begin{cases} 0 & \text{if } i > n \\ \max_{i \le j \le n} \left(\text{SCORE}(A[i..j]) + MaxScore(j+1) \right) & \text{otherwise} \end{cases}$$

This is essentially the same recurrence as the one we developed for *Splittable*; the only difference is that the boolean operations $\vee$ and $\wedge$ have been replaced by the numerical operations max and $+$.

2.6 Longest Increasing Subsequence

For any sequence S, a **subsequence** of S is another sequence obtained from S by deleting zero or more elements, without changing the order of the remaining elements; the elements of the subsequence need not be contiguous in S. For example, when you drive down a major street in any city, you drive through a *sequence* of intersections with traffic lights, but you only have to stop at a *subsequence* of those intersections, where the traffic lights are red. If you're very lucky, you never stop at all: the empty sequence is a subsequence of S. On the other hand, if you're very unlucky, you may have to stop at every intersection: S is a subsequence of itself.

As another example, the strings BENT, ACKACK, SQUARING, and SUBSEQUENT are all subsequences of the string SUBSEQUENCEBACKTRACKING, as are the empty string and the entire string SUBSEQUENCEBACKTRACKING, but the strings QUEUE and EQUUS and TALLYHO are not. A subsequence whose elements are contiguous in the original sequence is called a **substring**; for example, MASHER and LAUGHTER are both subsequences of MANSLAUGHTER, but only LAUGHTER is a substring.

Now suppose we are given a sequence of *integers*, and we need to find the longest subsequence whose elements are in increasing order. More concretely, the input is an integer array $A[1..n]$, and we need to compute the longest possible sequence of indices $1 \le i_1 < i_2 < \cdots < i_\ell \le n$ such that $A[i_k] < A[i_{k+1}]$ for all k.

One natural approach to building this **longest increasing subsequence** is to *decide*, for each index j in order from 1 to n, whether or not to include $A[j]$ in the subsequence. Jumping into the middle of this decision sequence, we might imagine the following picture:

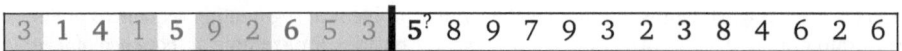

| 3 | 1 | 4 | 1 | 5 | 9 | 2 | 6 | 5 | 3 | 5? | 8 | 9 | 7 | 9 | 3 | 2 | 3 | 8 | 4 | 6 | 2 | 6 |

As in our earlier text segmentation examples, the black bar separates our past decisions from the portion of the input we have not yet processed. Numbers we have already decided to include are highlighted and bold; numbers we have already decided to exclude are grayed out. (Notice that the numbers we've decided to include are increasing!) Our algorithm must decide whether or not to include the number immediately after the black bar.

In this example, we definitely *cannot* include 5, because then the selected numbers would no longer be in increasing order. So let's skip ahead to the next decision:

| 3 | 1 | 4 | 1 | 5 | 9 | 2 | 6 | 5 | 3 | 5 ‖ 8⁷ 9 7 9 3 2 3 8 4 6 2 6 |

Now we *can* include 8, but it's not obvious whether we *should*. Rather than trying to be "smart", our backtracking algorithm will use simple brute force.

- First *tentatively* include the 8, and let the Recursion Fairy make the rest of the decisions.

- Then *tentatively* exclude the 8, and let the Recursion Fairy make the rest of the decisions.

Whichever choice leads to a longer increasing subsequence is the right one. (This is precisely the same recursion pattern we used to solve SUBSETSUM.)

Now for the key question: *What do we need to remember about our past decisions?* We can only include $A[j]$ if the resulting subsequence is in increasing order. If we assume (inductively!) that the numbers previously selected from $A[1..j-1]$ are in increasing order, then we can include $A[j]$ if and only if $A[j]$ is larger than the last number selected from $A[1..j-1]$. Thus, the only information we need about the past is **the last number selected so far**. We can now revise our pictures by erasing everything we don't need:

| 6 ‖ 5⁷ 8 9 7 9 3 2 3 8 4 6 2 6 |

| 6 ‖ 8⁷ 9 7 9 3 2 3 8 4 6 2 6 |

So the problem our recursive strategy is *actually* solving is the following:

> Given an integer *prev* and an array $A[1..n]$, find the longest increasing subsequence of A in which every element is larger than *prev*.

As usual, our recursive strategy requires a base case. Our current strategy breaks down when we get to the end of the array, because there is no "next number" to consider. But an empty array has exactly one subsequence, namely, the *empty* sequence. Vacuously, every element in the empty sequence is larger than whatever value you want, and every pair of elements in the empty sequence appears in increasing order. Thus, the longest increasing subsequence of the empty array has length 0.

Here's the resulting recursive algorithm:

```
LISBIGGER(prev, A[1 .. n]):
    if n = 0
        return 0
    else if A[1] ≤ prev
        return LISBIGGER(prev, A[2 .. n])
    else
        skip ← LISBIGGER(prev, A[2 .. n])
        take ← LISBIGGER(A[1], A[2 .. n]) + 1
        return max{skip, take}
```

Okay, but remember that passing arrays around on the call stack is expensive; let's try to rephrase everything in terms of array indices, assuming that the array $A[1 .. n]$ is a global variable. The integer *prev* is typically an array element $A[i]$, and the remaining array is always a suffix $A[j .. n]$ of the original input array. So we can reformulate our recursive *problem* as follows:

> Given two indices i and j, where $i < j$, find the longest increasing subsequence of $A[j .. n]$ in which every element is larger than $A[i]$.

Let $LISbigger(i, j)$ denote the *length* of the longest increasing subsequence of $A[j .. n]$ in which every element is larger than $A[i]$. Our recursive strategy gives us the following recurrence:

$$
LISbigger(i, j) = \begin{cases} 0 & \text{if } j > n \\ LISbigger(i, j + 1) & \text{if } A[i] \geq A[j] \\ \max \left\{ \begin{array}{c} LISbigger(i, j + 1) \\ 1 + LISbigger(j, j + 1) \end{array} \right\} & \text{otherwise} \end{cases}
$$

Alternatively, if you prefer pseudocode:

```
LISBIGGER(i, j):
    if j > n
        return 0
    else if A[i] ≥ A[j]
        return LISBIGGER(i, j + 1)
    else
        skip ← LISBIGGER(i, j + 1)
        take ← LISBIGGER(j, j + 1) + 1
        return max{skip, take}
```

Finally, we need to connect our recursive strategy to the original problem: Finding the longest increasing subsequence of an array *with no other constraints*. The simplest approach is to add an artificial sentinel value $-\infty$ to the beginning of the array.

$$\boxed{\begin{aligned}&\underline{\text{LIS}(A[1..n]):}\\&\quad A[0] \leftarrow -\infty\\&\quad \text{return LISBIGGER}(0,1)\end{aligned}}$$

The running time of LISBIGGER satisfies the Hanoi recurrence $T(n) \leq 2T(n-1)+O(1)$, which as usual implies that $T(n) = O(2^n)$. We really shouldn't be surprised by this running time; in the worst case, the algorithm examines each of the 2^n subsequences of the input array.

2.7 Longest Increasing Subsequence, Take 2

This is not the only backtracking strategy we can use to find longest increasing subsequences. Instead of considering the *input* sequence one element at a time, we could try to construct the *output* sequence one element at a time. That is, instead of asking "Is $A[i]$ the next element of the output sequence?", we could ask directly, "Where is the next element of the output sequence, if any?"

Jumping into the middle of this strategy, we might be faced with the following picture. Suppose we just decided to include the 6 just left of the black bar in our output sequence, and we need to decide which element to the right of the bar to include next.

$$\boxed{3 \;\; 1 \;\; 4 \;\; 1 \;\; 5 \;\; 9 \;\; 2 \;\; 6 \;\Big|\; 5^? \; 3^? \; 5^? \; 8^? \; 9^? \; 7^? \; 9^? \; 3^? \; 2^? \; 3^? \; 8^? \; 4^? \; 6^? \; 2^? \; 6^?}$$

Of course, we can only include numbers on the right that are greater than 6; otherwise, our output sequence would not be increasing.

$$\boxed{3 \;\; 1 \;\; 4 \;\; 1 \;\; 5 \;\; 9 \;\; 2 \;\; 6 \;\Big|\; 5 \; 3 \; 5 \; 8^? \; 9^? \; 7^? \; 9^? \; 3 \; 2 \; 3 \; 8^? \; 4 \; 6 \; 2 \; 6}$$

But we have no idea *which* of those larger numbers is the best choice, and trying to cleverly *figure out* the best choice is too much work, and it's only going to get us into trouble anyway. Instead, we enumerate all possibilities by brute force, and let the Recursion Fairy evaluate each one.

$$\boxed{3 \;\; 1 \;\; 4 \;\; 1 \;\; 5 \;\; 9 \;\; 2 \;\; 6 \;\; 5 \;\; 3 \;\; 5 \;\; 8 \;\Big|\; 9 \; 7 \; 9 \; 3 \; 2 \; 3 \; 8 \; 4 \; 6 \; 2 \; 6}$$

$$\boxed{3 \;\; 1 \;\; 4 \;\; 1 \;\; 5 \;\; 9 \;\; 2 \;\; 6 \;\; 5 \;\; 3 \;\; 5 \;\; 8 \;\; 9 \;\Big|\; 7 \; 9 \; 3 \; 2 \; 3 \; 8 \; 4 \; 6 \; 2 \; 6}$$

$$\boxed{3 \;\; 1 \;\; 4 \;\; 1 \;\; 5 \;\; 9 \;\; 2 \;\; 6 \;\; 5 \;\; 3 \;\; 5 \;\; 8 \;\; 9 \;\; 7 \;\Big|\; 9 \; 3 \; 2 \; 3 \; 8 \; 4 \; 6 \; 2 \; 6}$$

$$\boxed{3 \;\; 1 \;\; 4 \;\; 1 \;\; 5 \;\; 9 \;\; 2 \;\; 6 \;\; 5 \;\; 3 \;\; 5 \;\; 8 \;\; 9 \;\; 7 \;\; 9 \;\Big|\; 3 \; 2 \; 3 \; 8 \; 4 \; 6 \; 2 \; 6}$$

$$\boxed{3 \;\; 1 \;\; 4 \;\; 1 \;\; 5 \;\; 9 \;\; 2 \;\; 6 \;\; 5 \;\; 3 \;\; 5 \;\; 8 \;\; 9 \;\; 7 \;\; 9 \;\; 3 \;\; 2 \;\; 3 \;\; 8 \;\Big|\; 4 \; 6 \; 2 \; 6}$$

The subset of numbers we can consider as the next element depends *only* on the last number we decided to include. Thus, we can simplify our picture of the decision process by discarding everything to the left of the bar *except* the last number we decided to include.

6	5 3 5 8 9 7 9 3 2 3 8 4 6 2 6

The remaining sequence of numbers is just a suffix of the original input array. Thus, if we think of the input array $A[1..n]$ as a global variable, we can formally express our recursive problem in terms of indices as follows:

> Given an index i, find the longest increasing subsequence of $A[i..n]$ that begins with $A[i]$.

Let $LISfirst(i)$ denote the length of the longest increasing subsequence of $A[i..n]$ that begins with $A[i]$. We can now formulate our recursive backtracking strategy as the following recursive definition:

$$LISfirst(i) = 1 + \max\left\{LISfirst(j) \mid j > i \text{ and } A[j] > A[i]\right\}$$

Because we are dealing with sets of natural numbers, we define $\max \varnothing = 0$. Then we automatically have $LISfirst(i) = 1$ if $A[j] \leq A[i]$ for all $j > i$; in particular, $LISfirst(n) = 1$. These are the base cases for our recurrence.

We can also express this recursive definition in pseudocode as follows:

```
LISFIRST(i):
    best ← 0
    for j ← i + 1 to n
        if A[j] > A[i]
            best ← max{best, LISFIRST(j)}
    return 1 + best
```

Finally, we need to reconnect this recursive algorithm to our original problem—finding the longest increasing subsequence without knowing its first element. One natural approach that works is to try all possible first elements by brute force. Equivalently, we can add a sentinel element $-\infty$ to the beginning of the array, find the longest increasing subsequence that starts with the sentinel, and finally ignore the sentinel.

```
LIS(A[1..n]):
    best ← 0
    for i ← 1 to n
        best ← max{best, LISFIRST(i)}
    return best
```

```
LIS(A[1..n]):
    A[0] ← −∞
    return LISFIRST(0) − 1
```

2.8 Optimal Binary Search Trees

Our final example combines recursive backtracking with the divide-and-conquer strategy. Recall that the running time for a successful search in a binary search tree is proportional to the number of ancestors of the target node.[13] As a result, the worst-case search time is proportional to the depth of the tree. Thus, to minimize the worst-case search time, the height of the tree should be as small as possible; by this metric, the ideal tree is perfectly balanced.

In many applications of binary search trees, however, it is more important to minimize the total cost of several searches rather than the worst-case cost of a single search. If x is a more frequent search target than y, we can save time by building a tree where the depth of x is smaller than the depth of y, even if that means increasing the overall depth of the tree. A perfectly balanced tree is *not* the best choice if some items are significantly more popular than others. In fact, a totally unbalanced tree with depth $\Omega(n)$ might actually be the best choice!

This situation suggests the following problem. Suppose we are given a sorted array of **keys** $A[1..n]$ and an array of corresponding **access frequencies** $f[1..n]$. Our task is to build the binary search tree that minimizes the *total* search time, assuming that there will be exactly $f[i]$ searches for each key $A[i]$.

Before we think about how to solve this problem, we should first come up with a good recursive definition of the function we are trying to optimize! Suppose we are also given a binary search tree T with n nodes. Let $v_1, v_2, \ldots, v_n$ be the nodes of T, indexed in sorted order, so that each node v_i stores the corresponding key $A[i]$. Then ignoring constant factors, the total cost of performing all the binary searches is given by the following expression:

$$Cost(T, f[1..n]) := \sum_{i=1}^{n} f[i] \cdot \#\text{ancestors of } v_i \text{ in } T \qquad (*)$$

Now suppose v_r is the root of T; by definition, v_r is an ancestor of every node in T. If $i < r$, then all ancestors of v_i except the root are in the left subtree of T. Similarly, if $i > r$, then all ancestors of v_i except the root are in the right subtree of T. Thus, we can partition the cost function into three parts as follows:

$$Cost(T, f[1..n]) = \sum_{i=1}^{n} f[i] + \sum_{i=1}^{r-1} f[i] \cdot \#\text{ancestors of } v_i \text{ in } left(T)$$

$$+ \sum_{i=r+1}^{n} f[i] \cdot \#\text{ancestors of } v_i \text{ in } right(T)$$

The second and third summations look exactly like our original definition $(*)$

---

[13]An *ancestor* of a node v is either the node itself or an ancestor of the parent of v. A *proper* ancestor of v is either the parent of v or a proper ancestor of the parent of v.

for $Cost(T, f[1..n])$. Simple substitution now gives us a recurrence for $Cost$:

$$Cost(T, f[1..n]) = \sum_{i=1}^{n} f[i] + Cost(left(T), f[1..r-1]) \\ + Cost(right(T), f[r+1..n])$$

The base case for this recurrence is, as usual, $n = 0$; the cost of performing no searches in the empty tree is zero.

Now our task is to compute the tree T_{opt} that minimizes this cost function. Suppose we somehow magically knew that the root of T_{opt} is v_r. Then the recursive definition of $Cost(T, f)$ immediately implies that the left subtree $left(T_{opt})$ must be the optimal search tree for the keys $A[1..r-1]$ and access frequencies $f[1..r-1]$. Similarly, the right subtree $right(T_{opt})$ must be the optimal search tree for the keys $A[r+1..n]$ and access frequencies $f[r+1..n]$. **Once we choose the correct key to store at the root, the Recursion Fairy will construct the rest of the optimal tree.**

More generally, let $OptCost(i, k)$ denote the total cost of the optimal search tree for the interval of frequencies $f[i..k]$. This function obeys the following recurrence.

$$OptCost(i, k) = \begin{cases} 0 & \text{if } i > k \\ \displaystyle\sum_{j=i}^{k} f[i] + \min_{i \le r \le k} \left\{ \begin{array}{l} OptCost(i, r-1) \\ + OptCost(r+1, k) \end{array} \right\} & \text{otherwise} \end{cases}$$

The base case correctly indicates that the minimum possible cost to perform zero searches into the empty set is zero! Our original problem is to compute $OptCost(1, n)$.

This recursive definition can be translated mechanically into a recursive backtracking algorithm to compute $OptCost(1, n)$. Not surprisingly, the running time of this algorithm is exponential. In the next chapter, we'll see how to reduce the running time to polynomial, so there's not much point in computing the precise running time...

♥ Analysis

...unless you're into that sort of thing. Just for the fun of it, let's figure out how slow this backtracking algorithm actually is. The running time satisfies the recurrence

$$T(n) = \sum_{k=1}^{n} \left(T(k-1) + T(n-k) \right) + O(n).$$

The $O(n)$ term comes from computing the total number of searches $\sum_{i=1}^{n} f[i]$. Yeah, that's one ugly recurrence, but we can solve it using exactly the same subtraction trick we used before. We replace the $O(\,)$ notation with an explicit constant, regroup and collect identical terms, subtract the recurrence for $T(n-1)$ to get rid of the summation, and then regroup again.

$$T(n) \;=\; 2\sum_{k=0}^{n-1} T(k) + an$$

$$T(n-1) \;=\; 2\sum_{k=0}^{n-2} T(k) + a(n-1)$$

$$T(n) - T(n-1) \;=\; 2T(n-1) + a$$

$$T(n) \;=\; 3T(n-1) + a$$

Hey, that doesn't look so bad after all. The recursion tree method immediately gives us the solution $T(n) = O(3^n)$ (or we can just guess and confirm by induction).

This analysis implies that our recursive algorithm does *not* examine all possible binary search trees! The number of binary search trees with n vertices satisfies the recurrence

$$N(n) = \sum_{r=1}^{n-1}\bigl(N(r-1)\cdot N(n-r)\bigr),$$

which has the closed-form solution $N(n) = \Theta(4^n/\sqrt{n})$. (No, that's not obvious.) Our algorithm saves considerable time by searching *independently* for the optimal left and right subtrees for each root. A full enumeration of binary search trees would consider all possible *pairs* of left and right subtrees; hence the product in the recurrence for $N(n)$.

Exercises

1. Describe recursive algorithms for the following generalizations of the SUB-SETSUM problem:

    (a) Given an array $X[1..n]$ of positive integers and an integer T, compute the *number* of subsets of X whose elements sum to T.

    (b) Given two arrays $X[1..n]$ and $W[1..n]$ of positive integers and an integer T, where each $W[i]$ denotes the *weight* of the corresponding element $X[i]$, compute the *maximum weight* subset of X whose elements sum to T. If no subset of X sums to T, your algorithm should return $-\infty$.

2. Describe recursive algorithms for the following variants of the text segmentation problem. Assume that you have a subroutine IsWord that takes an

array of characters as input and returns TRUE if and only if that string is a "word".

(a) Given an array $A[1..n]$ of characters, compute the number of partitions of A into words. For example, given the string ARTISTOIL, your algorithm should return 2, for the partitions ARTIST·OIL and ART·IS·TOIL.

(b) Given two arrays $A[1..n]$ and $B[1..n]$ of characters, decide whether A and B can be partitioned into words at the same indices. For example, the strings BOTHEARTHANDSATURNSPIN and PINSTARTRAPSANDRAGSLAP can be partitioned into words at the same indices as follows:

$$\text{BOT·HEART·HAND·SAT·URNS·PIN}$$
$$\text{PIN·START·RAPS·AND·RAGS·LAP}$$

(c) Given two arrays $A[1..n]$ and $B[1..n]$ of characters, compute the number of different ways that A and B can be partitioned into words at the same indices.

3. An *addition chain* for an integer n is an increasing sequence of integers that starts with 1 and ends with n, such that each entry after the first is the sum of two earlier entries. More formally, the integer sequence $x_0 < x_1 < x_2 < \cdots < x_\ell$ is an addition chain for n if and only if

- $x_0 = 1$,
- $x_\ell = n$, and
- for every index $k > 0$, there are indices $i \le j < k$ such that $x_k = x_i + x_j$.

The ℓength of an addition chain is the number of elements minus 1; we don't bother to count the first entry. For example, $\langle 1, 2, 3, 5, 10, 20, 23, 46, 92, 184, 187, 374 \rangle$ is an addition chain for 374 of length 11.

(a) Describe a recursive backtracking algorithm to compute a minimum-length addition chain for a given positive integer n. **Don't** analyze or optimize your algorithm's running time, except to satisfy your own curiosity. A correct algorithm whose running time is exponential in n is sufficient for full credit. [*Hint: This problem is a lot more like n Queens than text segmentation.*]

♥(b) Describe a recursive backtracking algorithm to compute a minimum-length addition chain for a given positive integer n *in time that is sub-exponential in n. [Hint: You may find the results of certain Egyptian rope-fasteners, Indus-River prosodists, and Russian peasants helpful.]*

4. (a) Let $A[1..m]$ and $B[1..n]$ be two arbitrary arrays. A *common subsequence* of A and B is both a subsequence of A and a subsequence of B. Give a simple recursive definition for the function $lcs(A, B)$, which gives the length of the *longest* common subsequence of A and B.

(b) Let $A[1..m]$ and $B[1..n]$ be two arbitrary arrays. A *common super-sequence* of A and B is another sequence that contains both A and B as subsequences. Give a simple recursive definition for the function $scs(A, B)$, which gives the length of the *shortest* common supersequence of A and B.

(c) Call a sequence $X[1..n]$ of numbers **bitonic** if there is an index i with $1 < i < n$, such that the prefix $X[1..i]$ is increasing and the suffix $X[i..n]$ is decreasing. Give a simple recursive definition for the function $lbs(A)$, which gives the length of the longest bitonic subsequence of an arbitrary array A of integers.

(d) Call a sequence $X[1..n]$ *oscillating* if $X[i] < X[i+1]$ for all even i, and $X[i] > X[i+1]$ for all odd i. Give a simple recursive definition for the function $los(A)$, which gives the length of the longest oscillating subsequence of an arbitrary array A of integers.

(e) Give a simple recursive definition for the function $sos(A)$, which gives the length of the shortest oscillating supersequence of an arbitrary array A of integers.

(f) Call a sequence $X[1..n]$ *convex* if $2 \cdot X[i] < X[i-1] + X[i+1]$ for all i. Give a simple recursive definition for the function $lxs(A)$, which gives the length of the longest convex subsequence of an arbitrary array A of integers.

5. For each of the following problems, the input consists of two arrays $X[1..k]$ and $Y[1..n]$ where $k \le n$.

(a) Describe a recursive backtracking algorithm to determine whether X is a subsequence of Y. For example, the string PPAP is a subsequence of the string PENPINEAPPLEAPPLEPEN.

(b) Describe a recursive backtracking algorithm to find the smallest number of symbols that can be removed from Y so that X is no longer a subsequence. Equivalently, your algorithm should find the longest subsequence of Y that is *not* a supersequence of X. For example, after removing removing two symbols from the string PENPINEAPPLEAPPLEPEN, the string PPAP is no longer a subsequence.

♥(c) Describe a recursive backtracking algorithm to determine whether X occurs as two *disjoint* subsequences of Y. For example, the string PPAP appears as two disjoint subsequences in the string PENPINEAPPLEAPPLEPEN.

Don't analyze the running times of your algorithms, except to satisfy your own curiosity. All three algorithms run in exponential time; we'll improve that later, so the precise running time isn't particularly important.

6. This problem asks you to design backtracking algorithms to find the cost of an optimal binary search tree that satisfies additional balance constraints. Your input consists of a sorted array $A[1..n]$ of search keys and an array $f[1..n]$ of frequency counts, where $f[i]$ is the number of searches for $A[i]$. This is exactly the same cost function as described in Section 2.8. But now your task is to compute an optimal tree that satisfies some additional constraints.

   (a) **AVL trees** were the earliest self-balancing balanced binary search trees, first described in 1962 by Georgy Adelson-Velsky and Evgenii Landis. An AVL tree is a binary search tree where for every node v, the height of the left subtree of v and the height of the right subtree of v differ by at most one.

   Describe a recursive backtracking algorithm to construct an optimal AVL tree for a given set of search keys and frequencies.

   (b) **Symmetric binary B-trees** are another self-balancing binary trees, first described by Rudolf Bayer in 1972; these are better known by the name **red-black trees**, after a somewhat simpler reformulation by Leo Guibas and Bob Sedgwick in 1978. A red-black tree is a binary search tree with the following additional constraints:

   • Every node is either red or black.
   • Every red node has a black parent.
   • Every root-to-leaf path contains the same number of black nodes.

   Describe a recursive backtracking algorithm to construct an optimal red-black tree for a given set of search keys and frequencies.

   (c) **AA trees** were proposed by proposed by Arne Andersson in 1993 and slightly simplified (and named) by Mark Allen Weiss in 2000. AA trees are also known as *left-leaning red-black trees*, after a symmetric reformulation (with different rebalancing algorithms) by Bob Sedgewick in 2006. An AA tree is a red-black tree with one additional constraint:

   • No left child is red.[14]

   Describe a recursive backtracking algorithm to construct an optimal AA tree for a given set of search keys and frequencies.

   Don't analyze the running times of your algorithms, except to satisfy your own curiosity. All three algorithms run in exponential time; we'll improve that later, so the precise running times aren't particularly important.

For more backtracking exercises, see the next chapter!

---

[14]Sedgwick's reformulation requires that no *right* child is red. Whatever. Andersson and Sedgwick are strangely silent on which end of the egg to eat first.

*Potes enim videre in hac margine, qualiter hoc operati fuimus, scilicet quod
iunximus primum numerum cum secundo, videlicet 1 cum 2; et secundum cum
tercio; et tercium cum quarto; et quartum cum quinto, et sic deinceps....*

*[You can see in the margin here how we have worked this; clearly, we combined the
first number with the second, namely 1 with 2, and the second with the third, and
the third with the fourth, and the fourth with the fifth, and so forth....]*

— Leonardo Pisano, *Liber Abaci* (1202)

Those who cannot remember the past are condemned to repeat it.

— Jorge Agustín Nicolás Ruiz de Santayana y Borrás,
The Life of Reason, Book I: Introduction and Reason in Common Sense (1905)

*You know what a learning experience is?
A learning experience is one of those things that says,
"You know that thing you just did? Don't do that."*

— Douglas Adams, *The Salmon of Doubt* (2002)

3

Dynamic Programming

3.1 Mātrāvṛtta

One of the earliest examples of recursion arose in India more than 2000 years ago,
in the study of poetic meter, or prosody. Classical Sanskrit poetry distinguishes
between two types of syllables (*akṣara*): *light* (*laghu*) and *heavy* (*guru*). In
one class of meters, variously called *mātrāvṛtta* or *mātrāchandas*, each line of
poetry consists of a fixed number of "beats" (*mātrā*), where each light syllable
lasts one beat and each heavy syllable lasts two beats. The formal study of
mātrā-vṛtta dates back to the *Chandaḥśāstra*, written by the scholar Piṅgala
between 600BCE and 200BCE. Piṅgala observed that there are exactly five
4-beat meters: ——, —••, •—•, ••—, and ••••. (Here each "—"
represents a long syllable and each "•" represents a short syllable.)[1]

---

[1]In Morse code, a "dah" lasts three times as long as a "dit", but each "dit" or "dah" is followed
by a pause with the same duration as a "dit". Thus, each "dit-pause" is a *laghu akṣara*, each

Although Piṅgala's text *hints* at a systematic rule for counting meters with a given number of beats,[2] it took about a millennium for that rule to be stated explicitly. In the 7th century CE, another Indian scholar named Virahāṅka wrote a commentary on Piṅgala's work, in which he observed that the number of meters with n beats is the sum of the number of meters with $(n-2)$ beats and the number of meters with $(n-1)$ beats. In more modern notation, Virahāṅka's observation implies a recurrence for the total number $M(n)$ of n-beat meters:

$$M(n) = M(n-2) + M(n-1)$$

It is not hard to see that $M(0) = 1$ (there is only one empty meter) and $M(1) = 1$ (the only one-beat meter consists of a single short syllable).

The same recurrence reappeared in Europe about 500 years after Virahāṅka, in Leonardo of Pisa's 1202 treatise *Liber Abaci*, one of the most influential early European works on "algorism". In full compliance with Stigler's Law of Eponymy,[3] the modern *Fibonacci numbers* are defined using Virahāṅka's recurrence, but with different base cases:

$$F_n = \begin{cases} 0 & \text{if } n = 0 \\ 1 & \text{if } n = 1 \\ F_{n-1} + F_{n-2} & \text{otherwise} \end{cases}$$

In particular, we have $M(n) = F_{n+1}$ for all n.

Backtracking Can Be Slow

The recursive definition of Fibonacci numbers immediately gives us a recursive algorithm for computing them. Here is the same algorithm written in pseudocode:

"dah-pause" is a *guru akṣara*, and there are exactly five letters (M, D, R, U, and H) whose codes last four *mātrā*.

[2] The *Chandaḥśāstra* contains *two* systematic rules for listing all meters with a given number of *syllables*, which correspond roughly to writing numbers in binary from left to right (like Greeks) or from right to left (like Egyptians). The same text includes a recursive algorithm to compute 2^n (the number of meters with n syllables) by repeated squaring, and (arguably) a recursive algorithm to compute binomial coefficients (the number of meters with k short syllables and n syllables overall).

[3] *"No scientific discovery is named after its original discoverer."* In his 1980 paper that gives the law its name, the statistician Stephen Stigler jokingly claimed that this law was first proposed by sociologist Robert K. Merton. However, similar statements were previously made by Vladimir Arnol'd in the 1970's ("Discoveries are rarely attributed to the correct person."), Carl Boyer in 1968 ("Clio, the muse of history, often is fickle in attaching names to theorems!"), Alfred North Whitehead in 1917 ("Everything of importance has been said before by someone who did not discover it."), and even Stephen's father George Stigler in 1966 ("If we should ever encounter a case where a theory is named for the correct man, it will be noted."). We will see *many* other examples of Stigler's law in this book.

```
RECFIBO(n):
    if n = 0
        return 0
    else if n = 1
        return 1
    else
        return RECFIBO(n − 1) + RECFIBO(n − 2)
```

Unfortunately, this naive recursive algorithm is horribly slow. Except for the recursive calls, the entire algorithm requires only a constant number of steps: one comparison and possibly one addition. Let $T(n)$ denote the number of recursive calls to RECFIBO; this function satisfies the recurrence

$$T(0) = 1, \quad T(1) = 1, \quad T(n) = T(n-1) + T(n-2) + 1,$$

which looks an awful lot like the recurrence for Fibonacci numbers themselves! Writing out the first several values of $T(n)$ suggests the closed-form solution $T(n) = 2F_{n+1} - 1$, which we can verify by induction (hint, hint). So computing F_n using this algorithm takes about twice as long as just counting to F_n. Methods beyond the scope of this book[4] imply that $F_n = \Theta(\phi^n)$, where $\phi = (\sqrt{5} + 1)/2 \approx 1.61803$ is the so-called *golden ratio*. In short, the running time of this recursive algorithm is exponential in n.

We can actually see this exponential growth directly as follows. Think of the recursion tree for RECFIBO as a binary tree of additions, with only 0s and 1s at the leaves. Since the eventual output is F_n, exactly F_n of the leaves must have value 1; these leaves represent the calls to RECRIBO(1). An easy inductive argument (hint, hint) implies that RECFIBO(0) is called exactly F_{n-1} times. (If we just want an asymptotic bound, it's enough to observe that the number of calls to RECFIBO(0) is at most the number of calls to RECFIBO(1).) Thus, the recursion tree has exactly $F_n + F_{n-1} = F_{n+1} = O(F_n)$ leaves, and therefore, because it's a full binary tree, $2F_{n+1} - 1 = O(F_n)$ nodes altogether.

Memo(r)ization: Remember Everything

The obvious reason for the recursive algorithm's lack of speed is that it computes the same Fibonacci numbers over and over and over. A single call to RECFIBO(n) results in one recursive call to RECFIBO($n-1$), two recursive calls to RECFIBO($n-2$), three recursive calls to RECFIBO($n-3$), five recursive calls to RECFIBO($n-4$), and in general F_{k-1} recursive calls to RECFIBO($n-k$) for any integer $0 \le k < n$. Each call is recomputing some Fibonacci number from scratch.

We can speed up our recursive algorithm considerably by writing down the results of our recursive calls and looking them up again if we need them later.

---

[4]See http://algorithms.wtf for notes on solving backtracking recurrences.

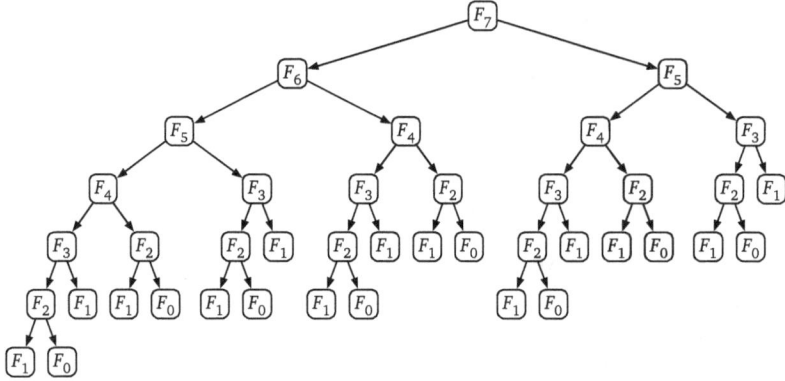

Figure 3.1. The recursion tree for computing F_7; arrows represent recursive calls.

This optimization technique, now known as *memoization* (yes, without an R), is usually credited to Donald Michie in 1967, but essentially the same technique was proposed in 1959 by Arthur Samuel.[5]

```
MemFibo(n):
    if n = 0
        return 0
    else if n = 1
        return 1
    else
        if F[n] is undefined
            F[n] ← MemFibo(n − 1) + MemFibo(n − 2)
        return F[n]
```

Memoization clearly decreases the running time of the algorithm, but by how much? If we actually trace through the recursive calls made by MemFibo, we find that the array $F[\ ]$ is filled from the bottom up: first $F[2]$, then $F[3]$, and so on, up to $F[n]$. This pattern can be verified by induction: Each entry $F[i]$ is filled only after its predecessor $F[i-1]$. If we ignore the time spent in recursive calls, it requires only constant time to evaluate the recurrence for each Fibonacci number F_i. But by design, the recurrence for F_i is evaluated only once for each index i. We conclude that MemFibo performs only $O(n)$ additions, an *exponential* improvement over the naïve recursive algorithm!

---

[5]Michie proposed that programming languages should support an abstraction he called a "memo function", consisting of both a standard function ("rule") and a dictionary ("rote"), instead of separately supporting arrays and functions. Whenever a memo function computes a function value for the first time, it "memorises" (yes, with an R) that value into its dictionary. Michie was inspired by Samuel's use of "rote learning" to speed up the recursive evaluation of checkers game trees; Michie describes his more general proposal as "enabling the programmer to 'Samuelize' any functions he pleases." (As far as I can tell, Michie never used the term "memoisation" himself.) Memoization was used even earlier by Claude Shannon's maze-solving robot "Theseus", which he designed and constructed in 1950.

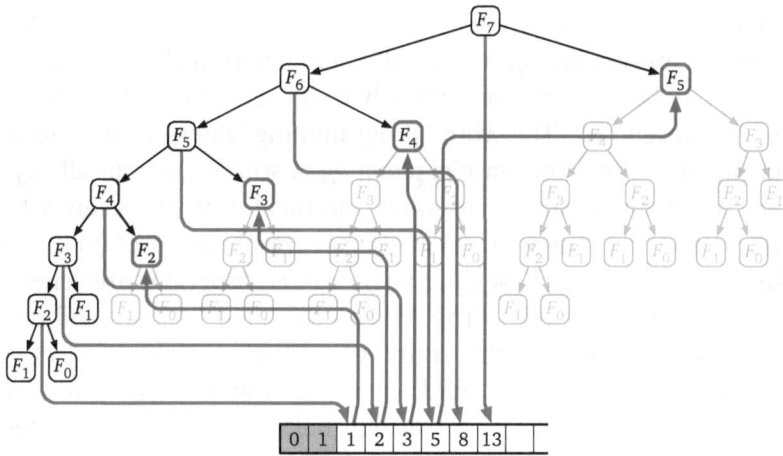

Figure 3.2. The recursion tree for F_7 trimmed by memoization. Downward green arrows indicate writing into the memoization array; upward red arrows indicate reading from the memoization array.

Dynamic Programming: Fill Deliberately

Once we see how the array $F[\ ]$ is filled, we can replace the memoized recurrence with a simple for-loop that *intentionally* fills the array in that order, instead of relying on a more complicated recursive algorithm to do it for us accidentally.

```
ITERFIBO(n):
    F[0] ← 0
    F[1] ← 1
    for i ← 2 to n
        F[i] ← F[i − 1] + F[i − 2]
    return F[n]
```

Now the time analysis is immediate: ITERFIBO clearly uses $O(n)$ *additions* and stores $O(n)$ *integers*.

This is our first explicit **dynamic programming** algorithm. The dynamic programming paradigm was formalized and popularized by Richard Bellman in the mid-1950s, while working at the RAND Corporation, although he was far from the first to use the technique. In particular, this iterative algorithm for Fibonacci numbers was already proposed by Virahāṅka and later Sanskrit prosodists in the 12th century, and again by Fibonacci at the turn of the 13th century![6]

---

[6]More general dynamic programming techniques were independently deployed several times in the late 1930s and early 1940s. For example, Pierre Massé used dynamic programming algorithms to optimize the operation of hydroelectric dams in France during the Vichy regime. John von Neumann and Oskar Morgenstern developed dynamic programming algorithms to determine the winner of any two-player game with perfect information (for example, checkers). Alan Turing and his cohorts used similar methods as part of their code-breaking efforts at

Many years after the fact, Bellman claimed that he deliberately chose the name "dynamic programming" to hide the mathematical character of his work from his military bosses, who were actively hostile toward anything resembling mathematical research.[7] The word "programming" does not refer to writing code, but rather to the older sense of *planning* or *scheduling*, typically by filling in a table. For example, sports programs and theater programs are schedules of important events (with ads); television programming involves filling each available time slot with a show (and ads); degree programs are schedules of classes to be taken (with ads). The Air Force funded Bellman and others to develop methods for constructing training and logistics schedules, or as they called them, "programs". The word "dynamic" was not only a reference to the multistage, time-varying processes that Bellman and his colleagues were attempting to optimize, but also a marketing buzzword that would resonate with the Futuristic Can-Do Zeitgeist™ of post-WW II America.[8] Thanks in part to Bellman's proselytizing, dynamic programming is now a standard tool for multistage planning in economics, robotics, control theory, and several other disciplines.

Don't Remember Everything After All

In many dynamic programming algorithms, it is not necessary to retain *all* intermediate results through the entire computation. For example, we can significantly reduce the space requirements of our algorithm IterFibo by maintaining only the two newest elements of the array:

Bletchley Park. Both Massé's work and von Neumann and Mergenstern's work were first published in 1944, six years before Bellman coined the phrase "dynamic programming". The details of Turing's "Banburismus" were kept secret until the mid-1980s.

[7]Charles Erwin Wilson became Secretary of Defense in January 1953, after a dozen years as the president of General Motors. "Engine Charlie" reorganized the Department of Defense and significantly decreased its budget in his first year in office, with the explicit goal of running the Department much more like an industrial corporation. Bellman described Wilson in his 1984 autobiography as follows:

> We had a very interesting gentleman in Washington named Wilson. He was secretary of Defense, and he actually had a pathological fear and hatred of the word *"research"*. I'm not using the term lightly; I'm using it precisely. His face would suffuse, he would turn red, and he would get violent if people used the term *"research"* in his presence. You can imagine how he felt, then, about the term *"mathematical"*. ... I felt I had to do something to shield Wilson and the Air Force from the fact that I was really doing mathematics inside the RAND Corporation. What title, what name, could I choose?

However, Bellman's first published use of the term "dynamic programming" already appeared in 1952, several months before Wilson took office, so this story is at least *slightly* embellished.

[8]. . . and just possibly a riff on the iconic brand name "Dynamic-Tension" for Charles Atlas's famous series of exercises, which Charles Roman coined in 1928. Hero of the Beach!

```
ITERFIBO2(n):
    prev ← 1
    curr ← 0
    for i ← 1 to n
        next ← curr + prev
        prev ← curr
        curr ← next
    return curr
```

(This algorithm uses the non-standard but consistent base case $F_{-1} = 1$ so that ITERFIBO2(0) returns the correct value 0.) Although saving space can be absolutely crucial in practice, we won't focus on space issues in this book.

♥3.2   Aside: Even Faster Fibonacci Numbers

Although the previous algorithm is simple and attractive, it is *not* the fastest algorithm to compute Fibonacci numbers. We can derive a faster algorithm by exploiting the following matrix reformulation of the Fibonacci recurrence:

$$\begin{bmatrix} 0 & 1 \\ 1 & 1 \end{bmatrix} \begin{bmatrix} x \\ y \end{bmatrix} = \begin{bmatrix} y \\ x + y \end{bmatrix}$$

In other words, multiplying a two-dimensional vector by the matrix $\begin{bmatrix} 0 & 1 \\ 1 & 1 \end{bmatrix}$ has exactly the same effect as one iteration of the inner loop of ITERFIBO2. It follows that multiplying by the matrix n times is the same as iterating the loop n times:

$$\begin{bmatrix} 0 & 1 \\ 1 & 1 \end{bmatrix}^n \begin{bmatrix} 1 \\ 0 \end{bmatrix} = \begin{bmatrix} F_{n-1} \\ F_n \end{bmatrix}.$$

So if we want the nth Fibonacci number, we only need to compute the nth power of the matrix $\begin{bmatrix} 0 & 1 \\ 1 & 1 \end{bmatrix}$. If we use repeated squaring,[9] computing the nth power of something requires only $O(\log n)$ multiplications. Here, because "something" is a 2×2 matrix, that means $O(\log n)$ 2×2 matrix multiplications, each of which reduces to a constant number of integer multiplications and additions. Thus, we can compute F_n in only $O(\log n)$ *integer arithmetic operations*.

We can achieve the same speedup using the identity $F_n = F_m F_{n-m-1} + F_{m+1} F_{n-m}$, which holds (by induction!) for all integers m and n. In particular, this identity implies the following mutual recurrence for pairs of adjacent Fibonacci numbers, first proposed by Édouard Lucas in 1898:

$$F_{2n-1} = F_{n-1}^2 + F_n^2$$

$$F_{2n} = F_n(F_{n-1} + F_{n+1}) = F_n(2F_{n-1} + F_n)$$

---

[9]as suggested by Pingala for powers of 2 elsewhere in *Chandaḥśāstra*

(We can also derive this mutual recurrence directly from the matrix-squaring algorithm.) These recurrences translate directly into the following algorithm:

```
⟨⟨Compute the pair Fₙ₋₁, Fₙ⟩⟩
FastRecFibo(n):
    if n = 1
        return 0, 1
    m ← ⌊n/2⌋
    hprv, hcur ← FastRecFibo(m)      ⟨⟨Fₘ₋₁, Fₘ⟩⟩
    prev ← hprv² + hcur²             ⟨⟨F₂ₘ₋₁⟩⟩
    curr ← hcur · (2 · hprv + hcur)  ⟨⟨F₂ₘ⟩⟩
    next ← prev + curr               ⟨⟨F₂ₘ₊₁⟩⟩
    if n is even
        return prev, curr
    else
        return curr, next
```

Our standard recursion tree technique implies that this algorithm performs only $O(\log n)$ integer arithmetic operations.

This is an exponential speedup over the standard iterative algorithm, which was already an exponential speedup over our original recursive algorithm. Right?

Whoa! Not so fast!

Well, not exactly. Fibonacci numbers grow exponentially fast. The nth Fibonacci number is approximately $n \log_{10} \phi \approx n/5$ decimal digits long, or $n \log_2 \phi \approx 2n/3$ bits. So we can't possibly compute F_n in logarithmic *time* — we need $\Omega(n)$ time just to write down the answer!

The way out of this apparent paradox is to observe that *we can't perform arbitrary-precision arithmetic in constant time.* Let $M(n)$ denote the time required to multiply two n-digit numbers. The running time of FastRecFibo satisfies the recurrence $T(n) = T(\lfloor n/2 \rfloor) + M(n)$, which solves to $T(n) = O(M(n))$ via recursion trees. The fastest integer multiplication algorithm known (as of 2019) runs in $O(n \log n)$ time, so that is also the running time of the fastest algorithm known (as of 2019) to compute Fibonacci numbers.

Is this algorithm slower than our "linear-time" iterative algorithms? Actually, no—addition isn't free, either! Adding two n-digit numbers requires $O(n)$ time, so the iterative algorithms IterFibo and IterFibo2 actually run in $O(n^2)$ *time.* (Do you see why?) So FastRecFibo is significantly faster than the iterative algorithms, just not *exponentially* faster.

In the original recursive algorithm, the extra cost of arbitrary-precision arithmetic is overwhelmed by the huge number of recursive calls. The correct recurrence is $T(n) = T(n-1) + T(n-2) + O(n)$, which still has the solution $T(n) = O(\phi^n)$.

3.3 *Interpunctio Verborum Redux*

For our next dynamic programming algorithm, let's consider the text segmentation problem from the previous chapter. We are given a string $A[1..n]$ and a subroutine IsWord that determines whether a given string is a word (whatever that means), and we want to know whether A can be partitioned into a sequence of words.

We solved this problem by defining a function *Splittable(i)* that returns True if and only if the suffix $A[i..n]$ can be partitioned into a sequence of words. We need to compute *Splittable(1)*. This function satisfies the recurrence

$$Splittable(i) = \begin{cases} \text{True} & \text{if } i > n \\ \bigvee_{j=i}^{n} \big(IsWord(i,j) \wedge Splittable(j+1)\big) & \text{otherwise} \end{cases}$$

where $IsWord(i,j)$ is shorthand for $IsWord(A[i..j])$. This recurrence translates directly into a recursive backtracking algorithm that calls the IsWord subroutine $O(2^n)$ times in the worst case.

But for any fixed string $A[1..n]$, there are only n different ways to call the recursive function *Splittable(i)*—one for each value of i between 1 and $n+1$—and only $O(n^2)$ different ways to call IsWord(i,j)—one for each pair (i,j) such that $1 \le i \le j \le n$. Why are we spending exponential time computing only a polynomial amount of stuff?

Each recursive subproblem is specified by an integer between 1 and $n+1$, so we can memoize the function *Splittable* into an array *SplitTable*$[1..n+1]$. Each subproblem *Splittable(i)* depends only on results of subproblems *Splittable(j)* where $j > i$, so the memoized recursive algorithm fills the array in *decreasing* index order. If we fill the array in this order deliberately, we obtain the dynamic programming algorithm shown in Figure 3.3. The algorithm makes $O(n^2)$ calls to IsWord, an exponential improvement over our earlier backtracking algorithm.

3.4 The Pattern: Smart Recursion

In a nutshell, dynamic programming is *recursion without repetition*. Dynamic programming algorithms store the solutions of intermediate subproblems, often *but not always* in some kind of array or table. Many algorithms students

```
FASTSPLITTABLE(A[1..n]):
    SplitTable[n + 1] ← TRUE
    for i ← n down to 1
        SplitTable[i] ← FALSE
        for j ← i to n
            if ISWORD(i, j) and SplitTable[j + 1]
                SplitTable[i] ← TRUE
    return SplitTable[1]
```

Figure 3.3. Interpunctio verborum velox

(and instructors, and textbooks) make the mistake of focusing on the table—because tables are easy and familiar—instead of the *much* more important (and difficult) task of finding a correct recurrence. As long as we memoize the correct recurrence, an explicit table isn't really necessary, but if the recurrence is incorrect, we are well and truly hosed.

> ## Dynamic programming is *not* about filling in tables.
> ## It's about smart recursion!

Dynamic programming algorithms are best developed in two distinct stages.

1. **Formulate the problem recursively.** Write down a recursive formula or algorithm for the whole problem in terms of the answers to smaller subproblems. This is the hard part. A complete recursive formulation has two parts:

   (a) **Specification.** Describe the problem that you want to solve recursively, in coherent and precise English—not *how* to solve that problem, but *what* problem you're trying to solve. Without this specification, it is impossible, even in principle, to determine whether your solution is correct.

   (b) **Solution.** Give a clear recursive formula or algorithm for the whole problem in terms of the answers to smaller instances of *exactly* the same problem.

2. **Build solutions to your recurrence from the bottom up.** Write an algorithm that starts with the base cases of your recurrence and works its way up to the final solution, by considering intermediate subproblems in the correct order. This stage can be broken down into several smaller, relatively mechanical steps:

   (a) **Identify the subproblems.** What are all the different ways your recursive algorithm can call itself, starting with some initial input? For example, the argument to RECFIBO is always an integer between 0 and n.

(b) **Choose a memoization data structure.** Find a data structure that can store the solution to *every* subproblem you identified in step (a). This is usually *but not always* a multidimensional array.

(c) **Identify dependencies.** Except for the base cases, every subproblem depends on other subproblems—which ones? Draw a picture of your data structure, pick a generic element, and draw arrows from each of the other elements it depends on. Then formalize your picture.

(d) **Find a good evaluation order.** Order the subproblems so that each one comes *after* the subproblems it depends on. You should consider the base cases first, then the subproblems that depends only on base cases, and so on, eventually building up to the original top-level problem. The dependencies you identified in the previous step define a partial order over the subproblems; you need to find a linear extension of that partial order. *Be careful!*

(e) **Analyze space and running time.** The number of distinct subproblems determines the space complexity of your memoized algorithm. To compute the total running time, add up the running times of all possible subproblems, *assuming deeper recursive calls are already memoized.* You can actually do this immediately after step (a).

(f) **Write down the algorithm.** You know what order to consider the subproblems, and you know how to solve each subproblem. So do that! If your data structure is an array, this usually means writing a few nested for-loops around your original recurrence, and replacing the recursive calls with array look-ups.

Of course, you have to prove that each of these steps is correct. If your recurrence is wrong, or if you try to build up answers in the wrong order, your algorithm won't work!

3.5 Warning: Greed is Stupid

If we're incredibly lucky, we can bypass all the recurrences and tables and so forth, and solve the problem using a *greedy* algorithm. Like a backtracking algorithm, a greedy algorithm constructs a solution through a series of decisions, but it makes those decisions directly, *without* solving at any recursive subproblems. While this approach seems very natural, it almost never works; optimization problems that can be solved correctly by a greedy algorithm are quite rare. Nevertheless, for many problems that should be solved by backtracking or dynamic programming, many students' first intuition is to apply a greedy strategy.

For example, a greedy algorithm for the text segmentation problem might find the shortest (or, if you prefer, longest) prefix of the input string that is a word, accept that prefix as the first word in the segmentation, and then recursively segment the remaining suffix of the input string. Similarly, a greedy algorithm for the longest increasing subsequence problem might look for the smallest element of the input array, accept that element as the start of the target subsequence, and then recursively look for the longest increasing subsequence to the right of that element. If these sound like stupid hacks to you, pat yourself on the back; these aren't even *close* to correct solutions.

Everyone should tattoo the following sentence on the back of their hands, right under all the rules about logarithms and big-Oh notation:

> # Greedy algorithms never work!
> ## Use dynamic programming instead!

What, never?
No, never!
What, *never*?
Well. . . hardly ever.[10]

Because the greedy approach is so incredibly tempting, but so rarely correct, I strongly advocate the following policy in any algorithms course, even (or perhaps *especially*) for courses that do not normally ask for proofs of correctness.[11]

> **You will not receive *any* credit for *any* greedy algorithm,**
> **on *any* homework or exam, even if the algorithm is correct,**
> **without a *formal* proof of correctness.**

Moreover, the vast majority of problems for which students are tempted to submit a greedy algorithm are actually best solved using dynamic programming. So I always offer the following advice to my algorithms students.

> **Whenever you write—or even *think*—the word "greeDY",**
> **your subconscious is telling you to use DYnamic programming.**

Even for problems that *can* be correctly solved by greedy algorithms, it's usually more productive to develop a backtracking or dynamic programming algorithm first. First make it work, then make it fast. We will see techniques for proving greedy algorithms correct in the next chapter.

---

[10]They hardly ever ever work! Then give three cheers, and one cheer more, for the rigorous Captain of the *Pinafore*! Then give three cheers, and one cheer more, for the Captain of the *Pinafore*!

[11]Introducing this policy in my own algorithms courses significantly improved students' grades, because it significantly reduced the frequency of incorrect greedy algorithms.

3.6 Longest Increasing Subsequence

Another problem we considered in the previous chapter was computing the length of the longest increasing subsequence of a given array $A[1..n]$ of numbers. We developed two different recursive backtracking algorithms for this problem. Both algorithms run in $O(2^n)$ time in the worst case; both algorithms can be sped up significantly via dynamic programming.

First Recurrence: Is This Next?

Our first backtracking algorithm evaluated the function $LISbigger(i, j)$, which we defined as the length of the longest increasing subsequence of $A[j..n]$ in which every element is larger than $A[i]$. We derived the following recurrence for this function:

$$
LISbigger(i, j) = \begin{cases} 0 & \text{if } j > n \\ LISbigger(i, j+1) & \text{if } A[i] \geq A[j] \\ \max \begin{cases} LISbigger(i, j+1) \\ 1 + LISbigger(j, j+1) \end{cases} & \text{otherwise} \end{cases}
$$

To solve the original problem, we can add a sentinel value $A[0] = -\infty$ to the array and compute $LISbigger(0, 1)$.

Each recursive subproblem is identified by two indices i and j, so there are only $O(n^2)$ distinct recursive subproblems to consider. We can memoize the results of these subproblems into a two-dimensional array **$LISbigger[0..n, 1..n]$**.[12] Moreover, each subproblem can be solved in $O(1)$ time, not counting recursive calls, so we should expect the final dynamic programming algorithm to run in $O(n^2)$ *time*.

The order in which the memoized recursive algorithm fills this array is not immediately clear; all we can tell from the recurrence is that each entry $LISbigger[i, j]$ is filled in *after* the entries $LISbigger[i, j+1]$ and $LISbigger[j, j+1]$ in the next column, as indicated on the left in Figure 3.4.

Fortunately, this partial information is enough to give us a *valid* evaluation order. If we fill the table one column at a time, from right to left, then whenever we reach an entry in the table, the entries it depends on are already available. This may not be the order that the recursive algorithm would use, but it works, so we'll go with it. The right figure in Figure 3.4 illustrates this evaluation order, with a double arrow indicating the outer loop and single arrows indicating the

---

[12]In fact, we only need half of this array, because we always have $i < j$. But even if we cared about constant factors in this book (we don't), this would be the wrong time to worry about them. First make it work; then make it better.

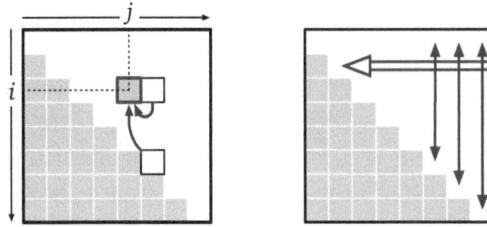

Figure 3.4. Subproblem dependencies for longest increasing subsequence, and a valid evaluation order

inner loop. In this case, the single arrows are bidirectional, because the order that we use to fill each column doesn't matter.

And we're done! Pseudocode for our dynamic programming algorithm is shown below; as expected, our algorithm clearly runs in $O(n^2)$ time. If necessary, we can reduce the space bound from $O(n^2)$ to $O(n)$ by maintaining only the two most recent columns of the table, $LISbigger[\cdot, j]$ and $LISbigger[\cdot, j+1]$.[13]

$$
\begin{array}{l}
\underline{\text{FASTLIS}(A[1..n]):} \\
\quad A[0] \leftarrow -\infty \qquad\qquad\qquad \langle\!\langle \text{Add a sentinel}\rangle\!\rangle \\
\quad \text{for } i \leftarrow 0 \text{ to } n \qquad\qquad\quad \langle\!\langle \text{Base cases}\rangle\!\rangle \\
\quad\quad LISbigger[i, n+1] \leftarrow 0 \\
\quad \text{for } j \leftarrow n \text{ down to } 1 \\
\quad\quad \text{for } i \leftarrow 0 \text{ to } j-1 \qquad \langle\!\langle \dots \text{or whatever}\rangle\!\rangle \\
\quad\quad\quad keep \leftarrow 1 + LISbigger[j, j+1] \\
\quad\quad\quad skip \leftarrow LISbigger[i, j+1] \\
\quad\quad\quad \text{if } A[i] \geq A[j] \\
\quad\quad\quad\quad LISbigger[i, j] \leftarrow skip \\
\quad\quad\quad \text{else} \\
\quad\quad\quad\quad LISbigger[i, j] \leftarrow \max\{keep, skip\} \\
\quad \text{return } LISbigger[0, 1]
\end{array}
$$

Second Recurrence: What's Next?

Our second backtracking algorithm evaluated the function $LISfirst(i)$, which we defined as the length of the longest increasing subsequence of $A[i..n]$ that begins with $A[i]$. We derived the following recurrence for this function:

$$LISfirst(i) = 1 + \max\left\{LISfirst(j) \mid j > i \text{ and } A[j] > A[i]\right\}$$

Here, we assume that $\max\varnothing = 0$, so that the base cases like $LISfirst(n) = 1$ fall out of the recurrence automatically. To solve the original problem, we can add a sentinel value $A[0] = -\infty$ to the array and compute $LISfirst(0) - 1$.

In this case, recursive subproblems are indicated by a single index i, so we can memoize the recurrence into a one-dimensional array $LISfirst[1..n]$. Each

---

[13] See, I told you not to worry about constant factors yet!

entry *LISfirst*[*i*] depends only on entries *LISfirst*[*j*] with $j > i$, so we can fill the array in decreasing index order. To compute each *LISfirst*[*i*], we need to consider *LISfirst*[*j*] for *all* indices $j > i$, but we don't need to consider those indices *j* in any particular order. The resulting dynamic programming algorithm runs in $O(n^2)$ *time* and uses $O(n)$ space.

$$\boxed{\begin{aligned}
&\underline{\text{FASTLIS2}(A[1\mathbin{..}n]):}\\
&\quad A[0] = -\infty \qquad\qquad \langle\!\langle \textit{Add a sentinel}\rangle\!\rangle\\
&\quad \text{for } i \leftarrow n \text{ downto } 0\\
&\qquad LISfirst[i] \leftarrow 1\\
&\qquad \text{for } j \leftarrow i+1 \text{ to } n \qquad \langle\!\langle \textit{\ldots or whatever}\rangle\!\rangle\\
&\qquad\quad \text{if } A[j] > A[i] \text{ and } 1+LISfirst[j] > LISfirst[i]\\
&\qquad\qquad LISfirst[i] \leftarrow 1 + LISfirst[j]\\
&\quad \text{return } LISfirst[0] - 1 \qquad \langle\!\langle \textit{Don't count the sentinel}\rangle\!\rangle
\end{aligned}}$$

3.7 Edit Distance

The *edit distance* between two strings is the minimum number of letter insertions, letter deletions, and letter substitutions required to transform one string into the other. For example, the edit distance between FOOD and MONEY is at most four:

$$\text{F\underline{O}OD} \rightarrow \text{MO\underline{O}D} \rightarrow \text{MON\,D} \rightarrow \text{MONE\underline{D}} \rightarrow \text{MONEY}$$

This distance function was independently proposed by Vladimir Levenshtein in 1965 (working on coding theory), Taras Vintsyuk in 1968 (working on speech recognition), and Stanislaw Ulam in 1972 (working with biological sequences). For this reason, edit distance is sometimes called *Levenshtein distance* or *Ulam distance* (but strangely, never "Vintsyuk distance").

We can visualize this editing process by aligning the strings one above the other, with a gap in the first word for each insertion and a gap in the second word for each deletion. Columns with two *different* characters correspond to substitutions. In this representation, the number of editing steps is just the number of columns that do *not* contain the same character twice.

$$\begin{array}{ccccc}
\text{F} & \text{O} & \text{O} & & \text{D} \\
\text{M} & \text{O} & \text{N} & \text{E} & \text{Y}
\end{array}$$

It's fairly obvious that we can't transform FOOD into MONEY in three steps, so the edit distance between FOOD and MONEY is exactly four. Unfortunately, it's not so easy in general to tell when a sequence of edits is as short as possible. For example, the following alignment shows that the distance between the strings ALGORITHM and ALTRUISTIC is *at most* 6. Is that the best we can do?

```
A  L  G  O  R     I     T  H  M
A  L     T  R  U  I  S  T  I  C
```

Recursive Structure

To develop a dynamic programming algorithm to compute edit distance, we first need to formulate the problem recursively. Our alignment representation for edit sequences has a crucial "optimal substructure" property. Suppose we have the gap representation for the shortest edit sequence for two strings. **If we remove the last column, the remaining columns must represent the shortest edit sequence for the remaining prefixes.** We can easily prove this observation by contradiction: If the prefixes had a shorter edit sequence, gluing the last column back on would gives us a shorter edit sequence for the original strings. So once we figure out what should happen in the last column, the Recursion Fairy can figure out the rest of the optimal gap representation.

Said differently, the alignment we are looking for represents a sequence of editing operations, ordered (for no particular reason) from right to left. Solving the edit distance problem requires making a sequence of decisions, one for each column in the output alignment. In the middle of this sequence of decisions, we have already aligned a suffix of one string with a suffix of the other.

AL GOR	I		T	H	M
AL TRU	I	S	T	I	C

Because the cost of an alignment is just the number of mismatched columns, our remaining decisions don't depend on the editing operations we've already chosen; they only depend on the prefixes we haven't aligned yet.

ALGOR
ALTRU

Thus, for any two input strings $A[1..m]$ and $B[1..n]$, we can formulate the edit distance problem recursively as follows: For any indices i and j, let **Edit(i, j)** denote the edit distance between the prefixes $A[1..i]$ and $B[1..j]$. We need to compute $Edit(m, n)$.

Recurrence

When i and j are both positive, there are exactly three possibilities for the last column in the optimal alignment of $A[1..i]$ and $B[1..j]$:

- **Insertion:** The last entry in the top row is empty. In this case, the edit distance is equal to $Edit(i, j-1)+1$. The +1 is the cost of the final insertion, and the recursive expression gives the minimum cost for the remaining alignment.

AL GOR	
AL TR	U

- **Deletion:** The last entry in the bottom row is empty. In this case, the edit distance is equal to $Edit(i-1, j) + 1$. The +1 is the cost of the final deletion, and the recursive expression gives the minimum cost for the remaining alignment.

AL GO	R
AL TRU	

- **Substitution:** Both rows have characters in the last column. If these two characters are different, then the edit distance is equal to $Edit(i-1, j-1) + 1$. If these two characters are equal, the substitution is free, so the edit distance is $Edit(i-1, j-1)$.

AL GO	R		AL GO	R
AL TR	U		AL T	R

This generic case analysis breaks down if either $i = 0$ or $j = 0$, but those boundary cases are easy to handle directly.

- Transforming the empty string into a string of length j requires j insertions, so $Edit(0, j) = j$.

- Transforming a string of length i into the empty string requires i deletions, so $Edit(i, 0) = i$.

As a sanity check, both of these base cases correctly indicate that the edit distance between the empty string and the empty string is zero!

We conclude that the *Edit* function satisfies the following recurrence:

$$Edit(i, j) = \begin{cases} i & \text{if } j = 0 \\ j & \text{if } i = 0 \\ \min \begin{cases} Edit(i, j-1) + 1 \\ Edit(i-1, j) + 1 \\ Edit(i-1, j-1) + [A[i] \neq B[j]] \end{cases} & \text{otherwise} \end{cases}$$

Dynamic Programming

Now that we have a recurrence, we can transform it into a dynamic programming algorithm following our usual mechanical recipe.

- **Subproblems:** Each recursive subproblem is identified by two indices $0 \leq i \leq m$ and $0 \leq j \leq n$.

- **Memoization structure:** So we can memoize all possible values of $Edit(i, j)$ in a two-dimensional array $Edit[0 .. m, 0 .. n]$.

- **Dependencies:** Each entry $Edit[i, j]$ depends only on its three neighboring entries $Edit[i-1, j]$, $Edit[i, j-1]$, and $Edit[i-1, j-1]$.

- **Evaluation order:** If we fill this array in standard row-major order—row by row from top down, each row from left to right—then whenever we reach an entry in the array, all the entries it depends on are already available. (This isn't the *only* evaluation order we could use, but it works, so let's go with it.)

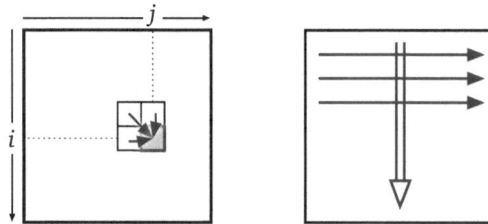

- **Space and time:** The memoization structure uses $O(mn)$ space. We can compute each entry $Edit[i, j]$ in $O(1)$ time once we know its predecessors, so the overall algorithm runs in $O(mn)$ **time.**

Here is the resulting dynamic programming algorithm:

```
EDITDISTANCE(A[1 .. m], B[1 .. n]):
    for j ← 0 to n
        Edit[0, j] ← j

    for i ← 1 to m
        Edit[i, 0] ← i
        for j ← 1 to n
            ins ← Edit[i, j − 1] + 1
            del ← Edit[i − 1, j] + 1
            if A[i] = B[j]
                rep ← Edit[i − 1, j − 1]
            else
                rep ← Edit[i − 1, j − 1] + 1
            Edit[i, j] ← min {ins, del, rep}
    return Edit[m, n]
```

This algorithm is most commonly attributed to Robert Wagner and Michael Fischer, who described the algorithm in 1974. However, in full compliance with Stigler's Law of Eponymy, either identical or more general algorithms were independently discovered by Taras Vintsyuk in 1968, V. M. Velichko and N. G. Zagoruyko in 1970, David Sankoff in 1972, Peter Sellers in 1974, and almost certainly several others.[14] Interestingly, *none* of these authors cite either Levenshtein or Ulam!

The memoization table for the input strings ALGORITHM and ALTRUISTIC is shown below. Bold numbers indicate places where characters in the two strings are equal. The edit distance between ALGORITHM and ALTRUISTIC is indeed six!

	A	L	G	O	R	I	T	H	M
	0	1	2	3	4	5	6	7	8	9
A	1	**0**	1	2	3	4	5	6	7	8
L	2	1	**0**	1	2	3	4	5	6	7
T	3	2	1	1	2	3	4	**4**	5	6
R	4	3	2	2	2	**2**	3	4	5	6
U	5	4	3	3	3	3	3	4	5	6
I	6	5	4	4	4	4	**3**	4	5	6
S	7	6	5	5	5	5	4	4	5	6
T	8	7	6	6	6	6	5	**4**	5	6
I	9	8	7	7	7	7	**6**	5	5	6
C	10	9	8	8	8	8	7	6	6	6

The arrows in this table indicate which predecessor(s) actually define each entry. Each direction of arrow corresponds to a different edit operation: horizontal=deletion, vertical=insertion, and diagonal=substitution. Bold red diagonal arrows indicate "free" substitutions of a letter for itself. Any path of arrows from the top left corner to the bottom right corner of this table represents an optimal edit sequence between the two strings. The example memoization array contains exactly three directed paths from the top left corner to the bottom right corner, each indicating a different sequence of six edits transforming ALGORITHM into ALTRUISTIC, as shown on the next page.

---

[14]This algorithm is sometimes also *incorrectly* attributed to Saul Needleman and Christian Wunsch in 1970. "The Needleman-Wunsch algorithm" more commonly refers to the standard dynamic programming algorithm for computing the longest common subsequence of two strings (or equivalently, the edit distance where only insertions and deletions are permitted) in $O(mn)$ time, but that attribution is *also* incorrect! In fact, Needleman and Wunsch's algorithm computes (weighted) longest common subsequences (possibly with gap costs) in $O(m^2n^2)$ time, using a different recurrence. Sankoff explicitly describes his $O(mn)$-time algorithm as an improvement of Needleman and Wunsch's algorithm.

```
A L G O R I     T H M
A L T R U I S T I C

A L G O R     I     T H M
A L   T R U I S T I C

A L G O R     I     T H M
A L T     R U I S T I C
```

Our EDITDISTANCE algorithm does not actually compute or store any arrows in the table, but the arrow(s) leading into any entry in the table can be reconstructed on the fly in $O(1)$ time from the numerical values. Thus, once we've filled in the table, we can reconstruct the shortest edit sequence in $O(n+m)$ additional time.

3.8   Subset Sum

Recall that the *Subset Sum* problem asks whether any subset of a given array $X[1..n]$ of positive integers sums to a given integer T. In the previous chapter, we developed a recursive Subset Sum algorithm that can be reformulated as follows. Fix the original input array $X[1..n]$ and define the boolean function

$$SS(i, t) = \text{TRUE} \text{ if and only if some subset of } X[i..n] \text{ sums to } t.$$

We need to compute $SS(1, T)$. This function satisfies the following recurrence:

$$SS(i, t) = \begin{cases} \text{TRUE} & \text{if } t = 0 \\ \text{FALSE} & \text{if } t < 0 \text{ or } i > n \\ SS(i+1, t) \lor SS(i+1, t - X[i]) & \text{otherwise} \end{cases}$$

We can transform this recurrence into a dynamic programming algorithm following the usual boilerplate.

- **Subproblems:** Each subproblem is described by an integer i such that $1 \le i \le n+1$, and an integer $t \le T$. However, subproblems with $t < 0$ are trivial, so it seems rather silly to memoize them.[15] Indeed, we can modify the recurrence so that those subproblems never arise:

$$SS(i, t) = \begin{cases} \text{TRUE} & \text{if } t = 0 \\ \text{FALSE} & \text{if } i > n \\ SS(i+1, t) & \text{if } t < X[i] \\ SS(i+1, t) \lor SS(i+1, t - X[i]) & \text{otherwise} \end{cases}$$

---

[15]Yes, I'm breaking my own rule against premature optimization.

- **Data structure:** We can memoize our recurrence into a two-dimensional array $S[1..n+1, 0..T]$, where $S[i, t]$ stores the value of $SS(i, t)$.

- **Evaluation order:** Each entry $S[i, t]$ depends on at most two other entries, both of the form $SS[i+1, \cdot]$. So we can fill the array by considering rows from bottom to top in the outer loop, and considering the elements in each row in arbitrary order in the inner loop.

- **Space and time:** The memoization structure uses $O(nT)$ space. If $S[i+1, t]$ and $S[i+1, t-X[i]]$ are already known, we can compute $S[i, t]$ in constant time, so the algorithm runs in $O(nT)$ **time.**

Here is the resulting dynamic programming algorithm:

$\underline{\text{FastSubsetSum}(X[1..n], T):}$
    $S[n+1, 0] \leftarrow \text{True}$
    for $t \leftarrow 1$ to T
        $S[n+1, t] \leftarrow \text{False}$

    for $i \leftarrow n$ downto 1
        $S[i, 0] = \text{True}$
        for $t \leftarrow 1$ to $X[i]-1$
            $S[i, t] \leftarrow S[i+1, t]$ 《Avoid the case $t < 0$》
        for $t \leftarrow X[i]$ to T
            $S[i, t] \leftarrow S[i+1, t] \vee S[i+1, t-X[i]]$

    return $S[1, T]$

The worst-case running time $O(nT)$ for this algorithm is a significant improvement over the $O(2^n)$-time recursive backtracking algorithm when T is small.[16] However, if the target sum T is significantly larger than 2^n, this iterative algorithm is actually slower than the naïve recursive algorithm, because it's wasting time solving subproblems that the recursive algorithm never considers. Dynamic programming isn't *always* an improvement![17]

3.9 Optimal Binary Search Trees

The final problem we considered in the previous chapter was the optimal binary search tree problem. The input is a sorted array $A[1..n]$ of search keys and an array $f[1..n]$ of frequency counts, where $f[i]$ is the number of times we will

---

[16]Even though the subset sum problem is NP-hard, this time bound does *not* imply that P=NP, because T is not necessarily bounded by a polynomial function of the input size.

[17]In the 1967 research memorandum(!) where he proposed memo functions, Donald Michie wrote, "To tabulate values of a function which will not be needed is a waste of space, and to recompute the same values more than once is a waste of time." But in fact, tabulating values of a function that will **not** be needed is also a waste of *time*!

search for $A[i]$. Our task is to construct a binary search tree for that set such that the total cost of all the searches is as small as possible.

Fix the frequency array f, and let $OptCost(i, k)$ denote the total search time in the optimal search tree for the subarray $A[i..k]$. We derived the following recurrence for the function $OptCost$:

$$OptCost(i,k) = \begin{cases} 0 & \text{if } i > k \\ \displaystyle\sum_{j=i}^{k} f[j] + \min_{i \leq r \leq k} \left\{ \begin{array}{l} OptCost(i, r-1) \\ + OptCost(r+1, k) \end{array} \right\} & \text{otherwise} \end{cases}$$

You can probably guess what we're going to do with this recurrence eventually, but let's rid of that ugly summation first.

For any pair of indices $i \leq k$, let $F(i, k)$ denote the total frequency count for all the keys in the interval $A[i..k]$:

$$F(i, k) := \sum_{j=i}^{k} f[j]$$

This function satisfies the following simple recurrence:

$$F(i,k) = \begin{cases} f[i] & \text{if } i = k \\ F(i, k-1) + f[k] & \text{otherwise} \end{cases}$$

We can compute all possible values of $F(i, k)$ in $O(n^2)$ time using—you guessed it!—dynamic programming! The usual mechanical steps give us the following dynamic programming algorithm:

```
INITF(f[1..n]):
    for i ← 1 to n
        F[i, i-1] ← 0
        for k ← i to n
            F[i, k] ← F[i, k-1] + f[k]
```

We will use this short algorithm as an initialization subroutine. This initialization allows us to simplify the original $OptCost$ recurrence as follows:

$$OptCost(i,k) = \begin{cases} 0 & \text{if } i > k \\ F[i,k] + \min_{i \leq r \leq k} \left\{ \begin{array}{l} OptCost(i, r-1) \\ + OptCost(r+1, k) \end{array} \right\} & \text{otherwise} \end{cases}$$

Now let's turn the crank.

- **Subproblems:** Each recursive subproblem is specified by two integers i and k, such that $1 \le i \le n+1$ and $0 \le k \le n$.

- **Memoization:** We can store all possible values of *OptCost* in a two-dimensional array $OptCost[1..n+1, 0..n]$. (Only the entries $OptCost[i, j]$ with $j \ge i - 1$ will actually be used, but whatever.)

- **Dependencies:** Each entry $OptCost[i, k]$ depends on the entries $OptCost[i, j-1]$ and $OptCost[j+1, k]$, for all j such that $i \le j \le k$. In other words, each table entry depends on all entries either directly to the left or directly below.

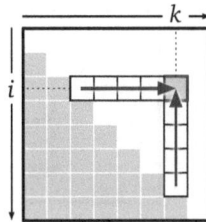

The following subroutine fills the entry $OptCost[i, k]$, assuming all the entries it depends on have already been computed.

```
COMPUTEOPTCOST(i, k):
    OptCost[i, k] ← ∞
    for r ← i to k
        tmp ← OptCost[i, r − 1] + OptCost[r + 1, k]
        if OptCost[i, k] > tmp
            OptCost[i, k] ← tmp
    OptCost[i, k] ← OptCost[i, k] + F[i, k]
```

- **Evaluation order:** There are at least three different orders that can be used to fill the array. The first one that occurs to most students is to scan through the table one diagonal at a time, starting with the trivial base cases $OptCost[i, i-1]$ and working toward the final answer $OptCost[1, n]$, like so:

```
OPTIMALBST(f[1..n]):
    INITF(f[1..n])
    for i ← 1 to n + 1
        OptCost[i, i − 1] ← 0
    for d ← 0 to n − 1
        for i ← 1 to n − d        ⟨⟨... or whatever⟩⟩
            COMPUTEOPTCOST(i, i + d)
    return OptCost[1, n]
```

We could also traverse the array row by row from the bottom up, traversing each row from left to right, or column by column from left to right, traversing each columns from the bottom up.

```
OPTIMALBST2(f[1..n]):              OPTIMALBST3(f[1..n]):
  INITF(f[1..n])                     INITF(f[1..n])
  for i ← n + 1 downto 1             for j ← 0 to n + 1
    OptCost[i, i − 1] ← 0              OptCost[j + 1, j] ← 0
    for j ← i to n                    for i ← j downto 1
      COMPUTEOPTCOST(i, j)              COMPUTEOPTCOST(i, j)
  return OptCost[1, n]               return OptCost[1, n]
```

As before, we can illustrate these evaluation orders using a double-lined arrow to indicate the outer loop and single-lined arrows to indicate the inner loop. The bidirectional arrows in the first evaluation order indicate that the order of the inner loops doesn't matter.

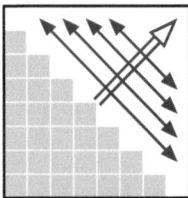

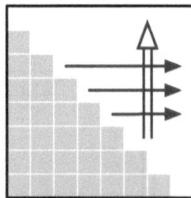

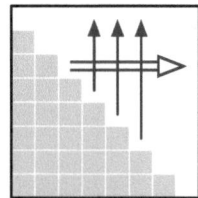

- **Time and space:** The memoization structure uses $O(n^2)$ space. No matter which evaluation order we choose, we need $O(n)$ time to compute each entry $OptCost[i, k]$, so our overall algorithm runs in $O(n^3)$ **time**.

As usual, we could have predicted the final space and time bounds directly from the original recurrence:

$$
OptCost(i, k) = \begin{cases} 0 & \text{if } i > k \\ F[i, k] + \min_{i \leq r \leq k} \left\{ \begin{aligned} &OptCost(i, r - 1) \\ &+ OptCost(r + 1, k) \end{aligned} \right\} & \text{otherwise} \end{cases}
$$

The $OptCost$ function has two arguments, each of which can take on roughly n different values, so we probably need a data structure of size $O(n^2)$. On the other hand, there are *three* variables in the body of the recurrence (i, k, and r), each of which can take roughly n different values, so it should take $O(n^3)$ time to compute everything.

3.10 Dynamic Programming on Trees

So far, all of our dynamic programming examples use multidimensional arrays to store the results of recursive subproblems. However, as the next example shows, this is not always the most appropriate data structure to use.

An *independent set* in a graph is a subset of the vertices with no edges between them. Finding the largest independent set in an arbitrary graph is extremely hard; in fact, this is one of the canonical NP-hard problems we will study in Chapter 12. But in some special classes of graphs, we can find largest independent sets quickly. In particular, when the input graph is a *tree* with n vertices, we can actually compute the largest independent set in $O(n)$ time.

Suppose we are given a tree T. Without loss of generality, suppose T is a rooted tree; that is, there is a special node in T called the *root*, and all edges are implicitly directed away from this vertex. (If T is an unrooted tree—a connected acyclic undirected graph—we can choose an arbitrary vertex as the root.) We call vertex w a *descendant* of vertex v if the unique path from w to the root includes v; equivalently, the descendants of v are v itself and the descendants of the children of v. The *subtree rooted at* v consists of all the descendants of v and the edges between them.

For any node v in T, let $MIS(v)$ denote the size of the largest independent set in the subtree rooted at v. Any independent set in this subtree that excludes v itself is the union of independent sets in the subtrees rooted at the children of v. On the other hand, any independent set that *includes* v necessarily excludes all of v's children, and therefore includes independent sets in the subtrees rooted at v's grandchildren. Thus, the function MIS obeys the following recurrence, where the nonstandard notation $w \downarrow v$ means "w is a child of v":

$$MIS(v) = \max\left\{\sum_{w \downarrow v} MIS(w),\ 1 + \sum_{w \downarrow v}\sum_{x \downarrow w} MIS(x)\right\}$$

We need to compute $MIS(r)$, where r is the root of T.

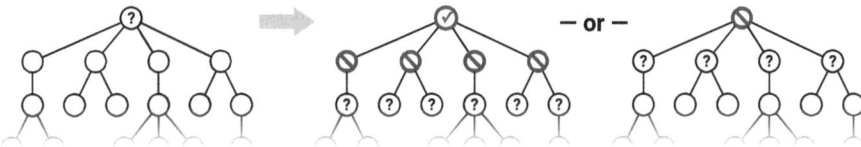

Figure 3.5. Computing the maximum independent set in a tree

What data structure should we use to memoize this recurrence? The most natural choice is **the tree T itself!** Specifically, for each vertex v in T, we store the result of $MIS(v)$ in a new field $v.MIS$. (In principle, we *could* use an array instead, but then we'd need pointers back and forth between each node and its corresponding array entry, so why bother?)

What's a good order to consider the subproblems? The subproblem associated with any node v depends on the subproblems associated with the children and grandchildren of v. So we can visit the nodes in any order we like, provided that every vertex is visited before its parent; in particular, we can use a standard *post-order* traversal.

What's the running time of the algorithm? The non-recursive time associated with each node v is proportional to the number of children and grandchildren of v; this number can be very different from one vertex to the next. But we can turn the analysis around: Each vertex contributes a constant amount of time to its parent and its grandparent! Because each vertex has at most one parent and at most one grandparent, the algorithm runs in $O(n)$ *time*.

Here is the resulting dynamic programming algorithm. Yes, it's still recursive, because that's the most natural way to implement a post-order tree traversal.

$\underline{\text{TREEMIS}(v)\text{:}}$
 $skipv \leftarrow 0$
 for each child w of v
  $skipv \leftarrow skipv + \text{TREEMIS}(w)$
 $keepv \leftarrow 1$
 for each grandchild x of v
  $keepv \leftarrow keepv + x.MIS$
 $v.MIS \leftarrow \max\{keepv, skipv\}$
 return $v.MIS$

We can derive an even simpler linear-time algorithm by defining two separate functions over the nodes of T:

- Let $MISyes(v)$ denote the size of the largest independent set of the subtree rooted at v that *includes* v.

- Let $MISno(v)$ denote the size of the largest independent set of the subtree rooted at v that *excludes* v.

Again, we need to compute $\max\{MISyes(r), MISno(r)\}$, where r is the root of T. The first two functions satisfy the following mutual recurrence:

$$MISyes(v) = 1 + \sum_{w \downarrow v} MISno(w)$$

$$MISno(v) = \sum_{w \downarrow v} \max\{MISyes(w), MISno(w)\}$$

Again, we can memoize these functions into the tree itself, by defining two new fields for each vertex. A straightforward post-order tree traversal evaluates both functions at every node in $O(n)$ time. The following algorithm not only memoizes both function values at v, it also returns the larger of those two values.

$\underline{\text{TREEMIS2}(v)\text{:}}$
 $v.MISno \leftarrow 0$
 $v.MISyes \leftarrow 1$
 for each child w of v
  $v.MISno \leftarrow v.MISno + \text{TREEMIS2}(w)$
  $v.MISyes \leftarrow v.MISyes + w.MISno$
 return $\max\{v.MISyes, v.MISno\}$

In the second line of the inner loop, we are using the value $w.MISno$ that was memoized by the recursive call in the previous line.

Exercises

For all of the following exercises—and more generally when developing *any* new dynamic programming algorithm—I strongly recommend following the steps outlined in Section 3.4. In particular, don't even *start* thinking about tables or for-loops until you have a complete recursive solution, including a clear English specification of the recursive subproblems you are actually solving.[18] **First make it work, then make it fast.**

Sequences/Arrays

1. In a previous life, you worked as a cashier in the lost Antarctican colony of Nadiria, spending the better part of your day giving change to your customers. Because paper is a very rare and valuable resource in Antarctica, cashiers were required by law to use the fewest bills possible whenever they gave change. Thanks to the numerological predilections of one of its founders, the currency of Nadiria, called Dream-Dollars, was available in the following denominations: $1, $4, $7, $13, $28, $52, $91, and $365.[19]

   ♣(a) The greedy change algorithm repeatedly takes the largest bill that does not exceed the target amount. For example, to make $122 using the greedy algorithm, we first take a $91 bill, then a $28 bill, and finally three $1 bills. Give an example where this greedy algorithm uses more Dream-Dollar bills than the minimum possible. *[Hint: It may be easier to write a small program than to work this out by hand.]*

   (b) Describe and analyze a recursive algorithm that computes, given an integer k, the minimum number of bills needed to make k Dream-Dollars. (Don't worry about making your algorithm fast; just make sure it's correct.)

   (c) Describe a dynamic programming algorithm that computes, given an integer k, the minimum number of bills needed to make k Dream-Dollars. (This one needs to be fast.)

---

[18]In my algorithms classes, any dynamic programming solution that does *not* include an English specification of the underlying recursive subproblems automatically gets a score of *zero*, even if the solution is otherwise perfect. Introducing this policy significantly improved students' grades, because it significantly reduced the number of times they submitted incorrect (or incoherent) dynamic programming algorithms.

[19]For more details on the history and culture of Nadiria, including images of the various denominations of Dream-Dollars, see http://moneyart.biz/dd/.

2. Describe efficient algorithms for the following variants of the text segmentation problem. Assume that you have a subroutine IsWord that takes an array of characters as input and returns True if and only if that string is a "word". Analyze your algorithms by bounding the number of calls to IsWord.

    (a) Given an array $A[1..n]$ of characters, compute the number of partitions of A into words. For example, given the string ARTISTOIL, your algorithm should return 2, for the partitions ARTIST·OIL and ART·IS·TOIL.

    (b) Given two arrays $A[1..n]$ and $B[1..n]$ of characters, decide whether A and B can be partitioned into words at the same indices. For example, the strings BOTHEARTHANDSATURNSPIN and PINSTARTRAPSANDRAGSLAP can be partitioned into words at the same indices as follows:

    $$BOT · HEART · HAND · SAT · URNS · PIN$$
    $$PIN · START · RAPS · AND · RAGS · LAP$$

    (c) Given two arrays $A[1..n]$ and $B[1..n]$ of characters, compute the number of different ways that A and B can be partitioned into words at the same indices.

3. Suppose you are given an array $A[1..n]$ of numbers, which may be positive, negative, or zero, and which are **not** necessarily integers.

    (a) Describe and analyze an algorithm that finds the largest sum of elements in a contiguous subarray $A[i..j]$.

    (b) Describe and analyze an algorithm that finds the largest *product* of elements in a contiguous subarray $A[i..j]$.

    For example, given the array $[-6, 12, -7, 0, 14, -7, 5]$ as input, your first algorithm should return 19, and your second algorithm should return 504.

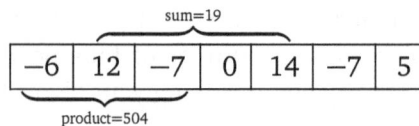

Given the one-element array $[-374]$ as input, your first algorithm should return 0, and your second algorithm should return 1. (The empty interval is still an interval!) For the sake of analysis, assume that comparing, adding, or multiplying any pair of numbers takes $O(1)$ time.

> *[Hint: Part (a) has been a standard computer science interview question since at least the mid-1980s. You can find many correct solutions on the web; the problem even has its own Wikipedia page! But at least in 2016, a significant fraction of the solutions I found on the web for part (b) were either slower than necessary or actually incorrect.]*

4. This exercise explores variants of the maximum-subarray problem (Problem 3). In all cases, your input consists of an array $A[1..n]$ of real numbers (which could be positive, negative, or zero) and possibly an additional integer $X \geq 0$.

   (a) *Wrapping around:* Suppose A is a *circular* array. In this setting, a "contiguous subarray" can be either an interval $A[i..j]$ or a suffix followed by a prefix $A[i..n] \cdot A[1..j]$. Describe and analyze an algorithm that finds a contiguous subarray of A with the largest sum.

   (b) *Long subarrays only:* Describe and analyze an algorithm that finds a contiguous subarray of A *of length at least X* that has the largest sum. (Assume $X \leq n$.)

   (c) *Short subarrays only:* Describe and analyze an algorithm that finds a contiguous subarray of A *of length at most X* that has the largest sum.

   (d) *The Price Is Right:* Describe and analyze an algorithm that finds a contiguous subarray of A with the largest sum *less than or equal to X*.

   (e) Describe a faster algorithm for Problem 4(d) when every number in the array A is non-negative.

5. This exercise asks you to develop efficient algorithms to find optimal *subsequences* of various kinds. A subsequence is anything obtained from a sequence by extracting a subset of elements, but keeping them in the same order; the elements of the subsequence need not be contiguous in the original sequence. For example, the strings C, DAMN, YAIOAI, and DYNAMICPROGRAMMING are all subsequences of the string DYNAMICPROGRAMMING.

   [Hint: Exactly one of these problems can be solved in $O(n)$ time using a greedy algorithm.]

   (a) Let $A[1..m]$ and $B[1..n]$ be two arbitrary arrays. A *common subsequence* of A and B is another sequence that is a subsequence of both A and B. Describe an efficient algorithm to compute the length of the *longest* common subsequence of A and B.

   (b) Let $A[1..m]$ and $B[1..n]$ be two arbitrary arrays. A *common supersequence* of A and B is another sequence that contains both A and B as subsequences. Describe an efficient algorithm to compute the length of the *shortest* common supersequence of A and B.

   (c) Call a sequence $X[1..n]$ of numbers *bitonic* if there is an index i with $1 < i < n$, such that the prefix $X[1..i]$ is increasing and the suffix $X[i..n]$ is decreasing. Describe an efficient algorithm to compute the length of the longest bitonic subsequence of an arbitrary array A of integers.

(d) Call a sequence $X[1..n]$ of numbers *oscillating* if $X[i] < X[i+1]$ for all even i, and $X[i] > X[i+1]$ for all odd i. Describe an efficient algorithm to compute the length of the longest oscillating subsequence of an arbitrary array A of integers.

(e) Describe an efficient algorithm to compute the length of the shortest oscillating supersequence of an arbitrary array A of integers.

(f) Call a sequence $X[1..n]$ of numbers *convex* if $2 \cdot X[i] < X[i-1]+X[i+1]$ for all i. Describe an efficient algorithm to compute the length of the longest convex subsequence of an arbitrary array A of integers.

(g) Call a sequence $X[1..n]$ of numbers *weakly increasing* if each element is larger than the average of the two previous elements; that is, $2 \cdot X[i] > X[i-1]+X[i-2]$ for all $i > 2$. Describe an efficient algorithm to compute the length of the longest weakly increasing subsequence of an arbitrary array A of integers.

(h) Call a sequence $X[1..n]$ of numbers *double-increasing* if $X[i] > X[i-2]$ for all $i > 2$. (In other words, a double-increasing sequence is a perfect shuffle of two increasing sequences.) Describe an efficient algorithm to compute the length of the longest double-increasing subsequence of an arbitrary array A of integers.

(i) Recall that a sequence $X[1..n]$ of numbers is *increasing* if $X[i] < X[i+1]$ for all i. Describe an efficient algorithm to compute the length of the *longest common increasing subsequence* of two given arrays of integers. For example, $\langle 1,4,5,6,7,9 \rangle$ is the longest common increasing subsequence of the sequences $\langle 3,1,4,1,5,9,2,6,5,3,5,8,9,7,9,3 \rangle$ and $\langle 1,4,1,4,2, 1,3,5,6,2,3,7,3,0,9,5 \rangle$.

6. A *shuffle* of two strings X and Y is formed by interspersing the characters into a new string, keeping the characters of X and Y in the same order. For example, the string BANANAANANAS is a shuffle of the strings BANANA and ANANAS in several different ways.

BANANA~ANANAS~~~~~~BAN~ANA~ANANAS~~~~~~B~ANAN~A~ANA~NA~S

Similarly, the strings PRODGYRNAMAMMIINCG and DYPRONGARMAMMICING are both shuffles of DYNAMIC and PROGRAMMING:

PRO~D~GY~R~NAM~AMMI~I~NCG~~~~~~~~DY~PRON~GAR~M~AMM~IC~ING

(a) Given three strings $A[1..m]$, $B[1..n]$, and $C[1..m+n]$, describe and analyze an algorithm to determine whether C is a shuffle of A and B.

(b) A *smooth* shuffle of X and Y is a shuffle of X and Y that never uses more than two consecutive symbols of either string. For example,

- PR$_D$O$_Y$G$_N$A$_R$A$_M$MM$_I$I$_C$NG is a smooth shuffle of the strings DYNAMIC and PROGRAMMING.
- D$_Y$PR$_N$OGR$_A$A$_M$MM$_I$C$_I$NG is a shuffle of DYNAMIC and PROGRAMMING, but it is not a smooth shuffle (because of the substrings OGR and ING).
- XX$_X$X$_X$X$_X$XX$_X$X$_X$XX$_X$X$_X$XX is a smooth shuffle of the strings XXXXXXX and XXXXXXXXXXX.
- There is no smooth shuffle of the strings XXXX and XXXXXXXXXXXX.

Describe and analyze an algorithm to decide, given three strings X, Y, and Z, whether Z is a smooth shuffle of X and Y.

7. For each of the following problems, the input consists of two arrays $X[1..k]$ and $Y[1..n]$ where $k \leq n$.

   (a) Describe and analyze an algorithm to decide whether X is a subsequence of Y. For example, the string PPAP is a subsequence of the string PENPINEAPPLEAPPLEPEN.

   (b) Describe and analyze an algorithm to find the smallest number of symbols that can be removed from Y so that X is no longer a subsequence. Equivalently, your algorithm should find the longest subsequence of Y that is *not* a supersequence of X. For example, after removing removing two symbols from the string PENPINEAPPLEAPPLEPEN, the string PPAP is no longer a subsequence.

   ♥(c) Describe and analyze an algorithm to determine whether X occurs as two *disjoint* subsequences of Y. For example, the string PPAP appears as two disjoint subsequences in the string PENPINEAPPLEAPPLEPEN.

   (d) Suppose the input also includes a third array $C[1..n]$ of numbers, which may be positive, negative, or zero, where $C[i]$ is the *cost* of $Y[i]$. Describe and analyze an algorithm to compute the minimum-cost occurrence of X as a subsequence of Y. That is, we want to find an array $I[1..k]$ such that $I[j] < I[j+1]$ and $X[I[j]] = Y[j]$ for every index j, and the total cost $\sum_{j=1}^{k} C[j]$ is as small as possible.

   (e) Describe and analyze an algorithm to compute the total number of (possibly overlapping) occurrences of X as a subsequence of Y. For purposes of analysis, assume that we can add two arbitrary integers in $O(1)$ time. For example, the string PPAP appears exactly 23 times as a subsequence of the string PENPINEAPPLEAPPLEPEN. If all characters in X and Y are equal, your algorithm should return $\binom{n}{k}$.

   (f) What is the running time of your algorithm for part (d) if adding two ℓ-bit integers requires $O(\ell)$ time?

8. Describe and analyze an efficient algorithm to find the length of the longest contiguous substring that appears both forward and backward in an input string $T[1..n]$. The forward and backward substrings must not overlap. Here are several examples:

   - Given the input string ALGORITHM, your algorithm should return 0.
   - Given the input string RECURSION, your algorithm should return 1, for the substring R.
   - Given the input string REDIVIDE, your algorithm should return 3, for the substring EDI. (The forward and backward substrings must not overlap!)
   - Given the input string DYNAMICPROGRAMMINGMANYTIMES, your algorithm should return 4, for the substring YNAM. (In particular, it should *not* return 6, for the subsequence YNAMIR).

9. A palindrome is any string that is exactly the same as its reversal, like I, or DEED, or RACECAR, or AMANAPLANACATACANALPANAMA.

   (a) Describe and analyze an algorithm to find the length of the *longest subsequence* of a given string that is also a palindrome.

   For example, the longest palindrome subsequence of the string MAHDYNAMICPROGRAMZLETMESHOWYOUTHEM is MHYMRORMYHM; thus, given that string as input, your algorithm should return 11.

   (b) Describe and analyze an algorithm to find the length of the *shortest supersequence* of a given string that is also a palindrome. For example, the shortest palindrome supersequence of TWENTYONE is TWENTOYOTNEWT, so given the string TWENTYONE as input, your algorithm should return 13.

   (c) Any string can be decomposed into a sequence of palindromes. For example, the string BUBBASEESABANANA ("Bubba sees a banana.") can be broken into palindromes in the following ways (and 65 others):

   BUB • BASEESAB • ANANA

   B • U • BB • ASEESA • B • ANANA

   BUB • B • A • SEES • ABA • N • ANA

   B • U • BB • A • S • EE • S • A • B • A • NAN • A

   B • U • B • B • A • S • E • E • S • A • B • A • N • A • N • A

   Describe and analyze an efficient algorithm to find the smallest number of palindromes that make up a given input string. For example, given the input string BUBBASEESABANANA, your algorithm should return 3.

   (d) Describe and analyze an efficient algorithm to find the largest integer k such that a given string can be split into palindromes of length at least k. For example:

- Given the string PALINDROME, your algorithm should return 1.
- Given the string BUBBASEESABANANA, your algorithm should return 3, for the partition BUB • BASEESAB • ANANA.
- Given a string of n identical symbols, your algorithm should return n.

(e) Describe and analyze an efficient algorithm to find the number of different ways that a given string can be decomposed into palindromes. For example:

- Given the string PALINDROME, your algorithm should return 1.
- Given the string BUBBASEESABANANA, your algorithm should return 70.
- Given a string of n identical symbols, your algorithm should return 2^{n-1}.

♥(f) A *metapalindrome* is a decomposition of a string into a sequence of palindromes, such that the sequence of palindrome lengths is itself a palindrome. For example:

$$\text{BOB • S • MAM • ASEESA • UKU • L • ELE}$$

is a metapalindrome for the string BOBSMAMASEESAUKULELE, whose length sequence is the palindrome $(3, 1, 3, 6, 3, 1, 3)$. Describe and analyze an efficient algorithm to find the length of the shortest metapalindrome for a given string. For example, given the input string BOBSMAMASEESAUKULELE, your algorithm should return 11.

10. Suppose you are given an array $A[1..n]$ of positive integers. An *increasing back-and-forth subsequence* is an sequence of indices $I[1..\ell]$ with the following properties:

- $1 \le I[j] \le n$ for all j.
- $A[I[j]] < A[I[j+1]]$ for all $j < \ell$.
- If $I[j]$ is even, then $I[j+1] > I[j]$.
- If $I[j]$ is odd, then $I[j+1] < I[j]$.

Less formally, suppose we are given an array of n squares, each containing a positive integer. Suppose we place a token on one of the squares, and then repeatedly move the token left (if it's on an odd-indexed square) or right (if it's on an even-indexed square), always moving from a smaller number to a larger number. Then the sequence of token positions is an increasing back-and-forth subsequence.

Describe an algorithm to compute the length of the longest increasing back-and-forth subsequence of a given array of n integers. For example, given the input array

1	1	8	7	5	6	3	6	4	4	8	3	9	1	2	2	3	9	4	0
1<	2>	3<	4>	5<	6>	7<	8>	9<	10>	11<	12>	13<	14>	15<	16>	17<	18>	19<	20>

your algorithm should return the integer 9, which is the length of the following increasing back-and-forth subsequence:

0	1	2	3	4	6	7	8	9
20>	1<	15<	18>	10>	6>	4>	3<	13<

11. Suppose we want to typeset a paragraph of text onto a piece of paper (or if you insist, a computer screen). The text consists of a sequence of n words, where the ith word has length $\ell[i]$. We want to break the paragraph into several lines of total length exactly L. For example, according to TEX, the program used to typeset these notes, *the paragraph you are reading right now* is approximately 11.94794 cm $\approx$ 4.7055 inches wide.

Depending on how the paragraph is broken into lines of text, we must insert different amounts of white space between the words. The paragraph should be fully justified, meaning that the first character on each line starts at the left margin, and *except for the last line*, the last character on each line ends at the right margin. There must be at least one unit of white space between any two words on the same line. See *the paragraph you are reading right now*? Just like that.

Define the *slop* of a paragraph layout as the sum over all lines, *except the last*, of the cube of the amount of extra white-space in each line, not counting the one unit of required space between each adjacent pair of words. Specifically, if a line contains words i through j, then the slop of that line is defined to be $\left(L - j + i - \sum_{k=i}^{j} \ell[k]\right)^3$. Describe a dynamic programming algorithm to print the paragraph with minimum slop.

12. You and your eight-year-old nephew Elmo decide to play a simple card game. At the beginning of the game, the cards are dealt face up in a long row. Each card is worth a different number of points. After all the cards are dealt, you and Elmo take turns removing either the leftmost or rightmost card from the row, until all the cards are gone. At each turn, you can decide which of the two cards to take. The winner of the game is the player that has collected the most points when the game ends.

Having never taken an algorithms class, Elmo follows the obvious greedy strategy—when it's his turn, Elmo *always* takes the card with the higher point value. Your task is to find a strategy that will beat Elmo whenever possible. (It might seem mean to beat up on a little kid like this, but Elmo absolutely *hates* it when grown-ups let him win.)

(a) Prove that you should not also use the greedy strategy. That is, show that there is a game that you can win, but only if you do *not* follow the same greedy strategy as Elmo.

(b) Describe and analyze an algorithm to determine, given the initial sequence of cards, the maximum number of points that you can collect playing against Elmo.

*(c) When Elmo was four, he used an even simpler strategy—on his turn, he always chose his next card uniformly at random. That is, if there was more than one card left on his turn, he would take the leftmost card with probability $1/2$, and the rightmost card with probability $1/2$. Describe an algorithm to determine, given the initial sequence of cards, the maximum *expected* number of points you can collect playing against four-year-old-Elmo.

(d) Five years later, thirteen-year-old Elmo has become a *much* stronger player. Describe and analyze an algorithm to determine, given the initial sequence of cards, the maximum number of points that you can collect playing against a *perfect* opponent.

13. It's almost time to show off your flippin' sweet dancing skills! Tomorrow is the big dance contest you've been training for your entire life, except for that summer you spent with your uncle in Alaska hunting wolverines. You've obtained an advance copy of the list of n songs that the judges will play during the contest, in chronological order. Yesssssssss!

You know all the songs, all the judges, and your own dancing ability extremely well. For each integer k, you know that if you dance to the kth song on the schedule, you will be awarded exactly $Score[k]$ points, but then you will be physically unable to dance for the next $Wait[k]$ songs (that is, you cannot dance to songs $k + 1$ through $k + Wait[k]$). The dancer with the highest total score at the end of the night wins the contest, so you want your total score to be as high as possible.

Describe and analyze an efficient algorithm to compute the maximum total score you can achieve. The input to your sweet algorithm is the pair of arrays $Score[1..n]$ and $Wait[1..n]$.

14. The new swap-puzzle game *Candy Swap Saga XIII* involves n cute animals numbered from 1 to n. Each animal holds one of three types of candy: circus peanuts, Heath bars, and Cioccolateria Gardini chocolate truffles. You also have a candy in your hand; at the start of the game, you have a circus peanut.

To earn points, you visit each of the animals in order from 1 to n. For each animal, you can either keep the candy in your hand or exchange it with the candy the animal is holding.

- If you swap your candy for another candy of the *same* type, you earn one point.

- If you swap your candy for a candy of a *different* type, you lose one point. (Yes, your score can be negative.)

- If you visit an animal and decide not to swap candy, your score does not change.

You *must* visit the animals in order, and once you visit an animal, you can never visit it again.

Describe and analyze an efficient algorithm to compute your maximum possible score. Your input is an array $C[1..n]$, where $C[i]$ is the type of candy that the ith animal is holding.

15. Lenny Rutenbar, the founding dean of the new Maksymilian R. Levchin College of Computer Science, has commissioned a series of snow ramps on the south slope of the Orchard Downs sledding hill[20] and challenged Bill Kudeki, head of the Department of Electrical and Computer Engineering, to a sledding contest. Bill and Lenny will both sled down the hill, each trying to maximize their air time. The winner gets to expand their department/college into both Siebel Center and the new ECE Building; the loser has to move their entire department/college in the Boneyard culvert next to Loomis Lab.

    Whenever Lenny or Bill reaches a ramp *while on the ground*, they can either use that ramp to jump through the air, possibly flying over one or more ramps, or sled past that ramp and stay on the ground. Obviously, if someone flies over a ramp, they cannot use that ramp to extend their jump.

    (a) Suppose you are given a pair of arrays $Ramp[1..n]$ and $Length[1..n]$, where $Ramp[i]$ is the distance from the top of the hill to the ith ramp, and $Length[i]$ is the distance that any sledder who takes the ith ramp will travel through the air. Describe and analyze an algorithm to determine the maximum total distance that Lenny or Bill can spend in the air.

    (b) The university lawyers heard about Lenny and Bill's little bet and immediately objected. To protect the university from either lawsuits or sky-rocketing insurance rates, they impose an upper bound on the number of jumps that either sledder can take. Describe and analyze an algorithm to determine the maximum total distance that Lenny or Bill can spend in the air *with at most k jumps*, given the original arrays $Ramp[1..n]$ and $Length[1..n]$ and the integer k as input.

    ♥(c) When the lawyers realized that imposing their restriction didn't immediately shut down the contest, they added a new restriction: No ramp can be used more than once! Disgusted by the legal interference, Lenny and Bill give up on their bet and decide to cooperate to put on a good show

---

[20]The north slope is faster, but too short for an interesting contest.

for the spectators. Describe and analyze an algorithm to determine the maximum total distance that Lenny and Bill can spend in the air, each taking at most k jumps (so at most $2k$ jumps total), and with each ramp used at most once.

16. Farmers Boggis, Bunce, and Bean have set up an obstacle course for Mr. Fox. The course consists of a long row of booths, each with a number painted on the front with bright red paint. Formally, Mr. Fox is given an array $A[1..n]$, where $A[i]$ is the number painted on the front of the ith booth. Each number $A[i]$ could be positive, negative, or zero. Everyone agrees with the following rules:

    - At each booth, Mr. Fox *must* say either "Ring!" or "Ding!".

    - If Mr. Fox says "Ring!" at the ith booth, he earns a reward of $A[i]$ chickens. (If $A[i] < 0$, Mr. Fox pays a penalty of $-A[i]$ chickens.)

    - If Mr. Fox says "Ding!" at the ith booth, he pays a penalty of $A[i]$ chickens. (If $A[i] < 0$, Mr. Fox earns a reward of $-A[i]$ chickens.)

    - Mr. Fox is forbidden to say the same word more than three times in a row. For example, if he says "Ring!" at booths 6, 7, and 8, then he must say "Ding!" at booth 9.

    - All accounts will be settled at the end, after Mr. Fox visits every booth and the umpire calls "Hot box!" Mr. Fox does not actually have to carry chickens through the obstacle course.

    - Finally, if Mr. Fox violates any of the rules, or if he ends the obstacle course owing the farmers chickens, the farmers will shoot him.

    Describe and analyze an algorithm to compute, the largest number of chickens that Mr. Fox can earn by running the obstacle course, given the array $A[1..n]$ of numbers as input. *[Hint: Watch out for the burning pine cone!]*

17. *Dance Dance Revolution* is a dance video game, first introduced in Japan by Konami in 1998. Players stand on a platform marked with four arrows, pointing forward, back, left, and right, arranged in a cross pattern. During play, the game plays a song and scrolls a sequence of n arrows (←, ↑, ↓, or →) from the bottom to the top of the screen. At the precise moment each arrow reaches the top of the screen, the player must step on the corresponding arrow on the dance platform. (The arrows are timed so that you'll step with the beat of the song.)

    You are playing a variant of this game called "Vogue Vogue Revolution", where the goal is to play perfectly but move as little as possible. When an arrow reaches the top of the screen, if one of your feet is already on the correct arrow, you are awarded one style point for maintaining your current pose. If neither foot is on the right arrow, you must move one (and *only* one) foot from its current location to the correct arrow on the platform. If you ever step on the wrong arrow, or fail to step on the correct arrow, or move more than one foot at a time, or move either foot when you are already standing on the correct arrow, all your style points are taken away and you lose the game.

How should you move your feet to maximize your total number of style points? For purposes of this problem, assume you always start with your left foot on ← and your right foot on →, and that you've memorized the entire sequence of arrows. For example, if the sequence is ↑↑↓↓←→←→, you can earn 5 style points by moving your feet as shown below:

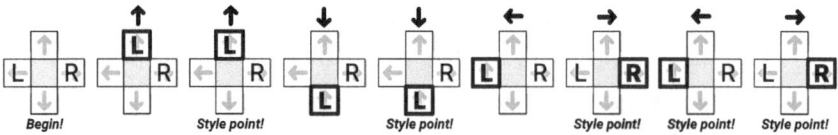

(a) **Prove** that for *any* sequence of n arrows, it is possible to earn at least $n/4 - 1$ style points.

(b) Describe an efficient algorithm to find the maximum number of style points you can earn during a given VVR routine. The input to your algorithm is an array $Arrow[1..n]$ containing the sequence of arrows.

18. Consider the following solitaire form of Scrabble. We begin with a fixed, finite sequence of tiles; each tile has both a letter and a numerical value. At the start of the game, we draw the first seven tiles from the sequence and put them into our hand. In each turn, we form an English word from some or all of the tiles in our hand, place those tiles on the table, and receive the total value of those tiles as points. (If no English word can be formed from the tiles in our hand, the game immediately ends.) Then we repeatedly draw the next tile from the start of the sequence until either (a) we have seven tiles in our hand, or (b) the sequence is empty. (Sorry, no double/triple word/letter scores, bingos, blanks, or passing.) Our goal is to obtain as many points as possible.

For example, consider the following sequence of 20 tiles:

Given this sequence of tiles at the beginning of the game, we can earn 68 points as follows:

- We initially draw I_2 N_2 X_8 A_1 N_2 A_1 D_3.
- Play the word N_2 A_1 I_2 A_1 D_3 for 9 points, leaving N_2 X_8 in hand.

- Draw the next five tiles U_5 D_3 I_2 D_3 K_8.
- Play the word U_5 N_2 D_3 I_2 D_3 for 15 points, leaving K_8 X_8 in hand.
- Draw the next five tiles U_5 B_4 L_2 A_1 K_8.
- Play the word B_4 U_5 L_2 K_8 for 19 points, leaving K_8 X_8 A_1 in hand.
- Draw the last three tiles H_5 A_1 N_2.
- Play the word A_1 N_2 K_8 H_5 for 16 points, leaving X_8 A_1 in hand.
- Play the word A_1 X_8 for 9 points, emptying our hand and ending the game.

(a) Suppose the sequence of tiles is represented by two arrays $Letter[1..n]$, containing a sequence of letters between A and Z, and $Value[A..Z]$, where $Value[\ell]$ is the value of any tile with letter ℓ. Design and analyze an efficient algorithm to compute the maximum number of points that can be earned from the given sequence of tiles.

(b) Now suppose two tiles with the same letter might have different values. Now the tile sequence is represented by two arrays $Letter[1..n]$ and $Value[1..n]$, where $Value[i]$ is the value of the ith tile. Design and analyze an efficient algorithm to compute the maximum number of points that can be earned from the given sequence of tiles.

In both problems, the output is a single number: the maximum possible score. Assume (because it's true) that you can find all English words that can be made from any set of at most seven tiles, along with the point values of those words, in $O(1)$ time.

19. Suppose we are given a set L of n line segments in the plane, where each segment has one endpoint on the line $y = 0$ and one endpoint on the line $y = 1$, and all $2n$ endpoints are distinct.

(a) Describe and analyze an algorithm to compute the largest subset of L in which no pair of segments intersects.

(b) Describe and analyze an algorithm to compute the largest subset of L in which *every* pair of segments intersects.

Now suppose we are given a set L of n line segments in the plane, where both endpoints of each segment lie on the unit circle $x^2 + y^2 = 1$, and all $2n$ endpoints are distinct.

(c) Describe and analyze an algorithm to compute the largest subset of L in which no pair of segments intersects.

(d) Describe and analyze an algorithm to compute the largest subset of L in which *every* pair of segments intersects.

20. Let P be a set of n points evenly distributed on the unit circle, and let S be a set of m line segments with endpoints in P. The endpoints of the m segments are *not* necessarily distinct; n could be significantly smaller than $2m$.

    (a) Describe an algorithm to find the size of the largest subset of segments in S such that every pair is disjoint. Two segments are disjoint if they do not intersect even at their endpoints.

    (b) Describe an algorithm to find the size of the largest subset of segments in S such that every pair is interior-disjoint. Two segments are interior-disjoint if their intersection is either empty or an endpoint of both segments.

    (c) Describe an algorithm to find the size of the largest subset of segments in S such that every pair intersects.

    (d) Describe an algorithm to find the size of the largest subset of segments in S such that every pair crosses. Two segments cross if they intersect but not at their endpoints.

    For full credit, all four algorithms should run in $O(mn)$ time.

21. You are driving a bus along a highway, full of rowdy, hyper, thirsty students and a soda fountain machine. Each minute that a student is on your bus, that student drinks one ounce of soda. Your goal is to drop the students off quickly, so that the total amount of soda consumed by all students is as small as possible.

    You know how many students will get off of the bus at each exit. Your bus begins somewhere along the highway (probably not at either end) and moves at a constant speed of 37.4 miles per hour. You must drive the bus along the highway; however, you may drive forward to one exit then backward to an exit in the opposite direction, switching as often as you like. (You can stop the bus, drop off students, and turn around instantaneously.)

    Describe an efficient algorithm to drop the students off so that they drink as little soda as possible. Your input consists of the bus route (a list of the exits, together with the travel time between successive exits), the number of students you will drop off at each exit, and the current location of your bus (which you may assume is an exit).

22. Let's define a *summary* of two strings A and B to be a concatenation of substrings of the following form:

    - ▲SNA indicates a substring SNA of only the first string A.
    - ◆FOO indicates a common substring FOO of both strings.
    - ▼BAR indicates a substring BAR of only the second string B.

A summary is *valid* if we can recover the original strings A and B by concatenating the appropriate substrings of the summary in order and discarding the delimiters ▲, ◆, and ▼. Each regular character has length 1, and each delimiter ▲, ◆, or ▼ has some fixed non-negative length Δ. The *length* of a summary is the sum of the lengths of its symbols.

For example, each of the following strings is a valid summary of the strings KITTEN and KNITTING:

- ◆K▼N◆ITT▲E▼I◆N▼G has length $9 + 7\Delta$.
- ◆K▼N◆ITT▲EN▼ING has length $10 + 5\Delta$.
- ◆K▲ITTEN▼NITTING has length $13 + 3\Delta$.
- ▲KITTEN▼KNITTING has length $14 + 2\Delta$.

Describe and analyze an algorithm that computes the length of the shortest summary of two given strings $A[1..m]$ and $B[1..n]$. The delimiter length Δ is also part of the input to your algorithm. For example:

- Given strings KITTEN and KNITTING and $\Delta = 0$, your algorithm should return 9.
- Given strings KITTEN and KNITTING and $\Delta = 1$, your algorithm should return 15.
- Given strings KITTEN and KNITTING and $\Delta = 2$, your algorithm should return 18.

23. *Vankin's Mile* is an American solitaire game played on an $n \times n$ square grid. The player starts by placing a token on any square of the grid. Then on each turn, the player moves the token either one square to the right or one square down. The game ends when player moves the token off the edge of the board. Each square of the grid has a numerical value, which could be positive, negative, or zero. The player starts with a score of zero; whenever the token lands on a square, the player adds its value to his score. The object of the game is to score as many points as possible.

For example, given the grid below, the player can score $8-6+7-3+4 = 10$ points by placing the initial token on the 8 in the second row, and then moving down, down, right, down, down. (This is *not* the best possible score for this grid of numbers.)

−1	7	−8	10	−5
−4	−9	8	−6	0
5	−2	−6	−6	7
−7	4	7→−3	−3
7	1	−6	4	−9

(a) Describe and analyze an efficient algorithm to compute the maximum possible score for a game of Vankin's Mile, given the $n \times n$ array of values as input.

(b) In the European version of this game, appropriately called *Vankin's Kilometer*, the player can move the token either one square down, one square right, *or one square left* in each turn. However, to prevent infinite scores, the token cannot land on the same square more than once. Describe and analyze an efficient algorithm to compute the maximum possible score for a game of Vankin's Kilometer, given the $n \times n$ array of values as input.[21]

24. Suppose you are given an $m \times n$ bitmap as an array $M[1..n, 1..n]$ of 0s and 1s. A *solid block* in M is a subarray of the form $M[i..i', j..j']$ in which all bits are equal. A solid block is square if it has the same number of rows and columns.

   (a) Describe an algorithm to find the maximum area of a solid *square* block in M in $O(n^2)$ time.

   (b) Describe an algorithm to find the maximum area of a solid block in M in $O(n^3)$ time.

   (c) Describe an algorithm to find the maximum area of a solid block in M in $O(n^2 \log n)$ time. [*Hint: Divide and conquer.*]

   ♥(d) Describe an algorithm to find the maximum area of a solid block in M in $O(n^2)$ time.

25. Suppose you are given an array $M[1..n, 1..n]$ of numbers, which may be positive, negative, or zero, and which are *not* necessarily integers. Describe an algorithm to find the largest sum of elements in any rectangular subarray of the form $M[i..i', j..j']$. For full credit, your algorithm should run in $O(n^3)$ time. [*Hint: See problem 3.*]

26. Describe and analyze an algorithm that finds the maximum-area rectangular pattern that appears more than once in a given bitmap. Specifically, given a two-dimensional array $M[1..n, 1..n]$ of bits as input, your algorithm should output the area of the largest repeated rectangular pattern in M. For example, given the bitmap shown on the left in the figure below, your algorithm should return the integer 195, which is the area of the 15×13 doggo. (Although it doesn't happen in this example, the two copies of the repeated pattern might overlap.)

---

[21]If we also allowed *upward* movement, the resulting game (Vankin's Fathom?) would be NP-hard.

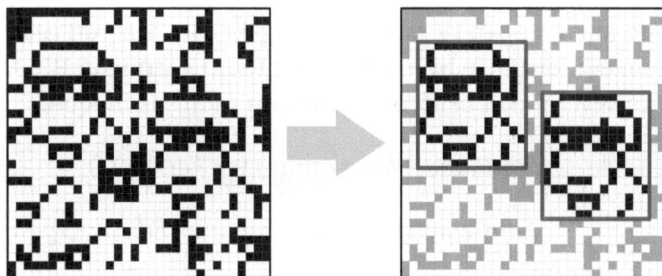

(a) For full credit, describe an algorithm that runs in $O(n^5)$ time.

♥(b) For extra credit, describe an algorithm that runs in $O(n^4)$ time.

♣♥(c) For extra extra credit, describe an algorithm that runs in $O(n^3 \text{polylog } n)$ time.

27. Let P be a set of points in the plane in *convex position*. Intuitively, if a rubber band were wrapped around the points, then every point would touch the rubber band. More formally, for any point p in P, there is a line that separates p from the other points in P. Moreover, suppose the points are indexed $P[1], P[2], \ldots, P[n]$ in counterclockwise order around the "rubber band", starting with the leftmost point $P[1]$.

This problem asks you to solve a special case of the traveling salesman problem, where the salesman must visit every point in P, and the cost of moving from one point $p \in P$ to another point $q \in P$ is the Euclidean distance $|pq|$.

(a) Describe a simple algorithm to compute the shortest *cyclic* tour of P.

(b) A *simple* tour is one that never crosses itself. Prove that the shortest tour of P must be simple.

(c) Describe and analyze an efficient algorithm to compute the shortest tour of P that starts at the leftmost point $P[1]$ and ends at the rightmost point $P[r]$.

(d) Describe and analyze an efficient algorithm to compute the shortest tour of P, with no restrictions on the endpoints.

♥28. Describe and analyze an algorithm to solve the traveling salesman problem in $O(2^n \text{poly}(n))$ time. Given an undirected n-vertex graph G with weighted edges, your algorithm should return the weight of the lightest cycle in G that visits every vertex exactly once, or ∞ if G has no such cycles. [*Hint: The obvious recursive backtracking algorithm takes $O(n!)$ time.*]

29. Let $W = \{w_1, w_2, \ldots, w_n\}$ be a finite set of strings over some fixed alphabet Σ. An *edit center* for W is a string $C \in \Sigma^*$ such that the maximum edit distance

from C to any string in W is as small as possible. The *edit radius* of W is the maximum edit distance from an edit center to a string in W. A set of strings may have several edit centers, but its edit radius is unique.

$$EditRadius(W) := \min_{C \in \Sigma^*} \max_{w \in W} Edit(w, C)$$

$$EditCenter(W) := \arg\min_{C \in \Sigma^*} \max_{w \in W} Edit(w, C)$$

(a) Describe and analyze an efficient algorithm to compute the edit radius of three given strings.

♣♥(b) Describe and analyze an efficient algorithm to approximate the edit radius of an arbitrary set of strings within a factor of 2. (Computing the *exact* edit radius is NP-hard unless the number of strings is fixed.)

♥30. Let $D[1..n]$ be an array of digits, each an integer between 0 and 9. A *digital subsequence* of D is a sequence of positive integers composed in the usual way from disjoint substrings of D. For example, the sequence 3, 4, 5, 6, 8, 9, 32, 38, 46, 64, 83, 279 is a digital subsequence of the first several digits of π:

$$3,1,4,1,5,9,2,6,5,3,5,8,9,7,9,3,2,3,8,4,6,2,6,4,3,3,8,3,2,7,9$$

The *length* of a digital subsequence is the number of integers it contains, *not* the number of digits; the preceding example has length 12. As usual, a digital subsequence is *increasing* if each number is larger than its predecessor.

Describe and analyze an efficient algorithm to compute the longest increasing digital subsequence of D. [*Hint: Be careful about your computational assumptions. How long does it take to compare two k-digit numbers?*]

For full credit, your algorithm should run in $O(n^4)$ time; faster algorithms are worth extra credit. The fastest algorithm I know for this problem runs in $O(n^{3/2} \log n)$ time; achieving this bound requires several tricks, both in the design of the algorithm and in its analysis, but nothing outside the scope of this class.[22]

♥31. Consider the following variant of the classical Tower of Hanoi problem. As usual, there are n disks with distinct sizes, placed on three pegs numbered 0, 1, and 2. Initially, all n disks are on peg 0, sorted by size from smallest on top to largest on bottom. Our goal is to move all the disks to peg 2. In a single step, we can move the highest disk on any peg to a different peg,

---

[22]With more advanced techniques, I believe the running time can be reduced to $O(n^{3/2} \log \log n)$, but I haven't worked through the details.

provided we satisfy two constraints. First, we must never place a smaller disk on top of a larger disk. Second—and this is the non-standard part—*we must never move a disk directly from peg 0 to peg 2.*

Describe and analyze an algorithm to compute the exact number of moves required to move all n disks from peg 0 to peg 2, subject to the stated restrictions. For full credit, your algorithm should use only $O(\log n)$ arithmetic operations in the worst case. For the sake of analysis, assume that adding or multiplying two k-digit numbers requires $O(k)$ time. *[Hint: Matrices!]*

Splitting Sequences/Arrays

32. A *basic arithmetic expression* is composed of characters from the set $\{1, +, \times\}$ and parentheses. Almost every integer can be represented by more than one basic arithmetic expression. For example, all of the following basic arithmetic expression represent the integer 14:

$$1+1+1+1+1+1+1+1+1+1+1+1+1+1$$
$$((1+1) \times (1+1+1+1+1)) + ((1+1) \times (1+1))$$
$$(1+1) \times (1+1+1+1+1+1+1)$$
$$(1+1) \times (((1+1+1) \times (1+1)) + 1)$$

Describe and analyze an algorithm to compute, given an integer n as input, the minimum number of 1s in a basic arithmetic expression whose value is equal to n. The number of parentheses doesn't matter, just the number of 1s. For example, when $n = 14$, your algorithm should return 8, for the final expression above. The running time of your algorithm should be bounded by a small polynomial function of n.

33. Suppose you are given a sequence of integers separated by $+$ and $-$ signs; for example:
$$1+3-2-5+1-6+7$$

You can change the value of this expression by adding parentheses in different places. For example:

$$1+3-2-5+1-6+7 = -1$$
$$(1+3-(2-5)) + (1-6) + 7 = 9$$
$$(1+(3-2)) - (5+1) - (6+7) = -17$$

Describe and analyze an algorithm to compute, given a list of integers separated by $+$ and $-$ signs, the maximum possible value the expression can take by adding parentheses. Parentheses must be used only to group additions and subtractions; in particular, do not use them to create implicit multiplication as in $1 + 3(-2)(-5) + 1 - 6 + 7 = 33$.

34. Suppose you are given a sequence of integers separated by $+$ and $\times$ signs; for example:

$$1 + 3 \times 2 \times 0 + 1 \times 6 + 7$$

You can change the value of this expression by adding parentheses in different places. For example:

$$(1 + (3 \times 2)) \times 0 + (1 \times 6) + 7 = 13$$
$$((1 + (3 \times 2 \times 0) + 1) \times 6) + 7 = 19$$
$$(1 + 3) \times 2 \times (0 + 1) \times (6 + 7) = 104$$

(a) Describe and analyze an algorithm to compute the maximum possible value the given expression can take by adding parentheses, assuming all integers in the input are *positive*. [Hint: This is easy.]

(b) Describe and analyze an algorithm to compute the maximum possible value the given expression can take by adding parentheses, assuming all integers in the input are *non-negative*.

(c) Describe and analyze an algorithm to compute the maximum possible value the given expression can take by adding parentheses, with no restrictions on the input numbers.

Assume any arithmetic operation takes $O(1)$ time.

35. After graduating from Sham-Poobanana University, you decide to interview for a position at the Wall Street bank **Long Live Boole**. The managing director of the bank, Eloob Egroeg, poses a 'solve-or-die' problems to each new employee, which they must solve within 24 hours. Those who fail to solve the problem are fired immediately!

Entering the bank for the first time, you notice that the employee offices are organized in a straight row, with a large T or F printed on the door of each office. Furthermore, between each adjacent pair of offices, there is a board marked by one of the symbols $\wedge, \vee,$ or $\oplus$. When you ask about these arcane symbols, Eloob confirms that T and F represent the boolean values TRUE and FALSE, and the symbols on the boards represent the standard boolean operators AND, OR, and XOR. He also explains that these letters and symbols describe whether certain combinations of employees can work together successfully. At the start of any new project, Eloob hierarchically clusters his employees by adding parentheses to the sequence of symbols, to obtain an unambiguous boolean expression. The project is successful if this parenthesized boolean expression evaluates to T.

For example, if the bank has three employees, and the sequence of symbols on and between their doors is $T \wedge F \oplus T$, there is exactly one successful parenthesization scheme: $(T \wedge (F \oplus T))$. However, if the list of door symbols is $F \wedge T \oplus F$, there is no way to add parentheses to make the project successful.

Eloob finally poses your solve-or-die interview question: Describe an algorithm to decide whether a given sequence of symbols can be parenthesized so that the resulting boolean expression evaluates to T. Your input is an array $S[0..2n]$, where $S[i] \in \{T, F\}$ when i is even, and $S[i] \in \{\vee, \wedge, \oplus\}$ when i is odd.

36. Every year, as part of its annual meeting, the Antarctican Snail Lovers of Upper Glacierville hold a Round Table Mating Race. Several high-quality breeding snails are placed at the edge of a round table. The snails are numbered in order around the table from 1 to n. During the race, each snail wanders around the table, leaving a trail of slime behind it. The snails have been specially trained never to fall off the edge of the table or to cross a slime trail, even their own. If two snails meet, they are declared a breeding pair, removed from the table, and whisked away to a romantic hole in the ground to make little baby snails. Note that some snails may never find a mate, even if the race goes on forever.

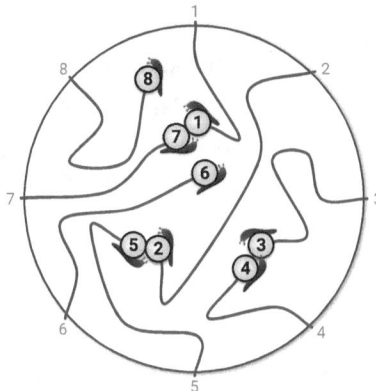

Figure 3.6. The end of a typical Antarctican SLUG race. Snails 6 and 8 never find mates. The organizers must pay $M[3,4] + M[2,5] + M[1,7]$.

For every pair of snails, the Antarctican SLUG race organizers have posted a monetary reward, to be paid to the owners if that pair of snails meets during the Mating Race. Specifically, there is a two-dimensional array $M[1..n, 1..n]$ posted on the wall behind the Round Table, where $M[i,j] = M[j,i]$ is the reward to be paid if snails i and j meet.

Describe and analyze an algorithm to compute the maximum total reward that the organizers could be forced to pay, given the array M as input.

37. You have mined a large slab of marble from a quarry. For simplicity, suppose the marble slab is a rectangle measuring n inches in height and m inches in width. You want to cut the slab into smaller rectangles of various sizes—some for kitchen counter tops, some for large sculpture projects, others for memorial headstones. You have a marble saw that can make either horizontal or vertical cuts across any rectangular slab. At any time, you can query the spot price $P[x, y]$ of an x-inch by y-inch marble rectangle, for any positive integers x and y. These prices depend on customer demand, and people who buy marble counter tops are weird, so don't make any assumptions about them; in particular, larger rectangles may have significantly smaller spot prices. Given the array of spot prices and the integers m and n as input, describe an algorithm to compute how to subdivide an $n \times m$ marble slab to maximize your profit.

38. This problem asks you to design efficient algorithms to construct optimal binary search trees that satisfy additional balance constraints. Your input consists of a sorted array $A[1..n]$ of search keys and an array $f[1..n]$ of frequency counts, where $f[i]$ is the number of searches for $A[i]$. This is exactly the same cost function as described in Section 3.9. But now your task is to compute an optimal tree that satisfies some additional constraints.

    (a) **AVL trees** were the earliest self-balancing balanced binary search trees, first described in 1962 by Georgy Adelson-Velsky and Evgenii Landis. An AVL tree is a binary search tree where for every node v, the height of the left subtree of v and the height of the right subtree of v differ by at most one.

    Describe and analyze an algorithm to construct an optimal AVL tree for a given set of search keys and frequencies.

    (b) **Symmetric binary B-trees** are another self-balancing binary trees, first described by Rudolf Bayer in 1972; these are better known by the name **red-black trees**, after a somewhat simpler reformulation by Leo Guibas and Bob Sedgwick in 1978. A red-black tree is a binary search tree with the following additional constraints:
    - Every node is either red or black.
    - Every red node has a black parent.
    - Every root-to-leaf path contains the same number of black nodes.

Describe a recursive backtracking algorithm to construct an optimal red-black tree for a given set of search keys and frequencies.

(c) **AA trees** were proposed by proposed by Arne Andersson in 1993 and slightly simplified (and named) by Mark Allen Weiss in 2000. AA trees are also known as *left-leaning red-black trees*, after a symmetric reformulation (with different rebalancing algorithms) by Bob Sedgewick in 2006. An AA tree is a red-black tree with one additional constraint:

- No left child is red.[23]

Describe and analyze an algorithm to construct an optimal AA tree for a given set of search keys and frequencies.

39. Suppose you are given an $m \times n$ bitmap as an array $M[1..m, 1..n]$ of 0s and 1s. A *solid block* in M is a subarray of the form $M[i..i', j..i']$ in which all bits are equal. Suppose you want to decompose M into as few disjoint blocks as possible.

One natural recursive partitioning strategy is called a *guillotine subdivision*. If the entire bitmap M is a solid block, there is nothing to do. Otherwise, we cut M into two smaller bitmaps along a horizontal or vertical line, and then recursively decompose the two smaller bitmaps into solid blocks.

Any guillotine subdivision can be represented as a binary tree, where each internal node stores the position and orientation of a cut, and each leaf stores a single but 0 or 1 indicting the contents of the corresponding block. The *size* of a guillotine subdivision is the number of leaves in the corresponding binary tree (that is, the final number of solid blocks), and the *depth* of a guillotine subdivision is the depth of the corresponding binary tree.

(a) Describe and analyze an algorithm to compute a guillotine subdivision of M of minimum possible size.

(b) Show that a guillotine subdivision does *not* always yield a partition into the smallest number of solid blocks.

(c) Describe and analyze an algorithm to compute a guillotine subdivision for M with the smallest possible depth.

(d) Describe and analyze an algorithm to determine $M[i, j]$, given the tree representing a guillotine decomposition for M and two indices i and j.

---

[23] Sedgewick's reformulation requires that no *right* child is red. Whatever. Andersson and Sedgewick are strangely silent about whether to measure angles clockwise or counterclockwise, whether Pluto is a planet, whether "lower rank" means "better" or "worse", and whether it's better to fight a hundred duck-sized horses or a single horse-sized duck.

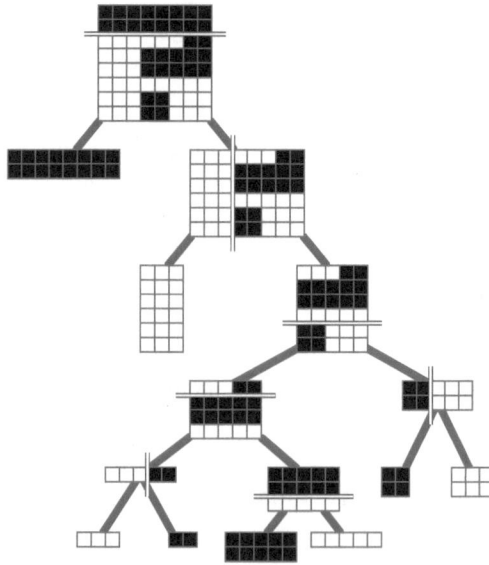

Figure 3.7. A guillotine subdivision with size 8 and depth 5.

(e) Define the *depth* of a pixel $M[i, j]$ in a guillotine subdivision to be the depth of the leaf that contains that pixel. Describe and analyze an algorithm to compute a guillotine subdivision for M such that the sum of the depths of the pixels as small as possible.

(f) Describe and analyze an algorithm to compute a guillotine subdivision for M such that the sum of the depths of the *black* pixels as small as possible.

♣40. Congratulations! You've been hired by the giant online bookstore DeNile ("Not just a river in Egypt!") to optimize their warehouse robots. Each book that DeNile sells has a unique ISBN (International Standard Book Number), which is just a numerical value. Each of DeNile's warehouses contains a long row of bins, each containing multiple copies of a single book. These bins are arranged in sorted order by ISBN; each bin's ISBN is printed on the front of the bin in machine-readable form. Books are retrieved from these bins by robots, which run along rails parallel to the row of bins.

DeNile does not maintain a list of which bins contain which ISBN numbers; that would be too simple! Instead, to retrieve a desired book, the robot must first find that book's bin using a binary search. Because the search requires physical motion by the robot, we can no longer assume that each step of the binary search requires $O(1)$ time. Specifically:

- The robot always starts at the "0th bin" (where the books are loaded into boxes to ship to customers).

- Moving the robot from the ith bin to the jth bin requires $\alpha|i-j|$ seconds for some constant α.

- The robot must be directly in front of a bin in order to read that bin's ISBN. Reading an ISBN requires β seconds, for some constant β.

- Reversing the robot's direction of motion (from increasing to decreasing or vice versa) requires γ additional seconds, for some constant γ.

- When the robot finds the target bin, it extracts one book from that bin and returns to "the 0th bin".

Design and analyze an algorithm to compute a binary search tree over the bins that minimizes the total time the robot spends searching for books. Your input is an array $f[1..n]$ of integers, where $f[i]$ is the number of times that the robot will be asked to retrieve a book from the ith bin, along with the time parameters α, β, and γ.

♠41. A standard method to improve the cache performance of search trees is to pack more search keys and subtrees into each node. A **B-tree** is a rooted tree in which each internal node stores up to B keys and pointers to up to $B+1$ children, each the root of a smaller B-tree. Specifically, each node v stores three fields:

- a positive integer $v.d \le B$,

- a *sorted* array $v.key[1..v.d]$, and

- an array $v.child[0..v.d]$ of child pointers.

In particular, the number of child pointers is always exactly one more than the number of keys.[24]

Each pointer $v.child[i]$ is either NULL or a pointer to the root of a B-tree whose keys are all larger than $v.key[i]$ and smaller than $v.key[i+1]$. In particular, all keys in the leftmost subtree $v.child[0]$ are smaller than $v.key[1]$, and all keys in the rightmost subtree $v.child[v.d]$ are larger than $v.key[v.d]$.

Intuitively, you should have the following picture in mind:

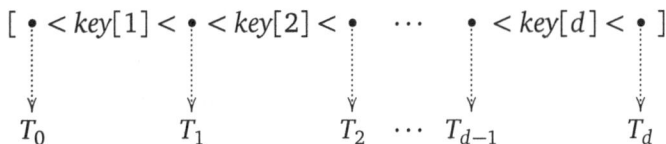

$$[\ \bullet < key[1] < \bullet < key[2] < \bullet \quad \cdots \quad \bullet < key[d] < \bullet\ ]$$

$$T_0 \qquad T_1 \qquad T_2 \quad \cdots \quad T_{d-1} \qquad T_d$$

[24]Normally, B-trees are required to satisfy two additional constraints, which guarantee a worst-case search cost of $O(\log_B n)$: Every leaf must have exactly the same depth, and every node except possibly the root must contain at least $B/2$ keys. However, in this problem, we are not interested in optimizing the *worst-case* search cost, but rather the *total* cost of a sequence of searches, so we will not impose these additional constraints.

Here T_i is the subtree pointed to by *child*[i].

The **cost** of searching for a key x in a B-tree is the number of nodes in the path from the root to the node containing x as one of its keys. A 1-tree is just a standard binary search tree.

Fix an arbitrary positive integer $B > 0$. (I suggest $B = 8$.) Suppose your are given a sorted array $A[1,\ldots,n]$ of search keys and a corresponding array $F[1,\ldots,n]$ of frequency counts, where $F[i]$ is the number of times that we will search for $A[i]$. Your task is to describe and analyze an efficient algorithm to find a B-tree that minimizes the total cost of searching for the given keys with the given frequencies.

(a) Describe a polynomial-time algorithm for the special case $B = 2$.

(b) Describe an algorithm for arbitrary B that runs in $O(n^{B+c})$ time for some fixed integer c.

♥(c) Describe an algorithm for arbitrary B that runs in $O(n^c)$ time for some fixed integer c that does *not* depend on B.

42. A string w of parentheses (and) and brackets [and] is **balanced** if it satisfies one of the following conditions:

   - w is the empty string.
   - $w = (x)$ for some balanced string x
   - $w = [x]$ for some balanced string x
   - $w = xy$ for some balanced strings x and y

   For example, the string

$$w = ([()[]()) [()()] ()$$

   is balanced, because $w = xy$, where

$$x = ([()] [] ()) \qquad \text{and} \qquad y = [() ()] ().$$

   (a) Describe and analyze an algorithm to determine whether a given string of parentheses and brackets is balanced.

   (b) Describe and analyze an algorithm to compute the length of a longest balanced subsequence of a given string of parentheses and brackets.

   (c) Describe and analyze an algorithm to compute the length of a shortest balanced supersequence of a given string of parentheses and brackets.

   (d) Describe and analyze an algorithm to compute the minimum edit distance from a given string of parentheses and brackets to a balanced string of parentheses and brackets.

▾(e) Describe and analyze an algorithm to compute the longest common balanced subsequence of two given strings of parentheses and brackets.

▾(f) Describe and analyze an algorithm to compute the longest palindromic balanced subsequence of a given string of parentheses and brackets.

▾(g) Describe and analyze an algorithm to compute the longest common palindromic balanced subsequence (whew!) of two given strings of parentheses and brackets.

For each problem, your input is an array $w[1..n]$, where $w[i] \in \{(,),[,]\}$ for every index i. (You may prefer to use different symbols instead of parentheses and brackets—for example, L, R, l, r or $\triangleleft, \triangleright, \blacktriangleleft, \blacktriangleright$—but please tell your grader what symbols you're using!)

▾43. Congratulations! Your research team has just been awarded a $50M multi-year project, jointly funded by DARPA, Google, and McDonald's, to produce DWIM: The first compiler to read programmers' minds! Your proposal and your numerous press releases all promise that DWIM will automatically correct errors in any given piece of code, while modifying that code as little as possible. Unfortunately, now it's time to start actually making the damn thing work.

As a warmup exercise, you decide to tackle the following necessary subproblem. Recall that the *edit distance* between two strings is the minimum number of single-character insertions, deletions, and replacements required to transform one string into the other. An *arithmetic expression* is a string w such that

- w is a string of one or more decimal digits,
- $w = (x)$ for some arithmetic expression x, or
- $w = x \diamond y$ for some arithmetic expressions x and y and some binary operator $\diamond$.

Suppose you are given a string of tokens from the alphabet $\{\#, \diamond, (,)\}$, where $\#$ represents a decimal digit and $\diamond$ represents a binary operator. Describe and analyze an algorithm to compute the minimum edit distance from the given string to an arithmetic expression.

44. Ribonucleic acid (RNA) molecules are long chains of millions of nucleotides or *bases* of four different types: adenine (A), cytosine (C), guanine (G), and uracil (U). The *sequence* of an RNA molecule is a string $b[1..n]$, where each character $b[i] \in \{A, C, G, U\}$ corresponds to a base. In addition to the chemical bonds between adjacent bases in the sequence, hydrogen bonds can form between certain pairs of bases. The set of bonded base pairs is called the *secondary structure* of the RNA molecule.

We say that two base pairs (i, j) and (i', j') with $i < j$ and $i' < j'$ *overlap* if $i < i' < j < j'$ or $i' < i < j' < j$. In practice, most base pairs are non-overlapping. Overlapping base pairs create so-called *pseudoknots* in the secondary structure, which are essential for some RNA functions, but are more difficult to predict.

Suppose we want to predict the best possible secondary structure for a given RNA sequence. We will adopt a drastically simplified model of secondary structure:

- Each base can bond with at most one other base.
- Only A–U pairs and C–G pairs can bond.
- Pairs of the form $(i, i + 1)$ and $(i, i + 2)$ cannot bond.
- Bonded base pairs cannot overlap.

The last (and least realistic) restriction allows us to visualize RNA secondary structure as a sort of fat tree, as shown below.

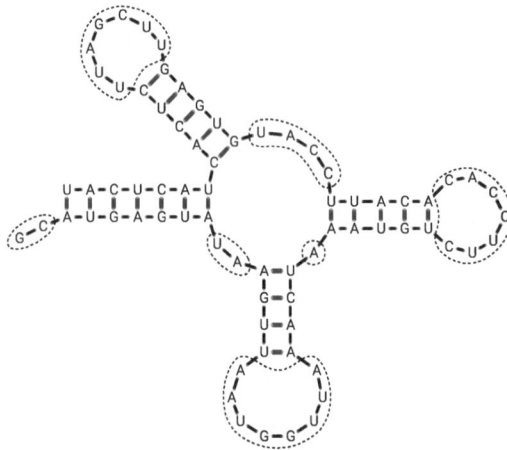

Figure 3.8. Example RNA secondary structure with 21 bonded base pairs, indicated by heavy red lines. Gaps are indicated by dotted curves. This structure has score $2^2 + 2^2 + 8^2 + 1^2 + 7^2 + 4^2 + 7^2 = 187$.

(a) Describe and analyze an algorithm that computes the maximum possible *number* of bonded base pairs in a secondary structure for a given RNA sequence.

(b) A *gap* in a secondary structure is a maximal substring of unpaired bases. Large gaps lead to chemical instabilities, so secondary structures with smaller gaps are more likely. To account for this preference, let's define the *score* of a secondary structure to be the sum of the *squares* of the gap lengths; see Figure 3.8. (This score function is utterly fictional; real RNA structure prediction requires *much* more complicated scoring functions.)

Describe and analyze an algorithm that computes the minimum possible score of a secondary structure for a given RNA sequence.

*45. (a) Describe and analyze an efficient algorithm to determine, given a string w and a regular expression R, whether $w \in L(R)$.

(b) *Generalized* regular expressions allow the binary operator $\cap$ (intersection) and the unary operator $\neg$ (complement), in addition to the usual • (concatenation), + (or), and * (Kleene closure) operators. NFA constructions and Kleene's theorem imply that any generalized regular expression E represents a regular language $L(E)$.

Describe and analyze an efficient algorithm to determine, given a string w and a generalized regular expression E, whether $w \in L(E)$.

In both problems, assume that you are actually given a parse tree for the (generalized) regular expression, not just a string.

Trees and Subtrees

46. You've just been appointed as the new organizer of the first annual mandatory holiday party at Giggle (a subsidiary of Abugida). Giggle employees are organized into a strict hierarchy—a tree with the company president at the root. The all-knowing oracles in Human Resources have assigned a real number to each employee measuring how "fun" the employee is. To keep things social, there is one restriction on the guest list: an employee cannot attend the party if their immediate supervisor is also present. On the other hand, the president of the company *must* attend the party, even though she has a negative fun rating; it's her company, after all. Give an algorithm that makes a guest list for the party that maximizes the sum of the "fun" ratings of the guests.

47. Since so few people came to last year's holiday party, the president of Giggle decides to give each employee a present instead this year. Specifically, each employee must receive on the three gifts: (1) an all-expenses-paid six-week vacation anywhere in the world, (2) an all-the-pancakes-you-can-sort breakfast for two at Jumping Jack Flash's Flapjack Stack Shack, or (3) a burning paper bag full of dog poop. Corporate regulations prohibit any employee from receiving exactly the same gift as his/her direct supervisor. Any employee who receives a better gift than his/her direct supervisor will almost certainly be fired in a fit of jealousy.

As Giggle's official party czar, it's *your* job to decide which gift each employee receives. Describe an algorithm to distribute gifts so that the minimum number of people are fired. Yes, you may send the president a flaming bag of dog poop.

More formally, you are given a rooted tree T, representing the company hierarchy, and you want to label the nodes of T with integers 1, 2, or 3, so that every node has a different label from its parent. The *cost* of an labeling is the number of nodes with smaller labels than their parents. See Figure 3.9 for an example. Describe and analyze an algorithm to compute the minimum-cost labeling of T.

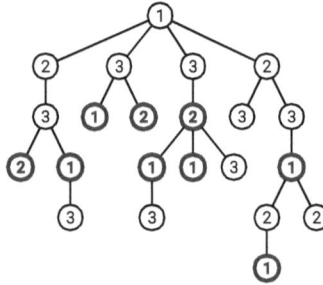

Figure 3.9. A tree labeling with cost 9. The nine bold nodes have smaller labels than their parents. This is *not* the optimal labeling for this tree.

48. After the Flaming Dog Poop Holiday Debacle, you were strongly encouraged to seek other employment, and so you left Giggle for rival company Twitbook. Unfortunately, the new president of Twitbook just decided to imitate Giggle by throwing her own holiday party, and in light of your past experience, appointed you as the official party organizer. The president demands that you invite exactly k employees, including the president herself, and everyone who is invited is required to attend. Yeah, that'll be fun.

Just like at Giggle, employees at Twitbook are organized into a strict hierarchy: a tree with the company president at the root. The all-knowing oracles in Human Resources have assigned a real number to each employee indicating the *awkwardness* of inviting both that employee and their immediate supervisor; a negative value indicates that the employee and their supervisor actually like each other. Your goal is to choose a subset of exactly k employees to invite, so that the total awkwardness of the resulting party is as small as possible. For example, if the guest list does not include both an employee and their immediate supervisor, the total awkwardness is zero. The input to your algorithm is the tree T, the integer k, and the awkwardness of each node in T.

(a) Describe an algorithm that computes the total awkwardness of the least awkward subset of k employees, assuming the company hierarchy is described by a *binary* tree. That is, assume that each employee directly supervises at most two others.

♥(b) Describe an algorithm that computes the total awkwardness of the least awkward subset of k employees, with no restrictions on the company hierarchy.

49. Suppose we need to broadcast a message to all the nodes in a rooted tree. Initially, only the root node knows the message. In a single round, any node that knows the message can forward it to at most one of its children. See Figure 3.10 for an example.

    (a) Design an algorithm to compute the minimum number of rounds required to broadcast the message to all nodes in a *binary* tree.

    ◆(b) Design an algorithm to compute the minimum number of rounds required to broadcast the message to all nodes in an *arbitrary* rooted tree. [Hint: *You may find techniques in the next chapter useful to prove your algorithm is correct, even though it's not a greedy algorithm.*]

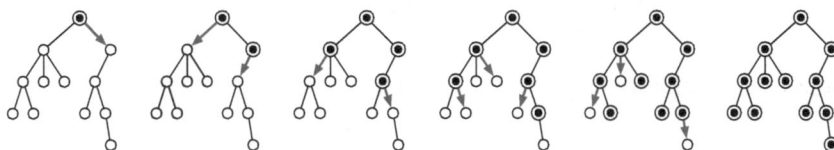

Figure 3.10. A message being distributed through a tree in five rounds.

50. One day, Alex got tired of climbing in a gym and decided to take a very large group of climber friends outside to climb. The climbing area where they went, had a huge wide boulder, not very tall, with various marked hand and foot holds. Alex quickly determined an "allowed" set of moves that her group of friends can perform to get from one hold to another.

    The overall system of holds can be described by a rooted tree T with n vertices, where each vertex corresponds to a hold and each edge corresponds to an allowed move between holds. The climbing paths converge as they go up the boulder, leading to a unique hold at the summit, represented by the root of T.[25]

    Alex and her friends (who are all excellent climbers) decided to play a game, where as many climbers as possible are simultaneously on the boulder and each climber needs to perform a sequence of *exactly k* moves. Each climber can choose an arbitrary hold to start from, and all moves must move away from the ground. Thus, each climber traces out a path of k edges in the tree T, all directed toward the root. However, no two climbers are allowed to touch the same hold; the paths followed by different climbers cannot intersect at all.

    Describe and analyze an efficient algorithm to compute the maximum number of climbers that can play this game. More formally, you are given a rooted tree T and an integer k, and you want to find the largest possible

---

[25] Q: Why do computer science professors think trees have their roots at the top?
A: Because they've never been outside!

number of disjoint paths in T, where each path has length k. Do **not** assume that T is a binary tree. For example, given the tree T below and $k = 3$ as input, your algorithm should return the integer 8.

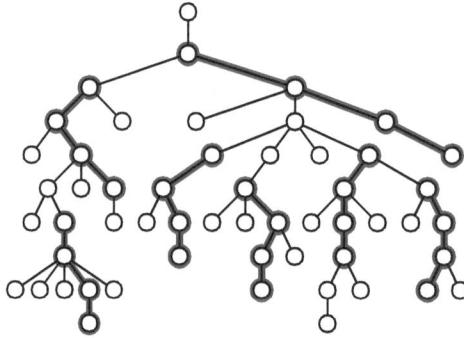

Figure 3.11. Seven disjoint paths of length $k = 3$. This is *not* the largest such set of paths in this tree.

51. Let T be a rooted binary tree with n vertices, and let $k \le n$ be a positive integer. We would like to mark k vertices in T so that every vertex has a nearby marked ancestor. More formally, we define the *clustering cost* of any subset K of vertices as

$$cost(K) = \max_v cost(v, K),$$

where the maximum is taken over all vertices v in the tree, and $cost(v, K)$ is the distance from v to its nearest ancestor in K:

$$cost(v, K) = \begin{cases} 0 & \text{if } v \in K \\ \infty & \text{if } v \text{ is the root of } T \text{ and } v \notin K \\ 1 + cost(parent(v)) & \text{otherwise} \end{cases}$$

In particular, $cost(K) = \infty$ if K excludes the root of T.

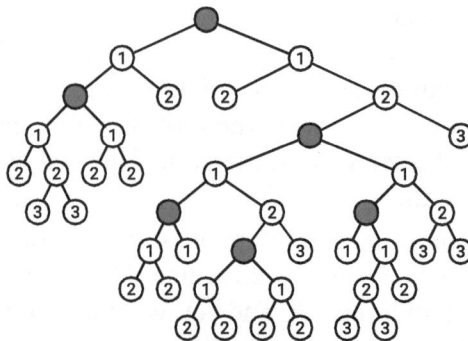

Figure 3.12. A subset of five vertices in a binary tree, with clustering cost 3.

▼(a) Describe a dynamic programming algorithm to compute, given the tree T and an integer k, the minimum clustering cost of any subset of k vertices in T. For full credit, your algorithm should run in $O(n^2 k^2)$ time.

(b) Describe a dynamic programming algorithm to compute, given the tree T and an integer r, the size of the smallest subset of vertices whose clustering cost is at most r. For full credit, your algorithm should run in $O(nr)$ time.

(c) Show that your solution for part (b) implies an algorithm for part (a) that runs in $O(n^2 \log n)$ time.

52. This question asks you to find efficient algorithms to compute the **largest common rooted subtree** of two given rooted trees. Recall that a *rooted tree* is a connected acyclic graph with a designated node called the root. A rooted subtree of a rooted tree consists of an arbitrary node and all its descendants. The precise definition of "common" depends on which pairs of rooted trees we consider isomorphic.

(a) Recall that a *binary* tree is a rooted tree in which every node has a (possibly empty) *left* subtree and a (possibly empty) *right* subtree. Two binary trees are isomorphic if and only if they are both empty, or their left subtrees are isomorphic and their right subtrees are isomorphic. Describe an algorithm to find the largest common *binary* subtree of two given *binary* trees.

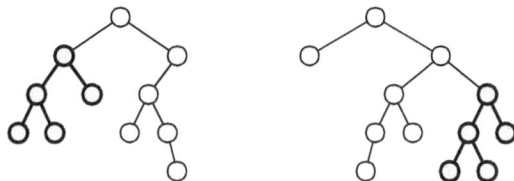

Figure 3.13. Two binary trees, with their largest common (rooted) subtree emphasized.

(b) In an *ordered* rooted tree, each node has a *sequence* of children, which are the roots of ordered rooted subtrees. Two ordered rooted trees are isomorphic if they are both empty, or if their ith subtrees are isomorphic for every index i. Describe an algorithm to find the largest common ordered subtree of two ordered trees T_1 and T_2.

◆▼(c) In an *unordered* rooted tree, each node has an unordered *set* of children, which are the roots of unordered rooted subtrees. Two unordered rooted trees are isomorphic if they are both empty, or the subtrees of each root *can be ordered so that* their ith subtrees are isomorphic for every index i. Describe an algorithm to find the largest common unordered subtree of two unordered trees T_1 and T_2.

53. This question asks you to find efficient algorithms to compute optimal subtrees in *unrooted* trees—connected acyclic undirected graphs. A *subtree* of an unrooted tree is any connected subgraph.

    (a) Suppose you are given an unrooted tree T with weights on its *edges*, which may be positive, negative, or zero. Describe an algorithm to find a *path* in T with maximum total weight.

    (b) Suppose you are given an unrooted tree T with weights on its *vertices*, which may be positive, negative, or zero. Describe an algorithm to find a *subtree* of T with maximum total weight. *[This was a 2016 Google interview question.]*

    (c) Let T_1 and T_2 be arbitrary *ordered* unrooted trees, meaning that the neighbors of every node have a well-defined cyclic order. Describe an algorithm to find the largest common *ordered* subtree of T_1 and T_2.

    ♦♥(d) Let T_1 and T_2 be arbitrary *unordered* unrooted trees. Describe an algorithm to find the largest common *unordered* subtree of T_1 and T_2.

54. **Rooted minors** of rooted trees are a natural generalization of subsequences. A rooted minor of a rooted tree T is any tree obtained by *contracting* one or more edges. When we contract an edge $u \rightarrow v$, where u is the parent of v, the children of v become new children of u and then v is deleted. In particular, the root of T is also the root of every rooted minor of T.

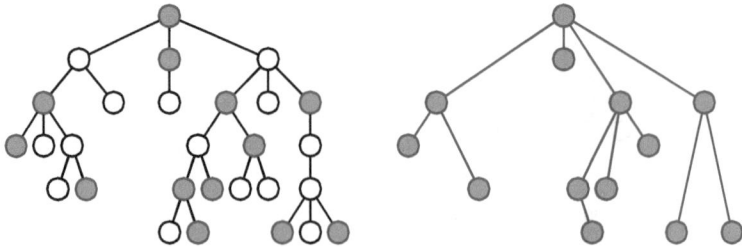

Figure 3.14. A rooted tree and one of its rooted minors.

    (a) Let T be a rooted tree with labeled nodes. We say that T is *boring* if, for each node x, all children of x have the same label; children of different nodes may have different labels. Describe an algorithm to find the largest boring rooted minor of a given labeled rooted tree.

    (b) Suppose we are given a rooted tree T whose nodes are labeled with numbers. Describe an algorithm to find the largest *heap-ordered rooted minor* of T. That is, your algorithm should return the largest rooted minor M such that every node in M has a smaller label than its children in M.

(c) Suppose we are given a *binary* tree T whose nodes are labeled with numbers. Describe an algorithm to find the largest *binary-search-ordered rooted minor* of T. That is, your algorithm should return a rooted minor M such that every node in M has at most two children, and an inorder traversal of M is an increasing subsequence of an inorder traversal of T.

(d) Recall that a rooted tree is *ordered* if the children of each node have a well-defined left-to-right order. Describe an algorithm to find the largest binary-search-ordered minor of an *arbitrary* ordered tree T whose nodes are labeled with numbers. Again, the left-to-right order of nodes in M should be consistent with their order in T.

♥(e) Describe an algorithm to find the largest common *ordered* rooted minor of two *ordered* labeled rooted trees.

♦♥(f) Describe an algorithm to find the largest common *unordered* rooted minor of two *unordered* labeled rooted trees. *[Hint: Combine dynamic programming with maximum flows.]*

4

Greedy Algorithms

4.1 Storing Files on Tape

Suppose we have a set of n files that we want to store on magnetic tape.[1] In the future, users will want to read those files from the tape. Reading a file from tape isn't like reading a file from disk; first we have to fast-forward past all the other files, and that takes a significant amount of time. Let $L[1..n]$ be an array listing the lengths of each file; specifically, file i has length $L[i]$. If the files are stored in order from 1 to n, then the cost of accessing the kth file is

$$cost(k) = \sum_{i=1}^{k} L[i].$$

---

[1]Readers who are tempted to object that magnetic tape has been obsolete for decades are cordially invited to tour your nearest supercomputer facility; ask to see the tape robots. Alternatively, consider filing a sequence of books on a library bookshelf. You know, those strange brick-like objects made of dead trees and ink?

The cost reflects the fact that before we read file k we must first scan past all the earlier files on the tape. If we assume for the moment that each file is equally likely to be accessed, then the *expected* cost of searching for a random file is

$$E[cost] = \sum_{k=1}^{n} \frac{cost(k)}{n} = \frac{1}{n} \sum_{k=1}^{n} \sum_{i=1}^{k} L[i].$$

If we change the order of the files on the tape, we change the cost of accessing the files; some files become more expensive to read, but others become cheaper. Different file orders are likely to result in different expected costs. Specifically, let $\pi(i)$ denote the index of the file stored at position i on the tape. Then the expected cost of the permutation π is

$$E[cost(\pi)] = \frac{1}{n} \sum_{k=1}^{n} \sum_{i=1}^{k} L[\pi(i)].$$

Which order should we use if we want this expected cost to be as small as possible? The answer *seems* intuitively clear: Sort the files by increasing length. But intuition is a tricky beast. The only way to be *sure* that this order works is to ~~take off and nuke the entire site from orbit~~ actually *prove* that it works!

Lemma 4.1. $E[cost(\pi)]$ *is minimized when* $L[\pi(i)] \leq L[\pi(i+1)]$ *for all* i.

Proof: Suppose $L[\pi(i)] > L[\pi(i+1)]$ for some index i. To simplify notation, let $a = \pi(i)$ and $b = \pi(i+1)$. If we swap files a and b, then the cost of accessing a increases by $L[b]$, and the cost of accessing b decreases by $L[a]$. Overall, the swap changes the expected cost by $(L[b] - L[a])/n$. But this change is an improvement, because $L[b] < L[a]$. Thus, if the files are out of order, we can decrease the expected cost by swapping some mis-ordered pair of files. $\square$

This is our first example of a correct *greedy algorithm*. To minimize the *total* expected cost of accessing the files, we put the file that is cheapest to access first, and then recursively write everything else; no backtracking, no dynamic programming, just make the best local choice and blindly plow ahead. If we use an efficient sorting algorithm, the running time is clearly $O(n \log n)$, plus the time required to actually write the files. To show that the greedy algorithm is actually correct, we proved that the output of any other algorithm can be improved by some sort of exchange

Let's generalize this idea further. Suppose we are also given an array $F[1..n]$ of *access frequencies* for each file; file i will be accessed exactly $F[i]$ times over the lifetime of the tape. Now the *total* cost of accessing all the files on the tape is

$$\Sigma cost(\pi) = \sum_{k=1}^{n} \left(F[\pi(k)] \cdot \sum_{i=1}^{k} L[\pi(i)] \right) = \sum_{k=1}^{n} \sum_{i=1}^{k} \left(F[\pi(k)] \cdot L[\pi(i)] \right).$$

As before, reordering the files can change this total cost. So what order should we use if we want the total cost to be as small as possible? (This question is similar in spirit to the optimal binary search tree problem, but the target data structure and the cost function are both different, so the algorithm must be different, too.)

We already proved that if all the frequencies are equal, we should sort the files by increasing size. If the frequencies are all different but the file lengths $L[i]$ are all equal, then intuitively, we should sort the files by *decreasing* access frequency, with the most-accessed file first. In fact, this is not hard to prove (hint, hint) by modifying the proof of Lemma 4.1. But what if the sizes and the frequencies both vary? In this case, we should sort the files by the *ratio L/F*.

Lemma 4.2. *$\Sigma cost(\pi)$ is minimized when* $\dfrac{L[\pi(i)]}{F[\pi(i)]} \leq \dfrac{L[\pi(i+1)]}{F[\pi(i+1)]}$ *for all i.*

Proof: Suppose $L[\pi(i)]/F[\pi(i)] > L[\pi(i+1)]/F[\pi(i+i)]$ for some index i. To simplify notation, let $a = \pi(i)$ and $b = \pi(i+1)$. If we swap files a and b, then the cost of accessing a increases by $L[b]$, and the cost of accessing b decreases by $L[a]$. Overall, the swap changes the total cost by $L[b]F[a] - L[a]F[b]$. But this change is an improvement, because

$$\frac{L[a]}{F[a]} > \frac{L[b]}{F[b]} \quad \Longleftrightarrow \quad L[b]F[a] - L[a]F[b] < 0.$$

Thus, if any two adjacent files are out of order, we can improve the total cost by swapping them. □

4.2 Scheduling Classes

The next example is slightly more complex. Suppose you decide to drop out of computer science and change your major to Applied Chaos. The Applied Chaos department offers all of its classes on the same day every week, called "Soberday" by the students (but interestingly, *not* by the faculty). Every class has a different start time and a different ending time: AC 101 ("Toilet Paper Landscape Architecture") starts at 10:27pm and ends at 11:51pm; AC 666 ("Immanentizing the Eschaton") starts at 4:18pm and ends at 4:22pm, and so on. In the interest of graduating as quickly as possible, you want to register for as many classes as possible. (Applied Chaos classes don't require any actual *work*.) The university's registration computer won't let you register for overlapping classes, and no one in the department knows how to override this "feature". Which classes should you take?

More formally, suppose you are given two arrays $S[1..n]$ and $F[1..n]$ listing the start and finish times of each class; to be concrete, we can assume that

$0 \le S[i] < F[i] \le M$ for each i, for some value M (for example, the number of picoseconds in Soberday). Your task is to choose the largest possible subset $X \in \{1, 2, \ldots, n\}$ so that for any pair $i, j \in X$, either $S[i] > F[j]$ or $S[j] > F[i]$. We can illustrate the problem by drawing each class as a rectangle whose left and right x-coordinates show the start and finish times. The goal is to find a largest subset of rectangles that do not overlap vertically.

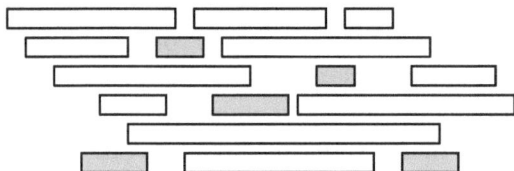

Figure 4.1. A maximum conflict-free schedule for a set of classes.

This problem has a fairly simple recursive solution, based on the observation that either you take class 1 or you don't. Let B denote the set of classes that *end before* class 1 starts, and let A denote the set of classes that *start after* class 1 ends:

$$B := \{i \mid 2 \le i \le n \text{ and } F[i] < S[1]\}$$
$$A := \{i \mid 2 \le i \le n \text{ and } S[i] > F[1]\}$$

If class 1 is in the optimal schedule, then so are the optimal schedules for B and A, which we can find recursively. If not, we can find the optimal schedule for $\{2, 3, \ldots, n\}$ recursively. So we should try both choices and take whichever one gives the better schedule. Evaluating this recursive algorithm from the bottom up gives us a dynamic programming algorithm that runs in $O(n^3)$ time. I won't bother to go through the details, because we can do better.[2]

Intuitively, we'd like the first class to finish as early as possible, because that leaves us with the largest number of remaining classes. This intuition suggests the following simple greedy algorithm. Scan through the classes in order of finish time; whenever you encounter a class that doesn't conflict with your latest class so far, take it! See Figure 4.2 for a visualization of the resulting greedy schedule.

We can write the greedy algorithm somewhat more formally as shown in in Figure 4.3. (Hopefully the first line is understandable.) After the initial sort, the algorithm is a simple linear-time loop, so the entire algorithm runs in $O(n \log n)$ *time*.

---

[2]But you should still work out the details yourself. The dynamic programming algorithm can be used to find the "best" schedule for several different definitions of "best", but the greedy algorithm I'm describing here only works when "best" means "biggest". Also, you can improve the running time to $O(n^2)$ using a different recurrence.

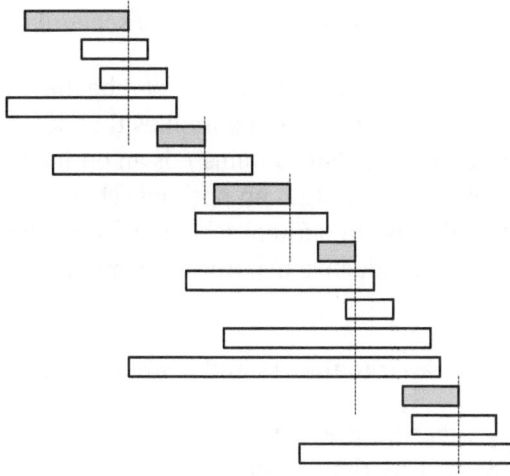

Figure 4.2. The same classes sorted by finish times and the greedy schedule.

```
GREEDYSCHEDULE(S[1..n], F[1..n]):
    sort F and permute S to match
    count ← 1
    X[count] ← 1
    for i ← 2 to n
        if S[i] > F[X[count]]
            count ← count + 1
            X[count] ← i
    return X[1..count]
```

Figure 4.3. A greedy algorithm for finding a maximum set of non-overlapping classes

To prove that GREEDYSCHEDULE actually computes the largest conflict-free schedule, we use an exchange argument, similar to the one we used for tape sorting. We are not claiming that the greedy schedule is the *only* maximal schedule; there could be others. (Compare Figures 4.1 and 4.2!) All we can claim is that at least one of the optimal schedules is the one produced by the greedy algorithm.

Lemma 4.3. *At least one maximal conflict-free schedule includes the class that finishes first.*

Proof: Let f be the class that finishes first. Suppose we have a maximal conflict-free schedule X that does not include f. Let g be the first class in X to finish. Since f finishes before g does, f cannot conflict with any class in the set $X \setminus \{g\}$. Thus, the schedule $X' = X \cup \{f\} \setminus \{g\}$ is also conflict-free. Since X' has the same size as X, it is also maximal. ☐

To finish the proof, we call on our old friend induction.

Theorem 4.4. *The greedy schedule is an optimal schedule.*

Proof: Let f be the class that finishes first, and let A be the subset of classes that start after f finishes. The previous lemma implies that some optimal schedule contains f, so the best schedule that contains f is an optimal schedule. The best schedule that includes f must contain an optimal schedule for the classes that do not conflict with f, that is, an optimal schedule for A. The greedy algorithm chooses f and then, by the inductive hypothesis, computes an optimal schedule of classes from A. □

The proof might be easier to understand if we unroll the induction slightly.

Proof: Let $\langle g_1, g_2, \ldots, g_k \rangle$ be the sequence of classes chosen by the greedy algorithm, sorted by starting time. Suppose we have a maximal conflict-free schedule

$$S = \langle g_1, g_2, \ldots, g_{j-1}, c_j, c_{j+1}, \ldots, c_m \rangle,$$

again sorted by starting time, where c_j is different from the class g_j chosen by the greedy algorithm. (We could have $j = 1$, in which case this schedule starts with a non-greedy choice c_1.) By construction, the jth greedy choice g_j does not conflict with any earlier class $g_1, g_2, \ldots, g_{j-1}$, and because our schedule S is conflict-free, neither does c_j. Moreover, g_j has the *earliest* finish time among all classes that don't conflict with the earlier classes; in particular, g_j finishes before c_j. It follows that g_j does not conflict with any of the later classes $c_{j+1}, \ldots, c_m$. Thus, the modified schedule

$$S' = \langle g_1, g_2, \ldots, g_{j-1}, g_j, c_{j+1}, \ldots, c_m \rangle,$$

is also conflict-free. (This argument is a direct generalization of Lemma 4.3, which considers the case $j = 1$.)

By induction, it now follows that there is an optimal schedule $\langle g_1, g_2, \ldots, g_k, c_{k+1}, \ldots, c_m \rangle$ that includes *every* class chosen by the greedy algorithm. But this is impossible unless $k = m$; if some class c_{k+1} does not conflict with any of the first k greedy classes, then the greedy algorithm would choose more than k classes! □

4.3 General Pattern

The basic structure of this correctness proof is exactly the same as for the tape-sorting problem: an inductive exchange argument.

- Assume that there is an optimal solution that is different from the greedy solution.
- Find the "first" difference between the two solutions.

- Argue that we can exchange the optimal choice for the greedy choice without making the solution worse (although the exchange might not make it better).

This argument implies by induction that some optimal solution *contains* the entire greedy solution, and therefore *equals* the greedy solution. Sometimes, as in the scheduling problem, an additional step is required to show no optimal solution *strictly* improves the greedy solution.

4.4 Huffman Codes

A *binary code* assigns a string of 0s and 1s to each character in the alphabet. A binary code is *prefix-free* if no code is a prefix of any other. (Confusingly, prefix-free codes are also commonly called *prefix codes*.) 7-bit ASCII and Unicode's UTF-8 are both prefix-free binary codes. Morse code is a binary code with symbols • and —, but it is *not* prefix-free, because the code for E (•) is a prefix of the codes for I (••), S (•••), and H (••••).[3]

Any prefix-free binary code can be visualized as a binary tree with the encoded characters stored at the leaves. The code word for any symbol is given by the path from the root to the corresponding leaf; 0 for left, 1 for right. Thus, the length of any symbol's codeword is the depth of the corresponding leaf in the code tree. Although they are superficially similar, binary code trees are *not* binary search trees; we don't care at all about the order of symbols at the leaves.

Suppose we want to encode a message written in an n-character alphabet so that the encoded message is as short as possible. Specifically, given an array of frequency counts $f[1..n]$, we want to compute a prefix-free binary code that minimizes the total encoded length of the message:

$$\sum_{i=1}^{n} f[i] \cdot depth(i).$$

This is exactly the same cost function we considered for optimizing binary search trees, but the optimization problem is different, because code trees are not required to keep the keys in any particular order.

---

[3]For this reason, Morse code is arguably better described as a prefix-free *ternary* code, with three symbols: •, —, and pause. Alternatively, Morse code can be considered a prefix-free binary code, with one beat of sound/light/current/high voltage/smoke/gas (■) and one beat of silence/darkness/ground/low voltage/air/liquid (□) as the two symbols. Then each "dit" is encoded as ■□, each "dah" as ■■■□, and each pause as □□. In standard Morse code, each letter is followed by one pause, and each word is followed by two additional pauses; however, □s at the end of the entire coded message are omitted. For example, the string "MORSE CODE" is unambiguously encoded as the following bit string:

■·■■·■□□□■■·■·■■□□···■··■■□□■·■■·■■·■□□··■·□□□■·■■·■■·■□□■■·□□■·■■·■·□□··■□□■·■■·■■·■.

In 1951, as a PhD student at MIT, David Huffman developed the following greedy algorithm to produce such an optimal code:[4]

> HUFFMAN: Merge the two least frequent letters and recurse.

Huffman's algorithm is best illustrated through an example. Suppose we want to encode the following helpfully self-descriptive sentence, discovered by Lee Sallows:[5]

> This sentence contains three a's, three c's, two d's, twenty-six e's, five f's, three g's, eight h's, thirteen i's, two l's, sixteen n's, nine o's, six r's, twenty-seven s's, twenty-two t's, two u's, five v's, eight w's, four x's, five y's, and only one z.

To keep things simple, let's ignore the forty-four spaces, nineteen apostrophes, nineteen commas, three hyphens, and only one period, and encode only the letters, as though the message were written in *scriptio continua*:

THISSENTENCECONTAINSTHREEASTHREECSTWODSTWENTYSIXESFIVEFST
HREEGSEIGHTHSTHIRTEENISTWOLSSIXTEENNSNINEOSSIXRSTWENTYSEV
ENSSTWENTYTWOTSTWOUSFIVEVSEIGHTWSFOURXSFIVEYSANDONLYONEZ[6]

Here is the frequency table for Sallows' sentence:

A	C	D	E	F	G	H	I	L	N	O	R	S	T	U	V	W	X	Y	Z
3	3	2	26	5	3	8	13	2	16	9	6	27	22	2	5	8	4	5	1

Huffman's algorithm picks out the two least frequent letters, breaking ties arbitrarily—in this case, say, Z and D—and merges them together into a single

---

[4]Huffman was a student in an information theory class taught by Robert Fano, who was a close colleague of Claude Shannon, the father of information theory. Fano and Shannon had previously developed a different greedy algorithm for producing prefix codes—split the frequency array into two subarrays as evenly as possible, and then recursively build a code for each subarray—but these Fano-Shannon codes were known not to be optimal. Fano posed the problem of finding an optimal prefix code to his class. Huffman decided to solve the problem as a class project, instead of taking a final exam, not realizing that the problem was open, or that Fano and Shannon had already tried and failed to solve it. After several months of fruitless effort, Huffman eventually gave up and decided to take the final exam after all. As he was throwing his notes in the trash, the solution dawned on him. Huffman would later describe the epiphany as "the absolute lightning of sudden realization".

[5]This sentence was first reported by Alexander Dewdney in his October 1984 "Computer Recreations" column in *Scientific American*. Sallows himself published the remarkable story of its discovery in 1985, along with several other self-descriptive sentences; you can find Sallows' paper on his web site. Frustrated with the slow progress of his code running on a VAX 11/780, Sallows designed and built dedicated hardware to perform a brute-force search for self-descriptive sentences with various flavor text ("This pangram has...", "This sentence contains exactly...", and so on). Careful theoretical analysis limited the search space to just over six billion possibilities, which his 1-MHz Pangram Machine enumerated in just under two hours.

[6]... and he talked for forty-five minutes, and nobody understood a word that he said, but we had fun fillin' out the forms and playin' with the pencils on the bench there.

new character ☒ with frequency 3. This new character becomes an internal node in the code tree we are constructing, with Z and D as its children; it doesn't matter which child is which. The algorithm then recursively constructs a Huffman code for the new frequency table

A	C	E	F	G	H	I	L	N	O	R	S	T	U	V	W	X	Y	☒
3	3	26	5	3	8	13	2	16	9	6	27	22	2	5	8	4	5	3

After 19 merges, all 20 letters have been merged together. The record of merges gives us our code tree. The algorithm makes a number of arbitrary choices; as a result, there are actually several different Huffman codes. One such Huffman code is shown below; numbers in non-leaf nodes are frequencies for merged characters. For example, the code for A is 101000, and the code for S is 111.

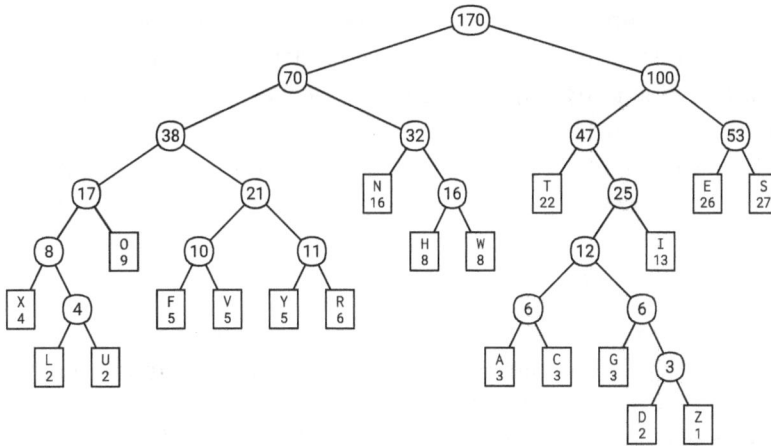

Encoding Sallows' sentence with this particular Huffman code would yield a bit string that starts like so:

```
100 0110 1011 111 111 110 010 100 110 010 101001 110 101001 0001 010 100 ···
 T   H    I    S   S   E   N   T   E   N    C     E     C     O   N   T
```

Here is the list of costs for encoding each character in Sallows' sentence, along with that character's contribution to the total length of the encoded sentence:

char	A	C	D	E	F	G	H	I	L	N	O	R	S	T	U	V	W	X	Y	Z
freq	3	3	2	26	5	3	8	13	2	16	9	6	27	22	2	5	8	4	5	1
depth	6	6	7	3	5	6	4	4	6	3	4	5	3	3	6	5	4	5	5	7
total	18	18	14	78	25	18	32	52	12	48	36	30	81	66	12	25	32	20	25	7

Altogether, the encoded message is 649 bits long. Different Huffman codes encode the same characters differently, possibly with code words of different length, but the overall length of the encoded message is the same for *every* Huffman code: 649 bits.

Given the simple structure of Huffman's algorithm, it's rather surprising that it produces an *optimal* prefix-free binary code.[7] Encoding Sallows' sentence using *any* prefix-free code requires at least 649 bits! Fortunately, the recursive structure makes this claim easy to prove using an exchange argument, similar to our earlier optimality proofs. We start by proving that the algorithm's very first choice is correct.

Lemma 4.5. *Let x and y be the two least frequent characters (breaking ties between equally frequent characters arbitrarily). There is an optimal code tree in which x and y are siblings.*

Proof: I'll actually prove a stronger statement: There is an optimal code in which x and y are siblings *and* have the largest depth of any leaf.

Let T be an optimal code tree, and suppose this tree has depth d. Because T is a full binary tree, it has at least two leaves at depth d that are siblings. (Verify this claim by induction!) Suppose those two leaves are *not* x and y, but some other characters a and b.

Let T' be the code tree obtained by swapping x and a, and let $\Delta = d - depth_T(x)$. This swap increases the depth of x by Δ and decreases the depth of a by Δ, so

$$cost(T') = cost(T) + \Delta \cdot (f[x] - f[a]).$$

Our assumption that x is one of the two least frequent characters but a is not implies $f[x] \leq f[a]$, and our assumption that a has maximum depth implies $\Delta \geq 0$. It follows that $cost(T') \leq cost(T)$. On the other hand, T is an optimal code tree, so we must also have $cost(T') \geq cost(T)$. We conclude that T' is *also* an optimal code tree.

Similarly, swapping y and b must give yet another optimal code tree. In this final optimal code tree, x and y are maximum-depth siblings, as required. □

Now optimality is guaranteed by our dear friend the Recursion Fairy! Our recursive argument relies on the following non-standard recursive definition: *A full binary tree is either a single node, or a full binary tree where some leaf has been replaced by an internal node with two leaf children.*

Theorem 4.6. *Every Huffman code is an optimal prefix-free binary code.*

Proof: If the message has only one or two distinct characters, the theorem is trivial, so assume otherwise.

Let $f[1..n]$ be the original input frequencies, and assume without loss of generality that $f[1]$ and $f[2]$ are the two smallest frequencies. To set up the

---

[7]It was certainly surprising to both Huffman and Fano!

recursive subproblem, define $f[n+1] = f[1] + f[2]$. Our earlier exchange argument implies that 1 and 2 are (deepest) siblings in some optimal code for $f[1..n]$.

Let T' be the Huffman tree for $f[3..n+1]$; the inductive hypothesis implies that T' is an optimal code tree for the smaller set of frequencies. To obtain the final code tree T, we replace the leaf labeled $n+1$ with an internal node with two children, labelled 1 and 2. I claim that T is optimal for the original frequency array $f[1..n]$.

To prove this claim, we can express the cost of T in terms of the cost of T' as follows. (In these equations, $depth(i)$ denotes the depth of the leaf labelled i in either T or T'; each leaf that appears in both T and T' has the same depth in both trees.)

$$
\begin{aligned}
cost(T) &= \sum_{i=1}^{n} f[i] \cdot depth(i) \\
&= \sum_{i=3}^{n+1} f[i] \cdot depth(i) \;+\; f[1] \cdot depth(1) + f[2] \cdot depth(2) \\
&\qquad\qquad\qquad - f[n+1] \cdot depth(n+1) \\
&= cost(T') + (f[1] + f[2]) \cdot depth(T) \;-\; f[n+1] \cdot (depth(T) - 1) \\
&= cost(T') + f[1] + f[2] \;+\; (f[1] + f[2] - f[n+1]) \cdot (depth(T) - 1) \\
&= cost(T') + f[1] + f[2]
\end{aligned}
$$

This equation implies that minimizing the cost of T is equivalent to minimizing the cost of T'; in particular, attaching leaves labeled 1 and 2 to the leaf in T' labeled $n+1$ gives an optimal code tree for the original frequencies. □

To efficiently construct a Huffman code, we keep the characters in a priority queue, using the character frequencies as priorities. We can represent the code tree as three arrays of indices, listing the *Left* and *Right* children and the *Parent* of each node. The leaves of the final code tree are nodes at indices 1 through n, and the root is the node with index $2n - 1$. Pseudocode for the algorithm is shown in Figure 4.4. BUILDHUFFMAN performs $O(n)$ priority-queue operations: exactly $2n - 1$ INSERTS and $2n - 2$ EXTRACTMINS. If we implement the priority queue as a standard binary heap, each of these operations requires $O(\log n)$ time, and thus the entire algorithm runs in $O(n \log n)$ *time*.

Finally, simple algorithms to encode and decode messages using a fixed Huffman code are shown in Figure 4.5; both algorithms run in $O(m)$ time, where m is the length of the encoded message.

```
BUILDHUFFMAN(f[1..n]):
    for i ← 1 to n
        L[i] ← 0;  R[i] ← 0
        INSERT(i, f[i])
    for i ← n to 2n − 1
        x ← EXTRACTMIN( )      ⟨⟨find two rarest symbols⟩⟩
        y ← EXTRACTMIN( )
        f[i] ← f[x] + f[y]     ⟨⟨merge into a new symbol⟩⟩
        INSERT(i, f[i])
        L[i] ← x;  P[x] ← i    ⟨⟨update tree pointers⟩⟩
        R[i] ← y;  P[y] ← i
    P[2n − 1] ← 0
```

Figure 4.4. Building a Huffman code.

```
HUFFMANENCODE(A[1..k]):
    m ← 1
    for i ← 1 to k
        HUFFMANENCODEONE(A[i])


HUFFMANENCODEONE(x):
    if x < 2n − 1
        HUFFMANENCODEONE(P[x])
        if x = L[P[x]]
            B[m] ← 0
        else
            B[m] ← 1
        m ← m + 1
```

```
HUFFMANDECODE(B[1..m]):
    k ← 1
    v ← 2n − 1
    for i ← 1 to m
        if B[i] = 0
            v ← L[v]
        else
            v ← R[v]
        if L[v] = 0
            A[k] ← v
            k ← k + 1
            v ← 2n − 1
```

Figure 4.5. Encoding and decoding algorithms for Huffman codes

4.5 Stable Matching

Every year, thousands of new doctors must obtain internships at hospitals around the United States. During the first half of the 20th century, competition among hospitals for the best doctors led to earlier and earlier offers of internships, sometimes as early as the second year of medical school, along with tighter deadlines for acceptance. In the 1940s, medical schools agreed not to release information until a common date during their students' fourth year. In response, hospitals began demanding faster decisions. By 1950, hospitals would regularly call doctors, offer them internships, and demand *immediate* responses. Interns were forced to gamble if their third-choice hospital called first—accept and risk losing a better opportunity later, or reject and risk having no position at all.[8]

---

[8]The American academic job market involves similar gambles, at least in computer science. Some departments start making offers in February with two-week decision deadlines; other departments don't even start interviewing until March; MIT notoriously waits until May, when all

Finally, a central clearinghouse for internship assignments, now called the National Resident Matching Program (NRMP), was established in the early 1950s. Each year, doctors submit a ranked list of all hospitals where they would accept an internship, and each hospital submits a ranked list of doctors they would accept as interns. The NRMP then computes an matching between doctors and hospitals that satisfies the following *stability* requirement. A matching is **unstable** if there is a doctor α and hospital B that would be both happier with each other than with their current match; that is,

- α is matched with some other hospital A, even though she prefers B.
- B is matched with some other doctor β, even though they prefer α.

In this case, we call (α, B) an *unstable pair* for the matching. The goal of the Resident Match is a **stable matching**, which is a matching with no unstable pairs.

For simplicity, I'll assume from now on that there are exactly the same number of doctors and hospitals; each hospital offers exactly one internship; each doctor ranks all hospitals and vice versa; and finally, there are no ties in the doctors' or hospitals' rankings.[9]

Some Bad Ideas

At first glance, it is not even clear that a stable matching always exists! Certainly not *every* matching of doctors and hospitals is stable. Suppose there are three doctors (Dr. Quincy, Dr. Rotwang, Dr. Shephard, represented by lower-case letters) and three hospitals (Arkham Asylum, Bethlem Royal Hospital, and County General Hospital, represented by upper-case letters), who rank each other as follows:

q	r	s		A	B	C
A	C	A		r	s	q
C	A	B		q	q	r
B	B	C		s	r	s

The matching $\{Aq, Br, Cs\}$ is unstable, because Arkham would rather hire Dr. Rotwang than Dr. Quincy, and Dr. Rotwang would rather work at Arkham than at Bedlam. (A, r) is an unstable pair for this matching.

---

its interviews are over, before making *any* faculty offers. Needless to say, the mishmash of offer dates and decision deadlines causes tremendous stress, for candidates and departments alike. For similar reasons, since 1965, most American universities have agreed to a common April 15 deadline for prospective graduate students to accept offers of financial support (and by extension, offers of admission).

[9]In reality, most hospitals offer multiple internships, each doctor ranks only a subset of the hospitals and vice versa, and there are typically more internships than interested doctors. And then it starts getting complicated.

One might imagine using an incremental algorithm that starts with an arbitrary matching, and then greedily performs exchanges to resolve instabilities. Unfortunately, resolving one instability can create new ones; in fact, this incremental "improvement" can lead to an infinite loop. For example, if we start with our earlier unstable matching $\{Aq, Br, Cs\}$, each of the following exchanges resolves one unstable pair (indicated over the arrow), but the sequence of exchanges leads back to the original matching:[10]

$$\{Aq, Br, Cs\} \xrightarrow{Ar} \{Ar, Bq, Cs\} \xrightarrow{Cr} \{As, Bq, Cr\} \xrightarrow{Cq} \{As, Br, Cq\} \xrightarrow{Aq} \{Aq, Br, Cs\}$$

Alternatively, we might try the following multi-round greedy protocol. In each round, every unmatched hospital makes an offer to their favorite unmatched doctor, then every unmatched doctor with an offer accepts their favorite offer. It's not hard to prove that at least one new doctor-hospital pair is matched in each round, so the algorithm always ends with a matching. For the previous example input, we already have a stable matching $\{Ar, Bs, Cq\}$ at the end of the first round! But consider the following input instead:

q	r	s		A	B	C
C	A	A		q	q	s
B	C	B		s	r	r
A	B	C		r	s	q

In the first round, Dr. Shephard accepts an offer from County, and Dr. Quincy accepts an offer from Bedlam (rejecting Arkham's offer), leaving only Dr. Rotwang and Arkham unmatched. Thus, the protocol ends with the matching $\{Ar, Bq, Cs\}$ after two rounds. Unfortunately, this matching is unstable; Arkham and Dr. Shephard prefer each other to their matches.

The Boston Pool and Gale-Shapley Algorithms

In 1952, the NRMP adopted the "Boston Pool" algorithm to assign interns, so named because it had been previously used by a regional clearinghouse in the Boston area. Ten years later, David Gale and Lloyd Shapley described and formally analyzed a generalization of the Boston Pool algorithm and proved that it computes a stable matching. Gale and Shapley used the metaphor of college admissions. Essentially the same algorithm was independently developed by Elliott Peranson in 1972 for use in medical school admissions. Similar algorithms have since been adopted for many other matching markets, including faculty hiring in France, hiring of new economics PhDs in the United States, university admission in Germany, public school admission in New York and Boston, billet assignments for US Navy sailors, and kidney-matching programs.

---

[10]This example was discovered by Donald Knuth.

Shapley was awarded the 2012 Nobel Prize in Economics for his research on stable matchings, together with Alvin Roth, who significantly extended Shapley's work and used it to develop several real-world exchanges. (Gale did not share the prize, because he died in 2008.)

Like our last failed greedy algorithm, the Gale-Shapley algorithm proceeds in rounds until every position has been accepted. Each round has two stages:

1. An arbitrary unmatched hospital A offers its position to the best doctor α (according to A's preference list) who has not already rejected it.

2. If α is unmatched, she (tentatively) accepts A's offer. If α already has a match but prefers A, she rejects her current match and (tentatively) accepts the new offer from A. Otherwise, α rejects the new offer.

Each doctor ultimately accepts the best offer that she receives, according to her preference list.[11] In short, hospitals make offers greedily, and doctors accept offers greedily. The doctors' ability to reject their current matches in favor of better offers is the key to making this mutual greedy strategy work.

For example, suppose that there are four doctors (Dr. Quincy, Dr. Rotwang, Dr. Shephard, and Dr. Tam) and four hospitals (Arkham Asylum, Bethlem Royal Hospital, County General Hospital, and The Dharma Initiative), who rank each other as follows:

q	r	s	t		A	B	C	D
A	A	B	D		t	r	t	s
B	D	A	B		s	t	r	r
C	C	C	C		r	q	s	q
D	B	D	A		q	s	q	t

Given these preference lists as input, the Gale-Shapley algorithm might proceed as follows:

1. Arkham makes an offer to Dr. Tam.

2. Bedlam makes an offer to Dr. Rotwang.

3. County makes an offer to Dr. Tam, who rejects her earlier offer from Arkham.

4. Dharma makes an offer to Dr. Shephard. (From this point on, there is only one unmatched hospital, so the algorithm has no more choices.)

5. Arkham makes an offer to Dr. Shephard, who rejects her earlier offer from Dharma.

---

[11]The 1952 Boston Pool algorithm is a special case of the Gale-Shapley algorithm that executes offers in a particular order. Roughly speaking, each offer is made by a hospital X whose favorite doctor (among those who haven't rejected X already) ranks X highest. Because the order of offers depends on the entire set of preference lists, this algorithm *must* be executed by a central authority; in contrast, the Gale-Shapley algorithm does not even require each participant to know their own preferences in advance, as long as they behave consistently with some fixed rankings.

6. Dharma makes an offer to Dr. Rotwang, who rejects her earlier offer from Bedlam.

7. Bedlam makes an offer to Dr. Tam, who rejects her earlier offer from County.

8. County makes an offer to Dr. Rotwang, who rejects it.

9. County makes an offer to Dr. Shephard, who rejects it.

10. County makes an offer to Dr. Quincy.

After the tenth round, all pending offers are accepted, and the algorithm returns the matching $\{As, Bt, Cq, Dr\}$. You can (and should) verify by brute force that this matching is stable, even though no doctor was hired by her favorite hospital, and no hospital hired their favorite doctor; in fact, County ended up hiring their *least* favorite doctor. This is not the only stable matching for these preference lists; the matching $\{Ar, Bs, Cq, Dt\}$ is also stable.

Running Time

Analyzing the number of offers performed by the algorithm is relatively straightforward (which is why we're doing it first). Each hospital makes an offer to each doctor at most once, so the algorithm makes at most n^2 offers.

To analyze the actual *running time*, however, we need to specify the algorithm in more detail. How are the preference lists given to the algorithm? How does the algorithm decide whether any hospital is unmatched, and if so, how does it find an unmatched hospital? How does the algorithm store the tentative matchings? How does the algorithm decide whether a doctor prefers her new offer to her current match? Most fundamentally: *How does the algorithm actually represent doctors and hospitals?*

One possibility is to represent each doctor and hospital by a unique integer between 1 and n, and to represent preferences as two arrays $Dpref[1..n, 1..n]$ and $Hpref[1..n, 1..n]$, where $Dpref[i, r]$ represents the rth hospital in doctor i's preference list, and $HPref[j, r]$ represents the rth doctor in hospital j's preference list. With the input in this form, the Boston Pool algorithm can execute each offer in constant time, after some initial preprocessing; the overall implementation runs in $O(n^2)$ *time*. We leave the remaining details as a straightforward exercise.

A somewhat harder exercise is to prove that there are inputs (and choices of who makes offers when) that force $\Omega(n^2)$ offers to be made before the algorithm halts. Thus, our $O(n^2)$ upper bound on the worst-case running time is *tight*.

Correctness

But why is the algorithm *correct* at all? How do we know that it always computes a stable matching, or *any* complete matching for that matter?

Once a doctor receives an offer, she has at least a tentative match for the rest of time. Equivalently, if any doctor is unmatched, then no hospital has offered that doctor a job, which implies that the hospitals have not exhausted their preference lists. It follows that when the algorithm terminates (after at most n^2 rounds), every doctor is matched, and therefore every position is filled. In other words, the algorithm always computes a perfect matching between doctors and hospitals. (Whew!) It remains only to prove that the resulting matching is stable.

Suppose the algorithm matches some doctor α to some hospital A, even though she prefers another hospital B. Because every doctor accepts the best offer she receives, α received no offer she liked more than A; in particular, B never made an offer to α. On the other hand, B made offers to every doctor they prefer over their final match β. It follows that B prefers β over α, which means (α, B) is *not* an unstable pair. We conclude that there are no unstable pairs; the matching is stable!

Optimality!

Surprisingly, the correctness of the Gale-Shapley algorithm does not depend on which hospital makes its offer in each round. In fact, no matter which unassigned hospital makes an offer in each round, *the algorithm always computes the same matching*! Let's say that α is a *feasible* doctor for A if there is a stable matching that assigns doctor α to hospital A.

Lemma 4.7. *During the Gale-Shapley algorithm, each hospital A is rejected only by doctors that are infeasible for A.*

Proof: We prove the lemma by induction on the number of rounds. Consider an arbitrary round of the algorithm, in which doctor α rejects one hospital A for another hospital B. The rejection implies that α prefers B to A. Each doctor that appears higher than α in B's preference list already rejected B in an earlier round and therefore, by the inductive hypothesis, is infeasible for B.

Now consider an arbitrary matching (of the same doctors and hospitals) that assigns α to A. We already established that α prefers B to A. If B prefers α to its partner, the matching is unstable. On the other hand, if B prefers its partner to α, then (by our earlier argument) its partner is infeasible, and again the matching is unstable. We conclude that there is no stable matching that assigns α to A. ☐

Now let ***best(A)*** denote the highest-ranked *feasible* doctor on A's preference list. Lemma 4.7 implies that every doctor that A prefers to its final match is infeasible for A. On the other hand, the final matching is stable, so the doctor assigned to A must be feasible for A. The following result is now immediate:

Corollary 4.8. *The Gale-Shapley algorithm matches best(A) with A, for every hospital A.*

In other words, the Gale-Shapley algorithm computes the *best possible* stable matching from the hospitals' point of view. It turns out that this matching is also the *worst* possible from the doctors' point of view! Let **worst(α)** denote the lowest-ranked feasible hospital on doctor α's preference list.

Corollary 4.9. *The Gale-Shapley algorithm matches α with worst(α), for every doctor α.*

Proof: Suppose Gale and Shapley assign doctor α to hospital A; we need to show that $A = worst(\alpha)$. Consider an arbitrary stable matching where A is *not* matched with α but with another doctor β. The previous corollary implies that A prefers $\alpha = best(A)$ to β. Because the matching is stable, α must therefore prefer her assigned hospital to A. This argument works for *any* stable matching, so α prefers *every* other feasible match to A; in other words, $A = worst(\alpha)$. $\square$

A subtle consequence of these two corollaries, discovered by Lester Dubins and David Freedman in 1981, is that a doctor can potentially improve her match by lying about her preferences, but a hospital cannot. (However, a set of hospitals can collude so that *some* of their matches improve.) Partly for this reason, the National Residency Matching Program reversed its matching algorithm in 1998, so that potential residents offer to work for hospitals, according to their preference orders, and each hospital accepts its best offer. Thus, the new algorithm computes the best possible stable matching for the doctors, and the worst possible stable matching for the hospitals. In practice, however, this reversal altered less than 1% of the residents' matches. As far as I know, the precise effect of this change on the *patients* is an open problem.

Exercises

Caveat lector: Some of these exercises *cannot* be solved using greedy algorithms! Whenever you describe and analyze a greedy algorithm, you *must* also include a proof that your algorithm is correct; this proof will typically take the form of an exchange argument. These proofs are especially important in classes (like mine) that do *not* normally require proofs of correctness.

1. The GreedySchedule algorithm we described for the class scheduling problem is not the only greedy strategy we could have tried. For each of the following alternative greedy strategies, either prove that the resulting algorithm always constructs an optimal schedule, or describe a small input

example for which the algorithm does *not* produce an optimal schedule. Assume that all algorithms break ties arbitrarily (that is, in a manner that is completely out of your control). *[Hint: **Three** of these algorithms are actually correct.]*

(a) Choose the course x that *ends last*, discard classes that conflict with x, and recurse.

(b) Choose the course x that *starts first*, discard all classes that conflict with x, and recurse.

(c) Choose the course x that *starts last*, discard all classes that conflict with x, and recurse.

(d) Choose the course x with *shortest duration*, discard all classes that conflict with x, and recurse.

(e) Choose a course x that *conflicts with the fewest other courses*, discard all classes that conflict with x, and recurse.

(f) If no classes conflict, choose them all. Otherwise, discard the course with *longest duration* and recurse.

(g) If no classes conflict, choose them all. Otherwise, discard a course that *conflicts with the most other courses* and recurse.

(h) Let x be the class with the *earliest start time*, and let y be the class with the *second earliest start time*.
   - If x and y are disjoint, choose x and recurse on everything but x.
   - If x completely contains y, discard x and recurse.
   - Otherwise, discard y and recurse.

(i) If any course x completely contains another course, discard x and recurse. Otherwise, choose the course y that *ends last*, discard all classes that conflict with y, and recurse.

2. Now consider a weighted version of the class scheduling problem, where different classes offer different number of credit hours (totally unrelated to the duration of the class lectures). Your goal is now to choose a set of non-conflicting classes that give you the largest possible number of credit hours, given arrays of start times, end times, and credit hours as input.

(a) Prove that the greedy algorithm described at the beginning of this chapter—Choose the class that ends first and recurse—does *not* always return an optimal schedule.

(b) Prove that **none** of the greedy algorithms described in Exercise 1 always return an optimal schedule. *[Hint: Solve Exercise 1 first; the algorithms that don't work there don't work here, either.]*

(c) Describe and analyze an algorithm that always computes an optimal schedule. *[Hint: Your algorithm will not be greedy.]*

3. Let X be a set of n intervals on the real line. We say that a subset of intervals $Y \subseteq X$ *covers* X if the union of all intervals in Y is equal to the union of all intervals in X. The *size* of a cover is just the number of intervals.

   Describe and analyze an efficient algorithm to compute the smallest cover of X. Assume that your input consists of two arrays $L[1..n]$ and $R[1..n]$, representing the left and right endpoints of the intervals in X. If you use a greedy algorithm, you must prove that it is correct.

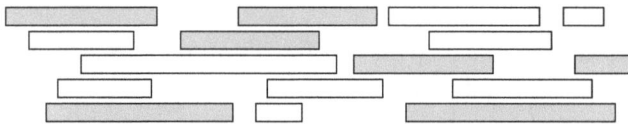

A set of intervals, with a cover (shaded) of size 7.

4. Let X be a set of n intervals on the real line. We say that a set P of points *stabs* X if every interval in X contains at least one point in P. Describe and analyze an efficient algorithm to compute the smallest set of points that stabs X. Assume that your input consists of two arrays $L[1..n]$ and $R[1..n]$, representing the left and right endpoints of the intervals in X. As usual, If you use a greedy algorithm, you must prove that it is correct.

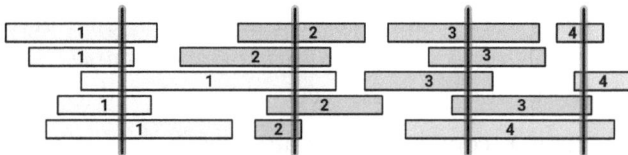

A set of intervals stabbed by four points (shown here as vertical segments)

5. Let X be a set of n intervals on the real line. A *proper coloring* of X assigns a color to each interval, so that any two overlapping intervals are assigned different colors. Describe and analyze an efficient algorithm to compute the minimum number of colors needed to properly color X. Assume that your input consists of two arrays $L[1..n]$ and $R[1..n]$, representing the left and right endpoints of the intervals in X. As usual, if you use a greedy algorithm, you must prove that it is correct.

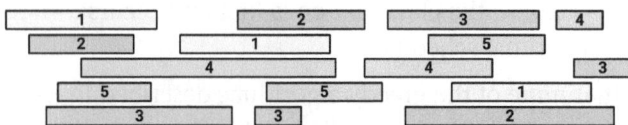

A proper coloring of a set of intervals using five colors.

6. (a) For every integer n, find a frequency array $f[1..n]$ whose Huffman code tree has depth $n-1$, such that the largest frequency is as small as possible.

   (b) Suppose the total length N of the *unencoded* message is bounded by a polynomial in the alphabet size n. Prove that the any Huffman tree for the frequencies $f[1..n]$ has depth $O(\log n)$.

♥7. Call a frequency array $f[1..n]$ *α-heavy* if it satisfies two conditions:

   - $f[1] > f[i]$ for all $i > 1$; that is, 1 is the *unique* most frequent symbol.
   - $f[1] \geq \alpha \sum_{i=1}^{n} f[i]$; that is, at least an α fraction of the symbols are 1s.

   Find the largest real number α such that in every Huffman code for every α-heavy frequency array, symbol 1 is represented by a single bit. *[Hint: First prove that $1/3 \leq \alpha \leq 1/2$.]*

8. Describe and analyze an algorithm to compute an optimal *ternary* prefix-free code for a given array of frequencies $f[1..n]$. Don't forget to prove that your algorithm is correct for *all* n.

9. Describe in detail how to implement the Gale-Shapley stable matching algorithm, so that the worst-case running time is $O(n^2)$, as claimed earlier in this chapter.

10. (a) Prove that it is possible for the Gale-Shapley algorithm to perform $\Omega(n^2)$ offers before termination. (You need to describe both a suitable input and a sequence of $\Omega(n^2)$ valid offers.)

    (b) Describe for any integer n a set of preferences for n doctors and n hospitals that forces the Gale-Shapley algorithm to execute $\Omega(n^2)$ rounds, *no matter which valid proposal is made in each round*. *[Hint: Part (b) implies part (a).]*

11. Describe and analyze an efficient algorithm to determine whether a given set of hospital and doctor preferences has to a *unique* stable matching.

12. Consider a generalization of the stable matching problem, where some doctors do not rank all hospitals and some hospitals do not rank all doctors, and a doctor can be assigned to a hospital only if each appears in the other's preference list. In this case, there are three additional unstable situations:

    - A matched hospital prefers an unmatched doctor to its assigned match.
    - A matched doctor prefers an unmatched hospital to her assigned match.
    - An unmatched doctor and an unmatched hospital appear in each other's preference lists.

A stable matching in this setting may leave some doctors and/or hospitals unmatched, even though their preference lists are non-empty. For example, if every doctor lists Harvard as their only acceptable hospital, and every hospital lists Dr. House as their only acceptable intern, then only House and Harvard will be matched.

Describe and analyze an efficient algorithm that computes a stable matching in this more general setting. *[Hint: Reduce to an instance where every doctor ranks every hospital and vice versa, and then invoke Gale-Shapley.]*

13. The Scandinavian furniture company Fürni has hired n drivers to deliver n identical orders to n different addresses in Wilmington, Delaware. Each driver has their own well-established delivery route through Wilmington that visits all n addresses. Assuming they follow their routes as they always do, two drivers never visit the same addresses at the same time.

    In principle, each of the n drivers can deliver their furniture to any of the n addresses, but there's a complication. One of the drivers has secretly wired proximity sensors and explosives to the Johannshamn sofas (with the Strinne green stripe pattern). If two sofas are ever at the same address at the same time, both will explode, destroying both the delivery truck and the building at that address. This can only happen if one driver delivers an order to that address, and then later another driver visits that same address *while the furniture is still on their truck.*

    Your job as the Fürni dispatcher is to assign each driver to a delivery address. Describe an algorithm to assign addresses to drivers so that each of the n addresses receives their furniture order and there are no explosions.

    For example, suppose Jack's route visits 537 Paper Street at 6pm and 1888 Franklin Street at 8pm, and Marla's route visits 537 Paper at 7pm and 1888 Franklin at 9pm. Then Jack should deliver to 1888 Franklin, and Marla should deliver to 537 Paper; otherwise, there would be an explosion at 1888 Franklin at 8pm. (Cue the Pixies.) *[Hint: Jack and Marla are a bit unstable.]*

14. Suppose you are a simple shopkeeper living in a country with n different types of coins, with values $1 = c[1] < c[2] < \cdots < c[n]$. (In the U.S., for example, $n = 6$ and the values are 1, 5, 10, 25, 50 and 100 cents.) Your beloved and benevolent dictator, El Generalissimo, has decreed that whenever you give a customer change, you must use the smallest possible number of coins, so as not to wear out the image of El Generalissimo lovingly engraved on each coin by servants of the Royal Treasury.

    (a) In the United States, there is a simple greedy algorithm that always results in the smallest number of coins: subtract the largest coin and recursively give change for the remainder. El Generalissimo does not approve of American capitalist greed. Show that there is a set of coin values for which the greedy algorithm does *not* always give the smallest possible of coins.

(b) Now suppose El Generalissimo decides to impose a currency system where the coin denominations are consecutive powers $b^0, b^1, b^2, \ldots, b^k$ of some integer $b \geq 2$. Prove that despite El Generalissimo's disapproval, the greedy algorithm described in part (a) does make optimal change in this currency system.

(c) Describe and analyze an efficient algorithm to determine, given a target amount T and a sorted array $c[1..n]$ of coin denominations, the smallest number of coins needed to make T cents in change. Assume that $c[1] = 1$, so that it is possible to make change for any amount T.

15. Suppose you are given an array $A[1..n]$ of integers, each of which may be positive, negative, or zero. A contiguous subarray $A[i..j]$ is called a *positive interval* if the sum of its entries is greater than zero. Describe and analyze an algorithm to compute the minimum number of positive intervals that cover every positive entry in A. For example, given the following array as input, your algorithm should output 3. If every entry in the input array is negative, your algorithm should output 0.

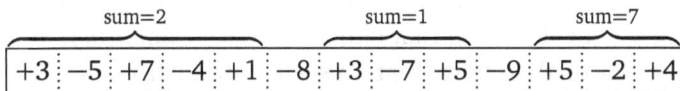

	sum=2					sum=1					sum=7	
+3	−5	+7	−4	+1	−8	+3	−7	+5	−9	+5	−2	+4

16. Consider the following process. At all times you have a single positive integer x, which is initially equal to 1. In each step, you can either *increment* x or *double* x. Your goal is to produce a target value n. For example, you can produce the integer 10 in four steps as follows:

$$1 \xrightarrow{+1} 2 \xrightarrow{\times 2} 4 \xrightarrow{+1} 5 \xrightarrow{\times 2} 10$$

Obviously you can produce any integer n using exactly $n-1$ increments, but for almost all values of n, this is horribly inefficient. Describe and analyze an algorithm to compute the *minimum* number of steps required to produce any given integer n.

17. Suppose we have n skiers with heights given in an array $P[1..n]$, and n skis with heights given in an array $S[1..n]$. Describe an efficient algorithm to assign a ski to each skier, so that the average difference between the height of a skier and her assigned ski is as small as possible. The algorithm should

compute a permutation σ such that the expression

$$\frac{1}{n}\sum_{i=1}^{n}\left|P[i]-S[\sigma(i)]\right|$$

is as small as possible.

18. Alice wants to throw a party and she is trying to decide who to invite. She has n people to choose from, and she knows which pairs of these people know each other. She wants to invite as many people as possible, subject to two constraints:

    - For each guest, there should be at least five other guests that they already know.

    - For each guest, there should be at least five other guests that they *don't* already know.

    Describe and analyze an algorithm that computes the largest possible number of guests Alice can invite, given a list of n people and the list of pairs who know each other.

19. Suppose we are given two arrays $C[1..n]$ and $R[1..n]$ of positive integers. An $n \times n$ matrix of 0s and 1s *agrees with R and C* if, for every index i, the ith row contains $R[i]$ 1s, and the ith column contains $C[i]$ 1s. Describe and analyze an algorithm that either constructs a matrix that agrees with R and C, or correctly reports that no such matrix exists.

20. You've just accepted a job from Elon Musk, delivering burritos from San Francisco to New York City. You get to drive a Burrito-Delivery Vehicle through Elon's new Transcontinental Underground Burrito-Delivery Tube, which runs in a direct line between these two cities.[12]

    Your Burrito-Delivery Vehicle runs on single-use batteries, which must be replaced after at most 100 miles. The actual fuel is virtually free, but the batteries are expensive and fragile, and therefore must be installed only by official members of the Transcontinental Underground Burrito-Delivery Vehicle Battery-Replacement Technicians' Union.[13] Thus, even if you replace your battery early, you must still pay full price for each new battery to be installed. Moreover, your Vehicle is too small to carry more than one battery at a time.

---

[12] ... and which was clearly modeled after Maciej Cegłowski's fictional "Alameda-Weehauken Burrito Tunnel"

[13] or as they call themselves in German, Die Transkontinentaluntergrundburritolieferfahrzeug-batteriewechseltechnikervereinigung.

There are several fueling stations along the Tube; each station charges a different price for installing a new battery. Before you start your trip, you carefully print the Wikipedia page listing the locations and prices of every fueling station along the Tube. Given this information, how do you decide the best places to stop for fuel?

More formally, suppose you are given two arrays $D[1..n]$ and $C[1..n]$, where $D[i]$ is the distance from the start of the Tube to the ith station, and $C[i]$ is the cost to replace your battery at the ith station. Assume that your trip starts and ends at fueling stations (so $D[1] = 0$ and $D[n]$ is the total length of your trip), and that your car starts with an empty battery (so you must install a new battery at station 1).

(a) Describe and analyze a greedy algorithm to find the minimum number of refueling stops needed to complete your trip. Don't forget to prove that your algorithm is correct.

(b) But what you really want to minimize is the total *cost* of travel. Show that your greedy algorithm in part (a) does *not* produce an optimal solution when extended to this setting.

(c) Describe an efficient algorithm to compute the locations of the fuel stations you should stop at to minimize the total cost of travel.

21. You've been hired to store a sequence of n books on shelves in a library. The order of the books is fixed by the cataloging system and cannot be changed; each shelf must store a contiguous interval of the given sequence of books. You are given two arrays $H[1..n]$ and $T[1..n]$, where $H[i]$ and $T[i]$ are respectively the height and thickness of the ith book in the sequence. All shelves in this library have the same length L; the total thickness of all books on any single shelf cannot exceed L.

(a) Suppose all the books have the same height h and the shelves have height larger than h, so every book fits on every shelf. Describe and analyze a greedy algorithm to store the books in as few shelves as possible. *[Hint: The algorithm is obvious, but why is it correct?]*

(b) That was a nice warmup, but now here's the real problem. In fact the books have different heights, but you can adjust the height of each shelf to match the tallest book on that shelf. (In particular, you can change the height of any empty shelf to zero.) Now your task is to store the books so that the sum of the heights of the shelves is as small as possible. Show that your greedy algorithm from part (a) does *not* always give the best solution to this problem.

(c) Describe and analyze an algorithm to find the best matching between books and shelves as described in part (b).

22. A string w of parentheses (and) is **balanced** if it satisfies one of the following conditions:

    - w is the empty string.
    - $w = (x)$ for some balanced string x
    - $w = xy$ for some balanced strings x and y

    For example, the string

    $$w = ((())()()) (()()) ()$$

    is balanced, because $w = xy$, where

    $$x = ((())()()) \quad \text{and} \quad y = (()()) ().$$

    (a) Describe and analyze an algorithm to determine whether a given string of parentheses is balanced.

    (b) Describe and analyze a greedy algorithm to compute the length of a longest balanced subsequence of a given string of parentheses. As usual, don't forget to prove your algorithm is correct.

    For both problems, your input is an array $w[1..n]$, where for each i, either $w[i] = ($ or $w[i] =)$. Both of your algorithms should run in $O(n)$ time.

23. One day Alex got tired of climbing in a gym and decided to take a large group of climber friends outside to climb. They went to a climbing area with a huge wide boulder, not very tall, with several marked hand and foot holds. Alex quickly determined an "allowed" set of moves that her group of friends can perform to get from one hold to another.

    The overall system of holds can be described by a rooted tree T with n vertices, where each vertex corresponds to a hold and each edge corresponds to an allowed move between holds. The climbing paths converge as they go up the boulder, leading to a unique hold at the summit, represented by the root of T.

    Alex and her friends (who are all excellent climbers) decided to play a game, where as many climbers as possible are simultaneously on the boulder and each climber needs to perform a sequence of *exactly* k moves. Each climber can choose an arbitrary hold to start from, and all moves must move away from the ground. Thus, each climber traces out a path of k edges in the tree T, all directed toward the root. However, no two climbers are allowed to touch the same hold; the paths followed by different climbers cannot intersect at all.

    (a) Describe and analyze a greedy algorithm to compute the maximum number of climbers that can play this game. Your algorithm is given a rooted tree T and an integer k as input, and it should compute the largest possible number of disjoint paths in T, where each path has length k. Do **not** assume that T is a binary tree. For example, given the tree below as input, your algorithm should return the integer 8.

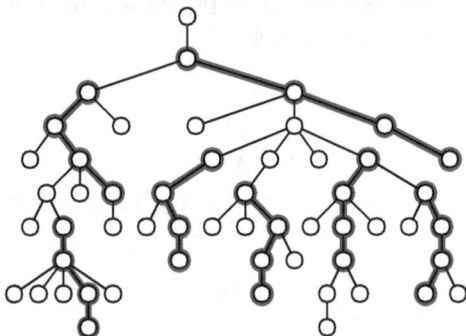

Figure 4.6. Seven disjoint paths of length $k = 3$. This is *not* the largest such set of paths in this tree.

(b) Now suppose each vertex in T has an associated *reward*, and your goal is to maximize the total reward of the vertices in your paths, instead of the total number of paths. Show that your greedy algorithm does *not* always return the optimal reward.

(c) Describe an efficient algorithm to compute the maximum possible reward, as described in part (b).

24. Congratulations! You have successfully conquered Camelot, transforming the former battle-scarred hereditary monarchy into an anarcho-syndicalist commune, where citizens take turns to act as a sort of executive-officer-for-the-week, but with all the decisions of that officer ratified at a special bi-weekly meeting, by a simple majority in the case of purely internal affairs, but by a two-thirds majority in the case of more major. . . .

As a final symbolic act, you order the Round Table (surprisingly, an actual circular table) to be split into pizza-like wedges and distributed to the citizens of Camelot as trophies. Each citizen has submitted a request for an angular wedge of the table, specified by two angles—for example: Sir Robin the Brave might request the wedge from 17.23° to 42°, and Sir Lancelot the Pure might request the 2° wedge from 359° to 1°. Each citizen will be happy if and only if they receive *precisely* the wedge that they requested. Unfortunately, some of these ranges overlap, so satisfying *all* the citizens' requests is simply impossible. Welcome to politics.

Describe and analyze an algorithm to find the maximum number of requests that can be satisfied. [*Hint: The output of your algorithm should not change if you rotate the table. Do not assume that angles are integers.*]

25. Suppose you are standing in a field surrounded by several large balloons. You want to use your brand new Acme Brand Zap-O-Matic™ to pop all the balloons, without moving from your current location. The Zap-O-Matic™ shoots a high-powered laser beam, which pops all the balloons it hits. Since each shot requires enough energy to power a small country for a year, you want to fire as few shots as possible.

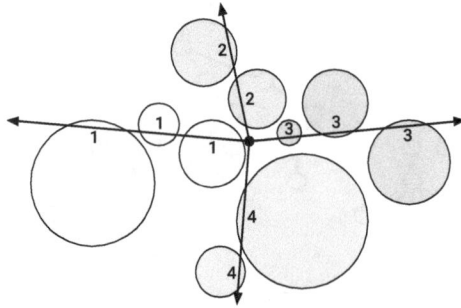

Figure 4.7. Nine balloons popped by four shots of the Zap-O-Matic™

The *minimum zap* problem can be stated more formally as follows. Given a set C of n circles in the plane, each specified by its radius and the (x, y) coordinates of its center, compute the minimum number of rays from the origin that intersect every circle in C. Your goal is to find an efficient algorithm for this problem.

(a) Suppose it is possible to shoot a ray that does not intersect any balloons. Describe and analyze a greedy algorithm that solves the minimum zap problem in this special case. *[Hint: See Exercise 4.]*

(b) Describe and analyze a greedy algorithm whose output is within 1 of optimal. That is, if m is the minimum number of rays required to hit every balloon, then your greedy algorithm must output either m or $m+1$. (Of course, you must prove this fact.)

(c) Describe an algorithm that solves the minimum zap problem in $O(n^2)$ time.

♥(d) Describe an algorithm that solves the minimum zap problem in $O(n \log n)$ time.

Assume you have a subroutine that tells you the range of angles of rays that intersects an arbitrary circle c in $O(1)$ time. This subroutine is not difficult to write, but it's not the interesting part of the problem.

[T]he distributions and partitions of knowledge are not like several lines that meet in one angle, and so touch but in a point, but are like branches of a tree that meet in a stem, which hath a dimension and quantity of entireness and continuance before it come to discontinue and break itself into arms and boughs.

— Francis Bacon, *The Advancement of Learning* (1605)

Thus you see, most noble Sir, how this type of solution bears little relationship to mathematics, and I do not understand why you expect a mathematician to produce it, rather than anyone else.

— Leonhard Euler, describing the Königsburg bridge problem
in a letter to Carl Leonhard Gottlieb Ehler (April 3, 1736)

Well, ya turn left by the fire station in the village and take the old post road by the reservoir and…no, that won't do.

Best to continue straight on by the tar road until you reach the schoolhouse and then turn left on the road to Bennett's Lake until…no, that won't work either.

East Millinocket, ya say? Come to think of it, you can't get there from here.

— Robert Bryan and Marshall Dodge,
Bert and I and Other Stories from Down East (1961)

5

Basic Graph Algorithms

5.1 Introduction and History

A graph is a collection of pairs—pairs of integers, pairs of people, pairs of cities, pairs of stars, pairs of countries, pairs of scientific papers, pairs of web pages, pairs of game positions, pairs of recursive subproblems, even pairs of graphs. Mirroring the most common method for visualizing graphs, the underlying objects being paired are usually called **vertices** or **nodes**, and the pairs themselves are called **edges** or **arcs**, but in fact the objects and pairs can be anything at all.

One of the earliest examples of graphs are *road networks* and maps thereof. Roman engineers constructed a network of more than 400 000 km of public roads across Europe, western and central Asia, and northern Africa during the height of the Roman empire. Travelers on the road network would carry *itineraria*, which were either simple lists or more pictorial representations of the landmarks and distances along various roads. The *Tabula Peutingeriana*, a 13th-century scroll depicting the entire Roman *cursus publicus*, is widely believed to be a medieval copy of a 5th-century revision of a 1st-century *itinerarium pictum*, commissioned during the reign of Augustus Caesar. The Peutinger Table is not a geographically accurate map—historians debate whether it qualifies as a "map" at all!—but an abstract representation of the road network, similar to a modern subway map. Cities along each road are indicated by kinks in the curve representing that road; the names of these cites and the lengths of road segments between them are also indicated on the map. Thus, the map contains enough information to find the shortest route between any two cities in the 5th-century Roman empire. See Figure 5.1.

Figure 5.1. A small excerpt of Konrad Miller's 1872 restoration of the *Tabula Peutingeriana*, showing the Roman road from modern-day Birten (*Veteribus*, top left) through Köln (*Agripina*) and Bonn (*Bonnae*) to Mainz (*Mogontiaco*, top right), with branches to Trier (*Avg Tresvirorvm*, center) and Metz (*Matricorvm*, bottom center). (See Image Credits at the end of the book.)

One of the oldest classical applications of graphs—and specifically trees—is in representing genealogies. Complex family "trees" have been used for centuries to settle legal questions about marriage, inheritance, and royal succession. Civil law in the Roman empire, later adopted as canon law by the early Catholic Church, forbade marriage between first cousins or closer relatives. In the early ninth century, the Church changed both the required distance and the method of computation. Where the Roman *computatio legalis* required the sum of the distances to the nearest common ancestor to be at least four, the newer *computatio canonica* required the maximum of the two distances to be at least seven. In 1215, bowing to practical considerations (and actual practice), the Church relaxed the minimum required distance for marriage to four.[1] The left diagram in Figure 5.2 illustrates a particularly convoluted case: Tirius and Theburga marry and have a son Gaius, after which Tirius dies; Theburga then

---

[1]During the 11th and 12th centuries, this restriction gradually expanded to include up to four links by affinity, initially through marriage, and later through extra-marital sex, betrothal, and even godparenting. For example, marriage between a man and his sister's husband's sister's husband's sister was formally forbidden, as was a marriage between a widower and his son's wife's widowed mother. These affinity requirements were significantly reduced but not eliminated in 1215; the Church only abandoned the concept of affinity *ex copula illicita* in 1917.

marries Lothar, bears him a son, and dies; finally, Lothar and Bertha marry and have a daughter Gemma. Can Gaius's son legally marry Gemma's daughter?

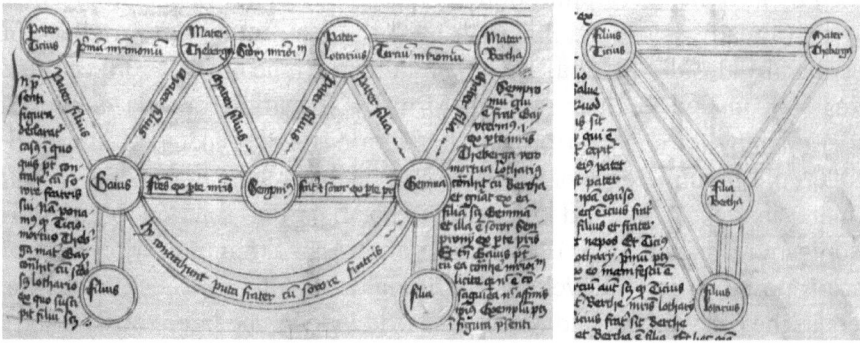

Figure 5.2. Two diagrams describing a complex marriage case, from an anonymous 15th-century treatise on Johannes Andreae's *Super arboribus consanguinitatis et affinitatis*, an early 14th-century treatise on canon law. (See Image Credits at the end of the book.)

In the late 1600s, French mathematician Pierre Varignon developed a graphical method for finding the equilibrium position of a tree-like network of ropes under tension, building on earlier work by Simon Stevin published a century earlier. Varignon observed that when the ropes are at equilibrium, one can draw a graph whose edges are segments parallel to the ropes, with lengths equal to the forces along those ropes, such that the ropes meeting at any point in the network define a closed cycle in the graph. Varignon's method of "graphical statics" was not published in complete detail until 1725, two years after his death. These graphs are now known as *reciprocal force diagrams* or *Maxwell-Cremona diagrams*, after James Clerk Maxwell and Luigi Cremona, who (along with Carl Culmann and others) developed a rich theory of reciprocal diagrams in the late 1800s.

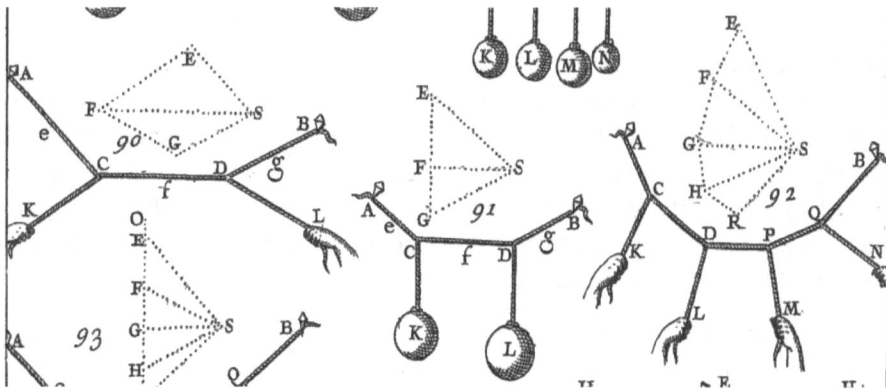

Figure 5.3. Reciprocal force diagrams (dotted), from Varignon's posthumous *Nouvelle mécanique, ou statique, dont le projet fut donné en MDCLXXXVII [New mechanics, or statics, whose project was given in 1687]* (See Image Credits at the end of the book.)

Of course, there are many other familiar examples of graphs, like board games (dating to antiquity); vertices and edges of convex polyhedra (formally studied by ancient Greek philosophers, but much older); visualizations of star patterns (already developed in East Asia by the 7th century CE); knight's tours (described by al-Adli, Rudraṭa, al-Suli, and others in the 9th and 10th centuries), mazes (introduced in their modern form by Giovanni Fontana circa 1420); geodetic triangulations (introduced by Gemma Frisius in 1533, and used to calculate the circumference of the earth by Willebrod Snell in 1615 and to define the meter in 1799), Leonhard Euler's well-known partial[2] solution to the Bridges of Königsburg puzzle (1735); telegraph and other communication networks (first proposed in 1753, developed by Ronalds, Schilling, Gauss, Weber, and others in the early 1800s, and deployed worldwide by the late 1800s); electrical circuits (formalized in the early 1800s by Ohm, Maxwell, Kirchhoff, and others); molecular structural formulas (introduced independently by August Kekulé in 1857 and Archibald Couper in 1858); social networks (first studied in the mid-1930s by sociologist Jacob Moreno); digital electronic circuits (proposed by Charles Sanders Peirce in 1886, and cast into their modern form by Claude Shannon in 1937); and yeah, okay, if you insist, the modern internet.

The word "graph" for the abstract mathematical was coined by James Sylvester in 1878, who adapted Kekulé's "chemicographs" to describe certain algebraic invariants, at the suggestion of his colleague William Clifford. The word "tree" was first used for connected acyclic graphs by Arthur Cayley in 1857, although the abstract concept of trees had already been used by Gustav Kirchhoff and Karl von Staudt ten years earlier. The zeroth book on graph theory was published by André Sainte-Laguë in 1926; Dénes Kőnig published the first graph theory book ten years later.

5.2 Basic Definitions

Formally, a (simple) **graph** is a pair of sets (V, E), where V is an arbitrary non-empty finite set, whose elements are called **vertices**[3] or **nodes**, and E is a set of pairs of elements of V, which we call **edges**. In an **undirected** graph, the edges are unordered pairs, or just sets of size two; I usually write uv instead of $\{u, v\}$ to denote the undirected edge between u and v. In a **directed** graph, the edges are ordered pairs of vertices; I usually write $u \to v$ instead of (u, v) to denote the directed edge from u to v.

---

[2]Euler dismissed the final step of his argument—actually finding an Euler tour of a graph when every vertex has even degree—as obvious. Euler also failed to notice that a graph with an Euler tour must be connected. The first complete proof that a graph has an Euler tour if and only if it is connected and every vertex has even degree was published by Carl Hierholzer in 1873.

[3]The singular of the English word "vertices" is **vertex**. Similarly, the singular of "matrices" is **matrix**, and the singular of "indices" is **index**. Unless you're speaking Italian, there is no such

Following standard (but admittedly confusing) practice, I will also use V to denote the *number* of vertices in a graph, and E to denote the *number* of edges. Thus, in any undirected graph we have $0 \le E \le \binom{V}{2}$, and in any directed graph we have $0 \le E \le V(V-1)$.

The ***endpoints*** of an edge uv or $u\rightarrow v$ are its vertices u and v. We distinguish the endpoints of a directed edge $u\rightarrow v$ by calling u the ***tail*** and v the ***head***.

The definition of a graph as a pair of *sets* forbids multiple undirected edges with the same endpoints, or multiple directed edges with the same head and the same tail. (The same directed graph can contain both a directed edge $u\rightarrow v$ and its reversal $v\rightarrow u$.) Similarly, the definition of an undirected edge as a *set* of vertices forbids an undirected edge from a vertex to itself. Graphs *without* loops and parallel edges are often called ***simple*** graphs; non-simple graphs are sometimes called ***multigraphs***. Despite the formal definitional gap, most algorithms for simple graphs extend to multigraphs with little or no modification, and for that reason, I see no need for a formal definition here.

For any edge uv in an undirected graph, we call u a ***neighbor*** of v and vice versa, and we say that u and v are ***adjacent***. The ***degree*** of a node is its number of neighbors. In directed graphs, we distinguish two kinds of neighbors. For any directed edge $u\rightarrow v$, we call u a ***predecessor*** of v, and we call v a ***successor*** of u. The ***in-degree*** of a vertex is its number of predecessors; the ***out-degree*** is its number of successors.

A graph $G' = (V', E')$ is a ***subgraph*** of $G = (V, E)$ if $V' \subseteq V$ and $E' \subseteq E$. A ***proper subgraph*** of G is any subgraph other than G itself.

A ***walk*** in an undirected graph G is a sequence of vertices, where each adjacent pair of vertices are adjacent in G; informally, we can also think of a walk as a sequence of edges. A walk is called a ***path*** if it visits each vertex at most once. For any two vertices u and v in a graph G, we say that v is ***reachable*** from u if G contains a walk (and therefore a path) between u and v. An undirected graph is ***connected*** if every vertex is reachable from every other vertex. Every undirected graph consists of one or more ***components***, which are its maximal connected subgraphs; two vertices are in the same component if and only if there is a path between them.[4]

A walk is ***closed*** if it starts and ends at the same vertex; a ***cycle*** is a closed walk that enters and leaves each vertex at most once. An undirected graph is ***acyclic*** if no subgraph is a cycle; acyclic graphs are also called ***forests***. A ***tree*** is a connected acyclic graph, or equivalently, one component of a forest. A ***spanning***

---

thing as a vertice, matrice, indice, appendice, helice, apice, vortice, radice, simplice, codice, directrice, dominatrice, Unice, Kleenice, Asterice, Obelice, Dogmatice, Getafice, Cacofonice, Vitalstatistice, Geriatrice, or Jimi Hendrice! If you have trouble remembering this rule, stick to "node".

[4]Components are often called "connected components", but this usage is redundant; components are connected by definition.

tree of an undirected graph G is a subgraph that is a tree and contains every vertex of G. A graph has a spanning tree if and only if it is connected. A *spanning forest* of G is a collection of spanning trees, one for each component of G.

Directed graphs require slightly different definitions. A **directed walk** is a sequence of vertices $v_0 \to v_1 \to v_2 \to \cdots \to v_\ell$ such that $v_{i-1} \to v_i$ is a directed edge for every index i; directed paths and directed cycles are defined similarly. Vertex v is **reachable** from vertex u in a directed graph G if and only if G contains a directed walk (and therefore a directed path) from u to v. A directed graph is **strongly connected** if every vertex is reachable from every other vertex. A directed graph is **acyclic** if it does not contain a directed cycle; directed acyclic graphs are often called **dags**.

5.3 Representations and Examples

The most common way to visually represent graphs is by **drawing** them. A drawing of a graph maps each vertex to a point in the plane (typically drawn as a small circle or some other shape) and each edge to a curve or straight line segment between the two vertices. A graph is **planar** if it has a drawing where no two edges cross; such a drawing is also called an **embedding**.[5] The same graph can have many different drawings, so it is important not to confuse a particular drawing with the graph itself. In particular, planar graphs can have non-planar drawings!

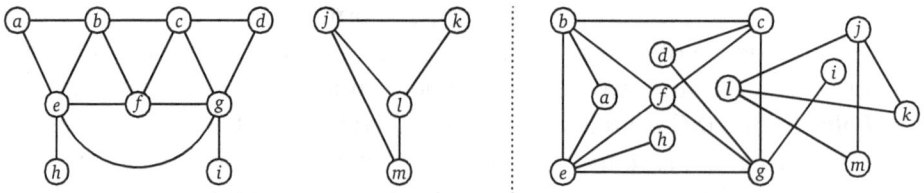

Figure 5.4. Two drawings of the same disconnected planar graph with 13 vertices, 19 edges, and two components. Only the drawing on the left is an embedding.

However, drawings are far from the only useful representation of graphs. For example, the **intersection graph** of a collection of geometric objects has a node for every object and an edge for every intersecting pair of objects. Whether a particular graph can be represented as an intersection graph depends on what kind of object you want to use for the vertices. Different types of objects—line segments, rectangles, circles, etc.—define different classes of graphs. One particularly useful type of intersection graph is an *interval graph*, whose vertices

---

[5]Confusingly, the word "embedding" is often used as a synonym for "drawing", even when the edges intersect. Please don't do that.

are intervals on the real line, with an edge between any two intervals that overlap.

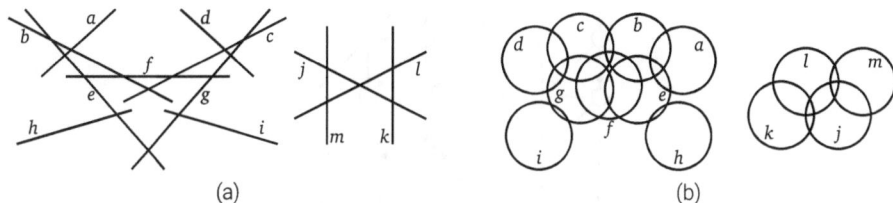

Figure 5.5. The graph in Figure 5.4 is also the intersection graph of (a) a set of line segments and (b) a set of circles.

Another good example is the ***dependency graph*** of a recursive algorithm. Dependency graphs are directed acyclic graphs. The vertices are all the distinct recursive subproblems that arise when executing the algorithm on a particular input. There is an edge from one subproblem to another if evaluating the second subproblem requires a recursive evaluation of the first. For example, for the Fibonacci recurrence

$$F_n = \begin{cases} 0 & \text{if } n = 0, \\ 1 & \text{if } n = 1, \\ F_{n-1} + F_{n-2} & \text{otherwise,} \end{cases}$$

the vertices of the dependency graph are the integers $0, 1, 2, \ldots, n$, and the edges are the pairs $(i-1){\to}i$ and $(i-2){\to}i$ for every integer i between 2 and n.

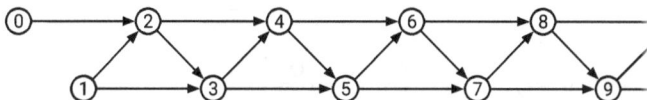

Figure 5.6. The dependency graph of the Piṅgala-Fibonacci recurrence.

As a more complex example, recall the recurrence for the *edit distance* problem from Chapter 3:

$$Edit(i, j) = \begin{cases} i & \text{if } j = 0 \\ j & \text{if } i = 0 \\ \min \begin{cases} Edit(i-1, j) + 1 \\ Edit(i, j-1) + 1 \\ Edit(i-1, j-1) + [A[i] \neq B[j]] \end{cases} & \text{otherwise} \end{cases}$$

The dependency graph of this recurrence is an $m \times n$ grid of vertices (i, j) connected by vertical edges $(i-1, j){\to}(i, j)$, horizontal edges $(i, j-1){\to}(i, j)$, and diagonal edges $(i-1, j-1){\to}(i, j)$. Dynamic programming works efficiently for any recurrence that has a reasonably small dependency graph; a proper evaluation order ensures that each subproblem is visited *after* its predecessors.

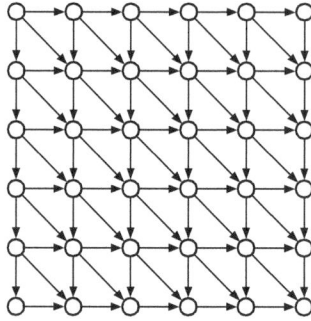

Figure 5.7. The dependency graph of the edit distance recurrence.

Another interesting example is the ***configuration graph*** of a game, puzzle, or mechanism like tic-tac-toe, checkers, the Rubik's Cube, the Tower of Hanoi, or a Turing machine. The vertices of the configuration graph are all the valid configurations of the puzzle; there is an edge from one configuration to another if it is possible to transform one configuration into the other with a single simple "move". (Obviously, the precise definition depends on what moves are allowed.) Even for reasonably simple mechanisms, the configuration graph can be extremely complex, and we typically only have access to local information about the configuration graph.

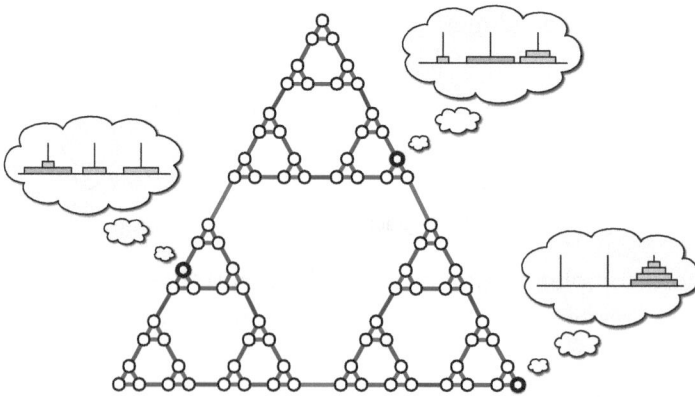

Figure 5.8. The configuration graph of the 4-disk Tower of Hanoi.

Configuration graphs are close relatives of the *game trees* we considered in Chapter 2, but with one crucial difference. Each state of a game appears *exactly once* in its configuration graph, but can appear many times in its game tree. In short, configuration graphs are *memoized* game trees!

Finite-state automata used in formal language theory can be modeled as labeled directed graphs. Recall that a deterministic finite-state automaton is formally defined as a 5-tuple $M = (\Sigma, Q, s, A, \delta)$, where Σ is a finite set called the *alphabet*, Q is a finite set of *states*, $s \in Q$ is the *start state*, $A \subseteq Q$ is the set of *accepting states*, and $\delta : Q \times \Sigma \to Q$ is a *transition function*. But it is often more useful to think of M as a directed graph G_M whose vertices are the states Q, and whose edges have the form $q \to \delta(q, a)$ for every state $q \in Q$ and symbol $a \in \Sigma$. Basic questions about the language $L(M)$ accepted by M can then be phrased as questions about the graph G_M. For example, $L(M) = \emptyset$ if and only if no accepting state/vertex is reachable from the start state/vertex s.

Finally, sometimes one graph can be used to implicitly represent other larger graphs. A good example of this implicit representation is the *subset construction*, which is normally used to convert NFAs into DFAs, but can be applied to *arbitrary* directed graphs as follows. Given *any* directed graph $G = (V, E)$, we can define a new directed graph $G' = (2^V, E')$ whose vertices are all *subsets* of vertices in V, and whose edges E' are defined as follows:

$$E' := \{A \to B \mid u \to v \in E \text{ for some } u \in A \text{ and } v \in B\}$$

We can mechanically translate this definition into an algorithm to construct G' from G, but strictly speaking, this construction is unnecessary, because G is *already* an *implicit* representation of G'.

It's important not to confuse any of these examples/representations with the actual formal *definition*: A graph is a pair of sets (V, E), where V is an *arbitrary* non-empty finite set, and E is a set of pairs (either ordered or unordered) of elements of V. In short: A graph is a set of pairs of things.

5.4 Data Structures

In practice, graphs are usually represented by one of two standard data structures: *adjacency lists* and *adjacency matrices*. At a high level, both data structures are arrays indexed by vertices; this requires that each vertex has a unique integer identifier between 1 and V. In a formal sense, these integers *are* the vertices.

Adjacency Lists

By far the most common data structure for storing graphs is the **adjacency list**. An adjacency list is an array of lists, each containing the neighbors of one of the vertices (or the out-neighbors if the graph is directed).[6] For undirected graphs, each edge uv is stored twice, once in u's neighbor list and once in v's neighbor list; for directed graphs, each edge $u \to v$ is stored only once, in the neighbor list of the tail u. For both types of graphs, the overall space required for an adjacency list is $O(V + E)$.

---

[6]Attentive students might notice that despite is name, an adjacency list is not a list. This nomenclature is an example of the Red Herring Principle: In computer science, as in mathematics, a red herring is neither necessarily red nor necessarily a fish.

There are several different ways to represent these neighbor lists, but the standard implementation uses a simple singly-linked list. The resulting data structure allows us to list the (out-)neighbors of a node v in $O(1 + \deg(v))$ time; just scan v's neighbor list. Similarly, we can determine whether $u{\to}v$ is an edge in $O(1 + \deg(u))$ time by scanning the neighbor list of u. For undirected graphs, we can improve the time to $O(1 + \min\{\deg(u), \deg(v)\})$ by simultaneously scanning the neighbor lists of both u and v, stopping either when we locate the edge or when we fall of the end of a list.

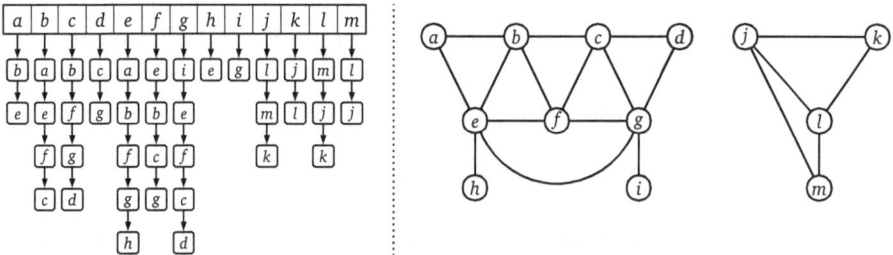

Figure 5.9. An adjacency list for our example graph.

Of course, linked lists are not the only data structure we could use; any other structure that supports searching, listing, insertion, and deletion will do. For example, we can reduce the time to determine whether uv is an edge to $O(1 + \log(\deg(u)))$ by using a balanced binary search tree to store the neighbors of u, or even to $O(1)$ time by using an appropriately constructed hash table.[7]

One common implementation of adjacency lists is the **adjacency array**, which uses a single array to store all edge records, with the records of edges incident to each vertex in a contiguous interval, and with a separate array storing the index of the first edge incident to each vertex. Moreover, it is useful to keep the intervals for each vertex in sorted order, as shown in Figure 5.10, so that we can check in $O(\log \deg(u))$ time whether two vertices u and v are adjacent.

Adjacency Matrices

The other standard data structure for graphs is the **adjacency matrix**,[8] first proposed by Georges Brunel in 1894. The adjacency matrix of a graph G is a $V \times V$ matrix of 0s and 1s, normally represented by a two-dimensional array $A[1..V, 1..V]$, where each entry indicates whether a particular edge is present in G. Specifically, for all vertices u and v:

- if the graph is undirected, then $A[u, v] := 1$ if and only if $uv \in E$, and

---

[7]This is a *lot* more subtle than it sounds. Most popular hashing techniques do *not* guarantee fast query times, and even most *good* hashing methods can guarantee only $O(1)$ *expected* time. See http://algorithms.wtf for a more thorough discussion of hashing.

[8]See footnote 3.

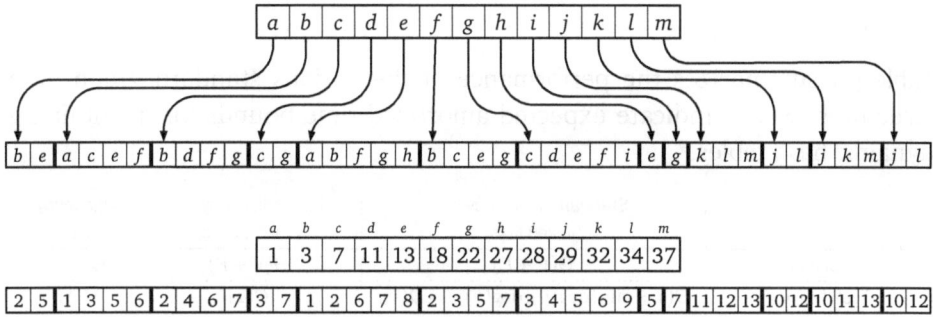

| a | b | c | d | e | f | g | h | i | j | k | l | m |

| b | e | a | c | e | f | b | d | f | g | c | g | a | b | f | g | h | b | c | e | g | c | d | e | f | i | e | g | k | l | m | j | l | j | k | m | j | l |

a	b	c	d	e	f	g	h	i	j	k	l	m
1	3	7	11	13	18	22	27	28	29	32	34	37

| 2 | 5 | 1 | 3 | 5 | 6 | 2 | 4 | 6 | 7 | 3 | 7 | 1 | 2 | 6 | 7 | 8 | 2 | 3 | 5 | 7 | 3 | 4 | 5 | 6 | 9 | 5 | 7 | 11 | 12 | 13 | 10 | 12 | 10 | 11 | 13 | 10 | 12 |

Figure 5.10. An abstract adjacency array for our example graph, and its actual implementation as a pair of integer arrays.

- if the graph is directed, then $A[u, v] := 1$ if and only if $u \rightarrow v \in E$.

For undirected graphs, the adjacency matrix is always *symmetric*, meaning $A[u, v] = A[v, u]$ for all vertices u and v, because uv and vu are just different names for the same edge, and the diagonal entries $A[u, u]$ are all zeros. For directed graphs, the adjacency matrix may or may not be symmetric, and the diagonal entries may or may not be zero.

	a b c d e f g h i j k l m
a	0 1 0 0 1 0 0 0 0 0 0 0 0
b	1 0 1 0 1 1 0 0 0 0 0 0 0
c	0 1 0 1 0 1 1 0 0 0 0 0 0
d	0 0 1 0 0 0 1 0 0 0 0 0 0
e	1 1 0 0 0 1 1 1 0 0 0 0 0
f	0 1 1 0 1 0 1 0 0 0 0 0 0
g	0 0 1 1 1 1 0 0 1 0 0 0 0
h	0 0 0 0 1 0 0 0 0 0 0 0 0
i	0 0 0 0 0 0 1 0 0 0 0 0 0
j	0 0 0 0 0 0 0 0 0 0 1 1 1
k	0 0 0 0 0 0 0 0 0 1 0 1 0
l	0 0 0 0 0 0 0 0 0 1 1 0 1
m	0 0 0 0 0 0 0 0 0 1 0 1 0

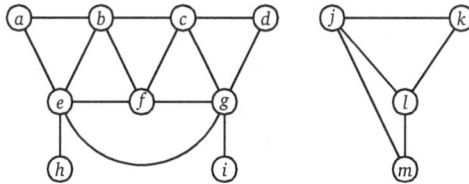

Figure 5.11. An adjacency matrix for our example graph.

Given an adjacency matrix, we can decide in $\Theta(1)$ time whether two vertices are connected by an edge just by looking in the appropriate slot in the matrix. We can also list all the neighbors of a vertex in $\Theta(V)$ time by scanning the corresponding row (or column). This running time is optimal in the worst case, but even if a vertex has few neighbors, we still have to scan the entire row to find them all. Similarly, adjacency matrices require $\Theta(V^2)$ space, regardless of how many edges the graph actually has, so they are only space-efficient for very *dense* graphs.

Comparison

Table 5.1 summarizes the performance of the various standard graph data structures. Stars* indicate expected amortized time bounds for maintaining dynamic hash tables.[9]

	Standard adjacency list (linked lists)	Fast adjacency list (hash tables)	Adjacency matrix
Space	$\Theta(V+E)$	$\Theta(V+E)$	$\Theta(V^2)$
Test if $uv \in E$	$O(1+\min\{\deg(u),\deg(v)\}) = O(V)$	$O(1)$	$O(1)$
Test if $u{\rightarrow}v \in E$	$O(1+\deg(u)) = O(V)$	$O(1)$	$O(1)$
List v's (out-)neighbors	$\Theta(1+\deg(v)) = O(V)$	$\Theta(1+\deg(v)) = O(V)$	$\Theta(V)$
List all edges	$\Theta(V+E)$	$\Theta(V+E)$	$\Theta(V^2)$
Insert edge uv	$O(1)$	$O(1)^*$	$O(1)$
Delete edge uv	$O(\deg(u)+\deg(v)) = O(V)$	$O(1)^*$	$O(1)$

Table 5.1. Times for basic operations on standard graph data structures.

In light of this comparison, one might reasonably wonder why anyone would *ever* use an adjacency matrix; after all, adjacency lists with hash tables support the same operations in the same time, using less space. The main reason is that for sufficiently dense graphs, adjacency matrices are simpler and more efficient in practice, because they avoid the overhead of chasing pointers and computing hash functions; they're just contiguous blocks of memory.

Similarly, why would anyone use *linked lists* in an adjacency list structure to store neighbors, instead of balanced binary search trees or hash tables? Although the primary reason in practice is almost surely *tradition*—If they were good enough for Donald Knuth's code, they should be good enough for yours!—there are more principled arguments. One is that standard adjacency lists are in fact *good enough* for most applications. Most standard graph algorithms never (or rarely) actually ask whether an arbitrary edge is present or absent, or attempt to insert or delete edges, and so optimizing the data structures to support those operations is unnecessary.

But in my opinion, the most compelling reason for *both* standard data structures is that many graphs are *implicitly* represented by adjacency matrices and standard adjacency lists. For example:

- Intersection graphs are usually represented as a list of the underlying geometric objects. As long as we can test whether two objects intersect in constant time, we can apply any graph algorithm to an intersection graph by *pretending* that the input graph is stored explicitly as an adjacency matrix.

- Any data structure composed from records with pointers between them can be seen as a directed graph. Graph algorithms can be applied to these data structures by *pretending* that the graph is stored in a standard adjacency list.

---

[9]Don't worry if you don't understand the phrase "expected amortized".

- Similarly, we can apply any graph algorithm to a configuration graph *as though* it were represented as a standard adjacency list, provided we can enumerate all possible moves from a given configuration in constant time each.

For the last two examples, we can enumerate the edges leaving any vertex in time proportional to its degree, but we *cannot* necessarily determine in constant time if two vertices are adjacent. (Is there a pointer from this record to that record? Can we get from this configuration to that configuration in one move?) Moreover, we usually don't have the luxury of reorganizing the pointers in each record or the moves out of a given configuration into a more efficient data structure. Thus, a standard adjacency list, with neighbors stored in linked lists, is the appropriate model data structure.

In the rest of this book, unless explicitly stated otherwise, all time bounds for graph algorithms assume that the input graph is represented by a standard adjacency list. Similarly, unless explicitly stated otherwise, when an exercise asks you to design and analyze a graph algorithm, you should assume that the input graph is represented in a standard adjacency list.

5.5 Whatever-First Search

So far we have only discussed *local* operations on graphs; arguably the most fundamental *global* question we can ask about graphs is **reachability**. Given a graph G and a vertex s in G, the reachability question asks which vertices are reachable from s; that is, for which vertices v is there a path from s to v? For now, let's consider only undirected graphs; I'll consider directed graphs briefly at the end of this section. For undirected graphs, the vertices reachable from s are precisely the vertices in the same component as s.

Perhaps the most natural reachability algorithm—at least for people like us who are used to thinking recursively—is *depth-first search*. This algorithm can be written either recursively or iteratively. It's exactly the same algorithm either way; the only difference is that we can actually see the "recursion" stack in the non-recursive version.

$\underline{\text{RECURSIVEDFS}(v):}$
  if v is unmarked
    mark v
    for each edge vw
      RECURSIVEDFS(w)

$\underline{\text{ITERATIVEDFS}(s):}$
  PUSH(s)
  while the stack is not empty
    $v \leftarrow$ POP
    if v is unmarked
      mark v
      for each edge vw
        PUSH(w)

Depth-first search is just one (perhaps the most common) species of a general family of graph traversal algorithms that I call ***whatever-first search***. The generic traversal algorithm stores a set of candidate edges in some data structure that I'll call a "bag". The only important properties of a "bag" are that we can put stuff into it and then later take stuff back out. A stack is a particular type of bag, but certainly not the only one. Here is the generic algorithm:

WhateverFirstSearch(s):
  put s into the bag
  while the bag is not empty
    take v from the bag
    if v is unmarked
      mark v
      for each edge vw
        put w into the bag

I claim that WhateverFirstSearch marks every node reachable from s and nothing else. The algorithm clearly marks each vertex in G *at most* once. To show that it visits every node in a connected graph *at least* once, we modify the algorithm slightly; the modifications are in bold red. Instead of keeping vertices in the bag, the modified algorithm stores pairs of vertices. This modification allows us to remember, whenever we visit a vertex v for the first time, which previously-visited neighbor vertex put v into the bag. We call this earlier vertex the *parent* of v.

WhateverFirstSearch(s):
  put $(\varnothing, s)$ in bag
  while the bag is not empty
    take (p, v) from the bag   ($\star$)
    if v is unmarked
      mark v
      parent(v) $\leftarrow p$
      for each edge vw ($\dagger$)
        put (v, w) into the bag   ($\star\star$)

Lemma 5.1. *WhateverFirstSearch(s) marks every vertex reachable from s and only those vertices. Moreover, the set of all pairs $(v, parent(v))$ with $parent(v) \neq \varnothing$ defines a spanning tree of the component containing s.*

Proof: First we argue that the algorithm marks every vertex v that is reachable from s, by induction on the shortest-path distance from s to v. The algorithm marks s. Let v be any other vertex reachable from s, and let $s\to\cdots\to u\to v$ be any path from s to v with the minimum number of edges. (There must be such a path, because v is reachable from s.) The prefix path $s\to\cdots\to u$ is shorter than the shortest path from s to u, so the inductive hypothesis implies that the algorithm marks u. When the algorithm marks u, it must immediately put the pair (u, v) into the bag, so it must later take (u, v) out of the bag, at which point the algorithm immediately marks v, unless it was already marked.

Every pair $(v, parent(v))$ with $parent(v) \neq \varnothing$ is actually an edge in the underlying graph G. We claim that for any marked vertex v, the path of parent edges $v \to parent(v) \to parent(parent(v)) \to \cdots$ eventually leads back to s; we prove this claim by induction on the order in which vertices are marked. Trivially s is reachable from s, so let v be any other marked vertex. The parent of v must be marked before v is marked, so the inductive hypothesis implies that the parent path $parent(v) \to parent(parent(v)) \to \cdots$ leads to s; adding one more parent edge $s \to parent(s)$ establishes the claim.

The previous claim implies that every vertex marked by the algorithm is reachable from s, and that the set of all parent edges forms a connected graph. Because every marked node except s has a unique parent, the number of parent edges is exactly one less than the number of marked vertices. We conclude that the parent edges form a tree. □

Analysis

The running time of the traversal algorithm depends on what data structure we use for the "bag", but we can make a few general observations. Let T is the time required to insert a single item into the bag or delete a single item from the bag. The for loop (†) is executed exactly once for each marked vertex, and therefore at most V times. Each edge uv in the component of s is put into the bag exactly twice; once as the pair (u, v) and once as the pair (v, u), so line (★★) is executed at most $2E$ times. Finally, we can't take more things out of the bag than we put in, so line (★) is executed at most $2E + 1$ times. Thus, assuming the underlying graph G is stored in a standard adjacency list, WHATEVERFIRSTSEARCH runs in $O(V + ET)$ **time**. (If G is stored in an adjacency matrix, the running time of WHATEVERFIRSTSEARCH increases to $O(V^2 + ET)$.)

5.6 Important Variants

Stack: Depth-First

If we implement the "bag" using a *stack*, we recover our original depth-first search algorithm. Stacks support insertions (push) and deletions (pop) in $O(1)$ time each, so the algorithm runs in $O(V + E)$ **time**. The spanning tree formed by the parent edges is called a **depth-first spanning tree**. The exact shape of the tree depends on the start vertex and on the order that neighbors are visited inside the for loop (†), but in general, depth-first spanning trees are long and skinny. We will consider several important properties and applications of depth-first search in Chapter 6.

Queue: Breadth-First

If we implement the "bag" using a *queue*, we get a different graph-traversal algorithm called **breadth-first search**. Queues support insertions (push) and deletions (pull) in $O(1)$ time each, so the algorithm runs in $O(V + E)$ **time**. In this case, the **breadth-first spanning tree** formed by the parent edges contains **shortest paths** from the start vertex s to every other vertex in its component; we will consider shortest paths in detail in Chapter 8. Again, the exact shape of a breadth-first spanning tree depends on the start vertex and on the order that neighbors are visited in the for loop (†), but in general, breadth-first spanning trees are short and bushy.

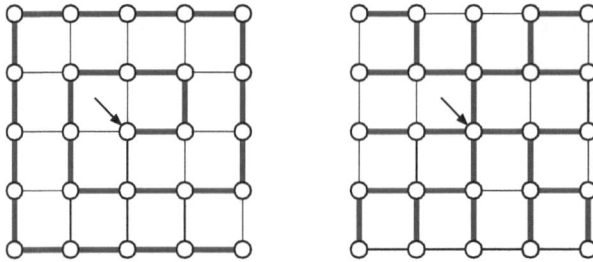

Figure 5.12. A depth-first spanning tree and a breadth-first spanning tree of the same graph, both starting at the center vertex.

Priority Queue: Best-First

Finally, if we implement the "bag" using a *priority queue*, we get yet another family of algorithms called **best-first search**. Because the priority queue stores at most one copy of each edge, inserting an edge or extracting the minimum-priority edge requires $O(\log E)$ time, which implies that best-first search runs in $O(V + E \log E)$ **time**.

I describe best-first search as a "family of algorithms", rather than a single algorithm, because there are different methods to assign priorities to the edges, and these choices lead to different algorithmic behavior. I'll describe three well-known variants below, but there are many others. In all three examples, we assume that every edge uv or $u \to v$ in the input graph has a non-negative weight $w(uv)$ or $w(u \to v)$.

First, if the input graph is undirected and we use the weight of each edge as its priority, best-first search constructs the **minimum spanning tree** of the component of s. Surprisingly, as long as all the edge weights are distinct, the resulting tree does *not* depend on the start vertex or the order that neighbors are visited; in this case, the minimum spanning tree is actually unique. This instantiation of best-first search is commonly (but, as usual, incorrectly) known as *Prim's algorithm*; we'll discuss this and other minimum-spanning-trees in more detail in Chapter 7.

Define the *length* of a path to be the sum of the weights of its edges. We can also compute **shortest paths** in weighted graphs using best-first search, as follows. Every marked vertex v stores a distance $dist(v)$. Initially we set $dist(s) = 0$. For every other vertex v, when we set $parent(v) \leftarrow p$, we also set $dist(v) \leftarrow dist(p) + w(p \rightarrow v)$, and when we insert the edge $v \rightarrow w$ into the priority queue, we use the priority $dist(v) + w(v \rightarrow w)$. Assuming all edge weights are positive, $dist(v)$ is the length of the shortest path from s to v. This instantiation of best-first search is commonly (but, as usual, strictly speaking, incorrectly) known as *Dijkstra's algorithm*; we'll see this algorithm again in Chapter 8.

Finally, define the *width* of a path to be the *minimum* weight of any edge in the path. A simple modification of "Dijkstra's" best-first search algorithm computes **widest paths** from s to every other reachable vertex; widest paths are also called **bottleneck shortest paths**. Every marked vertex v stores a value $width(v)$. Initially we set $width(s) = \infty$. For every other vertex v, when we set $parent(v) \leftarrow p$, we also set $width(v) \leftarrow \min\{width(p), w(p \rightarrow v)\}$, and when we insert the edge $v \rightarrow w$ into the priority queue, we use the priority $\min\{width(v), w(v \rightarrow w)\}$. Widest paths are useful in algorithms for computing *maximum flows*, which (you guessed it) we'll consider in Chapter 10.

Disconnected Graphs

WHATEVERFIRSTSEARCH(s) only visits the vertices reachable from a single start vertex s. To visit *every* vertex in G, we can use the following simple "wrapper" function.

```
WFSALL(G):
    for all vertices v
        unmark v
    for all vertices v
        if v is unmarked
            WHATEVERFIRSTSEARCH(v)
```

Wait, I hear you ask, why are you making this so complicated? Why not just[10] scan the vertex array?

```
MARKEVERYVERTEXDUH(G):
    for all vertices v
        mark v
```

---

[10]This word is almost always a signal that you are missing something important.

Well, sure, *if* you have an complete list of vertices, then you can do that, but remember that not all graphs are represented so explicitly.[11] More importantly, even if we do have an explicit vertex list, the order in which this naive algorithm visits vertices is determined by their order in the *data structure*, not by the abstract structure of the graph.

In particular, unlike a naive scan through the vertices, WFSALL visits all the vertices in one component, and then all the vertices in the next component, and so on through each component of the input graph. This component-by-component traversal allows us, for example, to count the components of a disconnected graph using a single counter.

$$
\begin{array}{l}
\underline{\text{COUNTCOMPONENTS}(G):} \\
\quad count \leftarrow 0 \\
\quad \text{for all vertices } v \\
\quad\quad \text{unmark } v \\
\quad \text{for all vertices } v \\
\quad\quad \text{if } v \text{ is unmarked} \\
\quad\quad\quad count \leftarrow count + 1 \\
\quad\quad\quad \text{WHATEVERFIRSTSEARCH}(v) \\
\quad return\ count
\end{array}
$$

With just a bit more work, we can record which component contains each vertex, instead of merely marking it.

$$
\begin{array}{l}
\underline{\text{COUNTANDLABEL}(G):} \\
\quad count \leftarrow 0 \\
\quad \text{for all vertices } v \\
\quad\quad \text{unmark } v \\
\quad \text{for all vertices } v \\
\quad\quad \text{if } v \text{ is unmarked} \\
\quad\quad\quad count \leftarrow count + 1 \\
\quad\quad\quad \text{LABELONE}(v, count) \\
\quad return\ count
\end{array}
$$

$$
\begin{array}{l}
\lang\langle\textit{Label one component}\rang\rangle \\
\underline{\text{LABELONE}(v, count):} \\
\quad \text{while the bag is not empty} \\
\quad\quad \text{take } v \text{ from the bag} \\
\quad\quad \text{if } v \text{ is unmarked} \\
\quad\quad\quad \text{mark } v \\
\quad\quad\quad comp(v) \leftarrow count \\
\quad\quad\quad \text{for each edge } vw \\
\quad\quad\quad\quad \text{put } w \text{ into the bag}
\end{array}
$$

WFSALL marks every vertex once, puts every edge into the bag once, and takes every edge out of the bag once, so the overall running time is $O(V + ET)$, where T is the time for a bag operation. In particular, if we run depth-first search or breadth-first search at every vertex, the resulting algorithm still requires only $O(V + E)$ time.

Moreover, because WHATEVERFIRSTSEARCH computes a spanning tree of one component, we can use WFSALL to compute a spanning *forest* of the entire

---

[11]On the other hand, if we store a time-stamp at every vertex indicating the last time it was "marked", then we can "unmark every vertex" in $O(1)$ time by recording the start time of our traversal, and considering a vertex "marked" if its time stamp is later than the recorded start time.

graph. In particular, best-first search with edge weights as priorities computes the minimum-weight spanning forest in $O(V + E \log E)$.

Shockingly, at least one *extremely* popular algorithms textbook claims that this wrapper can only be used with depth-first search.[12] This claim is flatly incorrect. In fact, the *very first* implementation of breadth-first search, written around 1945 by Konrad Zuse in his proto-language *Plankalkül*, was developed for the specific purpose of counting and labeling the components of an undirected graph.

Directed Graphs

Whatever-first search is easy to adapt to directed graphs; the only difference is that when we mark a vertex, we put all of its *out*-neighbors into the bag. In fact, if we are using standard adjacency lists or adjacency matrices, we do not have to change the code at all!

WHATEVERFIRSTSEARCH(s):
  put s into the bag
  while the bag is not empty
    take v from the bag
    if v is unmarked
      mark v
      for each edge $v \rightarrow w$
        put w into the bag

Our earlier proof implies that the algorithm marks every vertex reachable from s, and the directed edges $parent(v) \rightarrow p$ define a rooted tree, with all edges directed away from the root s. However, even if the graph is connected, we no longer necessarily obtain a *spanning* tree of the graph, because reachability is no longer symmetric.

On the gripping hand, WHATEVERFIRSTSEARCH does define a spanning tree of the vertices reachable from s. Moreover, by varying the instantiation of the "bag", we can obtain a depth-first spanning tree, a breadth-first spanning tree, a minimum-weight directed spanning tree, a shortest-path tree, or a widest-path tree of those reachable vertices.

5.7 Graph Reductions: Flood Fill

One of the earliest modern examples of whatever-first search was proposed by Edward Moore in the mid-1950s. A *pixel map* is a two-dimensional array

---

[12]To quote directly: "Unlike breadth-first search, whose predecessor subgraph forms a tree, the predecessor subgraph produced by a depth-first search may be composed of several trees, because the search may repeat from multiple sources."

whose value represent colors; the individual entries in the array are called *pixels*, an abbreviation of *picture elements*.[13] A *connected region* in a pixel map is a connected subset of pixels that all have the same color, where two pixels are considered adjacent if they are immediate horizontal or vertical neighbors. The *flood fill* operation, commonly represented by a paint can in raster-graphics editing software, changes every pixel in a connected region to a new color; the input to the operation consists of the indices i and j of one pixel in the target region and the new color.

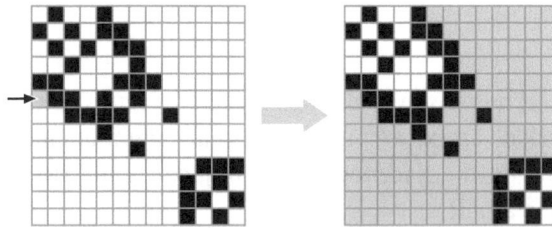

Figure 5.13. An example of flood fill

The flood-fill problem can be reduced to the reachability problem by chasing the definitions. We define an undirected graph $G = (V, E)$, whose vertices are the individual pixels, and whose edges connect neighboring pixels with the same color. Each connected region in the pixel map is a component of G; thus, the flood-fill problem **reduces** to a reachability problem in G. We can solve this reachability problem using whatever-first search in G, starting at the given pixel (i, j), with one minor modification; whenever we mark a vertex, we immediately change its color. For an $n \times n$ pixel map, the graph G has n^2 vertices and at most $2n^2$ edges, so whatever-first search runs in $O(V + E) = \boldsymbol{O(n^2)}$ **time**.

This simple example demonstrates the essential ingredients of a **reduction**. Rather than solving the flood-fill problem from scratch, we use an existing algorithm as a black-box subroutine. *How* whatever-first search works is utterly irrelevant here; all that matters is its *specification*: Given a graph G and a starting vertex s, mark every vertex in G that is reachable from s. Like any other subroutine, we still have to describe how to construct the input and how to use its output. We also have to analyze *our* resulting algorithm in terms of *our* input parameters, not the vertices and edges of whatever intermediate graph our algorithm constructs.

Now that we have an algorithm that works—but *only* now—we can apply two easy optimizations to make it faster, one practical and the other theoretical:

---

[13]Before the advent of modern raster display devices in the 1960s, pixels were more commonly known as *stitches* or *tesserae*, depending on whether they were made of thread or very small rocks. The word *pix* became a standard abbreviation for *picture(s)* in the early 20th century—not long after *sox* became a common plural of *sock*—supplanting the earlier colloquialism *piccy*. See also voxel (volume element), texel (texture element), and taxel (tactile element and/or badger).

- In an actual implementation, we would not actually build a separate graph data structure for G. Instead, we can use the pixel map directly *as though* it were a standard adjacency list, because we can list the same-color neighbors of any pixel in $O(1)$ time each. In particular, there is no need to separately "mark" vertices; we can use the color of the pixels instead.

- More careful analysis implies that the running time is proportional to the number of pixels in the region being filled—equivalently, the number of vertices in component of G containing vertex (i, j)—which could be considerably smaller than $O(n^2)$.

Exercises

Graphs

1. Prove that the following definitions are all equivalent.

    - A tree is a connected acyclic graph.

    - A tree is one component of a forest. (A forest is an acyclic graph.)

    - A tree is a connected graph with *at most* $V - 1$ edges.

    - A tree is a minimally connected graph; removing any edge disconnects the graph.

    - A tree is an acyclic graph with *at least* $V - 1$ edges.

    - A tree is a maximally acyclic graph; adding an edge between any two vertices creates a cycle.

    - A tree is a graph that contains a unique path between each pair of vertices.

2. Prove that any connected acyclic graph with $n \geq 2$ vertices has at least two vertices with degree 1. Do not use the words "tree" or "leaf", or any well-known properties of trees; your proof should follow entirely from the definitions of "connected" and "acyclic".

3. A graph (V, E) is *bipartite* if the vertices V can be partitioned into two subsets L and R, such that every edge has one vertex in L and the other in R.

    (a) Prove that every tree is a bipartite graph.

    (b) Prove that a graph G is bipartite if and only if every cycle in G has an even number of edges.

    (c) Describe and analyze an efficient algorithm that determines whether a given undirected graph is bipartite.

4. Whenever groups of pigeons gather, they instinctively establish a *pecking order*. For any pair of pigeons, one pigeon always pecks the other, driving it away from food or potential mates. The same pair of pigeons always chooses the same pecking order, even after years of separation, no matter what other pigeons are around. Surprisingly, the overall pecking order can contain cycles—for example, pigeon i pecks pigeon j, which pecks pigeon k, which pecks pigeon ℓ, which pecks pigeon i.

   (a) Prove that any finite population of pigeons can be placed in a procession (perhaps a parade?) so that each pigeon pecks the preceding pigeon's posterior. Pretty please.

   (b) Suppose you are given a directed graph representing the pecking relationships among a set of n pigeons. The graph contains one vertex per pigeon, and it contains an edge $i{\rightarrow}j$ if and only if pigeon i pecks pigeon j. Describe and analyze an algorithm to compute a pecking order for the pigeons, as guaranteed by part (a).

   (c) Prove that for any set of at least three pigeons, either the pecking order described in part (a) is unique, or there are three pigeons i, j, and k, such that pigeon i pecks pigeon j, which pecks pigeon k, which pecks pigeon i.

5. An **Euler tour** of a graph G is a closed walk through G that traverses every edge of G exactly once.

   (a) Prove that if a connected graph G has an Euler tour, then every vertex in G has even degree. (Euler proved this.)

   (b) Prove that if every vertex in a connected graph G has even degree, then G has an Euler tour. (Euler did *not* prove this.)

   (c) Describe and analyze an algorithm to compute an Euler tour in a given graph, or correctly report that no such tour exists. (Euler vaguely waved his hands at this.)

6. The d-dimensional hypercube is the graph defined as follows. There are 2^d vertices, each labeled with a different string of d bits. Two vertices are joined by an edge if their labels differ in exactly one bit.

   (a) A Hamiltonian cycle in a graph G is a cycle of edges in G that enters each vertex of G exactly once. Prove that for all $d \geq 2$, the d-dimensional hypercube has a Hamiltonian cycle.

   (b) Which hypercubes have an Euler tour (a closed walk that traverses every edge exactly once)? [*Hint: This is very easy.*]

Traversal Algorithms

7. Recall that a directed graph G is *strongly connected* if, for any two vertices u and v, there is a path in G from u to v and a path in G from v to u.

   Describe an algorithm to determine, given an *undirected* graph G as input, whether it is possible to direct each edge of G so that the resulting directed graph is strongly connected.

8. Let G be a connected graph, and let T be a depth-first spanning tree of G rooted at some node v. Prove that if T is also a breadth-first spanning tree of G rooted at v, then $G = T$.

9. Professors Epprich and Goodstein propose the following optimization of the generic whatever-first search algorithm. Instead of checking whether the vertices we take out of the bag are marked, their algorithm checks before it even puts the vertex into the bag, thereby ensuring that each vertex is put into the bag at most once. Their algorithm also assigns the parent of each vertex when that vertex is marked.

   ```
   EAGERWFS(s):
       mark s
       put s into the bag
       while the bag is not empty
           take v from the bag
           for each edge vw
               if w is unmarked
                   mark w
                   parent(w) ← v
                   put w into the bag
   ```

   (a) Prove that EAGERWFS(s) marks every node reachable from s and nothing else. Equivalently, prove that the parent edges $v \rightarrow parent(v)$ computed by EAGERWFS(s) define a spanning tree of the component containing s.

   (b) Prove that if the bag is implemented as a queue, EAGERWFS is equivalent to breadth-first search, meaning the two algorithms mark the same vertices in the same order and construct the same spanning tree. *[Hint: What is the definition of a queue?]*

   (c) Prove that EAGERWFS is *never* equivalent to depth-first search, no matter what data structure is used as the bag (and thus, in particular, when the bag is a stack).

   Neither EAGERWFS nor RECURSIVEDFS specify the order that edges vw at each vertex v are considered, and different edge orders may lead to different spanning trees. Thus, you need to argue, for some explicit graph G, that no spanning tree of G produced by RECURSIVEDFS can be constructed by EAGERWFS (using *any* bag data structure), or vice versa.

10. One of the earliest published descriptions of whatever-first search as a generic class of algorithms was by Edsger Dijkstra, Leslie Lamport, Alain Martin, Carel Scholten, and Elisabeth Steffens in 1975, as part of the design of an automatic garbage collector. Instead of maintaining marked and unmarked vertices, their algorithm maintains a color for each vertex, which is either white, gray, or black. As usual, in the following algorithm, we imagine a fixed underlying graph G.

THREECOLORSEARCH(s):
   color all nodes white
   color s gray
   while at least one vertex is gray
      THREECOLORSTEP( )

THREECOLORSTEP( ):
   $v \leftarrow$ any gray vertex
   if v has no white neighbors
      color v black
   else
      $w \leftarrow$ any white neighbor of v
      $parent(w) \leftarrow v$
      color w gray

(a) Prove that THREECOLORSEARCH maintains the following invariant at all times: No black vertex is a neighbor of a white vertex. [Hint: This should be easy.]

(b) Prove that after THREECOLORSEARCH(s) terminates, all vertices reachable from s are black, all vertices not reachable from s are white, and that the parent edges $v \rightarrow parent(v)$ define a rooted spanning tree of the component containing s.

    [Hint: Intuitively, black nodes are "marked" and gray nodes are "in the bag". Unlike our formulation of WHATEVERFIRSTSEARCH, however, the three-color algorithm is not required to process all edges out of a node at the same time.]

(c) Prove that the following variant of THREECOLORSEARCH, which maintains the set of gray vertices in a standard stack, is equivalent to depth-first search. [Hint: The order of the last two lines of THREE-COLORSTACKSTEP matters!]

THREECOLORSTACKSEARCH(s):
   color all nodes white
   color s gray
   push s onto the stack
   while at least one vertex is gray
      THREECOLORSTACKSTEP( )

THREECOLORSTACKSTEP( ):
   pop v from the stack
   if v has no white neighbors
      color v black
   else
      $w \leftarrow$ any white neighbor of v
      $parent(w) \leftarrow v$
      color w gray
      push v onto the stack
      push w onto the stack

(d) Prove that the following variant of THREECOLORSEARCH, which maintains the set of gray vertices in a standard queue, is **not** equivalent

to breadth-first search. *[Hint: The order of the last two lines of*
THREECOLORQUEUESTEP *doesn't matter!]*

THREECOLORQUEUESEARCH(*s*):
  color all nodes white
  color *s* gray
  push *s* into the queue
  while at least one vertex is gray
    THREECOLORQUEUESTEP( )

THREECOLORQUEUESTEP( ):
  pull *v* from the queue
  if *v* has no white neighbors
    color *v* black
  else
    w ← any white neighbor of *v*
    parent(w) ← *v*
    color *w* gray
    push *v* into the queue
    push *w* into the queue

▼(e) Now suppose that another process is adding edges to *G* while THREE-
COLORSEARCH is running. These new edges could violate the color
invariant described in part (a) and therefore destroy the correctness
of the algorithm—in particular, when THREECOLORSEARCH terminates,
some vertices reachable from *s* could be white. This would be disastrous
if we are relying on "white" to mean "unreachable and therefore safe to
delete".

However, if the other process explicitly preserves the color invariant,
we can still use the three-color algorithm to safely identify unreachable
vertices. We model the two concurrent algorithms as follows; the
either/or choice in GARBAGECOLLECT and the choice of which vertices *u*
and *w* to MUTATE are entirely out of the main algorithm's control.[14]

GARBAGECOLLECT(*s*):
  color all vertices white
  color *s* gray
  while at least one vertex is gray
    either
      COLLECTSTEP( )
    or
      MUTATE( )

COLLECTSTEP( ):
  v ← any gray vertex
  if *v* has no white neighbors
    color *v* black
  else
    w ← any white neighbor of *v*
    color *w* gray

---

[14]This is a *dramatic* oversimplification of the "mark and sweep" garbage-collection algorithms
actually used in multi-threaded languages like Lua and Go. A more thorough discussion of
multi-threaded dynamic memory management is unfortunately beyond the scope of this book,
except for the First Commandment: **Thou Shalt Not Roll Thine Own Garbage Collector.**

```
Mutate():
    u ← any vertex
    w ← any vertex
    if uw is not an edge
        add edge uw
        if u is black and w is white
            color u gray
        if u is white and w is black
            color w gray
```

Prove that GarbageCollect eventually terminates with every vertex reachable from s colored black and every vertex not reachable from s colored white.

♥(f) Suppose instead of recoloring black vertices gray, Mutate maintains the color invariant by coloring some *white* vertices gray:

```
Mutate():
    u ← any vertex
    w ← any vertex
    if uw is not an edge
        add edge uw
        if u is black and w is white
            color w gray
        if u is white and w is black
            color u gray
```

Prove that GarbageCollect eventually terminates with s colored black, every vertex reachable from a black vertex colored black, and every vertex not reachable from a black vertex colored white.

Reductions

11. A **number maze** is an $n \times n$ grid of positive integers. A token starts in the upper left corner; your goal is to move the token to the lower-right corner. On each turn, you are allowed to move the token up, down, left, or right; the distance you may move the token is determined by the number on its current square. For example, if the token is on a square labeled 3, then you may move the token three steps up, three steps down, three steps left, or three steps right. However, you are never allowed to move the token off the edge of the board.

    Describe and analyze an efficient algorithm that either returns the minimum number of moves required to solve a given number maze, or correctly reports that the maze has no solution. For example, given the number maze in Figure 5.14, your algorithm should return the integer 8.

12. **Snakes and Ladders** is a classic board game, originating in India no later than the 16th century. The board consists of an $n \times n$ grid of squares,

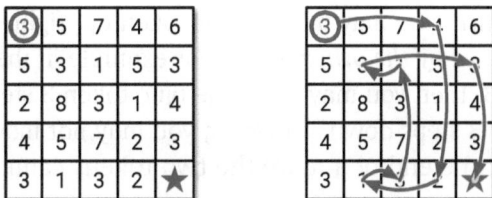

Figure 5.14. A 5 × 5 number maze that can be solved in eight moves.

numbered consecutively from 1 to n^2, starting in the bottom left corner and proceeding row by row from bottom to top, with rows alternating to the left and right. Certain pairs of squares in this grid, always in different rows, are connected by either "snakes" (leading down) or "ladders" (leading up). Each square can be an endpoint of at most one snake or ladder.

You start with a token in cell 1, in the bottom left corner. In each move, you advance your token up to k positions, for some fixed constant k. If the token ends the move at the *top* end of a snake, it slides down to the bottom of that snake. Similarly, if the token ends the move at the *bottom* end of a ladder, it climbs up to the top of that ladder.

Describe and analyze an algorithm to compute the smallest number of moves required for the token to reach the last square of the grid.

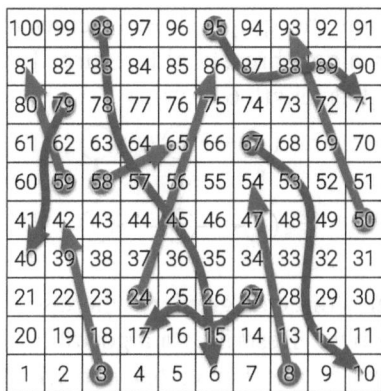

Figure 5.15. A Snakes and Ladders board. Upward straight arrows are ladders; downward wavy arrows are snakes.

13. The infamous Mongolian puzzle-warrior Vidrach Itky Leda invented the following puzzle in the year 1473. The puzzle consists of an $n \times n$ grid of squares, where each square is labeled with a positive integer, and two tokens, one red and the other blue. The tokens always lie on distinct squares of the grid. The tokens start in the top left and bottom right corners of the grid; the goal of the puzzle is to swap the tokens.

In a single turn, you may move either token up, right, down, or left *by a distance determined by the **other** token*. For example, if the red token is on a square labeled 3, then you may move the blue token 3 steps up, 3 steps left, 3 steps right, or 3 steps down. However, you may not move either token off the grid, and at the end of a move the two tokens cannot lie on the same square.

Describe and analyze an efficient algorithm that either returns the minimum number of moves required to solve a given Vidrach Itky Leda puzzle, or correctly reports that the puzzle has no solution. For example, given the puzzle in Figure 5.16, your algorithm would return the number 5.

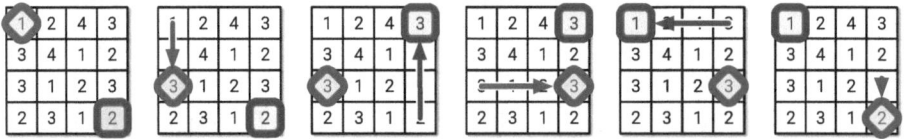

Figure 5.16. A five-move solution for a 4 × 4 Vidrach Itky Leda puzzle.

14. Suppose you are given a directed graph $G = (V, E)$ and two vertices s and t. Describe and analyze an algorithm to determine if there is a walk in G from s to t (possibly repeating vertices and/or edges) whose length is divisible by 3.

    For example, given the graph shown below, with the indicated vertices s and t, your algorithm should return TRUE, because the walk $s \to w \to y \to x \to s \to w \to t$ has length 6.

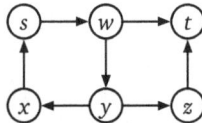

15. Suppose you are given a directed graph G where some edges are red and the remaining edges are blue. Describe an algorithm to find the shortest walk in G from one vertex s to another vertex t in which no three consecutive edges have the same color. That is, if the walk contains two red edges in a row, the next edge must be blue, and if the walk contains two blue edges in a row, the next edge must be red.

    For example, given the following graph as input, your algorithm should return the integer 7, because $s \to a \to b \Rightarrow d \to c \Rightarrow a \to b \to t$ is the shortest legal walk from s to t.

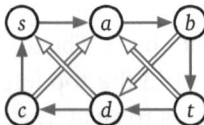

16. Consider a directed graph G, where each edge is colored either red, white, or blue. A walk in G is called a *French flag walk* if its sequence of edge colors is red, white, blue, red, white, blue, and so on. More formally, a walk $v_0 \to v_1 \to \cdots \to v_k$ is a French flag walk if, for every integer i, the edge $v_i \to v_{i+1}$ is red if $i \bmod 3 = 0$, white if $i \bmod 3 = 1$, and blue if $i \bmod 3 = 2$.

    Describe an algorithm to find all vertices in G that can be reached from a given vertex v through a French flag walk.

17. There are n galaxies connected by m intergalactic teleport-ways. Each teleport-way joins two galaxies and can be traversed in both directions. Also, each teleport-way e has an associated cost of $c(e)$ dollars, where $c(e)$ is a positive integer. A teleport-way can be used multiple times, but the toll must be paid every time it is used.

    Judy wants to travel from galaxy s to galaxy t, but teleportation is not very pleasant and she would like to minimize the number of times she needs to teleport. However, she wants the total cost to be a multiple of five dollars, because carrying small change is not pleasant either.

    (a) Describe and analyze an algorithm to compute the smallest number of times Judy needs to teleport to travel from galaxy s to galaxy t so that the total cost is a multiple of five dollars.

    (b) Solve part (a), but now assume that Judy has a coupon that allows her to use exactly one teleport-way for free.

18. Three Seashells is a solitaire game, played on a connected undirected graph G. Initially, three tokens are placed on distinct start vertices a, b, c. In each turn, you *must* move *all three* tokens, by moving each token along an edge from its current vertex to an adjacent vertex. At the end of each turn, the three tokens *must* lie on three different vertices. Your goal is to move the tokens onto three goal vertices x, y, z; it does not matter which token ends up on which goal vertex.

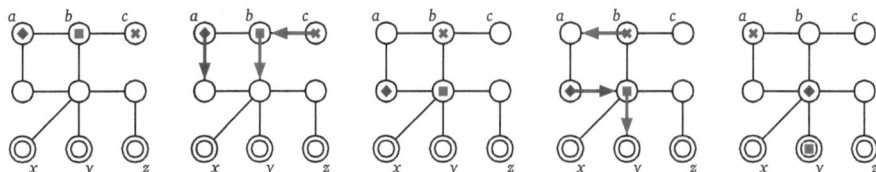

Figure 5.17. The initial configuration of the Three Seashells puzzle and the first two turns of a solution.

    Describe and analyze an algorithm to determine whether a given Three Seashells puzzle is solvable. Your input consists of the graph G, the start vertices a, b, c, and the goal vertices x, y, z. Your output is a single bit: TRUE or FALSE.

19. Let G be a connected undirected graph. Suppose we start with two coins on two arbitrarily chosen vertices of G, and we want to move the coins so that they lie on the same vertex using as few moves as possible. At every step, each coin *must* move to an adjacent vertex.

    (a) Describe and analyze an algorithm to compute the minimum number of steps to reach a configuration where both coins are on the same vertex, or to report correctly that no such configuration is reachable. The input to your algorithm consists of a graph $G = (V, E)$ and two vertices $u, v \in V$ (which may or may not be distinct).

    (b) Now suppose there are three coins. Describe and analyze an algorithm to compute the minimum number of steps to reach a configuration where both coins are on the same vertex, or to report correctly that no such configuration is reachable.

    (c) Finally, suppose there are *forty-two* coins. Describe and analyze an algorithm to determine whether it is possible to move all 42 coins to the same vertex. Again, *every* coin must move at *every* step. For full credit, your algorithm should run in $O(V + E)$ time.

20. One of my daughter's elementary-school math workbooks[15] contains several puzzles of the following type:

    Complete each angle maze below by tracing a path from start to finish that has only acute angles.

    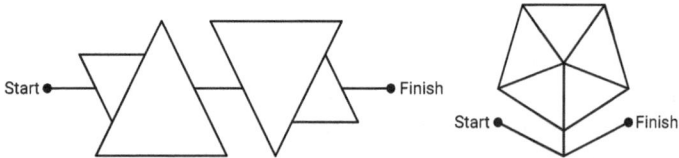

    Describe and analyze an algorithm to solve arbitrary acute-angle mazes.

    You are given a connected undirected graph G, whose vertices are points in the plane and whose edges are line segments. Edges do not intersect, except at their endpoints. For example, a drawing of the letter X would have five vertices and four edges, and the first maze above has 18 vertices and 21 edges. You are also given two vertices Start and Finish.

    Your algorithm should return TRUE if G contains a walk from Start to Finish that has only acute angles, and FALSE otherwise. Formally, a walk through G is valid if, for any two consecutive edges $u \rightarrow v \rightarrow w$ in the walk, either $\angle uvw = \pi$ or $0 < \angle uvw < \pi/2$. Assume you have a subroutine that can determine in $O(1)$ time whether the angle between two given segments is straight, obtuse, right, or acute.

    ---

    [15] Jason Batterson and Shannon Rogers, *Beast Academy Math: Practice 3A*, 2012. See https://www.beastacademy.com/resources/printables.php for several more examples.

21. Suppose you are given a set of n horizontal and vertical line segments and two points s and t in the plane. Describe an efficient algorithm to determine if there is a path from s to t that does not intersect any of the given line segments.

    Each horizontal line segment is specified by its left and right x-coordinates and its unique y-coordinate; similarly, each vertical line segment is specified by its unique x-coordinate and its top and bottom y-coordinates. Finally, the points s and t are each specified by their x- and y-coordinates.

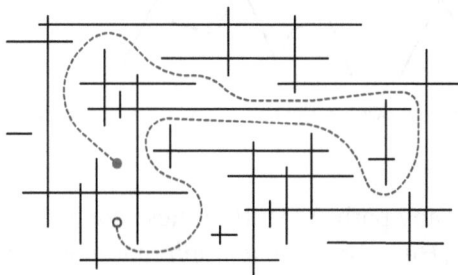

Figure 5.18. A path between two points in a maze of horizontal and vertical line segments.

22. Every cheesy romance movie has a scene where the romantic couple, after a long and frustrating separation, suddenly see each other across a long distance, and then slowly approach one another with unwavering eye contact as the music rolls in and the rain lifts and the sun shines through the clouds and the music swells and everyone starts dancing with rainbows and kittens and chocolate unicorns and. . . .[16]

    Suppose a romantic couple—in grand computer science tradition, named Alice and Bob—enters their favorite park at the east and west entrances and immediately establish eye-contact. They can't just run directly to each other; instead, they must stay on the path that zig-zags through the park between the east and west entrances. To maintain the proper dramatic tension, Alice and Bob must traverse the path so that they always lie on a direct east-west line.

    We can describe the zigzag path as two arrays $X[0..n]$ and $Y[0..n]$, containing the x- and y-coordinates of the corners of the path, in order from the southwest endpoint to the southeast endpoint. The X array is sorted in increasing order, and $Y[0] = Y[n]$. The path is a sequence of straight line segments connecting these corners.

    (a) Suppose $Y[0] = Y[n] = 0$ and $Y[i] > 0$ for every other index i; that is, the endpoints of the path are strictly below every other point on the path.

---

[16]Fun fact: Damien Chazelle, the director of *Whiplash* and *La La Land*, is the son of Princeton computer science professor and electric guitarist Bernard Chazelle.

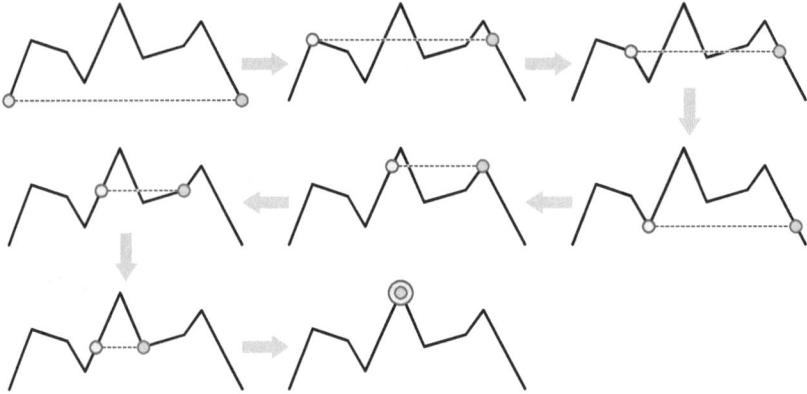

Figure 5.19. Alice and Bob meet. Alice walks backward in step 2, and Bob walks backward in steps 5 and 6.

Prove that for any path P meeting these conditions, Alice and Bob can *always* meet. *[Hint: Describe a graph that models all possible locations of the couple along the path. What are the vertices of this graph? What are the edges? Use the* **Handshake Lemma**: *Every graph has an even number of vertices with odd degree.]*

(b) If the endpoints of the path are *not* below every other vertex, Alice and Bob might still be able to meet, or they might not. Describe an algorithm to decide whether Alice and Bob can meet, without either breaking east-west eye contact or stepping off the path, given the arrays $X[0..n]$ and $Y[0..n]$ as input.

♥(c) Describe an algorithm for part (b) that runs in $O(n)$ time.

23. The famous puzzle-maker Kaniel the Dane invented a solitaire game played with two tokens on an $n \times n$ square grid. Some squares of the grid are marked as *obstacles*, and one grid square is marked as the *target*. In each turn, the player must move one of the tokens from is current position *as far as possible* upward, downward, right, or left, stopping just before the token hits (1) the edge of the board, (2) an obstacle square, or (3) the other token. The goal is to move either of the tokens onto the target square.

For example, we can solve the puzzle shown in Figure 5.20 by moving the red token down until it hits the obstacle, then moving the green token left until it hits the red token, and then moving the red token left, down, right, and up. The red token stops at the target on the 6th move *because* the green token is just above the target square.

Describe and analyze an algorithm to determine whether an instance of this puzzle is solvable. Your input consist of the integer n, a list of obstacle locations, the target location, and the initial locations of the tokens. The

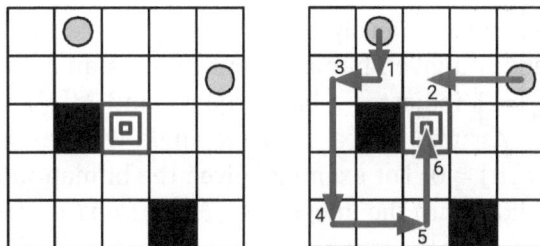

Figure 5.20. An instance of Kaniel the Dane's puzzle that can be solved in six moves. Circles indicate initial token positions; black squares are obstacles; the center square is the target.

output of your algorithm is a single boolean: TRUE if the given puzzle is solvable and FALSE otherwise. *[Hint: Don't forget about the time required to construct the graph.]*

♥24. **Rectangle Walk** is a new abstract puzzle game, available for only 99¢ on Steam, iOS, Android, Xbox One, Playstation 5, Nintendo Wii U, Atari 2600, Palm Pilot, Commodore 64, TRS-80, Sinclair ZX-1, DEC PDP-8, PLATO, Zuse Z3, Duramesc, Odhner Arithmometer, Analytical Engine, Jacquard Loom, Horologium Mirabile Lundense, Leibniz Stepped Reckoner, Al-Jazari's Robot Band, Yan Shi's Automaton, Antikythera Mechanism, Knotted Rope, Ishango Bone, and Pile of Rocks.

The game is played on an $n \times n$ grid of black and white squares. The player moves a rectangle through this grid, subject to the following conditions:

- The rectangle must be aligned with the grid; that is, the top, bottom, left, and right coordinates must be integers.

- The rectangle must fit within the $n \times n$ grid, and it must contain at least one grid cell.

- The rectangle must not contain a black square.

- In a single move, the player can replace the current rectangle r with any rectangle r' that either contains r or is contained in r.

Initially, the player's rectangle is a 1×1 square in the upper right corner. The player's goal is to reach a 1×1 square in the bottom left corner using as few moves as possible.

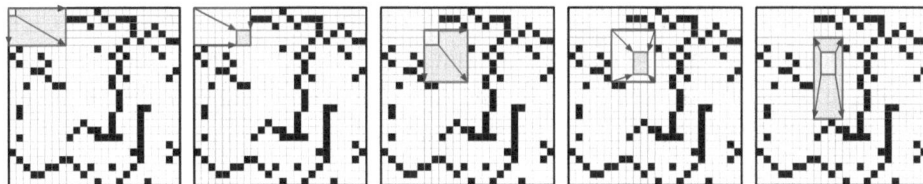

Figure 5.21. The first five steps of a Rectangle Walk.

Describe and analyze an algorithm to compute the length of the shortest Rectangle Walk in a given bitmap. Your input is an array $M[1..n, 1..n]$, where $M[i,j] = 1$ indicates a black square and $M[i,j] = 0$ indicates a white square. Assume that a valid rectangle walk exists; in particular, $M[1,1] = M[n,n] = 0$. For example, given the bitmap shown above, your algorithm should return the integer 18. [Hint: Don't forget about the time required to construct the graph!!]

25. **Racetrack** (also known as *Graph Racers* and *Vector Rally*) is a two-player paper-and-pencil racing game that Jeff played on the bus in 5th grade.[17] The game is played with a track drawn on a sheet of graph paper. The players alternately choose a sequence of grid points that represent the motion of a car around the track, subject to certain constraints explained below.

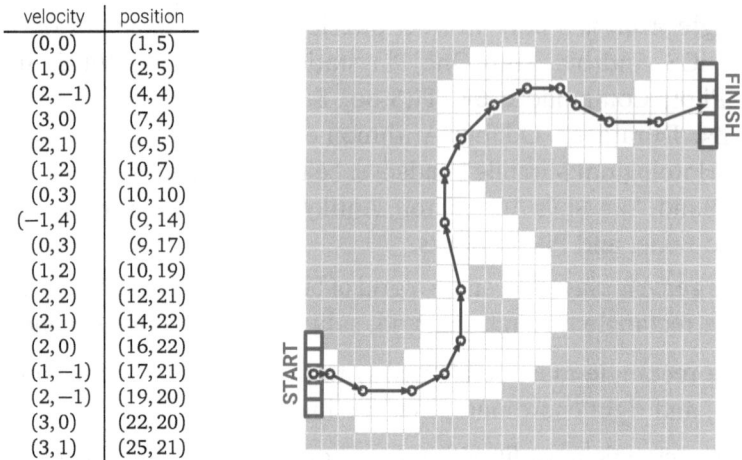

velocity	position
$(0,0)$	$(1,5)$
$(1,0)$	$(2,5)$
$(2,-1)$	$(4,4)$
$(3,0)$	$(7,4)$
$(2,1)$	$(9,5)$
$(1,2)$	$(10,7)$
$(0,3)$	$(10,10)$
$(-1,4)$	$(9,14)$
$(0,3)$	$(9,17)$
$(1,2)$	$(10,19)$
$(2,2)$	$(12,21)$
$(2,1)$	$(14,22)$
$(2,0)$	$(16,22)$
$(1,-1)$	$(17,21)$
$(2,-1)$	$(19,20)$
$(3,0)$	$(22,20)$
$(3,1)$	$(25,21)$

Figure 5.22. A 16-step Racetrack run, on a 25 × 25 track. This is *not* the shortest run on this track.

Each car has a *position* and a *velocity*, both with integer x- and y-coordinates. A subset of grid squares is marked as the *starting area*, and another subset is marked as the *finishing area*. The initial position of each car is chosen by the player somewhere in the starting area; the initial velocity of each car is always $(0,0)$. At each step, the player optionally increments or decrements either or both coordinates of the car's velocity; in other words, each component of the velocity can change by at most 1 in a single step. The car's new position is then determined by adding the new velocity to the car's previous position. The new position must be inside the track; otherwise, the car crashes and that player loses the race. The race ends when the first car reaches a position inside the finishing area.

---

[17]The actual game is a bit more complicated than the version described here. See http://harmmade.com/vectorracer/ for an excellent online version.

Suppose the racetrack is represented by an $n \times n$ array of bits, where each 0 bit represents a grid point inside the track, each 1 bit represents a grid point outside the track, the "starting area" is the first column, and the "finishing area" is the last column.

Describe and analyze an algorithm to find the minimum number of steps required to move a car from the starting line to the finish line of a given racetrack.

26. A *rolling die maze* is a puzzle involving a standard six-sided die (a cube with numbers on each side) and a grid of squares. You should imagine the grid lying on a table; the die always rests on and exactly covers one square of the grid. In a single step, you can *roll* the die 90 degrees around one of its bottom edges, moving it to an adjacent square one step north, south, east, or west.

Some squares in the grid may be *blocked*; the die can never rest on a blocked square. Other squares may be *labeled* with a number; whenever the die rests on a labeled square, the number on the *top* face of the die must equal the label. Squares that are neither labeled nor marked are *free*. You may not roll the die off the edges of the grid. A rolling die maze is *solvable* if it is possible to place a die on the lower left square and roll it to the upper right square under these constraints.

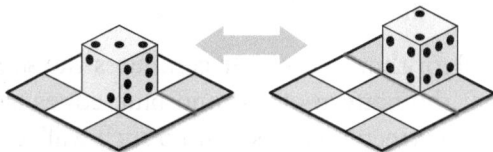

Figure 5.23. Rolling a die

Figure 5.24 shows four rolling die mazes. Assuming we use a standard die with 1 and 6 on opposite sides, only the first two mazes are solvable. For example, the first maze is solvable by by placing the die on the lower left square with 1 on the top face, and then rolling the die east, then north, then north, then east.

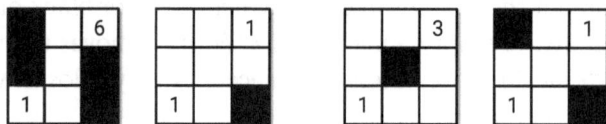

Figure 5.24. Four rolling die mazes; only the first two are solvable.

(a) Suppose the input is a two-dimensional array $L[1..n, 1..n]$, where each entry $L[i, j]$ stores the label of the square in the ith row and jth column, where 0 means the square is free and -1 means the square is blocked.

Describe and analyze a polynomial-time algorithm to determine whether the given rolling die maze is solvable.

♥(b) Now suppose the maze is specified *implicitly* by a list of labeled and blocked squares. Specifically, suppose the input consists of an integer M, specifying the height and width of the maze, and an array $S[1..n]$, where each entry $S[i]$ is a triple (x, y, L) indicating that square (x, y) has label L. As in the explicit encoding, label -1 indicates that the square is blocked; free squares are not listed in S at all. Describe and analyze an efficient algorithm to determine whether the given rolling die maze is solvable. For full credit, the running time of your algorithm should be polynomial in the input size n.

[*Hint: You have some freedom in how to place the initial die. There are rolling die mazes that can be solved only if the initial position is chosen correctly.*]

♥27. Suppose you are given an arbitrary directed graph G in which each edge is colored either red or blue, along with two special vertices s and t.

(a) Describe an algorithm that either computes a walk from s to t such that the pattern of red and blue edges along the walk is a palindrome, or correctly reports that no such walk exists.

(b) Describe an algorithm that either computes the *shortest* walk from s to t such that the pattern of red and blue edges along the walk is a palindrome, or correctly reports that no such walk exists.

[*Hint: Where did we last see palindromes?*]

♠♥28. Draughts, also known in the United States as "checkers", is a game played on an $m \times m$ grid of squares, alternately colored light and dark.[18] The game is usually played on an 8×8 or 10×10 board, but the rules easily generalize to any board size. Each dark square is occupied by at most one game piece (usually called a *checker* in the U.S.), which is either black or white; light squares are always empty. One player ("White") moves the white pieces; the other ("Black") moves the black pieces. A player loses when her last piece is taken off the board.

---

[18]The counting tables used by medieval English government accountants were covered by a green cloth with black squares in a checker pattern; disk-shaped counters were placed in these squares to represent values. For this reason, the British government's accountants have been collectively known since the 10th century as the *Exchequer*. The actual counting tables were used by the Exchequer to tally tax payments well into the 19th century.

Consider the following simple version of the game, essentially American checkers or British draughts, but where every piece is a king.[19] Pieces can be moved in any of the four diagonal directions. On each turn, a player either *moves* one of her pieces one step diagonally into an empty square, or makes a series of *jumps* with one of her pieces. In each jump, the piece moves to an empty square two steps away in any diagonal direction, but only if the intermediate square is occupied by a piece of the opposite color; this enemy piece is *captured* and immediately removed from the board. All jumps in the same turn must be made with the same piece.

Describe an algorithm to decide whether White can capture every black piece, thereby winning the game, *in a single turn*. The input consists of the width of the board (m), a list of positions of white pieces, and a list of positions of black pieces. For full credit, your algorithm should run in $O(n)$ time, where n is the total number of pieces. [*Hint: The greedy strategy—make arbitrary jumps until you get stuck—does **not** always find a winning sequence of jumps even when one exists. See problem 5. Parity, parity, parity.*]

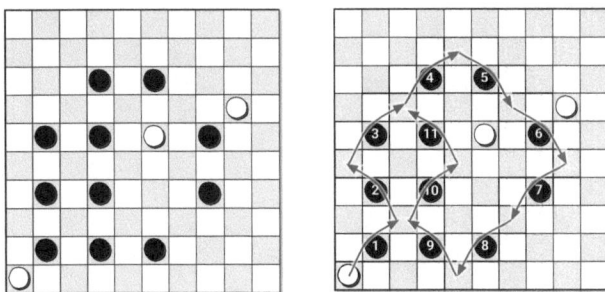

Figure 5.25. White wins in one turn.

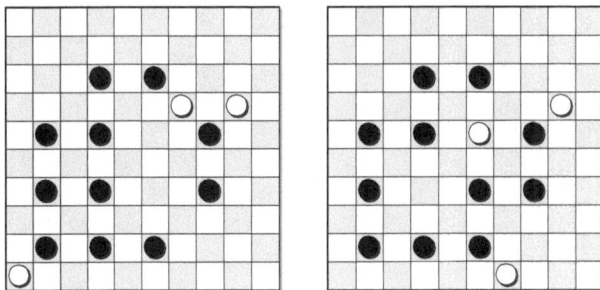

Figure 5.26. White cannot win in one turn from either of these positions.

---

[19]Most other variants of draughts have "flying kings", which behave *very* differently than kings in the British/American game, and which make this problem *much* more difficult, as we will see in Chapter 12.

And, for the hous is crinkled to and fro,
And hath so queinte weyes for to go—
For hit is shapen as the mase is wroght—
Therto have I a remedie in my thoght,
That, by a clewe of twyne, as he hath goon,
The same wey he may returne anoon,
Folwing alwey the threed, as he hath come.

— Geoffrey Chaucer, *The Legend of Good Women* (c. 1385)

"Com'è bello il mondo e come sono brutti i labirinti!" dissi sollevato.
"Come sarebbe bello il mondo se ci fosse una regola per girare nei labirinti,"
rispose il mio maestro.

[*"How beautiful the world is, and how ugly labyrinths are," I said, relieved.*
"How beautiful the world would be if there were a procedure for moving through
labyrinths," my master replied.]

— Umberto Eco, *Il nome della rosa* (1980)
English translation (*The Name of the Rose*) by William Weaver (1983)

6

Depth-First Search

In the previous chapter, we considered a generic algorithm—whatever-first search—for traversing arbitrary graphs, both undirected and directed. In this chapter, we focus on a particular instantiation of this algorithm called *depth-first search*, and primarily on the behavior of this algorithm in directed graphs.

Although depth-first search can be accurately described as "whatever-first search with a stack", the algorithm is normally implemented recursively, rather than using an explicit stack:

$\underline{\text{DFS}(v):}$
    if v is unmarked
        mark v
        for each edge $v \rightarrow w$
            DFS(w)

We can make this algorithm slightly faster (in practice) by checking whether a node is marked *before* we recursively explore it. This modification ensures that we call DFS(v) only once for each vertex v. We can further modify the algorithm to compute other useful information about the vertices and edges, by introducing two black-box subroutines, PreVisit and PostVisit, which we leave unspecified for now.

$$
\begin{array}{|l|}
\hline
\text{DFS}(v)\text{:} \\
\quad \text{mark } v \\
\quad \text{PreVisit}(v) \\
\quad \text{for each edge } vw \\
\quad\quad \text{if } w \text{ is unmarked} \\
\quad\quad\quad parent(w) \leftarrow v \\
\quad\quad\quad \text{DFS}(w) \\
\quad \text{PostVisit}(v) \\
\hline
\end{array}
$$

Recall that a node w is *reachable* from another node v in a directed graph G—or more simply, v can reach w—if and only if G contains a directed path from v to w. Let **reach(v)** denote the set of vertices reachable from v (including v itself). If we unmark all vertices in G, and then call DFS(v), the set of marked vertices is precisely *reach(v)*.

Reachability in undirected graphs is symmetric: v can reach w if and only if w can reach v. As a result, after unmarking all vertices of an undirected graph G, calling DFS(v) traverses the entire component of v, and the parent pointers define a spanning tree of that component.

The situation is more subtle with directed graphs, as shown in the figure below. Even though the graph is "connected", different vertices can reach different, and potentially overlapping, portions of the graph. The parent pointers assigned by DFS(v) define a tree rooted at v whose vertices are precisely *reach(v)*, but this is not necessarily a spanning tree of the graph.

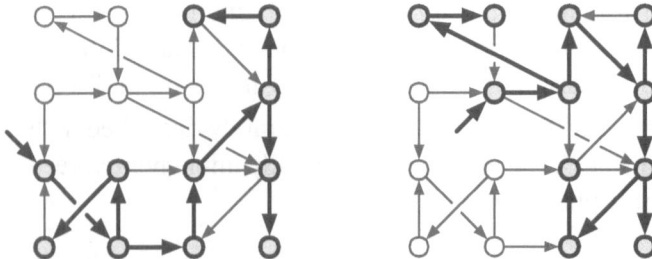

Figure 6.1. Depth-first trees rooted at different vertices in the same directed graph.

As usual, we can extend our reachability algorithm to traverse the *entire* input graph, even if it is disconnected, using the standard wrapper function shown on the left in Figure 6.2. Here we add a generic black-box subroutine

PREPROCESS to perform any necessary preprocessing for the PREVISIT and POSTVISIT functions.

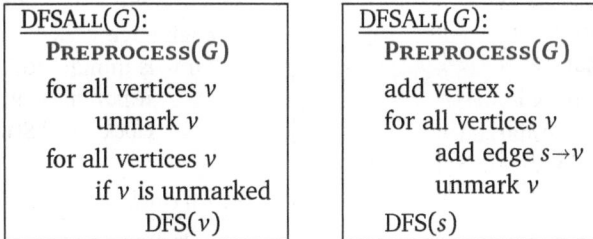

DFSALL(G):	DFSALL(G):
PREPROCESS(G)	PREPROCESS(G)
for all vertices v	add vertex s
unmark v	for all vertices v
for all vertices v	add edge $s{\rightarrow}v$
if v is unmarked	unmark v
DFS(v)	DFS(s)

Figure 6.2. Two formulations of the standard wrapper algorithm for depth-first search

Alternatively, if we are allowed to modify the graph, we can add a new *source* vertex s, with edges to every other vertex in G, and then make a single call to DFS(s), as shown on the right of Figure 6.2. Now the resulting parent pointers always define a spanning tree of the *augmented* input graph, but not of the *original* input graph. Otherwise, the two wrapper functions have essentially identical behavior; choosing one or the other is entirely a matter of convenience.[1]

Again, this algorithm behaves slightly differently for undirected and directed graphs. In undirected graphs, as we saw in the previous chapter, it is easy to adapt DFSALL to count the components of a graph; in particular, the parent pointers computed by DFSALL define a spanning forest of the input graph, containing a spanning tree for each component. When the graph is directed, however, DFSALL may discover any number of "components" between 1 and V, even when the graph is "connected", depending on the precise structure of the graph and the order in which the wrapper algorithm visits the vertices.

6.1 Preorder and Postorder

Hopefully you are already familiar with preorder and postorder traversals of rooted *trees*, both of which can be computed using depth-first search. Similar traversal orders can be defined for arbitrary directed graphs—even if they are disconnected—by passing around a counter, as shown in Figure 6.3. Equivalently, we can use our generic depth-first-search algorithm with the following subroutines PREPROCESS, PREVISIT, and POSTVISIT.

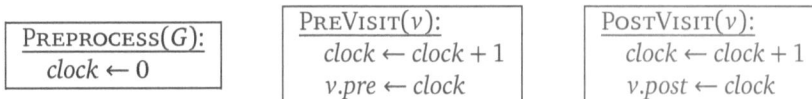

PREPROCESS(G):	PREVISIT(v):	POSTVISIT(v):
$clock \leftarrow 0$	$clock \leftarrow clock + 1$	$clock \leftarrow clock + 1$
	$v.pre \leftarrow clock$	$v.post \leftarrow clock$

---

[1]The equivalence of these two wrapper functions is a specific feature of **depth**-first search. In particular, wrapping *breadth*-first search in a for-loop to visit every vertex does *not* yield the same traversal order as adding a source vertex and invoking breadth-first search at s.

$$\boxed{\begin{array}{l} \text{DFSALL}(G)\text{:} \\ \quad clock \leftarrow 0 \\ \quad \text{for all vertices } v \\ \quad\quad \text{unmark } v \\ \quad \text{for all vertices } v \\ \quad\quad \text{if } v \text{ is unmarked} \\ \quad\quad\quad clock \leftarrow \text{DFS}(v, clock) \end{array}}$$

$$\boxed{\begin{array}{l} \text{DFS}(v, clock)\text{:} \\ \quad \text{mark } v \\ \quad clock \leftarrow clock + 1; \ \ v.pre \leftarrow clock \\ \quad \text{for each edge } v{\rightarrow}w \\ \quad\quad \text{if } w \text{ is unmarked} \\ \quad\quad\quad w.parent \leftarrow v \\ \quad\quad\quad clock \leftarrow \text{DFS}(w, clock) \\ \quad clock \leftarrow clock + 1; \ \ v.post \leftarrow clock \\ \quad \text{return } clock \end{array}}$$

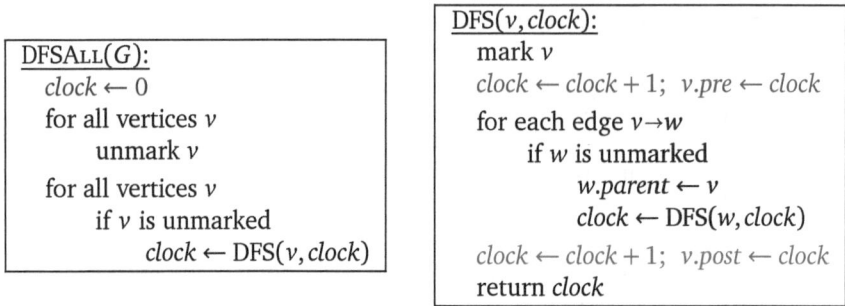

Figure 6.3. Defining preorder and postorder via depth-first search.

In either formulation, this algorithm assigns assigns $v.pre$ (and advances the clock) just after pushing v onto the recursion stack, and it assigns $v.post$ (and advances the clock) just before popping v off the recursion stack. It follows that for any two vertices u and v, the intervals $[u.pre, u.post]$ and $[v.pre, v.post]$ are either disjoint or nested. Moreover, $[u.pre, u.post]$ contains $[v.pre, v.post]$ if and only if DFS(v) is called during the execution of DFS(u), or equivalently, if and only if u is an ancestor of v in the final forest of parent pointers.

After DFSALL labels every node in the graph, the labels $v.pre$ define a **preordering** of the vertices, and the labels $v.post$ define a **postordering** of the vertices.[2] With a few trivial exceptions, every graph has several different pre- and postorderings, depending on the order that DFS considers edges leaving each vertex, and the order that DFSALL considers vertices.

For the rest of this chapter, we refer to $v.pre$ as the *starting time* of v (or less formally, "when v starts"), $v.post$ as the *finishing time* of v (or less formally, "when v finishes"), and the interval between the starting and finishing times as the *active interval* of v (or less formally, "while v is active").

Classifying Vertices and Edges

During the execution of DFSALL, each vertex v of the input graph has one of three states:

- *new* if DFS(v) has not been called, that is, if $clock < v.pre$;
- *active* if DFS(v) has been called but has not returned, that is, if $v.pre \leq clock < v.post$;
- *finished* if DFS(v) has returned, that is, if $v.post \leq clock$.

Because starting and finishing times correspond to pushes and pops on the recursion stack, a vertex is active if and only if it is on the recursion stack. It follows that the active nodes always comprise a directed path in G.

---

[2]Confusingly, *both* of these orders are sometimes called "depth-first ordering". Please don't do that.

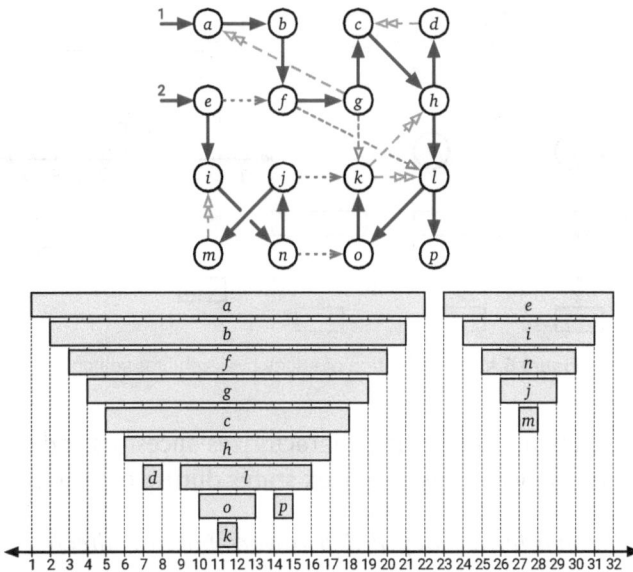

Figure 6.4. A depth-first forest of a directed graph, and the corresponding active intervals of its vertices, defining the preordering *abfgchdlokpeinjm* and the postordering *dkoplhcgfbamjnie*. Forest edges are solid; dashed edges are explained in Figure 6.5.

The edges of the input graph fall into four different classes, depending on how their active intervals intersect. Fix your favorite edge $u{\to}v$.

- If v is new when DFS(u) begins, then DFS(v) must be called during the execution of DFS(u), either directly or through some intermediate recursive calls. In either case, u is a proper ancestor of v in the depth-first forest, and $u.pre < v.pre < v.post < u.post$.

  – If DFS(u) calls DFS(v) directly, then $u = v.parent$ and $u{\to}v$ is called a **tree edge**.

  – Otherwise, $u{\to}v$ is called a **forward edge**.

- If v is active when DFS(u) begins, then v is already on the recursion stack, which implies the opposite nesting order $v.pre < u.pre < u.post < v.post$. Moreover, G must contain a directed path from v to u. Edges satisfying this condition are called **back edges**.

- If v is finished when DFS(u) begins, we immediately have $v.post < u.pre$. Edges satisfying this condition are called **cross edges**.

- Finally, the fourth ordering $u.post < v.pre$ is impossible.

These edge classes are illustrated in Figure 6.5. Again, the actual classification of edges depends on the order in which DFSALL considers vertices and the order in which DFS considers the edges leaving each vertex.

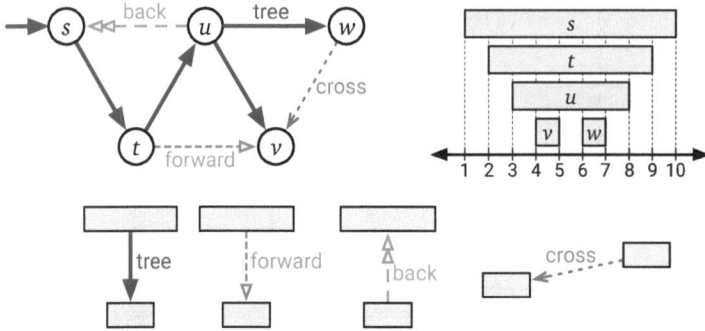

Figure 6.5. Classification of edges by depth-first search.

Finally, the following key lemma characterizes ancestors and descendants in any depth-first forest according to vertex states during the traversal.

Lemma 6.1. *Fix an arbitrary depth-first traversal of any directed graph G. The following statements are equivalent for all vertices u and v of G.*

(a) *u is an ancestor of v in the depth-first forest.*

(b) $u.pre \leq v.pre < v.post \leq u.post$.

(c) *Just after DFS(v) is called, u is active.*

(d) *Just before DFS(u) is called, there is a path from u to v in which every vertex (including u and v) is new.*

Proof: First, suppose u is an ancestor of v in the depth-first forest. Then by definition there is a path P of tree edges u to v. By induction on the path length, we have $u.pre \leq w.pre < w.post \leq u.post$ for every vertex w in P, and thus every vertex in P is new before DFS(u) is called. In particular, we have $u.pre \leq v.pre < v.post \leq u.post$, which implies that u is active while DFS(v) is executing.

Because parent pointers correspond to recursive calls, $u.pre \leq v.pre < v.post \leq u.post$ implies that u is an ancestor of v.

Suppose u is active just after DFS(v) is called. Then $u.pre \leq v.pre < v.post \leq u.post$, which implies that there is a path of (zero or more) tree edges from u, through the intermediate nodes on the recursion stack (if any), to v.

Finally, suppose u is not an ancestor of v. Fix an arbitrary path P from u to v, let x be the first vertex in P that is not a descendant of u, and let w be the predecessor of x in P. The edge $w{\to}x$ guarantees that $x.pre < w.post$, and $w.post < u.post$ because w is a descendant of u, so $x.pre < u.post$. It follows that $x.pre < u.pre$, because otherwise x would be a descendant of u. Because active intervals are properly nested, there are only two possibilities:

- If $u.post < x.post$, then x is active when DFS(u) is called.
- If $x.post < u.pre$, then x is already finished when DFS(u) is called.

We conclude that *every* path from u to v contains a vertex that is not new when DFS(u) is called. □

6.2 Detecting Cycles

A *directed acyclic graph* or *dag* is a directed graph with no directed cycles. Any vertex in a dag that has no incoming vertices is called a *source*; any vertex with no outgoing edges is called a *sink*. An isolated vertex with no incident edges at all is both a source and a sink. Every dag has at least one source and one sink, but may have more than one of each. For example, in the graph with n vertices but no edges, every vertex is a source and every vertex is a sink.

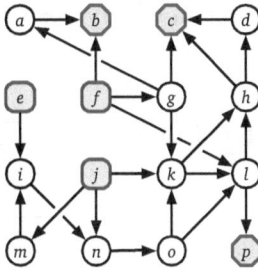

Figure 6.6. A directed acyclic graph. Vertices e, f, and j are sources; vertices b, c, and p are sinks.

Recall from our earlier case analysis that if $u.post < v.post$ for any edge $u{\to}v$, the graph contains a directed path from v to u, and therefore contains a directed *cycle* through the edge $u{\to}v$. Thus, we can determine whether a given directed graph G is a dag in $O(V + E)$ time by computing a postordering of the vertices and then checking each edge by brute force.

Alternatively, instead of numbering the vertices, we can explicitly maintain the status of each vertex and immediately return FALSE if we ever discover an edge to an active vertex. This algorithm also runs in $O(V + E)$ time; see Figure 6.7.

<u>ISACYCLIC(G):</u>
   for all vertices v
      $v.status \leftarrow$ NEW
   for all vertices v
      if $v.status =$ NEW
         if ISACYCLICDFS(v) = FALSE
            return FALSE
   return TRUE

<u>ISACYCLICDFS(v):</u>
   $v.status \leftarrow$ ACTIVE
   for each edge $v{\to}w$
      if $w.status =$ ACTIVE
         return FALSE
      else if $w.status =$ NEW
         if ISACYCLICDFS(w) = FALSE
            return FALSE
   $v.status \leftarrow$ FINISHED
   return TRUE

Figure 6.7. A linear-time algorithm to determine if a graph is acyclic.

6.3 Topological Sort

A *topological ordering* of a directed graph G is a total order $\prec$ on the vertices such that $u \prec v$ for every edge $u{\rightarrow}v$. Less formally, a topological ordering arranges the vertices along a horizontal line so that all edges point from left to right. A topological ordering is clearly impossible if the graph G has a directed cycle—the rightmost vertex of the cycle would have an edge pointing to the left!

On the other hand, consider an arbitrary postordering of an arbitrary directed graph G. Our earlier analysis implies that $u.post < v.post$ for any edge $u{\rightarrow}v$, then G contains a directed path from v to u, and therefore contains a directed cycle through $u{\rightarrow}v$. Equivalently, if G is acyclic, then $u.post > v.post$ for every edge $u{\rightarrow}v$. It follows that every directed acyclic graph G has a topological ordering; in particular, the reversal of any postordering of G is a topological ordering of G.

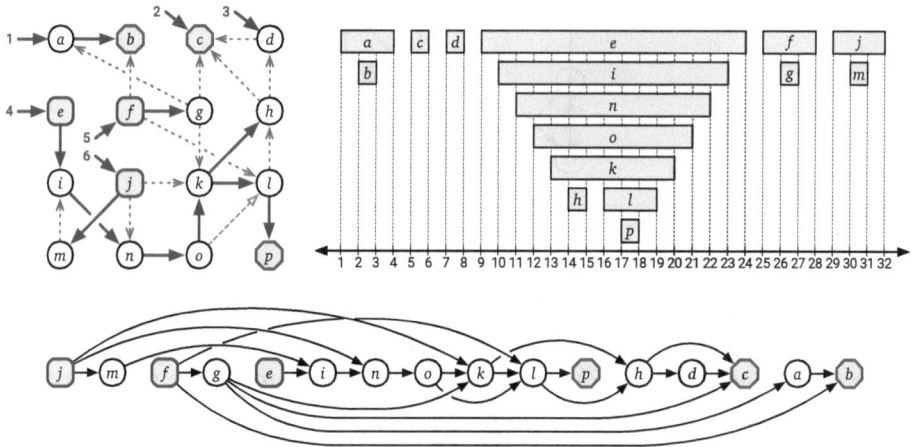

Figure 6.8. Reversed postordering of the dag from Figure 6.6.

If we require the topological ordering in a separate data structure, we can simply write the vertices into an array in reverse postorder, in $O(V + E)$ time, as shown in Figure 6.9.

Implicit Topological Sort

But recording the topological order into a separate data structure is usually overkill. In most applications of topological sort, the ordered list of the vertices is not our actual goal; rather, we want to perform some fixed computation at each vertex of the graph, either in topological order or in reverse topological order. For these applications, it is not necessary to *record* the topological order at all!

```
TOPOLOGICALSORT(G):
    for all vertices v
        v.status ← NEW
    clock ← V
    for all vertices v
        if v.status = NEW
            clock ← TOPSORTDFS(v, clock)
    return S[1 .. V]
```

```
TOPSORTDFS(v, clock):
    v.status ← ACTIVE
    for each edge v→w
        if w.status = NEW
            clock ← TOPSORTDFS(v, clock)
        else if w.status = ACTIVE
            fail gracefully
    v.status ← FINISHED
    S[clock] ← v
    clock ← clock − 1
    return clock
```

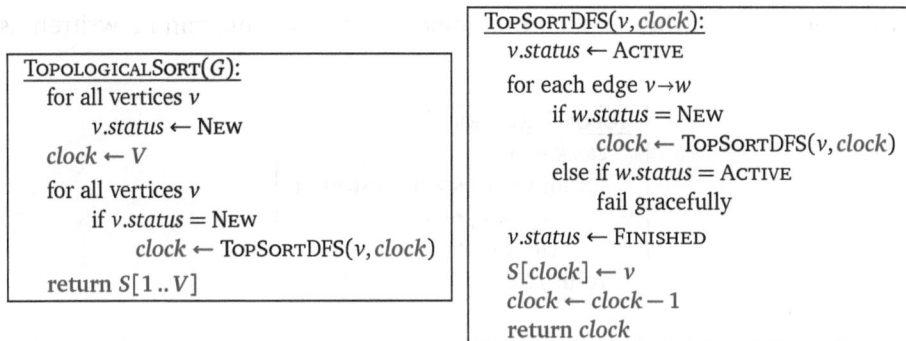

Figure 6.9. Explicit topological sort

If we want to process a directed acyclic graph in *reverse* topological order, it suffices to process each vertex at the end of its recursive depth-first search. After all, topological order is the same as reversed postorder!

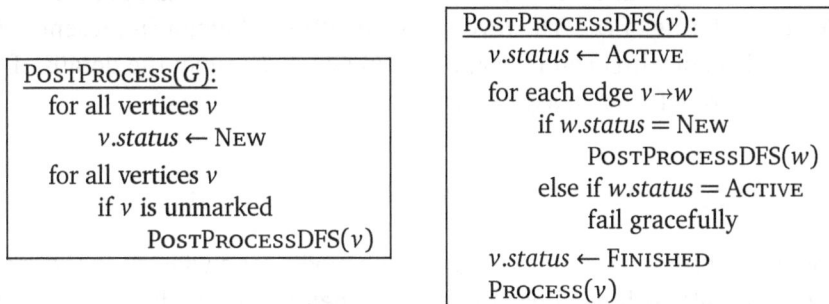

```
POSTPROCESS(G):
    for all vertices v
        v.status ← NEW
    for all vertices v
        if v is unmarked
            POSTPROCESSDFS(v)
```

```
POSTPROCESSDFS(v):
    v.status ← ACTIVE
    for each edge v→w
        if w.status = NEW
            POSTPROCESSDFS(w)
        else if w.status = ACTIVE
            fail gracefully
    v.status ← FINISHED
    PROCESS(v)
```

If we already *know* that the input graph is acyclic, we can further simplify the algorithm by simply marking vertices instead of recording their search status.

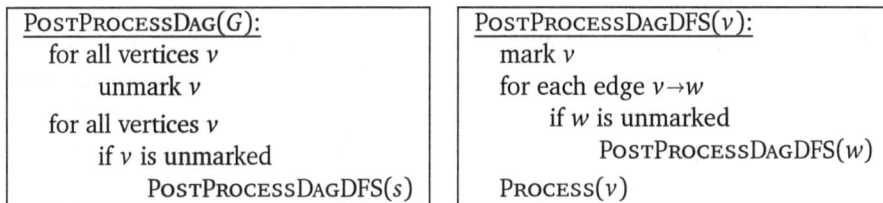

```
POSTPROCESSDAG(G):
    for all vertices v
        unmark v
    for all vertices v
        if v is unmarked
            POSTPROCESSDAGDFS(s)
```

```
POSTPROCESSDAGDFS(v):
    mark v
    for each edge v→w
        if w is unmarked
            POSTPROCESSDAGDFS(w)
    PROCESS(v)
```

This is just the standard depth-first search algorithm, with POSTVISIT renamed to PROCESS!

Because it is such a common operation on directed acyclic graphs, I sometimes express postorder processing of a dag idiomatically as follows:

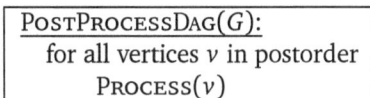

```
POSTPROCESSDAG(G):
    for all vertices v in postorder
        PROCESS(v)
```

For example, our earlier explicit topological sort algorithm can be written as follows:

$$
\boxed{
\begin{array}{l}
\underline{\text{TOPOLOGICALSORT}(G):} \\
\quad clock \leftarrow V \\
\quad \text{for all vertices } v \text{ in postorder} \\
\quad\quad S[clock] \leftarrow v \\
\quad\quad clock \leftarrow clock - 1 \\
\quad \text{return } S[1..V]
\end{array}
}
$$

To process a dag in *forward* topological order, we can record a topological ordering of the vertices into an array and then run a simple for-loop. Alternatively, we can apply depth-first search to the ***reversal*** of G, denoted ***rev(G)***, obtained by replacing each each $v \rightarrow w$ with its reversal $w \rightarrow v$. Reversing a directed cycle gives us another directed cycle with the opposite orientation, so the reversal of a dag is another dag. Every source in G is a sink in $rev(G)$ and vice versa; it follows inductively that every topological ordering of $rev(G)$ is the reversal of a topological ordering of G.[3] The reversal of any directed graph (represented in a standard adjacency list) can be computed in $O(V + E)$ time; the details of this construction are left as an easy exercise.

6.4 Memoization and Dynamic Programming

Our topological sort algorithm is arguably the model for a wide class of dynamic programming algorithms. Recall that the ***dependency graph*** of a recurrence has a vertex for every recursive subproblem and an edge from one subproblem to another if evaluating the first subproblem requires a recursive evaluation of the second. The dependency graph must be acyclic, or the naïve recursive algorithm would never halt.

Evaluating any recurrence with memoization is *exactly* the same as performing a depth-first search of the dependency graph. In particular, a vertex of the dependency graph is "marked" if the value of the corresponding subproblem has already been computed. The black-box subroutines PREVISIT and POSTVISIT are proxies for the actual value computation. See Figure 6.10.

Carrying this analogy further, evaluating a recurrence *using dynamic programming* is the same as evaluating all subproblems in the dependency graph of the recurrence in reverse topological order—every subproblem is considered *after* the subproblems it depends on. Thus, *every* dynamic programming algorithm is equivalent to a postorder traversal of the dependency graph of its underlying recurrence!

---

[3]A postordering of the reversal of G is not necessarily the reversal of a postordering of G, even though both are topological orderings of G.

```
MEMOIZE(x):
    if value[x] is undefined
        initialize value[x]

    for all subproblems y of x
        MEMOIZE(y)
        update value[x] based on value[y]
    finalize value[x]
```

```
DFS(v):
    if v is unmarked
        mark v
        PREVISIT(x)
        for all edges v→w
            DFS(w)

        POSTVISIT(x)
```

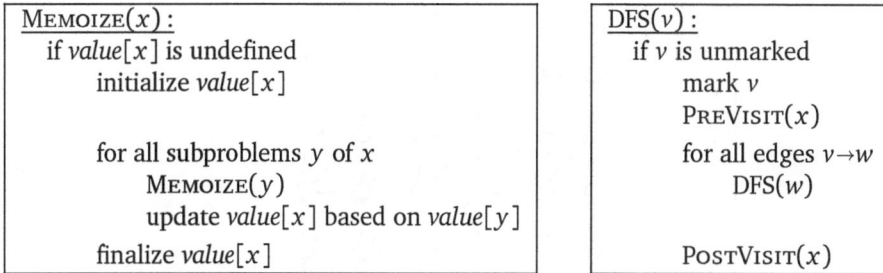

Figure 6.10. Memoized recursion is depth-first search. Depth-first search is memoized recursion.

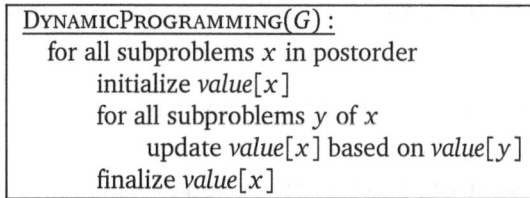

```
DYNAMICPROGRAMMING(G):
    for all subproblems x in postorder
        initialize value[x]
        for all subproblems y of x
            update value[x] based on value[y]
        finalize value[x]
```

Figure 6.11. Dynamic programming is postorder traversal.

However, there are some minor differences between most dynamic programming algorithms and topological sort. First, in most dynamic programming algorithms, the dependency graph is *implicit*—the nodes and edges are not explicitly stored in memory, but rather are encoded by the underlying recurrence. But this difference really is minor; as long as we can enumerate recursive subproblems in constant time each, we can traverse the dependency graph exactly *as if* it were explicitly stored in an adjacency list.

More significantly, most dynamic programming recurrences have highly structured dependency graphs. For example, as we discussed in Chapter 5, the dependency graph for the edit distance recurrence is a regular grid with diagonals, and the dependency graph for optimal binary search trees is an upper triangular grid with all possible rightward and upward edges. This regular structure allows us to hard-wire a suitable evaluation order directly into the algorithm, typically as a collection of nested loops, so there is no need to topologically sort the dependency graph at run time. We previously called the reverse topological order an *evaluation order*.

Dynamic Programming in Dags

Conversely, we can use depth-first search to build dynamic programming algorithms for problems with less structured dependency graphs. For example, consider the **longest path** problem, which asks for the path of *maximum* total weight from one node s to another node t in a directed graph G with weighted edges. In general directed graphs, the longest path problem is NP-hard (by an easy reduction from the traveling salesman problem; see Chapter 12), but it is

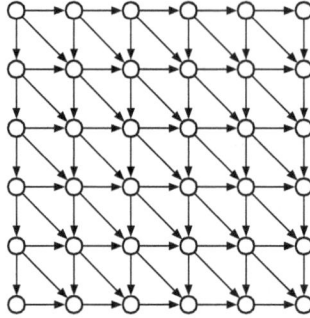

Figure 6.12. The dependency **dag** of the edit distance recurrence.

easy to if the input graph G is acyclic, we can compute the longest path in G in linear time, as follows.

Fix the target vertex t, and for any node v, let **LLP(v)** denote the Length of the Longest Path in G from v to t. If G is a dag, this function satisfies the recurrence

$$LLP(v) = \begin{cases} 0 & \text{if } v = t, \\ \max\left\{\ell(v{\to}w) + LLP(w) \mid v{\to}w \in E\right\} & \text{otherwise,} \end{cases}$$

where $\ell(v{\to}w)$ denotes the given weight ("length") of edge $v{\to}w$, and $\max\varnothing = -\infty$. In particular, if v is a *sink* but not equal to t, then $LLP(v) = -\infty$.

The dependency graph for this recurrence is the input graph G itself: subproblem $LLP(v)$ depends on subproblem $LLP(w)$ if and only if $v{\to}w$ is an edge in G. Thus, we can evaluate this recursive function in $O(V + E)$ time by performing a depth-first search of G, starting at s. The algorithm memoizes each length $LLP(v)$ into an extra field in the corresponding node v.

LONGESTPATH(v, t):
    if $v = t$
        return 0
    if $v.LLP$ is undefined
        $v.LLP \leftarrow -\infty$
        for each edge $v{\to}w$
            $v.LLP \leftarrow \max\left\{v.LLP, \ell(v{\to}w) + \text{LONGESTPATH}(w, t)\right\}$
        return $v.LLP$

In principle, we can transform this memoized recursive algorithm into a dynamic programming algorithm via topological sort:

```
LONGESTPATH(s, t):
    for each node v in postorder
        if v = t
            v.LLP ← 0
        else
            v.LLP ← −∞
            for each edge v→w
                v.LLP ← max {v.LLP, ℓ(v→w) + w.LLP}
    return s.LLP
```

These two algorithms are arguably identical—the recursion in the first algorithm and the for-loop in the second algorithm represent the "same" depth-first search! Choosing one of these formulations over the other is entirely a matter of convenience.

Almost any dynamic programming problem that asks for an optimal *sequence* of decisions can be recast as finding an optimal *path* in some associated dag. For example, the text segmentation, subset sum, longest increasing subsequence, and edit distance problems we considered in Chapters 2 and 3 can all be reformulated as finding either a longest path or a shortest path in a dag, possibly with weighted vertices or edges. In each case, the dag in question is the dependency graph of the underlying recurrence. On the other hand, "tree-shaped" dynamic programming problems, like finding optimal binary search trees or maximum independent sets in trees, cannot be recast as finding an optimal *path* in a dag.

6.5 Strong Connectivity

Let's go back to the proper definition of connectivity in directed graphs. Recall that one vertex u can *reach* another vertex v in a directed graph G if G contains a directed path from u to v, and that $reach(u)$ denotes the set of all vertices that u can reach. Two vertices u and v are **strongly connected** if u can reach v and v can reach u. A directed graph is strongly connected if and only if every pair of vertices is strongly connected.

Tedious definition-chasing implies that strong connectivity is an equivalence relation over the set of vertices of any directed graph, just like connectivity in undirected graphs. The equivalence classes of this relation are called the **strongly connected components**—or more simply, the **strong components**—of G. Equivalently, a strong component of G is a maximal strongly connected subgraph of G. A directed graph G is strongly connected if and only if G has exactly one strong component; at the other extreme, G is a dag if and only if every strong component of G consists of a single vertex.

The **strong component graph scc(G)** is another directed graph obtained from G by contracting each strong component to a single vertex and collapsing parallel edges. (The strong component graph is sometimes also called the *meta-graph* or *condensation* of G.) It's not hard to prove (hint, hint) that $scc(G)$ is always a dag. Thus, at least in principle, it is possible to topologically order the strong components of G; that is, the vertices can be ordered so that every *back* edge joins two edges in the same strong component.

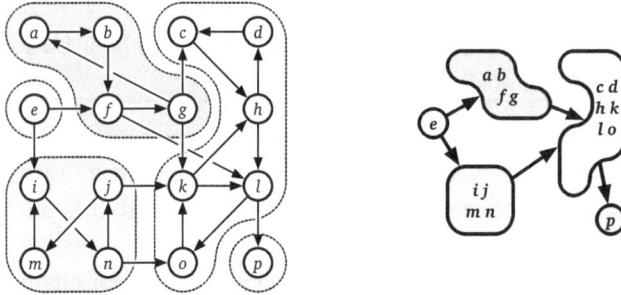

Figure 6.13. The strong components of a graph G and the strong component graph $scc(G)$.

It is straightforward to compute the strong component of a single vertex v in $O(V + E)$ time. First we compute $reach(v)$ via whatever-first search. Then we compute $reach^{-1}(v) = \{u \mid v \in reach(u)\}$ by searching the reversal of G. Finally, the strong component of v is the intersection $reach(v) \cap reach^{-1}(v)$. In particular, we can determine whether the entire graph is strongly connected in $O(V + E)$ time.

Similarly, we can compute *all* the strong components in a directed graph by combining the previous algorithm with our standard wrapper function. However, the resulting algorithm runs in $O(VE)$ time; there are at most V strong components, and each requires $O(E)$ time to discover, even when the graph is a dag. Surely we can do better! After all, we only need $O(V + E)$ time to decide whether every strong component is a single vertex.

6.6 Strong Components in Linear Time

In fact, there are several algorithms to compute strong components in $O(V + E)$ time, all of which rely on the following observation.

Lemma 6.2. *Fix a depth-first traversal of any directed graph G. Each strong component C of G contains exactly one node that does not have a parent in C. (Either this node has a parent in another strong component, or it has no parent.)*

Proof: Let C be an arbitrary strong component of G. Consider any path from one vertex $v \in C$ to another vertex $w \in C$. Every vertex on this path can reach w, and thus can reach every vertex in C; symmetrically, every node on this path can be reached by v, and thus can be reached by every vertex in C. We conclude that every vertex on this path is also in C.

Let v be the vertex in C with the earliest starting time. If v has a parent, then $parent(v)$ starts before v and thus cannot be in C.

Now let w be another vertex in C. Just before DFS(v) is called, every vertex in C is new, so there is a path of new vertices from v to w. Lemma 6.1 now implies that w is a descendant of v in the depth-first forest. Every vertex on the path of tree edges v to w lies in C; in particular, $parent(w) \in C$. □

The previous lemma implies that each strong component of a directed graph G defines a connected subtree of any depth-first forest of G. In particular, for any strong component C, the vertex in C with the earliest starting time is the lowest common ancestor of all vertices in C; we call this vertex the **root** of C.

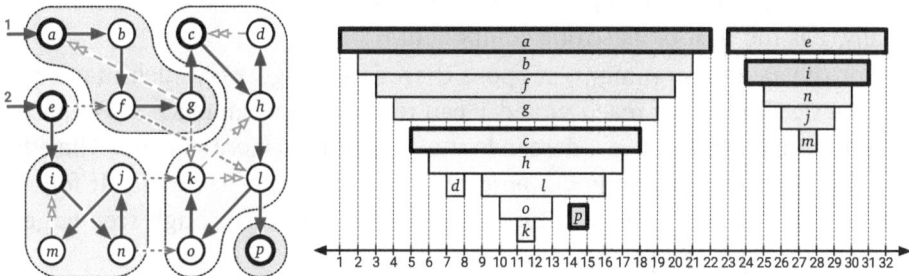

Figure 6.14. Strong components are contiguous in the depth-first forest.

I'll present two algorithms, both of which follow the same intuitive outline. Let C be any strong component of G that is a sink in $scc(G)$; we call C a **sink component**. Equivalently, C is a sink component if the reach of any vertex in C is precisely C. We can find all the strong components in G by repeatedly finding a vertex v in some sink component (somehow), finding the vertices reachable from v, and removing that sink component from the input graph, until no vertices remain. This isn't quite an algorithm yet, because it's not clear how to find a vertex in a sink component!

```
STRONGCOMPONENTS(G):
    count ← 0
    while G is non-empty
        C ← ∅
        count ← count + 1
        v ← any vertex in a sink component of G    ⟨⟨Magic!⟩⟩
        for all vertices w in reach(v)
            w.label ← count
            add w to C
        remove C and its incoming edges from G
```

Figure 6.15. Almost an algorithm to compute strong components.

Kosaraju and Sharir's Algorithm

At first glance, finding a vertex in a sink component *quickly* seems quite difficult. However, it's actually quite easy to find a vertex in a *source* component—a strong component of G that corresponds to a *source* in $scc(G)$—using depth-first search.

Lemma 6.3. *The last vertex in any postordering of G lies in a source component of G.*

Proof: Fix a depth-first traversal of G, and let v be the last vertex in the resulting postordering. Then DFS(v) must be the last direct call to DFS made by the wrapper algorithm DFSALL. Moreover, v is the root of one of the trees in the depth-first forest, so any node x with $x.post > v.pre$ is a descendant of v. Finally, v is the root of its strong component C.

For the sake of argument, suppose there is an edge $x \rightarrow y$ such that $x \notin C$ and $y \in C$. Then x can reach y, and y can reach v, so x can reach v. Because v is the root of C, vertex y is a descendant of v, and thus $v.pre < y.pre$. The edge $x \rightarrow y$ guarantees that $y.pre < x.post$ and therefore $v.pre < x.post$. It follows that x is a descendant of v. But then v can reach x (through tree edges), contradicting our assumption that $x \notin C$. □

It is easy to check (hint, hint) that $rev(scc(G)) = scc(rev(G))$ for any directed graph G. Thus, the *last* vertex in a postordering of $rev(G)$ lies in a *sink* component of the original graph G. Thus, if we traverse the graph a second time, where the wrapper function follows a reverse postordering of $rev(G)$, then each call to DFS visits exactly one strong component of G.[4]

Putting everything together, we obtain the algorithm shown in Figure 6.16, which counts and labels the strong components of any directed graph in $O(V+E)$ time. This algorithm was discovered (but never published) by Rao Kosaraju in 1978, and later independently rediscovered by Micha Sharir in 1981.[5] The Kosaraju-Sharir algorithm has two phases. The first phase performs a depth-first search of $rev(G)$, pushing each vertex onto a stack when it is finished. In the second phase, we perform a *whatever*-first traversal of the original graph G, considering vertices in the order they appear on the stack. The algorithm labels each vertex with the root of its strong component (with respect to the second depth-first traversal).

Figure 6.17 shows the Kosaraju-Sharir algorithm running on our example graph. With only minor modifications to the algorithm, we can also compute the strong component graph $scc(G)$ in $O(V + E)$ time.

---

[4]Again: A reverse postordering of $rev(G)$ is not the same as a postordering of G.

[5]There are rumors that the same algorithm appears in the Russian literature even before Kosaraju, but I haven't found a reliable source for that rumor yet.

```
KOSARAJUSHARIR(G):
    S ← new empty stack
    for all vertices v
        unmark v
        v.root ← NONE

    《Phase 1: Push in postorder in rev(G)》
    for all vertices v
        if v is unmarked
            PUSHPOSTREVDFS(v, S)

    《Phase 2: DFS again in stack order》
    while S is non-empty
        v ← POP(S)
        if v.root = NONE
            LABELONEDFS(v, v)
```

```
PUSHPOSTREVDFS(v, S):
    mark v
    for each edge u→v    《Reversed!》
        if u is unmarked
            PUSHPOSTREVDFS(u, S)
    PUSH(v, S)
```

```
LABELONEDFS(v, r):
    v.root ← r
    for each edge v→w
        if w.root = NONE
            LABELONEDFS(w, r)
```

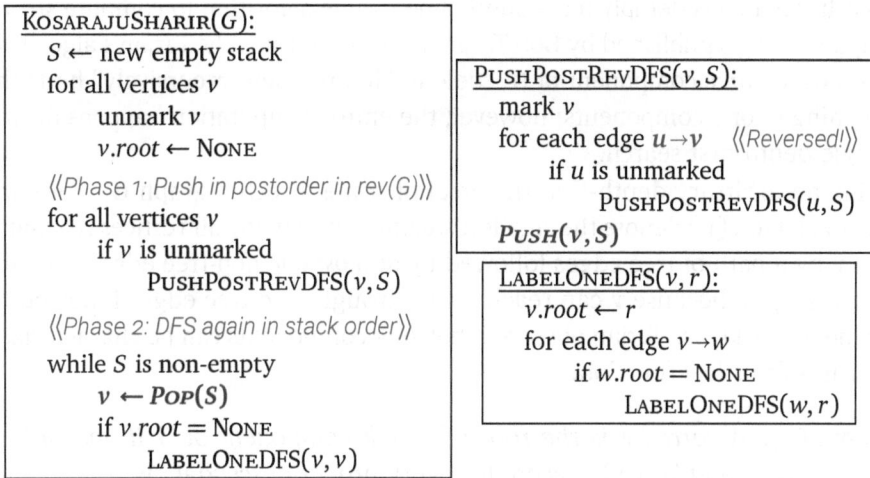

Figure 6.16. The Kosaraju-Sharir strong components algorithm

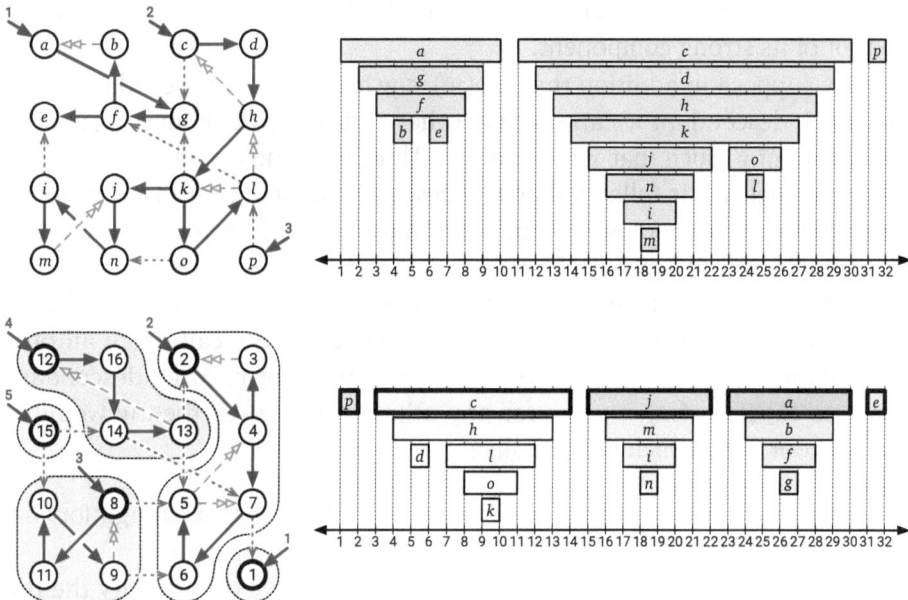

Figure 6.17. The Kosaraju-Sharir algorithm in action. Top: Depth-first traversal of the reversed graph. Bottom: Depth-first traversal of the original graph, visiting root vertices in reversed postorder from the first traversal.

♥Tarjan's Algorithm

An earlier but considerably more subtle linear-time algorithm to compute strong components was published by Bob Tarjan in 1972.[6] Intuitively, Tarjan's algorithm identifies a *source* component of G, "deletes" it, and then "recursively" finds the remaining strong components; however, the entire computation happens during a single depth-first search.

Fix an arbitrary depth-first traversal of some directed graph G. For each vertex v, let ***low(v)*** denote the smallest *starting time* among all vertices reachable from v by a path of tree edges followed by *at most one* non-tree edge. Trivially, $low(v) \leq v.pre$, because v can reach itself through zero tree edges followed by zero non-tree edges. Tarjan observed that sink components can be characterized in terms of this *low* function.

Lemma 6.4. *A vertex v is the root of a sink component of G if and only if $low(v) = v.pre$ and $low(w) < w.pre$ for every proper descendant w of v.*

Proof: First, let v be a vertex such that $low(v) = v.pre$. Then there is no edge $w \rightarrow x$ where w is a descendant of v and $x.pre < v.pre$. On the other hand, v cannot reach any vertex y such that $y.pre > v.post$. It follows that v can reach only its descendants, and therefore any descendant of v can reach only descendants of v. In particular, v cannot reach its parent (if it has one), so v is the root of its strong component.

Now suppose in addition that $low(w) < w.pre$ for every descendant w of v. Then each descendant w can reach another vertex x (which must be another descendant of v) such that $x.pre < w.pre$. Thus, by induction, every descendant of v can reach v. It follows that the descendants of v comprise the strong component C whose root is v. Moreover, C must be a sink component, because v cannot reach any vertex outside of C.

On the other hand, suppose v is the root of a sink component C. Then v can reach another vertex w if and only if $w \in C$. But v can reach all of its descendants, and every vertex in C is a descendant of v, so v's descendants comprise C. If $low(w) = w.pre$ for any other node $w \in C$, then w would be another root of C, which is impossible. □

Computing $low(v)$ for every vertex v via depth-first search is straightforward; see Figure 6.18.

Lemma 6.4 implies that after running FindLow, we can identify the root of *every* sink component in $O(V + E)$ time (by a global whatever-first search),

---

[6]According to legend, Kosaraju apparently discovered his algorithm *during* an algorithms lecture. He was supposed to present Tarjan's algorithm, but he forgot his notes, so he had to make up something else on the fly. The only aspect of this story that I find surprising is that nobody tells it about Sharir or Tarjan.

```
FINDLOWDFS(v):
    mark v
    clock ← clock + 1
    v.pre ← clock
    v.low ← v.pre
    for each edge v→w
        if w is unmarked
            FINDLOWDFS(w)
            v.low ← min{v.low, w.low}
        else
            v.low ← min{v.low, w.pre}
```

```
FINDLOW(G):
    clock ← 0
    for all vertices v
        unmark v
    for all vertices v
        if v is unmarked
            FINDLOWDFS(v)
```

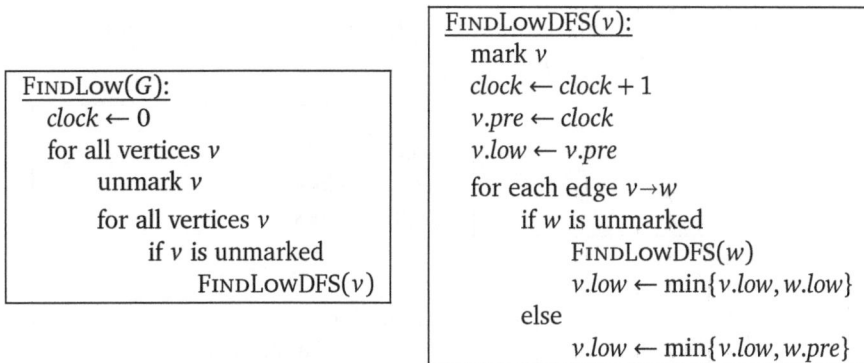

Figure 6.18. Computing *low(v)* for every vertex *v*.

and then mark and delete those sink components in $O(V + E)$ additional time (by calling whatever-first search at each root), and then recurse. Unfortunately, the resulting algorithm might require V iterations, each removing only a single vertex, naively giving us a total running time of $O(VE)$.

To speed up this strategy, Tarjan's algorithm maintains an auxiliary stack of vertices (separate from the recursion stack). Whenever we start a new vertex v, we push it onto the stack. Whenever we finish a vertex v, we compare $v.low$ with $v.pre$. Then the *first* time we discover that $v.low = v.pre$, we know three things:

- Vertex v is the root of a sink component C.
- All vertices in C appear consecutively at the top of the auxiliary stack.
- The *deepest* vertex in C on the auxiliary stack is v.

At this point, we can identify the vertices in C by popping them off the auxiliary stack one by one, stopping when we pop v.

We could delete the vertices in C and recursively compute the strong components of the remaining graph, but that would be wasteful, because we would repeat *verbatim* all computation done before visiting v. Instead, we *label* each vertex in C, identifying v as the root of its strong component, and then ignore labeled vertices for the rest of the depth-first search. Formally, this modification changes the definition of *low(v)* to the smallest starting time among all vertices **in the same strong component as v** that v can reach by a path of tree edges followed by at most one non-tree edge. But to prove correctness, it's easier to observe that ignoring labeled vertices leads the algorithm to exactly the same behavior as actually deleting them.

Finally, Tarjan's algorithm is shown in Figure 6.19, with the necessary modifications from FINDLOW (Figure 6.18) indicated in bold red. The running time of the algorithm can be split into two parts. Each vertex is pushed onto S once and popped off S once, so the total time spent maintaining the auxiliary stack (the red stuff) is $O(V)$. If we ignore the auxiliary stack maintenance, the rest of the algorithm is just a standard depth-first search. We conclude that the algorithm runs in $O(V + E)$ *time*.

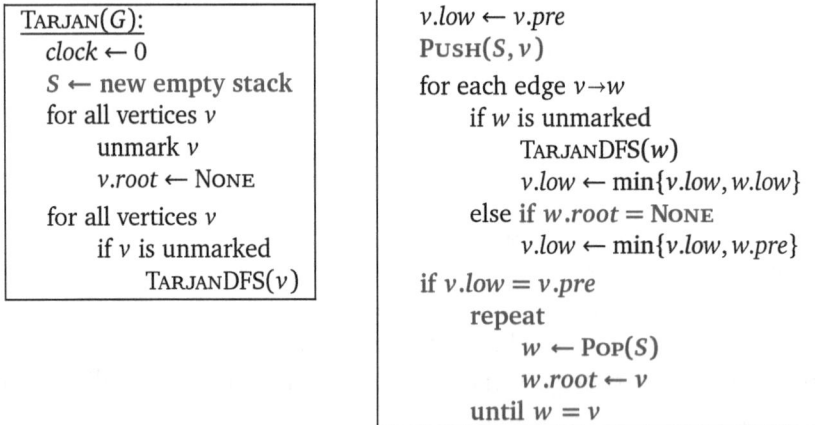

```
TARJAN(G):
    clock ← 0
    S ← new empty stack
    for all vertices v
        unmark v
        v.root ← NONE
    for all vertices v
        if v is unmarked
            TARJANDFS(v)
```

```
TARJANDFS(v):
    mark v
    clock ← clock + 1
    v.pre ← clock
    v.low ← v.pre
    PUSH(S, v)
    for each edge v→w
        if w is unmarked
            TARJANDFS(w)
            v.low ← min{v.low, w.low}
        else if w.root = NONE
            v.low ← min{v.low, w.pre}
    if v.low = v.pre
        repeat
            w ← POP(S)
            w.root ← v
        until w = v
```

Figure 6.19. Tarjan's strong components algorithm.

Exercises

Depth-first search, topological sort, and strong components

0. (a) Describe an algorithm to compute the reversal $rev(G)$ of a directed graph in $O(V + E)$ time.

   (b) Prove that for every directed graph G, the strong component graph $scc(G)$ is acyclic.

   (c) Prove that $scc(rev(G)) = rev(scc(G))$ for every directed graph G.

   (d) Fix an arbitrary directed graph G. For any vertex v of G, let $S(v)$ denote the strong component of G that contains v. For all vertices u and v of G, prove that u can reach v in G if and only if $S(u)$ can reach $S(v)$ in $scc(G)$.

1. A directed graph G is *semi-connected* if, for every pair of vertices u and v, either u is reachable from v or v is reachable from u (or both).

   (a) Give an example of a directed acyclic graph with a unique source that is *not* semi-connected.

   (b) Describe and analyze an algorithm to determine whether a given directed *acyclic* graph is semi-connected.

  (c) Describe and analyze an algorithm to determine whether an arbitrary directed graph is semi-connected.

2. The police department in the city of Sham-Poobanana has made every street in the city one-way. Despite widespread complaints from confused motorists, the mayor claims that it is possible to legally drive from any intersection in Sham-Poobanana to any other intersection.

  (a) The city needs to either verify or refute the mayor's claim. Formalize this problem in terms of graphs, and then describe and analyze an algorithm to solve it.

  (b) After running your algorithm from part (a), the mayor reluctantly admits that she was ~~lying~~ misinformed. Call an intersection x *good* if, for any intersection y that one can legally reach from x, it is possible to legally drive from y back to x. Now the mayor claims that over 95% of the intersections in Sham-Poobanana are good. Describe and analyze an efficient algorithm to verify or refute her claim.

  For full credit, both algorithms should run in linear time.

3. Suppose we are given a directed acyclic graph G with a unique source s and a unique sink t. A vertex $v \notin \{s, t\}$ is called an **(s, t)-cut vertex** if every path from s to t passes through v, or equivalently, if deleting v makes t unreachable from s. Describe and analyze an algorithm to find every (s, t)-cut vertex in G.

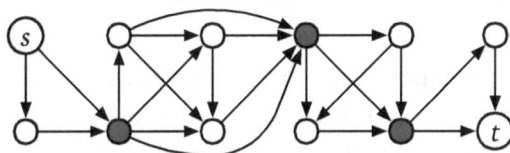

Figure 6.20. A directed acyclic graph with three (s, t)-cut vertices.

4. A vertex v in a connected undirected graph G is called a **cut vertex** if the subgraph $G - v$ (obtained by removing v from G) is disconnected.

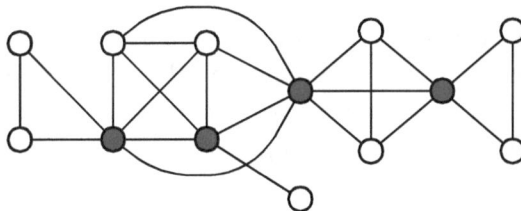

Figure 6.21. An undirected graph with four cut vertices.

(a) Describe a linear-time algorithm that determines, given an undirected graph G and a vertex v, whether v is a cut vertex in G. What is the running time to find all cut vertices by trying your algorithm for each vertex?

(b) Let T be a depth-first spanning tree of an undirected graph G.

    i. Prove that the root of T is a cut vertex of G if and only if it has more than one child in T.

    ii. Prove that a non-root vertex v is a cut vertex of G if and only if at least one descendant (in T) of each child of v (in T) is a neighbor (in G) of some proper ancestor of v (in T).

    [Hint: These claims no longer hold if T not a depth-first spanning tree and/or G is a directed graph.]

(c) Describe an algorithm that identifies every cut vertex in a given undirected graph in $O(V + E)$ time.

5. An edge e in a connected undirected graph G is called a *bridge* (or a *cut edge*) if the subgraph $G - e$ (obtained by removing e from G) is disconnected.

(a) Given G and edge e describe a linear-time algorithm that determines whether e is a bridge or not. What is the running time to find all bridges by trying your algorithm for each edge?

(b) Let T be an arbitrary spanning tree of G. Prove that *every* bridges of G is also an edge in T. This claim implies that G has at most $V - 1$ bridges. How does this information improve your algorithm from part (a) to find all bridges?

(c) Now suppose we root T at an arbitrary vertex r. For any vertex v, let T_v denote the subtree of T rooted at v; for example, $T_r = T$. Let uv be an arbitrary edge of T, where u is the parent of v. Prove that uv is a bridge of G if and only if uv is the only edge in G with exactly one endpoint in T_v.

(d) Describe a linear-time algorithm to identify every bridge in G. *[Hint: Let T be a depth-first spanning tree of G.]*

6. The ***transitive closure*** G^T of a directed graph G is a directed graph with the same vertices as G, that contains any edge $u \rightarrow v$ if and only if there is a directed path from u to v in G. A ***transitive reduction*** of G is a graph with the smallest possible number of edges whose transitive closure is G^T. The same graph may have several transitive reductions.

(a) Describe an efficient algorithm to compute the transitive closure of a given directed graph.

(b) Prove that a directed graph G has a *unique* transitive reduction if and only if G is acyclic.

(c) Describe an efficient algorithm to compute a transitive reduction of a given directed graph.

7. One of the oldest algorithms for exploring arbitrary connected graphs was proposed by Gaston Tarry in 1895, as a systematic procedure for solving mazes.[7] The input to Tarry's algorithm is an undirected graph G; however, for ease of presentation, we formally split each undirected edge uv into two directed edges $u \rightarrow v$ and $v \rightarrow u$. (In an actual implementation, this split is trivial; the algorithm simply uses the given adjacency list for G *as though G were directed*.)

$\underline{\text{TARRY}(G):}$
    unmark all vertices of G
    color all edges of G white
    $s \leftarrow$ any vertex in G
    $\text{RECTARRY}(s)$

$\underline{\text{RECTARRY}(v):}$
    mark v ⟨⟨"visit v"⟩⟩
    if there is a white arc $v \rightarrow w$
        if w is unmarked
            color $w \rightarrow v$ green
        color $v \rightarrow w$ red   ⟩⟨⟨"traverse $v \rightarrow w$"⟩⟩
        $\text{RECTARRY}(w)$
    else if there is a green arc $v \rightarrow w$
        color $v \rightarrow w$ red   ⟩⟨⟨"traverse $v \rightarrow w$"⟩⟩
        $\text{RECTARRY}(w)$

We informally say that Tarry's algorithm "visits" vertex v every time it marks v, and it "traverses" edge $v \rightarrow w$ when it colors that edge red and recursively calls $\text{RECTARRY}(w)$. Unlike our earlier graph traversal algorithm, Tarry's algorithm can mark same vertex multiple times.

(a) Describe how to implement Tarry's algorithm so that it runs in $O(V + E)$ time.

(b) Prove that no directed edge in G is traversed more than once.

(c) When the algorithm visits a vertex v for the kth time, exactly how many edges into v are red, and exactly how many edges out of v are red? *[Hint: Consider the starting vertex s separately from the other vertices.]*

(d) Prove each vertex v is visited at most $\deg(v)$ times, except the starting vertex s, which is visited at most $\deg(s)+1$ times. This claim immediately implies that $\text{TARRY}(G)$ terminates.

(e) Prove that the last vertex visited by $\text{TARRY}(G)$ is the starting vertex s.

---

[7]Even older graph-traversal algorithms were described by Charles Trémaux in 1882, by Christian Wiener in 1873, by Carl Hierholzer in 1873, and (implicitly) by Leonhard Euler in 1736. In particular, Wiener's algorithm is equivalent to depth-first search in connected undirected graphs.

(f) For every vertex v that Tarry(G) visits, prove that all edges into v and out of v are red when Tarry(G) halts. *[Hint: Consider the vertices in the order that they are marked for the first time, starting with s, and prove the claim by induction.]*

(g) Prove that Tarry(G) visits every vertex of G. This claim and the previous claim imply that Tarry(G) traverses every edge of G exactly once.

8. Consider the following variant of Tarry's graph-traversal algorithm; this variant traverses green edges without recoloring them red and assigns two numerical labels to every vertex:

RecTarry2($v, clock$):
  if v is unmarked
    $v.pre \leftarrow clock$; $clock \leftarrow clock + 1$
    mark v
  if there is a white arc $v \to w$
    if w is unmarked
      color $w \to v$ green
    color $v \to w$ red
    RecTarry2($w, clock$)
  else if there is a green arc $v \to w$
    $v.post \leftarrow clock$; $clock \leftarrow clock + 1$
    RecTarry2($w, clock$)

Tarry2(G):
  unmark all vertices of G
  color all edges of G white
  $s \leftarrow$ any vertex in G
  RecTarry2($s, 1$)

Prove or disprove the following claim: When Tarry2(G) halts, the green edges define a spanning tree and the labels $v.pre$ and $v.post$ define a preorder and postorder labeling that are all consistent with a single depth-first search of G. In other words, prove or disprove that Tarry2 produces the same *output* as depth-first search, even though it visits the edges in a completely different order.

9. You have a collection of n lock-boxes and m gold keys. Each key unlocks *at most* one box. However, each box might be unlocked by one key, by multiple keys, or by no keys at all. There are only two ways to open each box once it is locked: Unlock it properly (which requires having one matching key in your hand), or smash it to bits with a hammer.

Your baby brother, who loves playing with shiny objects, has somehow managed to lock all your keys inside the boxes! Luckily, your home security system recorded everything, so you know exactly which keys (if any) are inside each box. You need to get all the keys back out of the boxes, because they are made of gold. Clearly you have to smash at least one box.

(a) Your baby brother has found the hammer and is eagerly eyeing one of the boxes. Describe and analyze an algorithm to determine if it is possible to retrieve all the keys without smashing any box except the one your brother has chosen.

(b) Describe and analyze an algorithm to compute the minimum number of boxes that must be smashed to retrieve all the keys.

10. Suppose you are teaching an algorithms course. In your second midterm, you give your students a drawing of a graph and ask then to indicate a breadth-first search tree and a depth-first search tree rooted at a particular vertex. Unfortunately, once you start grading the exam, you realize that the graph you gave the students has several such spanning trees—far too many to list. Instead, you need a way to tell whether each student's submission is correct!

   In each of the following problems, suppose you are given a connected graph G, a start vertex s, and a spanning tree T of G.

   (a) Suppose G is *undirected*. Describe and analyze an algorithm to decide whether T is a *depth*-first spanning tree rooted at s.

   (b) Suppose G is *undirected*. Describe and analyze an algorithm to decide whether T is a *breadth*-first spanning tree rooted at s. [*Hint: It's not enough for T to be an unweighted shortest-path tree. Yes, this is the right chapter for this problem!*]

   (c) Suppose G is *directed*. Describe and analyze an algorithm to decide whether T is a *breadth*-first spanning tree rooted at s. [*Hint: Solve part (b) first.*]

   (d) Suppose G is *directed*. Describe and analyze an algorithm to decide whether T is a *depth*-first spanning tree rooted at s.

11. Several modern programming languages, including JavaScript, Python, Perl, and Ruby, include a feature called **parallel assignment**, which allows multiple assignment operations to be encoded in a single line of code. For example, the Python code x,y = 0,1 simultaneously sets x to 0 and y to 1. The values of the right-hand side of the assignment are all determined by the *old* values of the variables. Thus, the Python code a,b = b,a swaps the values of a and b, and the following Python code computes the nth Fibonacci number:

```
def fib(n):
    prev, curr = 1, 0
    while n > 0:
        prev, curr, n = curr, prev+curr, n-1
    return curr
```

   Suppose the interpreter you are writing needs to convert every parallel assignment into an equivalent sequence of individual assignments. For example, the parallel assignment a,b = 0,1 can be serialized in either order—either a=0; b=1 or a=0; b=1—but the parallel assignment x,y = x+1,x+y can only be serialized as y=x+y; x=x+1. Serialization may require one or more additional temporary variables; for example, serializing a,b = b,a requires one temporary variable, and serializing x,y = x+y,x-y requires two temporary variables.

(a) Describe an algorithm to determine whether a given parallel assignment can be serialized without additional temporary variables.

(b) Describe an algorithm to determine whether a given parallel assignment can be serialized with *exactly one* additional temporary variable.

Assume that the given parallel assignment involves only simple integer variables (no indirection via pointers or arrays); no variable appears on the left side more than once; and expressions on the right side have no side effects. Don't worry about the details of parsing the assignment statement; just assume (but describe!) an appropriate graph representation.

Dynamic Programming

12. Suppose we are given a directed acyclic graph G whose nodes represent jobs and whose edges represent precedence constraints; that is. each edge $u \to v$ indicates the job u must be completed before job v begins. Each node v also has a weight $T(v)$ indicating the time required to execute job v.

(a) Describe an algorithm to determine the shortest interval of time in which all jobs in G can be executed.

(b) Suppose the first job starts at time 0. Describe an algorithm to determine, for each vertex v, the earliest time when job v can begin.

(c) Now describe an algorithm to determine, for each vertex v, the *latest* time when job v can begin without violating the precedence constraints or increasing the overall completion time (computed in part (a)), assuming that every job except v starts at its earliest start time (computed in part (b)).

13. Let G be a directed acyclic graph with a unique source s and a unique sink t.

(a) A *Hamiltonian path* in G is a directed path in G that contains every vertex in G. Describe an algorithm to determine whether G has a Hamiltonian path.

(b) Suppose the *vertices* of G have weights. Describe an efficient algorithm to find the path from s to t with maximum total weight.

(c) Suppose we are also given an integer ℓ. Describe an efficient algorithm to find the maximum-weight path from s to t that contains at most ℓ edges. (Assume there is at least one such path.)

(d) Suppose some of the vertices of G are marked as *important*, and we are also given an integer k. Describe an efficient algorithm to find the maximum-weight path from s to t that visits at least k important vertices. (Assume there is at least one such path.)

(e) Describe an algorithm to compute the number of paths from s to t in G. (Assume that you can add arbitrarily large integers in $O(1)$ time.)

14. Let G be a directed acyclic graph whose vertices have labels from some fixed alphabet, and let $A[1 .. \ell]$ be a string over the same alphabet. Any directed path in G has a label, which is a string obtained by concatenating the labels of its vertices.

(a) Describe an algorithm that either finds a path in G whose label is A or correctly reports that there is no such path.

(b) Describe an algorithm to find the *number* of paths in G whose label is A. (Assume that you can add arbitrarily large integers in $O(1)$ time.)

(c) Describe an algorithm to find the longest path in G whose label is a subsequence of A.

(d) Describe an algorithm to find the *shortest* path in G whose label is a *supersequence* of A.

(e) Describe an algorithm to find a path in G whose label has minimum edit distance from A.

15. A *polygonal path* is a sequence of line segments joined end-to-end; the endpoints of these line segments are called the **vertices** of the path. The **length** of a polygonal path is the sum of the lengths of its segments. A polygonal path with vertices $(x_1, y_1), (x_2, y_2), \ldots, (x_k, y_k)$ is **monotonically increasing** if $x_i < x_{i+1}$ and $y_i < y_{i+1}$ for every index i—informally, each vertex of the path is above and to the right of its predecessor.

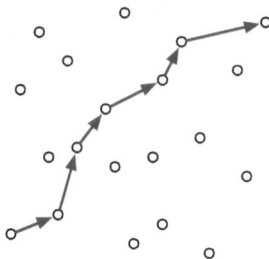

Figure 6.22. A monotonically increasing polygonal path with seven vertices through a set of points

Suppose you are given a set S of n points in the plane, represented as two arrays $X[1..n]$ and $Y[1..n]$. Describe and analyze an algorithm to compute the length of the longest monotonically increasing path with vertices in S. Assume you have a subroutine LENGTH(x, y, x', y') that returns the length of the segment from (x, y) to (x', y').

16. For any two nodes u and w in a directed acyclic graph G, the *interval* $G[u, w]$ is the union of all directed paths in G from u to v. Equivalently, $G[u, w]$ consists of all vertices v such that $v \in reach(u)$ and $w \in reach(x)$, together with all the edges in G connecting those vertices.

    Suppose we are given a directed acyclic graph G, in which every vertex has a numerical weight, which may be positive, negative, or zero.

    (a) Describe an efficient algorithm to find the maximum-weight interval in G, where the weight of each interval is the sum of the weights of its vertices.

    (b) Describe an efficient algorithm to find the largest vertex weight in every interval in G. Your algorithm should compute a two-dimensional array $MaxWt[1..V, 1..V]$ where each entry $MaxWt[u, w]$ is the maximum weight among all vertices in the interval $G[u, w]$. In particular, if $G[u, w]$ is empty, then $MaxWt[u, w]$ should be $-\infty$.

17. Let G be a directed acyclic graph whose vertices have labels from some fixed alphabet. Any directed path in G has a label, which is a string obtained by concatenating the labels of its vertices. Recall that a *palindrome* is a string that is equal to its reversal.

    (a) Describe and analyze an algorithm to find the length of the longest palindrome that is the label of a path in G. For example, given the graph in Figure 6.23, your algorithm should return the integer 6, which is the length of the palindrome HANNAH.

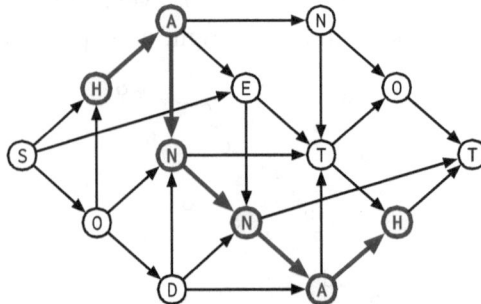

Figure 6.23. A dag whose longest palindrome path label has length 6.

(b) Describe an algorithm to find the longest palindrome that is a sub-sequence of the label of a path in G.

(c) Suppose G has a single source s and a single sink t. Describe an algorithm to find the shortest palindrome that is a supersequence of the label of a path in G from s to t.

18. Suppose you are given two directed acyclic graphs G and H in which every node has a *label* from some finite alphabet; different nodes may have the same label. The label of a *path* in either dag is the string obtained by concatenating the labels of its vertices.

(a) Describe and analyze an algorithm to compute the length of the longest string that is both the label of a path in G and the label of a path in H.

(b) Describe and analyze an algorithm to compute the length of the longest string that is both a subsequence of the label of a path in G and a subsequence of the label of a path in H.

(c) Describe and analyze an algorithm to compute the length of the shortest string that is both a supersequence of the label of a path in G and a supersequence of the label of a path in H. [*Hint: This is easier than it looks.*]

19. Let G be an arbitrary (*not* necessarily acyclic) directed graph in which every vertex v has an integer weight $w(v)$.

(a) Describe an algorithm to find the longest directed path in G whose vertex weights define an increasing sequence.

(b) Describe and analyze an algorithm to determine the maximum-weight vertex reachable from each vertex in G. That is, for each vertex v, your algorithm needs to compute $maxreach(v) := \max\{w(x) \mid x \in reach(v)\}$.

20. (a) Suppose you are given a directed acyclic graph G with n vertices and an integer $k \leq n$. Describe an efficient algorithm to find a set of at most k vertex-disjoint paths that visit every vertex in G.

(b) Now suppose the edges of the input dag G have weights, which may be positive, negative, or zero. Describe an efficient algorithm to find a set of at most k vertex-disjoint paths *with minimum total weight* that visit every vertex in G.

Your algorithms should run in $O(n^{k+c})$ time for some small constant c. A single vertex is a path with weight zero. (We will see a more efficient algorithm for part (a) in Chapter 11.)

21. Kris is a professional rock climber who is competing in the U.S. climbing nationals. The competition requires Kris to use as many holds on the climbing wall as possible, using only transitions that have been explicitly allowed by the route-setter.

    The climbing wall has n holds. Kris is given a list of m pairs (x, y) of holds, each indicating that moving directly from hold x to hold y is allowed; however, moving directly from y to x is not allowed unless the list also includes the pair (y, x). Kris needs to figure out a sequence of allowed transitions that uses as many holds as possible, since each new hold increases his score by one point. The rules allow Kris to choose the first and last hold in his climbing route. The rules also allow him to use each hold as many times as he likes; however, only the first use of each hold increases Kris's score.

    (a) Define the natural graph representing the input. Describe and analyze an algorithm to solve Kris's climbing problem if you are guaranteed that the input graph is a dag.

    (b) Describe and analyze an algorithm to solve Kris's climbing problem with no restrictions on the input graph.

    Both of your algorithms should output the maximum possible score that Kris can earn.

22. There are n galaxies connected by m intergalactic teleport-ways. Each teleport-way joins two galaxies and can be traversed in both directions. However, the company that runs the teleport-ways has established an extremely lucrative cost structure: Anyone can teleport *further* from their home galaxy at no cost whatsoever, but teleporting *toward* their home galaxy is prohibitively expensive.

    Judy has decided to take a sabbatical tour of the universe by visiting as many galaxies as possible, starting at her home galaxy. To save on travel expenses, she wants to teleport away from her home galaxy at every step, except for the very last teleport home.

    (a) Describe and analyze an algorithm to compute the maximum number of galaxies that Judy can visit. Your input consists of an undirected graph G with n vertices and m edges describing the teleport-way network, an integer $1 \le s \le n$ identifying Judy's home galaxy, and an array $D[1..n]$ containing the distances of each galaxy from s.

    ♥(b) Just before embarking on her universal tour, Judy wins the space lottery, giving her just enough money to afford *two* teleports toward her home galaxy. Describe a new algorithm to compute the maximum number of distinct galaxies Judy can visit. She can visit the same galaxy more than once, but crucially, only the first visit counts toward her total.

23. The Doctor and River Song decide to play a game on a directed acyclic graph G, which has one source s and one sink t.[8]

    Each player has a token on one of the vertices of G. At the start of the game, The Doctor's token is on the source vertex s, and River's token is on the sink vertex t. The players alternate turns, with The Doctor moving first. On each of his turns, the Doctor moves his token forward along a directed edge; on each of her turns, River moves her token *backward* along a directed edge.

    If the two tokens ever meet on the same vertex, River wins the game. ("Hello, Sweetie!") If the Doctor's token reaches t or River's token reaches s before the two tokens meet, then the Doctor wins the game.

    Describe and analyze an algorithm to determine who wins this game, assuming both players play perfectly. That is, if the Doctor can win *no matter how River moves*, then your algorithm should output "Doctor", and if River can win *no matter how the Doctor moves*, your algorithm should output "River". (Why are these the only two possibilities?) The input to your algorithm is the graph G.

♣♥24. Let $x = x_1 x_2 \ldots x_n$ be a given n-character string over some finite alphabet Σ, and let A be a deterministic finite-state machine with m states over the same alphabet.

    (a) Describe and analyze an algorithm to compute the length of the longest subsequence of x that is accepted by A. For example, if A accepts the language (AR)* and $x =$ ABRACADABRA, your algorithm should output the number 4, which is the length of the subsequence ARAR.

    (b) Describe and analyze an algorithm to compute the length of the shortest supersequence of x that is accepted by A. For example, if A accepts the language (ABCDR)* and $x =$ ABRACADABRA, your algorithm should output the number 25, which is the length of the supersequence ABCDRABCDRABCDRABCDRABCDR.

    Analyze your algorithms in terms of the length n of the input string, the number m of states in the finite-state machine, and the size of the alphabet Σ.

25. Not *every* dynamic programming algorithm can be modeled as finding an optimal path through a directed acyclic graph, but every dynamic programming algorithm does process some underlying dependency graph in postorder.

---

[8]The labels s and t are abbreviations for the Untempered **S**chism and the **T**ime Vortex, or the **S**hining World of the Seven Systems (also known as Gallifrey) and **T**renzalore, or **S**karo and **T**elos, or **S**omething else **T**imey-wimey. It's all very complicated, never mind.

(a) Suppose we are given a directed acyclic graph G where every node stores a numerical search key. Describe and analyze an algorithm to find the largest binary search tree that is a subgraph of G.

(b) Suppose we are given a directed acyclic graph G and two vertices s and t. Describe an algorithm to compute the number of directed paths in G from s to t. (Assume that any arithmetic operation requires $O(1)$ time.)

(c) Let G be a directed acyclic graph with the following features:

- G has a single source s and several sinks $t_1, t_2, \ldots, t_k$.
- Each edge $v \rightarrow w$ has an associated weight $p(v \rightarrow w)$ between 0 and 1.
- For each non-sink vertex v, the total weight of all edges leaving v is 1; that is, $\sum_w p(v \rightarrow w) = 1$.

The weights $p(v \rightarrow w)$ define a random walk in G from the source s to some sink t_i; after reaching any non-sink vertex v, the walk follows edge $v \rightarrow w$ with probability $p(v \rightarrow w)$. All probabilities are mutually independent. Describe and analyze an algorithm to compute the probability that this random walk reaches sink t_i, for every index i. (Assume that each arithmetic operation takes only $O(1)$ time.)

We must all hang together, gentlemen,
or else we shall most assuredly hang separately.

— Benjamin Franklin, at the signing of the
Declaration of Independence (July 4, 1776)

I remember seeking advice from someone—who could it have been?—about
whether this work was worth submitting for publication; the reasoning it uses is so
very simple.... Fortunately he advised me to go ahead, and many years passed
before another of my publications became as well-known as this very simple one.

— Joseph Kruskal, describing his shortest-spanning-subtree algorithm (1997)

Clean ALL the things!

— Allie Brosh, "This is Why I'll Never be an Adult",
Hyperbole and a Half, June 17, 2010.

7

Minimum Spanning Trees

Suppose we are given a connected, undirected, *weighted* graph. This is a
graph $G = (V, E)$ together with a function $w \colon E \to \mathbb{R}$ that assigns a real *weight*
$w(e)$ to each edge e, which may be positive, negative, or zero. This chapter
describes several algorithms to find the *minimum spanning tree* of G, that is,
the spanning tree T that minimizes the function

$$w(T) := \sum_{e \in T} w(e).$$

See Figure 7.1 for an example.

7.1 Distinct Edge Weights

An annoying subtlety in the problem statement is that weighted graphs can
have more than one spanning tree with the same minimum weight; in particular,
if every edge in G has weight 1, then *every* spanning tree of G is a minimum

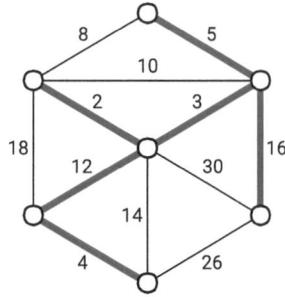

Figure 7.1. A weighted graph and its minimum spanning tree.

spanning tree, with weight $V - 1$. This ambiguity complicates the development of our algorithms; everything would be much simpler if we could simply *assume* that minimum spanning trees are unique.

Fortunately, there is an easy condition that implies the uniqueness we want.

Lemma 7.1. *If all edge weights in a connected graph G are distinct, then G has a unique minimum spanning tree.*[1]

Proof: Let G be an arbitrary connected graph with two minimum spanning trees T and T'; we need to prove that some pair of edges in G have the same weight. The proof is essentially a greedy exchange argument.

Each of our spanning trees must contain an edge that the other tree omits. Let e be a minimum-weight edge in $T \setminus T'$, and let e' be a minimum-weight edge in $T' \setminus T$ (breaking ties arbitrarily). Without loss of generality, suppose $w(e) \le w(e')$.

The subgraph $T' \cup \{e\}$ contains exactly one cycle C, which passes through the edge e. Let e'' be *any* edge of this cycle that is *not* in T. At least one such edge must exist, because T is a tree. (We may or may not have $e'' = e'$.) Because $e \in T$, we immediately have $e'' \ne e$ and therefore $e'' \in T' \setminus T$. It follows that $w(e'') \ge w(e') \ge w(e)$.

Now consider the spanning tree $T'' = T' + e - e''$. (This new tree T'' *might* be equal to T.) We immediately have $w(T'') = w(T') + w(e) - w(e'') \le w(T')$. But T' is a *minimum* spanning tree, so we must have $w(T'') = w(T')$; in other words, T'' is also a minimum spanning tree. We conclude that $w(e) = w(e'')$, which completes the proof. □

If we already have an algorithm that assumes distinct edge weights, we can still run it on graphs where some edges have equal weights, as long as we have a consistent method for breaking ties. One such method uses the following

---

[1] The converse of this lemma is false; a connected graph with repeated edge weights can still have a unique minimum spanning tree. As a trivial example, suppose G is a tree!

algorithm in place of simple weight comparisons. SHORTEREDGE takes as input four integers i, j, k, l, representing four (not necessarily distinct) vertices, and decides which of the two edges (i, j) and (k, l) has "smaller" weight. (Because the input graph undirected, the pairs (i, j) and (j, i) represent the same edge.)

SHORTEREDGE(i, j, k, l)	
if $w(i, j) < w(k, l)$	then return (i, j)
if $w(i, j) > w(k, l)$	then return (k, l)
if $\min(i, j) < \min(k, l)$	then return (i, j)
if $\min(i, j) > \min(k, l)$	then return (k, l)
if $\max(i, j) < \max(k, l)$	then return (i, j)
$\langle\langle$if $\max(i,j) > \max(k,l)\,\rangle\rangle$	return (k, l)

In light of Lemma 7.1 and this tie-breaking rule, we will safely assume for the rest of this chapter that edge weights are *always* distinct, and therefore minimum spanning trees are *always* unique. In particular, we can freely discuss *the* minimum spanning tree with no confusion.

7.2 The Only Minimum Spanning Tree Algorithm

There are many algorithms to compute minimum spanning trees, but almost all of them are instances of the following generic strategy. The situation is similar to graph traversal, where several different algorithms are all variants of the generic traversal algorithm whatever-first search.

The generic minimum spanning tree algorithm maintains an acyclic subgraph F of the input graph G, which we will call the *intermediate spanning forest*. At all times, F satisfies the following invariant:

> F is a subgraph of the minimum spanning tree of G.

Initially, F consists of V one-vertex trees. The generic algorithm connects trees in F by adding certain edges between them. When the algorithm halts, F consists of a single spanning tree; our invariant implies that this must be the minimum spanning tree of G. Obviously, we have to be careful about *which* edges we add to the evolving forest, because not every edge is in the minimum spanning tree.

At any stage of its evolution, the intermediate spanning forest F induces two special types of edges in the rest of the graph.

- An edge is **useless** if it is not an edge of F, but both its endpoints are in the same component of F.
- An edge is **safe** if it is the minimum-weight edge with exactly one endpoint in some component of F.

The same edge could be safe for two different components of F. Some edges of $G \setminus F$ are neither safe nor useless; we call these edges *undecided*.

All minimum spanning tree algorithms are based on two simple observations. The first observation was proved by Robert Prim in 1957 (although it is implicit in several earlier algorithms), and the second is immediate.

Lemma 7.2 (Prim). *The minimum spanning tree of G contains every safe edge.*

Proof: In fact we prove the following stronger statement: For *any* subset S of the vertices of G, the minimum spanning tree of G contains the minimum-weight edge with exactly one endpoint in S. Like the previous lemma, we prove this claim using a greedy exchange argument.

Let S be an arbitrary subset of vertices of G, and let e be the lightest edge with exactly one endpoint in S. (Our assumption that all edge weights are distinct implies that e is unique.) Let T be an arbitrary spanning tree that does *not* contain e; we need to prove that T is *not* the minimum spanning tree of G.

Because T is connected, it contains a path from one endpoint of e to the other. Because this path starts at a vertex of S and ends at a vertex not in S, it must contain at least one edge with exactly one endpoint in S; let e' be *any* such edge. Because T is acyclic, removing e' from T yields a spanning *forest* with exactly two components, one containing each endpoint of e. Thus, adding e to this forest gives us a new spanning tree $T' = T - e' + e$. The definition of e implies $w(e') > w(e)$, which implies that T' has smaller total weight than T. Thus, T is not the minimum spanning tree of G, which completes the proof. □

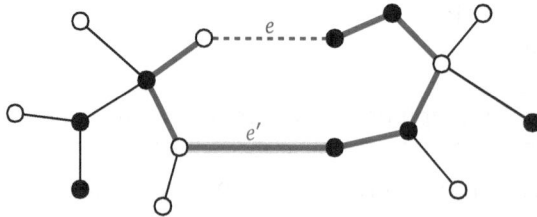

Figure 7.2. Every safe edge is in the minimum spanning tree. Black vertices are in the subset S.

Lemma 7.3. *The minimum spanning tree contains no useless edge.*

Proof: Adding any useless edge to F would introduce a cycle. □

Our generic minimum spanning tree algorithm repeatedly adds *safe* edges to the evolving forest F. If F is not yet connected, there must be at least one safe edge, because the input graph G is connected. Thus, no matter which safe edges we add in each iteration, our generic algorithm eventually connects F. By induction, Lemma 7.2 implies that the resulting tree is in fact the minimum spanning tree. Whenever we add new edges to F, some undecided edges may become safe, and other undecided edges may become useless. (Once an edge becomes useless, it stays useless forever.) To fully specify a particular algorithm, we must describe *which* safe edge(s) to add in each iteration, and how to find those edges.

7.3 Borůvka's Algorithm

The oldest and arguably simplest minimum spanning tree algorithm was discovered by the Czech mathematician Otakar Borůvka in 1926, about a year after Jindřich Saxel asked him how to construct an electrical network connecting several cities using the least amount of wire.[2] The algorithm was rediscovered by Gustav Choquet in 1938, rediscovered again by a team of Polish mathematicians led by Józef Łukaszewicz in 1951, and rediscovered again by George Sollin in 1961. Although Sollin never published his rediscovery, it was carefully described and credited in one of the first textbooks on graph algorithms; as a result, this algorithm is sometimes called "Sollin's algorithm".

The Borůvka / Choquet / Florek-Łukaziewicz-Perkal-Steinhaus-Zubrzycki / Prim / Sollin / Brosh[3] algorithm can be summarized in one line:

> BORŮVKA: Add **ALL** the safe edges and recurse.

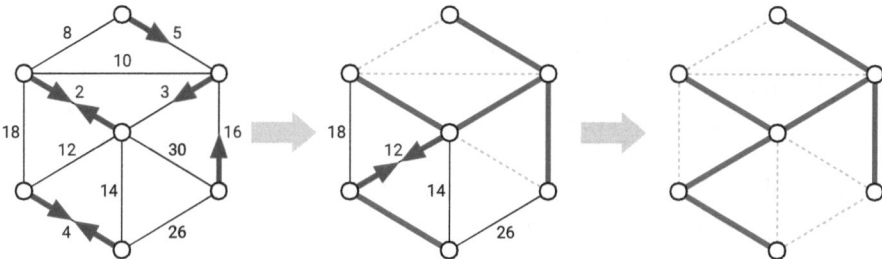

Figure 7.3. Borůvka's algorithm run on the example graph. Thick red edges are in F; dashed edges are useless. Arrows point along each component's safe edge. The algorithm ends after just two iterations.

Here is Borůvka's algorithm in more detail. The algorithm calls the COUNT-ANDLABEL algorithm from Chapter 5 (on page 204) to count the components of F and label each vertex v with an integer $comp(v)$ indicating its component.

---

[2]Saxel was an employee of the West Moravian Power Company, described by Borůvka as "very talented and hard-working", who was later executed by the Nazis as a person of Jewish descent.

[3]Go read everything in *Hyperbole and a Half*. And then go buy the book. And an extra copy for your cat. What's that? You don't have a cat? What kind of a monster are you? Go get a cat, and then buy it an extra copy of *Hyperbole and a Half*.

```
Borůvka(V, E):
    F = (V, ∅)
    count ← CountAndLabel(F)
    while count > 1
        AddAllSafeEdges(E, F, count)
        count ← CountAndLabel(F)
    return F
```

It remains only to describe how to identify and add all the safe edges to F. Suppose F has more than one component, since otherwise we're already done. The following subroutine computes an array $safe[1 .. V]$ of safe edges, where $safe[i]$ is the minimum-weight edge with one endpoint in the ith component of F, by a brute force examination of every edge in G. For each edge uv, if u and v are in the same component, then uv is either useless or already an edge in F. Otherwise, we compare the weight of uv to the weights of $safe[comp(u)]$ and $safe[comp(v)]$ and update the array entries if necessary. Once we have identified all the safe edges, we add each edge $safe[i]$ to F.

```
AddAllSafeEdges(E, F, count):
    for i ← 1 to count
        safe[i] ← Null
    for each edge uv ∈ E
        if comp(u) ≠ comp(v)
            if safe[comp(u)] = Null or w(uv) < w(safe[comp(u)])
                safe[comp(u)] ← uv
            if safe[comp(v)] = Null or w(uv) < w(safe[comp(v)])
                safe[comp(v)] ← uv
    for i ← 1 to count
        add safe[i] to F
```

Each call to CountAndLabel runs in $O(V)$ time, because the forest F has at most $V - 1$ edges. AddAllSafeEdges runs in $O(V + E)$ time, because we spend constant time on each vertex, each edge of G, and each component of F. Because the input graph is connected, we have $V \leq E + 1$. It follows that each iteration of the while loop of Borůvka takes $O(E)$ time.

Each iteration reduces the number of components of F by at least a factor of two—in the worst case, the components of F coalesce in pairs. Because F initially has V components, the while loop iterates at most $O(\log V)$ times. We conclude that the overall running time of Borůvka's algorithm is $O(E \log V)$.

This is the MST Algorithm You Want

Despite its relatively obscure origin, early Western algorithms researchers were aware of Borůvka's algorithm, but dismissed it as being "too complicated".

As a result, despite its simplicity and efficiency, most algorithms and data structures textbooks unfortunately do not even mention Borůvka's algorithm. This omission is a serious mistake; Borůvka's algorithm has several distinct advantages over other classical MST algorithms.

- Borůvka's algorithm often runs faster than its $O(E \log V)$ worst-case running time. The number of components in F can drop by significantly more than a factor of 2 in a single iteration, reducing the number of iterations below the worst-case $\lceil \log_2 V \rceil$.

- A slight reformulation of Borůvka's algorithm (actually closer to Borůvka's original presentation) actually runs in $O(E)$ time for a broad class of interesting graphs, including graphs that can be drawn in the plane without edge crossings. In contrast, the time analysis for the other two algorithms applies to *all* graphs.

- Borůvka's algorithm allows for significant parallelism; in each iteration, each component of F can be handled in a separate independent thread. This implicit parallelism allows for even faster performance on multicore or distributed systems. In contrast, the other two classical MST algorithms are intrinsically serial.

- Several more recent minimum-spanning-tree algorithms are faster even in the worst case than the classical algorithms described here. *All* of these faster algorithms are generalizations of Borůvka's algorithm.

In short, if you ever need to implement a minimum-spanning-tree algorithm, use Borůvka. On the other hand, if you want to *prove things about* minimum spanning trees effectively, you really need to know the next two algorithms as well.

7.4 Jarník's ("Prim's") Algorithm

The next oldest minimum spanning tree algorithm was first described by the Czech mathematician Vojtěch Jarník in a 1929 letter to Borůvka; Jarník published his discovery the following year. The algorithm was independently rediscovered by Joseph Kruskal in 1956, (arguably) by Robert Prim in 1957, by Harry Loberman and Arnold Weinberger in 1957, and finally by Edsger Dijkstra in 1958. Prim, Lobermand and Weinberger, and Dijkstra all (eventually) knew of and even cited Kruskal's paper, but since Kruskal also described two other minimum-spanning-tree algorithms in the same paper, *this* algorithm is usually called "Prim's algorithm", or sometimes "the Prim/Dijkstra algorithm", even though by 1958 Dijkstra already had another algorithm (inappropriately) named after him.

In Jarník's algorithm, the intermediate forest F has only one nontrivial component T; all the other components are isolated vertices. Initially, T consists of a single arbitrary vertex of the graph. The algorithm repeats the following step until T spans the whole graph:

> JARNÍK: Repeatedly add T's safe edge to T.

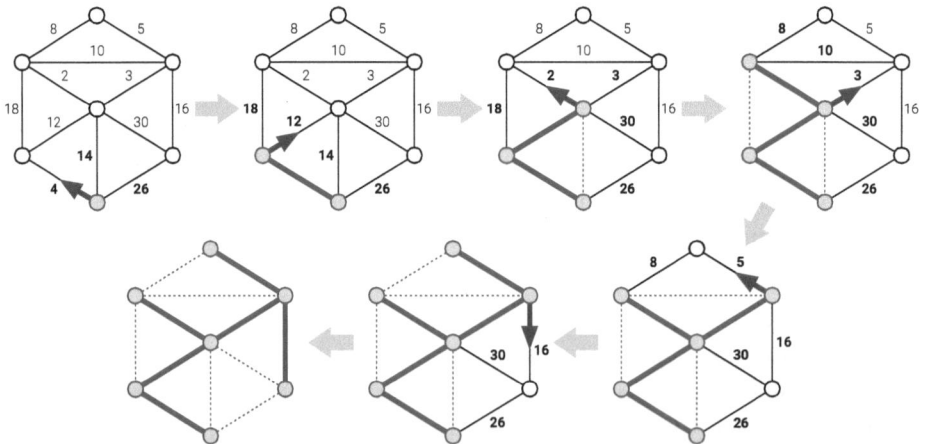

Figure 7.4. Jarník's algorithm run on the example graph, starting with the bottom vertex. At each stage, thick red edges are in T, an arrow points along T's safe edge; and dashed edges are useless.

To implement Jarník's algorithm, we keep all the edges adjacent to T in a priority queue. When we pull the minimum-weight edge out of the priority queue, we first check whether both of its endpoints are in T. If not, we add the edge to T and then add the new neighboring edges to the priority queue. In other words, Jarník's algorithm is a variant of "best-first search", as described at the end of Chapter 5! If we implement the underlying priority queue using a standard binary heap, Jarník's algorithm runs in $O(E \log E) = \boldsymbol{O(E \log V)}$ time.

♥Improving Jarník's Algorithm

We can improve Jarník's algorithm using a more complex priority queue data structure called a *Fibonacci heap*, first described by Michael Fredman and Robert Tarjan in 1984. Just like binary heaps, Fibonacci heaps support the standard priority queue operations INSERT, EXTRACTMIN, and DECREASEKEY. However, unlike standard binary heaps, which require $O(\log n)$ time for every operation, Fibonacci heaps support INSERT and DECREASEKEY in constant *amortized* time. The amortized cost of EXTRACTMIN is still $O(\log n)$.[4]

---

[4]Amortized time is an accounting trick that allows us to ignore infrequent fluctuations in the time for a single data structure operation. A Fibonacci heap can execute any intermixed sequence of I INSERTS, D DECREASEKEYS, and X EXTRACTMINS in $O(I + D + X \log n)$ time, in the worst case. So the *average* INSERT and the *average* DECREASEKEY each take constant time, and the *average* EXTRACTMIN takes $O(\log n)$ time; however, some individual operations may take

To apply this faster data structure, we keep the *vertices* of G in the priority queue instead of edges, where the priority of each vertex v is either the minimum-weight edge between v and the evolving tree T, or ∞ if there is no such edge. We can INSERT all the vertices into the priority queue at the beginning of the algorithm; then, whenever we add a new edge to T, we may need to decrease the priorities of some neighboring vertices.

To make the description easier, we break the algorithm into two parts. JARNÍKINIT initializes the priority queue; JARNÍKLOOP is the main algorithm. The input consists of the vertices and edges of the graph, along with the start vertex s. For each vertex v, we maintain both its priority $priority(v)$ and the incident edge $edge(v)$ such that $w(edge(v)) = priority(v)$.

```
JARNÍK(V, E, s):
    JARNÍKINIT(V, E, s)
    JARNÍKLOOP(V, E, s)
```

```
JARNÍKINIT(V, E, s):
    for each vertex v ∈ V \ {s}
        if vs ∈ E
            edge(v) ← vs
            priority(v) ← w(vs)
        else
            edge(v) ← NULL
            priority(v) ← ∞
        INSERT(v)
```

```
JARNÍKLOOP(V, E, s):
    T ← ({s}, ∅)
    for i ← 1 to |V| − 1
        v ← EXTRACTMIN
        add v and edge(v) to T
        for each neighbor u of v
            if u ∉ T and priority(u) > w(uv)
                edge(u) ← uv
                DECREASEKEY(u, w(uv))
```

Figure 7.5. Jarník's minimum spanning tree algorithm, ready to be used with a Fibonacci heap

The operations INSERT and EXTRACTMIN are each called $O(V)$ times once for each vertex except s, and DECREASEKEY is called $O(E)$ times, at most twice for each edge. Thus, if we use a Fibonacci heap, the improved algorithm runs in $O(E + V \log V)$ *time*, which is faster than Borůvka's algorithm unless $E = O(V)$.

In practice, however, this improvement is rarely faster than the naive implementation using a binary heap, unless the graph is extremely large and dense. The Fibonacci heap algorithms are quite complex, and the hidden constants in both the running time and space are significant—not outrageous, but certainly bigger than the hidden constant 1 in the $O(\log n)$ time bound for binary heap operations.

7.5 Kruskal's Algorithm

The last minimum spanning tree algorithm we'll consider was first described by Joseph Kruskal in 1956, in the same paper where he rediscovered Jarnik's algo-

---

longer in the worst case. Amortization uses *statistical* averaging over the sequence of operations; there is no assumption of randomness here, either in the input data or in the algorithm.

rithm. Kruskal was motivated by "a typewritten translation (of obscure origin)" of Borůvka's original paper that had been "floating around" the Princeton math department. Kruskal found Borůvka's algorithm "unnecessarily elaborate".[5] The same algorithm was rediscovered in 1957 by Harry Loberman and Arnold Weinberger, but somehow avoided being renamed after them.

Like our earlier minimum-spanning tree algorithms, Kruskal's algorithm has a memorable one-line description:

KRUSKAL: Scan all edges by increasing weight; if an edge is safe, add it to F.

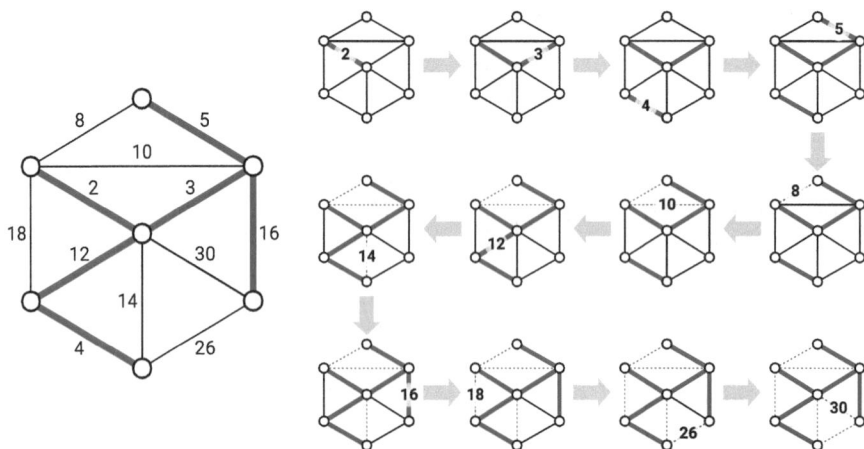

Figure 7.6. Kruskal's algorithm run on the example graph. Thick red edges are in F; thin dashed edges are useless.

The simplest method to scan the edges in increasing weight order is to *sort* the edges by weight, in $O(E \log E)$ time, and then use a simple for-loop over the sorted edge list. As we will see shortly, this preliminary sorting dominates the running time of the algorithm.

Because we examine the edges in order from lightest to heaviest, any edge we examine is safe if and only if its endpoints are in different components of the forest F. Suppose we encounter an edge e that joins two components A and B but is not safe. Then there must be a lighter edge e' with exactly one endpoint in A. But this is impossible, because (inductively) every previously examined edge has both endpoints in the same component of F.

Just as in Borůvka's algorithm, each vertex of F needs to "know" which component of F contains it. Unlike Borůvka's algorithm, however, we do

---

[5]To be fair, Borůvka's first paper *was* unnecessarily elaborate, in part because it was written for mathematicians in the formal language of (linear) algebra, rather than in the language of graphs. Borůvka's followup paper, also published in 1927 but in an electrotechnical journal, was written in plain language for a much broader audience, essentially in its current modern form. Kruskal was apparently unaware of Borůvka's second paper. Stupid Iron Curtain.

not recompute all component labels from scratch every time we add an edge. Instead, when two components are joined by an edge, the smaller component inherits the label of the larger component; that is, we traverse the smaller component (via whatever-first search). This traversal requires $O(1)$ time for each vertex in the smaller component. Each time the component label of a vertex changes, the component of F containing that vertex grows by at least a factor of 2; thus, each vertex label changes at most $O(\log V)$ times. It follows that the *total* time spent updating vertex labels is only $O(V \log V)$.

More generally, Kruskal's algorithm maintains a partition of the vertices of G into disjoint subsets (in our case, the components of F), using a data structure that supports the following operations:

- MAKESET(v) — Create a set containing only the vertex v.
- FIND(v) — Return an identifier unique to the set containing v.
- UNION(u, v) — Replace the sets containing u and v with their union. (This operation decreases the number of sets.)

Here's a complete description of Kruskal's algorithm in terms of these operations:

KRUSKAL(V, E):
    sort E by increasing weight
    $F \leftarrow (V, \varnothing)$
    for each vertex $v \in V$
        MAKESET(v)
    for $i \leftarrow 1$ to $|E|$
        $uv \leftarrow$ ith lightest edge in E
        if FIND(u) $\neq$ FIND(v)
            UNION(u, v)
            add uv to F
    return F

After the initial sort, the algorithm performs exactly V MAKESET operations (one for each vertex), $2E$ FIND operations (two for each edge), and $V - 1$ UNION operations (one for each edge in the minimum spanning tree). We just described a disjoint-set data structure for which MAKESET and FIND require $O(1)$ time, and UNION runs in $O(\log V)$ *amortized* time. Using this implementation, the total time spent maintaining the set partition is $O(E + V \log V)$.[6]

But recall that we already need $O(E \log E) = O(E \log V)$ time just to sort the edges. Because this is larger than the time spent maintaining the UNION-FIND data structure, the overall running time of Kruskal's algorithm is $O(E \log V)$,

---

[6] A different disjoint-set data structure, which uses a strategy called *union-by-rank with path compression*, performs each UNION or FIND in $O(\alpha(V))$ amortized time, where α is the almost-but-not-quite-constant *inverse Ackerman function*. If you don't feel like consulting Wikipedia, just think of $\alpha(V)$ as 4. Using this implementation, the total time spent maintaining the set partition is $O(E\alpha(V))$, which is slightly faster when V is large and E is very close to V.

exactly the same as Borůvka's algorithm, or Jarník's algorithm with a normal (non-Fibonacci) heap.

Exercises

1. Let $G = (V, E)$ be an arbitrary connected graph with weighted edges.

   (a) Prove that for any cycle in G, the minimum spanning tree of G *excludes* the maximum-weight edge in that cycle.

   (b) Prove or disprove: The minimum spanning tree of G includes the minimum-weight edge in *every* cycle in G.

2. Throughout this chapter, we assumed that no two edges in the input graph have equal weights, which implies that the minimum spanning tree is unique. In fact, a weaker condition on the edge weights implies MST uniqueness.

   (a) Describe an edge-weighted graph that has a unique minimum spanning tree, even though two edges have equal weights.

   (b) Prove that an edge-weighted graph G has a *unique* minimum spanning tree if and only if the following conditions hold:

   - For any partition of the vertices of G into two subsets, the minimum-weight edge with one endpoint in each subset is unique.
   - The maximum-weight edge in any cycle of G is unique.

   (c) Describe and analyze an algorithm to determine whether or not a graph has a unique minimum spanning tree.

3. Most classical minimum-spanning-tree algorithms use the notions of "safe" and "useless" edges described in the text, but there is an alternate formulation. Let G be a weighted undirected graph, where the edge weights are distinct. We say that an edge e is ***dangerous*** if it is the longest edge in some cycle in G, and ***useful*** if it does not lie in any cycle in G.

   (a) Prove that the minimum spanning tree of G contains every useful edge.

   (b) Prove that the minimum spanning tree of G does not contain any dangerous edge.

   (c) Describe and analyze an efficient implementation of the following algorithm, first described by Joseph Kruskal in the same 1956 paper where he proposed "Kruskal's algorithm". Examine the edges of G in *decreasing* order; if an edge is dangerous, remove it from G. [*Hint: It won't be as fast as Kruskal's usual algorithm.*]

4. (a) Describe and analyze an algorithm to compute the *maximum*-weight spanning tree of a given edge-weighted graph.

(b) A *feedback edge set* of an undirected graph G is a subset F of the edges such that every cycle in G contains at least one edge in F. In other words, removing every edge in F makes the graph G acyclic. Describe and analyze a fast algorithm to compute the minimum-weight feedback edge set of a given edge-weighted graph.

5. Suppose we are given both an undirected graph G with weighted edges and a minimum spanning tree T of G.

   (a) Describe an algorithm to update the minimum spanning tree when the weight of a single edge e is decreased.

   (b) Describe an algorithm to update the minimum spanning tree when the weight of a single edge e is increased.

   In both cases, the input to your algorithm is the edge e and its new weight; your algorithms should modify T so that it is still a minimum spanning tree. [*Hint: Consider the cases $e \in T$ and $e \notin T$ separately.*]

6. (a) Describe and analyze an algorithm to find the *second smallest spanning tree* of a given graph G, that is, the spanning tree of G with smallest total weight except for the minimum spanning tree.

   ♥(b) Describe and analyze an efficient algorithm to compute, given a weighted undirected graph G and an integer k, the k spanning trees of G with smallest weight.

7. A graph $G = (V, E)$ is *dense* if $E = \Theta(V^2)$. Describe a modification of Jarník's minimum-spanning tree algorithm that runs in $O(V^2)$ time (independent of E) when the input graph is dense, using only elementary data structures—in particular, *without* using Fibonacci heaps. This variant of Jarník's algorithm was first described by Edsger Dijkstra in 1958.

8. Minimum-spanning tree algorithms are often formulated using an operation called *edge contraction*. To contract the edge uv, we insert a new node, redirect any edge incident to u or v (except uv) to this new node, and then delete u and v. After contraction, there may be multiple parallel edges between the new node and other nodes in the graph; we remove all but the lightest edge between any two nodes.

   The three classical minimum-spanning tree algorithms described in this chapter can all be expressed cleanly in terms of contraction as follows. All three algorithms start by making a clean copy G' of the input graph G and then repeatedly contract safe edges in G'; the minimum spanning tree consists of the contracted edges.

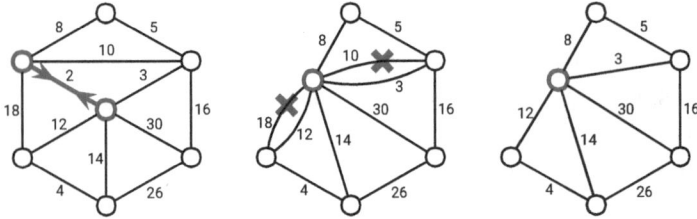

Figure 7.7. Contracting an edge and removing redundant parallel edges.

- Borůvka: Mark the lightest edge leaving each vertex, contract all marked edges, and recurse.
- Jarník: Repeatedly contract the lightest edge incident to some fixed root vertex.
- Kruskal: Repeatedly contract the lightest edge in the graph.

(a) Describe an algorithm to execute a single pass of Borůvka's contraction algorithm in $O(V + E)$ time. The input graph is represented in an adjacency list.

(b) Consider an algorithm that first performs k passes of Borůvka's contraction algorithm, and then runs Jarník's algorithm (*with* a Fibonacci heap) on the resulting contracted graph.

    i. What is the running time of this hybrid algorithm, as a function of V, E, and k?

    ii. For which value of k is this running time minimized? What is the resulting running time?

(c) Call a family of graphs *nice* if it has the following properties:
- Contracting an edge of a nice graph yields another nice graph.
- Every nice graph with V vertices has only $O(V)$ edges.

For example, planar graphs—graphs that can be drawn in the plane with no crossing edges—are nice. Contracting any edge of a planar graph leaves a smaller planar graph, and Euler's formula implies that every planar graph with V vertices has at most $3V - 6$ edges.

Prove that Borůvka's contraction algorithm computes the minimum spanning tree of any nice graph in $O(V)$ time.

9. Consider a path between two vertices s and t in a undirected weighted graph G. The *width* of this path is the minimum weight of any edge in the path. The *bottleneck distance* between s and t is the width of the widest path from s to t. (If there are no paths from s to t, the bottleneck distance is $-\infty$; on the other hand, the bottleneck distance from s to itself is ∞.)

(a) Prove that the *maximum* spanning tree of G contains widest paths between *every* pair of vertices.

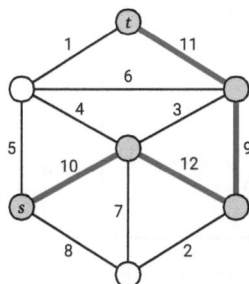

The bottleneck distance between s and t is 9.

(b) Describe an algorithm to solve the following problem in $O(V + E)$ time: Given a undirected weighted graph G, two vertices s and t, and a weight W, is the bottleneck distance between s and t at most W?

(c) Suppose B is the bottleneck distance between s and t.

   i. Prove that deleting any edge with weight less than B does not change the bottleneck distance between s and t.

   ii. Prove that *contracting* any edge with weight *greater* than B does not change the bottleneck distance between s and t. (If contraction creates parallel edges, delete all but the *heaviest* edge between each pair of nodes.)

♥(d) Describe an algorithm to compute a minimum-bottleneck path between s and t in $O(V + E)$ time. [*Hint: Start by finding the median-weight edge in G.*]

10. Borůvka's algorithm can be reformulated to use a standard disjoint-set data structure to identify safe edges, just like Kruskal's algorithm, instead of explicitly counting and labeling components of the evolving spanning forest F in each iteration.

   In this variant, each component of F is represented by an *up-tree*; each vertex v stores a pointer *parent*(v) to its parent, or to v itself if v is the root of its up-tree. The subroutine FIND(v) returns the root of v's up-tree, but also applies *path compression*, reassigning all parent pointers from v to the root to point directly to the root, to speed up future FIND operations.[7] The subroutine UNION combines two up-trees into one by making one of the two root nodes the parent of the other.[8]

---

[7] Path compression is a form of memoization!
[8] Normally, UNION is implemented more carefully to ensure that the root of the larger or older up-tree does not change; however, those details don't matter here.

```
FIND(v):
    if parent(v) = v
        return v
    else
        v̄ ← FIND(parent(v))
        parent(v) ← v̄
        return v̄
```

```
UNION(u, v):
    ū ← FIND(u)
    v̄ ← FIND(v)
    either
        parent(ū) ← v̄
    or
        parent(v̄) ← ū
```

In the modified version of Borůvka's algorithm, in addition to the parent pointers, the root vertex $\bar{v}$ of each component of F maintains an edge $safe(\bar{v})$, which (at the end of FINDSAFEEDGES) is the lightest edge with one endpoint in that component.

```
FINDSAFEEDGES(V, E):
    for each vertex v ∈ V
        safe(v) ← NULL
    found ← FALSE
    for each edge uv ∈ E
        ū ← FIND(u)
        v̄ ← FIND(v)
        if ū ≠ v̄
            if safe(ū) = NULL or w(uv) < w(safe(ū))
                safe(ū) ← uv
            if safe(v̄) = NULL or w(uv) < w(safe(v̄))
                safe(v̄) ← uv
            found ← TRUE
    return found
```

```
ADDSAFEEDGES(V, E, F):
    for each vertex v ∈ V
        if safe(v) ≠ NULL
            xy ← safe(v)
            if FIND(x) ≠ FIND(y)
                UNION(x, y)
                add xy to F
```

```
BORŮVKA(V, E):
    F = ∅
    for each vertex v ∈ V
        parent(v) ← v
    while FINDSAFEEDGES(V, E)
        ADDSAFEEDGES(V, E, F)
    return F
```

Prove that each call to FINDSAFEEDGES and ADDSAFEEDGES requires only $O(E)$ time. *[Hint: What is the depth of the up-trees when FINDSAFEEDGES ends?]* It follows that this variant of BORŮVKA also runs in $O(E \log V)$ time.

I study my Bible as I gather apples. First I shake the whole tree, that the ripest might fall. Then I climb the tree and shake each limb, and then each branch and then each twig, and then I look under each leaf.

— attributed to Martin Luther (c. 1500)

Life is an unfoldment, and the further we travel the more truth we can comprehend. To understand the things that are at our door is the best preparation for understanding those that lie beyond.

— attributed to Hypatia of Alexandria (c. 400) by Elbert Hubbard
in *Little Journeys to the Homes of Great Teachers* (1908)

Your mind will answer most questions if you learn to relax and wait for the answer. Like one of those thinking machines, you feed in your question, sit back, and wait …

— William S. Burroughs, *Naked Lunch* (1959)

The methods given in this paper require no foresight or ingenuity, and hence deserve to be called algorithms.

— Edward R. Moore, "The Shortest Path Through a Maze" (1959)

8

Shortest Paths

Suppose we are given a weighted *directed* graph $G = (V, E, w)$ with two special vertices, and we want to find the shortest path from a *source* vertex s to a *target* vertex t. That is, we want to find the directed path P starting at s and ending at t that minimizes the function

$$w(P) := \sum_{u \to v \in P} w(u \to v).$$

For example, if I want to answer the question "What's the fastest way to drive from my old apartment in Champaign, Illinois to my wife's old apartment in Columbus, Ohio?", I might use a graph whose vertices are cities, edges are roads, weights are driving times, s is Champaign, and t is Columbus.[1] The graph is directed, because driving times along the same road might be different

---

[1]West on Church, north on Prospect, east on I-74, south on I-465, east on Airport Expressway, north on I-65, east on I-70, north on Grandview, east on 5th, north on Olentangy River, east on Dodridge, north on High, west on Kelso, south on Neil. Depending on traffic. We live in Urbana now.

in different directions. (At one time, there was a speed trap on I-70 just east of the Indiana/Ohio border, but only for eastbound traffic.)

8.1 Shortest Path Trees

Almost every algorithm known for computing shortest paths from one vertex to another actually solves (large portions of) the following more general *single source shortest path* or *SSSP* problem: Find shortest paths from the source vertex *s* to *every* other vertex in the graph. This problem is usually solved by finding a *shortest path tree* rooted at *s* that contains all the desired shortest paths.

It's not hard to see that if shortest paths are unique, then they form a tree, because any subpath of a shortest path is itself a shortest path. If there are multiple shortest paths to some vertices, we can always choose one shortest path to each vertex so that the union of the paths is a tree. If there are shortest paths from *s* to two vertices *u* and *v* that diverge, then meet, then diverge again, we can modify one of the paths without changing its length, so that the two paths only diverge once.

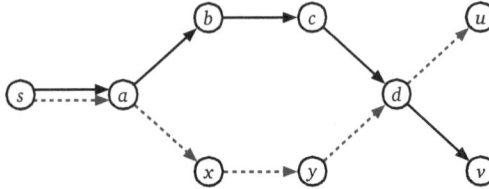

Figure 8.1. If $s{\to}a{\to}b{\to}c{\to}d{\to}v$ (solid) and $s{\to}a{\to}x{\to}y{\to}d{\to}u$ (dashed) are shortest paths, then $s{\to}a{\to}b{\to}c{\to}d{\to}u$ (along the top) is also a shortest path.

Although they are both optimal spanning trees, shortest-path trees and minimum spanning trees are very different creatures. Shortest-path trees are rooted and directed; minimum spanning trees are unrooted and undirected. Shortest-path trees are most naturally defined for directed graphs; minimum spanning trees are more naturally defined for undirected graphs. If edge weights are distinct, there is only one minimum spanning tree, but every source vertex induces a different shortest-path tree; moreover, it is possible for *every* shortest path tree to use a different set of edges from the minimum spanning tree.

♥8.2 Negative Edges

For most shortest-path problems, where the edge weights correspond to distance or length or time, it is natural to assume that all edge weights are non-negative, or even positive. However, for many applications of shortest-path algorithms, it is natural to consider edges with negative weight. For example, the weight

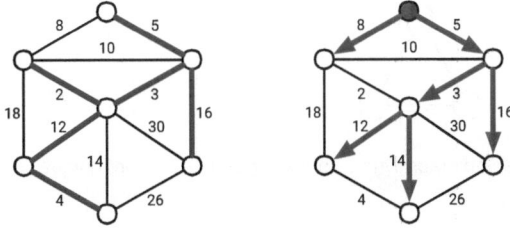

Figure 8.2. A minimum spanning tree and a shortest path tree of the same undirected graph.

of an edge might represent the *cost* of moving from one vertex to another, so negative-weight edges represent transitions with negative cost, or equivalently, transitions that earn a profit.

Negative edges are a thorn in the side of most shortest-path problems, because the presence of a negative *cycle* might imply that shortest paths may not be well-defiend. To be precise, a shortest path from s to t exists if and only if there is at least one path from s to t, but there is no path from s to t that touches a negative cycle. For *any* path from s to t that touches a negative cycle, there is a shorter path from s to t that goes around the cycle one more time.[2] Thus, if at least one path from s to t touches a negative cycle, there is no shortest path from s to t.

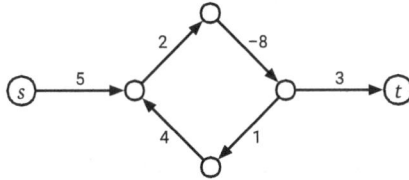

Figure 8.3. There is no shortest walk from s to t.

In part because we need to consider negative edge weights, this chapter explicitly considers *only* directed graphs. All of the algorithms described here also work for undirected graphs with essentially trivial modifications, *if and only if* negative edges are prohibited. Correctly handling negative edges in undirected graphs is considerably more subtle. We cannot simply replace every undirected edge with a pair of directed edges, because this would transform any negative edge into a short negative cycle. Subpaths of an *undirected* shortest path that contains a negative edge are *not* necessarily shortest paths; consequently, the set of all undirected shortest paths from a single source vertex may not define a tree, even if shortest paths are unique.

---

[2]Technically, we should be discussing shortest *walks* here, rather than shortest *paths*, but the abuse of terminology is standard. If s can reach t, there must be a shortest simple path from s to t; it's just NP-hard to compute (when there are negative cycles), by an easy reduction from the Hamiltonian path problem. On the other hand, if there is a shortest *walk* from s to t, that walk must be a simple path, and therefore must be the shortest simple path from s to t. Blerg.

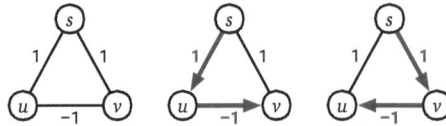

Figure 8.4. An undirected graph where shortest paths from s are unique but do not define a tree.

A complete treatment of undirected graphs with negative edges is beyond the scope of this book. I will only mention, for people who want to follow up via Google, that a *single* shortest path in an undirected graph with negative edges can be computed in $O(VE + V^2 \log V)$ time, by a reduction to maximum weighted matching.

8.3 The Only SSSP Algorithm

Just like graph traversal and minimum spanning trees, many different SSSP algorithms can be described as special cases of a single generic algorithm, first proposed by Lester Ford in 1956 and independently described by George Dantzig in 1957[3] and again by George Minty in 1958. Each vertex v in the graph stores two values, which (inductively) describe a *tentative* shortest path from s to v.

- $dist(v)$ is the length of the tentative shortest $s \leadsto v$ path, or ∞ if there is no such path.

- $pred(v)$ is the predecessor of v in the tentative shortest $s \leadsto v$ path, or NULL if there is no such vertex.

The predecessor pointers automatically define a tentative shortest-path *tree* rooted at s; these pointers are exactly the same as the parent pointers in our generic graph traversal algorithm. At the beginning of the algorithm, we initialize the distances and predecessors as follows:

$$
\boxed{
\begin{array}{l}
\underline{\text{InitSSSP}(s):} \\
\quad dist(s) \leftarrow 0 \\
\quad pred(s) \leftarrow \text{Null} \\
\quad \text{for all vertices } v \neq s \\
\quad\quad dist(v) \leftarrow \infty \\
\quad\quad pred(v) \leftarrow \text{Null}
\end{array}
}
$$

During the execution of the algorithm, an edge $u \rightarrow v$ is *tense* if $dist(u) + w(u \rightarrow v) < dist(v)$. If $u \rightarrow v$ is tense, the tentative shortest path $s \leadsto v$ is clearly incorrect, because the path $s \leadsto u \rightarrow v$ is shorter. We can correct (or at least improve) this obvious overestimate by *relaxing* the edge as follows:

---

[3]Specifically, Dantzig showed that the shortest path problem can be phrased as a linear programming problem, and then described an interpretation of his simplex method in terms of the original graph. His description is (morally) equivalent to Ford's relaxation strategy.

$$\underline{\text{Relax}(u \rightarrow v):}$$
$$dist(v) \leftarrow dist(u) + w(u \rightarrow v)$$
$$pred(v) \leftarrow u$$

Now that everything is set up, Ford's generic algorithm has a simple one-line description:

Repeatedly relax tense edges, until there are no more tense edges.

$$\underline{\text{FordSSSP}(s):}$$
$$\text{InitSSSP}(s)$$
while there is at least one tense edge
$$\text{Relax any tense edge}$$

If FordSSSP eventually terminates (because there are no more tense edges), then the predecessor pointers correctly define a shortest-path tree, and each value $dist(v)$ is the actual shortest-path distance from s to v. In particular, if s cannot reach v, then $dist(v) = \infty$, and if any negative cycle is reachable from s, then the algorithm never terminates.

The correctness of Ford's generic algorithm follows from the following series of simpler claims:

1. At any moment during the execution of the algorithm, for every vertex v, the distance $dist(v)$ is either ∞ or the length of a walk from s to v. This claim can be proved by induction on the number of relaxations.

2. If the graph has no negative cycles, then $dist(v)$ is either ∞ or the length of some *simple path* from s to v. Specifically, if $dist(v)$ is the length of a walk from s to v that contains a directed cycle, that cycle must have negative length. This claim implies that if G has no negative cycles, the relaxation algorithm eventually halts, because there are only a finite number of simple paths in G.

3. If no edge in G is tense, then for every vertex v, the distance $dist(v)$ is the length of the predecessor path $s \rightarrow \cdots pred(pred(v)) \rightarrow pred(v) \rightarrow v$. Specifically, if v violates this condition but its predecessor $pred(v)$ does not, the edge $pred(v) \rightarrow v$ is tense.

4. If no edge in G is tense, then for every vertex v, the path of predecessor edges $s \rightarrow \cdots \rightarrow pred(pred(v)) \rightarrow pred(v) \rightarrow v$ is in fact a shortest path from s to v. Specifically, if v violates this condition but its predecessor u *in some shortest path* does not, the edge $u \rightarrow v$ is tense. This claim also implies that if G has a negative cycle, then some edge is *always* tense, so the generic algorithm never halts.

So far I haven't said anything about how to find tense edges, or which tense edge(s) to relax if there is more than one. Just like whatever-first search, there are several different instantiations of Ford's generic relaxation algorithm. Unlike whatever-first search, however, the efficiency and correctness of each search strategy depends on the structure of the input graph.

The rest of this chapter considers the four most common instantiations of Ford's algorithm, each of which is the best choice for a different class of input graphs. I'll leave the remaining details of the generic correctness proof as exercises, and instead give (more informative, self-contained) correctness proofs for each of these four specific algorithms.

8.4 Unweighted Graphs: Breadth-First Search

In the simplest special case of the shortest path problem, all edges have weight 1, and the length of a path is just the number of edges. This special case can be solved by a species of our generic graph-traversal algorithm called ***breadth-first search***. Breadth-first search is often attributed to Edward Moore, who described it in 1957 (as "Algorithm A") as the first published method to find the shortest path through a maze.[4] Especially in the context of VLSI wiring and robot path planning, breadth-first search is sometimes attributed to Chin Yang Lee, who described several applications of Moore's "Algorithm A" (with proper credit to Moore) in 1961. However, in 1945, more than a decade before Moore considered mazes, Konrad Zuse described an implementation of breadth-first search, as a method to count and label the components of a disconnected graph.[6]

---

[4]Moore was motivated by a weakness in Claude Shannon's maze-solving robot "Theseus", which Shannon designed and constructed in 1950. (Theseus used a memoized version of depth-first search, implemented using electromechanical relays; this was almost certainly the first *implementation* of depth-first search in graphs.) According to Moore, "When this machine was used with a maze which had more than one solution, a visitor asked why it had not been built to always find the shortest path. Shannon and I each attempted to find economical methods of doing this by machine. He found several methods suitable for analog computation,[5] and I obtained these algorithms."

[5]Analog methods for computing shortest paths through mazes have been proposed using ball bearings, fluid/plasma flow, chemical reaction waves, chemotaxis, resistor networks, electric circuits with LEDs, memristor networks, glow discharge in microfluidic chips, growing plants, slime mold, amoebas, ants, bees, nematodes, and tourists.

[6]Konrad Zuse was one of the early pioneers of computing; he designed and built his first programmable computer (later dubbed the Z1) in the late 1930s from metal strips and rods in his parents' living room; the Z1 and its original blueprints were destroyed by a British air raid in 1944. Zuse's 1945 PhD thesis describes the very first high-level programming language, called *Plankalkül*. The first complete example of a Plankalkül program in Zuse's thesis is an implementation of breadth-first search to count components, along with a pseudocode explanation and an illustrated step-by-step trace of the algorithm's execution on a disconnected graph with eight vertices. Due to the collapse of the Nazi government, Zuse was unable to submit his PhD thesis, and Plankalkül remained unpublished until 1972. The first Plankalkül compiler was finally implemented in 1975 by Joachim Hohmann.

Breadth-first search maintains a first-in-first-out queue of vertices, which initially contains only the source vertex s. At each iteration, the algorithm PULLS a vertex u from the front of the queue and examines each of its outgoing edges $u \rightarrow v$. Whenever the algorithm discovers an outgoing tense edge $u \rightarrow v$, it relaxes that edge and PUSHES vertex v onto the queue. The algorithm ends when the queue becomes empty.

BFS(s):

   INITSSSP(s)

   PUSH(s)

   while the queue is not empty

      $u \leftarrow$ PULL( )

      for all edges $u \rightarrow v$

         if $dist(v) > dist(u) + 1$ ⟨⟨*if $u \rightarrow v$ is tense*⟩⟩

            $dist(v) \leftarrow dist(u) + 1$

            $pred(v) \leftarrow u$ ⟨⟨*relax $u \rightarrow v$*⟩⟩

            PUSH(v)

Breadth-first search is somewhat easier to analyze if we break its execution into *phases*, by introducing an imaginary *token*. Before we PULL any vertices, we PUSH the token into the queue. The current phase ends when we PULL the token out of the queue; we begin the next phase when we PUSH the token into the queue again. Thus, the first phase consists entirely of scanning the source vertex s. The algorithm ends when the queue contains *only* the token. The modified algorithm is shown in Figure 8.5, and Figure 8.6 shows an example of this algorithm in action. Let me emphasize that these modifications are merely a convenience for analysis; with or without the token, the algorithm PUSHES and PULLS vertices in the same order, scans edges in the same order, and outputs exactly the same distances and predecessors.

BFSWITHTOKEN(s):

   INITSSSP(s)

   PUSH(s)

   PUSH(✷)   ⟨⟨*start the first phase*⟩⟩

   while the queue contains at least one vertex

      $u \leftarrow$ PULL( )

      if $u = $ ✷

         PUSH(✷)   ⟨⟨*start the next phase*⟩⟩

      else

         for all edges $u \rightarrow v$

            if $dist(v) > dist(u) + 1$ ⟨⟨*if $u \rightarrow v$ is tense*⟩⟩

              $dist(v) \leftarrow dist(u) + 1$

              $pred(v) \leftarrow u$ ⟨⟨*relax $u \rightarrow v$*⟩⟩

              PUSH(v)

Figure 8.5. Breadth-first search with an end-of-phase token (✷); bold red lines are only for analysis.

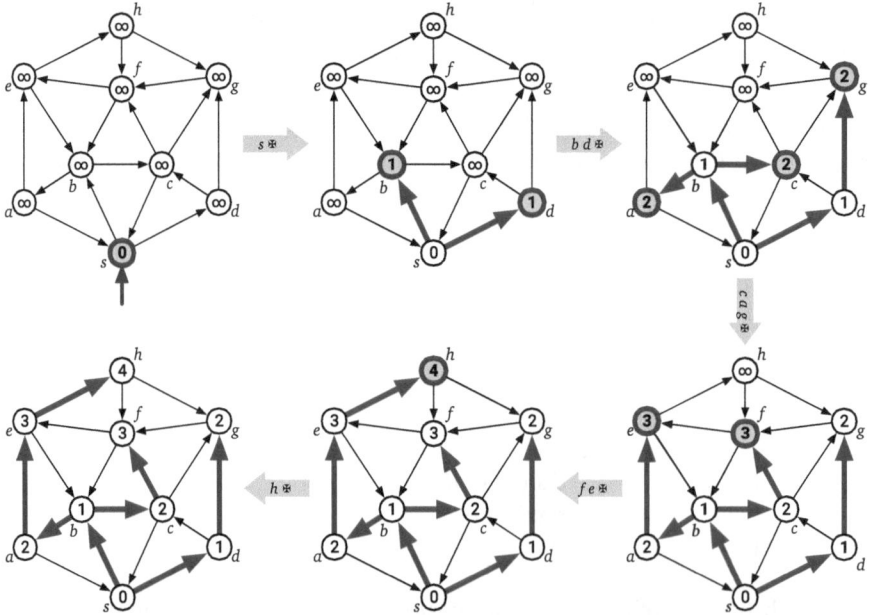

Figure 8.6. A complete run of breadth-first search in a directed graph. Vertices are pulled from the queue in the order $s \maltese b d \maltese c a g \maltese f e \maltese h \maltese \maltese$, where $\maltese$ is the end-of-phase token. Bold vertices are in the queue at the end of each phase. Bold edges describe the evolving shortest path tree.

Let me emphasize that in the following lemma, $dist(v)$ is just a variable maintained by the algorithm. While $dist(v)$ *intuitively* represents a tentative shortest-path distance, we cannot assume (yet) that $dist(v)$ is ever actually equal to the true shortest-path distance from s to v. Don't worry; we'll get there.

Lemma 8.1. *For every integer $i \geq 0$ and every vertex v, at the end of the ith phase, either $dist(v) = \infty$ or $dist(v) \leq i$, and v is in the queue if and only if $dist(v) = i$.*

Proof: The proof proceeds by induction on i. The base case $i = 0$ is straightforward: At the start of the first phase ("at the end of the zeroth phase"), the queue contains only the start vertex s and the token $\maltese$, and INITSSSP just set $dist(s) \leftarrow 0$ and $dist(v) \leftarrow \infty$ for all $v \neq s$.

So fix an integer $i > 0$. The inductive hypothesis implies that at the *start* of the ith phase, the queue contains every vertex u with $dist(u) = i - 1$, followed by the token $\maltese$. In other words, the queue looks like this:

$$\rightarrow \quad \maltese \quad i-1 \quad i-1 \quad \cdots \quad i-1 \quad \rightarrow$$

Thus, before we PULL the token $\maltese$ from the queue, ending the ith phase, we PULL *every* vertex u with $dist(u) = i - 1$.

For each such vertex u, we consider every outgoing edge $u \rightarrow v$. If $u \rightarrow v$ is tense, we set $dist(v) \leftarrow dist(u) + 1$, so that $dist(v) = i$, and then immediately

PUSH v into the queue. These are the only assignments to distance labels during the ith phase. Thus, by induction, during the entire ith phase, the queue contains some vertices with distance label $i-1$, followed by the token, followed by some vertices with distance label i:

$$\rightarrow \quad i \quad \cdots \quad i \quad \divideontimes \quad i-1 \quad \cdots \quad i-1 \quad \rightarrow$$

In particular, just before the ith phase ends, the queue contains the token, followed by some vertices with distance label i.

$$\rightarrow \quad i \quad i \quad \cdots \quad i \quad \divideontimes \quad \rightarrow$$

Moreover, vertex v appears in this final queue if and only if $dist(v)$ was changed during the ith phase. Thus, at the end of the ith phase, the queue contains *every* vertex v with $dist(v) = i$. □

Lemma 8.1 implies that the main body of BFS assigns distance labels in non-decreasing order; on the other hand, the distance label $dist(v)$ of each vertex v never increases. It follows that for each vertex v, the line "$dist(v) \leftarrow dist(u)+1$" is executed *at most once*, during phase $dist(v)$. Similarly:

- Each predecessor pointer $pred(v)$ is changed at most once, during phase $dist(v)$.
- Each vertex v is PUSHed into the queue at most once, during phase $dist(v)$.
- Each vertex u is PULLed from the queue at most once, during phase $dist(u)+1$.
- For each edge $u \rightarrow v$, the comparison "is $dist(v) > dist(u) + 1$" is performed at most once, during phase $dist(u) + 1$.

Altogether, these observations imply that breadth-first search runs in $O(V + E)$ *time*. Intuitively, we can think of the vertices in the queue as a "wavefront" expanding monotonically outward from the source vertex s, passing over each vertex and edge of the graph at most once. This expanding wavefront analogy was already proposed by Chin Yang Lee in 1961, inspired by visualizations produced by his implementation of Moore's Algorithm A.

These observations also imply that we can replace the condition "if $dist(v) > dist(u) + 1$" by the (arguably) simpler test "if $dist(v) = \infty$". Then distances play the same role as the marks maintained by other graph-traversal algorithms, which ensure that each vertex is visited only once. Specifically, a vertex is "marked" if and only if its distance label is finite.

But we still need to prove that the final distance labels are correct!

Theorem 8.2. *When BFS ends, $dist(v)$ is the length of the shortest path in G from s to v, for every vertex v.*

Proof: Fix an arbitrary vertex v, and consider an arbitrary path $v_0 \rightarrow v_1 \rightarrow \cdots \rightarrow v_\ell$ in G, where $v_0 = s$ and $v_\ell = v$. I claim that $dist(v_j) \leq j$ for each index j; in particular $dist(v) \leq \ell$. We can prove this claim by induction on j as follows.

- Trivially $dist(v_0) = dist(s) = 0$.

- For any index $j > 0$, the induction hypothesis implies $dist(v_{j-1}) \leq j - 1$. Immediately after we Pull vertex v_{j-1} from the queue, either $dist(v_j) \leq dist(v_{j-1}) + 1$ already, or we set $dist(v_j) \leftarrow dist(v_{j-1}) + 1$. In either case, we have $dist(v_j) \leq dist(v_{j-1}) + 1 \leq j$.

We just proved that $dist(v)$ is at most the length of an *arbitrary* path from s to v; it follows that $dist(v)$ is at most the length of the *shortest* path from s to v.

A similar induction proof implies that $dist(v)$ is the length of the predecessor path $s \rightarrow \cdots \rightarrow pred(pred(v)) \rightarrow pred(v) \rightarrow v$, so this must be the shortest path. □

8.5 Directed Acyclic Graphs: Depth-First Search

Shortest paths are also easy to compute in directed acyclic graphs, even when the edges are weighted, and in particular, even when some edges have negative weight. (We don't have to worry about negative cycles, because by definition, dags don't have *any* cycles!) Indeed, this is a completely standard dynamic programming algorithm.

Let G be a directed graph with weighted edges, and let s be the fixed start vertex. For any vertex v, let $dist(v)$ denote the length of the shortest path in G from s to v. This function satisfies the following simple recurrence:

$$dist(v) = \begin{cases} 0 & \text{if } v = s \\ \min_{u \rightarrow v} (dist(u) + w(u \rightarrow v)) & \text{otherwise} \end{cases}$$

In fact, this identity holds for *all* directed graphs, but it is only a *recurrence* for directed acyclic graphs. If the input graph G contained a cycle, a recursive evaluation of this function would fall into an infinite loop; however, because G is a dag, each recursive call visits an earlier vertex in topological order.

The dependency graph for this recurrence is the reversal of the input graph G: subproblem $dist(v)$ depends on $dist(u)$ if and only if $u \rightarrow v$ is an edge in G. Thus, we compute the distance of every in $O(V + E)$ *time* by performing a depth-first search in the reversal of G and considering vertices in postorder. Equivalently, we can consider the vertices in the original graph G in topological order, as shown in Figure 8.7.

The resulting dynamic-programming algorithm is another example of Ford's generic relaxation algorithm! To make this connection clearer, we can move the initialization $dist(v)$ outside the main loop and add computation of predecessor pointers, as shown in Figure 8.8. Figure 8.9 shows this algorithm in action.

DAGSSSP(s):
    for all vertices v in topological order
        if $v = s$
            $dist(v) \leftarrow 0$
        else
            $dist(v) \leftarrow \infty$
            for all edges $u \rightarrow v$
                if $dist(v) > dist(u) + w(u \rightarrow v)$ 《if $u \rightarrow v$ is tense》
                   $dist(v) \leftarrow dist(u) + w(u \rightarrow v)$ 《relax $u \rightarrow v$》

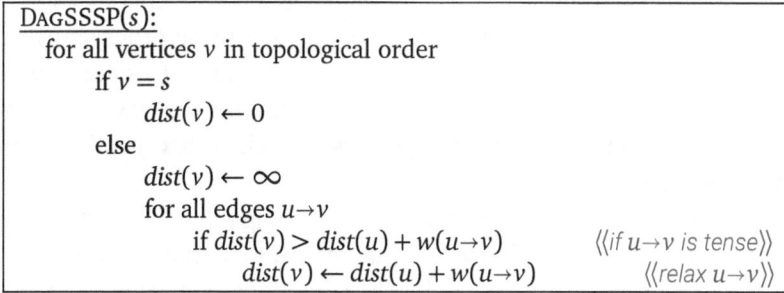

Figure 8.7. Computing shortest paths in a dag using dynamic programming

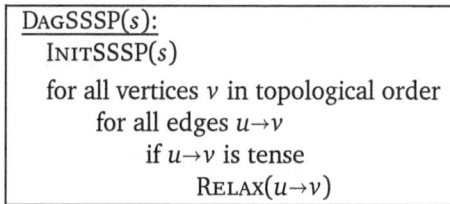

DAGSSSP(s):
    INITSSSP(s)

    for all vertices v in topological order
        for all edges $u \rightarrow v$
            if $u \rightarrow v$ is tense
                RELAX(u \rightarrow v)

Figure 8.8. Computing shortest paths in a dag using Ford's algorithm. (These are the same algorithm.)

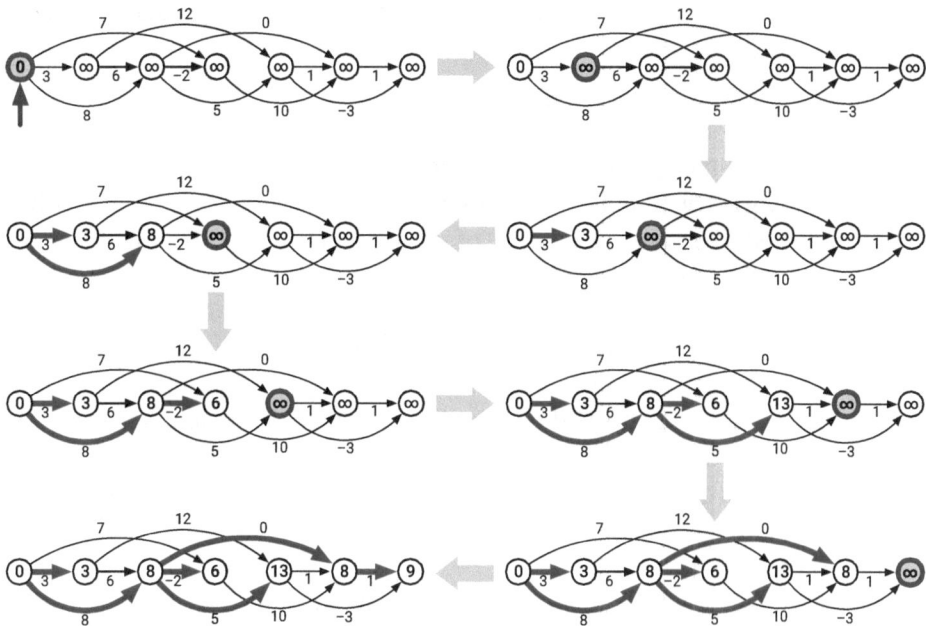

Figure 8.9. Computing shortest paths in a dag, by relaxing **incoming** edges in topological order. In each iteration, bold edges indicate predecessors, and the bold vertex is about to be scanned. Compare with Figure 8.10.

DAGSSSP differs from breadth-first search and other instances of Ford's relaxation strategy in one minor respect. Whenever these other shortest-path algorithms consider a vertex, they attempt to relax each of its *outgoing* edges, intuitively *pushing* the wavefront forward from the source; whereas, DAGSSSP attempts to relax each of the *incoming* edges of each vertex, intuitively *pulling* the wavefront forward.

However, if we modify DAGSSSP to relax outgoing edges instead of incoming edges, we obtain another algorithm that computes shortest paths in dags in $O(V + E)$ *time* and that more closely resembles our other shortest-path algorithms.

PUSHDAGSSSP(s):
  INITSSSP(s)
  for all vertices u in topological order
    for all **outgoing** edges $u{\to}v$
      if $u{\to}v$ is tense
        RELAX($u{\to}v$)

Figure 8.10 shows an execution of this modified algorithm on the same graph as Figure 8.9. The correctness of PUSHDAGSSSP follows immediately from the correctness of Ford's general relaxation strategy, but it's not hard to prove correctness directly, by induction over the vertices in topological order.

8.6 Best-First: Dijkstra's Algorithm

If we replace the FIFO queue in breadth-first search with a priority queue, where the key of a vertex v is its tentative distance $dist(v)$, we obtain an algorithm first "published" in 1957 by a team of researchers at the Case Institute of Technology led by Michael Leyzorek, in an annual project report for the Combat Development Department of the US Army Electronic Proving Ground. The same algorithm was independently discovered by Edsger Dijkstra in 1956 (but not published until 1959), again by George Minty some time before 1960, and again by Peter Whiting and John Hillier in 1960. A nearly identical algorithm was also described by George Dantzig in 1958. Although several early sources called it "Minty's algorithm", this approach is now universally known as "Dijkstra's algorithm", in full accordance with Stigler's Law.[7] Pseudocode for this algorithm is shown in Figure 8.11.

An easy induction proof implies that, at all times during the execution of this algorithm, an edge $u{\to}v$ is tense if and only if vertex u is either in the priority

---

[7]I will follow this common convention, despite the historical inaccuracy, partly because I don't think anybody wants to read about the "Leyzorek-Gray-Johnson-Ladew-Meaker-Petry-Seitz-Dantzig-Dijkstra-Minty-Whiting-Hillier algorithm", and partly because papers that aren't *actually published* don't count.

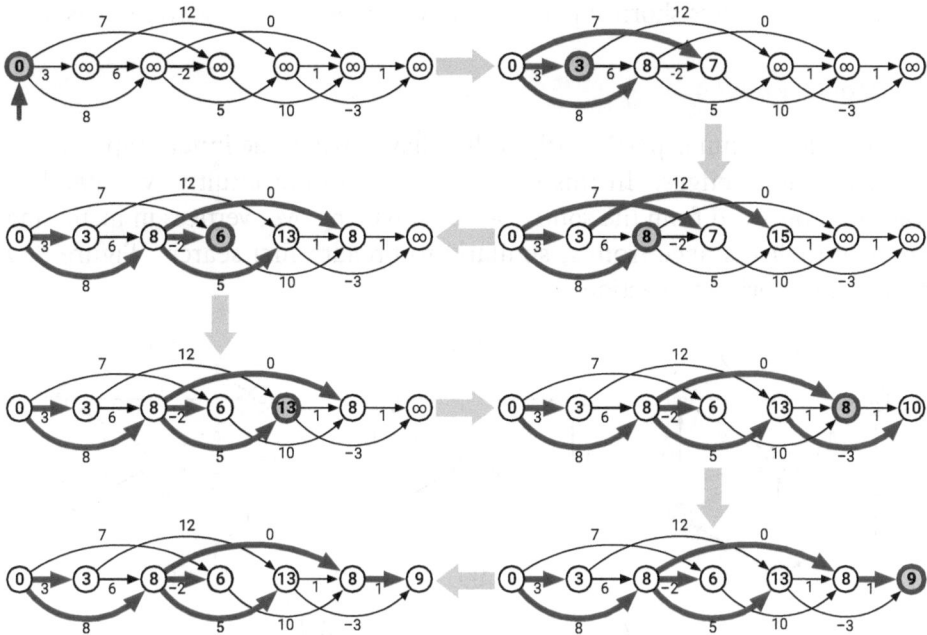

Figure 8.10. Computing shortest paths in a dag, by relaxing **outgoing** edges in topological order. In each iteration, bold edges indicate predecessors, and the bold vertex is about to be scanned. Compare with Figure 8.9.

```
DIJKSTRA(s):
    INITSSSP(s)
    INSERT(s, 0)
    while the priority queue is not empty
        u ← EXTRACTMIN( )
        for all edges u→v
            if u→v is tense
                RELAX(u→v)
                if v is in the priority queue
                    DECREASEKEY(v, dist(v))
                else
                    INSERT(v, dist(v))
```

Figure 8.11. Dijkstra's algorithm.

queue or is the vertex most recently EXTRACTed from the priority queue. Thus, Dijkstra's algorithm is an instance of Ford's general strategy, which implies that it correctly computes shortest paths, provided there are no negative cycles in G.

No Negative Edges

Dijkstra's algorithm is particularly well-behaved when the input graph has no negative-weight edges. In this setting, the algorithm intuitively expands a wavefront outward from the source vertex s, passing over vertices in increasing order of their distance from s, similarly to breadth-first search. Figure 8.12 shows the algorithm in action.

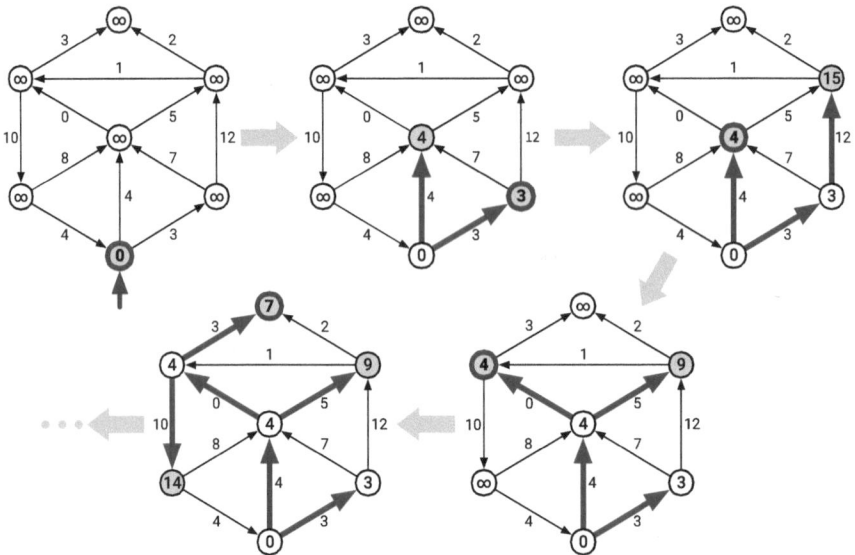

Figure 8.12. The first four iterations of Dijkstra's algorithm on a graph with no negative edges. In each iteration, bold edges indicate predecessors; shaded vertices are in the priority queue; and the bold vertex is about to be scanned. The remaining iterations do not change the distances or the shortest-path tree.

We can derive a self-contained proof of correctness for Dijkstra's algorithm in this setting by formalizing this wavefront intuition. For each integer i, let u_i denote the vertex returned by the ith call to EXTRACTMIN, and let d_i be the value of $dist(u_i)$ just after this EXTRACTion. In particular, we have $u_1 = s$ and $d_1 = 0$. We cannot assume at this point that the vertices u_i are distinct; in principle, the same vertex might be EXTRACTed more than once.

Lemma 8.3. *If G has no negative-weight edges, then for all $i < j$, we have $d_i \leq d_j$.*

Proof: Assume G has no negative weight edges. Fix an arbitrary index i; to prove the lemma, it suffices to prove that $d_{i+1} \geq d_i$. There are two cases to consider.

- If G contains the edge $u_i \rightarrow u_{i+1}$, and this edge is relaxed during the ith iteration of the main loop, then at the end of the ith iteration, we have $dist(u_{i+1}) = dist(u_i) + w(u_i \rightarrow u_{i+1}) \geq dist(u_i)$, because all edge weights are non-negative.

- Otherwise, at the start of the ith iteration, u_{i+1} must already be in the priority queue, and it must have priority $dist(u_{i+1}) \geq dist(u_i)$, because u_i is the vertex returned by EXTRACTMIN. Moreover, $dist(u_{i+1})$ does not change during the ith iteration.

In both cases, we conclude that $d_{i+1} \geq d_i$. The lemma now follows immediately by induction on i. □

Lemma 8.4. *If G has no negative-weight edges, each vertex of G is EXTRACTed from the priority queue at most once.*

Proof: Suppose v is EXTRACTed more than once. Specifically, suppose v is EXTRACTed in the ith iteration of the main loop, reINSERTed during the jth iteration, and reEXTRACTed during the kth iteration, for some indices $i < j < k$. Then in the notation of the previous proof, we have $v = u_i = u_k$.

The distance label $dist(v)$ never increases. Moreover, $dist(v)$ strictly decreases during the jth iteration, just before v is reINSERTed. It follows that $d_i > d_k$. Therefore, by the previous lemma, G has at least one negative-weight edge. □

Lemma 8.4 immediately implies that each vertex is scanned at most once, and thus that each edge is relaxed at most once. However, unlike in breadth-first search, each distance label $dist(v)$ can change multiple times. The first time $dist(v)$ changes from ∞, we INSERT v into the priority queue; after that, each change to $dist(v)$ is followed by a call to DECREASEKEY. After v is EXTRACTed from the priority queue, its distance label never changes.

The rest of the correctness proof is almost identical to breadth-first search.

Theorem 8.5. *If G has no negative-weight edges, then when DIJKSTRA ends, $dist(v)$ is the length of the shortest path in G from s to v, for every vertex v.*

Proof: Fix an arbitrary vertex v, and consider an arbitrary path $v_0 \rightarrow v_1 \rightarrow \cdots \rightarrow v_\ell$ in G, where $v_0 = s$ and $v_\ell = v$. For any index j, let L_j denote the length of the subpath $v_0 \rightarrow v_1 \rightarrow \cdots \rightarrow v_j$. We prove by induction that $dist(v_j) \leq L_j$ for all j.

- Trivially $dist(v_0) = dist(s) = 0 = L_0$.

- For any index $j > 0$, the induction hypothesis implies $dist(v_{j-1}) \leq L_{j-1}$. Immediately after we PULL vertex v_{j-1} from the queue, either $dist(v_i) \leq dist(v_{j-1}) + w(v_{j-1} \rightarrow v_j)$ already, or we set $dist(v_i) \leftarrow dist(v_{j-1}) + w(v_{j-1} \rightarrow v_j)$. In either case, we have

$$dist(v_j) \leq dist(v_{j-1}) + w(v_{j-1} \rightarrow v_j) \leq L_{j-1} + w(v_{j-1} \rightarrow v_j) = L_j.$$

We just proved that $dist(v)$ is at most the length of *every* path from s to v; it follows that $dist(v)$ is at most the length of the *shortest* path from s to v.

On the other hand, a similar induction proof implies that $dist(v)$ is the length of the predecessor path $s\rightarrow\cdots\rightarrow pred(pred(v))\rightarrow pred(v)\rightarrow v$. □

It remains only to bound the algorithm's running time. Altogether DIJKSTRA performs at most E DECREASEKEY operations, and at most V INSERT and EXTRACTMIN operations. Thus, if we implement the underlying priority queue using a standard binary heap, which supports each operation in $O(\log V)$ time, DIJKSTRA runs in $O(E \log V)$ *time*.[8]

If we know in advance that our input graphs will *never* have negative edges, we can simplify Dijkstra's algorithm slightly, by INSERTing every vertex into the priority queue in the initialization phase, and then only calling DECREASEKEY in the main loop, as shown in Figure 8.13. This is the version of Dijkstra's algorithm presented by most algorithms textbooks, Wikipedia, and even Dijkstra's original paper; it's also the version of Dijkstra's algorithm that I described as "best-first search" in Chapter 5.

NONNEGATIVEDIJKSTRA(s):
  INITSSSP(s)
  for all vertices v
    INSERT($v, dist(v)$)
  while the priority queue is not empty
    $u \leftarrow$ EXTRACTMIN( )
    for all edges $u\rightarrow v$
      if $u\rightarrow v$ is tense
        RELAX($u\rightarrow v$)
        DECREASEKEY($v, dist(v)$)

Figure 8.13. Dijkstra's algorithm very slightly simplified for graphs without negative edges. Differences from DIJKSTRA are bold red.

♥Negative Edges

However, NONNEGATIVEDIJKSTRA does *not* correctly compute shortest paths in graphs with negative edges. Moreover, even when all edge weights are

---

[8]Shortest-path papers from the 1950s never mentioned priority queues. Dijkstra proposed a brute-force scan of all vertices on the wavefront at every iteration; his original algorithm runs in $O(V^2)$ *time*, which is actually faster than the binary-heap implementation when $E = \Omega(V^2)$! Minty proposed a brute-force scan of all *edges* $u\rightarrow v$ such that $dist(u)$ is finite but $dist(v)$ is not; thus, his original algorithm runs in $O(VE)$ time. The use of a priority queue, implemented as a binary heap, to obtain near-linear running time was proposed by Donald Johnson in 1977. The running time can be improved to $O(E + V \log V)$ using a more complex priority queue data structure called a *Fibonacci heaps*. There are even faster algorithms, using even more sophisticated priority queues, for the special case of integer edge weights.

positive, NONNEGATIVEDIJKSTRA is no faster than DIJKSTRA (either in theory or in practice). For both of these reasons, I think DIJKSTRA is more deserving of the name "Dijkstra's algorithm" than NONNEGATIVEDIJKSTRA. Even Edsger Dijkstra would have agreed that a correct algorithm that is sometimes (and in practice, rarely) slow is better than a fast algorithm that doesn't always work!

Unfortunately, when the input graph has negative edges, the familiar "expanding wavefront" intuition is no longer accurate. The same vertex can be EXTRACTed multiple times; the same edge can be relaxed multiple times; and distances might not be discovered in increasing order. Figure 8.15 shows an example execution where the top left vertex is EXTRACTED six times, and the top three edges are each relaxed twice.

For graphs without negative cycles, but no other restrictions on edge weights, the worst-case running time of DIJKSTRA is actually exponential. Figure 8.14 shows particularly simple family of graphs (due to Douglas Shier and Christoph Witzgall) that forces DIJKSTRA to perform $\Theta(2^{V/2})$ relaxations.[9] A more complex family of graphs (which I'll leave as an exercise) forces $\Theta(2^V)$ relaxations, which is the worst possible. *In practice*, however, Dijkstra's algorithm is usually fast even for graphs with negative edges.

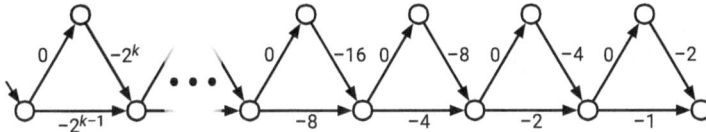

Figure 8.14. A directed graph with negative edges that forces DIJKSTRA to run in exponential time.

8.7 Relax ALL the Edges: Bellman-Ford

The simplest implementation of Ford's generic shortest-path algorithm was first sketched by Alfonso Shimbel in 1954, described in more detail by Edward Moore in 1957, and independently rediscovered by Max Woodbury and George Dantzig in 1957, by Richard Bellman in 1958, and by George Minty in 1958. (Neither Woodbury and Dantzig nor Minty published their algorithms.) In full compliance with Stigler's Law, the algorithm is almost universally known as *Bellman-Ford*,[10] because Bellman explicitly used Ford's 1956 formulation of

---

[9]Amusingly, Shier and Witzgall's example is a dag with only $O(V)$ edges, which implies that shortest paths can be computed in only $O(V)$ time, even if we *didn't* already notice that the zig-zag path along the top *is* the shortest path tree.

[10]I will follow this common convention, despite the historical inaccuracy, partly because I don't think anyone really wants read about the "Shimbel/Moore/Woodbury-Dantzig/Bellman-Ford/Kalaba/Minty algorithm", and partly because I'm tired of people looking at me funny when I talk about "Shimbel's algorithm".

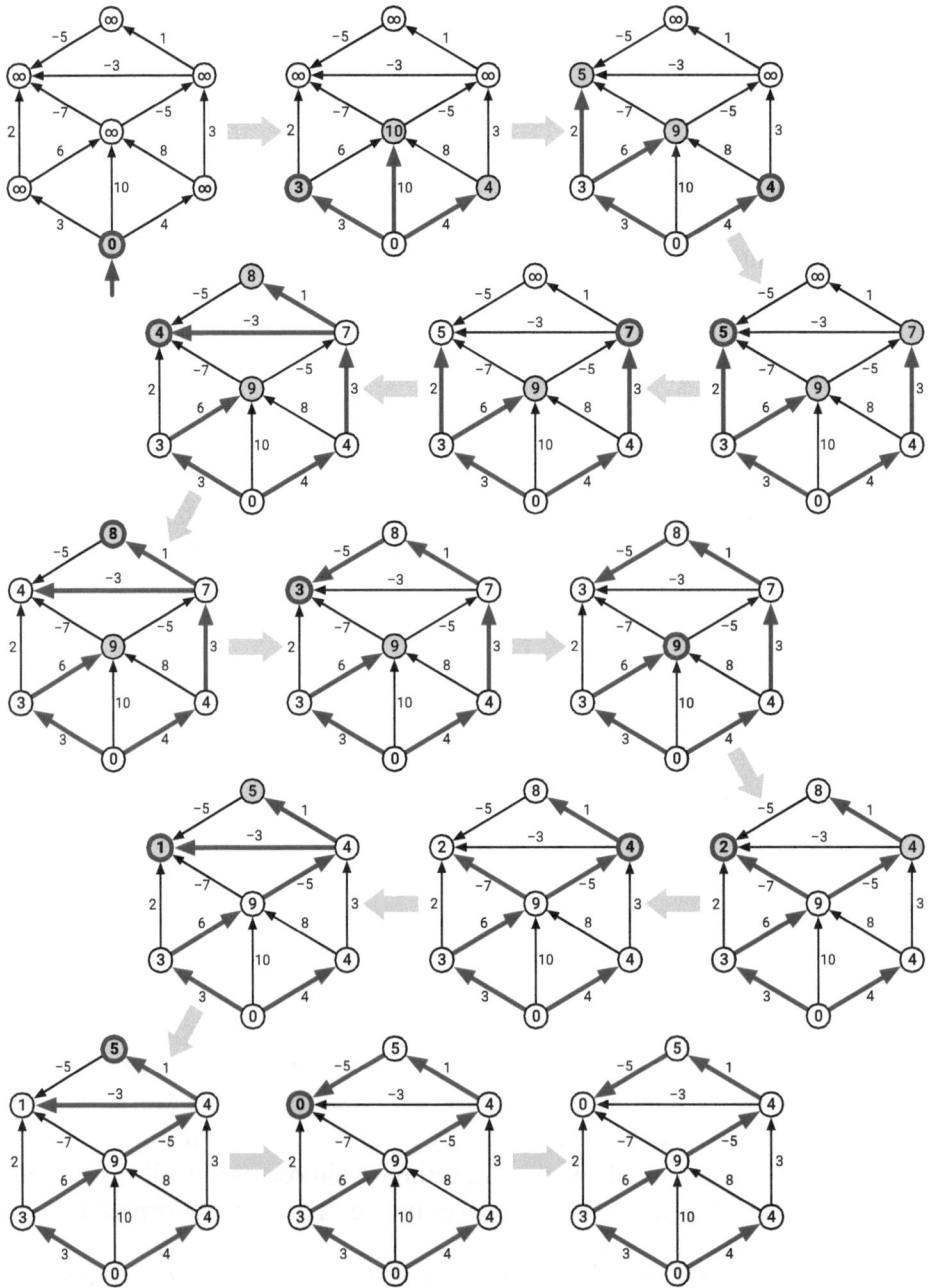

Figure 8.15. A complete run of Dijkstra's algorithm on a graph with negative edges. At each iteration, bold edges indicate predecessors; shaded vertices are in the priority queue; and the bold vertex is the next to be scanned. Compare with Figure 8.17.

relaxing edges, although some authors refer to "Bellman-Kalaba"[11] and a few early sources refer to "Bellman-Shimbel".

The Shimbel / Moore / Woodbury-Dantzig / Bellman-Ford / Kalaba / Minty / Brosh[12] algorithm can be summarized in one line:

BELLMAN-FORD: Relax **ALL** the tense edges, then recurse.

$$
\begin{array}{l}
\underline{\text{BELLMANFORD}(s)} \\
\quad \text{INITSSSP}(s) \\
\quad \text{while there is at least one tense edge} \\
\qquad \text{for every edge } u{\to}v \\
\qquad\quad \text{if } u{\to}v \text{ is tense} \\
\qquad\qquad \text{RELAX}(u{\to}v)
\end{array}
$$

The following lemma is the key to proving both correctness and efficiency of Bellman-Ford. For every vertex v and non-negative integer i, let $dist_{\leq i}(v)$ denote the length of the shortest *walk* in G from s to v consisting of *at most* i edges. In particular, $dist_{\leq 0}(s) = 0$ and $dist_{\leq 0}(v) = \infty$ for all $v \neq s$.

Lemma 8.6. *For every vertex v and non-negative integer i, after i iterations of the main loop of BELLMANFORD, we have $dist(v) \leq dist_{\leq i}(v)$.*

Proof: The proof proceeds by induction on i. The base case $i = 0$ is trivial, so assume $i > 0$. Fix a vertex v, and let W be the shortest walk from s to v consisting of at most i edges (breaking ties arbitrarily). By definition, W has length $dist_{\leq i}(v)$. There are two cases to consider.

- Suppose W has no edges. Then W must be the trivial walk from s to s, so $v = s$ and $dist_{\leq i}(s) = 0$. We set $dist(s) \leftarrow 0$ in INITSSSP, and $dist(s)$ can never increase, so we always have $dist(s) \leq 0$.

- Otherwise, let $u{\to}v$ be the last edge of W. The induction hypothesis implies that after $i-1$ iterations, $dist(u) \leq dist_{\leq i-1}(u)$. During the ith iteration of the outer loop, when we consider the edge $u{\to}v$ in the inner loop, either $dist(v) < dist(u) + w(u{\to}v)$ already, or we set $dist(v) \leftarrow dist(u) + w(u{\to}v)$. In both cases, we have $dist(v) \leq dist_{\leq i-1}(u) + w(u{\to}v) = dist_{\leq i}(v)$. As usual, $dist(v)$ cannot increase (although $dist(v)$ might decrease further before the ith iteration of the outer loop ends).

---

[11]This name is most likely a reference to Richard Bellman and Robert Kalaba's 1965 monograph on dynamic programming and control theory, which describes Bellman's algorithm. Bellman and Kalaba also published an extension of Bellman's algorithm in 1960 that computes kth shortest paths, for any constant k.

[12]Go read everything in *Hyperbole and a Half* again. And then adopt another cat, so you can buy it another copy of the book.

In both cases, we conclude that $dist(v) \leq dist_{\leq i}(v)$ at the end of the ith iteration. □

If the input graph has no negative cycles, the shortest walk from s to any other vertex is a simple path with at most $V - 1$ edges; it follows that BELLMAN-FORD halts with the correct shortest-path distances after at most $V - 1$ iterations. Said differently, if any edge is still tense after $V - 1$ iterations, then the input graph must contain a negative cycle! Thus, we can rewrite the algorithm more concretely as follows:

$\underline{\text{BELLMANFORD}(s)}$
  INITSSSP(s)
  repeat $V - 1$ times
    for every edge $u \rightarrow v$
      if $u \rightarrow v$ is tense
        RELAX($u \rightarrow v$)
  for every edge $u \rightarrow v$
    if $u \rightarrow v$ is tense
      return "Negative cycle!"

Each iteration of the inner loop trivially requires $O(E)$ time, so the overall algorithm runs in $O(VE)$ **time**. Thus, Bellman-Ford is *always* efficient, even if the graph has negative edges, and in fact even if the graph has negative *cycles*.

If all edge weights are non-negative, however, Dijkstra's algorithm is faster, at least in the worst case. (In practice, Dijkstra's algorithm is often faster than Bellman-Ford even for graphs with negative edges.)

Moore's Improvement

Neither Moore nor Bellman described the Bellman-Ford algorithm in the form I've presented here. Moore presented his version of the algorithm ("Algorithm D") in the same paper that proposed breadth-first search ("Algorithm A") for unweighted graphs; indeed, the two algorithms are nearly identical. Although Moore's algorithm has the same $O(VE)$ worst-case running time as BELLMANFORD, it is often significantly faster in practice, intuitively because it avoids checking edges that are "obviously" not tense.

Moore derived his weighted shortest-path algorithm by making two modifications to breadth-first search. First, replace each "+1" with "+$w(u \rightarrow v)$" in the innermost loop, to take the edge weights into account. Second, check whether a vertex is already in the FIFO queue before INSERTING it, so that the queue always contains at most one copy of each vertex.[13]

---

[13]Moore's algorithm is still *correct* without this check, but the $O(VE)$ time bound is not.

Following our earlier analysis of breadth-first search, I'll introduce a "token" ✸ to break the execution of the algorithm into phases. Just like breadth-first search, each phase begins when the token is PUSHed into the queue, and ends when the token is PULLed out of the queue again. Just like BFS, the algorithm ends when the queue contains *only* the token. The resulting algorithm is shown in Figure 8.16.

<u>MOORE(s):</u>
  INITSSSP(s)
  PUSH(s)
  PUSH(✸)   ⟨⟨*start the first phase*⟩⟩
  while the queue contains at least one vertex
      $u \leftarrow$ PULL( )
      if $u = $ ✸
          PUSH(✸)   ⟨⟨*start the next phase*⟩⟩
      else
          for all edges $u \rightarrow v$
             if $u \rightarrow v$ is tense
                RELAX($u \rightarrow v$)
                if v is not already in the queue
                    PUSH(v)

Figure 8.16. Moore's shortest-path algorithm. Bold red lines involving the token ✸ are only for analysis.

Because the queue contains at most one copy of each vertex at any time, each vertex is PULLed from the queue at most once in each phase, and therefore each edge $u \rightarrow v$ is checked for tenseness at most once in each phase. Moreover, every edge that is tense when a phase begins is relaxed during that phase. (Some edges that become tense during the phase might also be relaxed during that phase, and some relaxed edges might become tense again in the same phase.) Thus, MOORE can be viewed as a refinement of BELLMANFORD that uses a queue to maintain tense edges, rather than testing every edge by brute force. In particular, a similar inductive proof establishes the following analogue of Lemma 8.6:

Lemma 8.7. *For every vertex v and non-negative integer i, after i phases of* MOORE, *we have $dist(v) \le dist_{\le i}(v)$.*

Thus, if the input graph has no negative cycles, MOORE halts after at most $V - 1$ phases. In each phase, we scan each vertex at most once, so we relax each edge at most once, so the worst-case running time of a single phase is $O(E)$. Thus, the overall running time of MOORE is $O(VE)$. In practice, however, MOORE often computes shortest paths considerably faster than BELLMANFORD, because it only scans an edge $u \rightarrow v$ if $dist(u)$ was changed in the previous phase.

If the input graph contains a negative cycle, MOORE never halts. Fortunately, like BELLMANFORD, it is easy to modify Moore's algorithm to report negative

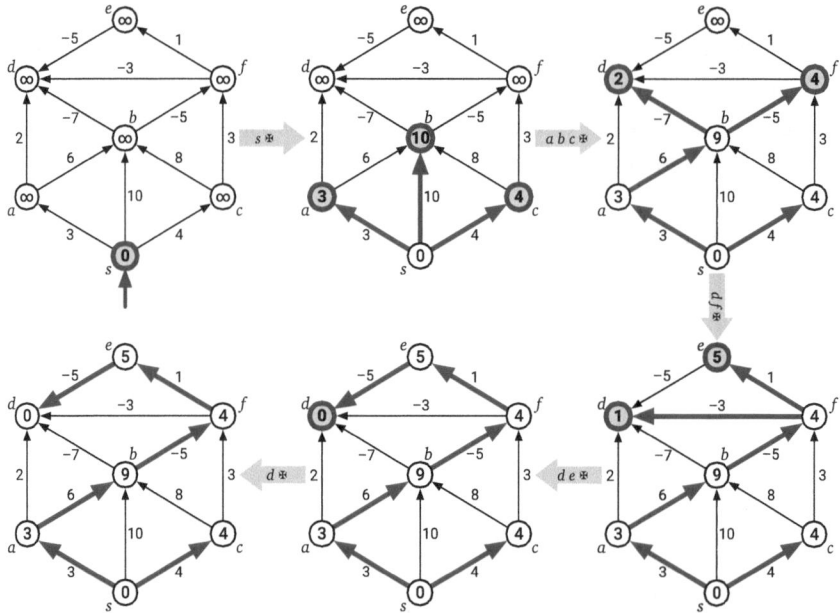

Figure 8.17. A complete run of Moore's algorithm on a directed graph with negative edges. Nodes are pulled from the queue in the order $s \maltese a\,b\,c \maltese d\,f \maltese d\,e \maltese d \maltese \maltese$, where $\maltese$ is the end-of-phase token. At the start of each phase, bold edges indicate predecessors, and shaded vertices are in the vertex queue. Compare with Figures 8.6 and 8.15.

cycles if they exist. Perhaps the easiest modification is to *actually* maintain a token, and count the number of times the token is Pulled from the queue. Then the input graph contains a negative cycle if and only if the queue is non-empty immediately after the token is Pulled for the $(V-1)$th time.

Dynamic Programming Formulation

Like almost everything else with his name on it, Richard Bellman derived the "Bellman-Ford" shortest-path algorithm via dynamic programming. As usual, we need to start with a recursive definition of shortest path distances. It's tempting to use the same identity that we exploited for directed acyclic graphs:

$$
dist(v) = \begin{cases} 0 & \text{if } v = s \\ \min_{u \to v}\left(dist(u) + w(u \to v)\right) & \text{otherwise} \end{cases}
$$

Unfortunately, if the input graph is not a dag, this recurrence doesn't work! Suppose the input graph contains the directed cycle $u \to v \to w \to u$. To compute $dist(w)$ we first need $dist(v)$, and to compute $dist(v)$ we first need $dist(u)$, but to compute $dist(u)$ we first need $dist(w)$. If the input graph has any directed cycles, we get stuck in an infinite loop!

To support a proper recurrence, we need to add an additional structural parameter to the distance function, which decreases monotonically at each recursive call, defined so that the function is trivial to evaluate when the parameter reaches 0. Bellman chose *the maximum number of edges* as this additional parameter.[14]

As in our earlier analysis, let $dist_{\leq i}(v)$ denote the length of the shortest walk from s to v consisting of at most i edges. Bellman observed that this function obeys the following ~~Bellman's equation~~ recurrence:

$$dist_{\leq i}(v) = \begin{cases} 0 & \text{if } i = 0 \text{ and } v = s \\ \infty & \text{if } i = 0 \text{ and } v \neq s \\ \min \left\{ \begin{array}{l} dist_{\leq i-1}(v) \\ \min_{u \to v} (dist_{\leq i-1}(u) + w(u \to v)) \end{array} \right\} & \text{otherwise} \end{cases}$$

Let's assume that the graph has no negative cycles, so our goal is to compute $dist_{\leq V-1}(v)$ for every vertex v. Here is a straightforward dynamic-programming evaluation of this recurrence, where $dist[i, v]$ stores the value of $dist_{\leq i}(v)$. Correctness of the final shortest-path distances follows from the correctness of the recurrence, and the $O(VE)$ running time is obvious. This is essentially how Bellman presented his shortest-path algorithm.

$\underline{\text{BELLMANFORDDP}(s)}$
  $dist[0, s] \leftarrow 0$
  for every vertex $v \neq s$
    $dist[0, v] \leftarrow \infty$
  for $i \leftarrow 1$ to $V - 1$
    for every vertex v
      $dist[i, v] \leftarrow dist[i - 1, v]$
      for every edge $u \to v$
        if $dist[i, v] > dist[i - 1, u] + w(u \to v)$
          $dist[i, v] \leftarrow dist[i - 1, u] + w(u \to v)$

We can transform this dynamic programming algorithm into our original formulation of BELLMANFORD through a short series of minor optimizations. First, each iteration of the outermost loop considers each edge $u \to v$ exactly once, but the order in which we consider those edges doesn't actually matter. Thus, we can safely remove one level of indentation from the last three lines! The modified algorithm may consider edges in a different *order*, but it still correctly computes $dist_{\leq i}(v)$ for all i and v.

---

[14]As we'll see in the next chapter, this is not the only reasonable choice.

```
BELLMANFORDDP2(s)
    dist[0, s] ← 0
    for every vertex v ≠ s
        dist[0, v] ← ∞
    for i ← 1 to V − 1
        for every vertex v
            dist[i, v] ← dist[i − 1, v]
        for every edge u→v
            if dist[i, v] > dist[i − 1, u] + w(u→v)
                dist[i, v] ← dist[i − 1, u] + w(u→v)
```

Next we change the indices in the last two lines from $i − 1$ to i. This change may cause the distances $dist[i, v]$ to approach the true shortest-path distances more quickly than before, but the algorithm correctly computes the true shortest path distances. Instead of $dist[i, v] = dist_{\le i}(v)$, we now have $dist[i, v] \le dist_{\le i}(v)$ for all i and v, mirroring Lemmas 8.6 and 8.7.

```
BELLMANFORDDP3(s)
    dist[0, s] ← 0
    for every vertex v ≠ s
        dist[0, v] ← ∞
    for i ← 1 to V − 1
        for every vertex v
            dist[i, v] ← dist[i − 1, v]
        for every edge u→v
            if dist[i, v] > dist[i, u] + w(u→v)      ⟨⟨not i − 1!⟩⟩
                dist[i, v] ← dist[i, u] + w(u→v)  ⟨⟨not i − 1!⟩⟩
```

But this algorithm is a little silly. In the ith iteration of the outermost loop, we first copy the $(i − 1)$th row of the array $dist[\cdot, \cdot]$ to the ith row, and then modify the elements of the ith row. So we really don't need a two-dimensional array at all; the iteration index i is completely redundant! In our final modification, we maintain only a one-dimensional array of tentative distances.

```
BELLMANFORDFINAL(s)
    dist[s] ← 0
    for every vertex v ≠ s
        dist[v] ← ∞
    for i ← 1 to V − 1
        for every edge u→v
            if dist[v] > dist[u] + w(u→v)
                dist[v] ← dist[u] + w(u→v)
```

This final dynamic programming algorithm is almost identical to our original formulation of BELLMANFORD! The first three lines initialize the shortest path distances, and the last two lines relax the edge $u→v$ if that edge is tense.

BELLMANFORDFINAL is missing only two features of our earlier formulation: It does not maintain predecessor pointers or detect negative cycles. Fortunately, adding those features is straightforward.

Exercises

0. Let G be a directed graph with arbitrary edge weights (which may be positive, negative, or zero), possibly with negative cycles, and let s be an arbitrary vertex of G.

    (a) Suppose every vertex v stores a number $dist(v)$ (but no predecessor pointers). Describe and analyze an algorithm to determine whether $dist(v)$ is the shortest-path distance from s to v, for every vertex v.

    (b) Suppose instead that every vertex $v \neq s$ stores a pointer $pred(v)$ to another vertex in G (but no distances). Describe and analyze an algorithm to determine whether these predecessor pointers define a single-source shortest path tree rooted at s.

1. A *looped tree* is a weighted, directed graph built from a binary tree by adding an edge from every leaf back to the root. Every edge has non-negative weight.

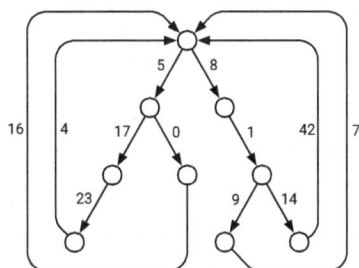

A looped tree.

    (a) How much time would Dijkstra's algorithm require to compute the shortest path between two vertices u and v in a looped tree with n nodes?

    (b) Describe and analyze a faster algorithm.

2. Suppose we are given a directed graph G with weighted edges and two vertices s and t.

    (a) Describe and analyze an algorithm to find the shortest path from s to t when exactly one edge in G has negative weight. [*Hint: Modify Dijkstra's algorithm. Or don't.*]

(b) Describe and analyze an algorithm to find the shortest path from s to t when exactly k edges in G have negative weight. How does the running time of your algorithm depend on k?

3. Suppose we are given an undirected graph G in which every *vertex* has a positive weight.

   (a) Describe and analyze an algorithm to find a *spanning tree* of G with minimum total weight. (The total weight of a spanning tree is the sum of the weights of its vertices.)

   (b) Describe and analyze an algorithm to find a *path* in G from one given vertex s to another given vertex t with minimum total weight. (The total weight of a path is the sum of the weights of its vertices.)

   [Hint: One of these problems is trivial.]

4. For any edge e in any graph G, let $G \setminus e$ denote the graph obtained by deleting e from G. Suppose we are given a graph G and two vertices s and t. The *replacement paths* problem asks us to compute the shortest-path distance from s to t in $G \setminus e$, for *every* edge e of G. The output is an array of E distances, one for each edge of G.

   (a) Suppose G is a *directed* graph, and the shortest path from vertex s to vertex t passes through *every* vertex of G. Describe an algorithm to solve this special case of the replacement paths problem in $O(E \log V)$ time.

   ♥(b) Describe an algorithm to solve the replacement paths problem for arbitrary *undirected* graphs in $O(E \log V)$ time.

   In both subproblems, you may assume that all edge weights are non-negative. *[Hint: If we delete an edge of the original shortest path, how do the old and new shortest paths overlap?]*

5. Let $G = (V, E)$ be a connected directed graph with non-negative edge weights, let s and t be vertices of G, and let H be a subgraph of G obtained by deleting some edges. Suppose we want to reinsert exactly one edge from G back into H, so that the shortest path from s to t in the resulting graph is as short as possible. Describe and analyze an algorithm that chooses the best edge to reinsert, in $O(E \log V)$ time.

6. (a) Describe and analyze a modification of Bellman-Ford that actually returns a negative cycle if any such cycle is reachable from s, or a shortest-path tree if there is no such cycle. The modified algorithm should still run in $O(VE)$ time.

(b) Describe and analyze a modification of Bellman-Ford that computes the correct shortest path distances from s to every other vertex of the input graph, even if the graph contains negative cycles. Specifically, if any walk from s to v contains a negative cycle, your algorithm should end with $dist(v) = -\infty$; otherwise, $dist(v)$ should contain the length of the shortest path from s to v. The modified algorithm should still run in $O(VE)$ time.

♥(c) Repeat parts (a) and (b), but for Ford's generic relaxation algorithm. You may assume that the unmodified algorithm halts in $O(2^V)$ steps if there is no negative cycle; your modified algorithms should also run in $O(2^V)$ time.

7. Consider the following even looser variant of Ford's generic relaxation algorithm:

> $\underline{\text{FELLMANBORED}(s):}$
> $\quad \text{INITSSSP}(s)$
> $\quad \text{for } i \leftarrow 1 \text{ to whatever, man, I don't care}$
> $\quad\quad e_i \leftarrow \text{any edge in } G$
> $\quad\quad \text{if } e_i \text{ is tense}$
> $\quad\quad\quad \text{RELAX}(e_i)$

Prove that if FELLMANBORED examines the edges of any walk W starting from s, in order along W, then the last distance label in W is at most the length of W. More formally: If the edges of any walk $v_0 \to v_1 \to \cdots \to v_\ell$, where $v_0 = s$, define a *subsequence* of the edges $e_1, e_2, e_3, \ldots$ examined by FELLMANBORED, then we have $dist(v_\ell) \le \sum_{i=1}^{\ell} w(v_{i-1} \to v_i)$. *[Hint: This property is almost easier to prove than it is to state correctly.]*

8. This problem considers several ways to detect negative cycles using Ford's generic relaxation algorithm.

(a) Prove that if $pred(s)$ ever changes after INITSSSP, then the input graph contains a negative cycle through s.

(b) Show that $pred(s)$ might never change after INITSSSP, even when the input graph contains a negative cycle through s.

(c) Let P denote the current graph of predecessor edges $pred(v) \to v$, and let X denote the set of all currently *tense* edges; both of these sets evolve as the algorithm executes. Prove that the input graph has no negative cycles if and only if $P \cup X$ is always a dag.

(d) Let R denote the set of all edges that have been relaxed so far; this set grows as the algorithm executes. Prove that the input graph has no negative cycles if and only if R is always a dag.

♥9. Prove that Dijkstra's algorithm performs $\Omega(2^V)$ relaxations in the worst case when edges are allowed to have negative weight, even if the underlying graph is acyclic. Specifically, for every positive integer n, construct a n-vertex dag G_n with weighted edges, such that Dijkstra's algorithm calls RELAX $\Omega(2^n)$ times when G_n is the input graph. [Hint: Binary counter.]

♥10. Prove that Ford's generic relaxation algorithm (and therefore Dijkstra's algorithm) halts after at most $O(2^V)$ relaxations, unless the input graph contains a negative cycle. [Hint: See Problem 8(d).]

11. Suppose you are given a directed graph G in which **every edge has negative weight**, and a source vertex s. Describe and analyze an efficient algorithm that computes the shortest-path distances from s to every other vertex in G. Specifically, for every vertex t:

   - If t is not reachable from s, your algorithm should report $dist(t) = \infty$.

   - If G has a cycle that is reachable from s, and t is reachable from that cycle, then the shortest-path distance from s to t is not well-defined, because there are paths (formally, walks) from s to t of arbitrarily large negative length. In this case, your algorithm should report $dist(t) = -\infty$.

   - If neither of the two previous conditions applies, your algorithm should report the correct shortest-path distance from s to t.

12. Although we typically speak of "the" shortest path between two nodes, single graph could contain several minimum-length paths with the same endpoints. Even for weighted graphs, it is often desirable to choose a minimum-weight path with the fewest edges; call this a **best path** from s to t. Suppose we are given a directed graph G with positive edge weights and a source vertex s in G. Describe and analyze an algorithm to compute *best* paths in G from s to every other vertex.

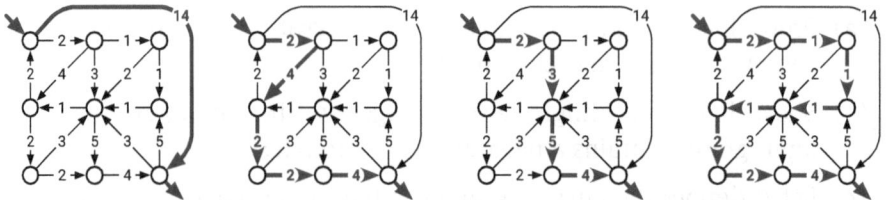

Figure 8.18. Four (of many) equal-length shortest paths. The first path is the "best" shortest path.

13. Describe and analyze an algorithm to determine the *number* of shortest paths from a source vertex s to a target vertex t in an arbitrary directed graph G with weighted edges. You may assume that all edge weights are positive and that all necessary arithmetic operations can be performed in

O(1) time. [*Hint: Compute shortest path distances from s to every other vertex. Throw away all edges that cannot be part of a shortest path from s to another vertex. What's left?*]

14. You just discovered your best friend from elementary school on Twitbook. You both want to meet as soon as possible, but you live in two different cites that are far apart. To minimize travel time, you agree to meet at an intermediate city, and then you simultaneously hop in your cars and start driving toward each other. But where *exactly* should you meet?

    You are given a weighted graph $G = (V, E)$, where the vertices V represent cities and the edges E represent roads that directly connect cities. Each edge e has a weight $w(e)$ equal to the time required to travel between the two cities. You are also given a vertex p, representing your starting location, and a vertex q, representing your friend's starting location.

    Describe and analyze an algorithm to find the target vertex t that allows you and your friend to meet as quickly as possible.

15. You are hired as a cyclist for the Giggle Highway View project, which will provide street-level images along the entire US national highway system. As a pilot project, you are asked to ride the Giggle Highway-View Fixed-Gear Carbon-Fiber Bicycle from "the Giggleplex" in Portland, Oregon to "Gigglesburg" in Williamsburg, Brooklyn, New York.

    You are a hopeless caffeine addict, but like most Giggle employees you are also a coffee snob; you only drink independently roasted, hand-pulled, direct-trade, organic, shade-grown, single-origin espresso, unadulterated by milk or sugar, thank you *very* much. After each espresso shot, you can bike up to L miles before suffering a caffeine-withdrawal migraine.

    Giggle helpfully provides you with a map of the United States, in the form of an undirected graph G, whose vertices represent coffee shops that sell independently roasted hand-pulled direct-trade organic shade-grown single-origin espresso, and whose edges represent highway connections between them. Each edge e is labeled with the length $\ell(e)$ of the corresponding stretch of highway. Naturally, there are acceptable espresso stands at both Giggle offices, represented by two specific vertices s and t in the graph G.

    (a) Describe and analyze an algorithm to determine whether it is possible to bike from the Giggleplex to Gigglesburg without suffering a caffeine-withdrawal migraine.

    (b) You discover that by wearing a more expensive fedora, you can increase the distance L that you can bike between espresso shots. Describe and analyze and algorithm to find the minimum value of L that allows you to bike from the Giggleplex to Gigglesburg without suffering a caffeine-withdrawal migraine.

(c) When you report to your supervisor (whom Giggle recently hired away from their competitor Ünter) that the ride is impossible, she demands to look at your map. "Oh, I see the problem; there are no *Starbucks* on this map!" As you look on in horror, she hands you an updated graph G' that includes a vertex for every Starbucks location in the United States, helpfully marked in Starbucks Green (Pantone® 3425 C).

Describe and analyze an algorithm to find the minimum number of Starbucks locations you must visit to bike from the Giggleplex to Gigglesburg without suffering a caffeine-withdrawal migraine. More formally, your algorithm should find the minimum number of green vertices on any path in G' from s to t that uses only edges of length at most L.

16. Suppose you are given a directed graph $G = (V, E)$ with non-negatively weighted edges and two vertices s and t. Describe and analyze an algorithm to find the shortest walk in G from s to t (possibly repeating vertices and/or edges) whose number of edges is divisible by 3.

For example, given the graph shown below, with the indicated vertices s and t, and with all edges having weight 1, your algorithm should return 6, which is the length of the walk $s \to w \to y \to x \to s \to w \to t$ has length 6.

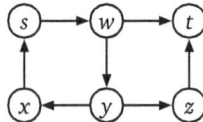

17. Suppose you are given a directed graph G with non-negatively weighted edges, where some edges are red and the remaining edges are blue. Describe an algorithm to find the shortest walk in G from one vertex s to another vertex t in which no three consecutive edges have the same color. That is, if the walk contains two red edges in a row, the next edge must be blue, and if the walk contains two blue edges in a row, the next edge must be red.

For example, given the following graph as input, where every red edge has weight 1 and every blue edge has weight 2, your algorithm should return the integer 9, because the shortest legal walk from s to t is $s \to a \to b \Rightarrow d \to c \Rightarrow a \to b \to c$.

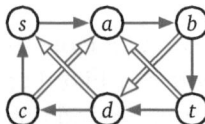

18. Consider a directed graph G, where each edge has a non-negative weight, and each edge is colored either red, white, or blue. A walk in G is called a *French flag walk* if its sequence of edge colors is red, white, blue, red, white, blue, and so on. More formally, a walk $v_0 \to v_1 \to \cdots \to v_k$ is a French flag walk if, for every integer i, the edge $v_i \to v_{i+1}$ is red if $i \bmod 3 = 0$, white if $i \bmod 3 = 1$, and blue if $i \bmod 3 = 2$.

    Describe an algorithm to find the *shortest* French flag walks from one starting vertex s to every other vertex in G.

19. There are n galaxies connected by m intergalactic teleport-ways. Each teleport-way joins two galaxies and can be traversed in both directions. Also, each teleport-way e has an associated cost of $c(e)$ dollars, where $c(e)$ is a positive integer. A teleport-way can be used multiple times, but the toll must be paid every time it is used.

    Judy wants to travel from galaxy s to galaxy t as cheaply as possible. However, she wants the total cost to be a multiple of five dollars, because carrying small change is not pleasant either.

    (a) Describe and analyze an algorithm to compute the minimum total cost of traveling from galaxy s to galaxy t, subject to the restriction that the total cost is a multiple of five dollars.

    (b) Solve part (a), but now assume that Judy has a coupon that allows her to use exactly one teleport-way for free.

20. After moving to a new city, you decide to choose a walking route from your home to your new office. To get a good daily workout, your route must consist of an uphill path (for exercise) followed by a downhill path (to cool down), or just an uphill path, or just a downhill path. (You'll walk the same path home, so you'll get exercise one way or the other.) But you also want the *shortest* path that satisfies these conditions, so that you actually get to work on time.

    Your input consists of an undirected graph G, whose vertices represent intersections and whose edges represent road segments, along with a start vertex s and a target vertex t. Every vertex v has an associated value $h(v)$, which is the height of that intersection above sea level, and each edge uv has an associated value $\ell(uv)$, which is the length of that road segment.

    (a) Describe and analyze an algorithm to find the shortest uphill–downhill walk from s to t. Assume all vertex heights are distinct.

    (b) Now suppose we allow some or all vertex heights to be equal. Describe and analyze an algorithm to find the shortest "uphill then downhill" walk from s to t; you may use flat edges in both the "uphill" and "downhill" portions of your walk.

(c) Finally, suppose you discover that there is no path from s to t with the structure you want. Describe an algorithm to find a path from s to t that alternates between "uphill" and "downhill" subpaths as few times as possible, and has minimum length among all such paths.

21. After graduating from Sham-Poobanana University you accept a job with Aerophobes-Я-Us, the leading traveling agency for people who hate to fly. Your job is to build a system to help customers plan airplane trips from one city to another. All of your customers are afraid of flying (and by extension, airports), so any trip you plan needs to be as short as possible. You know all the departure and arrival times of all the flights on the planet.

Suppose one of your customers wants to fly from city X to city Y. Describe an algorithm to find a sequence of flights that minimizes the *total time in transit*—the length of time from the initial departure to the final arrival, including time at intermediate airports waiting for connecting flights.

22. In Exercise 20 from Chapter 5, you designed an algorithm to decide whether a given *acute-angle maze* is solvable. In this problem, you will design algorithms to find the *shortest* walk through a given acute-angle maze, for two different definitions of "length".

Complete each angle maze below by tracing a path from start to finish that has only acute angles.

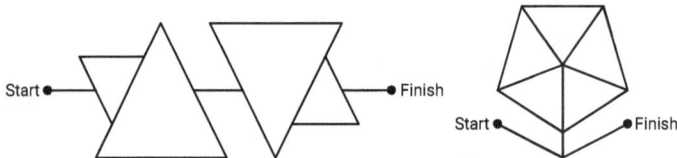

Your input is a connected undirected graph G whose vertices are points in the plane and whose edges are line segments. Edges do not intersect, except at their endpoints. For example, a drawing of the letter X would have five vertices and four edges; the first maze above has 14 vertices and 21 edges. You are also given two vertices Start and Finish.

A walk from Start to Finish in G is *valid* if it contains only acute angles, or more formally, for any two consecutive edges $u \to v \to w$, either $\angle uvw = \pi$ or $0 < \angle uvw < \pi/2$. Assume you can determine in $O(1)$ time whether the angle between two given segments is straight, obtuse, right, or acute.

(a) Describe an algorithm to compute a valid walk from Start to Finish that traverses as few segments as possible. (If your walk traverses the same segment twice, count it twice.)

(b) Describe an algorithm to compute a valid walk from Start to Finish that makes as few turns as possible. [Hint: This is **not** the same as part (a).]

(c) Describe an algorithm to compute a valid walk from Start to Finish whose total Euclidean length is as small as possible. (Assume you can also compute the length of any segment in $O(1)$ time.)

23. After a grueling midterm at the See-Bull Center for Fake News Detection, you decide to take the bus home. Since you planned ahead, you have a schedule that lists the times and locations of every stop of every bus in Sham-Poobanana. Unfortunately, no single bus visits both the See-Bull Center and your home; you must change buses at least once. There are exactly b different buses. Each bus starts at 12:00:01AM, makes exactly n stops, and finally stops running at 11:59:59PM. Buses always run exactly on schedule, and you have an accurate watch. Finally, you are far too tired to walk between bus stops.

    (a) Describe and analyze an algorithm to determine the sequence of bus rides that gets you home as early as possible. Your goal is to minimize your *arrival time*, not the time you spend traveling.

    (b) Oh, no! The midterm was held on Halloween, and the streets are infested with zombies! The Sham-Poobanana Mass Transit District doesn't have the funding to add additional buses or install zombie-proof bus stops, especially for only one night a year. Describe and analyze an algorithm to determine a sequence of bus rides that minimizes *the total time you spend waiting at bus stops*; you don't care how late you get home or how much time you spend on buses. (Assume you can wait inside the See-Bull Center until your first bus is just about to leave.)

24. The first morning after returning from a glorious spring break, Alice wakes to discover that her car won't start, so she has to get to her classes at Sham-Poobanana University by public transit. She has a complete transit schedule for Poobanana County. The bus routes are represented in the schedule by a directed graph G, whose vertices represent bus stops and whose edges represent bus routes between those stops. For each edge $u \rightarrow v$, the schedule records three positive real numbers:

    - $\ell(u \rightarrow v)$ is the length of the bus ride from stop u to stop v (in minutes)
    - $f(u \rightarrow v)$ is the first time (in minutes past 12am) that a bus leaves stop u for stop v.
    - $\Delta(u \rightarrow v)$ is the time between successive departures from stop u to stop v (in minutes).

    Thus, the first bus for this route leaves u at time $f(u \rightarrow v)$ and arrives at v at time $f(u \rightarrow v) + \ell(u \rightarrow v)$, the second bus leaves u at time $f(u \rightarrow v) + \Delta(u \rightarrow v)$ and arrives at v at time $f(u \rightarrow v) + \Delta(u \rightarrow v) + \ell(u \rightarrow v)$, the third bus leaves u at time

$f(u{\to}v)+2\cdot\Delta(u{\to}v)$ and arrives at v at time $f(u{\to}v)+2\cdot\Delta(u{\to}v)+\ell(u{\to}v)$, and so on.

Alice wants to leaves from stop s (her home) at a certain time and arrive at stop t (The See-Bull Center) as quickly as possible. If Alice arrives at a stop on one bus at the exact time that another bus is scheduled to leave, she can catch the second bus. Because she's a student at SPU, Alice can ride the bus for free, so she doesn't care how many times she has to change buses.

Describe and analyze an algorithm to find the earliest time Alice can reach her destination. Your input consists of the directed graph $G = (V, E)$, the vertices s and t, the values $\ell(e), f(e), \Delta(e)$ for each edge $e \in E$, and Alice's starting time (in minutes past 12am).

[*Hint: In this rare instance, it may be easier to modify the algorithm, instead of modifying the input graph.*]

25. Mulder and Scully have computed, for every road in the United States, the exact probability that someone driving on that road *won't* be abducted by aliens. Agent Mulder needs to drive from Langley, Virginia to Area 51, Nevada. What route should he take so that he has the least chance of being abducted?

More formally, you are given a directed graph $G = (V, E)$, where every edge e has an independent safety probability $p(e)$. The *safety* of a path is the product of the safety probabilities of its edges. Design and analyze an algorithm to determine the safest path from a given start vertex s to a given target vertex t. You may assume that all necessary arithmetic operations can be performed in $O(1)$ time.

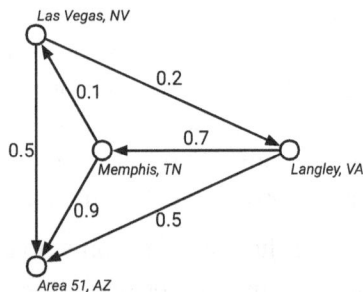

For example, with the probabilities shown above, if Mulder tries to drive directly from Langley to Area 51, he has a 50% chance of getting there without being abducted. If he stops in Memphis, he has a $0.7 \times 0.9 = 63\%$ chance of arriving safely. If he stops first in Memphis and then in Las Vegas, he has a $1 - 0.7 \times 0.1 \times 0.5 = 96.5\%$ chance of being abducted! (That's how they got Elvis, you know.)

*26. On an overnight camping trip in Sunnydale National Park, you are woken from a restless sleep by a scream. As you crawl out of your tent to investigate, a terrified park ranger runs out of the woods, covered in blood and clutching a crumpled piece of paper to his chest. As he reaches your tent, he gasps, "Get out... while... you...", thrusts the paper into your hands, and falls to the ground. Checking his pulse, you discover that the ranger is stone dead.

You look down at the paper and recognize a map of the park, drawn as an undirected graph, where vertices represent landmarks in the park, and edges represent trails between those landmarks. (Trails start and end at landmarks and do not cross.) You recognize one of the vertices as your current location; several vertices on the boundary of the map are labeled EXIT.

On closer examination, you notice that someone (perhaps the poor dead park ranger) has written a real number between 0 and 1 next to each vertex and each edge. A scrawled note on the back of the map indicates that a number next to an edge is the probability of encountering a vampire along the corresponding trail, and a number next to a vertex is the probability of encountering a vampire at the corresponding landmark. (Vampires can't stand each other's company, so you'll never see more than one vampire on the same trail or at the same landmark.) The note warns you that stepping off the marked trails will result in a slow and painful death.

You glance down at the corpse at your feet. Yes, his death certainly looked painful. Wait, was that a twitch? Are his teeth getting longer? After driving a tent stake through the undead ranger's heart, you wisely decide to *immediately* leave the park as fast as possible.

Describe and analyze an efficient algorithm to find a path from your current location to an arbitrary EXIT node, such that the total *expected number* of vampires encountered along the path is as small as possible. Be sure to account for *both* the vertex probabilities *and* the edge probabilities. [Hint: Even without the vertex probabilities, this is not the same as the previous problem!]

The tree which fills the arms grew from the tiniest sprout;
the tower of nine storeys rose from a (small) heap of earth;
the journey of a thousand li commenced with a single step.

> — Lao-Tzu, *Tao Te Ching*, chapter 64 (6th century BCE),
> translated by James Legge (1891)

And I would walk five hundred miles,
And I would walk five hundred more,
Just to be the man who walks a thousand miles
To fall down at your door.

> — The Proclaimers, "I'm Gonna Be (500 Miles)",
> *Sunshine on Leith* (2001)

Almost there... Almost there...

> — Red Leader [Drewe Henley], *Star Wars* (1977)

9

All-Pairs Shortest Paths

9.1 Introduction

In the previous chapter, we discussed several algorithms to find the shortest paths from a single source vertex s to every other vertex of the graph, by constructing a shortest path tree rooted at s. The shortest path tree specifies two pieces of information for each node v in the graph:

- $dist(v)$ is the length of the shortest path from s to v;
- $pred(v)$ is the second-to-last vertex in the shortest path from s to v.

In this chapter, we consider the more general *all pairs shortest path* problem, which asks for the shortest path from *every* possible source to every possible destination. For every pair of vertices u and v, we want to compute the following information:

- $dist(u, v)$ is the length of the shortest path from u to v;
- $pred(u, v)$ is the second-to-last vertex on the shortest path from u to v.

These intuitive definitions exclude a few boundary cases, all of which we already saw in the previous chapter.

- If there is no path from u to v, then there is no *shortest* path from u to v; in this case, we define $dist(u,v) = \infty$ and $pred(u,v) = \text{NULL}$.

- If there is a negative cycle between u and v, then there are paths[1] from u to v with arbitrarily negative length; in this case, we define $dist(u,v) = -\infty$ and $pred(u,v) = \text{NULL}$.

- Finally, if u does not lie on a negative cycle, then the shortest path from u to itself has no edges, and therefore doesn't have a last edge; in this case, we define $dist(u,u) = 0$ and $pred(u,u) = \text{NULL}$.

The desired output of the all-pairs shortest path problem is a pair of $V \times V$ arrays, one storing all V^2 shortest-path distances,[2] the other storing all V^2 predecessors. In this chapter, I'll focus almost exclusively on computing the distance array. The predecessor array, from which we can compute the actual shortest paths, can be computed with only minor modifications (hint, hint).

9.2 Lots of Single Sources

The most obvious solution to the all-pairs shortest path problem is to run a single-source shortest path algorithm V times, once for each possible source vertex. Specifically, to fill the one-dimensional subarray $dist[s,\cdot]$, we invoke a single-source algorithm starting at the source vertex s.

$\text{OBVIOUSAPSP}(V, E, w)$:
    for every vertex s
        $dist[s,\cdot] \leftarrow \text{SSSP}(V, E, w, s)$

The running time of this algorithm obviously depends on which single-source shortest path algorithm we use. Just as in the single-source setting, there are four natural options, depending on the structure of the graph and its edge weights:

- If the edges of the graph are unweighted, breadth-first search gives us an overall running time of $O(VE) = O(V^3)$.

- If the graph is acyclic, scanning the vertices in topological order also gives us an overall running time of $O(VE) = O(V^3)$.

---

[1]formally, walks

[2]Back when road maps used to be printed on paper and had to be searched manually, it was fairly common for them to include a triangular "distance table". To find the distance from Champaign to Columbus, for example, you would look in the row labeled "Champaign" and the column labeled "Columbus".

- If all edge weights are non-negative, Dijkstra's algorithm gives us a running time to $O(VE \log V) = O(V^3 \log V)$.[3]

- Finally, in the most general setting, the Bellman-Ford algorithm gives us an overall running time of $O(V^2 E) = O(V^4)$.

9.3   Reweighting

Negative edges slow us down significantly; can we get rid of them? One simple idea that occurs to many people is increasing the weights of all the edges by the same amount so that all the weights become positive, so that we can use Dijkstra's algorithm instead of Bellman-Ford. Unfortunately, this simple idea doesn't work, intuitively because our two natural notions of "length" are incompatible—paths with more edges can have smaller total weight than paths with fewer edges. If we increase all edge weights at the same rate, paths with more edges get longer faster than paths with fewer edges; as a result, the shortest path between two vertices might change.

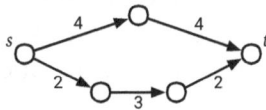

Figure 9.1. Increasing all the edge weights by 2 changes the shortest path from *s* to *t*.

However, there is a more subtle method for reweighting edges that does preserve shortest paths. This reweighting method is often attributed to Donald Johnson, who described its application to shortest path algorithms in 1973. But in fact, Johnson attributed the method to a 1972 paper of Jack Edmonds and Richard Karp. The same method was also described by Nobuaki Tomizawa in 1971, and in a slightly different form by Delbert Fulkerson in 1961.

Suppose each vertex v has some associated *price* $\pi(v)$, which might be positive, negative, or zero. We can define a new weight function w' as follows:

$$w'(u \to v) = \pi(u) + w(u \to v) - \pi(v)$$

To give some intuition, imagine that when we leave vertex u, we have to pay an exit tax of $\pi(u)$, and when we enter v, we get $\pi(v)$ as an entrance gift.

It's not hard to show that shortest paths with the new weight function w' are exactly the same as shortest paths with the original weight function w. In

---

[3]Again, if we replace the binary heap in our implementation of Dijkstra's algorithm with an unsorted array, the overall running time becomes $O(V^3)$ (no matter how many edges the graph has), and if we replace the binary heap with a Fibonacci heap, the running time drops to $O(V(E + V \log V)) = O(VE + V^2 \log V) = O(V^3)$.

fact, for *any* path $u \rightsquigarrow v$ from one vertex u to another vertex v, we have

$$w'(u \rightsquigarrow v) = \pi(u) + w(u \rightsquigarrow v) - \pi(v).$$

We pay $\pi(u)$ in exit fees, plus the original weight of of the path, minus the $\pi(v)$ entrance gift. At every intermediate vertex x on the path, we get $\pi(x)$ as an entrance gift, but then immediately pay it back as an exit tax! Since all paths from u to v change length by exactly the same amount, the shortest path from u to v does not change. (Paths between different pairs of vertices could change lengths by different amounts, so their order could change.)

9.4 Johnson's Algorithm

Johnson's all-pairs shortest path algorithm computes a cost $\pi(v)$ for each vertex, so that the new weight of every edge is non-negative, and then computes shortest paths with respect to the new weights using Dijkstra's algorithm.

First, suppose the input graph has a vertex s that can reach *all* the other vertices. Johnson's algorithm computes the shortest paths from s to the other vertices, using Bellman-Ford (which doesn't care if the edge weights are negative), and then reweights the graph using the price function $\pi(v) = dist(s, v)$. The new weight of every edge is

$$w'(u \rightarrow v) = dist(s, u) + w(u \rightarrow v) - dist(s, v).$$

These new weights are non-negative *because* Bellman-Ford halted! Recall that an edge $u \rightarrow v$ is *tense* if $dist(s, u) + w(u \rightarrow v) < dist(s, v)$, and that single-source shortest path algorithms eliminate all tense edges. (If Bellman-Ford detects a negative cycle, Johnson's algorithm aborts, because shortest paths are not well-defined.)

If there is no suitable vertex s that can reach everything, then no matter where we start Bellman-Ford, some of the resulting vertex prices will be infinite. To avoid this issue, we *always* add a new vertex s to the graph, with zero-weight edges from s to the other vertices, but *no* edges going back into s. This addition doesn't change the shortest paths between any pair of original vertices, because there are no paths into s.

Complete pseudocode for Johnson's algorithm is shown in Figure 9.2. The running time of this algorithm is dominated by the calls to Dijkstra's algorithm. Specifically, we spend $O(VE)$ time running BELLMANFORD once, $O(VE \log V)$ time running DIJKSTRA V times, and $O(V + E)$ time doing other bookkeeping. Thus, the overall running time is $O(VE \log V) = O(V^3 \log V)$.[4] Negative edges don't slow us down after all!

---

[4]...assuming the default binary-heap implementation; see the previous footnote.

```
JOHNSONAPSP(V, E, w) :
    ⟨⟨Add an artificial source⟩⟩
    add a new vertex s
    for every vertex v
        add a new edge s→v
        w(s→v) ← 0
    ⟨⟨Compute vertex prices⟩⟩
    dist[s, ·] ← BELLMANFORD(V, E, w, s)
    if BELLMANFORD found a negative cycle
        fail gracefully
    ⟨⟨Reweight the edges⟩⟩
    for every edge u→v ∈ E
        w'(u→v) ← dist[s, u] + w(u→v) − dist[s, v]
    ⟨⟨Compute reweighted shortest path distances⟩⟩
    for every vertex u
        dist'[u, ·] ← DIJKSTRA(V, E, w', u)
    ⟨⟨Compute original shortest-path distances⟩⟩
    for every vertex u
        for every vertex v
            dist[u, v] ← dist'[u, v] − dist[s, u] + dist[s, v]
```

Figure 9.2. Johnson's all-pairs shortest paths algorithm

9.5 Dynamic Programming

We can also solve the all-pairs shortest path problem directly using dynamic programming, instead of invoking a single-source algorithm. For *dense* graphs, where $E = \Omega(V^2)$, the dynamic programming approach eventually yields an algorithm that is both simpler and (slightly) faster than Johnson's algorithm. **For the rest of this chapter, I will assume that the input graph contains no negative cycles.**

As usual for dynamic programming algorithms, we first need a recurrence. Just as in the single-source setting, the "obvious" recursive definition

$$dist(u, v) = \begin{cases} 0 & \text{if } u = v \\ \min_{x \to v} \left(dist(u, x) + w(x \to v) \right) & \text{otherwise} \end{cases}$$

only works when the input graph is a dag; any directed cycles drive the recurrence into an infinite loop.

We can break this infinite loop by introducing as an additional parameter, exactly as we did for Bellman-Ford; let $dist(u, v, \ell)$ denote the length of the shortest path from u to v that uses *at most ℓ edges*. The shortest path between any two vertices traverses at most $V - 1$ edges, so the true shortest-path distance is $dist(u, v, V - 1)$. Bellman's single-source recurrence adapts to this setting immediately:

$$dist(u, v, \ell) = \begin{cases} 0 & \text{if } \ell = 0 \text{ and } u = v \\ \infty & \text{if } \ell = 0 \text{ and } u \neq v \\ \min \left\{ \begin{array}{l} dist(u, v, \ell - 1) \\ \min_{x \to v} (dist(u, x, \ell - 1) + w(x \to v)) \end{array} \right\} & \text{otherwise} \end{cases}$$

Turning this recurrence into a dynamic programming algorithm is straightforward; the resulting algorithm runs in $O(V^2 E) = O(V^4)$ time.

```
ShimbelAPSP(V, E, w):
    for all vertices u
        for all vertices v
            if u = v
                dist[u, v, 0] ← 0
            else
                dist[u, v, 0] ← ∞
    for ℓ ← 1 to V − 1
        for all vertices u
            for all vertices v ≠ u
                dist[u, v, ℓ] ← dist[u, v, ℓ − 1]
                for all edges x→v
                    if dist[u, v, ℓ] > dist[u, x, ℓ − 1] + w(x→v)
                        dist[u, v, ℓ] ← dist[u, x, ℓ − 1] + w(x→v)
```

This algorithm was first sketched by Alfonso Shimbel in 1954.[5] Just like Bellman's formulation of Bellman-Ford, we don't need the inner loop over vertices v or the iteration index ℓ. The modified algorithm is shown below.

```
AllPairsBellmanFord(V, E, w):
    for all vertices u
        for all vertices v
            if u = v
                dist[u, v] ← 0
            else
                dist[u, v] ← ∞
    for ℓ ← 1 to V − 1
        for all vertices u
            for all edges x→v
                if dist[u, v] > dist[u, x] + w(x→v)
                    dist[u, v] ← dist[u, x] + w(x→v)
```

---

[5]Shimbel assumed the input was a complete $V \times V$ matrix of distances, so his original algorithm actually runs in $O(V^4)$ time no matter how many edges the graph has.

Given how we derived it, it should come as no surprise that the resulting algorithm is exactly the same as interleaving V different executions of Bellman-Ford, each with a different source vertex. In particular, for all vertices u and v, after the ℓth iteration of the main for-loop, $dist[u, v]$ is *at most* the length of the shortest path from u to v containing at most ℓ edges.

9.6 Divide and Conquer

But we can make a more significant improvement, suggested by Michael Fischer and Albert Meyer in 1971. Bellman's recurrence breaks the shortest path into a slightly shorter path and a single edge, by considering all possible predecessors of the target vertex. Instead, let's break the shortest paths into two shorter shortest paths at the *middle* vertex. This idea gives us a different recurrence for the same function $dist(u, v, \ell)$. Here we need to stop at the base case $\ell = 1$ instead of $\ell = 0$, because a path with at most one edge has no "middle" vertex. To simplify the recurrence slightly, let's define $w(v \to v) = 0$ for every vertex v.

$$dist(u, v, \ell) = \begin{cases} w(u \to v) & \text{if } i = 1 \\ \min_{x} \big(dist(u, x, \ell/2) + dist(x, v, \ell/2)\big) & \text{otherwise} \end{cases}$$

As stated, this recurrence only works when ℓ is a power of 2, since otherwise we might try to find the shortest path with (at most) a fractional number of edges! But that's not really a problem; $dist(u, v, \ell)$ is the true shortest-path distance from u to v *for all* $\ell \geq V - 1$; in particular, we can use $\ell = 2^{\lceil \lg V \rceil} < 2V$.

Once again, a dynamic programming solution is straightforward. Even before we write down the algorithm, we can tell the running time is $O(V^3 \log V)$—we need to consider V possible values of u, v, and x, but only $\lceil \lg V \rceil$ possible values of ℓ. In the following pseudocode for Fischer and Meyer's algorithm, the array entry $dist[u, v, i]$ stores the value of $dist(u, v, 2^i)$.

$\underline{\text{FISCHERMEYERAPSP}(V, E, w)}$:
    for all vertices u
        for all vertices v
            $dist[u, v, 0] \leftarrow w(u \to v)$
    for $i \leftarrow 1$ to $\lceil \lg V \rceil$ $\langle\!\langle \ell = 2^i \rangle\!\rangle$
        for all vertices u
            for all vertices v
                $dist[u, v, i] \leftarrow \infty$
                for all vertices x
                    if $dist[u, v, i] > dist[u, x, i-1] + dist[x, v, i-1]$
                        $dist[u, v, i] \leftarrow dist[u, x, i-1] + dist[x, v, i-1]$

Unlike our earlier algorithms, FISCHERMEYERAPSP is *not* the same as V invocations of any single-source shortest-path algorithm; in particular, the innermost loop does *not* simply relax tense edges. Nevertheless, we can still remove the last dimension of the table, using $dist[u, v]$ everywhere in place of $dist[u, v, i]$, just as we did in Bellman-Ford and our earlier dynamic programming algorithm; this reduces the space from $O(V^3)$ to $O(V^2)$. This more polished algorithm was described by Leyzorek *et al.* in 1957, in the same paper where they describe Dijkstra's algorithm.

```
LeyzorekAPSP(V, E, w):
    for all vertices u
        for all vertices v
            dist[u, v] ← w(u→v)

    for i ← 1 to ⌈lg V⌉          ⟨⟨ℓ = 2^i⟩⟩
        for all vertices u
            for all vertices v
                for all vertices x
                    if dist[u, v] > dist[u, x] + dist[x, v]
                        dist[u, v] ← dist[u, x] + dist[x, v]
```

9.7 Funny Matrix Multiplication

There is a very close connection (first observed by Shimbel, and later independently by Bellman) between computing shortest paths in a directed graph and computing powers of a square matrix. Compare the following algorithm for squaring an $n \times n$ matrix A with the inner loop of FischerMeyerAPSP. (I've slightly modified the notation in the second algorithm to make the similarity clearer.)

```
MatrixSquare(A):
    for i ← 1 to n
        for j ← 1 to n
            A'[i, j] ← 0
            for k ← 1 to n
                A'[i, j] ← A'[i, j] + A[i, k] · A[k, j]
```

```
FischerMeyerInnerLoop(D):
    for all vertices u
        for all vertices v
            D'[u, v] ← ∞
            for all vertices x
                D'[u, v] ← min {D'[u, v], D[u, x] + D[x, v]}
```

The *only* difference between these two algorithms is that the second algorithm uses addition instead of multiplication, and minimization instead of addition. For this reason, the shortest path inner loop is sometimes referred to as "min-plus" or "distance" or "funny" matrix multiplication.

Our slower algorithm SHIMBELAPSP is the standard iterative algorithm for computing the $(V-1)$th "min-plus power" of the weight matrix w. The first set of loops sets up the min-plus identity matrix, with 0s on the main diagonal and ∞ everywhere else, and each iteration of the second main loop computes the next "min-plus power". FISCHERMEYERAPSP replaces this iterative method for computing powers with repeated squaring, exactly as we saw at the end of Chapter 1. Once again, we see the influence of ancient Egyptian ἀρπεδονάπται!

There are faster divide-and-conquer algorithms for (standard) matrix multiplication, similar to Karatsuba's divide-and-conquer algorithm for multiplying integers. The first such algorithm, described by Volker Strassen in 1969, reduces the problem of multiplying two $n \times n$ matrices to *seven* instances of multiplying two $n/2 \times n/2$ matrices; Strassen's algorithm runs in $O(n^{\lg 7}) = O(n^{2.807355})$. Strassen's algorithm has been improved many times over the last fifty years; as of 2018, the fastest matrix-multiplication algorithm known runs in $O(n^{2.372864})$ time.[6] Unfortunately, *all* of these faster algorithms use subtraction, and there's no "funny" equivalent of subtraction. (What's the inverse operation for min?) So at least for general graphs, there's no obvious way to speed up the inner loop of our dynamic programming algorithms.

But "not obvious" does not mean "impossible"! In fact, there are several significantly faster algorithms for *special cases* of the all-pairs shortest paths problem. One of the nicest is a simple randomized algorithm discovered in 1991 by Zvi Galil and Oded Margalit, and further simplified in 1992 by Raimund Seidel, that computes all-pairs shortest path *distances* in *unweighted, undirected* graphs in $O(M(V)\log V)$ *expected* time, where $M(n) = O(n^{2.372864})$ is the time required to (seriously) multiply two $n \times n$ integer matrices.[7] Galil, Margalit, and Seidel's approach has since been extended to compute actual shortest paths, deterministically, in directed graphs, with small integer edge weights, in strongly subcubic time.

On the other hand, despite considerable progress in the small-integer-weight setting, nobody knows how to compute all-pairs shortest paths for more general edge weights in $O(V^{2.999999})$ time, for any number of 9s. Moreover, there is some evidence that such an algorithm is impossible! So maybe "not obvious" does mean "impossible" after all.

---

[6]Determining the minimum time required to multiply two arbitrary $n \times n$ matrices is a long-standing open problem; many people believe there is an undiscovered algorithm that runs in $O(n^{2+\varepsilon})$ time for any $\varepsilon > 0$, or possibly even in $O(n^2)$ time.

[7]Raimund Seidel. On the all-pairs-shortest-path problem in unweighted undirected graphs. *Journal of Computer and System Sciences*, 51(3):400-403, 1995. This is one of the few algorithms papers where (in the 1992 conference version at least) the algorithm is completely described and analyzed *in the abstract* of the paper. See also: Noga Alon, Zvi Galil, Oded Margalit*. On the exponent of the all pairs shortest path problem. *Journal of Computer and System Sciences* 54(2):255–262, 1997.

9.8 (Kleene-Roy-)Floyd-Warshall(-Ingerman)

Our fast dynamic programming algorithm is still a factor of $O(\log V)$ slower in the worst case than the standard implementation of Johnson's algorithm. A different formulation of shortest paths that removes this logarithmic factor was proposed twice in 1962, first by Robert Floyd and later independently by Peter Ingerman, both slightly generalizing an algorithm of Stephen Warshall published earlier in the same year. In fact, Warshall's algorithm was previously discovered by Bernard Roy in 1959, and the underlying recursion pattern was used by Stephen Kleene[8] in 1951.

Warshall's (and Roy's and Kleene's) insight was to use a different third parameter in the dynamic programming recurrence. Instead of considering paths with a limited number of edges, they considered paths that can pass through only certain vertices. Here, "pass through" means "both enter and leave"; for example, the path $w \to x \to y \to z$ starts at w, *passes through* x and y, and ends at z.

Number the vertices arbitrarily from 1 to V. For every pair of vertices u and v and every integer r, we define a path $\pi(u, v, r)$ as follows:

> $\pi(u, v, r)$ is the shortest path (if any) from u to v that passes through only vertices numbered at most r.

In particular, $\pi(u, v, V)$ is the true shortest path from u to v. Kleene and Roy and Warshall all observed that these paths have a simple recursive structure.

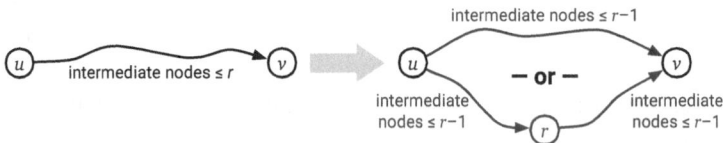

Figure 9.3. Recursive structure of the restricted shortest path $\pi(u, v, r)$.

- The path $\pi(u, v, 0)$ can't pass through any intermediate vertices, so it must be the edge (if any) from u to v.

- For any integer $r > 0$, either $\pi(u, v, r)$ passes through vertex r or it doesn't.

  - If $\pi(u, v, r)$ passes through vertex r, it consists of a subpath from u to r, followed by a subpath from r to v. Both of those subpaths pass through only vertices numbered at most $r - 1$; moreover, those subpaths are as short as possible with this restriction. So the two subpaths must be $\pi(u, r, r - 1)$ and $\pi(r, v, r - 1)$.

---

[8]Pronounced "clay knee", not "clean" or "clean-ee" or "clay-nuh" or "dimaggio". Specifically, Kleene described an inductive proof that every finite automata has an equivalent regular expression; Kleene's induction pattern is essentially identical to the Floyd-Warshall recurrence.

– On the other hand, if $\pi(u, v, r)$ does not pass through vertex r, then it passes through only vertices numbered at most $r - 1$, and it must be the *shortest* path with this restriction. So in this case, we must have $\pi(u, v, r) = \pi(u, v, r - 1)$.

Now let $dist(u, v, r)$ denote the *length* of the path $\pi(u, v, r)$. The recursive structure of $\pi(u, v, r)$ immediately implies the following recurrence:

$$dist(u, v, r) = \begin{cases} w(u \to v) & \text{if } r = 0 \\ \min \left\{ \begin{array}{l} dist(u, v, r - 1) \\ dist(u, r, r - 1) + dist(r, v, r - 1) \end{array} \right\} & \text{otherwise} \end{cases}$$

Our goal is to compute $dist(u, v, V)$ for all vertices u and v. Once again, this recurrence can be evaluated by a straightforward dynamic programming algorithm in $O(V^3)$ *time.*

$\underline{\text{KLEENEAPSP}}(V, E, w)$:
  for all vertices u
    for all vertices v
      $dist[u, v, 0] \leftarrow w(u \to v)$

  for $r \leftarrow 1$ to V
    for all vertices u
      for all vertices v
        if $dist[u, v, r - 1] < dist[u, r, r - 1] + dist[r, v, r - 1]$
          $dist[u, v, r] \leftarrow dist[u, v, r - 1]$
        else
          $dist[u, v, r] \leftarrow dist[u, r, r - 1] + dist[r, v, r - 1]$

Like all our previous dynamic programming algorithms for shortest paths, we can simplify KLEENEAPSP by removing the third dimension of the memoization table. Also, because we chose the vertex numbering arbitrarily, there's no reason to refer to it explicitly in the pseudocode. We finally arrive at Floyd's improvement of Warshall's algorithm:

$\underline{\text{FLOYDWARSHALL}}(V, E, w)$:
  for all vertices u
    for all vertices v
      $dist[u, v] \leftarrow w(u \to v)$

  for all vertices r
    for all vertices u
      for all vertices v
        if $dist[u, v] > dist[u, r] + dist[r, v]$
          $dist[u, v] \leftarrow dist[u, r] + dist[r, v]$

It's interesting to compare FLOYDWARSHALL with our earlier, slightly slower dynamic programming algorithm LEYZOREKAPSP. Instead of $O(\log V)$ passes through all triples of vertices, FLOYDWARSHALL requires only a single pass, but only because it uses a different nesting order for the three loops!

Exercises

1. (a) Describe a modification of LEYZOREKAPSP that returns an array of predecessor pointers, in addition to the array of shortest path distances, still in $O(V^3 \log V)$ time.

   (b) Describe a modification of FLOYDWARSHALL that returns an array of predecessor pointers, in addition to the array of shortest path distances, still in $O(V^3)$ time.

2. All of the algorithms discussed in this chapter fail if the graph contains a negative cycle. Johnson's algorithm detects the negative cycle in the initialization phase (via Bellman-Ford) and aborts; the dynamic programming algorithms just return incorrect results. However, *all* of these algorithms can be modified to return correct shortest-path distances, even in the presence of negative cycles. Specifically, for all vertices u and v:

   • If u cannot reach v, the algorithm should return $dist[u, v] = \infty$.

   • If u can reach a negative cycle that can reach v, the algorithm should return $dist[u, v] = -\infty$.

   • Otherwise, there is a shortest path from u to v, so the algorithm should return its length.

   (a) Describe how to modify Johnson's algorithm to return the correct shortest-path distances, even if the graph has negative cycles.

   (b) Describe how to modify LEYZOREKAPSP to return the correct shortest-path distances, even if the graph has negative cycles.

   (c) Describe how to modify Floyd-Warshall to return the correct shortest-path distances, even if the graph has negative cycles.

3. The algorithms described in this chapter can also be modified to return an explicit description of some negative cycle in the input graph G, if one exists, instead of only reporting whether or not G contains a negative cycle.

   (a) Describe how to modify Johnson's algorithm to return either the array of all shortest-path distances or a negative cycle.

   (b) Describe how to modify LEYZOREKAPSP to return either the array of all shortest-path distances or a negative cycle.

   (c) Describe how to modify Floyd-Warshall to return either the array of all shortest-path distances or a negative cycle.

In all cases, if the input graph contains more than one negative cycle, your algorithms may choose one arbitrarily.

4. Let $G = (V, E)$ be a directed graph with weighted edges; edge weights can be positive, negative, or zero, but there are no negative cycles.

   (a) Describe an efficient algorithm that either finds a cycle of length zero in G, or correctly reports that no such cycle exists.

   (b) Describe an efficient algorithm that constructs a subgraph H of G with the following properties:
       • Every vertex of G is a vertex of H.
       • Every directed cycle in H has length 0.
       • Every directed cycle of length 0 in G is also a cycle in H.
       In particular, if there are no zero-cycles in G, then H has no edges.

5. Let $G = (V, E)$ be a directed graph with weighted edges; edge weights can be positive, negative, or zero. Suppose the vertices of G are partitioned into k disjoint subsets $V_1, V_2, \ldots, V_k$; that is, every vertex of G belongs to exactly one subset V_i. For each i and j, let $\delta(i, j)$ denote the minimum shortest-path distance between vertices in V_i and vertices in V_j:

$$\delta(i, j) = \min \left\{ dist(v_i, v_j) \mid v_i \in V_i \text{ and } v_j \in V_j \right\}.$$

Describe an algorithm to compute $\delta(i, j)$ for all i and j. For full credit, your algorithm should run in $O(VE + kV \log V)$ time.

6. In this problem we will discover how you, yes *you*, can be employed by Wall Street and cause a major economic collapse! The *arbitrage* business is a money-making scheme that takes advantage of differences in currency exchange. In particular, suppose 1 US dollar buys 120 Japanese yen, 1 yen buys 0.01 euros, and 1 euro buys 1.2 US dollars. Then, a trader starting with $1 can convert their money from dollars to yen, then from yen to euros, and finally from euros back to dollars, ending with $1.44! The cycle of currencies $\$ \to ¥ \to € \to \$$ is called an **arbitrage cycle**. Of course, finding and exploiting arbitrage cycles before the prices are corrected requires extremely fast algorithms.

   Suppose n different currencies are traded in your currency market. You are given the matrix $Exch[1 .. n, 1 .. n]$ of exchange rates between every pair of currencies; for each i and j, one unit of currency i can be traded for $Exch[i, j]$ units of currency j. (Do *not* assume that $Exch[i, j] \cdot Exch[j, i] = 1$.)

   (a) Describe an algorithm that returns an array $MaxAmt[1 .. n]$, where $MaxAmt[i]$ is the maximum amount of currency i that you can obtain by trading, starting with one unit of currency 1, assuming there are no arbitrage cycles.

(b) Describe an algorithm to determine whether the given matrix of currency exchange rates creates an arbitrage cycle.

(c) Modify your algorithm from part (b) to actually return an arbitrage cycle, if it exists.

7. Morty needs to retrieve a stabilized plumbus from the Clackspire Labyrinth. He must enter the labyrinth using Rick's interdimensional portal gun, traverse the Labyrinth to a plumbus, then take that plumbus through the Labyrinth to a fleeb to be stabilized, and finally take the stabilized plumbus back to the original portal to return home. Plumbuses are stabilized by fleeb juice, which any fleeb will release immediately after being removed from its fleebhole. An unstabilized plumbus will explode if it is carried more than 137 flinks from its original storage unit. The Clackspire Labyrinth smells like farts, so Morty wants to spend as little time there as possible.

Rick has given Morty a detailed map of the Clackspire Labyrinth, which consist of a directed graph $G = (V, E)$ with non-negative edge weights (indicating distance in flinks), along with two disjoint subsets $P \subset V$ and $F \subset V$, indicating the plumbus storage units and fleebholes, respectively. Morty needs to identify a start vertex s, a plumbus storage unit $p \in P$, and a fleebhole $f \in F$, such that the shortest-path distance from p to f is at most 137 flinks long, and the length of the shortest walk $s \leadsto p \leadsto f \leadsto s$ is as short as possible.

Describe and analyze an algo(burp)rithm to so(burp)olve Morty's problem. You can assume that it is in fact possible for Morty to succeed.

8. Let $G = (V, E)$ be a directed graph with weighted edges; edge weights could be positive, negative, or zero.

(a) How would we delete an arbitrary vertex v from this graph, without changing the shortest-path distance between any other pair of vertices? Describe an algorithm that constructs a directed graph $G' = (V \setminus \{v\}, E')$ with weighted edges, such that the shortest-path distance between any two vertices in G' is equal to the shortest-path distance between the same two vertices in G, in $O(V^2)$ time.

(b) Now suppose we have already computed all shortest-path distances in G'. Describe an algorithm to compute the shortest-path distances in the original graph G from v to every other vertex, and from every other vertex to v, all in $O(V^2)$ time.

(c) Combine parts (a) and (b) into another all-pairs shortest path algorithm that runs in $O(V^3)$ time. (The resulting algorithm is *almost* the same as Floyd-Warshall!)

9. Suppose A and B are *boolean* $n \times n$ matrices. The *boolean* or *and-or* product of A and B is the $n \times n$ matrix C defined as follows:

$$C[i,j] := \bigvee_k \left(A[i,k] \wedge B[k,j] \right)$$

(a) Reduce boolean matrix multiplication to min-plus matrix multiplication. That is, given a subroutine MinPlusMultiply that computes the min-plus product of two $n \times n$ matrices in $T(n)$ time, describe and analyze an algorithm BooleanMatrixMultiply that multiplies two boolean matrices in $O(T(n))$ time.

(b) Reduce boolean matrix multiplication to standard matrix multiplication. That is, given a subroutine MatrixMultiply that computes the standard product of two $n \times n$ matrices in $T(n)$ time, describe and analyze an algorithm BooleanMatrixMultiply that multiplies two boolean matrices in $O(T(n))$ time.

10. The *transitive closure* of a directed graph G contains an edge $u \rightarrow v$ if and only if there is a directed path from u to v in G. For this problem, assume we can multiply two $n \times n$ boolean matrices in $O(n^\omega)$ time, for some constant $2 \le \omega < 3$. (Problem 9(b) implies $\omega \le 2.372864$.)

(a) Describe an algorithm to compute the transitive closure of an n-vertex directed graph in $O(n^\omega \log n)$ time.

(b) Now suppose G is a directed *acyclic* graph. Describe an algorithm to compute the transitive closure of G in $O(n^\omega)$ time. *[Hint: Do what you always do with dags, and then divide and conquer. Use the fact that $\omega \ge 2.]*

(c) Finally, describe an algorithm to compute the transitive closure of an *arbitrary* directed graph in $O(n^\omega)$ time. *[Hint: Do what you always do to turn an arbitrary directed graph into a dag.]*

(d) Now let's reverse the previous reduction. Given a subroutine Transitive-Closure that computes the transitive closure of an n-vertex directed graph in $O(n^\alpha)$ time, for some constant $2 \le \alpha < 3$, describe and analyze an algorithm for boolean matrix multiplication that runs in $O(n^\alpha)$ time.

11. Prove that the following recursive algorithm correctly computes all-pairs shortest-path distances in $O(n^3)$ time. For simplicity, you may assume n is a power of 2. As usual, the array D is passed *by reference* to the helper

function RecAPSP. *[Hint: This is a jumbled version of Floyd-Warshall, with significantly better cache behavior.[9]]*

RECURSIVEAPSP(V, E, w):
  $n \leftarrow |V|$
  for $i \leftarrow 1$ to n
    for $j \leftarrow 1$ to n
      if $i = j$
        $D[i,j] \leftarrow 0$
      if $i \rightarrow j \in E$
        $D[i,j] \leftarrow w(i \rightarrow j)$
      else
        $D[i,j] \leftarrow \infty$
  RecAPSP($D, n, 1, 1, 1$)
  return $D[1..n, 1..n]$

RECAPSP(D, n, i, j, k):
  if $n = 1$
    $D[i,j] \leftarrow \min \{D[i,j], D[i,k] + D[j,k]\}$
  else
    $m \leftarrow n/2$
    RecAPSP($D, n/2, i, \quad j, \quad k \quad$)
    RecAPSP($D, n/2, i, \quad j, \quad k+m$)
    RecAPSP($D, n/2, i, \quad j+m, k \quad$)
    RecAPSP($D, n/2, i, \quad j+m, k+m$)
    RecAPSP($D, n/2, i+m, j, \quad k \quad$)
    RecAPSP($D, n/2, i+m, j, \quad k+m$)
    RecAPSP($D, n/2, i+m, j+m, k \quad$)
    RecAPSP($D, n/2, i+m, j+m, k+m$)

♥12. Let $G = (V, E)$ be an undirected, unweighted, connected, n-vertex graph, represented by an adjacency matrix $A[1..n, 1..n]$. In this problem, we will derive Seidel's sub-cubic algorithm to compute the $n \times n$ matrix $D[1..n, 1..n]$ of shortest-path distances in G using fast matrix multiplication. Assume that we have a subroutine MatrixMultiply that computes the standard product of two $n \times n$ matrices in $O(n^\omega)$ time, for some unknown constant $\omega \geq 2$.

(a) Let G^2 denote the graph with the same vertices as G, where two vertices are connected by a edge if and only if they are connected by a path of length at most 2 in G. Describe an algorithm to compute the adjacency matrix of G^2 using a single call to MatrixMultiply and $O(n^2)$ additional time.

(b) Suppose we discover that G^2 is a complete graph. Describe an algorithm to compute the matrix D of shortest path distances in G in $O(n^2)$ additional time.

(c) Suppose we recursively compute the matrix D^2 of shortest-path distances in G^2. Prove that the shortest-path distance in G from node i to node j is either $2 \cdot D^2[i,j]$ or $2 \cdot D^2[i,j] - 1$.

(d) Now suppose G^2 is *not* a complete graph. Let $X = D^2 \cdot A$, and let $\deg(i)$ denote the degree of vertex i in the original graph G. Prove that the shortest-path distance from node i to node j in G is $2 \cdot D^2[i,j]$ if and only if $X[i,j] \geq D^2[i,j] \cdot \deg(i)$.

---

[9] Joon-Sang Park, Michael Penner, and Viktor K. Prasanna. Optimizing graph algorithms for improved cache performance. *IEEE Trans. Parallel and Distributed Systems* 15(9):769–782, 2004. For a significant generalization to a wider class of dynamic programming problems, see Rezaul Alam Chowdhury and Vijaya Ramachandran. Cache-oblivious dynamic programming. *Proc. 17th SODA* 591–600, 2006.

(e) Describe an algorithm to compute the matrix D of shortest-path distances in G in $O(n^\omega \log n)$ time.

13. Gideon Yuval proposed the following reduction from min-plus matrix multiplication to standard matrix multiplication in 1976. Suppose we are given two integers $n \times n$ matrices A and B of integers, each of whose entries is between 0 and M, and we want to compute their min-plus product matrix C, defined by setting

$$C[i,k] = \min_j(A[i,j] + B[j,k])$$

for all indices i and k. Define two new $n \times n$ matrices A' and B', where

$$A'[i,j] = n^{M-A[i,j]} \qquad \text{and} \qquad B'[i,j] = n^{M-B[i,j]}.$$

Finally, let C' be the (standard) product of A' and B', defined by setting $C'[i,k] = \sum_j A'[i,j] \cdot B'[j,k]$.

(a) Describe an algorithm to construct A' from A using only standard integer arithmetic operations $(+, -, \times)$.

(b) Describe an algorithm to extract the min-plus product C from C', using only standard integer arithmetic operations $(+, -, \times)$.[10]

(c) Suppose we can compute the standard product of two $n \times n$ integer matrices using $O(n^\omega)$ arithmetic operations, for some constant $2 \le \omega < 3$. How many arithmetic operations does Yuval's algorithm need to compute the min-plus product C?

(d) Given a single $n \times n$ integer matrix A, how many arithmetic operations are required to compute the nth "funny" power of A using Yuval's algorithm? (Recall that if A is the weighted adjacency matrix of a graph, then the nth "funny" power of A is the matrix of shortest-path distances.)

(e) Why doesn't Yuval's algorithm imply an all-pairs shortest path algorithm that is faster than Floyd-Warshall for *arbitrary* edge weights? How are we cheating?

---

[10]In particular, do *not* use logarithms or division or the floor function $\lfloor x \rfloor$. Trust me—this is a can of worms you do *not* want to open.

A process cannot be understood by stopping it. Understanding must move with the flow of the process, must join it and flow with it.

— The First Law of Mentat, in Frank Herbert's *Dune* (1965)

Contrary to expectation, flow usually happens not during relaxing moments of leisure and entertainment, but rather when we are actively involved in a difficult enterprise, in a task that stretches our mental and physical abilities.... Flow is hard to achieve without effort. Flow is not "wasting time."

— Mihaly Csíkszentmihályi, *Flow: The Psychology of Optimal Experience* (1990)

There's a difference between knowing the path and walking the path.

— Morpheus [Laurence Fishburne], *The Matrix* (1999)

10

Maximum Flows & Minimum Cuts

In the mid-1950s, U. S. Air Force researcher Theodore E. Harris and retired U. S. Army general Frank S. Ross wrote a classified report studying the rail network that linked the Soviet Union to its satellite countries in Eastern Europe. The network was modeled as a graph with 44 vertices, representing geographic regions, and 105 edges, representing links between those regions in the rail network. Each edge was given a weight, representing the rate at which material could be shipped from one region to the next. Essentially by trial and error, they determined both the maximum amount of stuff that could be moved from Russia into Europe, as well as the cheapest way to disrupt the network by removing links (or in less abstract terms, blowing up train tracks), which they called "the bottleneck". Their report, which included the drawing of the network in Figure 10.1, was only declassified in 1999.[1]

---

[1]I learned this story from Alexander Schrijver's fascinating survey "On the history of combinatorial optimization (till 1960)"; the Harris-Ross report was declassified at Schrijver's request. Ford and Fulkerson (who we will meet shortly) credit Harris for formulating the

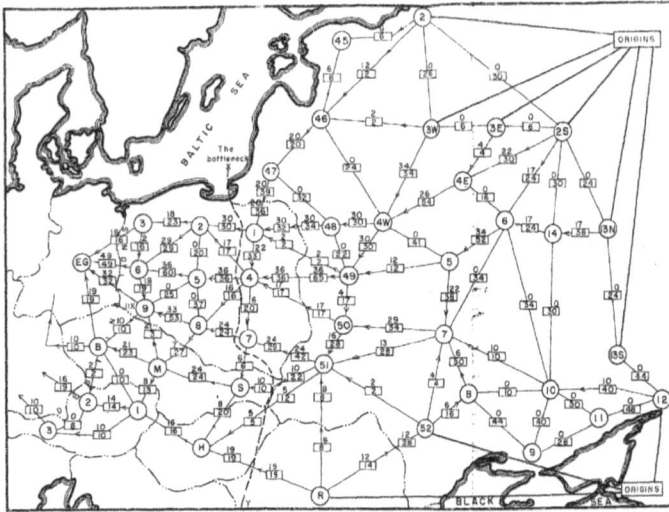

Figure 10.1. Harris and Ross's map of the Warsaw Pact rail network. (See Image Credits at the end of the book.)

This one of the first recorded applications of the **maximum flow** and **minimum cut** problems. For both problems, the input is a directed graph $G = (V, E)$ with two special vertices s and t, called the *source* and *target*. As in previous chapters, I will write $u \rightarrow v$ to denote the directed edge from vertex u to vertex v. Intuitively, the maximum flow problem asks for the maximum rate at which some resource can be moved from s to t; the minimum cut problem asks for the minimum damage needed to separate s from t.

10.1 Flows

An **(s, t)-flow** (or just a *flow* if the source and target vertices are clear from context) is a function $f : E \rightarrow \mathbb{R}$ that satisfies the following **conservation constraint** at every vertex v except possibly s and t:

$$\sum_u f(u \rightarrow v) = \sum_w f(v \rightarrow w).$$

In English, the total flow into v is equal to the total flow out of v. To keep the notation simple, we define $f(u \rightarrow v) = 0$ if there is no edge $u \rightarrow v$ in the graph.

The **value** of the flow f, denoted $|f|$, is the total net flow out of the source vertex s:

$$|f| := \sum_w f(s \rightarrow w) - \sum_u f(u \rightarrow s).$$

maximum-flow problem, although the precise chronology is somewhat muddled; Harris and Ross thank George Dantzig "for assistance in formulating the problem".

It's not hard to prove that $|f|$ is also equal to the total net flow *into* the target vertex t, as follows. To simplify notation, let $\partial f(v)$ denote the total net flow out of any vertex v:

$$\partial f(v) := \sum_u f(u{\to}v) - \sum_w f(v{\to}w).$$

The conservation constraint implies that $\partial f(v) = 0$ or every vertex v except s and t, so

$$\sum_v \partial f(v) = \partial f(s) + \partial f(t).$$

On the other hand, any flow that leaves one vertex must enter another vertex, so we must have $\sum_v \partial f(v) = 0$. It follows immediately that $|f| = \partial f(s) = -\partial f(t)$.

Now suppose we have another function $c : E \to \mathbb{R}_{\geq 0}$ that assigns a non-negative *capacity* $c(e)$ to each edge e. We say that a flow f is *feasible* (with respect to c) if $0 \leq f(e) \leq c(e)$ for every edge e. Most of the time we consider only flows that are feasible with respect to some fixed capacity function c. We say that a flow f *saturates* edge e if $f(e) = c(e)$, and *avoids* edge e if $f(e) = 0$. The *maximum flow problem* is to compute a feasible (s, t)-flow in a given directed graph, with a given capacity function, whose value is as large as possible.

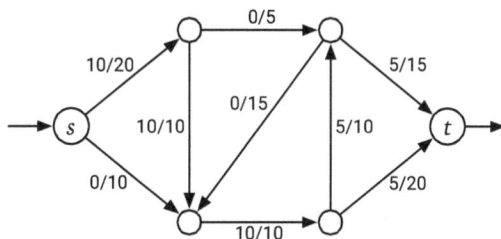

Figure 10.2. A feasible (s, t)-flow with value 10. Each edge is labeled with its flow/capacity.

10.2 Cuts

An (s, t)-*cut* (or just *cut* if the source and target vertices are clear from context) is a partition of the vertices into disjoint subsets S and T—meaning $S \cup T = V$ and $S \cap T = \emptyset$—where $s \in S$ and $t \in T$.

If we have a capacity function $c : E \to \mathbb{R}_{\geq 0}$, the *capacity* of a cut is the sum of the capacities of the edges that start in S and end in T:

$$\|S, T\| := \sum_{v \in S} \sum_{w \in T} c(v{\to}w).$$

(Again, if $v{\to}w$ is not an edge in the graph, we assume $c(v{\to}w) = 0$.) Notice that the definition is asymmetric; edges that start in T and end in S are unimportant.

The **minimum cut problem** is to compute an (s, t)-cut whose capacity is as small as possible.

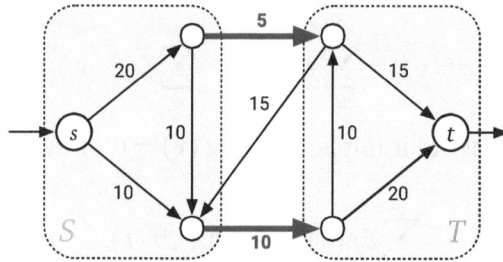

Figure 10.3. An (s, t)-cut with capacity 15. Each edge is labeled with its capacity.

Intuitively, the minimum cut is the cheapest way to disrupt all flow from s to t. Indeed, it is not hard to show the following relationship between flows and cuts:

Lemma 10.1. *Let f be **any** feasible (s, t)-flow, and let (S, T) be **any** (s, t)-cut. The value of f is at most the capacity of (S, T). Moreover, $|f| = \|S, T\|$ if and only if f saturates every edge from S to T and avoids every edge from T to S.*

Proof: Choose your favorite flow f and your favorite cut (S, T), and then follow the bouncing inequalities:

$$|f| = \partial f(s) \qquad \text{[by definition]}$$

$$= \sum_{v \in S} \partial f(v) \qquad \text{[conservation constraint]}$$

$$= \sum_{v \in S} \sum_{w} f(v \to w) - \sum_{v \in S} \sum_{u} f(u \to v) \qquad \text{[math, definition of } \partial\text{]}$$

$$= \sum_{v \in S} \sum_{w \notin S} f(v \to w) - \sum_{v \in S} \sum_{u \notin S} f(u \to v) \qquad \text{[removing edges from } S \text{ to } S\text{]}$$

$$= \sum_{v \in S} \sum_{w \in T} f(v \to w) - \sum_{v \in S} \sum_{u \in T} f(u \to v) \qquad \text{[definition of cut]}$$

$$\leq \sum_{v \in S} \sum_{w \in T} f(v \to w) \qquad \text{[because } f(u \to v) \geq 0\text{]}$$

$$\leq \sum_{v \in S} \sum_{w \in T} c(v \to w) \qquad \text{[because } f(v \to w) \leq c(v \to w)\text{]}$$

$$= \|S, T\| \qquad \text{[by definition]}$$

In the second step, we are just adding zeros, because $\partial f(v) = 0$ for every vertex $v \in S \setminus \{s\}$. In the fourth step, we are removing flow values $f(x \to y)$ where both x and y are in S, because they appear in both sums: positively when $v = x$ and $w = y$, and negatively when $v = y$ and $u = x$.

The first inequalities in this derivation is actually an equality if and only if f avoids every edge from T to S. Similarly, the second inequality is actually an equality if and only if f saturates every edge from S to T. □

This lemma immediately implies that if $|f| = \|S, T\|$, then f must be a maximum flow, and (S, T) must be a minimum cut.

10.3 The Maxflow-Mincut Theorem

Surprisingly, in every flow network, there is a feasible (s, t)-flow f and an (s, t)-cut (S, T) such that $|f| = \|S, T\|$. This is the famous *Maxflow-Mincut Theorem*, first proved by Lester Ford (of shortest-path fame) and Delbert Fulkerson in 1954 and independently by Peter Elias, Amiel Feinstein, and Claude Shannon (of information-theory and maze-solving-robot fame) in 1956.

The Maxflow-Mincut Theorem. *In every flow network with source s and target t, the value of the maximum (s, t)-flow is equal to the capacity of the minimum (s, t)-cut.*

Ford and Fulkerson proved this theorem as follows. Fix a graph G, vertices s and t, and a capacity function $c : E \to \mathbb{R}_{\geq 0}$. The proof will be easier if we assume that G is **reduced**, meaning there is at most one edge between any two vertices u and v. In particular, either $c(u \to v) = 0$ or $c(v \to u) = 0$. This assumption is easy to enforce: Subdivide each edge $u \to v$ in G with a new vertex x, replacing $u \to v$ with a path $u \to x \to v$, and define $c(u \to x) = c(x \to v) = c(u \to v)$. The modified graph has the same maximum flow value and minimum cut capacity as the original graph.

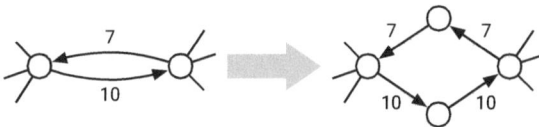

Figure 10.4. Enforcing the one-direction assumption.

Let f be an arbitrary feasible (s, t)-flow in G. We define a new capacity function $c_f : V \times V \to \mathbb{R}$, called the **residual capacity**, as follows:

$$c_f(u \to v) = \begin{cases} c(u \to v) - f(u \to v) & \text{if } u \to v \in E \\ f(v \to u) & \text{if } v \to u \in E \\ 0 & \text{otherwise} \end{cases}$$

Intuitively, the residual capacity of an edge indicates how much *more* flow can be pushed through that edge. Because $f \geq 0$ and $f \leq c$, these residual capacities are always non-negative. It is possible to have $c_f(u \to v) > 0$ even if $u \to v$ is not an edge in the original graph G. Thus, we define the **residual graph** $G_f = (V, E_f)$, where E_f is the set of edges whose residual capacity is positive. Most residual graphs are *not* reduced; in particular, if $0 < f(u \to v) < c(u \to v)$, then the residual graph G_f contains both $u \to v$ and its reversal $v \to u$.

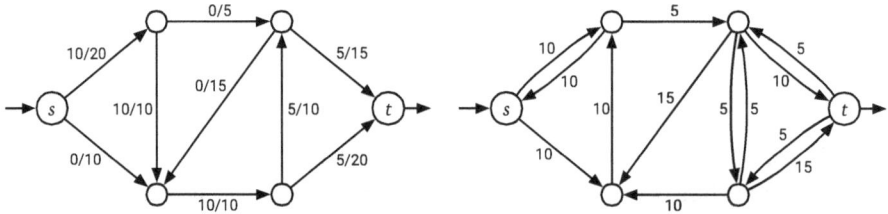

Figure 10.5. A flow f in a weighted graph G and the corresponding residual graph G_f.

Now we have two cases to consider: Either there is a directed path from the source vertex s to the target vertex t in the residual graph G^f, or there isn't.

First suppose the residual graph G_f contains a directed path P from s to t; we call P an **augmenting path**. Let $F = \min_{u \to v \in P} c_f(u \to v)$ denote the maximum amount of flow that we can push through P. We define a new flow $f' \colon E \to \mathbb{R}$ (in the original graph) as follows:

$$f'(u \to v) = \begin{cases} f(u \to v) + F & \text{if } u \to v \in P \\ f(u \to v) - F & \text{if } v \to u \in P \\ f(u \to v) & \text{otherwise} \end{cases}$$

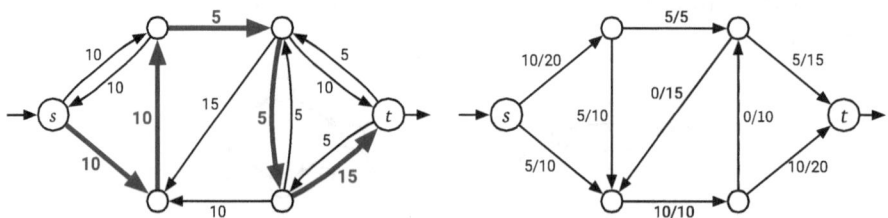

Figure 10.6. An augmenting path with value $F = 5$ and the resulting augmented flow f'.

I claim that this new flow f' is feasible with respect to the original capacities c, meaning $f' \geq 0$ and $f' \leq c$ everywhere. Consider an edge $u \to v$ in the original graph G. There are three cases to consider.

- If the augmenting path P contains $u \to v$, then

$$f'(u \to v) = f(u \to v) + F > f(u \to v) \geq 0$$

because f is feasible, and

$$
\begin{aligned}
f'(u\to v) &= f(u\to v) + F && \text{by definition of } f' \\
&\leq f(u\to v) + c_f(u\to v) && \text{by definition of } F \\
&= f(u\to v) + c(u\to v) - f(u\to v) && \text{by definition of } c_f \\
&= c(u\to v) && \text{Duh.}
\end{aligned}
$$

- If the augmenting path P contains the reversed edge $v\to u$, then

$$
f'(u\to v) = f(u\to v) - F < f(u\to v) \leq c(u\to v),
$$

again because f is feasible, and

$$
\begin{aligned}
f'(u\to v) &= f(u\to v) - F && \text{by definition of } f' \\
&\geq f(u\to v) - c_f(v\to u) && \text{by definition of } F \\
&= f(u\to v) - f(u\to v) && \text{by definition of } c_f \\
&= 0 && \text{Duh.}
\end{aligned}
$$

- Finally, if neither $u\to v$ nor $v\to u$ is in the augmenting path, then $f'(u\to v) = f(u\to v)$, and therefore $0 \leq f'(u\to v) \leq c(u\to v)$, because f is feasible.

So f is indeed feasible.

Finally, only the first edge in the augmenting path leaves s, which implies $|f'| = |f| + F > |f|$. Thus, f' is a feasible flow with larger value than f. We conclude that if there is a path from s to t in the residual graph G_f, then f is *not* a maximum flow.

On the other hand, suppose the residual graph G_f does *not* contain a directed path from s to t. Let S be the set of vertices that are reachable from s in G_f, and let $T = V \setminus S$. The partition (S, T) is clearly an (s, t)-cut. For every vertex $u \in S$ and $v \in T$, we have

$$
c_f(u\to v) = (c(u\to v) - f(u\to v)) + f(v\to u) = 0.
$$

The feasibility of f implies $c(u\to v) - f(u\to v) \geq 0$ and $f(v\to u) \geq 0$, so in fact we must have $c(u\to v) - f(u\to v) = 0$ and $f(v\to u) = 0$. In other words, our flow f saturates every edge from S to T and avoids every edge from T to S. Lemma 10.1 now implies that $|f| = \|S, T\|$, which means f is a maximum flow and (S, T) is a minimum cut.

This completes the proof! $\qquad\qquad\qquad\qquad\qquad\qquad\qquad\qquad\qquad\qquad$ $\square$

10.4 Ford and Fulkerson's augmenting-path algorithm

Ford and Fulkerson's proof of the Maxflow-Mincut Theorem immediately suggests an algorithm to compute maximum flows: Starting with the zero flow, repeatedly augment the flow along **any** path from s to t in the residual graph, until there is no such path.

This algorithm has an important but straightforward corollary:

Integrality Theorem. *If all capacities in a flow network are integers, then there is a maximum flow such that the flow through every edge is an integer.*

Proof: We argue by induction that after each iteration of the augmenting path algorithm, all flow values and all residual capacities are integers.

- Before the first iteration, all flow values are 0 (which is an integer), and all residual capacities are the original capacities, which are integers by definition.

- In each later iteration, the induction hypothesis implies that the capacity F of the augmenting path is an integer, so augmenting changes the flow on each edge, and therefore the residual capacity of each edge, by an integer.

In particular, each iteration of the augmenting path algorithm increases the value of the flow by a positive integer. It follows that the algorithm eventually halts and returns a maximum flow. □

If every edge capacity is an integer, then conservatively, the Ford-Fulkerson algorithm halts after at most $|f^*|$ iterations, where f^* is the actual maximum flow. In each iteration, we can build the residual graph G_f and perform a whatever-first-search to find an augmenting path in $O(E)$ time. Thus, in this setting, the algorithm runs in $O(E|f^*|)$ time in the worst case.

Jack Edmonds and Richard Karp observed that this running time analysis is essentially tight. Consider the 4-node network in Figure 10.7, where X is some large integer. The maximum flow in this network is clearly $2X$. However, Ford-Fulkerson might alternate between pushing one unit of flow along the augmenting path $s \to u \to v \to t$ and then pushing one unit of flow along the augmenting path $s \to v \to u \to t$, leading to a running time of $\Theta(X) = \Omega(|f^*|)$.

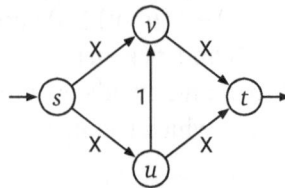

Figure 10.7. Edmonds and Karp's bad example for the Ford-Fulkerson algorithm.

Ford and Fulkerson's algorithm is usually fast in practice, and it is always fast when the maximum flow value $|f^*|$ is small, but without further constraints on the augmenting paths, this is *not* an efficient algorithm in worst case. Edmonds and Karp's bad example network can be described using only $O(\log X)$ bits; thus, the running time of Ford-Fulkerson is actually *exponential* in the input size.

♥Irrational Capacities

But what if the capacities are *not* integers? If we multiply all the capacities by the same (positive) constant, the maximum flow increases everywhere by the same constant factor. It follows that if all the edge capacities are *rational*, then the Ford-Fulkerson algorithm eventually halts, although still in exponential time (in the number of bits used to described the input).

However, if we allow *irrational* capacities, the algorithm can actually loop forever, always finding smaller and smaller augmenting paths. Worse yet, this infinite sequence of augmentations may not even converge to the maximum flow, or even to a significant fraction of the maximum flow! The smallest network that exhibits this bad behavior was discovered by Uri Zwick in 1993.[2]

Consider the six-node network shown in Figure 10.8. Six of the nine edges have some large integer capacity X, two have capacity 1, and one has capacity $\phi = (\sqrt{5} - 1)/2 \approx 0.618034$, chosen so that $1 - \phi = \phi^2$. To prove that the Ford-Fulkerson algorithm can get stuck, we can watch the residual capacities of the three horizontal edges as the algorithm progresses. (The residual capacities of the other six edges will always be at least $X - 3$.)

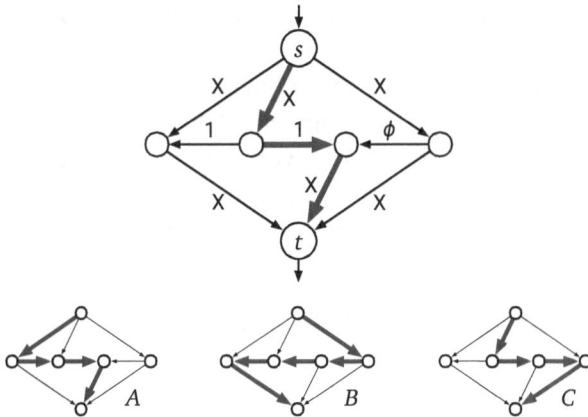

Figure 10.8. Uri Zwick's non-terminating flow example, and three augmenting paths.

Suppose the Ford-Fulkerson algorithm starts by choosing the central augmenting path, shown at the top of Figure 10.8. The three horizontal edges, in

[2]In 1962, Ford and Fulkerson described a more complex network, with 10 vertices and 48 edges, with the same bad behavior.

order from left to right, now have residual capacities 1, 0, and ϕ. Suppose inductively that the horizontal residual capacities are ϕ^{k-1}, 0, and ϕ^k for some non-negative integer k.

1. Augment along path B, adding ϕ^k to the flow; the residual capacities are now ϕ^{k+1}, ϕ^k, and 0.

2. Augment along path C, adding ϕ^k to the flow; the residual capacities are now ϕ^{k+1}, 0, and ϕ^k.

3. Augment along path B, adding ϕ^{k+1} to the flow; the residual capacities are now 0, ϕ^{k+1}, and ϕ^{k+2}.

4. Augment along path A, adding ϕ^{k+1} to the flow; the residual capacities are now ϕ^{k+1}, 0, and ϕ^{k+2}.

It follows by induction that after $4n+1$ augmentation steps, the horizontal edges have residual capacities ϕ^{2n-2}, 0, and ϕ^{2n-1}. As the number of augmentations grows to infinity, the value of the flow converges to

$$1 + 2\sum_{i=1}^{\infty} \phi^i = 1 + \frac{2}{1-\phi} = 4 + \sqrt{5} < 7,$$

even though the maximum flow value is clearly $2X + 1 \gg 7$.

Practically-minded readers might wonder why anyone should care about irrational capacities; after all, computers can't represent anything but (small) integers or (small dyadic) rationals exactly. Good question! The mathematician's answer is that the restriction to integer capacities is literally *artificial*; it's an *artifact* of digital computational hardware (or perhaps the otherwise irrelevant laws of physics), not an inherent feature of the abstract computational problem. But a more practical reason is that the behavior of the algorithm with irrational inputs tells us something about its worst-case behavior *in practice* with floating-point capacities—terrible! Even with very reasonable capacities, a careless implementation of Ford-Fulkerson could enter an infinite loop, simply because of round-off error, without ever coming close to the correct answer.

10.5 Combining and Decomposing Flows

Flows are normally defined as functions on the edges of a graph satisfying certain constraints at the vertices. However, flows have a second characterization that is more natural and useful in certain contexts.

Consider an arbitrary graph G with source vertex s and target vertex t. Fix any two (s, t)-flows f and g and any two real numbers α and β, and consider the function $h: E \to \mathbb{R}$ defined by setting

$$h(u{\to}v) := \alpha \cdot f(u{\to}v) + \beta \cdot g(u{\to}v)$$

for every edge $u \to v$; we can write this definition more simply as $h = \alpha f + \beta g$. Straightforward definition-chasing implies that h is also an (s, t)-flow with value $|h| = \alpha|f| + \beta|g|$. More generally, any linear combination of (s, t)-flows is also an (s, t)-flow.

It turns out that any (s, t)-flow can be written as a weighted sum of flows with a special structure. For any directed path P from s to t, we define a corresponding **path flow** as follows:

$$P(u \to v) = \begin{cases} 1 & \text{if } u \to v \in P, \\ -1 & \text{if } v \to u \in P, \\ 0 & \text{otherwise.} \end{cases}$$

Straightforward definition-chasing implies that the function $P \colon E \to \mathbb{R}$ is indeed an (s, t)-flow with value 1. I am deliberately overloading the variable P to mean both the path (a sequence of vertices and directed edges) and the unit flow along that path.

Similarly, for any directed cycle C, we define a corresponding **cycle flow** by setting

$$C(u \to v) = \begin{cases} 1 & \text{if } u \to v \in C, \\ -1 & \text{if } v \to u \in C, \\ 0 & \text{otherwise.} \end{cases}$$

Again, it is easy to verify that $C \colon E \to \mathbb{R}$ is an (s, t)-flow with value zero.

Our earlier argument implies that any linear combination of path flows and cycle flows is another flow; this weighted sum is called a **flow decomposition**. Moreover, *every* non-negative flow has a flow decomposition with the following special structure.

Flow Decomposition Theorem. *Every non-negative (s, t)-flow f can be written as a positive linear combination of directed (s, t)-paths and directed cycles. Moreover, a directed edge $u \to v$ appears in at least one of these paths or cycles if and only if $f(u \to v) > 0$, and the total number of paths and cycles is at most the number of edges in the network.*

Proof: We prove the theorem by induction on the number of edges carrying non-zero flow, intuitively by running the Ford-Fulkerson algorithm backward. As long as at least one edge in the graph carries positive flow, we can find either an (s, t)-path or a directed cycle that carries flow. Subtracting as much flow as possible from that path or cycle empties at least one edge, so the Recursion Fairy can give us the rest of the decomposition.

To formalize this argument, we first consider the special case of **circulations**; these are flows with value 0, where flow is conserved at *every* vertex. Fix an

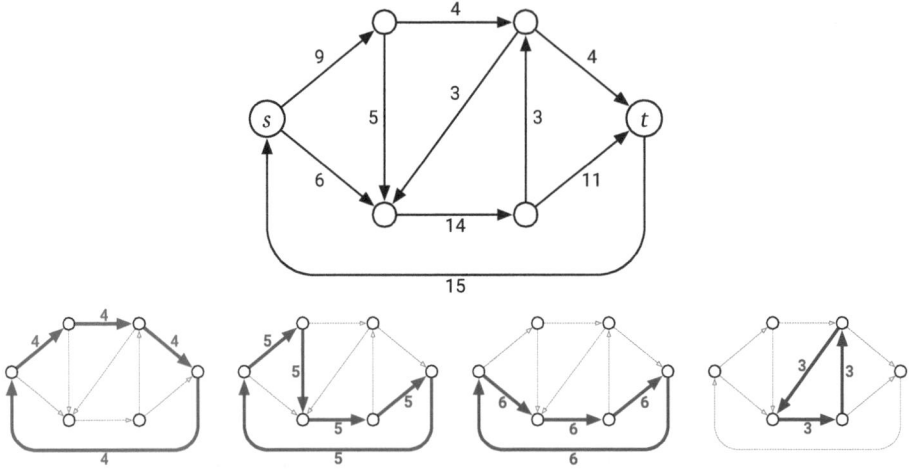

Figure 10.9. Decomposing a circulation into weighted directed cycles.

arbitrary circulation f in an arbitrary flow network, and let $\#f$ denote the number of edges $u{\to}v$ such that $f(u{\to}v) > 0$. We prove that f can be decomposed into a positive linear combination of at most $\max\{0, \#f - 1\}$ cycles, by induction on $\#f$. There are three cases to consider:

- If $\#f = 0$, then f is vacuously a linear combination of zero cycles.

- Suppose $f(u{\to}v) > 0$ for a single directed cycle of edges $u{\to}v$. Then $\#f \geq 2$, and f is trivially a linear combination of one cycle.

- Otherwise, pick an arbitrary edge $u{\to}v$ with $f(u{\to}v) > 0$. Consider an arbitrary walk $v_0{\to}v_1{\to}v_2{\to}\cdots$ with $v_0 = u$ and $v_1 = v$, such that $f(v_{i-1}{\to}v_i) > 0$ for every index i. The conservation constraint implies that every vertex with incoming flow also has outgoing flow, so we can make this walk arbitrarily long; in particular, the walk must eventually visit some vertex more than once. Let k be the smallest index such that $v_j = v_k$ for some index $j < k$. The subwalk $v_j{\to}v_{j-1}{\to}\cdots{\to}v_k$ is a simple directed cycle C.

  Define $F := \min_{e \in C} f(e)$, and consider the function $f' := f - F \cdot C$, or more verbosely,

$$f'(u{\to}v) := \begin{cases} f(u{\to}v) - F & \text{if } u{\to}v \in C, \\ f(u{\to}v) & \text{otherwise.} \end{cases}$$

Straightforward definition-chasing shows that f' is another feasible circulation in G. There is at least one edge $e \in C$ such that $f(e) = F$, and therefore $f'(e) = 0$, which implies $\#f' \leq \#f - 1$. Since fewer edges carry flow in f' than in f, the Recursion Fairy can decompose f' into at most $\#f' - 1 \leq \#f - 2$ cycles. Adding F units of flow around cycle C gives us a flow decomposition for f; more succinctly: $f = f' + F \cdot C$.

Now let f be an arbitrary (s, t)-flow in an arbitrary flow network, such that $|f| > 0$. Add an edge $t \to s$ to the network, and define a circulation f' by setting $f'(t \to s) = |f|$ and $f'(u \to v) = f(u \to v)$ for every original edge $u \to v$; observe that $\#f' = \#f + 1 \geq 2$. The previous argument implies that the circulation f' is a positive linear combination of at most $\#f' - 1$ directed cycles. Deleting the edge $t \to s$ gives us a decomposition of the original flow f into at most $\#f' - 1 = \#f$ paths and cycles. Specifically, cycles in f' that include $t \to s$ become (s, t)-paths in f, and cycles in f' that do not include $t \to s$ remain cycles in f. □

The proof of the Flow Decomposition Theorem implies stronger results in two interesting special cases.

- Any circulation can be decomposed into a weighted sum of cycles; no paths are necessary.

- Any *acyclic* (s, t)-flow can be decomposed into a weighted sum of (s, t)-paths; no cycles are necessary.

Moreover, by canceling flow cycles until no more remain, we can transform any flow into an acyclic flow with the same value. In particular, every flow network supports a maximum (s, t)-flow that is acyclic.

The proof also immediately translates directly into an algorithm, similar to Ford-Fulkerson, to decompose any (s, t)-flow into paths and cycles. The algorithm repeatedly seeks either a directed (s, t)-path or a directed cycle in the remaining flow, and then subtracts as much flow as possible along that path or cycle, until the flow is empty. We can find a flow path or cycle in $O(V)$ time as follows:

- If any edge leaving s has positive flow, follow an arbitrary walk from s in the flow graph until it either reaches t (giving us a flow path) or reaches some vertex for the second time (giving us a flow cycle).

- If no edge leaving s has positive flow, find any other vertex v with positive outflow, and follow an arbitrary walk from v in the flow graph until it reaches some vertex for the second time (giving us a flow cycle).

In both cases, the conservation constraint implies that this algorithm will never get stuck. Each iteration takes $O(V)$ time and removes at least one edge from the flow graph; thus, the entire decomposition algorithm runs in $O(VE)$ time.

Flow decompositions provide a natural lower bound on the running time of any maximum-flow algorithm that builds the flow one path or cycle at a time. Every flow can be decomposed into at most E paths and cycles, each of which uses at most V edges, so the overall complexity of the flow decomposition is $O(VE)$. Moreover, it is easy to construct flows for which *every* flow decomposition has complexity $\Omega(VE)$. Thus, any maximum-flow algorithm that explicitly constructs a flow one path or cycle at a time—in particular, any implementation of Ford and Fulkerson's augmenting path algorithm—must take $\Omega(VE)$ time in the worst case.

10.6 Edmonds and Karp's Algorithms

Ford and Fulkerson's algorithm does not specify which path in the residual graph to augment; the poor worst-case behavior of the algorithm can be blamed on poor choices for the augmenting path. In the early 1970s, Jack Edmonds and Richard Karp published two natural rules for choosing augmenting paths, both of which led to more efficient algorithms.

Fattest Augmenting Paths

Edmonds and Karp's first rule is essentially a greedy algorithm:

> Choose the augmenting path with largest bottleneck value.

It's not hard to show that the maximum-bottleneck (s, t)-path in a directed graph can be computed in $O(E \log V)$ time using a "best-first" traversal, similar to Jarník's minimum-spanning-tree algorithm or Dijkstra's shortest-path algorithm. The algorithm grows a directed tree T, rooted at s, one vertex at a time, by repeatedly adding the highest-capacity edge leaving T to T, until T contains a path from s to t. Alternately, one could emulate Kruskal's algorithm—insert edges one at a time in decreasing capacity order until there is a path from s to t—although this approach is less efficient, at least when the graph is directed.

To complete the running-time analysis of the flow algorithm, we need an upper bound on the number of iterations before the algorithm halts. In fact, for arbitrary real capacities, the algorithm may *never* halt; see Exercise 18. For integer capacities, however, we can bound the number of iterations as a function of the maximum flow value $|f^*|$, as follows.

Let f be any flow in G, and let f' be the maximum flow *in the current residual graph* G_f. (At the beginning of the algorithm, $G_f = G$ and $f' = f^*$.) We have already proved that f' can be decomposed into at most E paths and cycles. A simple averaging argument implies that at least one of the paths in this decomposition must carry at least $|f'|/E$ units of flow. It follows immediately that the *fattest* (s, t)-path in G_f carries at least $|f'|/E$ units of flow.

Thus, augmenting f along the maximum-bottleneck path in G_f multiplies the value of the remaining maximum flow in G_f by a factor of at most $1 - 1/E$. In other words, the residual maximum flow value *decays exponentially* with the number of iterations. After $E \cdot \ln|f^*|$ iterations, the maximum flow value in G_f is at most

$$|f^*| \cdot (1 - 1/E)^{E \cdot \ln|f^*|} < |f^*| e^{-\ln|f^*|} = 1.$$

(That's Euler's constant e, not the edge e. Sorry.) In particular, after $E \cdot \ln|f^*|$ iterations, the residual maximum flow value is less than 1. *If all capacities are integers*, the residual maximum flow value is also an integer, so it must be 0; in other words, f is a maximum flow!

We conclude that for graphs with integer capacities, the Edmonds-Karp "fattest path" algorithm runs in $O(E^2 \log E \log|f^*|)$ time. Unlike the worst-case running time of raw Ford-Fulkerson, this time bound is actually a polynomial function of the input size.

Just like the original Ford-Fulkerson algorithm, the "fattest path" algorithm can get stuck in an infinite loop in networks with arbitrary real capacities. However, our analysis implies that even if the algorithm never halts, it maintains a flow f that approaches a maximum flow in the limit.

Shortest Augmenting Paths

The second Edmonds-Karp rule was actually proposed as a practical heuristic by Ford and Fulkerson in their original maximum-flow paper; a variant of this rule was independently proposed in 1970 by the Russian mathematician Yefim Dinitz.[3]

> Choose the augmenting path with the smallest number of edges.

The shortest augmenting path can be found in $O(E)$ time by running breadth-first search in the residual graph. Surprisingly, the resulting algorithm halts after a polynomial number of iterations, independent of the actual edge capacities!

The proof of this polynomial upper bound relies on two observations about the evolution of the residual graph. Let f_i be the current flow after i augmentation steps, let G_i be the corresponding residual graph. In particular, f_0 is zero everywhere and $G_0 = G$. For each vertex v, let **$level_i(v)$** denote the unweighted shortest-path distance from s to v in G_i, or equivalently, the *level* of v in a breadth-first search tree of G_i rooted at s. In particular, if there is no path from s to v in G_i, then $level_i(v) = \infty$ (because $\min \emptyset = \infty$).

Our first observation is that the level of a vertex can only increase over time.

Lemma 10.2. $level_i(v) \geq level_{i-1}(v)$ *for all vertices v and all integers $i > 0$.*

Proof: Fix an arbitrary positive integer $i > 0$ and an arbitrary vertex v. We prove the claim by induction on $level_i(v)$ (and *not* on the integer i). As an inductive hypothesis, assume for every vertex u such that $level_i(u) < level_i(v)$, that $level_i(u) \geq level_{i-1}(u)$. There are three cases to consider.

---

[3]Specifically, Dinitz discovered a more complex maximum-flow algorithm, while he was a student in an algorithms class taught by Georgy Adelson-Velsky (the "AV" in AVL trees), in response to an in-class exercise. Dinitz's algorithm also pushes flows along shortest paths, but with additional bookkeeping to reduce the running time from $O(VE^2)$ to $O(V^2E)$.

- If $v = s$, we immediately have $level_i(s) = level_{i-1}(s) = 0$.
- If there is no path from s to v in G_i, then $level_i(v) = \infty \geq level_{i-1}(v)$.
- Otherwise, let $s \to \cdots \to u \to v$ be any unweighted shortest path from s to v in the graph G_i. Because this is a shortest path, we have $level_i(v) = level_i(u) + 1$, so the inductive hypothesis implies $level_i(u) \geq level_{i-1}(u)$. To complete the proof, we need to show that $level_{i-1}(u) \geq level_{i-1}(v) - 1$. We have two subcases to consider.

  - If $u \to v$ is an edge in G_{i-1}, then $level_{i-1}(v) \leq level_{i-1}(u) + 1$, because the levels are defined by breadth-first traversal.
  - On the other hand, if $u \to v$ is not an edge in G_{i-1}, then its reversal $v \to u$ must be an edge in the ith augmenting path, which by definition is the shortest path from s to t in G_{i-1}. It follows that $level_{i-1}(v) = level_{i-1}(u) - 1 \leq level_{i-1}(u) + 1$.

  In both subcases, we conclude that $level_i(v) = level_i(u) + 1 \geq level_{i-1}(u) + 1 \geq level_{i-1}(v)$. $\qquad\square$

Whenever we augment the flow, the bottleneck edge in the augmenting path disappears from the residual graph, and some edges in the *reversal* of the augmenting path may (re-)appear. Our second observation is that an edge cannot appear or disappear too many times.

Lemma 10.3. *During the execution of the Edmonds-Karp shortest-augmenting-path algorithm, each edge $u \to v$ disappears from the residual graph G_f at most $V/2$ times.*

Proof: Suppose $u \to v$ is in two residual graphs G_i and G_{j+1}, but not in any of the intermediate residual graphs $G_{i+1}, \dots, G_j$, for some $i < j$. Then $u \to v$ must be in the ith augmenting path, so $level_i(v) = level_i(u) + 1$, and $v \to u$ must be on the jth augmenting path, so $level_j(v) = level_j(u) - 1$. The previous lemma implies that

$$level_j(u) = level_j(v) + 1 \geq level_i(v) + 1 = level_i(u) + 2.$$

In other words, between the disappearance and reappearance of $u \to v$, the distance from s to u increased by at least 2. Because every level is either less than V or infinite, the number of disappearances is at most $V/2$. $\qquad\square$

Now we can derive an upper bound on the number of iterations. Because each edge disappears at most $V/2$ times, there are at most $EV/2$ edge disappearances overall. But at least one edge disappears on each iteration, so the algorithm must halt after at most $EV/2$ iterations. Finally, each iteration requires $O(E)$ time, so the overall algorithm runs in $O(VE^2)$ *time*.

10.7 Further Progress

This is nowhere near the end of the story for maximum-flow algorithms. Decades of further research have led to several faster algorithms, some of which are summarized in Figure 10.10.[4] All the listed algorithms listed compute a maximum flow in several iterations. Most of these algorithms have two variants: a simpler version that performs each iteration by brute force, and a faster variant that uses sophisticated data structures to maintain a spanning tree of the flow network, so that each iteration can be performed (and the spanning tree updated) in logarithmic time. There is no reason to believe that the best algorithms known so far are optimal; indeed, maximum flows are still a very active area of research.

Technique	Direct	With dynamic trees	Source(s)
Blocking flow	$O(V^2 E)$	$O(VE \log V)$	[Dinitz; Karzanov; Even and Itai; Sleator and Tarjan]
Network simplex	$O(V^2 E)$	$O(VE \log V)$	[Dantzig; Goldfarb and Hao; Goldberg, Grigoriadis, and Tarjan]
Push-relabel (generic)	$O(V^2 E)$	—	[Goldberg and Tarjan]
Push-relabel (FIFO)	$O(V^3)$	$O(VE \log(V^2/E))$	[Goldberg and Tarjan]
Push-relabel (highest label)	$O(V^2 \sqrt{E})$	—	[Cheriyan and Maheshwari; Tunçel]
Push-relabel-add games	—	$O(VE \log_{E/(V \log V)} V)$	[Cheriyan and Hagerup; King, Rao, and Tarjan]
Pseudoflow	$O(V^2 E)$	$O(VE \log V)$	[Hochbaum]
Pseudoflow (highest label)	$O(V^3)$	$O(VE \log(V^2/E))$	[Hochbaum and Orlin]
Incremental BFS	$O(V^2 E)$	$O(VE \log(V^2/E))$	[Goldberg, Held, Kaplan, Tarjan, and Werneck]
Compact networks	—	$O(VE)$	[Orlin]

Figure 10.10. Several purely combinatorial maximum-flow algorithms and their running times.

The fastest known (purely combinatorial) maximum-flow algorithm, announced by James Orlin in 2012, runs in $O(VE)$ *time*, exactly matching the worst-case complexity of a flow decomposition. The details of Orlin's algorithm are far beyond the scope of this book; in addition to his own new techniques, Orlin uses several older algorithms and data structures as black boxes, most of which are themselves quite complicated. In particular, Orlin's algorithm does *not* construct an explicit flow decomposition; in fact, for graphs with only $O(V)$ edges, an extension of his algorithm actually runs in only $O(V^2 / \log V)$ time! Nevertheless, for purposes of analyzing algorithms that *use* maximum flows,

---

[4]To keep this table short, I have deliberately omitted algorithms whose running time depends on edge capacities or the maximum flow value. Even with this restriction, the list is embarrassingly incomplete!

this is the time bound you should cite. So write the following sentence on your cheat sheets and cite it in your homeworks:

> **Maximum flows can be computed in $O(VE)$ time.**

Finally, faster maximum-flow algorithms are known for *unit-capacity* networks, where every edge has capacity 1. In 1973, Alexander Karzanov proved that Dinitz's blocking-flow algorithm—the first algorithm listed in the table above—runs in $O(\min\{V^{2/3}, E^{1/2}\} E)$ time in this setting. (This time bound appears to break the $\Omega(VE)$ flow decomposition barrier, but in fact Karzanov's analysis implies that any flow in a unit-capacity network can be decomposed into paths with total complexity $O(\min\{V^{2/3}, E^{1/2}\} E)$.) This was the fastest algorithm known in this setting for four decades. Karzanov's record was finally broken in 2013, when Aleksander Mądry announced a truly remarkable algorithm that computes maximum flows in unit-capacity networks in $O(E^{10/7} \operatorname{polylog} E)$ time. Again, the details of Mądry's algorithm are far beyond the scope of this book, or indeed the expertise of its author.

Exercises

0. Suppose you are given a directed graph $G = (V, E)$, two vertices s and t, a capacity function $c \colon E \to \mathbb{R}^+$, and a second function $f \colon E \to \mathbb{R}$. Describe an algorithm to determine whether f is a maximum (s, t)-flow in G.

1. Let f and f' be two feasible (s, t)-flows in a flow network G, such that $|f'| > |f|$. Prove that there is a feasible (s, t)-flow with value $|f'| - |f|$ in the residual network G_f.

2. Let $u \to v$ be an arbitrary edge in an arbitrary flow network G. Prove that if there is a minimum (s, t)-cut (S, T) such that $u \in S$ and $v \in T$, then there is *no* minimum cut (S', T') such that $u \in T'$ and $v \in S'$.

3. Let (S, T) and (S', T') be minimum (s, t)-cuts in some flow network G. Prove that $(S \cap S', T \cup T')$ and $(S \cup S', T \cap T')$ are also minimum (s, t)-cuts in G.

4. Let G be a flow network that contains an opposing pair of edges $u \to v$ and $v \to u$, both with positive capacity. Let G' be the flow network obtained from G by decreasing the capacities of both of these edges by $\min\{c(u \to v), c(v \to u)\}$. In other words:

   - If $c(u \to v) > c(v \to u)$, change the capacity of $u \to v$ to $c(u \to v) - c(v \to u)$ and delete $v \to u$.

- If $c(u \to v) < c(v \to u)$, change the capacity of $v \to u$ to $c(v \to u) - c(u \to v)$ and delete $u \to v$.
- Finally, if $c(u \to v) = c(v \to u)$, delete both $u \to v$ and $v \to u$.

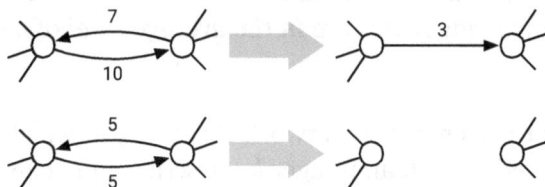

Figure 10.11. Enforcing the one-direction assumption.

(a) Prove that every maximum (s, t)-flow in G' is also a maximum (s, t)-flow in G. (Thus, by simplifying *every* opposing pair of edges in G, we obtain a new reduced flow network with the same maximum flow value as G.)

(b) Prove that every minimum (s, t)-cut in G is also a minimum (s, t)-cut in G' *and vice versa*.

(c) Prove that there is at least one maximum (s, t)-flow in G that is *not* a maximum (s, t)-flow in G'.

5. (a) Describe an efficient algorithm to determine whether a given flow network contains a *unique* maximum (s, t)-flow.

(b) Describe an efficient algorithm to determine whether a given flow network contains a *unique* minimum (s, t)-cut.

(c) Describe a flow network that contains a unique maximum (s, t)-flow but does not contain a unique minimum (s, t)-cut.

(d) Describe a flow network that contains a unique minimum (s, t)-cut but does not contain a unique maximum (s, t)-flow.

6. An (s, t)-flow in a network G is *acyclic* if there are no directed cycles where every edge has a positive flow value; that is, the subgraph of edges with positive flow value is a dag.

(a) Describe and analyze an algorithm to compute an *acyclic* maximum (s, t)-flow in a given flow network. Your algorithm should have the same asymptotic running time as Ford-Fulkerson.

(b) Describe and analyze an algorithm to determine whether *every* maximum (s, t)-flow in a given flow network is acyclic.

7. Let $G = (V, E)$ be a flow network in which every edge has capacity 1 and the shortest-path distance from s to t is at least d.

(a) Prove that the value of the maximum (s, t)-flow is at most E/d.

(b) Now suppose that G is *simple*, meaning that for all vertices u and v, there is at most one edge from u to v. (Flow networks can have parallel edges.) Prove that the value of the maximum (s, t)-flow is at most $O(V^2/d^2)$. [*Hint: How many nodes are in the average level of a BFS tree rooted at s?*]

8. Suppose we are given a flow network $G = (V, E)$ in which every edge has capacity 1, together with an integer k. Describe and analyze an algorithm to identify k edges in G such that after deleting those k edges, the value of the maximum (s, t)-flow in the remaining graph is as small as possible.

9. The analysis in our proof of the Flow Decomposition Theorem can be tightened. Let $G = (V, E)$ be an arbitrary flow network, and let f be an arbitrary (s, t)-flow in G.

(a) Prove that if $|f| = 0$, then f is the weighted sum of at most $E - V + 1$ directed cycles, where $f(e) > 0$ for every edge e in each of these cycles.

(b) Prove that if $|f| > 0$, then f is the weighted sum of at most $E - V + 2$ directed paths and directed cycles, where $f(e) > 0$ for every edge e in each of these paths and cycles.

(c) Prove that both of the previous upper bounds are tight: There are graphs in which some circulations cannot be decomposed into less than $E - V + 1$ cycles, and some flows cannot be decomposed into less than $E - V + 2$ paths and cycles. [*Hint: This is easy.*]

♣10. Our observation that any linear combination of (s, t)-flows is itself an (s, t)-flow implies that the set of all (not necessarily feasible) (s, t)-flows in any graph actually define a real *vector space*, which we can call the **flow space** of the graph.

(a) Prove that the flow space of any connected graph $G = (V, E)$ has dimension $E - V + 2$.

(b) Let T be any spanning tree of G. Prove that the following collection of paths and cycles define a basis for the flow space:
   • The unique path in T from s to t;
   • The unique cycle in $T \cup \{e\}$, for every edge $e \notin T$.

(c) Let T be any spanning tree of G, and let F be the forest obtained by deleting any single edge in T. Prove that the following collection of paths and cycles define a basis for the flow space:
   • The unique path in $F \cup \{e\}$ from s to t, for every edge $e \notin F$ that has one endpoint in each component of F;

- The unique cycle in $F \cup \{e\}$, for every edge $e \notin F$ with both endpoints in the same component of F.

(d) Prove or disprove the following claim: Every connected flow network has a flow basis that consists entirely of simple paths from s to t.

11. Cuts are sometimes defined as subsets of the edges of the graph, instead of as partitions of its vertices. In this problem, you will prove that these two definitions are *almost* equivalent.

    We say that a subset X of (directed) edges *separates s and t* if every directed path from s to t contains at least one (directed) edge in X. For any subset S of *vertices*, let δS denote the set of directed edges leaving S; that is, $\delta S := \{u \rightarrow v \mid u \in S, v \notin S\}$.

    (a) Prove that if (S, T) is an (s, t)-cut, then δS separates s and t.

    (b) Let X be an arbitrary subset of edges that separates s and t. Prove that there is an (s, t)-cut (S, T) such that $\delta S \subseteq X$.

    (c) Let X be a *minimal* subset of edges that separates s and t. (Such a set of edges is sometimes called a **bond**.) Prove that there is an (s, t)-cut (S, T) such that $\delta S = X$.

12. Suppose instead of capacities, we consider networks where each edge $u \rightarrow v$ has a non-negative **demand** $d(u \rightarrow v)$. Now an (s, t)-flow f is *feasible* if and only if $f(u \rightarrow v) \geq d(u \rightarrow v)$ for every edge $u \rightarrow v$. (Feasible flow values can now be arbitrarily large.) A natural problem in this setting is to find a feasible (s, t)-flow of *minimum* value.

    (a) Describe an efficient algorithm to compute a feasible (s, t)-flow, given the graph, the demand function, and the vertices s and t as input. [*Hint: Find a flow that is non-zero everywhere, and then scale it up to make it feasible.*]

    (b) Suppose you have access to a subroutine MaxFlow that computes *maximum* flows in networks with edge capacities. Describe an efficient algorithm to compute a *minimum* flow in a given network with edge demands; your algorithm should call MaxFlow exactly once.

    (c) State and prove an analogue of the max-flow min-cut theorem for this setting. (Do minimum flows correspond to maximum cuts?)

13. For any flow network G and any vertices u and v, let $bottleneck_G(u, v)$ denote the maximum, over all paths π in G from u to v, of the minimum-capacity edge along π.

(a) Describe and analyze an algorithm to compute $bottleneck_G(s, t)$ in $O(E \log V)$ time. This is the amount of flow that the Edmonds-Karp fattest-augmenting-paths algorithm pushes in the first iteration.

(b) Now suppose the flow network G is undirected; equivalently, suppose $c(u \to v) = c(v \to u)$ for every pair of vertices u and v. Describe and analyze an algorithm to compute $bottleneck_G(s, t)$ in $O(V + E)$ time. [*Hint: Find the median edge capacity.*] Why doesn't this speedup work for directed graphs?

♥(c) Again, suppose the flow network G is undirected. Describe and analyze an algorithm to construct a spanning tree T of G such that $bottleneck_T(u, v) = bottleneck_G(u, v)$ for *all* vertices u and v. (Edges in T inherit their capacities from G.) For full credit, your algorithm should run in $O(E)$ time.

14. Suppose you are given a flow network G with **integer** edge capacities and an **integer** maximum flow f^* in G. Describe algorithms for the following operations:

(a) INCREMENT(e): Increase the capacity of edge e by 1 and update the maximum flow.

(b) DECREMENT(e): Decrease the capacity of edge e by 1 and update the maximum flow.

Both algorithms should modify f^* so that it is still a maximum flow, more quickly than recomputing a maximum flow from scratch.

15. Let G be a network with integer edge capacities. An edge in G is *upper-binding* if increasing its capacity by 1 also increases the value of the maximum flow in G. Similarly, an edge is *lower-binding* if decreasing its capacity by 1 also decreases the value of the maximum flow in G.

(a) Does every network G have at least one upper-binding edge? Prove your answer is correct.

(b) Does every network G have at least one lower-binding edge? Prove your answer is correct.

(c) Describe an algorithm to find all upper-binding edges in G, given both G and a maximum flow in G as input, in $O(E)$ time.

(d) Describe an algorithm to find all lower-binding edges in G, given both G and a maximum flow in G as input, in $O(EV)$ time.

16. A given flow network G may have more than one minimum (s, t)-cut. Let's define the **best** minimum (s, t)-cut to be any minimum cut (S, T) with the smallest number of edges crossing from S to T.

(a) Describe an efficient algorithm to find the best minimum (s, t)-cut when the capacities are integers.

(b) Describe an efficient algorithm to find the best minimum (s, t)-cut for *arbitrary* edge capacities.

(c) Describe an efficient algorithm to determine whether a given flow network contains a unique *best* minimum (s, t)-cut.

17. A new assistant professor, teaching maximum flows for the first time, suggests the following greedy modification to the generic Ford-Fulkerson augmenting path algorithm. Instead of maintaining a residual graph, just[5] reduce the capacity of edges along the augmenting path! In particular, whenever we saturate an edge, just remove it from the graph. Who needs all that residual graph nonsense?

```
GREEDYFLOW(G, c, s, t):
    for every edge e in G
        f(e) ← 0

    while there is a path from s to t
        π ← an arbitrary path from s to t
        F ← minimum capacity of any edge in π
        for every edge e in π
            f(e) ← f(e) + F
            if c(e) = F
                remove e from G
            else
                c(e) ← c(e) − F
    return f
```

(a) Show that GREEDYFLOW does not always compute a maximum flow.

(b) Show that GREEDYFLOW is not even guaranteed to compute a good approximation to the maximum flow. That is, for any constant $\alpha > 1$, there is a flow network G such that the value of the maximum flow is more than α times the value of the flow computed by GREEDYFLOW. [*Hint: Assume that GREEDYFLOW chooses the worst possible path π at each iteration.*]

18. In 1980 Maurice Queyranne published an example of a flow network, shown below, where Edmonds and Karp's "fattest path" heuristic does not halt. As in Zwick's bad example for the original Ford-Fulkerson algorithm, ϕ denotes the inverse golden ratio $(\sqrt{5}-1)/2$. The three vertical edges play essentially the same role as the horizontal edges in Zwick's example.

---

[5]The adverb *just* is almost always subconscious shorthand for "I'm too lazy to figure out the details, but you should believe me anyway", or more succinctly, "This is probably wrong." See also *merely, simply, clearly,* and *obviously*.

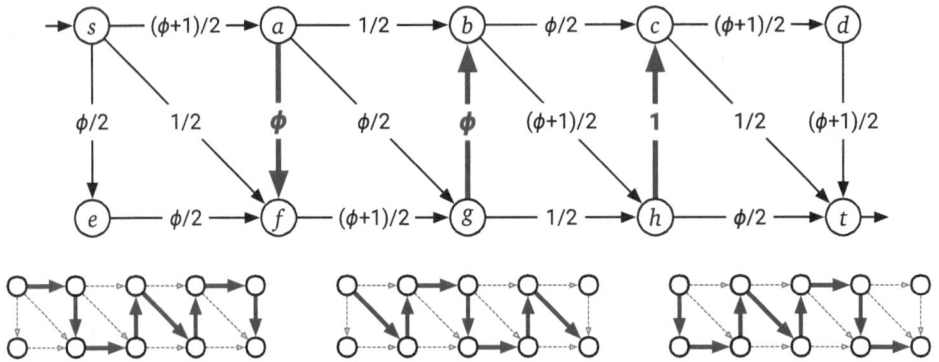

Figure 10.12. Queyranne's network, and a sequence of "fattest path" augmentations.

(a) Show that the following infinite sequence of path augmentations is a valid execution of the Edmonds-Karp "fattest path" algorithm. (See the bottom of Figure 10.12.)

> QUEYRANNEFATPATHS:
>   for $i \leftarrow 1$ to ∞
>   push ϕ^{3i-2} units of flow along $s \to a \to f \to g \to b \to h \to c \to d \to t$
>   push ϕ^{3i-1} units of flow along $s \to f \to a \to b \to g \to h \to c \to t$
>   push ϕ^{3i} units of flow along $s \to e \to f \to a \to g \to b \to c \to h \to t$

(b) Describe a sequence of $O(1)$ path augmentations that yields a maximum flow in Queyranne's network.

♥19. An **(s, t)-series-parallel** graph is a directed acyclic graph with two distinguished vertices s and t and with one of the following structures:

- **Base case:** A single directed edge from s to t.
- **Series:** The union of an (s, u)-series-parallel graph and a (u, t)-series-parallel graph that share a common vertex u but no other vertices or edges.
- **Parallel:** The union of two smaller (s, t)-series-parallel graphs with the same source s and target t, but with no other vertices or edges in common.

Every (s, t)-series-parallel graph G can be represented by a **decomposition tree**, which is a binary tree with three types of nodes: leaves (which corresponding to edges in G), series nodes (which correspond to vertices other than s and t), and parallel nodes. The same series-parallel graph could be represented by many different decomposition trees.

(a) Suppose you are given a directed graph G with two special vertices s and t. Describe and analyze an algorithm that either builds a decomposition tree for G or correctly reports that G is not (s, t)-series-parallel. [*Hint: Build the tree from the bottom up.*]

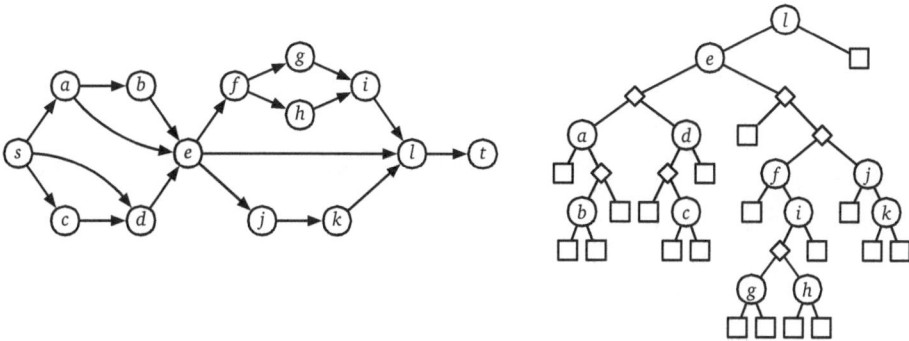

Figure 10.13. A series-parallel graph and a corresponding decomposition tree. Squares in the decomposition tree are leaves; diamonds are parallel nodes.

(b) Describe and analyze an algorithm to compute a maximum (s, t)-flow in a given (s, t)-series-parallel flow network with arbitrary edge capacities. [*Hint: In light of part (a), you can assume that you are actually given the decomposition tree. First compute the maximum-flow value, then compute an actual maximum flow.*]

20. We can speed up the Edmonds-Karp "fattest path" algorithm, at least for networks with small integer capacities, by relaxing our requirements for the next augmenting path. Instead of finding the augmenting path with maximum bottleneck capacity, we find a path whose bottleneck capacity is at least half of maximum, using the following *capacity scaling* algorithm. (This algorithm was actually proposed by Edmonds and Karp.)

Assume all the edge capacities are positive integers less than $U = 2^k$ for some integer k. The scaling algorithm maintains a bottleneck threshold Δ; initially, we set $\Delta \leftarrow U$. In each *phase*, the algorithm augments along paths from s to t in which every edge has residual capacity at least Δ. When there is no such path, the phase ends, we set $\Delta \leftarrow \lfloor \Delta/2 \rfloor$, and the next phase begins. The algorithm ends when $\Delta = 0$.

(a) How many phases will this algorithm execute in the worst case?

(b) Let f be the flow at the end of a phase for a particular value of Δ. Prove that the capacity of a minimum cut in the residual graph G_f is at most $E \cdot \Delta$.

(c) Prove that in each phase of the scaling algorithm, there are at most $2E$ augmentations.

(d) What is the overall running time of the capacity scaling algorithm?

11

Applications of Flows and Cuts

11.1 Edge-Disjoint Paths

One of the easiest applications of maximum flows is computing the maximum number of edge-disjoint paths between two specified vertices s and t in a directed graph G using maximum flows. A set of paths in G is *edge-disjoint* if each edge in G appears in at most one of the paths; several edge-disjoint paths may pass through the same vertex, however.

If we give each edge capacity 1, then the maximum flow from s to t pushes either 0 or 1 units of flow along each edge. The flow-decomposition theorem implies that the subgraph S of saturated edges is the union of several edge-disjoint paths and cycles. Moreover, the number of paths in this decomposition is exactly equal to the value of the flow. Extracting the actual paths from S is straightforward—follow any directed path in S from s to t, remove that path from S, and recurse.

Conversely, we can transform any collection of k edge-disjoint paths into a flow by pushing one unit of flow along each path from s to t; the value of the resulting flow is exactly k. It follows that any maximum flow algorithm actually computes the largest possible set of edge-disjoint paths.

If we use Orlin's algorithm to compute maximum flows, we can compute edge-disjoint paths in $O(VE)$ time, but Orlin's algorithm is overkill for this simple application. The cut $(\{s\}, V \setminus \{s\})$ has capacity at most $V - 1$, so the maximum flow has value at most $V - 1$. Thus, Ford and Fulkerson's original augmenting path algorithm already runs in $O(|f^*| E) = O(VE)$ *time*.

The same algorithm can also be used to find edge-disjoint paths in *undirected* graphs. First, replace every undirected edge uv in G with a pair of directed edges $u{\to}v$ and $v{\to}u$, each with unit capacity, and call the resulting directed graph G'. Next, compute a maximum (s, t)-flow f^* in G' using Ford-Fulkerson. For any edge uv in G, if f^* saturates both directed edges $u{\to}v$ and $v{\to}u$ in G', we can remove *both* edges from the flow without changing its value. (More generally, we can find an *acyclic* maximum flow in G' by canceling all cycles in f^*, not only cycles of length 2.) Thus, without loss of generality, f^* assigns a unique direction to each saturated edge. Finally, we can extract the edge-disjoint paths by searching the subgraph of directed edges saturated by f^*.

11.2 Vertex Capacities and Vertex-Disjoint Paths

Now suppose the vertices of the input graph G have capacities, not just the edges. In addition to our other constraints, for each vertex v other than s and t, we require the total flow into v (and therefore the total flow out of v) to be at most some non-negative value $c(v)$:

$$\sum_{u \to v} f(u{\to}v) \le c(v).$$

Can we still compute maximum flows with these new vertex constraints?

In 1962, Ford and Fulkerson proposed the following reduction to a flow network $\bar{G}$ with only edge capacities. Replace every vertex v with two vertices v_{in} and v_{out}, connected by an edge $v_{\text{in}}{\to}v_{\text{out}}$ with capacity $c(v)$, and then replace every directed edge $u{\to}v$ with the edge $u_{\text{out}}{\to}v_{\text{in}}$ (keeping the same capacity). Routine definition-chasing implies that every feasible $(s_{\text{out}}, t_{\text{in}})$-flow in $\bar{G}$ is equivalent to a feasible (s, t)-flow with the same value in the original graph G, and vice versa. In particular, every maximum flow in $\bar{G}$ is equivalent to a maximum flow in G. The reduction from G to $\bar{G}$ takes $O(E)$ time, after which we can compute the maximum flow in $\bar{G}$ using Orlin's algorithm. Altogether, computing the maximum flow in G requires $O(VE)$ *time*.

It is now easy to compute the maximum number of *vertex*-disjoint paths from s to t in $O(VE)$ time: Assign capacity 1 to every vertex and compute a maximum flow!

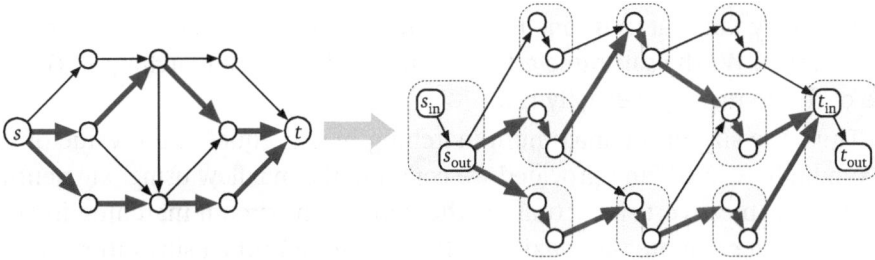

Figure 11.1. Reducing vertex-disjoint paths in G to edge-disjoint paths in $\bar{G}$.

11.3 Bipartite Matching

Another natural application of maximum flows is finding maximum *matchings* in bipartite graphs. A matching is a subgraph in which every vertex has degree at most one, or equivalently, a collection of edges such that no two share a vertex. The problem is to find a matching with the maximum number of edges.

For example, suppose we have a set of doctors who are looking for jobs, and a set of hospitals who are looking for doctors. Each doctor lists all hospitals where they are willing to work, and each hospital lists all doctors they are willing to hire. Our task is to find the largest subset of doctor-hospital hires that everyone is willing to accept.[1] This problem is equivalent to finding a maximum matching in a bipartite graph whose vertices are the doctors and hospitals, and there is an edge between a doctor and a hospital if and only if each find the other acceptable.

We can solve this problem by reducing it to a maximum flow problem, as follows. Let G be the given bipartite graph with vertex set $L \cup R$, such that every edge joins a vertex in L to a vertex in R. We create a new *directed* graph G' by (1) orienting each edge from L to R, (2) adding a new source vertex s with edges to every vertex in L, and (3) adding a new target vertex t with edges from every vertex in R. Finally, we assign every edge in G' a capacity of 1.

Any matching M in G can be transformed into a flow f_M in G' as follows: For each edge uw in M, push one unit of flow along the path $s \to u \to w \to t$. These paths are disjoint except at s and t, so the resulting flow satisfies the capacity constraints. Moreover, the value of the resulting flow is equal to the number of edges in M.

Conversely, consider any (s, t)-flow f in G', computed using the Ford-Fulkerson augmenting path algorithm. Because the edge capacities are integers, the Ford-Fulkerson algorithm assigns an integer flow to every edge. (This is easy to verify by induction, hint, hint.) Moreover, since each edge has *unit* capacity, the computed flow either saturates ($f(e) = 1$) or avoids ($f(e) = 0$) every edge

---

[1]This problem is very different from the stable matching problem we saw in Chapter 4, because we aren't trying to make each doctor and hospital as happy as possible.

in G'. Finally, since at most one unit of flow can enter any vertex in U or leave any vertex in W, the saturated edges from U to W form a matching in G. The size of this matching is exactly $|f|$.

Thus, the size of the maximum matching in G is equal to the value of the maximum flow in G', and provided we compute the maxflow using augmenting paths, we can convert the actual maxflow into a maximum matching in $O(E)$ time. We can compute the maximum flow in **$O(VE)$ time** using either Orlin's algorithm or off-the-shelf Ford-Fulkerson.

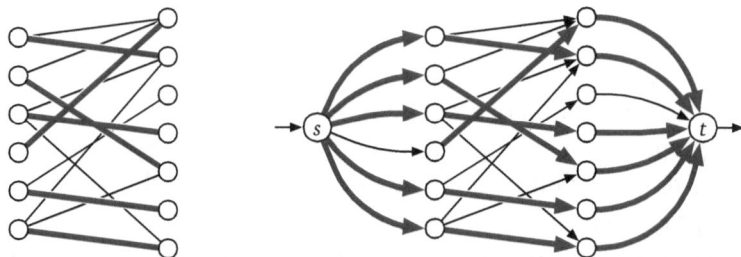

Figure 11.2. A maximum matching in a bipartite graph G, and the corresponding maximum flow in G'.

It is enlightening to interpret the behavior of Ford-Fulkerson in G' in terms of the original bipartite graph G. The algorithm maintains a matching M in G, which is initially empty; the edges of M correspond to edges in G' that carry flow. Call a vertex of G *matched* if is an endpoint of some edge in M, and *unmatched* otherwise. In each iteration of the algorithm, we look for an *alternating path* in G—a path from an unmatched vertex of L to an unmatched vertex in R that alternates between edges in M and edges not in M. (Alternating paths in G correspond exactly to augmenting paths for the current flow in G'.) If we find an augmenting path P, we update M to the symmetric difference $M \oplus P$, which increases the number of edges in M by 1, and continue to the next iteration. If there is no alternating path, the maxflow-mincut theorem implies that M is a maximum matching, so the algorithm ends. Finding a single alternating path requires $O(E)$ time, and the algorithm halts after at most V iterations, so the overall algorithm runs in **$O(VE)$ time**. Figure 11.3 shows this algorithm in action.

This characterization of maximum bipartite matchings in terms of alternating paths was proved by Claude Berge in 1957 (independently of the maxflow-mincut theorem), although it was already implicit in algorithms described by Harald Kuhn in 1955, by Dénes Kőnig in 1916, and by Carl Jacobi around 1836.

A more sophisticated algorithm, proposed by John Hopcroft and Richard Karp in 1973, computes maximum matchings in bipartite graphs in only $O(\sqrt{V}E)$ time, by finding several disjoint alternating paths in each iteration.

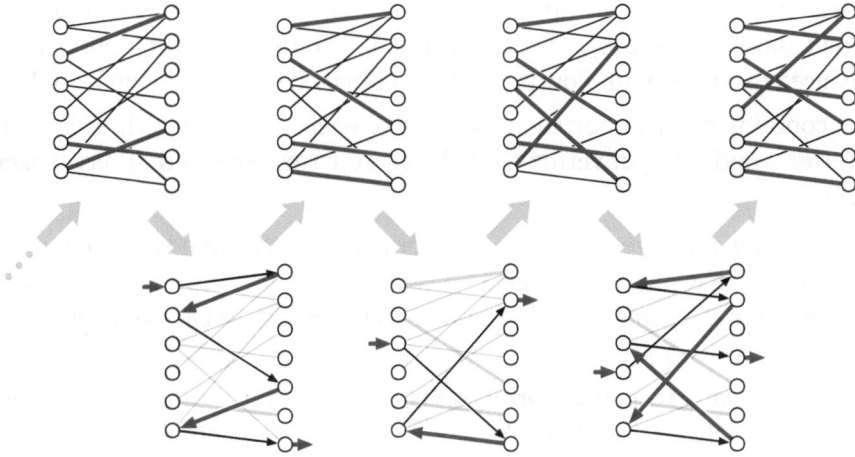

Figure 11.3. An increasing sequence of matchings connected by alternating paths.

11.4 Tuple Selection

The bipartite maximum matching problem is the simplest example of a broader class of problems that I call **tuple selection**.[2] The input to a tuple selection problem consists of several finite sets $X_1, X_2, \ldots, X_d$, each representing a different discrete resource. Our task is to select the largest possible set of d-tuples, each containing exactly one element from each set X_i, subject to several *capacity* constraints of the following form:

- For each index i, Each element $x \in X_i$ can appear in at most $c(x)$ selected tuples.

- For each index i, any two elements $x \in X_i$ and $y \in X_{i+1}$ can appear in at most $c(x, y)$ selected tuples.

Each of the upper bounds $c(x)$ and $c(x, y)$ is either a (typically small) non-negative integer or ∞.

In the maximum-matching problem, we have $d = 2$ resources, each element x has capacity $c(x) = 1$, and each pair (x, y) has capacity $c(x, y) = 1$ or $c(x, y) = 0$, depending on whether or not xy is an edge in the underlying bipartite graph.

---

[2]I couldn't find a standard name for these problems, so I made up my own. These are sometimes called "assignment problems", but it's more common for the phrase "the assignment problem" to refer to the problem of finding a maximum-*weight* bipartite matching in an edge-weighted bipartite graph.

Because the resources are linearly ordered, and only pairs of objects in *adjacent* subsets X_i and X_{i+1} are constrained,[3] the tuple selection problem can be reduced to a maximum-flow problem in a directed graph G defined as follows:

- G contains a vertex for each element of each set X_i, as well as a source vertex s and a target vertex t. Each vertex x (except s and t) has capacity $c(x)$.

- G contains an edge $s{\to}w$ for each element $w \in X_1$, an edge $z{\to}t$ for each element $z \in X_d$, and an edge $x{\to}y$ with capacity $c(x,y)$ for each pair of elements $x \in X_i$ and $y \in X_{i+1}$, for all i. (Optionally, we can omit edges $x{\to}y$ with $c(x,y) = 0$.)

Every path from s to t in G corresponds to (or "is") a d-tuple that we *could* select; conversely, every selectable d-tuple that satisfies the stated constraints corresponds to (or "is") a path from s to t in G.

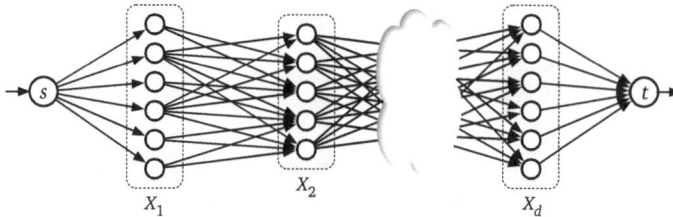

Figure 11.4. The flow network for a tuple selection problem.

More generally, let f be an arbitrary feasible integer (s,t)-flow in G. Because all capacities are integers or ∞, the Flow Decomposition Theorem implies that f is the sum of $|f|$ paths from s to t, each carrying exactly one unit of flow. Straightforward definition-chasing implies that the resulting set of tuples satisfies all the capacity constraints. Conversely, for any set of k tuples that satisfies the capacity constraints, the sum of the k corresponding paths is a feasible integer (s,t)-flow with value k.

Thus, we can select the maximum number of tuples that satisfy the given capacity constraints by computing a maximum (s,t)-flow f^* in G and then computing a flow decomposition of f^*. Because all finite capacities in G are integers, we can assume without loss of generality that f^* is an integer flow, and therefore (by the previous paragraph) corresponds to a valid set of $|f^*|$ tuples.

Exam Scheduling

The following "real world" scheduling problem might help clarify our general reduction.

---

[3]If pairs of objects from even one non-adjacent pair of subsets (X_i and X_j where $j > i+1$) are also constrained, the problem becomes NP-hard, by a straightforward reduction from EXACT-3DIMENSIONALMATCHING. We'll discuss NP-hardness in the next chapter.

Sham-Poobanana University has hired you to write an algorithm to schedule their final exams. There are n different classes, each of which needs to schedule a final exam in one of r rooms during one of t different time slots. At most one class's final exam can be scheduled in each room during each time slot; conversely, classes cannot be split into multiple rooms or multiple times. Moreover, each exam must be overseen by one of p proctors.[4] Each proctor can oversee at most one exam at a time; each proctor is available for only certain time slots; and no proctor is allowed oversee more than 5 exams total. The input to the scheduling problem consists of three arrays:

- An integer array $E[1..n]$ where $E[i]$ is the number of students enrolled in the ith class.

- An integer array $S[1..r]$, where $S[j]$ is the number of seats in the jth room. The ith class's final exam *can* be held in the jth room if and only if $E[i] \le S[j]$.

- A boolean array $A[1..t, 1..p]$ where $A[k, \ell] = \text{TRUE}$ if and only if the ℓth proctor is available during the kth time slot.[5]

let $N = n + r + tp$ denote the total size of the input. Your job is to design an algorithm that either schedules a room, a time slot, and a proctor for every class's final exam, or correctly reports that no such schedule is possible.

This is a standard tuple-selection problem with four resources: classes, rooms, time slots, and proctors. To solve this problem, we construct a flow network G with six types of vertices—a source vertex s', a vertex c_i for each class, a vertex r_j for each room, a vertex t_k for each time slot, a vertex p_ℓ for each proctor, and a target vertex t'—and five types of edges, as shown in Figure 11.5:

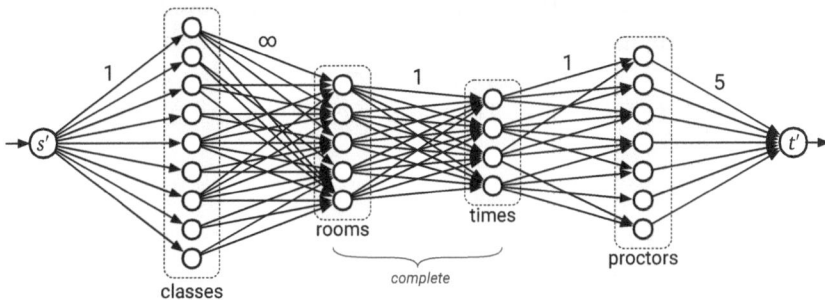

Figure 11.5. A flow network for the exam scheduling problem.

- An edge $s' \rightarrow c_i$ with capacity 1 for each class i. ("Each class can hold at most one final exam.")

---

[4]or as they are better known outside the US, invigilators
[5]Arguably, this information is better represented as a graph, but I thought that would make the reduction more confusing.

- An edge $c_i \rightarrow r_j$ with capacity ∞ for each class i and room j such that $E[i] \le S[j]$. ("Class i can hold exams in room j if and only if the room has enough seats.") This is the only place where the enrollments $E[i]$ and seat numbers $S[j]$ are used.

- An edge $r_j \rightarrow t_k$ with capacity 1 for each room j and time slot k. ("At most one exam can be held in room j at time k.")

- An edge $t_k \rightarrow p_\ell$ with capacity 1 for time slot k and proctor ℓ such that $A[\ell, k] = \text{TRUE}$. ("A proctor can oversee at most one exam at any time, and only during times that they are available.")

- An edge $p_\ell \rightarrow t'$ with capacity 5 for each proctor ℓ. ("Each proctor can oversee at most 5 exams.")

(I'm calling the source and target vertices s' and t' instead of s and t only because the problem statement already uses the variable t to denote the number of time slots.) Altogether, G has $n + r + t + p + 2 = O(N)$ vertices and $O(nr + rt + tp) = O(N^2)$ edges.

Each path from s' to t' in G represents a unique valid choice of class, room, time, and proctor for one final exam; specifically, the class fits into the room, and the proctor is available at that time. Conversely, for each valid choice (class, room, time, proctor), there is a corresponding path from s' to t' in G. Thus, we can construct a valid schedule for the maximum possible number of exams by computing an maximum (s', t')-flow f^* in G, decomposing f^* into paths from s' to t', and then transcribing each path into a class-room-time-proctor assignment. If $|f^*| = n$, we can return the resulting schedule; otherwise, we can correctly report that scheduling all n final exams is impossible.

Constructing G from the given input data by brute force takes $O(E)$ time. We can compute the maximum flow in $O(VE)$ time using either Ford-Fulkerson (because $|f^*| \le n < V$) or Orlin's algorithm, and we can compute the flow decomposition in $O(VE)$ time. Thus, the overall algorithm runs in $O(VE) = O(N^3)$ *time*.

11.5 Disjoint-Path Covers

A *path cover* of a directed graph G is a collection of directed paths in G such that every vertex of G lies on *at least* one path. A *disjoint*-path cover of G is a path cover such that every vertex of G lies on *exactly* one path. Every directed graph has a trivial disjoint-path cover consisting of several paths of length zero, but that's boring. Instead, let's look for disjoint-path covers that contain as few paths as possible. This problem is NP-hard in general—a graph has a disjoint-path cover of size 1 if and only if it contains a Hamiltonian path—but there is an efficient flow-based algorithm for directed *acyclic* graphs.

To solve this problem for a given directed acyclic graph $G = (V, E)$, we construct a new bipartite graph $G' = (V', E')$ as follows.

- H contains two vertices $v^\flat$ and $v^\sharp$ for every vertex v of G.
- H contains an undirected edge $u^\flat v^\sharp$ for every directed edge $u \to v$ in G.

(If G is represented as an adjacency matrix, then G' is the bipartite graph represented by the same adjacency matrix!)

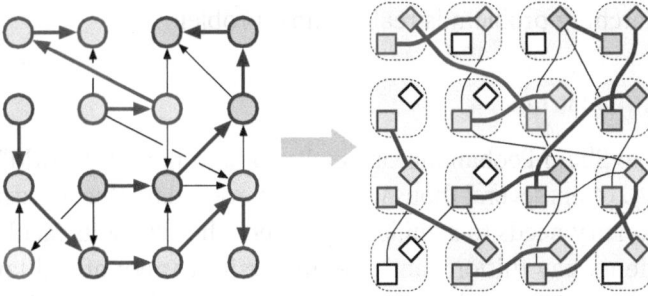

Figure 11.6. Reducing minimum disjoint-path cover of a dag to maximum bipartite matching; squares are flat$^\flat$ and diamonds are sharp$^\sharp$.

Now I claim that G can be covered by k disjoint paths if and only if the new graph G' has a matching of size $V - k$. As usual, we prove the equivalence in two stages:

$\Leftarrow$ Suppose G has a disjoint path cover P with k paths; think of P as a subgraph of G. Every vertex in P has in-degree either 0 or 1; moreover, there is exactly one vertex with in-degree 0 in each path in P. It follows that P has exactly $V - k$ edges. Now define a subset M of the edges of G' as follows:

$$M := \left\{ u^\flat v^\sharp \in E' \mid u \to v \in P \right\}.$$

By definition of disjoint-path cover, every vertex of G has at most one incoming edge in P and at most one outgoing edge in P. We conclude that every vertex of G' is incident to at most one edge in M; that is, M is a matching of size $V - k$.

$\Rightarrow$ Suppose G' has a matching M of size $V - k$. We project M' back to G by defining a subgraph $P = (V, M')$, where

$$M' := \left\{ u \to v \in E \mid u^\flat v^\sharp \in M \right\}.$$

By definition of matching, every vertex of G has at most one incoming edge in P and at most one outgoing edge in P. It follows that P is a collection of disjoint directed paths in G; since P includes every vertex, P defines an disjoint path cover with $V - k$ edges. The number of paths in P is equal to the number of vertices in G that have no incoming edge in M'. We conclude that P contains exactly k paths.

It follows immediately that we can find a minimum disjoint-path cover in G by computing a maximum matching in G', using Ford-Fulkerson's maximum-flow algorithm, in $O(V'E') = O(VE)$ *time*.

Despite its formulation in terms of dags and paths, this is really a maximum matching problem: We want to *match* as many vertices as possible to distinct *successors* in the graph. The number of paths required to cover the dag is equal to the number of vertices with no successor. (And of course, every bipartite maximum matching problem is really a flow problem.)

Minimal Faculty Hiring

Let's go back to Sham-Poobanana University for another "real-world" scheduling problem.[6] SPU offers several thousand courses every day. Due to extreme budget cuts, the university needs to significantly reduce the size of its faculty. However, because students pay tuition (and the university cannot afford lawyers), the university must retain enough professors to guarantee that every class advertised in the course catalog is actually taught. How few professors can SPU get away with? Each remaining faculty member will be assigned a sequence of classes to teach on any given day. The classes assigned to each professor must not overlap; moreover, there must be enough slack in each professor's schedule for them to walk from one class to the next. For purposes of this problem, let's assume that every professor is capable of teaching every class, and that professors will not have office hours, lunches, or bathroom breaks.[7]

Concretely, suppose there are n classes offered in m different locations. The input to our problem consists of the following data:

- An array $C[1..n]$ of classes, where each class $C[i]$ has three fields: the starting time $C[i].start$, the ending time $C[i].end$, and the location $C[i].loc$.

- A two-dimensional array $T[1..m, 1..m]$, where $T[u, v]$ is the time required to walk from location u to location v.

We want to find the minimum number of professors that can collectively teach every class, such that whenever a professor is assigned to teach two classes i and j where $C[j].start \geq C[i].start$, we actually have

$$C[j].start \geq C[i].end + T\big[C[i].loc, C[j].loc\big].$$

We can solve this problem by reducing it to a disjoint-path cover problem as follows. We construct a dag $G = (V, E)$ whose vertices are classes and whose edges represent pairs of classes that are scheduled far enough apart to be taught

---

[6]For a somewhat more realistic (and less depressing) formulation of this problem, consider airplanes and flights, or buses and bus routes, instead of professors and classes.

[7]They will, however, be expected to answer student emails as they walk between classes.

by the same professor. Specifically, a directed edge $i \rightarrow j$ indicates that the same professor can teach class i and then class j. It is easy to construct this dag in $O(n^2)$ time by brute force. Then we find a disjoint-path cover of G using the matching algorithm described above; each directed path in G represents a legal class schedule for one professor. The entire algorithm runs in $O(n^2 + VE) = O(n^3)$ time.[8]

Despite its initial description in terms of intervals and distances, this is really a maximum matching problem (which means it's *really* really a maximum-flow problem). Specifically, we want to *match* as many classes as possible to the *next* class taught by the same professor. The number of professors we need is equal to the number of classes with no assigned successor; each class without an assigned successor is the last class that some professor teaches.

11.6 Baseball Elimination

Every year millions of American baseball fans eagerly watch their favorite team, hoping they will win a spot in the playoffs, and ultimately the World Series. Sadly, most teams are "mathematically eliminated" days or even weeks before the regular season ends. Often, it is easy to spot when a team is eliminated—they can't win enough games to catch up to the current leader in their division. But sometimes the situation is more subtle. For example, here are the actual standings from the American League East on August 30, 1996.

Team	Won–Lost	Left	NYY	BAL	BOS	TOR	DET
New York Yankees	75–59	28		3	8	7	3
Baltimore Orioles	71–63	28	3		2	7	4
Boston Red Sox	69–66	27	8	2		0	0
Toronto Blue Jays	63–72	27	7	7	0		0
Detroit Tigers	49–86	27	3	4	0	0	

Detroit is clearly behind, but some die-hard Tigers fans may hold out hope that their team can still win. After all, if Detroit wins all 27 of their remaining games, they will end the season with 76 wins, more than any other team has now. So as long as every other team loses every game... but that's not possible,

---

[8]If we assume that every time interval $T[u, v]$ is equal,[9] this scheduling problem can actually be solved in $O(n \log n)$ time using a simple greedy algorithm.

[9]Many American universities schedule ten-minute breaks between classes, under the remarkable belief that a human being can walk from any classroom to any other classroom on the same campus in ten minutes. I invite anyone who thinks this belief is realistic to visit my campus and walk from one Siebel Center to the other.

because some of those other teams still have to play each other. Here is one complete argument:[10]

> By winning all of their remaining games, Detroit can finish the season with a record of 76 and 86. If the Yankees win just 2 more games, then they will finish the season with a 77 and 85 record which would put them ahead of Detroit. So, let's suppose the Tigers go undefeated for the rest of the season and the Yankees fail to win another game.
>
> The problem with this scenario is that New York still has 8 games left with Boston. If the Red Sox win all of these games, they will end the season with at least 77 wins putting them ahead of the Tigers. Thus, the only way for Detroit to even have a chance of finishing in first place, is for New York to win exactly one of the 8 games with Boston and lose all their other games. Meanwhile, the Sox must lose all the games they play against teams other than New York. This puts them in a 3-way tie for first place....
>
> Now let's look at what happens to the Orioles and Blue Jays in our scenario. Baltimore has 2 games left with with Boston and 3 with New York. So, if everything happens as described above, the Orioles will finish with at least 76 wins. So, Detroit can catch Baltimore only if the Orioles lose all their games to teams other than New York and Boston. In particular, this means that Baltimore must lose all 7 of its remaining games with Toronto. The Blue Jays also have 7 games left with the Yankees and we have already seen that for Detroit to finish in first place, Toronto must will all of these games. But if that happens, the Blue Jays will win at least 14 more games giving them at final record of 77 and 85 or better which means they will finish ahead of the Tigers. So, no matter what happens from this point in the season on, Detroit can not finish in first place in the American League East.

There has to be a better way to figure this out!

Here is a more abstract formulation of the problem. Our input consists of two arrays $W[1..n]$ and $G[1..n, 1..n]$, where $W[i]$ is the number of games team i has already won, and $G[i, j]$ is the number of upcoming games between teams i and j. We want to determine whether team n can end the season with the most wins (possibly tied with other teams).[11]

In the mid-1960s, Benjamin Schwartz observed that this question can be modeled as a maximum flow problem; about 20 years later, Dan Gusfield, Charles Martel, and David Fernández-Baca simplified Schwartz's flow formulation to a pair selection problem. Specifically, we want to know whether it is possible to **select** *a winner for each game*, so that team n comes in first place. Let $R[i] = \sum_j G[i, j]$ denote the number of remaining games for team i. We will assume that team n wins all $R[n]$ of its remaining games. Then team n can come in first place if and only if every other team i wins at most $W[n] + R[n] - W[i]$ of its $R[i]$ remaining games.

Since we want to **select** a winning team for each game, we start by building a bipartite graph, whose nodes represent the games and the teams. We have

---

[10]Both the example and this argument are taken from Eli Olinick's web site https://s2.smu.edu/~olinick/riot/detroit.html, which is based on Olinick's joint research with Ilan Adler, Alan Erera, and Dorit Hochbaum.

[11]We are implicitly assuming that no game ends in a tie and that every game is actually played. Both assumptions are consistent with Major League Baseball rules, at least for games that affect postseason standing, barring wars, natural disasters, or swarms of bees.

$\binom{n}{2}$ *game* nodes $g_{i,j}$, one for each pair $1 \le i < j < n$, and $n-1$ *team* nodes t_i, one for each $1 \le i < n$. For each pair i, j, we add edges $g_{i,j} \rightarrow t_i$ and $g_{i,j} \rightarrow t_j$ with *infinite* capacity. We add a source vertex s and edges $s \rightarrow g_{i,j}$ with capacity $G[i, j]$ for each pair i, j. Finally, we add a target node t and edges $t_i \rightarrow t$ with capacity $W[n] - W[i] + R[n]$ for each team i.

Figure 11.7 shows the graph derived from the 1996 American League East standings, where "team n" is the Detroit Tigers. All unlabeled edges have infinite capacity.

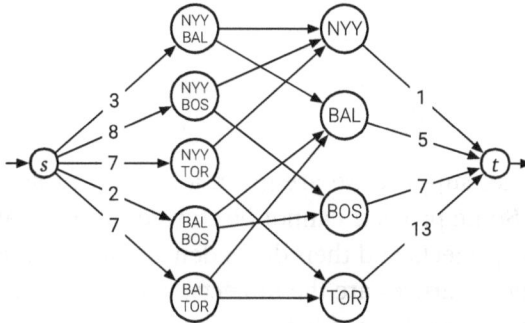

Figure 11.7. Cubs win! Cubs win!

Theorem. *Team n can end the season in first place if and only if there is a feasible flow in this graph that saturates every edge leaving s.*

Proof: Suppose it is possible for team n to end the season in first place. Then every team $i < n$ wins at most $W[n] + R[n] - W[i]$ of the remaining games. For each game between team i and team j that team i wins, add one unit of flow along the path $s \rightarrow g_{i,j} \rightarrow t_i \rightarrow t$. Because there are exactly $G[i, j]$ games between teams i and j, every edge leaving s is saturated. Because each team i wins at most $W[n] + R[n] - W[i]$ games, the resulting flow is feasible.

Conversely, let f be a feasible flow that saturates every edge out of s. Suppose team i wins exactly $f(g_{i,j} \rightarrow t_i)$ games against team j, for all i and j. Then teams i and j play $f(g_{i,j} \rightarrow t_i) + f(g_{i,j} \rightarrow t_j) = f(s \rightarrow g_{i,j}) = G[i, j]$ games, so every upcoming game is played. Moreover, each team i wins a total of $\sum_j f(g_{i,j} \rightarrow t_i) = f(t_i \rightarrow t) \le W[n] + R[n] - W[i]$ upcoming games, and therefore at most $W[n] + R[n]$ games overall. Thus, if team n win all their upcoming games, they end the season in first place. □

In summary, to decide whether our favorite team can win, we construct the flow network, compute a maximum flow, and report whether than maximum flow saturates every edge out of s. For example, in the graph in Figure 11.7, the total capacity of the edges leaving s is 27 (because there are 27 remaining games). On the other hand, the total capacity of the edges entering t is only 26, which implies that the maximum flow value is at most 26. We conclude that Detroit is mathematically eliminated.[12]

The flow network has $O(n^2)$ vertices and $O(n^2)$ edges, and it can be constructed in $O(n^2)$ time. Using Orlin's algorithm, we can compute the maximum flow in $O(VE) = O(n^4)$ *time*.

This is not the fastest algorithm for the baseball elimination problem. In 2001, Kevin Wayne proved that one can determine *all* teams that are mathematically eliminated in only $O(n^3)$ *time*, essentially using a single maximum-flow computation.

11.7 Project Selection

In our final example, suppose we are given a set of n projects that we could possibly perform. Some projects cannot be started until certain other projects are completed. The projects and their dependencies are described by a directed acyclic graph G whose vertices are the projects, where each edge $u \rightarrow v$ indicates that project u cannot be performed before project v. (This is exactly the form of dependency graphs we considered in Chapter 6.4.) Finally, each project v has an associated *profit* $\$(v)$ which will be given to us if the project is completed; some projects have negative profits, which we interpret as positive *costs*. We can choose to finish any subset X of the projects that includes all its dependents; that is, for every project $x \in X$, every project that x depends on is also in X. Our goal is to find a valid subset of the projects whose total profit is as large as possible. In particular, if all of the jobs have negative profit, the correct answer is to do nothing.

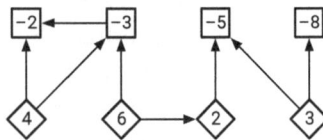

Figure 11.8. A dependency graph for a set of eight projects. Diamonds indicate profitable projects; squares indicate costly projects. Each edge $u \rightarrow v$ means u depends on v.

At a high level, our task to partition the projects into two subsets S and T, the jobs we *Select* and the jobs we *Turn down*. So intuitively, we'd like to model our problem as a minimum cut problem in a certain graph. But in which graph? How do we enforce prerequisites? We want to *maximize* profit, but we only know how to find *minimum* cuts. And how do we convert negative profits into positive capacities?

---

[12]We got (un)lucky here; it is possible for a team to be eliminated even if the total capacity of all edges into t is no smaller than the total capacity of edges out of s.

To transform our given constraint graph G into a flow network G', we add a source vertex s and a target vertex t to the dependency graph, with an edge $s{\to}v$ for every profitable job v (with $\$(v) > 0$), and an edge $u{\to}t$ for every costly job u (with $\$(u) < 0$). Intuitively, we can think of s as a new job ("Sleep!") with profit/cost 0 that we must perform last. We assign capacities to the edges of G' as follows:

- $c(s{\to}v) = \$(v)$ for every profitable job v;
- $c(u{\to}t) = -\$(u)$ for every costly job u;
- $c(u{\to}v) = \infty$ for every dependency edge $u{\to}v$.

All edge-capacities are positive, so this is a valid input to the maximum cut problem.

Now consider an arbitrary (s,t)-cut (S,T) in G'. For any edge $u{\to}v$ in the original dependency graph, if $u \in S$ and $v \in T$, then $\|S,T\| = \infty$. Thus, we can legally select the jobs in S if and only if the capacity of the cut (S,T) is finite.

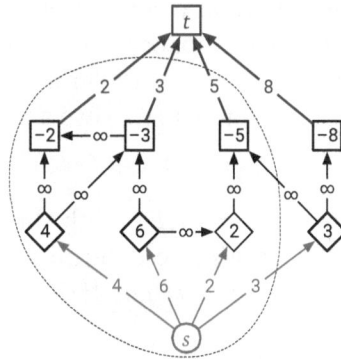

Figure 11.9. The flow network for the example dependency graph, along with its minimum cut. The cut has capacity 13 and $P = 15$, so the total profit for the selected jobs is 2.

In fact, it turns out that cuts with smaller capacity correspond to job selections with higher profit. Specifically, I claim that selecting the jobs in S earns a total profit of $P - \|S,T\|$, where P is the sum of all the positive profits:

$$P = \sum_v \max\{0, \$(v)\} = \sum_{\$(v)>0} \$(v).$$

We can prove this claim by straightforward definition-chasing, as follows. For any subset X of projects, we define three values. (Here, as usual, we define $c(u{\to}v) = 0$ when $u{\to}v$ is not an edge.)

$$cost(X) := \sum_{\substack{u \in X \\ \$(u)<0}} -\$(u) = \sum_{u \in X} c(u{\to}t)$$

$$yield(X) := \sum_{\substack{v \in X \\ \$(v)>0}} \$(v) = \sum_{v \in X} c(s{\to}v)$$

$$profit(X) := \sum_{v \in X} \$(v) = yield(X) - cost(X).$$

By definition, $P = yield(V) = yield(S) + yield(T)$. Because the cut (S, T) has finite capacity, only edges of the form $s \to v$ and $u \to t$ can cross the cut. By construction, every edge $s \to v$ points to a profitable job and each edge $u \to t$ points from a costly job. Thus, $\|S, T\| = cost(S) + yield(T)$. We immediately conclude that $P - \|S, T\| = yield(S) - cost(S) = profit(S)$, as claimed.

It follows immediately that we can *maximize* our total profit by computing a *minimum* cut in G'. We can easily construct G' from G in $O(V + E)$ time, and we can compute the minimum (s, t)-cut in G' in $O(VE)$ time using Orlin's algorithm. We conclude that the entire project-selection algorithm runs in $O(VE)$ **time**.

Exercises

1. Let $G = (V, E)$ be a directed graph where for each vertex v, the in-degree and out-degree of v are equal. Suppose G contains k edge-disjoint paths from some vertex u to another vertex v. Under these conditions, must G also contain k edge-disjoint paths from v to u? Give a proof or a counterexample with explanation.

2. Given an undirected graph $G = (V, E)$, with three vertices u, v, and w, describe and analyze an algorithm to determine whether there is a path from u to w that passes through v. [*Hint: If G were a directed graph, this problem would be NP-hard!*]

3. Consider a directed graph $G = (V, E)$ with several source vertices $s_1, s_2, \ldots, s_\sigma$ and target vertices $t_1, t_1, \ldots, t_\tau$, where no vertex is both a source and a target. A *multi-terminal flow* is a function $f : E \to \mathbb{R}_{\geq 0}$ that satisfies the flow conservation constraint at every vertex that is neither a source nor a target. The value $|f|$ of a multi-terminal flow is the total excess flow out of *all* the source vertices:

$$|f| := \sum_{i=1}^{\sigma} \left(\sum_w f(s_i \to w) - \sum_u f(u \to s_i) \right)$$

As usual, we are interested in finding flows with maximum value, subject to capacity constraints on the edges. (In particular, we don't care how much flow moves from any particular source to any particular target.)

(a) Consider the following algorithm for computing multi-terminal flows. The variables f and f' represent flow functions. The subroutine MAXFLOW(G, s, t) solves the standard maximum flow problem with source s and target t.

```
MAXMULTIFLOW(G, s[1..σ], t[1..τ]):
    f ← 0                           ⟨⟨Initialize the flow⟩⟩
    for i ← 1 to σ
        for j ← 1 to τ
            f' ← MAXFLOW(G_f, s[i], t[j])
            f ← f + f'              ⟨⟨Update the flow⟩⟩
    return f
```

Prove that this algorithm correctly computes a maximum multi-terminal flow in G.

(b) Describe a more efficient algorithm to compute a maximum multi-terminal flow in G.

4. The Island of Sodor is home to a large number of towns and villages, connected by an extensive rail network. Recently, several cases of a deadly contagious disease (either swine flu or zombies; reports are unclear) have been reported in the village of Skarloey. The controller of the Sodor railway plans to close down certain railway stations to prevent the disease from spreading to Tidmouth, his home town. No trains can pass through a closed station. To minimize expense (and public notice), he wants to close down as few stations as possible. However, he cannot close the Skarloey station, because that would expose him to the disease, and he cannot close the Tidmouth station, because then he couldn't visit his favorite pub.

   Describe and analyze an algorithm to find the minimum number of stations that must be closed to block all rail travel from Skarloey to Tidmouth. The Sodor rail network is represented by an undirected graph, with a vertex for each station and an edge for each rail connection between two stations. Two special vertices s and t represent the stations in Skarloey and Tidmouth.

   For example, given the following input graph, your algorithm should return the integer 2.

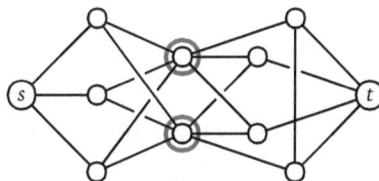

5. An $n \times n$ grid is an undirected graph with n^2 vertices organized into n rows and n columns. We denote the vertex in the ith row and the jth column by (i, j). Every vertex (i, j) has exactly four neighbors $(i - 1, j)$, $(i + 1, j)$, $(i, j - 1)$, and $(i, j + 1)$, except the boundary vertices, for which $i = 1$, $i = n$, $j = 1$, or $j = n$.

   Let $(x_1, y_1), (x_2, y_2), \ldots, (x_m, y_m)$ be distinct vertices, called terminals, in the $n \times n$ grid. The escape problem is to determine whether there are m

vertex-disjoint paths in the grid that connect the terminals to any m distinct boundary vertices.

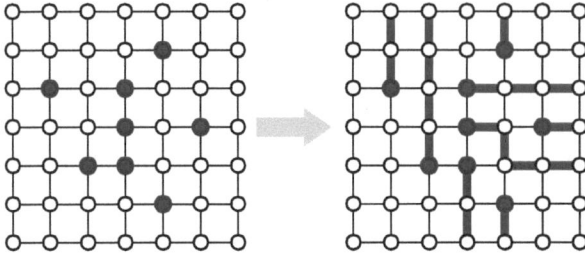

Figure 11.10. A positive instance of the escape problem, and its solution.

(a) Describe and analyze an efficient algorithm to solve the escape problem. The running time of your algorithm should be a small polynomial function of n.

(b) Now suppose the input to the escape problem consists of a single integer n and the list of m terminal vertices. If m is very small, the previous running time is actually *exponential* in the input size! Describe and analyze an algorithm to solve the escape problem in time *polynomial in m*.

♥(c) Modify the previous algorithm to output an explicit description of the escape paths (if they exist), still in time polynomial in m.

6. The SPU Commuter Silence Department is installing a mini-golf course in the basement of the See-Bull Center! The playing field is a closed polygon bounded by m horizontal and vertical line segments, meeting at right angles. The course has n *starting points* and n *holes*, in one-to-one correspondence. It is always possible hit the ball along a straight line directly from each starting point to the corresponding hole, without touching the boundary of the playing field. (Players are not allowed to bounce golf balls off the walls; too much glass.) The n starting points and n holes are all at distinct locations.

Sadly, the architect's computer crashed just as construction was about to begin. Thanks to the herculean efforts of their sysadmins, they were able to recover the *locations* of the starting points and the holes, but all information about which starting points correspond to which holes was lost!

Describe and analyze an algorithm to compute a one-to-one correspondence between the starting points and the holes that meets the straight-line requirement, or to report that no such correspondence exists. The input consists of the x- and y-coordinates of the m corners of the playing field, the n starting points, and the n holes. Assume you can determine in constant time whether two line segments intersect, given the x- and y-coordinates of their endpoints.

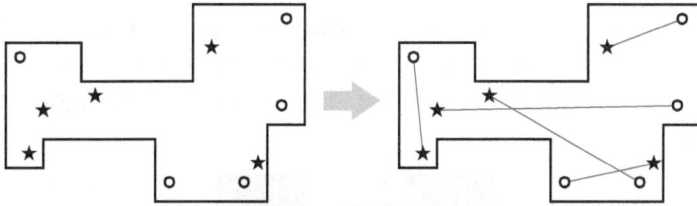

Figure 11.11. A mini-golf course with five starting points (★) and holes (○), and a legal correspondence between them.

7. A *cycle cover* of a given directed graph $G = (V, E)$ is a set of vertex-disjoint cycles that cover every vertex in G. Describe and analyze an efficient algorithm to find a cycle cover for a given graph, or correctly report that no cycle cover exists. *[Hint: Use bipartite matching!]*

8. Suppose you are given an $n \times n$ checkerboard with some of the squares deleted. You have a large set of dominos, just the right size to cover two squares of the checkerboard. Describe and analyze an algorithm to determine whether one tile the board with dominos—each domino must cover exactly two undeleted squares, and each undeleted square must be covered by exactly one domino.

   Your input is a boolean array $Deleted[1..n, 1..n]$, where $Deleted[i, j] =$ TRUE if and only if the square in row i and column j has been deleted. Your output is a single boolean; you do **not** have to compute the actual placement of dominos. For example, for the board shown in Figure 11.12, your algorithm should return TRUE.

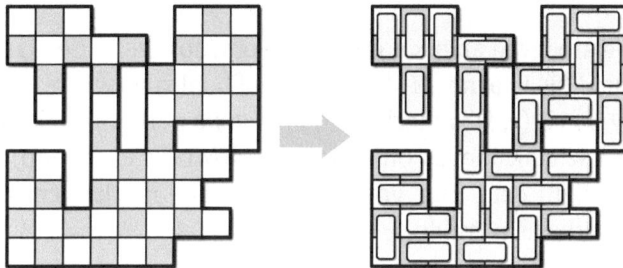

Figure 11.12. Covering a partial checkerboard with dominos.

9. Suppose we are given an $n \times n$ square grid, some of whose squares are colored black and the rest white. Describe and analyze an algorithm to determine whether tokens can be placed on the grid so that

   • every token is on a white square;
   • every row of the grid contains exactly one token; and
   • every column of the grid contains exactly one token.

Your input is a two dimensional array *IsWhite*[1..*n*,1..*n*] of booleans, indicating which squares are white. Your output is a single boolean. For example, given the grid in Figure 11.13 as input, your algorithm should return TRUE.

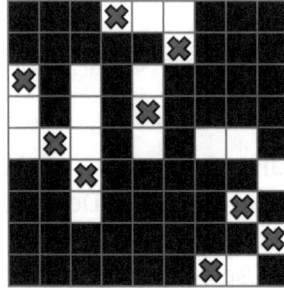

Figure 11.13. Marking every row and column in a grid.

10. Suppose we are given a set of boxes, each specified by their height, width, and depth in centimeters. All three side lengths of every box lie strictly between 10cm and 20cm. As you should expect, one box can be placed inside another if the first box can be rotated so that its height, width, and depth are respectively smaller than the height, width, and depth of the second box. Boxes can be nested recursively. Call a box is *visible* if it is not inside another box.

    Describe and analyze an algorithm to nest the boxes so that the number of visible boxes is as small as possible.

11. Suppose we are given an $n \times n$ grid, some of whose cells are marked; the grid is represented by an array $M[1..n, 1..n]$ of booleans, where $M[i, j] = \text{TRUE}$ if and only if cell (i, j) is marked. A *monotone* path through the grid starts at the top-left cell, moves only right or down at each step, and ends at the bottom-right cell. Our goal is to cover the marked cells with as few monotone paths as possible.

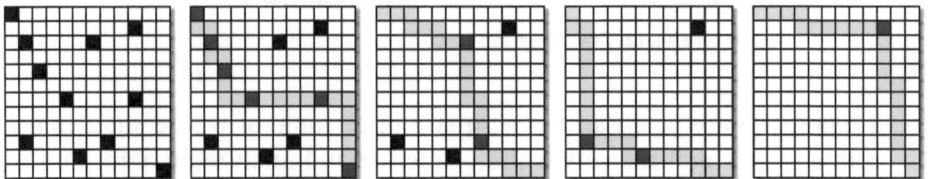

Figure 11.14. Greedily covering the marked cells in a grid with four monotone paths.

    (a) Describe an algorithm to find a monotone path that covers the largest number of marked cells.

(b) There is a natural greedy heuristic to find a small cover by monotone paths: If there are any marked cells, find a monotone path π that covers the largest number of marked cells, unmark any cells covered by π those marked cells, and recurse. Show that this algorithm does *not* always compute an optimal solution.

(c) Describe and analyze an efficient algorithm to compute the smallest set of monotone paths that covers every marked cell.

12. The Faculty Senate at Sham-Poobanana University has decided to convene a committee to determine whether Uncle Gabby, Professor Bobo Cornelius, or Mofo the Psychic Gorilla should replace the recently disgraced Baron Factotum as the new official ~~mascot~~ *symbol* of SPU's athletic teams (The Fighting Pooh-bahs). Exactly one faculty member must be chosen from each academic department to serve on this committee. Some faculty members have appointments in multiple departments, but each committee member can represent only one department. For example, if Prof. Blagojevich is affiliated with both the Department of Corruption and the Department of Stupidity, and he is chosen as the Stupidity representative, then someone else must represent Corruption. Finally, University policy requires that every faculty committee must contain exactly the same number of assistant professors, associate professors, and full professors. Fortunately, the number of departments is a multiple of 3.

Describe and analyze an algorithm to choose a subset of the SPU faculty to staff The Post-Factotum Simian ~~Mascot~~ *Symbol* Committee, or correctly report that no valid committee is possible. Your input is a bipartite graph indicating which professors belong to which departments; each professor vertex is labeled with that professor's rank (assistant, associate, or full).

13. The Department of Commuter Silence at Sham-Poobanana University has a flexible curriculum with a complex set of graduation requirements. The department offers n different courses, and there are m different requirements. Each requirement specifies a subset of the n courses and the number of courses that must be taken from that subset. The subsets for different requirements may overlap, but each course can be used to satisfy *at most one* requirement.

For example, suppose there are $n = 5$ courses A, B, C, D, E and $m = 2$ graduation requirements:

- You must take at least 2 courses from the subset $\{A, B, C\}$.
- You must take at least 2 courses from the subset $\{C, D, E\}$.

Then a student who has only taken courses B, C, D cannot graduate, but a student who has taken either A, B, C, D or B, C, D, E can graduate.

Describe and analyze an algorithm to determine whether a given student can graduate. The input to your algorithm is the list of m requirements (each specifying a subset of the n courses and the number of courses that must be taken from that subset) and the list of courses the student has taken.

14. You're organizing the First Annual SPU Commuter Silence 72-Hour Dance Exchange, to be held all day Friday, Saturday, and Sunday. Several 30-minute sets of music will be played during the event, and a large number of DJs have applied to perform. You need to hire DJs according to the following constraints.

    - Exactly k sets of music must be played each day, and thus $3k$ sets altogether.

    - Each set must be played by a single DJ in a consistent music genre (ambient, bubblegum, dubstep, horrorcore, K-pop, Kwaito, mariachi, straight-ahead jazz, trip-hop, Nashville country, parapara, ska, ...).

    - Each genre must be played at most once per day.

    - Each candidate DJ has given you a list of genres they are willing to play.

    - Each DJ can play at most three sets during the entire event.

    Suppose there are n candidate DJs and g different musical genres available. Describe and analyze an efficient algorithm that either assigns a DJ and a genre to each of the $3k$ sets, or correctly reports that no such assignment is possible.

15. Suppose you are running a web site that is visited by the same set of people every day. Each visitor claims membership in one or more *demographic groups*; for example, a visitor might describe himself as male, 40–50 years old, a father, a resident of Illinois, an academic, a blogger, and a fan of Gilbert and Sullivan.[13] Your site is supported by advertisers. Each advertiser has told you which demographic groups should see its ads and how many of its ads you must show each day. Altogether, there are n visitors, k demographic groups, and m advertisers.

    Describe an efficient algorithm to determine, given all the data described in the previous paragraph, whether you can show each visitor exactly *one* ad per day, so that every advertiser has its desired number of ads displayed, and every ad is seen by someone in an appropriate demographic group.

16. Suppose we are given an array $A[1 .. m][1 .. n]$ of non-negative real numbers. We want to *round* A to an integer matrix, by replacing each entry x in A

---

[13]I am a very good theoretical computer scientist, specifically, a geometric algorithm specialist.

with either $\lfloor x \rfloor$ or $\lceil x \rceil$, without changing the sum of entries in any row or column of A. For example:

$$
\begin{bmatrix}
1.2 & 3.4 & 2.4 \\
3.9 & 4.0 & 2.1 \\
7.9 & 1.6 & 0.5
\end{bmatrix}
\longmapsto
\begin{bmatrix}
1 & 4 & 2 \\
4 & 4 & 2 \\
8 & 1 & 1
\end{bmatrix}
$$

(a) Describe and analyze an efficient algorithm that either rounds A in this fashion, or reports correctly that no such rounding is possible.

(b) Prove that a legal rounding is possible *if and only if* the sum of entries in each row is an integer, and the sum of entries in each column is an integer. In other words, prove that either your algorithm from part (a) returns a legal rounding, or a legal rounding is *obviously* impossible.

♥(c) Suppose we are guaranteed that none of the entries in the input matrix A is an integer. Describe and analyze an even faster algorithm that either rounds A or reports correctly that no such rounding is possible. For full credit, your algorithm must run in $O(mn)$ time. [*Hint:* **Don't** *use flows.*]

17. ***Ad-hoc networks*** are made up of low-powered wireless devices. In principle[14], these networks can be used on battlefields, in regions that have recently suffered from natural disasters, and in other hard-to-reach areas. The idea is that a large collection of cheap, simple devices could be distributed through the area of interest (for example, by dropping them from an airplane); the devices would then automatically configure themselves into a functioning wireless network.

These devices can communicate only within a limited range. We assume all the devices are identical; there is a distance D such that two devices can communicate if and only if the distance between them is at most D.

We would like our ad-hoc network to be reliable, but because the devices are cheap and low-powered, they frequently fail. If a device detects that it is likely to fail, it should transmit its information to some other *backup* device within its communication range. We require each device x to have k potential backup devices, all within distance D of x; we call these k devices the ***backup set*** of x. Also, we do not want any device to be in the backup set of too many other devices; otherwise, a single failure might affect a large fraction of the network.

So suppose we are given the communication radius D, parameters b and k, and an array $d[1..n, 1..n]$ of distances, where $d[i, j]$ is the distance between device i and device j. Describe an algorithm that either computes

---

[14]but not so much in practice

a backup set of size k for each of the n devices, such that no device appears in more than b backup sets, or reports (correctly) that no good collection of backup sets exists.

18. Faced with the threat of brutally severe budget cuts, Potemkin University has decided to hire actors to sit in classes as "students", to ensure that every class they offer is completely full. Because actors are expensive, the university wants to hire as few of them as possible.

    Building on their previous leadership experience at the now-defunct Sham-Poobanana University, the administrators at Potemkin have given you a directed acyclic graph $G = (V, E)$, whose vertices represent classes, and where each edge $i \rightarrow j$ indicates that the same "student" can attend class i and then later attend class j. In addition, you are also given an array $cap[1..V]$ listing the maximum number of "students" who can take each class. Describe an analyze an algorithm to compute the minimum number of "students" that would allow every class to be filled to capacity.

19. Quentin, Alice, and the other Brakebills Physical Kids are planning an excursion through the Neitherlands to Fillory. The Neitherlands is a vast, deserted city composed of several plazas, each containing a single fountain that can magically transport people to a different world. Adjacent plazas are connected by gates, which have been cursed by the Beast. The gates between plazas are open only for five minutes every hour, all simultaneously—from 12:00 to 12:05, then from 1:00 to 1:05, and so on—and are otherwise locked. During those five minutes, if more than one person passes through any single gate, the Beast will detect their presence.[15] Moreover, anyone attempting to open a locked gate, or attempting to pass through more than one gate within the same five-minute period will turn into a niffin.[16] However, any number of people can safely pass through *different* gates at the same time and/or pass through the same gate at *different* times.

    You are given a map of the Neitherlands, which is a graph G with a vertex for each fountain and an edge for each gate, with the fountains to Earth and Fillory clearly marked.

    (a) Suppose you are also given a positive integer h. Describe and analyze an algorithm to compute the maximum number of people that can walk from the Earth fountain to the Fillory fountain in at most h hours—that is, after the gates have opened at most h times—without anyone alerting the Beast or turning into a niffin. The running time of your algorithm should depend on h. [Hint: Build a different graph.]

---

[15]This is very bad.
[16]This is very very bad.

(b) Describe an analyze an algorithm for part (a) whose running time is polynomial in V and E, with *no* dependence on h.

(c) On the other hand, suppose you are also given an integer k. Describe and analyze an algorithm to compute the minimum number of hours that allow k people to walk from the Earth fountain to the Fillory fountain, without anyone alerting the Beast or turning into a niffin. *[Hint: Use part (a).]*

20. Let $G = (L \sqcup R, E)$ be a bipartite graph, whose left vertices L are indexed $\ell_1, \ell_2, \ldots, \ell_n$ and whose right vertices are indexed $r_1, r_2, \ldots, r_n$. A matching M in G is **non-crossing** if, for every pair of edges $\ell_i r_j$ and $\ell_{i'} r_{j'}$ in M, we have $i < i'$ if and only if $j < j'$.

    (a) Describe and analyze an algorithm to find the largest non-crossing matching in G. *[Hint: This is not really a flow problem.]*

    (b) Describe and analyze an algorithm to find the smallest number of non-crossing matchings $M_1, M_2, \ldots, M_k$ such that each edge in G is in exactly one matching M_i. *[Hint: This is really a flow problem.]*

21. Let $G = (L \sqcup R, E)$ be a bipartite graph, whose left vertices L are indexed $\ell_1, \ell_2, \ldots, \ell_n$ in some arbitrary order.

    (a) A matching M in G is **dense** if there are no consecutive unmatched vertices in L; that is, for each index i, at least one of the vertices ℓ_i and ℓ_{i+1} is incident to an edge in M. Describe an algorithm to determine whether G has a dense matching.

    (b) A matching M in G is **sparse** if there are no consecutive *matched* vertices in L; that is, for each index i, at least one of the vertices ℓ_i and ℓ_{i+1} is *not* incident to an edge in M. (In particular, the empty matching is sparse.) Describe an algorithm to find the largest sparse matching in G.

    (c) A matching M in G is **palindromic** if, for every index i, either ℓ_i and ℓ_{n-i+1} are both incident to edges in M, or neither ℓ_i nor ℓ_{n-i+1} is incident to an edge in M. (In particular, the empty matching is palindromic.) Describe an algorithm to find the largest palindromic matching in G.

    None of these problems restrict which vertices in R are matched or unmatched.

22. A *rooted tree* is a directed acyclic graph, in which every vertex has exactly one incoming edge, except for the *root*, which has no incoming edges. Equivalently, a rooted tree consists of a root vertex, which has edges pointing to the roots of zero or more smaller rooted trees. Describe an efficient algorithm to compute, given two rooted trees A and B, the largest rooted

tree that is isomorphic to both a subgraph of A and a subgraph of B. More briefly, describe an algorithm to find the largest common subtree of two rooted trees.

[Hint: This would be a relatively straightforward dynamic programming problem if either every node had $O(1)$ children or the children of each node were ordered from left to right. But for unordered trees with large degree, you need another technique to combine recursive subproblems efficiently.]

12

NP-Hardness

12.1 A Game You Can't Win

Imagine that a salesman in a red suit, who looks suspiciously like Tom Waits, presents you with a black steel box with n binary switches on the front and a light bulb on top. The salesman tells you that the state of the light bulb is controlled by a complex *boolean circuit*—a collection of AND, OR, and NOT gates connected by wires, with one input wire for each switch and a single output wire for the bulb. He then asks you a simple question: Is it possible to set the switches so that the light bulb turns on? If you can answer this question correctly, he will give you ~~one million~~ one hundred billion dollars; if you answer incorrectly, or if you die without answering, he will take your soul.

Figure 12.1. An AND gate, an OR gate, and a NOT gate.

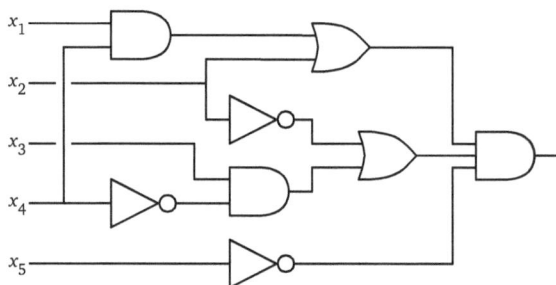

Figure 12.2. A boolean circuit. Inputs enter from the left, and the output leaves to the right.

As far as you can tell, the Adversary hasn't connected the switches to the light bulb at all, so no matter how you set the switches, the light bulb will stay off. If you declare that it *is* possible to turn on the light, the Adversary will open the box and reveal that there is no circuit at all. But if you declare that it is *not* possible to turn on the light, before testing all 2^n settings, the Adversary will magically create a circuit inside the box that turns on the light *if and only if* the switches are in one of the settings you haven't tested, and then flip the switches to that setting, turning on the light. (You can't detect the Adversary's cheating, because you can't see inside the box until the end.) The only way to *provably* answer the Adversary's question correctly is to try all 2^n possible settings. You quickly realize that this will take *far* longer than you expect to live, so you gracefully decline the Adversary's offer.

The Adversary smiles and says, in a growl like Heath Ledger's Joker after smoking a carton of Marlboros, "Ah, yes, of course, you have no reason to trust me. But perhaps I can set your mind at ease." He hands you a large roll of parchment—which you hope was made from *sheep* skin—with a circuit diagram drawn (or perhaps tattooed) on it. "Here are the complete plans for the circuit inside the box. Feel free to poke around inside the box to make sure the plans are correct. Or build your own circuit from these plans. Or write a computer program to simulate the circuit. Whatever you like. If you discover that the plans don't match the actual circuit in the box, you win the hundred billion bucks." A few spot checks convince you that the plans have no obvious flaws; subtle cheating appears to be impossible.

But you should still decline the Adversary's "generous" offer. The problem that the Adversary is posing is called **circuit satisfiability** or **CIRCUITSAT**: Given a boolean circuit, is there a set of inputs that makes the circuit output TRUE, or conversely, whether the circuit *always* outputs FALSE. For any *particular* input setting, we can calculate the output of the circuit in polynomial (actually, *linear*) time using depth-first-search. But nobody knows how to solve CIRCUITSAT faster than trying all 2^n possible inputs to the circuit by brute force, which requires exponential time. Admittedly, nobody has actually formally *proved* that we can't beat brute force—maybe, just *maybe*, there's a clever algorithm that just hasn't been discovered yet—but nobody has actually formally proved that anti-gravity unicorns don't exist, either. For all practical purposes, it's safe to assume that there is no fast algorithm for CIRCUITSAT.

You tell the salesman no. He smiles and says, "You're smarter than you look, kid," and then flies away on his anti-gravity unicorn.

12.2   P versus NP

A minimal requirement for an algorithm to be considered "efficient" is that its running time is bounded by a polynomial function of the input size: $O(n^c)$ for some constant c, where n is the size of the input.[1] Researchers recognized early on that not all problems can be solved this quickly, but had a hard time figuring out exactly which ones could and which ones couldn't. There are several so-called **NP-hard** problems, which most people believe *cannot* be solved in polynomial time, even though nobody can prove a super-polynomial lower bound.

A *decision problem* is a problem whose output is a single boolean value: YES or No. Let me define three classes of decision problems:

- **P** is the set of decision problems that can be solved in polynomial time. Intuitively, P is the set of problems that can be solved quickly.

- **NP** is the set of decision problems with the following property: If the answer is YES, then there is a *proof* of this fact that can be checked in polynomial time. Intuitively, NP is the set of decision problems where we can verify a YES answer quickly if we have the solution in front of us.

- **co-NP** is essentially the opposite of NP. If the answer to a problem in co-NP is No, then there is a proof of this fact that can be checked in polynomial time.

For example, the circuit satisfiability problem is in NP. If a given boolean circuit is satisfiable, then any set of m input values that produces TRUE output is a proof that the circuit is satisfiable; we can check the proof by evaluating the circuit in polynomial time. It is widely believed that circuit satisfiability is *not* in P or in co-NP, but nobody actually knows.

Every decision problem in P is also in NP. If a problem is in P, we can verify YES answers in polynomial time recomputing the answer from scratch! Similarly, every problem in P is also in co-NP.

---

[1]This notion of efficiency was independently formalized by Alan Cobham in 1965, Jack Edmonds in 1965, and Michael Rabin in 1966, although similar notions were considered more than a decade earlier by Kurt Gödel, John Nash, and John von Neumann.

Perhaps the single most important unanswered question in theoretical computer science—if not all of computer science—if not all of **science**—is whether the complexity classes P and NP are actually different. Intuitively, it seems obvious to most people that P ≠ NP; the homeworks and exams in your algorithms and data structures classes have (I hope) convinced you that problems can be incredibly hard to solve, even when the solutions are simple in retrospect. It's completely obvious; *of course* solving problems from scratch is harder than verifying that a given solution is correct. We can reasonably accept—and most algorithm designers *do* accept—the statement "P ≠ NP" as a law of nature, similar to other laws of nature like Maxwell's equations, general relativity, and the sun rising tomorrow morning that are strongly supported by evidence, but have no mathematical proof.

But if we're being mathematically rigorous, we have to admit that nobody knows how to *prove* that that P ≠ NP. In fact, there has been little or no real progress toward a proof for decades.[2] The Clay Mathematics Institute lists P-versus-NP as the first of its seven Millennium Prize Problems, offering a $1,000,000 reward for its solution. And yes, in fact, several people *have* lost their souls, or at least their sanity, attempting to solve this problem.

A more subtle but still open question is whether the complexity classes NP and co-NP are different. Even if we can verify every YES answer quickly, there's no reason to believe we can also verify No answers quickly. For example, as far as we know, there is no short proof that a boolean circuit is *not* satisfiable. It is generally believed that NP ≠ co-NP, but again, nobody knows how to prove it.

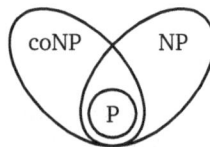

Figure 12.3. What we *think* the world looks like.

12.3 NP-hard, NP-easy, and NP-complete

A problem Π is **NP-hard** if a polynomial-time algorithm for Π would imply a polynomial-time algorithm for *every problem in NP*. In other words:

> Π is NP-hard ⟺ If Π can be solved in polynomial time, then P=NP

---

[2]Perhaps the most significant progress has taken the form of *barrier* results, which imply that entire avenues of attack are doomed to fail. In a very real sense, not only do we have no idea how to prove P ≠ NP, but we can actually *prove* that we have no idea how to prove P ≠ NP!

Intuitively, if we could solve one particular NP-hard problem quickly, then we could quickly solve *any* problem whose solution is easy to understand, using the solution to that one special problem as a subroutine. NP-hard problems are at least as hard as every problem in NP.

Finally, a problem is **NP-complete** if it is both NP-hard and an element of NP (or "NP-easy"). Informally, NP-complete problems are the hardest problems in NP. A polynomial-time algorithm for even one NP-complete problem would immediately imply a polynomial-time algorithm for *every* NP-complete problem. Literally *thousands* of problems have been shown to be NP-complete, so a polynomial-time algorithm for one (and therefore all) of them seems incredibly unlikely.

Calling a problem NP-hard is like saying "If I own a dog, then it can speak fluent English." You probably don't know whether or not I own a dog, but I bet you're pretty sure that I don't own a *talking* dog. Nobody has a mathematical *proof* that dogs can't speak English—the fact that no one has ever heard a dog speak English is *evidence*, as are the hundreds of examinations of dogs that lacked the proper mouth shape and brainpower, but mere evidence is not a mathematical *proof*. Nevertheless, no sane person would believe me if I said I owned a dog that spoke fluent English.[3] So the statement "If I own a dog, then it can speak fluent English" has a natural corollary: No one in their right mind should believe that I own a dog! Similarly, if a problem is NP-hard, no one in their right mind should believe it can be solved in polynomial time.

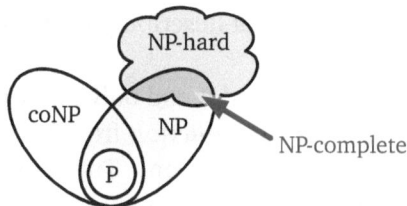

Figure 12.4. More of what we *think* the world looks like.

It is not immediately obvious that *any* problems are NP-hard. The following remarkable theorem was first published by Stephen Cook in 1971 and independently by Leonid Levin in 1973.[4]

---

[3] . . . The department chair shakes his head sadly and says, "Oh, come on, that just sounds like barking. Let *me* ask a question. Who was the greatest complexity theorist of all time?" The dog cocks his head, pauses for a few seconds, and then says "Karp!" After the chair chases them out of his office, the dog turns to its owner and says, "Maybe I should have said Impagliazzo?"

[4] Levin first reported his results at seminars in Moscow in 1971, while still a PhD student. News of Cook's result did not reach the Soviet Union until at least 1973, after Levin's announcement of his results had been published; in accordance with Stigler's Law, this result is often called "Cook's Theorem". Levin was denied his PhD at Moscow University for political reasons; he emigrated to the US in 1978 and earned a PhD at MIT a year later. Cook was denied tenure by the Berkeley

The Cook-Levin Theorem. *Circuit satisfiability is NP-hard.*

I won't even sketch a proof here, because I've been (deliberately) vague about the definitions.[5]

♥12.4 Formal Definitions (*HC SVNT DRACONES*)

Formally, the complexity classes P, NP, and co-NP are defined in terms of *languages* and *Turing machines*. A language is a set of strings over some finite alphabet Σ; without loss of generality, we can assume that $\Sigma = \{0, 1\}$. A Turing machine is a very restrictive type of computer—crudely, a finite-state machine with an unbounded memory tape—whose precise definition is surprisingly unimportant. P is the set of languages that can be decided in **P**olynomial time by a deterministic single-tape Turing machine. Similarly, NP is the set of all languages that can be decided in polynomial time by a nondeterministic Turing machine; NP is an abbreviation for **N**ondeterministic **P**olynomial-time.

The requirement of polynomial time is sufficiently crude that we do not have to specify the precise form of Turing machine (number of tapes, number of heads, number of tracks, size of the tape alphabet, and so on). In fact, any algorithm that runs on a random-access machine[6] in $T(n)$ time can be simulated by a single-tape, single-track, single-head Turing machine that runs in $O(T(n)^4)$ time. This simulation result allows us to argue formally about computational complexity in terms of standard high-level programming constructs like arrays and loops and recursion, instead of describing everything directly in terms of Turing machines.

Formally, a problem Π is NP-hard if and only if, for every language $\Pi' \in$ NP, there is a polynomial-time ***Turing reduction*** from Π' to Π. A Turing reduction means a reduction that can be executed on a Turing machine; that is, a Turing machine M that can solve Π' using another Turing machine M' for Π as a black-box subroutine. Turing reductions are also called *oracle reductions*; polynomial-time Turing reductions are also called *Cook reductions*.

---

mathematics department in 1970, just one year before publishing his seminal paper; he (but not Levin) later won the Turing award for his proof.

[5]Interested readers find a proof in my lecture notes on nondeterministic Turing machines at http://algorithms.wtf, or in Boaz Barak's excellent *Introduction to Theoretical Computer Science*.

[6]Random-access machines are a model of computation that more faithfully models physical computers. A standard random-access machine has unbounded random-access memory, modeled as an unbounded array $M[0..\infty]$ where each address $M[i]$ holds a single w-bit integer, for some fixed integer w, and can read to or write from any memory addresses in constant time. RAM algorithms are formally written in assembly-like language, using instructions like ADD i, j, k (meaning "$M[i] \leftarrow M[j] + M[k]$"), INDIR i, j (meaning "$M[i] \leftarrow M[M[j]]$"), and IF0GOTO i, ℓ (meaning "if $M[i] = 0$, go to line ℓ"), but the precise instruction set is surprisingly irrelevant. By definition, each instruction executes in unit time. In practice, RAM algorithms can be faithfully described using higher-level pseudocode, as long as we're careful about arithmetic precision.

Researchers in complexity theory prefer to define NP-hardness in terms of polynomial-time ***many-one reductions***, which are also called *Karp reductions*. A *many-one* reduction from one language $L' \subseteq \Sigma^*$ to another language $L \subseteq \Sigma^*$ is a function $f : \Sigma^* \to \Sigma^*$ such that $x \in L'$ if and only if $f(x) \in L$. Then we can define a *language L* to be NP-hard if and only if, for any language $L' \in$ NP, there is a many-one reduction from L' to L that can be computed in polynomial time.

Every Karp reduction "is" a Cook reduction, but not vice versa. Specifically, any Karp reduction from one decision problem Π to another decision Π' is equivalent to transforming the input to Π into the input for Π', invoking an oracle (that is, a subroutine) for Π', and then returning the answer verbatim. However, as far as we know, not every Cook reduction can be simulated by a Karp reduction.

Complexity theorists prefer Karp reductions primarily because NP is closed under Karp reductions, but is *not* closed under Cook reductions (unless NP=co-NP, which is considered unlikely). There are natural problems that are (1) NP-hard with respect to Cook reductions, but (2) NP-hard with respect to Karp reductions only if P=NP. One trivial example of such a problem is UNSAT: Given a boolean formula, is it *always false*? On the other hand, many-one reductions apply *only* to decision problems (or more formally, to languages); formally, no optimization or construction problem is Karp-NP-hard.

To make things even more confusing, both Cook and Karp originally defined NP-hardness in terms of ***logarithmic-space*** reductions. Every logarithmic-space reduction is a polynomial-time reduction, but (as far as we know) not vice versa. It is an open question whether relaxing the set of allowed (Cook or Karp) reductions from logarithmic-space to polynomial-time changes the set of NP-hard problems.

Fortunately, none of these subtleties rear their ugly heads in practice—in particular, every reduction described in this chapter can be formalized as a logarithmic-space many-one reduction—so you can wake up now.

12.5   Reductions and SAT

To prove that any problem other than circuit satisfiability is NP-hard, we use a *reduction argument*. Reducing problem A to another problem B means describing an algorithm to solve problem A under the assumption that an algorithm for problem B already exists. You've already been doing reduction for years, even before starting this book, only you probably called them something else, like subroutines or utility functions or modular programming or using a calculator. To prove something is NP-hard, we describe a similar transformation between problems, but not in the direction that most people expect.

You should tattoo the following rule of onto the back of your hand, right next to your mom's birthday and the *actual* rules of Monopoly.[7]

> **To prove that problem *A* is NP-hard,**
> **reduce a known NP-hard problem to *A*.**

In other words, to prove that your problem is hard, you need to describe an efficient algorithm to solve a *different* problem, which you already know is hard, using an hypothetical efficient algorithm for *your* problem as a black-box subroutine. The essential logic is a proof by contradiction. The reduction implies that if your problem were easy, then the other problem would be easy, which it ain't. Equivalently, since you know the other problem is hard, the reduction implies that your problem must also be hard; your hypothetical efficient algorithm does not actually exist.

As a canonical example, consider the *formula satisfiability* problem, usually just called **SAT**. The input to SAT is a boolean *formula* like

$$(a \vee b \vee c \vee \bar{d}) \Longleftrightarrow ((b \wedge \bar{c}) \vee \overline{(\bar{a} \Rightarrow d)} \vee (c \neq a \wedge b)),$$

and the question is whether it is possible to assign boolean values to the variables $a, b, c, \ldots$ so that the entire formula evaluates to TRUE.

To prove that SAT is NP-hard, we need to give a reduction from a known NP-hard problem. The only problem we know is NP-hard so far is CIRCUITSAT, so let's start there.

Let K be an arbitrary boolean circuit. We can transform (or more accurately, *transcribe*) K into a boolean formula Φ as follows. First, label each interior wire by a new variable y_j, and label the output wire with a new variable z. The formula Φ consists of a list of equations, one for each gate, separated by ANDs, followed by a final $\wedge z$. Figure 12.5 shows the resulting transcription for our example circuit.

Now we claim that the original circuit K is satisfiable **if and only if** the resulting formula Φ is satisfiable. Like every other "if and only if" statement, we prove this claim in two steps:

---

[7]If a player lands on an available property and declines (or is unable) to buy it, that property is immediately auctioned off to the highest bidder; the player who originally declined the property may bid, and bids may be arbitrarily higher or lower than the list price. Players in Jail can still buy and sell property, buy and sell houses and hotels, and collect rent. The game has 32 houses and 12 hotels; once they're gone, they're gone. In particular, if all houses are already on the board, you cannot downgrade a hotel to four houses; you must raze all the hotels in the group to the ground. Players can sell or exchange *undeveloped* properties with each other, but cannot sell property back to the bank; on the other hand, players can sell buildings to the bank (at half price), but cannot sell or exchange buildings with each other. All penalties are paid directly to the bank. A player landing on Free Parking does not win anything. A player landing on Go gets exactly $200, no more. Railroads are not magic transporters. Finally, Jeff *always* gets the boot. No, not the T-Rex or the penguin—the *boot*, dammit.

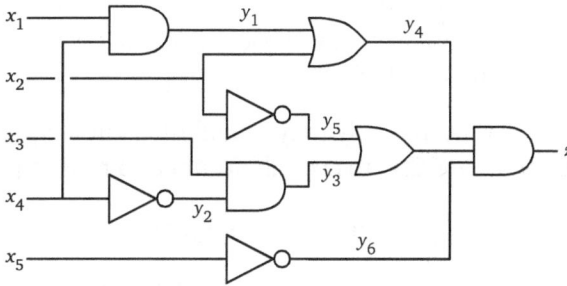

$$(y_1 = x_1 \wedge x_4) \wedge (y_2 = \overline{x_4}) \wedge (y_3 = x_3 \wedge y_2) \wedge (y_4 = y_1 \vee x_2) \wedge$$
$$(y_5 = \overline{x_2}) \wedge (y_6 = \overline{x_5}) \wedge (y_7 = y_3 \vee y_5) \wedge (z = y_4 \wedge y_7 \wedge y_6) \wedge z$$

Figure 12.5. Transcribing a boolean circuit as a boolean formula.

⇒ Given a set of inputs that satisfy the circuit K, we can derive a satisfying assignment for the formula Φ by computing the output of every gate in K.

⇐ Given a satisfying assignment for the formula Φ, we can obtain a satisfying input the circuit by simply ignoring the internal wire variables y_i and the output variable z.

The entire transformation from circuit to formula can be carried out in linear time. Moreover, the size of the resulting formula is at most a constant factor larger than any reasonable representation of the circuit.

Now suppose, for the sake of argument, there is an algorithm that can determine in polynomial time whether a given boolean formula is satisfiable. Then given any boolean circuit K, we can decide whether K is satisfiable by first transforming K into a boolean formula Φ as described above, and then asking our magical mystery SAT algorithm whether Φ is satisfiable, as suggested by the following cartoon. Each box represents an algorithm. The red box on the left is the transformation subroutine. The box on the right is the hypothetical magic SAT algorithm. It *must* be magic, because it has a *rainbow* on it.[8]

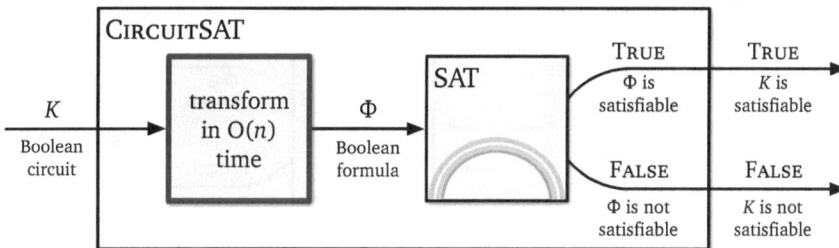

If you prefer magic pseudocode to magic boxes:

---

[8] Kay Erickson, personal communication, 2011. For those of you reading black-and-white printed copies: Yes, that round thing is a rainbow.

$$\boxed{\begin{array}{l} \text{C\textsc{ircuit}S\textsc{at}}(K):\\ \quad \text{transcribe } K \text{ into a boolean formula } \Phi \\ \quad \text{return S\textsc{at}}(\Phi) \qquad \langle\!\langle \;{\cdots}\star\star\textit{MAGIC}\star\star{\cdots}\; \rangle\!\rangle \end{array}}$$

Transcribing K into Φ requires only polynomial time (in fact, only *linear* time, but whatever), so the entire C\textsc{ircuit}S\textsc{at} algorithm also runs in polynomial time.

$$T_{\text{C\textsc{ircuit}S\textsc{at}}}(n) \le O(n) + T_{\text{S\textsc{at}}}(O(n))$$

We conclude that any polynomial-time algorithm for S\textsc{at} would give us a polynomial-time algorithm for C\textsc{ircuit}S\textsc{at}, which in turn would imply P=NP. So S\textsc{at} is NP-hard!

12.6 3S\textsc{at} (from C\textsc{ircuit}S\textsc{at})

A special case of S\textsc{at} that is particularly useful in proving NP-hardness results is called *3CNF-S\textsc{at}* or more often simply *3S\textsc{at}*.

A boolean formula is in *conjunctive normal form* (CNF) if it is a conjunction (AND) of several *clauses*, each of which is the disjunction (OR) of several *literals*, each of which is either a variable or its negation. For example:

$$\overbrace{(a \vee b \vee c \vee d)}^{\text{clause}} \wedge (b \vee \bar{c} \vee \bar{d}) \wedge (\bar{a} \vee c \vee d) \wedge (a \vee \bar{b})$$

A *3CNF* formula is a CNF formula with exactly three literals per clause; the previous example is not a 3CNF formula, since its first clause has four literals and its last clause has only two. 3S\textsc{at} is the restriction of S\textsc{at} to 3CNF formulas: Given a 3CNF formula, is there an assignment to the variables that makes the formula evaluate to T\textsc{rue}?

We could prove that 3S\textsc{at} is NP-hard by a reduction from the more general S\textsc{at} problem, but it's actually easier to start over from scratch, by reducing directly from C\textsc{ircuit}S\textsc{at}.

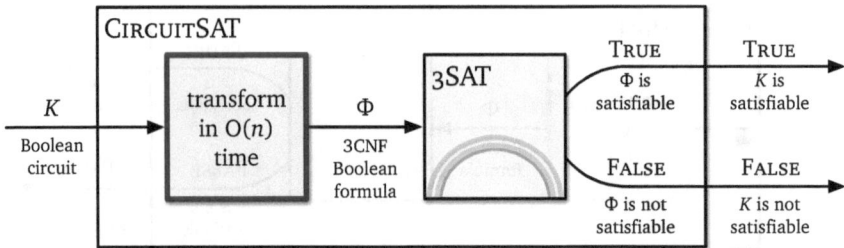

Figure 12.6. A polynomial-time reduction from C\textsc{ircuit}S\textsc{at} to 3S\textsc{at}.

Given an arbitrary boolean circuit K, we transform K into an equivalent 3CNF formula in several stages. Except for the very last stage, this reduction was actually described by Grigorii Tseitin in 1966, five years before Cook and Levin reported their proofs of the Cook-Levin Theorem. (In the same 1966 paper, Tseitin described the problem we now call CNF-SAT, possibly for the first time.) As we describe each stage, we will also prove that stage is correct.

- *Make sure every AND and OR gate in K has exactly two inputs.* If any gate has $k > 2$ inputs, replace it with a binary tree of $k - 1$ binary gates. Call the resulting circuit K'. The circuits K and K' are logically equivalent circuits, so every satisfying input for K is a satisfying input for K' and vice versa.

- *Transcribe K' into a boolean formula Φ_1 with one clause per gate,* exactly as in our previous reduction to SAT. We already proved that every satisfying input for K' can be transformed into a satisfying assignment for Φ_1 and vice versa.

- *Replace each clause in Φ_1 with a CNF formula.* There are only three types of clauses in Φ_1, one for each type of gate in K':

$$a = b \wedge c \longmapsto (a \vee \bar{b} \vee \bar{c}) \wedge (\bar{a} \vee b) \wedge (\bar{a} \vee c)$$
$$a = b \vee c \longmapsto (\bar{a} \vee b \vee c) \wedge (a \vee \bar{b}) \wedge (a \vee \bar{c})$$
$$a = \bar{b} \longmapsto (a \vee b) \wedge (\bar{a} \vee \bar{b})$$

Call the resulting CNF formula Φ_2. Because Φ_1 and Φ_2 are logically equivalent formulas, every satisfying assignment for Φ_1 is also a satisfying assignment for Φ_2, and vice versa.

- *Replace each clause in Φ_2 with a 3CNF formula.* Every clause in Φ_2 has *at most* three literals, but we need clauses with *exactly* three literals. To obtain a 3CNF formula, we expand each two-literal clause in Φ_2 into two three-literal clauses by introducing one new variable, and we expand the final one-literal clause in Φ_2 into four three-literal clauses by introducing two new variables.

$$a \vee b \longmapsto (a \vee b \vee x) \wedge (a \vee b \vee \bar{x})$$
$$z \longmapsto (z \vee x \vee y) \wedge (z \vee \bar{x} \vee y) \wedge (z \vee x \vee \bar{y}) \wedge (z \vee \bar{x} \vee \bar{y})$$

Call the resulting 3CNF formula Φ_3. Every satisfying assignment for Φ_2 can be transformed into a satisfying assignment for Φ_3 by assigning *arbitrary* values to the new variables (x and y). Conversely, every satisfying assignment for Φ_3 can be transformed into a satisfying assignment for Φ_2 by ignoring the new variables.

For example, our example circuit is transformed into the following 3CNF formula; compare with Figure 12.5.

$$(y_1 \vee \overline{x_1} \vee \overline{x_4}) \wedge (\overline{y_1} \vee x_1 \vee z_1) \wedge (\overline{y_1} \vee x_1 \vee \overline{z_1}) \wedge (\overline{y_1} \vee x_4 \vee z_2) \wedge (\overline{y_1} \vee x_4 \vee \overline{z_2})$$
$$\wedge (y_2 \vee x_4 \vee z_3) \wedge (y_2 \vee x_4 \vee \overline{z_3}) \wedge (\overline{y_2} \vee \overline{x_4} \vee z_4) \wedge (\overline{y_2} \vee \overline{x_4} \vee \overline{z_4})$$
$$\wedge (y_3 \vee \overline{x_3} \vee \overline{y_2}) \wedge (\overline{y_3} \vee x_3 \vee z_5) \wedge (\overline{y_3} \vee x_3 \vee \overline{z_5}) \wedge (\overline{y_3} \vee y_2 \vee z_6) \wedge (\overline{y_3} \vee y_2 \vee \overline{z_6})$$
$$\wedge (\overline{y_4} \vee y_1 \vee x_2) \wedge (y_4 \vee \overline{x_2} \vee z_7) \wedge (y_4 \vee \overline{x_2} \vee \overline{z_7}) \wedge (y_4 \vee \overline{y_1} \vee z_8) \wedge (y_4 \vee \overline{y_1} \vee \overline{z_8})$$
$$\wedge (y_5 \vee x_2 \vee z_9) \wedge (y_5 \vee x_2 \vee \overline{z_9}) \wedge (\overline{y_5} \vee \overline{x_2} \vee z_{10}) \wedge (\overline{y_5} \vee \overline{x_2} \vee \overline{z_{10}})$$
$$\wedge (y_6 \vee x_5 \vee z_{11}) \wedge (y_6 \vee x_5 \vee \overline{z_{11}}) \wedge (\overline{y_6} \vee \overline{x_5} \vee z_{12}) \wedge (\overline{y_6} \vee \overline{x_5} \vee \overline{z_{12}})$$
$$\wedge (\overline{y_7} \vee y_3 \vee y_5) \wedge (y_7 \vee \overline{y_3} \vee z_{13}) \wedge (y_7 \vee \overline{y_3} \vee \overline{z_{13}}) \wedge (y_7 \vee \overline{y_5} \vee z_{14}) \wedge (y_7 \vee \overline{y_5} \vee \overline{z_{14}})$$
$$\wedge (y_8 \vee \overline{y_4} \vee \overline{y_7}) \wedge (\overline{y_8} \vee y_4 \vee z_{15}) \wedge (\overline{y_8} \vee y_4 \vee \overline{z_{15}}) \wedge (\overline{y_8} \vee y_7 \vee z_{16}) \wedge (\overline{y_8} \vee y_7 \vee \overline{z_{16}})$$
$$\wedge (y_9 \vee \overline{y_8} \vee \overline{y_6}) \wedge (\overline{y_9} \vee y_8 \vee z_{17}) \wedge (\overline{y_9} \vee y_6 \vee z_{18}) \wedge (\overline{y_9} \vee y_6 \vee \overline{z_{18}}) \wedge (\overline{y_9} \vee y_8 \vee \overline{z_{17}})$$
$$\wedge (y_9 \vee z_{19} \vee z_{20}) \wedge (y_9 \vee \overline{z_{19}} \vee z_{20}) \wedge (y_9 \vee z_{19} \vee \overline{z_{20}}) \wedge (y_9 \vee \overline{z_{19}} \vee \overline{z_{20}})$$

Yikes! At first glance, this formula might look a *lot* more complicated than the original circuit, but in fact, it's only larger by a constant factor. Specifically, the simplified circuit K' has at most twice as many wires as the original circuit K, each binary gate in K' is transformed into at most five clauses in Φ_3. Even if the formula size were a large *polynomial* function (like n^{374}) of the circuit size, we would still have a valid reduction.

Our reduction transforms an arbitrary boolean circuit K into a 3CNF formula Φ_3 in polynomial time (in fact, in linear time). Moreover, any satisfying input for the input circuit K can be transformed into a satisfying assignment for Φ_3, and any satisfying assignment for Φ_3 can be transformed into a satisfying input for K. In other words, K is satisfiable if and only if Φ_3 is satisfiable. Thus, if 3SAT can be solved in polynomial time, then CIRCUITSAT can be solved in polynomial time, which implies that P = NP. We conclude that 3SAT is NP-hard.

12.7 Maximum Independent Set (from 3SAT)

For the next few problems we consider, the input is a simple, unweighted, undirected graph, and the problem asks for the size of the largest or smallest subgraph satisfying some structural property.

Let G be an arbitrary graph. An **independent set** in G is a subset of the vertices of G with no edges between them. The *maximum independent set* problem, which I'll abbreviate **MAXINDSET**, asks for the size of the largest independent set in a given graph. I will prove that MAXINDSET is NP-hard using a reduction from 3SAT, as suggested by Figure 12.7.

Given an arbitrary 3CNF formula Φ, we construct a graph G as follows. Let k denote the number of clauses in Φ. The graph G contains exactly $3k$ vertices, one for each literal in Φ. Two vertices in G are connected by an edge if and only if either (1) they correspond to literals in the same clause, or (2) they correspond to a variable and its inverse. For example, the formula $(a \vee b \vee c) \wedge (b \vee \bar{c} \vee \bar{d}) \wedge (\bar{a} \vee c \vee d) \wedge (a \vee \bar{b} \vee \bar{d})$ is transformed into the graph shown in Figure 12.8.

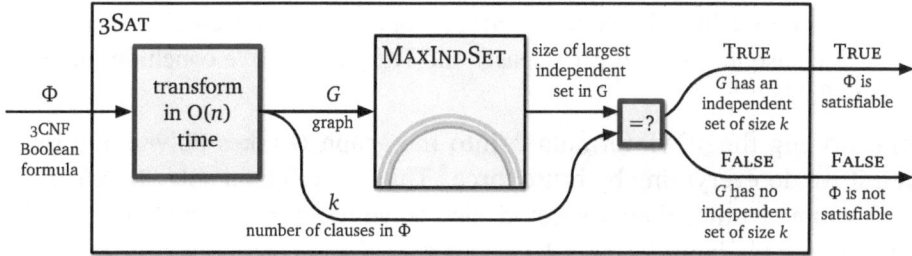

Figure 12.7. A polynomial-time reduction from 3SAT to MAXINDSET.

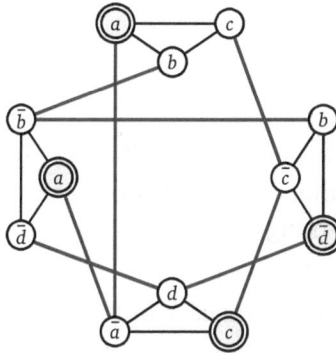

$$(a \vee b \vee c) \wedge (b \vee \bar{c} \vee \bar{d}) \wedge (\bar{a} \vee c \vee d) \wedge (a \vee \bar{b} \vee \bar{d})$$

Figure 12.8. A graph derived from the satisfiable 3CNF formula with 4 clauses, and an independent set of size 4.

Each independent set in G contains at most one vertex from each clause triangle, because any two vertices in each triangle are connected. Thus, the largest independent set in G has size *at most k*. I claim that G contains an independent set of size *exactly k* if and only if the original formula Φ is satisfiable. As usual for "if and only if" statements, the proof consists of two parts.

⇒ Suppose Φ is satisfiable. Fix an arbitrary satisfying assignment. By definition, each clause in Φ contains at least one TRUE literal. Thus, we can choose a subset S of k vertices in G that contains exactly one vertex per clause triangle, such that the corresponding k literals are all TRUE. Because each triangle contains at most one vertex in S, no two vertices in S are connected by a triangle edge. Because every literal corresponding to a vertex in S is TRUE, no two vertices in S are connected by a negation edge. We conclude that S is an independent set of size k in G.

⇐ On the other hand, suppose G contains an independent set S of size k. Each vertex in S must lie in a different clause triangle. Suppose we assign the value TRUE to each literal in S; because contradictory literals are connected by edges, this assignment is consistent. There may be variables x such that neither x nor $\bar{x}$ corresponds to a vertex in S; we can set these variables to any value we like. Because S contains one vertex in each clause triangle, each clause in Φ contains (at least) one TRUE literal. We conclude that Φ is satisfiable.

Transforming the 3CNF formula Φ into the graph G takes polynomial time, even if we do everything by brute force. Thus, if we could solve MaxIndSet in polynomial time, then we could also solve 3SAT in polynomial time, by transforming the input formula Φ into a graph G and comparing the size of the largest independent set in G with the number of clauses in Φ. But that would imply P=NP, which is ridiculous! We conclude that MaxIndSet is NP-hard.

12.8 The General Pattern

All NP-hardness proofs—and more generally, all polynomial-time reductions—follow the same general outline. To reduce problem X to problem Y in polynomial time, we need to do three things:

1. Describe a polynomial-time algorithm to transform an **arbitrary** instance of x of X into a *special* instance y of Y.
2. Prove that if x is a "good" instance of X, then y is a "good" instance of Y.
3. Prove that if y is a "good" instance of Y, then x is a "good" instance of X. (This is usually the part that causes the most trouble.)

Of course, *developing* a correct reduction doesn't mean handling these three tasks one at a time. *First* writing down an algorithm that *seems* to work and *then* trying prove that it *actually* works is rarely successful, especially in time-limited settings like exams. We *must* develop the algorithm, the "if" proof, and the "only if" proof simultaneously.

To quote the late great Ricky Jay:[9] This is an *acquired* skill.

One point that confuses many students is that the reduction algorithm only "works one way"—from X to Y—but the correctness proof needs to "work both ways". But the correctness proofs are not actually symmetric. The "if" proof needs to handle *arbitrary* instances of X, but the "only if" only needs to handle the *special* instances of Y produced by the reduction algorithm. Exploiting this asymmetry is the key to successfully designing correct reductions.

I find it useful to think in terms of transforming *certificates*—proofs that a given instance is "good"—along with the instances themselves. For example, a certificate for CircuitSat is a set of inputs that turns on the light bulb; a certificate for Sat or 3Sat is a satisfying assignment; a certificate for MaxIndSet is a large independent set. To reduce X to Y, we actually need to design *three* algorithms, one for each of the following tasks:

---

[9]from his 1996 off-Broadway show *Ricky Jay and his 52 Assistants*

- Transform an arbitrary instance x of X into a special instance y of Y in polynomial time.
- Transform an arbitrary certificate for x into a certificate for y, and
- Transform an arbitrary certificate for y into a certificate for x.

The second and third tasks refer to the input and output of the first algorithm. The *certificate* transformation needs to be reversible, not the *instance* transformation. We never have to transform instances of Y, and we don't need to think about *arbitrary* instances of Y at all. Only the first algorithm needs to run in polynomial time (although in practice, the second and third algorithms are almost always simpler than the first).

For example, our reduction from CIRCUITSAT to 3SAT consists of three algorithms:

- The first transforms an *arbitrary* boolean circuit K into a special 3CNF boolean formula Φ_3, in polynomial time. (Encode each wire as a variable and each gate as a sub-formula, and then expand each sub-formula into 3CNF.)
- The second transforms an *arbitrary* satisfying input for K into a satisfying assignment for Φ_3. (Trace the input through the circuit, transfer values from each wire to the corresponding variable, and give any additional variables arbitrary values.)
- The third transforms an *arbitrary* satisfying assignment for Φ_3 into a satisfying input for K. (Transfer values from each wire variable in Φ_3 to the corresponding wire in K.)

The reduction works because the first algorithm *encodes* any boolean circuit K into a highly structured 3CNF formula Φ_3. The specific structure of Φ_3 restricts *how* it can be satisfied; every satisfying assignment for Φ_3 must "come from" some satisfying input for K. We don't have to think about arbitrary 3CNF formulas at all.

Similarly, our reduction from 3SAT to MAXINDSET consists of three algorithms:

- The first transforms an *arbitrary* 3CNF formula Φ into a special graph G and a specific integer k, in polynomial time.
- The second transforms an *arbitrary* satisfying assignment for Φ into an independent set in G of size k.
- The third transforms an *arbitrary* independent set in G of size k into a satisfying assignment for Φ.

Again, our first transformation *encodes* the input formula Φ into a highly structured graph G and a specific integer k. The structure of G ensures that every independent set of size k "comes from" a satisfying assignment for Φ. We don't consider arbitrary graphs or arbitrary independent set sizes at all.

12.9 Clique and Vertex Cover (from Independent Set)

A *clique* is another name for a complete graph, that is, a graph where every pair of vertices is connected by an edge. The MAXCLIQUE problem asks for the number of nodes in its largest complete subgraph in a given graph. A *vertex cover* of a graph is a set of vertices that touches every edge in the graph. The MINVERTEXCOVER problem asks for the size of the smallest vertex cover in a given graph.

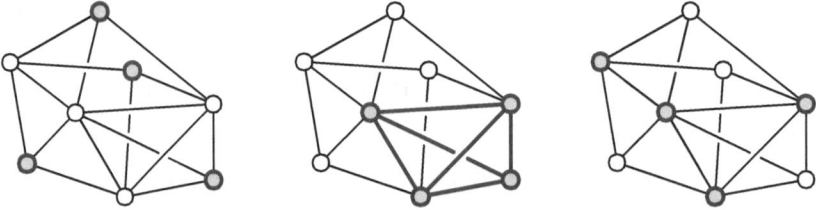

Figure 12.9. A graph whose largest independent set, largest clique, and smallest vertex cover all have size 4.

We can prove that MAXCLIQUE is NP-hard using the following easy reduction from MAXINDSET. Any graph G has an *edge-complement* $\overline{G}$ with the same vertices, but with exactly the opposite set of edges—uv is an edge in $\overline{G}$ if and only if uv is *not* an edge in G. A set of vertices is independent in G if and only if the same vertices define a clique in $\overline{G}$. Thus, the largest independent in G has the same vertices (and thus the same size) as the largest clique in the complement of G.

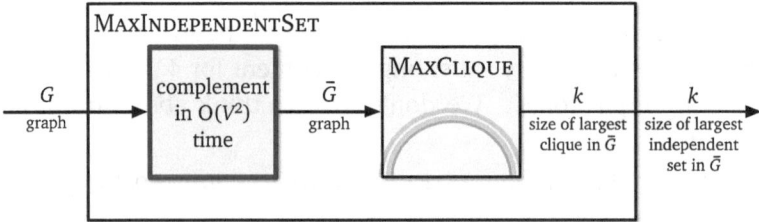

Figure 12.10. An easy reduction from MAXINDSET to MAXCLIQUE.

The proof that MINVERTEXCOVER is NP-hard is even simpler, because it relies on the following easy observation: I is an independent set in a graph $G = (V, E)$ if and only if its complement $V \setminus I$ is a vertex cover of the same graph G. Thus, the *largest* independent set in any graph is the complement of the *smallest* vertex cover of the same graph! Thus, if the smallest vertex cover in an n-vertex graph has size k, then the largest independent set has size $n - k$.

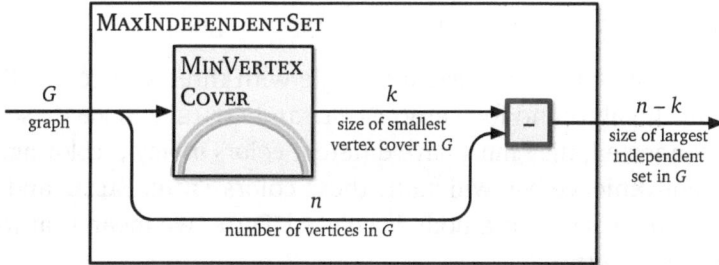

Figure 12.11. An even easier reductions from MaxIndSet to MinVertexCover.

12.10 Graph Coloring (from 3SAT)

A *proper k-coloring* of a graph $G = (V, E)$ is a function $C: V \to \{1, 2, \ldots, k\}$ that assigns one of k "colors" to each vertex, so that every edge has two different colors at its endpoints. (The "colors" are really arbitrary labels, which for simplicity we represent by small positive integers, rather than electromagnetic frequencies, CMYK vectors, or Pantone numbers, for example.) The graph coloring problem asks for the smallest possible number of colors in a legal coloring of a given graph.

To prove that graph coloring is NP-hard, it suffices to consider the decision problem **3COLOR**: Given a graph, does it have a proper 3-coloring? We prove 3COLOR is NP-hard using a reduction from 3SAT. (Why 3SAT? Because it has a 3 in it. You probably think I'm joking, but I'm not.) Given a 3CNF formula Φ, we construct a graph G that is 3-colorable if and only if Φ is satisfiable, as suggested by the usual diagram.

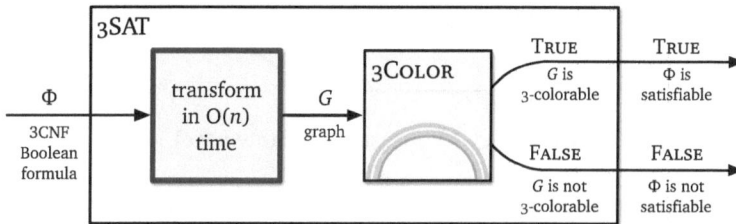

We describe the reduction using a standard strategy of decomposing the output graph G into *gadgets*, subgraphs that enforce various semantics of the input formula Φ in the language of graph coloring. Decomposing reductions into separate gadgets is not only helpful for understanding existing reductions and proving them correct, but for designing new NP-hardness reductions.[10]

---

[10]Our reduction from CircuitSat to Sat encoding each gate in the input circuit as a clause in the output formula; these clauses are "gate gadgets". Similarly, our reduction from 3Sat to MaxIndSet used two type of gadgets: "clause gadgets" (triangles) and "variable gadgets" (edges between contradicting literals).

Our formula-to-graph reduction uses three types of gadgets:

- There is a single *truth gadget*: a triangle with three vertices T, F, and X, which intuitively stand for TRUE, FALSE, and OTHER. Since these vertices are all connected, they must have different colors in any 3-coloring. For the sake of convenience, we will *name* those colors TRUE, FALSE, and OTHER. Thus, when we say that a node is colored TRUE, we mean that it has the same color as vertex T.

- For each variable a, the graph contains a *variable gadget*, which is a triangle joining two new nodes labeled a and $\bar{a}$ to node X in the truth gadget. Node a must be colored either TRUE or FALSE, and therefore node $\bar{a}$ must be colored either FALSE or TRUE, respectively.

Figure 12.12. The truth gadget and a variable gadget for a.

- Finally, for each clause in Φ, the graph contains a *clause gadget*. Each clause gadget joins three literal nodes (from the corresponding variable gadgets) to node T (from the truth gadget) using five new unlabeled nodes and ten edges, as shown below.

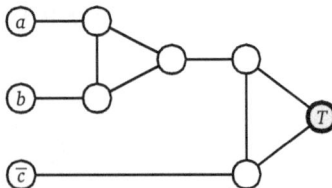

Figure 12.13. A clause gadget for $(a \lor b \lor \bar{c})$.

In effect, each triangle in the clause gadget behaves like a "majority gate". In any valid 3-coloring, if the two vertices to the left of the triangle have the same color, the rightmost vertex of the triangle must have the same color; on the other hand, if the two left vertices have different colors, the color of the right vertex can be chosen arbitrarily. See Figure 12.14.

It follows that there is no valid 3-coloring of a clause gadget where all three literal nodes are colored FALSE. On the other hand, any coloring of the literal nodes with more than one color can be extended to a valid 3-coloring of the clause gadget. The variable gadgets force each literal node to be colored either TRUE or FALSE; thus, in any valid 3-coloring of the clause gadget, at least one literal node is colored TRUE.

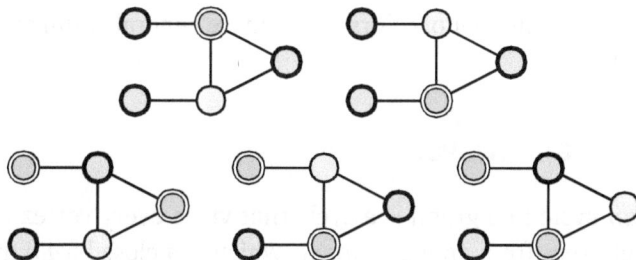

Figure 12.14. All valid 3-colorings of a "half-gadget", up to permutations of the colors

The final graph G contains exactly *one* node T, exactly *one* node F, and exactly *two* nodes a and $\bar{a}$ for each variable. For example, Figure 12.15 shows the graph that results from the same 3CNF formula $(a \vee b \vee c) \wedge (b \vee \bar{c} \vee \bar{d}) \wedge (\bar{a} \vee c \vee d) \wedge (a \vee \bar{b} \vee \bar{d})$ that we previously used to illustrate the MAXINDSET reduction in Figure 12.8. The 3-coloring is one of several that correspond to the satisfying assignment $a = c = \text{TRUE}$, $b = d = \text{FALSE}$.

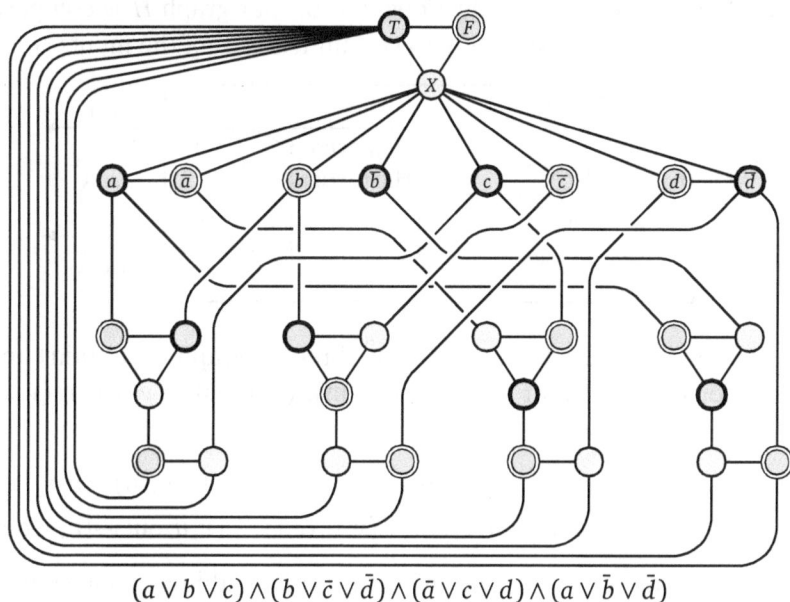

$$(a \vee b \vee c) \wedge (b \vee \bar{c} \vee \bar{d}) \wedge (\bar{a} \vee c \vee d) \wedge (a \vee \bar{b} \vee \bar{d})$$

Figure 12.15. The 3-colorable graph derived from a satisfiable 3CNF formula.

We've already done most of the work for a proof of correctness. If the formula is satisfiable, then we can color the literal nodes according to any satisfying assignment, and then (because each clause is satisfied) extend the coloring across every clause gadget. On the other hand, if the graph is 3-colorable, then we can extract a satisfying assignment from any 3-coloring—at least one of the three literal nodes in every clause gadget is colored TRUE.

Because 3COLOR is a special case of the more general graph coloring problem—

What is the minimum number of colors?—the more general optimization problem is also NP-hard.

12.11 Hamiltonian Cycle

A *Hamiltonian cycle* in a graph is a cycle that visits every vertex exactly once. (This is very different from an *Euler circuit*, which is a closed *walk* that traverses every *edge* exactly once; Euler circuits are easy to find and construct in linear time using depth-first search.) Here we consider two different proofs that the Hamiltonian cycle problem in *directed* graphs is NP-hard.

From Vertex Cover

Our first NP-hardness proof reduces from the decision version of the vertex cover problem. Given an *undirected* graph G and an integer k, we construct a *directed* graph H, such that H has a Hamiltonian cycle if and only if G has a vertex cover of size k. As in our previous reductions, the output graph H is composed of several gadgets, each corresponding to certain features of the inputs G and k.

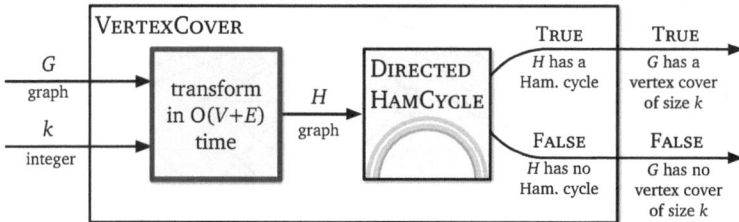

- For each undirected edge uv in G, the directed graph H contains an *edge gadget* consisting of four vertices (u, v, in), (u, v, out), (v, u, in), (v, u, out) and six directed edges

$$(u, v, \text{in}) \to (u, v, \text{out}) \qquad (u, v, \text{in}) \to (v, u, \text{in}) \qquad (v, u, \text{in}) \to (u, v, \text{in})$$
$$(v, u, \text{in}) \to (v, u, \text{out}) \qquad (u, v, \text{out}) \to (v, u, \text{out}) \qquad (v, u, \text{out}) \to (u, v, \text{out})$$

as shown in Figure 12.16. Each "in" vertex has an additional incoming edge, and each "out" vertex has an additional outgoing edge. Any Hamiltonian cycle in H must pass through an edge gadget in one of three ways—either straight through on both sides, or with a detour from one side to the other and back. Eventually, these options will correspond to both u and v, only u, or only v belonging to some vertex cover.

- For each vertex u in G, all the edge gadgets for incident edges uv are connected in H into a single directed path, which we call a *vertex chain*. Specifically, suppose vertex u has d neighbors $v_1, v_2, \ldots, v_d$. Then H has $d - 1$ additional edges $(u, v_i, \text{out}) \to (u, v_{i+1}, \text{in})$ for each i from 1 to $d - 1$.

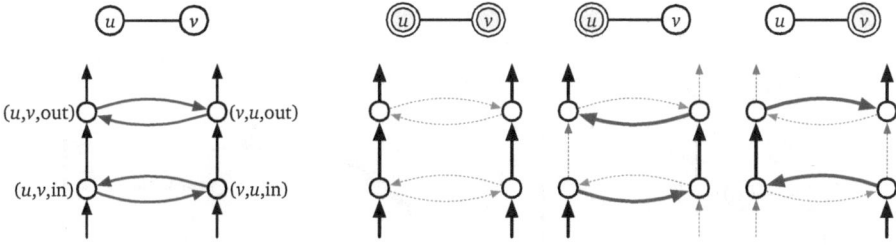

Figure 12.16. An edge gadget and its only possible intersections with a Hamiltonian cycle.

- Finally, H also contains k *cover vertices* $x_1, x_2, \ldots, x_k$. Each cover vertex has a directed edge to the first vertex in each vertex chain, and a directed edge from the last vertex in each vertex chain.

Figure 12.17 shows a complete example of our transformation; each double-arrowed blue segment represents a pair of directed edges.

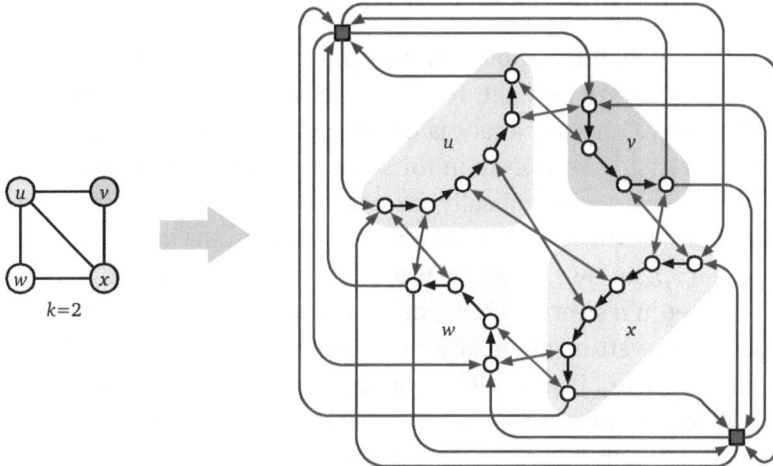

Figure 12.17. Example of our reduction from VERTEXCOVER to DIRECTEDHAMCYCLE.

As usual, we prove our reduction is correct in two stages.

⇒ First, suppose $C = \{u_1, u_2, \ldots, u_k\}$ is a vertex cover of G of size k. We can construct a Hamiltonian cycle in H that "encodes" C as follows. For each index i from 1 to k, we traverse a path from cover vertex x_i, through the vertex chain for u_i, to cover vertex x_{i+1} (or cover vertex x_1 if $i = k$). As we traverse the chain for each vertex u_i, we determine how to proceed from each node (u_i, v, in) as follows:

- If $v \in C$, follow the edge $(u_i, v, \text{in}) \rightarrow (u_i, v, \text{out})$.
- If $v \notin C$, detour through $(u_i, v, \text{in}) \rightarrow (v, u_i, \text{in}) \rightarrow (v, u_i, \text{out}) \rightarrow (u_i, v, \text{out})$.

Thus, for each edge uv of G, the Hamiltonian cycle visits (u, v, in) and (u, v, out) as part of u's vertex chain if $u \in C$ and as part of v's vertex chain otherwise. See Figure 12.18.

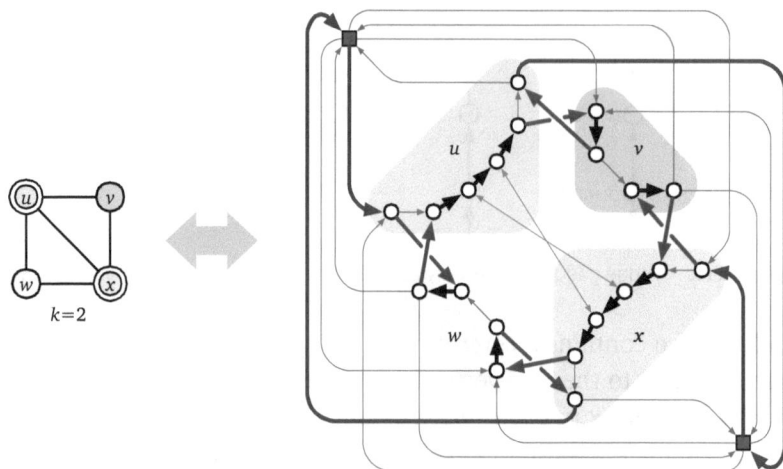

Figure 12.18. Every vertex cover of size k in G corresponds to a Hamiltonian cycle in H and vice versa.

$\Leftarrow$ On the other hand, suppose H contains a Hamiltonian cycle C. This cycle must contain an edge from each cover vertex to the start of some vertex chain. Our case analysis of edge gadgets inductively implies that after C enters the vertex chain for some vertex u, it must traverse the entire vertex chain. Specifically, at each vertex (u, v, in), the cycle must contain either the single edge $(u, v, \text{in}) \rightarrow (u, v, \text{out})$ or the detour path $(u, v, \text{in}) \rightarrow (v, u, \text{in}) \rightarrow (v, u, \text{out}) \rightarrow (u, v, \text{out})$, followed by an edge to the next edge gadget in u's vertex chain, or to a cover vertex if this is the last edge gadget in u's vertex chain. In particular, if C contains the detour edge $(u, v, \text{in}) \rightarrow (v, u, \text{in})$, it cannot contain edges between any cover vertex and v's vertex chain. It follows that C traverses exactly k vertex chains. Moreover, these vertex chains describe a vertex cover of the original graph G, because C visits the vertex (u, v, in) for every edge uv in G.

We conclude that G has a vertex cover of size k if and only if H contains a Hamiltonian cycle. The transformation from G to H takes at most $O(V^2)$ time; it follows that the directed Hamiltonian cycle problem is NP-hard.

From 3SAT

We can also prove that the directed Hamiltonian cycle problem is NP-hard by reducing directly from 3SAT. Given an arbitrary 3CNF formula Φ with n variables $x_1, x_2, \dots, x_n$ and k clauses $c_1, c_2, \dots, c_k$, we construct a directed graph H that contains a Hamiltonian cycle if and only if Φ is satisfiable, as follows.

For each variable x_i, we construct a *variable gadget*, which consists of a doubly-linked list of $2k$ vertices $(i, 0), (i, 1), \dots, (i, 2k)$, connected by edges $(i, j-1) \rightarrow (i, j)$ and $(i, j) \rightarrow (i, j-1)$ for each index j. We connect the first and last nodes in each adjacent pair of variable gadgets by adding edges

$$(i,0){\to}(i+1,0) \quad (i,2k){\to}(i+1,0) \quad (i,0){\to}(i+1,2k) \quad (i,2k){\to}(i+1,2k)$$

for each index i; we also connect the endpoints of the first and last variable gadgets with the edges

$$(n,0){\to}(1,0) \qquad (n,2k){\to}(1,0) \qquad (n,0){\to}(1,2k) \qquad (n,2k){\to}(1,2k).$$

The resulting graph G has exactly 2^n Hamiltonian cycles, one for each assignment of boolean values to the n variables of Φ. Specifically, for each i, we traverse the ith variable gadget from left to right if $x_i = $ TRUE and right to left if $x_i = $ FALSE. See Figure 12.19.

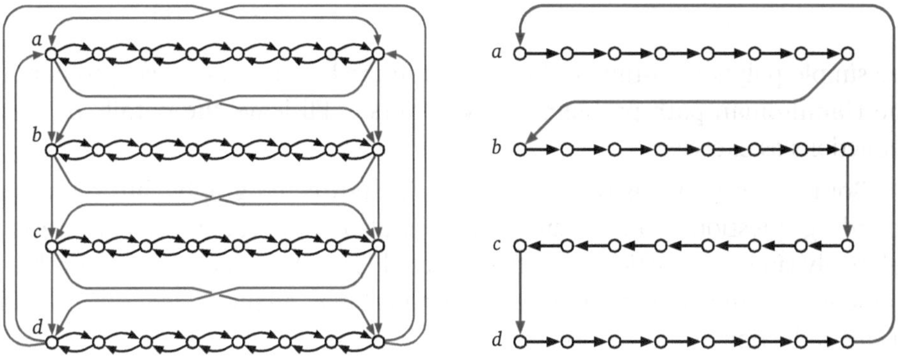

Figure 12.19. Left: Variable gadgets and connectors in G, for any formula with 4 variables and 4 clauses. Right: The Hamiltonian cycle in G corresponding to the assignment $a = b = d = $ TRUE and $c = $ FALSE

Now we extend G to a larger graph H by adding a *clause vertex* $[j]$ for each clause c_j, connected to the variable gadgets by six edges, as shown in Figure 12.20. For each positive literal x_i in c_j, we add the edges $(i,2j-1){\to}[j]{\to}(i,2j)$, and for each negative literal $\bar{x}_i$ in c_j, we add the edges $(i,2j){\to}[j]{\to}(i,2j-1)$. The connections to the clause vertices guarantee that a Hamiltonian cycle in G can be extended to a Hamiltonian cycle in H if and only if the corresponding variable assignment satisfies Φ. Exhaustive case analysis now implies that H has a Hamiltonian cycle if and only if Φ is satisfiable.

Transforming the formula Φ into the graph H takes $O(kn)$ time, which is at most quadratic in the total length of the formula; we conclude that the directed Hamiltonian cycle problem is NP-hard.

Variants and Extensions

Trivial modifications of the previous reductions imply that the Hamiltonian *path* problem in directed graphs is also NP-hard. A Hamiltonian path in a graph G is of course a simple path that visits every vertex of G exactly once. In fact, there

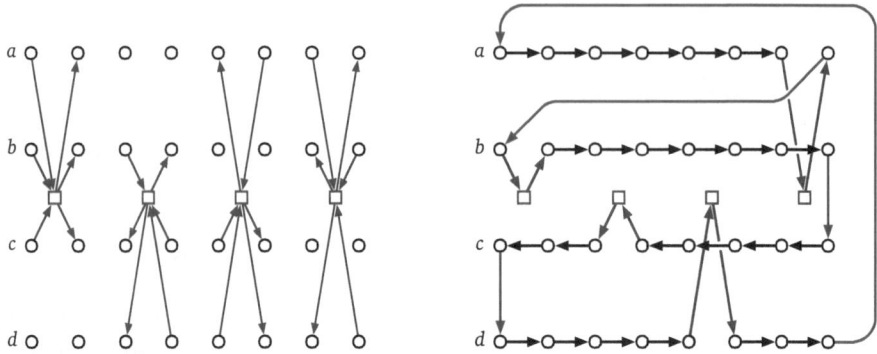

Figure 12.20. Left: Clause gadgets for the formula $(a \vee b \vee c) \wedge (b \vee \bar{c} \vee \bar{d}) \wedge (\bar{a} \vee c \vee d) \wedge (a \vee \bar{b} \vee \bar{d})$. Right: A hamiltonian cycle in H corresponding to the satisfying assignment $a = b = d = \text{TRUE}$ and $c = \text{FALSE}$.

are simple polynomial-time reductions from the Hamiltonian cycle problem to the Hamiltonian path problem and vice versa. I'll leave the details of these reductions as exercises.

Both of the previous reductions deal with directed graphs, but the corresponding question in undirected graph is also NP-hard. In fact, there is a relatively simple reduction from the directed Hamiltonian cycle/path problem to the undirected Hamiltonian cycle/path problem; again, I'll leave the details of this reduction as an exercise.

Finally, the infamous *traveling salesman problem* asks to find the shortest Hamiltonian cycle (or path) in a graph with weighted edges. Since finding the shortest cycle/path is obviously harder than determining if a cycle/path exists at all—Consider a graph where every edge has weight 1!—TravelingSalesman is also NP-hard.

12.12 Subset Sum (from Vertex Cover)

The next problem that we prove NP-hard is the SUBSETSUM problem considered in Chapter 2: Given a set X of positive integers and an integer T, determine whether X has a subset whose elements sum to T.

We once again reduce from VERTEXCOVER. Given a graph G and an integer k, we need to compute a set X of positive integers and an integer T, such that X has a subset that sums to T if and only if G has an vertex cover of size k. Our transformation uses only two types of "gadgets", which are *integers* representing the vertices and edges in G.

Number the *edges* of G arbitrarily from 0 to $E - 1$. Our set X contains the integer $b_i := 4^i$ for each edge i, and the integer

$$a_v := 4^E + \sum_{i \in \Delta(v)} 4^i$$

for each vertex v, where $\Delta(v)$ is the set of edges that have v has an endpoint. Alternately, we can think of each integer in X as an $(E+1)$-digit number written in base 4. The Eth digit is 1 if the integer represents a vertex, and 0 otherwise; and for each $i < E$, the ith digit is 1 if the integer represents edge i or one of its endpoints, and 0 otherwise. Finally, we set the target sum

$$T := k \cdot 4^E + \sum_{i=0}^{E-1} 2 \cdot 4^i.$$

Now let's prove that the reduction is correct.

$\Rightarrow$ First, suppose G has a vertex cover C of size k. Consider the subset

$$X' := \{a_v \mid v \in C\} \cup \{b_i \mid \text{edge } i \text{ has exactly one endpoint in } C\}$$

The sum of the elements of X', written in base 4, has most significant digit k and all other digits equal to 2. Thus, the elements of X' sum to exactly T.

$\Leftarrow$ On the other hand, suppose there is a subset $X' \subseteq X$ that sums to T. Specifically, we must have

$$\sum_{v \in V'} a_v + \sum_{i \in E'} b_i = t$$

for some subsets $V' \subseteq V$ and $E' \subseteq E$. Again, if we sum these base-4 numbers, there are no carries in the first E digits, because for each i there are only three numbers in X whose ith digit is 1. Each edge number b_i contributes only one 1 to the ith digit of the sum, but the ith digit of t is 2. Thus, for each edge in G, at least one of its endpoints must be in V'. In other words, V' is a vertex cover. On the other hand, only vertex numbers are larger than 4^E, and $\lfloor T/4^E \rfloor = k$, so V' has at most k elements. (In fact, it's not hard to see that V' has *exactly* k elements.)

For example, given the four-vertex graph $G = (V, E)$ where $V = \{u, v, w, x\}$ and $E = \{uv, uw, vw, vx, wx\}$, our set X might contain the following base-4 integers:

$$
\begin{aligned}
a_u &:= 11100_4 = 1344 & b_{uv} &:= 01000_4 = 256 \\
a_v &:= 11011_4 = 1300 & b_{uw} &:= 00100_4 = 64 \\
a_w &:= 10110_4 = 1105 & b_{vw} &:= 00010_4 = 16 \\
a_x &:= 10001_4 = 1029 & b_{vx} &:= 00001_4 = 4 \\
& & b_{wx} &:= 00000 1_4 = 1
\end{aligned}
$$

If we are looking for a vertex cover of size $k = 2$, our target sum would be $T := 222222_4 = 2730$. Indeed, the vertex cover $\{v, w\}$ corresponds to the subset $\{a_v, a_w, b_{uv}, b_{uw}, b_{vx}, b_{wx}\}$, whose sum is $1300 + 1105 + 256 + 64 + 4 + 1 = 2730$.

The reduction can clearly be performed in polynomial time. We've already proved that VERTEXCOVER is NP-hard, so it follows that SUBSETSUM is NP-hard.

Caveat Reductor!

One subtle point must be emphasized here. 300-something pages ago, back in Chapter 3, we developed a dynamic programming algorithm to solve SUBSETSUM in $O(nT)$ time. Isn't this a polynomial-time algorithm? Didn't we just prove that P=NP? Hey, where's my million dollars?!

Alas, life is not so simple. True, the running time is a polynomial function of the variables n and T, but to qualify as a true polynomial-time algorithm, the running time must be a polynomial function of the *input size*—the number of *bits* required to represent the input. The *values* of the elements of X and the target sum T could be exponentially larger than the number of input bits. Indeed, the reduction we just described produces a value of T that is exponentially larger than the size of our original input graph, which forces our dynamic programming algorithm to run in exponential time.

Algorithms like this are said to run in **pseudo-polynomial time**, and any NP-hard problem with such an algorithm is called **weakly NP-hard**. Equivalently, a weakly NP-hard problem is a problem that can be solved in polynomial time when all input numbers are represented in *unary* (as a sum of 1s), but becomes NP-hard when all input numbers are represented in *binary*. If a problem is NP-hard even when all the input numbers are represented in unary, we say that the problem is **strongly NP-hard**. A good example of a *strongly* NP-hard problem is TRAVELINGSALESMAN, which remains NP-hard even if the input graph is complete and all edge weights are equal to 1 or 2.

12.13 Other Useful NP-hard Problems

Literally thousands of problems have been proved to be NP-hard. Here I will list a few NP-hard problems that are useful in deriving reductions.[11] I won't describe the NP-hardness proofs for these problems in detail, but you can find most of them in Garey and Johnson's classic *Scary Black Book of NP-Completeness*.[12] All

---

[11] As someday it may happen a reduction must be found, I've got a little list. I've got a little list. Of some Herculean problems we can use to lower bound. Fast solutions don't exist. Our proofs they can assist.

[12] Michael Garey and David Johnson. *Computers and Intractability: A Guide to the Theory of NP-Completeness*. W. H. Freeman and Co., 1979. And yes, it really is black.

of the problems I've discussed so far, and most of the problems in the following list, were first proved NP-hard in a single landmark 1972 paper by Richard Karp.[13]

- **PLANARCIRCUITSAT:** Given a boolean circuit that can be embedded in the plane so that no two wires cross, is there an input that makes the circuit output TRUE? This problem can be proved NP-hard by reduction from the general circuit satisfiability problem, by replacing each crossing with a small assemblage of gates.

- **1-IN-3SAT:** Given a 3CNF formula, is there an assignment of values to the variables so that each clause contains *exactly* one TRUE literal? This problem can be proved NP-hard by reduction from the usual 3SAT.

- **NOTALLEQUAL3SAT:** Given a 3CNF formula, is there an assignment of values to the variables so that every clause contains at least one TRUE literal *and* at least one FALSE literal? This problem can be proved NP-hard by reduction from the usual 3SAT.

- **PLANAR3SAT:** Given a 3CNF boolean formula, consider a bipartite graph whose vertices are the clauses and variables, where an edge indicates that a variable (or its negation) appears in a clause. If this graph is planar, the 3CNF formula is also called planar. The PLANAR3SAT problem asks, given a planar 3CNF formula, whether it has a satisfying assignment. This problem can be proved NP-hard by reduction from PLANARCIRCUITSAT.[14]

- **EXACT3DIMENSIONALMATCHING** or **X3M:** Given a set S and a collection of three-element subsets of S, called *triples*, is there a sub-collection of disjoint triples that exactly cover S? This problem can be proved NP-hard by a reduction from 3SAT, because it has a 3 in it.

- **PARTITION:** Given a set S of n integers, are there subsets A and B such that $A \cup B = S, A \cap B = \emptyset$, and
$$\sum_{a \in A} a = \sum_{b \in B} b?$$

  This problem can be proved NP-hard by a simple reduction from SUBSETSUM. Like SUBSETSUM, the PARTITION problem is only weakly NP-hard.

- **3PARTITION:** Given a set S of $3n$ integers, can it be partitioned into n disjoint three-element subsets, such that every subset has exactly the same sum? Despite the similar names, this problem is *very* different from PARTITION; sorry, I didn't make up the names. This problem can be proved NP-hard by reduction from X3M, because it has a 3 in it. Unlike PARTITION, the 3PARTITION problem is *strongly* NP-hard; it remains NP-hard even if every input number is at most n^3.

---

[13]Later performed off-Broadway as *Richard Karp and his 21 Assistants*, for which Karp won a well-deserved ~~Tony~~ Turing award.

[14]Surprisingly, PLANARNOTALLEQUAL3SAT is solvable in polynomial time!

- **SetCover:** Given a collection of sets $\mathbf{S} = \{S_1, S_2, \ldots, S_m\}$, find the smallest sub-collection of S_i's that contains all the elements of $\bigcup_i S_i$. This problem is a generalization of both VertexCover and X3M.

- **HittingSet:** Given a collection of sets $\mathbf{S} = \{S_1, S_2, \ldots, S_m\}$, find the minimum number of elements of $\bigcup_i S_i$ that hit every set in $\mathbf{S}$. This problem is also a generalization of VertexCover.

- **LongestPath:** Given a non-negatively weighted graph G (either directed or undirected) and two vertices u and v, what is the longest simple path from u to v in the graph? A path is *simple* if it visits each vertex at most once. This problem is a generalization of the corresponding Hamiltonian path problem. Of course, the corresponding *shortest* path problem can be solved in polynomial time.

- **SteinerTree:** Given a weighted, undirected graph G with some of the vertices marked, what is the minimum-weight subtree of G that contains every marked vertex? If *every* vertex is marked, the minimum Steiner tree is the minimum spanning tree; if exactly two vertices are marked, the minimum Steiner tree is the shortest path between them. This problem can be proved NP-hard by reduction from VertexCover.

- **Max2Sat:** Given a Boolean formula in conjunctive normal form, with exactly *two* literals per clause, find a variable assignment that maximizes the number of clauses with at least one True literal. This problem can be proved NP-hard by reduction from 3Sat (yes, even though it doesn't have a 3 in it). The simpler decision problem 2Sat, which asks if there is an assignment that satisfies *every* clause, can actually be solved in polynomial time.

- **MaxCut:** Given an undirected graph $G = (V, E)$, find a subset $S \subset V$ that maximizes the number of edges with exactly one endpoint in S. Equivalently, find the largest bipartite subgraph of G. This problem can be proved NP-hard by reduction from Max2Sat.

In addition to these dry but useful problems, most interesting puzzles and solitaire games have been shown to be NP-hard, or to have NP-hard generalizations. (Arguably, if a game or puzzle isn't at least NP-hard, it isn't interesting!) Here are some examples you may find familiar:

- Minesweeper (from CircuitSat)[15]
- Sudoku (utlimately from 3Sat)[16]

---

[15] Richard Kaye. Minesweeper is NP-complete. *Mathematical Intelligencer* 22(2):9–15, 2000. But see also: Allan Scott, Ulrike Stege, and Iris van Rooij. Minesweeper may not be NP-complete but is hard nonetheless. *Mathematical Intelligencer* 33(4):5–17, 2011.

[16] Takayuki Yato and Takahiro Seta. Complexity and completeness of finding another solution and its application to puzzles. *IEICE Transactions on Fundamentals of Electronics, Communications and Computer Sciences* E86-A(5):1052–1060, 2003. http://www-imai.is.s.u-tokyo.ac.jp/~yato/data2/MasterThesis.pdf.

- Tetris (from 3Partition)[17]
- Klondike, aka "Solitaire" (from 3Sat)[18]
- Pac-Man (from HamiltonianCycle)[19]
- Super Mario Brothers (from 3Sat)[20]
- Candy Crush Saga (from a variant of 3Sat)[21]
- Threes/2048 (from 3Sat, of course)[22]
- Trainyard (from DominatingSet; see Exercise 26)[23]
- Shortest $n \times n \times n$ Rubik's cube solution (from 3Sat via a special case of PlanarUndirectedHamCycle).[24]
- Cookie Clicker (from Partition or 3Partition)[25]

This list is necessarily incomplete, thanks to a limited footnote budget.[26] As of June 2019, nobody has published a proof that a generalization of Ultimate Paperclips, Line Rider, Twister, or Cards Against Humanity is NP-hard, but I'm sure it's only a matter of time.

12.14 Choosing the Right Problem

One of the most difficult steps in proving that a problem is NP-hard is choosing the best problem to reduce from. The Cook-Levin Theorem implies that if there is a reduction from *any* NP-hard problem to problem X, then there is a reduction

---

[17]Ron Breukelaar, Erik D. Demaine, Susan Hohenberger, Hendrik J. Hoogeboom, Walter A. Kosters, and David Liben-Nowell. Tetris is hard, even to approximate. *International Journal of Computational Geometry and Applications* 14:41–68, 2004.

[18]Luc Longpré and Pierre McKenzie. The complexity of Solitaire. *Proceedings of the 32nd International Mathematical Foundations of Computer Science*, 182–193, 2007.

[19]Giovanni Viglietta. Gaming is a hard job, but someone has to do it! *Theory of Computing Systems*, 54(4):595–621, 2014. http://giovanniviglietta.com/papers/gaming2.pdf.

[20]Greg Aloupis, Erik D. Demaine, Alan Guo, and Giovanni Viglietta. Classic Nintendo games Are (computationally) hard. *Theoretical Computer Science* 586:135–160, 2015. http://arxiv.org/abs/1203.1895.

[21]Luciano Gualà, Stefano Leucci, Emanuele Natale. Bejeweled, Candy Crush and other match-three games are (NP-)hard. *Proc. 2014 IEEE Conference on Computational Intelligence and Games*, 2014. http://arxiv.org/abs/1403.5830.

[22]Stefan Langerman and Yushi Uno. Threes!, Fives, 1024!, and 2048 are Hard. *Proc. 8th International Conference on Fun with Algorithms*, 2016. https://arxiv.org/abs/1505.04274.

[23]Matteo Almanza, Stefano Leucci, and Alessandro Panconesi. Trainyard is NP-Hard. *Proc. 8th International Conference on Fun with Algorithms*, 2016. https://arxiv.org/abs/1603.00928.

[24]Erik D. Demaine, Sarah Eisenstat, and Mikhail Rudoy. Solving the Rubik's Cube optimally is NP-complete. *Proc. 35th Symposium on Theoretical Aspects of Computer Science*, 2018. https://arxiv.org/abs/1706.06708.

[25]Erik D. Demaine, Hiro Ito, Stefan Langerman, Jayson Lynch, Mikhail Rudoy, and Kai Xiao. Cookie Clicker. Preprint, August 2018. https://arxiv.org/abs/1808.07540.

[26]See https://xkcd.com/1208/

from *every* NP-complete problem to problem X, but some problems are easier to work with than others. There's no systematic method for choosing the right problem, but here are a few useful rules of thumb.

- If the problem asks how to assign bits to objects, or to choose a subset of objects, or to partition objects into two different subsets, try reducing from some version of SAT or PARTITION.

- If the problem asks how to assign labels to objects from a small fixed set, or to partition objects into a small number of subsets, try reducing from *k*COLOR or even 3COLOR.

- If the problem asks to arrange a set of objects in a particular order, try reducing from DIRECTEDHAMCYCLE or DIRECTEDHAMPATH or TRAVELING-SALESMAN.

- If the problem asks to find a *small* subset satisfying some constraints, try reducing from MINVERTEXCOVER.

- If the problem asks to find a *large* subset satisfying some constraints, try reducing from MAXINDSET or MAXCLIQUE or MAX2SAT.

- If the problem asks to partition objects into a large number of small subsets, try reducing from 3PARTITION.

- If the number 3 appears naturally in the problem, try 3SAT or 3COLOR or X3M or 3PARTITION. (No, this is not a joke.)

- If all else fails, try 3SAT or even CIRCUITSAT!

I do not recommend trying to reduce from TETRIS, SUPERMARIOBROS, or TRAINYARD. You really want to choose a starting problem that is as simple as possible, while still capturing *some* feature of your problem that makes it difficult to solve.

12.15 A Frivolous Real-World Example

Draughts is a family of board games that have been played for thousands of years. Most Americans are familiar with the version called *checkers* or *English draughts*, but the most common variant worldwide, known as **international draughts** or **Polish draughts**, originated in the Netherlands in the 16th century. For a complete set of rules, the reader should consult Wikipedia; here a few important differences from the Anglo-American game:

- **Flying kings:** As in checkers, a piece that ends a move in the row closest to the opponent becomes a *king* and gains the ability to move backward. Unlike in checkers, however, a king in international draughts can move any distance along a diagonal line in a single turn, as long as the intermediate squares are empty or contain exactly one opposing piece (which is captured).

- **Forced maximum capture:** In each turn, the moving player must capture as many opposing pieces as possible. This is distinct from the forced-capture rule in checkers, which requires only that each player must capture if possible, and that a capturing move ends only when the moving piece cannot capture further. In other words, checkers requires capturing a *locally maximal* set of opposing pieces on each turn; whereas, international draughts requires a *globally maximum* capture.

- **Capture subtleties:** As in checkers, captured pieces are removed from the board only at the end of the turn. Any piece can be captured at most once. Thus, when an opposing piece is jumped, that piece remains on the board *but cannot be jumped again* until the end of the turn.

For example, in the first position shown below, each circle represents a piece, and doubled circles represent kings. Black *must* make the first indicated move, capturing five white pieces, because it is not possible to capture more than five pieces, and there is no other move that captures five. Black cannot extend his capture further, either northeast or southeast, because the captured White pieces remain on the board until his turn is over. Then White *must* make the second indicated move, thereby winning the game.

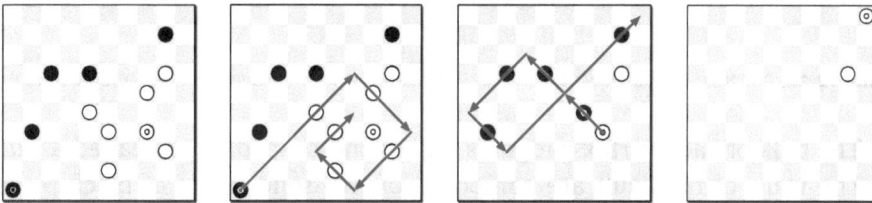

Figure 12.21. Two forced(!) moves in international draughts; doubled circles are kings.

The actual game, which is played on a 10 × 10 board with 20 pieces of each color, is computationally trivial; we can precompute the optimal move for both players in every possible board configuration and hard-code the results into a lookup table of constant size. Sure, it's a *big* constant, but it's still a constant!

But consider the natural generalization of international draughts to an $n \times n$ board. In this setting, *finding a legal move is actually NP-hard!* The following reduction from the Hamiltonian cycle problem in directed graphs was discovered by Bob Hearn in 2010.[27] In most two-player games, finding the *best* move is NP-hard (or worse). This is the only example I know of a game—and moreover a real game played by millions of people for centuries—where *merely following the rules* is NP-hard!

Given an undirected graph G with n vertices, we construct a board configuration for international draughts, such that White can capture a certain

---

[27] See Theoretical Computer Science Stack Exchange: http://cstheory.stackexchange.com/a/1999/111.

number of black pieces in a single move if and only if G has a Hamiltonian cycle. We treat G as a directed graph, with two arcs $u \to v$ and $v \to u$ in place of each undirected edge uv. Number the vertices arbitrarily from 1 to n. The final draughts configuration has several gadgets:

- The vertices of G are represented by rabbit-shaped *vertex gadgets*, which are evenly spaced along a horizontal line. Each arc $i \to j$ is represented by a path of two diagonal line segments from the "left ear" of vertex gadget i to the "right ear" of vertex gadget j. The path for arc $i \to j$ is located above the vertex gadgets if $i < j$, and below the vertex gadgets if $i > j$.

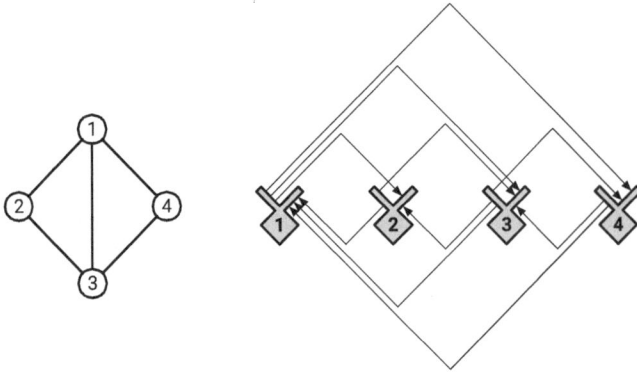

Figure 12.22. A high-level overview of the reduction from Hamiltonian cycle to international draughts.

- The bulk of each vertex gadget is a diamond-shaped region called a *vault*. The walls of the vault are composed of two solid layers of black pieces, which cannot be captured; these pieces are drawn as gray circles in the figures. There are N capturable black pieces inside each vault, for some large integer N to be determined later. A white king can enter the vault through the "right ear", capture every internal piece, and then exit through the "left ear". Both ears are hallways, again with walls two pieces thick, with gaps where the arc paths end to allow the white king to enter and leave. The lengths of the "ears" can easily be adjusted to align with the other gadgets.

- For each arc $i \to j$, we have a *corner gadget*, which allows a white king leaving vertex gadget i to be redirected to vertex gadget j.

- Finally, wherever two arc paths cross, we have a *crossing gadget*; these gadgets allow the white king to traverse either arc path, but forbid switching from one arc path to the other.

A single white king starts at the bottom corner of one of the vaults. In any legal move, this king must alternate between traversing entire arc paths and clearing vaults. The king can traverse the various gadgets backward, entering

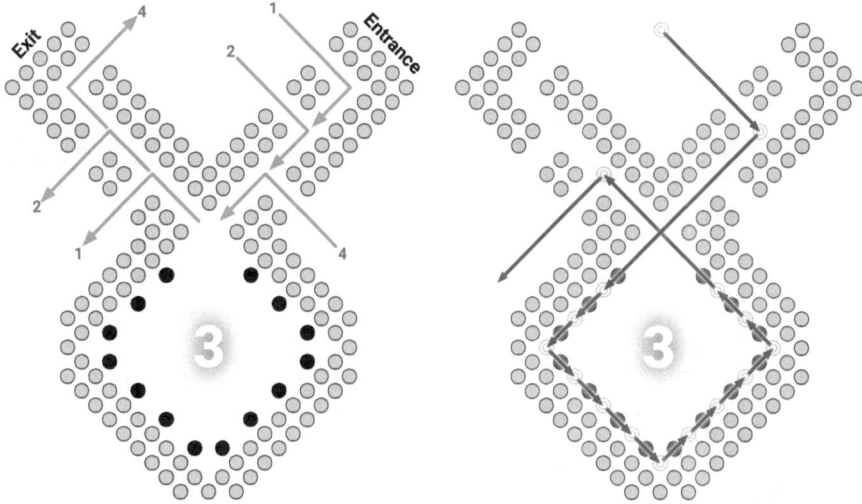

Figure 12.23. Left: A vertex gadget with three entrances and three exits. Right: A white king emptying the vault. Gray circles are black pieces that cannot be captured.

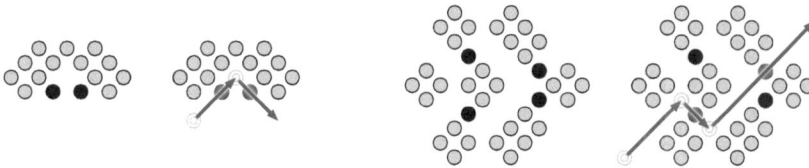

Figure 12.24. Left: One of two paths through a corner gadget. Right: One of two paths through a crossing gadget.

each vault through the exit and vice versa. But the reversal of a Hamiltonian cycle in G is another Hamiltonian cycle in G, so walking backward is fine.

If there is a Hamiltonian cycle in G, the white king can capture at least nN black pieces by visiting each of the other vaults and returning to the starting vault. On the other hand, if there is no Hamiltonian cycle in G, the white king can capture at most half of the pieces in the starting vault, and thus can capture at most $(n - 1/2)N + O(n^3)$ enemy pieces altogether. The $O(n^3)$ term accounts for the corner and crossing gadgets; each edge passes through one corner gadget and at most $n^2/2$ crossing gadgets.

To complete the reduction, we set $N = n^4$. Summing up, we obtain an $O(n^5) \times O(n^5)$ board configuration, with $O(n^5)$ black pieces and one white king. We can clearly construct this board configuration by brute force in polynomial time. Figure 12.25 shows a complete example of the construction.

It is still open whether the following related question is NP-hard: Given an $n \times n$ board configuration for international draughts, can (and therefore *must*) White capture *all* the black pieces (thereby winning the game) in a single turn?

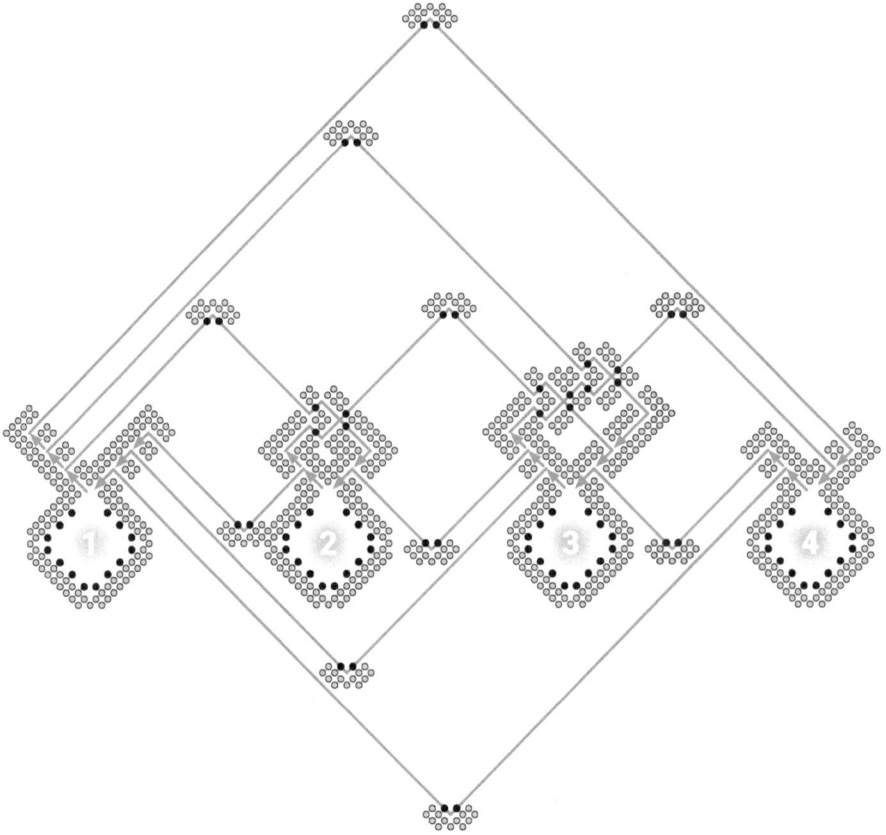

Figure 12.25. The final draughts configuration for the 4-vertex graph in Figure 12.22. (The green arrows are not actually part of the configuration.)

♥12.16 On Beyond Zebra

P and NP are only the first two steps in an enormous hierarchy of complexity classes. To close this chapter (and the book), let me describe a few more classes of interest.

Polynomial Space

PSPACE is the set of decision problems that can be solved using polynomial *space*. Every problem in NP (and therefore in P) is also in PSPACE. It is generally believed that NP ≠ PSPACE, but nobody can even prove that P ≠ PSPACE. A problem Π is *PSPACE-hard* if, for any problem Π′ that can be solved using polynomial *space*, there is a polynomial-*time* many-one reduction from Π′ to Π. If any PSPACE-hard problem is in NP, then PSPACE=NP; similarly, if any PSPACE-hard problem is in P, then PSPACE=P.

The canonical PSPACE-hard problem is the *quantified boolean formula problem*, or **QBF:** Given a boolean formula Φ that may include any number of universal or existential quantifiers, but no free variables, is Φ equivalent to TRUE? For example, the following expression is a valid input to QBF:

$$\exists a: \forall b: \exists c: (\forall d: a \vee b \vee c \vee \bar{d}) \Leftrightarrow ((b \wedge \bar{c}) \vee (\exists e: \overline{(\bar{a} \Rightarrow e)} \vee (c \neq a \wedge e))).$$

SAT is equivalent to the special case of QBF where the input formula contains only existential quantifiers ($\exists$). QBF remains PSPACE-hard even when the input formula must have all its quantifiers at the beginning, the quantifiers strictly alternate between $\exists$ and $\forall$, and the quantified proposition is in conjunctive normal form, with exactly three literals in each clause, for example:

$$\exists a: \forall b: \exists c: \forall d: \big((a \vee b \vee c) \wedge (b \vee \bar{c} \vee \bar{d}) \wedge (\bar{a} \vee c \vee d) \wedge (a \vee \bar{b} \vee \bar{d})\big)$$

This restricted version of QBF can also be phrased as a two-player strategy question. Suppose two players, Alice and Bob, are given a 3CNF predicate with free variables $x_1, x_2, \ldots, x_n$. The players alternately assign values to the variables in order by index—Alice assigns a value to x_1, Bob assigns a value to x_2, and so on. Alice eventually assigns values to every variable with an odd index, and Bob eventually assigns values to every variable with an even index. Alice wants to make the expression TRUE, and Bob wants to make it FALSE. Assuming Alice and Bob play perfectly, who wins this game? Not surprisingly, most two-player games[28] like tic-tac-toe, reversi, checkers, go, chess, and mancala—or more accurately, appropriate generalizations of these constant-size games to arbitrary board sizes—are PSPACE-hard.

Another canonical PSPACE-hard problem is *NFA totality*: Given a non-deterministic finite-state automaton M over some alphabet Σ, does M accept every string in Σ^*? The closely related problems *NFA equivalence* (Do two given NFAs accept the same language?) and *NFA minimization* (Find the smallest NFA that accepts the same language as a given NFA) are also PSPACE-hard, as are the corresponding questions about regular expressions. (The corresponding questions about *deterministic* finite-state automata are actually solvable in polynomial time.)

Exponential Time

The next significantly larger complexity class, **EXP** (also called EXPTIME), is the set of decision problems that can be solved in exponential time, that is, using at most 2^{n^c} steps for some constant $c > 0$. Every problem in PSPACE (and

---

[28] For a good (but inevitably aging) overview of known results on the computational complexity of games and puzzles, see Erik Demaine and Bob Hearn's monograph *Games, Puzzles, and Computation* (CRC Press, 2009).

therefore in NP (and therefore in P)) is also in EXP. It is generally believed that PSPACE $\subsetneq$ EXP, but nobody can even prove that NP $\neq$ EXP. A problem Π is **EXP-hard** if, for any problem Π' that can be solved in *exponential* time, there is a *polynomial*-time many-one reduction from Π' to Π. If any EXP-hard problem is in PSPACE, then EXP=PSPACE; similarly, if any EXP-hard problem is in NP, then EXP=NP. We *do* know that P $\neq$ EXP; in particular, no EXP-hard problem is in P.

Natural generalizations of many interesting 2-player games—like checkers, chess, mancala, and go—are actually EXP-hard. The boundary between PSPACE-complete games and EXP-hard games is rather subtle. For example, there are three ways to draw in chess (the standard 8×8 game): stalemate (the player to move is not in check but has no legal moves), repeating the same board position three times, or moving fifty times without capturing or moving a pawn. The $n \times n$ generalization of chess is either in PSPACE or EXP-hard depending on how we generalize these rules. If we declare a draw after (say) n^3 capture-free moves, then every game must end after a polynomial number of moves, so we can simulate all possible games from any given position using only polynomial space. On the other hand, if we ignore the capture-free move rule entirely, the resulting game can last an exponential number of moves, so there no obvious way to detect a repeating position using only polynomial space; indeed, this version of $n \times n$ chess is EXP-hard.

Excelsior!

Naturally, even exponential time is not the end of the story. **NEXP** is the class of decision problems that can be solve in *nondeterministic* exponential time; equivalently, a decision problem is in NEXP if and only if, for every YES instance, there is a *proof* of this fact that can be checked in exponential time. **EXPSPACE** is the set of decision problems that can be solved using exponential *space*. Even these larger complexity classes have hard problems; for example, if we add the intersection operator $\cap$ to the syntax of regular expressions, deciding whether two such expressions describe the same language is EXPSPACE-hard. Beyond EXPSPACE are complexity classes with *doubly*-exponential resource bounds (EEXP, NEEXP, and EEXPSPACE), then *triply* exponential resource bounds (EEEXP, NEEEXP, and EEEXPSPACE), and so on ad infinitum.

All these complexity classes can be ordered by inclusion:

$$P \subseteq NP \subseteq PSPACE \subseteq EXP \subseteq NEXP \subseteq EXPSPACE \subseteq EEXP \subseteq NEEXP \subseteq \cdots$$

Most complexity theorists strongly believe that every inclusion in this sequence is strict; that is, no two of these complexity classes are equal. However, the strongest result that has been proved is that every class in this sequence is strictly contained in the class *three* steps later in the sequence. For example, we have proofs that $P \neq EXP$ and $PSPACE \neq EXPSPACE$, but not whether $P \neq PSPACE$ or $NP \neq EXP$.

The limit of this series of increasingly exponential complexity classes is the class ***ELEMENTARY*** of decision problems that can be solved using time or space bounded by a function the form $2 \uparrow^k n$ for some constant integer k, where

$$2 \uparrow^k n := \begin{cases} n & \text{if } k = 0, \\ 2^{2 \uparrow^{k-1} n} & \text{otherwise.} \end{cases}$$

For example, $2 \uparrow^1 n = 2^n$ and $2 \uparrow^2 n = 2^{2^n}$.

It may be tempting to conjecture that *every* natural decidable problem can be solved in elementary time, but in fact this conjecture is incorrect. Consider the ***generalized regular expressions*** defined by recursively combining (possibly empty) strings over some finite alphabet by concatenation (xy), union $(x+y)$, Kleene closure (x^*), and negation $(\overline{x})$. For example, the generalized regular expression $\overline{(0+1)^*00(0+1)^*}$ represents the set of strings in $\{0,1\}^*$ that do *not* contain two 0s in a row. It is possible to determine algorithmically whether two generalized regular expressions describe identical languages, by recursively converting each expression into an equivalent NFA, converting each NFA into a DFA, and then minimizing the DFA. However, the running time of this algorithm has the non-elementary bound $2 \uparrow^{\Theta(n)} 2$, intuitively because each layer of recursive negation can exponentially increase the number of states. In fact, Larry Stockmeyer proved in 1974 that this problem *cannot* be solved in merely elementary time, even if we forbid Kleene closure.

Exercises

1. (a) Describe and analyze and algorithm to solve PARTITION in time $O(nM)$, where n is the size of the input set and M is the sum of the absolute values of its elements.

   (b) Why doesn't this algorithm imply that $P = NP$?

2. Consider the following problem, called BOXDEPTH: Given a set of n axis-aligned rectangles in the plane, how big is the largest subset of these rectangles that contain a common point?

   (a) Describe a polynomial-time reduction from BOXDEPTH to MAXCLIQUE.

   (b) Describe and analyze a polynomial-time algorithm for BOXDEPTH. [*Hint: $O(n^3)$ time should be easy, but $O(n \log n)$ time is possible.*]

   (c) Why don't these two results imply that $P = NP$?

3. A boolean formula is in *disjunctive normal form* (or *DNF*) if it consists of a *disjunction* (OR) or several *terms*, each of which is the conjunction (AND) of one or more literals. For example, the formula

$$(\overline{x} \wedge y \wedge \overline{z}) \vee (y \wedge z) \vee (x \wedge \overline{y} \wedge \overline{z})$$

is in disjunctive normal form. DNF-SAT asks, given a boolean formula in disjunctive normal form, whether that formula is satisfiable.

(a) Describe a polynomial-time algorithm to solve DNF-SAT.

(b) What is the error in the following argument that P=NP?

> Suppose we are given a boolean formula in conjunctive normal form with at most three literals per clause, and we want to know if it is satisfiable. We can use the distributive law to construct an equivalent formula in disjunctive normal form. For example,
>
> $$(x \vee y \vee \overline{z}) \wedge (\overline{x} \vee \overline{y}) \iff (x \wedge \overline{y}) \vee (y \wedge \overline{x}) \vee (\overline{z} \wedge \overline{x}) \vee (\overline{z} \wedge \overline{y})$$
>
> Now we can use the algorithm from part (a) to determine, in polynomial time, whether the resulting DNF formula is satisfiable. We have just solved 3SAT in polynomial time. Since 3SAT is NP-hard, we must conclude that P=NP!

4. The problem ALLORNOTHING3SAT asks, given a 3CNF boolean formula, whether there is an assignment to the variables such that each clause either has three TRUE literals or has three FALSE literals.

(a) Describe a polynomial-time algorithm to solve ALLORNOTHING3SAT.

(b) But 3SAT is NP-hard! Why doesn't the existence of this algorithm prove that P=NP?

5. (a) Suppose you are given a magic black box that can determine **in polynomial time**, given an arbitrary weighted graph G, the length of the shortest Hamiltonian cycle in G. Describe and analyze a **polynomial-time** algorithm that computes, given an arbitrary weighted graph G, the shortest Hamiltonian cycle in G, using this magic black box as a subroutine.

(b) Suppose you are given a magic black box that can determine **in polynomial time**, given an arbitrary graph G, the number of vertices in the largest complete subgraph of G. Describe and analyze a **polynomial-time** algorithm that computes, given an arbitrary graph G, a complete subgraph of G of maximum size, using this magic black box as a subroutine.

(c) Suppose you are given a magic black box that can determine **in polynomial time**, given an arbitrary graph G, whether G is 3-colorable. Describe and analyze a **polynomial-time** algorithm that either computes a proper 3-coloring of a given graph or correctly reports that no such coloring exists, using the magic black box as a subroutine. *[Hint: The input to the magic black box is a graph. Only a graph. Vertices and edges. Nothing else.]*

(d) Suppose you are given a magic black box that can determine **in polynomial time**, given an arbitrary boolean formula Φ, whether Φ is satisfiable. Describe and analyze a **polynomial-time** algorithm that either computes a satisfying assignment for a given boolean formula or correctly reports that no such assignment exists, using the magic black box as a subroutine.

(e) Suppose you are given a magic black box that can determine **in polynomial time**, given an arbitrary set X of positive integers, whether X can be partitioned into two sets A and B such that $\sum A = \sum B$. Describe and analyze a **polynomial-time** algorithm that either computes an equal partition of a given set of positive integers or correctly reports that no such partition exists, using the magic black box as a subroutine.

♣♥(f) Suppose you are given a magic black box that can determine **in polynomial time**, given an arbitrary generalized regular expression R (as defined just before the Exercises), whether R matches any string. Describe and analyze a **polynomial-time** algorithm that either finds a single string that matches a given generalized regular expression or correctly reports that no such string exists, using the magic black box as a subroutine.

6. **There's something special about the number 3.**

(a) Describe and analyze a polynomial-time algorithm for 2PARTITION. Given a set S of $2n$ positive integers, your algorithm will determine in polynomial time whether the elements of S can be split into n disjoint pairs whose sums are all equal.

(b) Describe and analyze a polynomial-time algorithm for 2COLOR. Given an undirected graph G, your algorithm will determine in polynomial time whether G has a proper coloring that uses only two colors.

(c) Describe and analyze a polynomial-time algorithm for 2SAT. Given a boolean formula Φ in conjunctive normal form, with exactly *two* literals per clause, your algorithm will determine in polynomial time whether Φ has a satisfying assignment. *[Hint: This problem is strongly connected to topics described in an earlier chapter.]*

7. **There's nothing special about the number 3.**

   (a) The problem 12PARTITION is defined as follows: Given a set S of $12n$ positive integers, determine whether the elements of S can be split into n subsets, each with 12 elements, whose sums are all equal. Prove that 12PARTITION is NP-hard. [*Hint: Reduce from 3PARTITION. It may be easier to consider multisets first.*]

   (b) The problem 12COLOR is defined as follows: Given an undirected graph G, determine whether we can color each vertex with one of twelve colors, so that every edge touches two different colors. Prove that 12COLOR is NP-hard. [*Hint: Reduce from 3COLOR.*]

   (c) The problem 12SAT is defined as follows: Given a boolean formula Φ in conjunctive normal form, with exactly twelve literals per clause, determine whether Φ has a satisfying assignment. Prove that 12SAT is NP-hard. [*Hint: Reduce from 3SAT.*]

8. There are two different versions of the Hamiltonian cycle problem, one for directed graphs and one for undirected graphs. Earlier in this chapter you can find two proofs that the *directed* Hamiltonian cycle problem is NP-hard.

   (a) Describe a polynomial-time reduction from the *undirected* Hamiltonian cycle problem to the *directed* Hamiltonian cycle problem. Prove your reduction is correct.

   (b) Describe a polynomial-time reduction from the *directed* Hamiltonian cycle problem to the *undirected* Hamiltonian cycle problem. Prove your reduction is correct.

   (c) Which of these two reductions implies that the *undirected* Hamiltonian cycle problem is NP-hard?

9. (a) Describe a polynomial-time reduction from UNDIRECTEDHAMILTONIANCYCLE to DIRECTEDHAMILTONIANCYCLE.

   (b) Describe a polynomial-time reduction from DIRECTEDHAMILTONIANCYCLE to UNDIRECTEDHAMILTONIANCYCLE.

10. (a) Describe a polynomial-time reduction from the HAMILTONIANPATH problem to HAMILTONIANCYCLE.

    (b) Describe a polynomial-time reduction from the HAMILTONIANCYCLE problem to HAMILTONIANPATH. [*Hint: A polynomial-time reduction can call the black-box subroutine more than once, but it doesn't have to.*]

11. Consider the following subtle variants of CNFSAT. For each problem, the input is a boolean formula Φ in conjunctive normal form, and the goal is to determine whether Φ has a satisfying assignment.

(a) Suppose every clause of Φ contains *at most* three literals and each variable appears in at most *three* clauses. Prove that this variant of CNFSAT is NP-hard.

(b) Suppose every clause of Φ contains *exactly* three literals and each variable appears in at most *four* clauses. Prove that this variant of 3SAT is NP-hard. *[Hint: Solve part (a) first.]*

♥(c) Suppose every clause of Φ can contain *any number of* literals, but each variable appears in at most *two* clauses. Describe a polynomial-time algorithm for this variant of CNFSAT.

♥(d) Suppose every clause of Φ contains *exactly* three literals and each variable appears in at most *three* clauses. Prove that Φ must be satisfiable. (So this variant of 3SAT is completely trivial!)

12. (a) Prove that NotAllEqual3SAT is NP-hard.

   (b) Prove that 1-in-3SAT is NP-hard.

13. A boolean formula in *exclusive-or conjunctive normal form* (XCNF) is a conjunction (AND) of several *clauses*, each of which is the *exclusive*-or of several literals; that is, a clause is true if and only if it contains an odd number of true literals. The XCNF-SAT problem asks whether a given XCNF formula is satisfiable. Either describe a polynomial-time algorithm for XCNF-SAT or prove that XCNF-SAT is NP-hard. *[Hint: Do not try to do both.]*

♥14. Consider the following variant of 3SAT, called MAJORITY3SAT. Just like 3SAT, the input to MAJORITY3SAT is a boolean formula Φ in conjunctive normal form, with exactly three literals er clause. MAJORITY3SAT asks whether there is an assignment to the variables of Φ, such that every clause contains *at least two* TRUE literals.

   Either describe an algorithm that solves MAJORITY3SAT in polynomial time or prove that MAJORITY3SAT is NP-hard. *[Hint: Do not try to do both.]*

♠♥15. For any subset $X \subseteq \{0, 1, 2, 3\}$, consider the following problem, which I'll call *X-3SAT*. The input is a boolean formula Φ in conjunctive normal form, with exactly three literals in each clause. The problem is to decide whether there is an assignment to the variables of Φ such that in each clause of Φ, the number of TRUE literals is in the set X. For example:

   - $\{1, 2, 3\}$-3SAT is the standard 3SAT problem.
   - $\{0, 3\}$-3SAT is the same as ALLORNOTHING3SAT. (See Exercise 4.)
   - $\{1, 2\}$-3SAT is usually called NOTALLEQUAL3SAT. (See Exercise 12(a).)
   - $\{1\}$-3SAT is usually called 1-IN-3SAT. (See Exercise 12(b).)

- $\{1,3\}$-3SAT is usually called XCNF-3SAT. (See Exercise 13.)
- $\{2,3\}$-3SAT is usually called MAJORITY3SAT. (See Exercise 14.)

Give a complete list of all subsets $X \subseteq \{0, 1, 2, 3\}$ such that X-3SAT is solvable in polynomial time, assuming P $\neq$ NP. [*Hint: Don't give 16 different arguments.*]

16. Prove that the following problems are NP-hard.

    (a) Given an undirected graph G, does G contain a simple path that visits all but 17 vertices?

    (b) Given an undirected graph G, does G have a spanning tree in which every node has degree at most 23?

    (c) Given an undirected graph G, does G have a spanning tree with at most 42 leaves?

    (d) Given an undirected graph $G = (V, E)$, what is the size of the largest subset of vertices $S \subseteq V$ such that at most 374 edges in E have both endpoints in S?

    (e) Given an undirected graph $G = (V, E)$, what is the size of the largest subset of vertices $S \subseteq V$ such that each vertex in S has at most 473 neighbors in S?

    (f) Given an undirected graph G, is it possible to color the vertices of G with three different colors, so that at most 31337 edges have both endpoints the same color?

17. Prove that the following variants of the minimum spanning tree problem are NP-hard.

    (a) Given a graph G, compute the *maximum-diameter* spanning tree of G. (The diameter of a tree T is the length of the longest path in T.)

    (b) Given a graph G with weighted edges, compute the minimum-weight *depth-first* spanning tree of G.

    (c) Given a graph G with weighted edges and a subset S of vertices of G, compute the minimum-weight spanning tree all of whose leaves are in S.

    (d) Given a graph G with weighted edges and an integer ℓ, compute the minimum-weight spanning tree with at most ℓ leaves.

    (e) Given a graph G with weighted edges and an integer Δ, compute the minimum-weight spanning tree where every node has degree at most Δ.

18. (a) Using the gadget in Figure 12.26(a), prove that deciding whether a given *planar* graph is 3-colorable is NP-hard. [*Hint: Show that the gadget can be 3-colored, and then replace any crossings in a planar embedding with the gadget appropriately.*]

(b) Using part (a) and the gadget in Figure 12.26(b), prove that deciding whether a planar graph *with maximum degree 4* is 3-colorable is NP-hard. *[Hint: Replace any vertex with degree greater than 4 with a collection of gadgets connected so that no degree is greater than four.]*

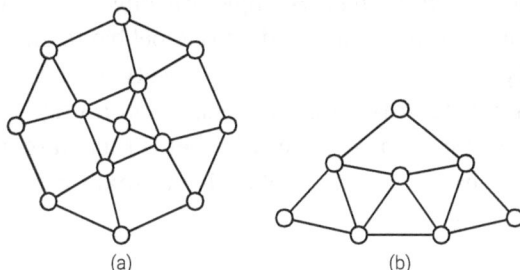

(a)   (b)

Figure 12.26. (a) Gadget for planar 3-colorability. (b) Gadget for degree-4 planar 3-colorability.

19. Prove that PLANARCIRCUITSAT is NP-hard. *[Hint: Construct a gadget for crossing wires.]*

20. (a) Describe a polynomial-time reduction from 3SAT to 4SAT.

    (b) Describe a polynomial-time reduction from 4SAT to 3SAT.

♥21. Describe a direct polynomial-time reduction from 4COLOR to 3COLOR. (This is a lot harder than the opposite direction.)

22. A *domino* is a 1×2 rectangle divided into two squares, each of which is labeled with an integer.[29] In a *legal arrangement* of dominos, the dominos are lined up end-to-end so that the numbers on adjacent ends match.

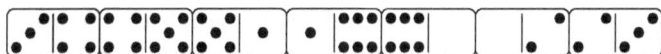

Figure 12.27. A legal arrangement of dominos in which every integer between 0 and 6 appears twice

For each of the following problems, either describe a polynomial-time algorithm or prove that the problem is NP-hard:

(a) Given an arbitrary bag D of dominos, is there a legal arrangement of *all* the dominos in D?

(b) Given an arbitrary bag D of dominos, is there a legal arrangement of a dominos from D in which every integer between 1 and n appears exactly twice?

---

[29]These integers are usually represented by pips, exactly like dice. On a standard domino, the number of pips on each side is between 0 and 6, although one can buy sets with up to 9 or even 12 pips on each side; we will allow arbitrary integer labels. A standard set of dominos contains exactly one domino for each possible unordered pair of labels; we do *not* assume that the inputs to our problems have this property.

▼(c) Given an arbitrary bag D of dominos, what is the largest number of dominos we can take from D to make a legal arrangement?

23. *Pebbling* is a solitaire game played on an undirected graph G, where each vertex has zero or more *pebbles*. A single *pebbling move* consists of removing two pebbles from a vertex v and adding one pebble to an arbitrary neighbor of v. (Obviously, the vertex v must have at least two pebbles before the move.) The PEBBLEDESTRUCTION problem asks, given a graph $G = (V, E)$ and a pebble count $p(v)$ for each vertex v, whether is there a sequence of pebbling moves that removes all but one pebble. Prove that PEBBLEDESTRUCTION is NP-hard.

24. Recall that a 5-coloring of a graph G is a function that assigns each vertex of G a "color" from the set $\{0, 1, 2, 3, 4\}$, such that for any edge uv, vertices u and v are assigned different "colors". A 5-coloring is *careful* if the colors assigned to adjacent vertices are not only distinct, but differ by more than 1 (mod 5). Prove that deciding whether a given graph has a careful 5-coloring is NP-hard. [*Hint: Reduce from the standard 5COLOR problem.*]

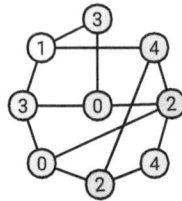

Figure 12.28. A careful 5-coloring.

25. (a) A subset S of vertices in an undirected graph G is *half-independent* if each vertex in S is adjacent to *at most one* other vertex in S. Prove that finding the size of the largest half-independent set of vertices in a given undirected graph is NP-hard.

(b) A subset S of vertices in an undirected graph G is *sort-of-independent* if if each vertex in S is adjacent to *at most 374* other vertices in S. Prove that finding the size of the largest sort-of-independent set of vertices in a given undirected graph is NP-hard.

(c) A subset S of vertices in an undirected graph G is *almost independent* if at most 374 edges in G have both endpoints in S. Prove that finding the size of the largest almost-independent set of vertices in a given undirected graph is NP-hard.

26. Let $G = (V, E)$ be a graph. A *dominating set* in G is a subset S of the vertices such that every vertex in G is either in S or adjacent to a vertex in S. The

DOMINATINGSET problem asks, given a graph G and an integer k as input, whether G contains a dominating set of size k. Prove that this problem is NP-hard.

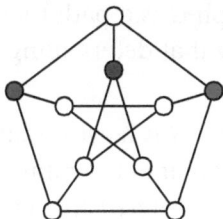

Figure 12.29. A dominating set of size 3 in the Petersen graph.

27. A subset S of vertices in an undirected graph G is *triangle-free* if, for every triple of vertices $u, v, w \in S$, at least one of the three edges uv, uw, vw is *absent* from G. Prove that finding the size of the largest triangle-free subset of vertices in a given undirected graph is NP-hard.

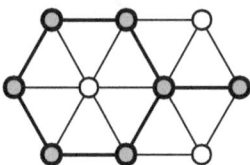

Figure 12.30. A triangle-free subset of 7 vertices. This is not the largest such subset in this graph.

28. The RECTANGLETILING problem is defined as follows: Given one large rectangle and several smaller rectangles, determine whether the smaller rectangles can be placed inside the large rectangle with no gaps or overlaps.

    (a) Prove that RECTANGLETILING is NP-hard.

    (b) Prove that RECTANGLETILING is *strongly* NP-hard.

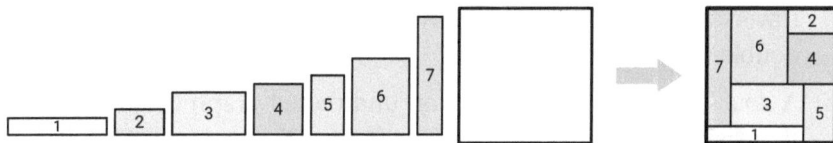

Figure 12.31. A positive instance of the RECTANGLETILING problem.

29. (a) A subset B of vertices in a graph G is a ***Burr set*** if removing every vertex in B from G leaves a subgraph that does not contain a Hamiltonian path. Prove that finding the smallest Burr set in a given graph is NP-hard.

    (b) A subset S of vertices in a graph G is a ***Schuyler set*** if removing every vertex in S from G leaves a subgraph that *does* contain a Hamiltonian path. Prove that finding the smallest Schuyler set in a given graph is NP-hard.

30. (a) A *tonian path* in a graph G is a path that goes through at least half of the vertices of G. Show that determining whether a graph has a tonian path is NP-hard.

    (b) A *tonian cycle* in a graph G is a cycle that goes through at least half of the vertices of G. Show that determining whether a graph has a tonian cycle is NP-hard. *[Hint: Use part (a). Or not.]*

31. Let G be an undirected graph with weighted edges. A *heavy Hamiltonian cycle* is a cycle C that passes through each vertex of G exactly once, such that the total weight of the edges in C is more than half of the total weight of all edges in G. Prove that deciding whether a graph has a heavy Hamiltonian cycle is NP-hard.

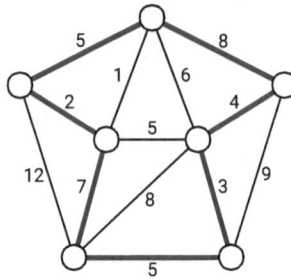

Figure 12.32. A heavy Hamiltonian cycle. The cycle has total weight 34; the graph has total weight 67.

32. For each of the following problems, either describe a polynomial-time algorithm or prove that the problem is NP-hard.

    (a) A *double-Eulerian tour* in an undirected graph G is a closed walk that traverses every edge in G exactly twice. Given a graph G, does G have a double-Eulerian tour?

    (b) A *double-Hamiltonian tour* in an undirected graph G is a closed walk that visits every vertex in G exactly twice. Given a graph G, does G have a double-Hamiltonian tour?

    (c) A *double-Hamiltonian **circuit*** in an undirected graph G is a closed walk that visits every vertex in G exactly twice *and traverses each edge in G at most once*. Given a graph G, does G have a double-Hamiltonian circuit?

    (d) A *triple-Eulerian tour* in an undirected graph G is a closed walk that traverses every edge in G exactly three times. Given a graph G, does G have a triple-Eulerian tour?

(e) A *triple-Hamiltonian tour* in an undirected graph G is a closed walk that visits every vertex in G exactly three times. Given a graph G, does G have a triple-Hamiltonian tour?

33. This exercise asks you to prove that a certain reduction from VERTEXCOVER to STEINERTREE is correct. Suppose we want to find the smallest vertex cover in a given undirected graph $G = (V, E)$. We construct a new graph $H = (V', E')$ as follows:

    • $V' = V \cup E \cup \{z\}$

    • $E' = \{ve \mid v \in V$ is an endpoint of $e \in E\} \cup \{vz \mid v \in V\}$.

    Equivalently, we construct H by subdividing each edge in G with a new vertex, and then connecting all the original vertices of G to a new *apex* vertex z.

    Prove that G has a vertex cover of size k if and only if there is a subtree of H with $k + |E| + 1$ vertices that contains every vertex in $E \cup \{z\}$.

34. Consider the following solitaire game. The puzzle consists of an $n \times m$ grid of squares, where each square may be empty, occupied by a red stone, or occupied by a blue stone. The goal of the puzzle is to remove some of the given stones so that the remaining stones satisfy two conditions: (1) every row contains at least one stone, and (2) no column contains stones of both colors. For some initial configurations of stones, reaching this goal is impossible.

    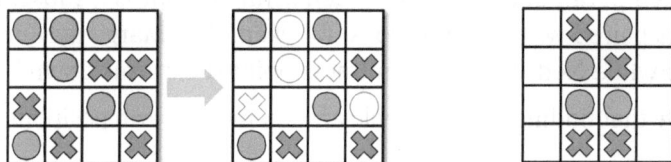

    A solvable puzzle and one of its many solutions.   An unsolvable puzzle.

    Prove that it is NP-hard to determine, given an initial configuration of red and blue stones, whether the puzzle can be solved.

35. Each of the following games involves an $n \times m$ grid of squares, where each square is either empty or occupied by a stone. In a single move, you can remove *all* the stones in an arbitrary column.

    (a) Prove that it is NP-hard to find the *smallest* subset of columns that can be cleared so that *at most* one stone remains in each row of the grid.

    (b) Prove that it is NP-hard to find the *largest* subset of columns that can be cleared so that *at least* one stone remains in each row of the grid.

▼(c) Prove that it is NP-hard to determine whether *any* subset of columns can be cleared so that *exactly* one stone remains in each row of the grid.

36. Jeff tries to make his students happy. At the beginning of class, he passes out a questionnaire that lists a number of possible course policies in areas where he is flexible. Every student is asked to respond to each possible course policy with one of "strongly favor", "mostly neutral", or "strongly oppose". Each student may respond with "strongly favor" or "strongly oppose" to at most five questions. Because Jeff's students are very understanding, each student is happy if (but only if) he or she prevails in at least one of their strong policy preferences. Either describe a polynomial-time algorithm for setting course policy to maximize the number of happy students, or show that the problem is NP-hard.

37. You're in charge of choreographing a musical for your local community theater, and it's time to figure out the final pose of the big show-stopping number at the end. ("Streetcar!") You've decided that each of the n cast members in the show will be positioned in a big line when the song finishes, all with their arms extended and showing off their best spirit fingers.

    The director has declared that during the final flourish, each cast member must either point both their arms up or point both their arms down; it's your job to figure out who points up and who points down. Moreover, the director has also given you a list of arrangements that will upset his delicate artistic temperament. Each forbidden arrangement is a subset of the cast members paired with arm positions; for example: "Marge may not point her arms up while Ned, Apu, and Smithers point their arms down."

    Prove that finding an acceptable arrangement of arm positions is NP-hard.

38. The next time you are at a party, one of the guests will suggest everyone play a round of Three-Way Mumbletypeg, a game of skill and dexterity that requires three teams and a knife. The official Rules of Three-Way Mumbletypeg (fixed during the Holy Roman Three-Way Mumbletypeg Council in 1625) require that (1) each team *must* have at least one person, (2) any two people on the same team *must* know each other, and (3) everyone watching the game *must* be on one of the three teams. Of course, it will be a really *fun* party; nobody will want to leave. There will be several pairs of people at the party who don't know each other. The host of the party, having heard thrilling tales of your prowess in all things algorithmic, will hand you a list of which pairs of party-goers know each other and ask you to choose the teams, while he sharpens the knife.

Either describe and analyze a polynomial time algorithm to determine whether the party-goers can be split into three legal Three-Way Mumbletypeg teams, or prove that the problem is NP-hard.

39. The party you are attending is going great, but now it's time to line up for *The Algorithm March* (アルゴリズムこうしん)! This dance was originally developed by the Japanese comedy duo Itsumo Kokokara (いつもここから) for the children's television show PythagoraSwitch (ピタゴラスイッチ). The Algorithm March is performed by a line of people; each person in line starts a specific sequence of movements one measure later than the person directly in front of them. Thus, the march is the dance equivalent of a musical round or canon, like "Row Row Row Your Boat" or "Frère Jacques".

    Proper etiquette dictates that each marcher must know the person directly in front of them in line, lest a minor mistake lead to horrible embarrassment between strangers. Suppose you are given a complete list of which people at your party know each other. Prove that it is NP-hard to determine the largest number of party-goers that can participate in the Algorithm March. You may assume without loss of generality that there are no ninjas at your party.

*40. Prove that the following problems about nondeterministic finite-state automata and regular expressions are NP-hard:

    (a) Given an NFA M over the alphabet $\Sigma = \{0, 1\}$, is there a string in Σ^* that M does *not* accept?

    (b) Given an *acyclic* NFA M over the alphabet $\Sigma = \{0, 1\}$, what is the length of the *shortest* string in Σ^* that M does *not* accept?

    (c) Given a regular expression R over the alphabet $\Sigma = \{0, 1\}$, is there a string in Σ^* that R does *not* match?

    (d) Given a *star-free* regular expression R over the alphabet $\Sigma = \{0, 1\}$, what is the length of the *shortest* string in Σ^* that R does *not* match?

    (In fact, problems (a) and (c) are PSPACE-complete; even proving that these problems are in PSPACE is nontrivial.)

*41. (a) Describe a polynomial-time algorithm for the following problem: Given an NFA M over the alphabet $\Sigma = \{0, 1\}$, is there a string in Σ^* that M *does* accept?

    (b) Describe a polynomial-time algorithm for the following problem: Given a regular expression R over the alphabet $\Sigma = \{0, 1\}$, is there a string in Σ^* that R *does* match?

(c) The complement of any regular language is another regular language. So why don't these two algorithms, together with the NP-hardness results in Problem 40, prove that P=NP?

42. Charon needs to ferry n recently deceased people across the river Acheron into Hades. Certain pairs of these people are sworn enemies, who cannot be together on either side of the river unless Charon is also present. (If two enemies are left alone, one will steal the obol from the other's mouth, leaving them to wander the banks of the Acheron as a ghost for all eternity. Let's just say this is a Very Bad Thing.) The ferry can hold at most k passengers at a time, including Charon, and only Charon can pilot the ferry.[30]

Prove that it is NP-hard to decide whether Charon can ferry all n people across the Acheron unharmed (aside from being, you know, dead). The input for Charon's problem consists of the integers k and n and an n-vertex graph G describing the pairs of enemies. The output is either TRUE or FALSE.

Please do not write your solution in classical Latin.

---

[30]This problem is a generalization of the well-known wolf-goat-and-cabbage puzzle, whose first known appearance is in the remarkable medieval manuscript *Propositiones ad Acuendos Juvenes* [*Problems to Sharpen the Young*].

XVIII. PROPOSITIO DE HOMINE ET CAPRA ET LVPO.
Homo quidam debebat ultra fluuium transferre lupum, capram, et fasciculum cauli. Et non potuit aliam nauem inuenire, nisi quae duos tantum ex ipsis ferre ualebat. Praeceptum itaque ei fuerat, ut omnia haec ultra illaesa omnino transferret. Dicat, qui potest, quomodo eis illaesis transire potuit?
Solutio. Simili namque tenore ducerem prius capram et dimitterem foris lupum et caulum. Tum deinde uenirem, lupumque transferrem: lupoque foris misso capram naui receptam ultra reducerem; capramque foris missam caulum transueherem ultra; atque iterum remigassem, capramque assumptam ultra duxissem. Sicque faciendo facta erit remigatio salubris, absque uoragine lacerationis.

For those few readers whose classical Latin is a little rusty, here is an English translation:

XVIII. THE PROBLEM OF THE MAN, THE GOAT, AND THE WOLF.
A man needed to transfer a wolf, a goat, and a bundle of cabbage across a river. However, he found that his boat could only bear the weight of two [objects at a time, including the man]. And he had to get everything across unharmed. Tell me if you can: How they were able to cross unharmed?
Solution. In a similar fashion [as an earlier problem], I would first take the goat across and leave the wolf and cabbage on the opposite bank. Then I would take the wolf across; leaving the wolf on shore, I would retrieve the goat and bring it back again. Then I would leave the goat and take the cabbage across. And then I would row across again and get the goat. In this way the crossing would go well, without any threat of slaughter.

The most likely author of the *Propositiones* is the prolific 8th-century English scholar Alcuin of York. The evidence for Alcuin's authorship of this treatise is somewhat circumstantial; however, we do know from his correspondence with Charlemagne that he sent the emperor some "simple arithmetical problems for fun". Most modern scholars believe that even if Alcuin did write the *Propositiones*, he did not invent all of the problems himself, but rather collected them from even earlier sources.

Some things never change.

If we had an index file, we could look it up in the index file under "index file".
— Tegan Jovanka [Janet Fielding], "Castrovalva (Part 1)",
Doctor Who, Season 19 (January 4, 1982)

I started with the phone book. Looking up "mensa" was not going to be easy, what with having to follow the strict alphabetizing rules that are so common nowadays. I prefer a softer, more fuzzy alphabetizing scheme, one that allows the mind to float free and "happen" upon the word. There is pride in that. The dictionary is a perfect example of over-alphabetization, with its harsh rules and every little word neatly in place. It almost makes me never want to eat again.
— Steve Martin, "How I Joined Mensa", *The New Yorker*, July 21, 1997.

Index

For some topics with multiple references, bold page numbers indicate the primary reference. Humans and pseudocode are indexed separately.

Dicebat Bernardus Carnotensis nos esse quasi nanos gigantium humeris insidentes, ut possimus plura eis et remotiora videre, non utique proprii visus acumine, aut eminentia corporis, sed quia in altum subvehimur et extollimur magnitudine gigantea.

[Bernard of Chartres used to say that we were like dwarfs seated on the shoulders of giants. He pointed out that we see more and farther than our predecessors, not because we have keener vision or greater height, but because we are lifted up and borne aloft on their gigantic stature.]

— John of Salisbury, *Metalogicon* (1159),
translated by Daniel D. McGarry (1955)

The secret to productivity is getting dead people to do your work for you.

— Robert J. Lang (2009)

Index of People

We should explain, before proceeding, that it is not our object to consider this
program with reference to the actual arrangement of the data on the Variables of
the engine, but simply as an abstract question of the nature and number of the
operations required to be performed during its complete solution.
> — Ada Augusta Byron King, Countess of Lovelace,
> translator's notes for Luigi F. Menabrea,
> "Sketch of the Analytical Engine invented by Charles Babbage, Esq." (1843)

How to play the flute. [picks up a flute] Well, here we are.
You blow there and you move your fingers up and down here.
> — Alan [John Cleese], "How to Do It",
> Monty Python's Flying Circus, episode 28 (aired October 26, 1972)

Index of Pseudocode

This index includes only algorithms with explicit pseudocode; see the main
index for other named algorithms.

A wisely chosen illustration is almost essential to fasten the truth upon the ordinary mind, and no teacher can afford to neglect this part of his preparation.

— Howard Crosby (c.1880)

One showing is worth a hundred sayings.

— Alan Watts (misquoting a Chinese proverb), *The Way of Zen* (1957)

Please do not think that this is a neutral matter and that the only advantage of doing without pictures is that of saving space. Pictures in textbooks actually interfere with the learning process.

— Neville Martin Gwynne, *Gwynne's Grammar* (2013)

Image Credits

All figures in this book, including the front cover, are original works of the author, except those listed below. All listed works are in the public domain unless otherwise indicated.

- Figure 0.1 (page 5) — Biblioteca nazionale Braidense (Milano)
  http://atena.beic.it/webclient/DeliveryManager?pid=2953344

- Figure 0.2 (page 5) — Internet Archive
  https://archive.org/details/archimedisopera05eutogoog/page/n377

- Figure 1.16 (page 45) — Internet Archive
  https://archive.org/details/p1rcrationsmoolucauoft/page/162

- Figure 1.25 (page 61) — Derived from a crayon portrait of the author by Tina Erickson (2000); included with permission of the artist.

- Figure 5.1 (page 188) — Wikimedia Commons
  https://commons.wikimedia.org/wiki/File:Tabula_Peutingeriana_-_Miller.jpg

- Figure 5.2 (page 189) — Gallery of "Legal Trees" published by the Yale Law Library under a Creative Commons Licence
  https://www.flickr.com/photos/yalelawlibrary/albums/72157621954683764

- Figure 5.3 (page 189) — Internet Archive
  https://archive.org/details/A077240124/page/n261

- Exercises 5.20 (page 216) and 8.22 (page 304) — Original puzzles by the author, inspired by Jason Batterson and Shannon Rogers, *Beast Academy Math: Practice 3A*, 2012.
  https://beastacademy.com/pdf/3A/printables/AngleMazes.pdf
  https://www.beastacademy.com/resources/printables.php

- Figure 10.1 (page 328) — T[homas] E. Harris and F[rank] S. Ross. Fundamentals of a method for evaluating rail net capacities. The RAND Corporation, Research Memorandum RM-1517, October 24, 1955. United States Government work in the public domain.
  http://www.dtic.mil/dtic/tr/fulltext/u2/093458.pdf

1. Have something to say.
2. Say it.
3. Stop when you have said it.
4. Give the paper a proper title.

     — John Shaw Billings, "An Address on Our Medical Literature",
International Medical Congress, London (1881)

You know, I could write a book.
And this book would be thick enough to stun an ox.

     — Laurie Anderson, "Let X=X", *Big Science* (1982)

Colophon

This book was edited in TeXShop (version 4.27) and typeset with pdfLATEX (MacTeX-2018) using the `memoir` document class (with madsen chapter style, komalike head style, and Ruled page style); several standard packages including amsmath, babel, enumitem, imakeidx, mathdesign, microtype, and standalone; and an embarrassing amount of customization and TEX-haXing. The text is typeset in Bitstream Charter, Ἀρτεμισία, Roboto, and Inconsolata. Except as indicated in the Image Credits, all figures were drawn by the author using OmniGraffle Pro, exported at PDF files, and included using the graphicx LATEX package.

    Portions of our programming have been mechanically reproduced, and we now conclude our broadcast day.

Made in United States
Troutdale, OR
12/26/2023